Jews, Sovereignty, and International Law

THE HISTORY AND THEORY OF INTERNATIONAL LAW

In the past few decades the understanding of the relationship between nations has undergone a radical transformation. The role of the traditional nation state is diminishing, along with many of the traditional vocabularies that were once used to describe what has been called, ever since Jeremy Bentham coined the phrase in 1780, 'international law'. The older boundaries between states are growing ever more fluid, new conceptions and new languages have emerged that are slowly coming to replace the image of a world of sovereign independent nation states that has dominated the study of international relations since the early nineteenth century. This redefinition of the international arena demands a new understanding of classical and contemporary questions in international and legal theory. It is the editors' conviction that the best way to achieve this is by bridging the traditional divide between international legal theory, intellectual history, and legal and political history. The aim of the series, therefore, is to provide a forum for historical studies, from classical antiquity to the twenty-first century, that are theoretically informed and for philosophical work that is historically conscious, in the hope that a new vision of the rapidly evolving international world, its past and its possible future, may emerge.

PREVIOUSLY PUBLISHED IN THIS SERIES

Remaking Central Europe
The League of Nations and the Former Habsburg Lands
Peter Becker and Natasha Wheatley

The Renaissance of Roman Colonization
Carlo Sigonio and the Making of Legal Colonial Discourse
Jeremia Pelgrom and Arthur Weststeijn

Britain and International Law in West Africa
The Practice of Empire
Inge Van Hulle

The Laws of War in International Thought
Pablo Kalmanovitz

A History of International Law in Italy
Edited by Giulio Bartolini

The New Histories of International Criminal Law ***Retrials***
Edited by Immi Tallgren and Thomas Skouteris

Jews, Sovereignty, and International Law

Ideology and Ambivalence in Early Israeli Legal Diplomacy

ROTEM GILADI

OXFORD
UNIVERSITY PRESS

OXFORD
UNIVERSITY PRESS

Great Clarendon Street, Oxford, OX2 6DP,
United Kingdom

Oxford University Press is a department of the University of Oxford.
It furthers the University's objective of excellence in research, scholarship,
and education by publishing worldwide. Oxford is a registered trade mark of
Oxford University Press in the UK and in certain other countries

First Edition published in 2021

Impression: 1

Published in the United States of America by Oxford University Press
198 Madison Avenue, New York, NY 10016, United States of America

British Library Cataloguing in Publication Data

Data available

Library of Congress Control Number: 2020952997

ISBN 978–0–19–885739–6

DOI: 10.1093/oso/9780198857396.001.0001

Printed and bound in the UK by
TJ Books Limited

Series Editors' Preface

Recent years have seen a surge in interest in "Jewish International Lawyers," and their contribution to 20th century international law. A 2019 edited volume devoted to *Jewish Lawyers and International Law*, profiles Kelsen, Lauterpacht, Henkin, Schwelb, and Cassin, among others,[1] while Philippe Sands' popular book *East West Street*, has drawn attention to the outsized significance of the Galician-Jewish community in Lvov/Lviv/Lemberg for international law from 1920. Loeffler's 2018 book, *Rooted Cosmopolitans*,[2] argues for a close affinity between European Jewry's experience of persecution and discrimination, culminating in the failure of the Minority Protection treaties and the Holocaust, and the project to institutionalize international human rights in the post-1945 world order. But the relationship between *Zionism* and international law, in particular after the creation of a sovereign Jewish State in Palestine, has received less attention. A quasi-official Israeli account published in 1956,[3] emphasized Israel's universalist outlook and cosmopolitan commitment to principles of the post-war international legal order, such as the prohibition on genocide, international human rights, and the Refugees' Convention.

In this deeply researched and original book, which draws extensively on Israeli state archives and private papers, Dr Giladi paints a very different picture of Israel's approach to the institutionalization of international human rights jurisdiction, to the Genocide Convention, and to the Refugees' Convention. He asks the question, did the "Zionist creed" of Israel's first foreign ministry legal advisor, Shabtai Rosenne (Sefton Rowson) and its first legal advisor to its UN Mission, Jacob Robinson (Jokubas Robinzonas), shape Israel's engagement with certain key developments in the post 1945 international legal order? Dr Giladi answers this question through a narrative which interweaves prosopography with a detailed reconstruction of debates within the Israel government about these legal commitments.

Rosenne (d.2010) went on to a distinguished career as an international legal academic, Ambassador and jurist, while Robinson retired from the Israeli Foreign Ministry in 1957, but would work as a scholar of the Holocaust based in the United States until his death in 1977. Giladi describes these two jurist diplomats as

[1] James Loeffler and Moria Paz, eds, *The Law of Strangers: Jewish Lawyers and International Law in the Twentieth Century* (Cambridge UP, 2019).

[2] James Loeffler, *Rooted Cosmpolitans: Jews and Human Rights in the Twentieth Century* (Yale UP, 2018).

[3] Nathan Feinberg, *Israel and the United Nations: Report of a Study Group Set Up by the Hebrew University of Jerusalem* (1956) discussed in this volume, 300-302.

"torchbearers" and "the engines of Israel's early international law diplomacy," each of which understood themselves by this stage of their lives as committed to political Zionism and the idea of the Jewish state.

In Giladi's argument, this Zionist creed leads to a different relationship with international law, than that evident in the work of pre-war Jewish advocacy organizations, or in the cosmopolitanism of a Lauterpacht or a Kelsen. He shows in great detail how political Zionism's posture towards international law was historically ambivalent, understanding the European law of nations as excluding Jews from statehood but also as a means through which Jews could become sovereign under the right diplomatic, political, and military conditions. Once sovereignty had been achieved, the critical political question was how international law could be a means to enhance the contested political and moral legitimacy of Israel, and to preserve its prerogatives to act as a homeland and safe haven for the Jewish people. Giladi shows that these imperatives were debated and pursued by Rosenne, Robinson, and their political superiors, leading to a combination of "disinterest, aversion and hostility towards the right of petition and the human rights project at large, the Genocide Convention and progenitor [Raphael Lemkin], and the Refugee Convention and the international refugee regime."[4] The book's bold claim is carefully substantiated, and vividly captures the at times turbulent internal Israeli government discussions, and the fascinating characters of the two main protagonists, Rosenne and Robinson. There is no doubt that this book will be an important contribution to Israeli and Jewish studies, to the history of Israel's foreign policy, and to the current debates about Jews, Zionism, and international law in the 20th century.

Nehal Bhuta, May 2021
Edinburgh

[4] This volume, 293.

Acknowledgements

I first encountered Jacob Robinson in Ann Arbor, Michigan, in James Hathaway's class on Refugee Law. His name, marked as a representative of Israel, appeared time and again in the voluminous *travaux préparatoires* of the 1951 Refugee Convention I had to read for nearly each class. I was intrigued: I had articled and practiced law, for a time, at the Legal Adviser's Office of Israel's Ministry of Foreign Affairs, where I met Shabtai Rosenne. Yet Robinson's name commanded no familiarity. What seemed like evidence of Israel's early investment in the Refugee Convention, moreover, did not cohere with media and civil society accounts of Israel's present-day treatment of asylum seekers. Nor did it seem congruent with what I thought I knew of Israel's outlook, in those early years, on the preferred destination of Jewish immigration. After completing my doctoral studies at the University of Michigan Law School, I began tracing Robinson and Rosenne's footsteps and, through their stories, exploring Israel's early attitude towards international law. This book is the result.

In the course of the journey I have accumulated debts that cannot be repaid. I can only acknowledge what I owe friends, colleagues, and mentors whose support made the book possible—and the journey as rewarding as it has been. I owe a particular debt to Martti Koskenniemi for his insightful advice and enthusiastic encouragement at a crucial point—preparing a book proposal and submitting it to the right publisher. Martti's work, besides, inspired my own turn to the history of international law and pointed at the vistas of political imagination it presented before the protagonists of this book, Jewish international lawyers invested in the Jewish national project. I am equally indebted to Yfaat Weiss, the director of the *Leibniz Institute for Jewish History and Culture—Simon Dubnow* in Leipzig, and not only for the generous grant that made completing the book possible. The Dubnow Institute, as it was known when I first was invited to join its ranks, became my home away from home. Its vibrant intellectual community and traditional interest in Jewish engagements with international law remain unique; no other place could provide me the kind of alchemist laboratory required for synthesizing modern Jewish history with the history of international law. For these, as for her unwavering support and thoughtful advice, I am most grateful.

At Dubnow, my work also benefited immensely from the invaluable expertise of Jörg Deventer, the Institute's Deputy-Director, and Elizabeth Gallas, head of the 'Law' research unit, and other *ressort* members. Other fora where segments of the book were presented are too numerous to recount here. I would however be remiss if I failed to mention the research seminars of the Dubnow Institute and the annual conferences of the Israeli Law and History Association. Each autumn, in Jerusalem and Saxony, I got to test my ideas—and so contend with rigorous critique that so often, if unacknowledged, informed the final shape things were to take.

Early research that found its way into this book was generously supported by the *Cherrick Center for the Study of Zionism, Yishuv and the State of Israel*; the *Minerva Center for Human Rights*; the *Aharon Barak Center for Interdisciplinary Legal Research*; and the *Nathan and Judith Feinberg Fund*, all at the Hebrew University of Jerusalem.

Many selflessly placed their time and knowledge at my disposal in countless conversations about international law and Jewish history; others read parts of the manuscript or commented on earlier versions of the research; more than a few willingly shared their archival findings, drafts of their work, or personal and family memories. I am immensely grateful to all, and to the too many I no doubt neglected to mention here. They are, in no particular order: Paul Mendes-Flohr, Ruth Lapidoth, Steve Ratner, Yuval Shany, Samuel Moyn, Tomer Broude, Philippe Sands, Louise Bethlehem, Gil Rubin, Iddo Nevo, Eliav Lieblich, Zohar Segev, Nathan Kurz, Orit Rozin, Nicholas Berg, Dmitry Shumsky, Donald Bloxham, Philipp Graf, Anat Stern (you were right: it was a book project), Piki Ish-Shalom, Gideon Shimoni, Gadi Heimann, Motti Golani, Leora Bilski, Dirk Moses, Moshe Hirsch, Marcos Silber, Michael Marrus, Hanna Yablonka, Laura Jockusch, Jochen von Bernstorff, Alon Confino, the late Nissim Bar-Yaacov, Manuela Consonni, Neri Horwitz, Scott Ury, Amos Goldberg, Nehal Bhuta, James Loeffler, Assaf Likovski, Arie Dubnov, Momme Schwarz, Yoram Shachar, Marcel Müller, Roni Mikel, Derek Penslar, Natasha Wheatley, Martin Jost, Mira Siegelberg, William Schabas, Eitan Bar-Yosef, Markus Kirchhoff, and James Hathaway.

I was fortunate to receive the help, along the way, of dedicated research assistants—Ayana Yacobovitch, Eitan Smith, Sara Cohen, Shani Dann, Irit Chen, Sophie Rabenow, and Maya Kreiner, and benefit from the useful advice and steadfast support of the staff of numerous archives and libraries in The Hague, Leipzig, Edinburgh, Jerusalem, New York, Washington, DC, Cincinnati, and elsewhere. I am particularly indebted to Shabtai Rosenne's family for sharing his papers, life, and person with me.

At Oxford University Press, I was treated with never-ending patience, good counsel, and boundless encouragement by the editorial team—Merel Alstein and John Smallman—and series editors Nehal Bhuta, Anthony Pagden, and Benjamin Straumann. I thank them for making the publishing experience so pain-free. Another debt to acknowledge goes to the tolerant staff and owners of countless laptop-friendly cafes in Edinburgh, Helsinki, Leipzig, Amsterdam and The Hague, and several other cities—but first and foremost Jerusalem—where large portions of this book were written. We all have our quirks and writing habits; mine seem to require an idiosyncratic type of background noise that you orchestrated. Whatever tips I left tried to but could never express enough my thanks.

As our girls—young women now—used say at a time when they were much younger and this book itself an infant: 'best for last'. Only you know the full measure of sacrifice this journey required from you and the vast tolerance you have shown me. My parents, Dahlia and Nissim, my beloved partner Lauren, and our darling daughters Daria, Rama, and Leila: this book is dedicated to you with infinite love and endless gratitude.

Jerusalem, Winter 2020

Chapter 4 draws on and develops some materials and analysis published in Rotem Giladi, 'Not Our Salvation: Israel, the Genocide Convention, and the World Court 1950–1951' (2015) 26 Diplomacy & Statecraft 473; Chapters 6–7 draw on and develop some materials and analysis published in Rotem Giladi, 'A "Historical Commitment"? Identity and Ideology in Israel's Attitude to the Refugee Convention 1951–4' (2014) 37 The International History Review 745.

A Note on Translation and Archives

Unless otherwise indicated, all translations from Hebrew are by the author. I preferred to cite English titles of Hebrew works, where existing, over cumbersome transliterations. The few Hebrew words used in this work, unaccompanied by translation, have acquired general recognition: these include *Gola* or *Galut* (Diaspora or exile); *Knesset* (Israel's parliament); and *Yishuv* (the organized Jewish community in mandatory Palestine).

Other than private archives—this is the case especially with Shabtai Rosenne's papers, which the Rosenne family kindly made available to me—this book draws on materials in the *Israel State Archive*; the *Central Zionist Archive*; the *Hebrew University Archive*; the *Abba Eban Archive* at the *Harry S Truman Research Institute for the Advancement of Peace*, Hebrew University; and the *National Library of Israel*—all in Jerusalem—as well as other archives and collections, including the *American Jewish Archives* (Cincinnati); the *American Jewish Historical Society* archive (New York); the *United States Holocaust Memorial Museum Archives* (Washington DC); and the *New York Public Library*.

Contents

PART V: CREED

Abbreviations

AIU	*Alliance Israélite Universelle*
AJA	American Jewish Archives (Cincinnati)
AJC	American Jewish Committee
AJHS	American Jewish Historical Society (New York)
AJIL	American Journal of International Law
ASIL Proc	Proceedings of the American Society of International Law
Brit YB Intl L	British Yearbook of International Law
CCJO	Consultative Council of Jewish Organizations
CDJ	*Comité des Délégations Juives auprès de la Conference de la Paix*
CP	International Law, Being the Collected Papers of Hersch Lauterpacht
CUP	Cambridge University Press
CV	*Centralverein deutscher Staatsbürger jüdischen Glaubens*
CZA	Central Zionist Archive (Jerusalem)
ECOSOC	United Nations Economic and Social Council
EJIL	European Journal of International Law
GA	United Nations General Assembly
GAOR	General Assembly Official Records
HUA	Hebrew University Archive (Jerusalem)
ICJ	International Court of Justice
ICJ Rep	International Court of Justice Reports
ICLQ	International and Comparative Law Quarterly
ICRC	International Committee of the Red Cross
IJA	Institute of Jewish Affairs (New York)
ILQ	International Law Quarterly
IOD	International Organizations Division, Israeli Ministry of Foreign Affairs
IRO	International Refugee Organization
ISA	Israel State Archive (Jerusalem)
JA	Jewish Agency for Palestine
MFA	Ministry of Foreign Affairs (Israel)
NGO	Non-Governmental Organization
NYPL	New York Public Library
OUP	Oxford University Press
PMC	Permanent Mandates Commission
RdC	*Recueil de cours de l'académie de droit international*
RGDIP	*Revue Générale de Droit International Public*
SCOR	Security Council Official Records
SG	United Nations Secretary-General
UK	United Kingdom
UN	United Nations

UNHCR	United Nations High Commissioner for Refugees
UNSCOP	United Nations Special Committee on Palestine
UNTS	United Nations Treaty Series
UP	University Press
US	United States
USHMM	United States Holocaust Memorial Museum Archives (Washington DC)
USSR	Union of Soviet Socialist Republics
WJC	World Jewish Congress
YB	Yearbook

PART I
THE SOVEREIGN TURN

Prologue

'With an Eye to the Past', But No Longer 'An Object of International Law'

The Late Birth and Early Demise of the *Jewish Yearbook of International Law*

In the spring of 1949, the 1948 volume of the *Jewish Yearbook of International Law* appeared. It was printed in the newly declared state of Israel, by a Jerusalem publishing house: civil strife, siege, and war had delayed the publication.[1] In February 1948, a car-bomb exploded in front of the offices of the Jerusalem Press. The resulting fire consumed 'some of the manuscripts which the editors had left there a few hours earlier'.[2] Written in English, not Hebrew, it aimed for readership exceeding the local.[3] This was the first volume of the *Jewish Yearbook*. Its purpose, the editors explained, was to finally redress

> The need for a periodical publication which would be devoted mainly to the study of questions of international law affecting or of particular interest to the Jewish people [which] has long been felt by all those who realized the *sui generis* character of those questions.[4]

To anyone acquainted with the international legal aspects of the Jewish Question—or with the engagement of Jewish jurists with international law—the names of many contributors rang familiar. Some stood out in wider international law circles. Two full-length articles were written by a former teacher and his former student at the Law Faculty of the University of Vienna. Long before 1948, both had found new, distant homes. Each would be described as the greatest international lawyer of the twentieth century.[5] The teacher, Hans Kelsen, now at the University

[1] 'Most of the contributions to this volume', the editors reported, 'were ready for print at the beginning of 1948'; it was 'originally intended' that 'the *Yearbook* would have appeared towards the middle of' 1948: emphasis in the original; 'Introduction' (1948) 1 Jewish YB Intl L v, vi; Nathan Feinberg, *Reminiscences* (Keter 1985) 150–1 (Hebrew).

[2] 'Introduction' (n 1) vi.

[3] Feinberg and Stoyanovsky to Jewish Agency Executive, 18 October 1946, A/306/6, Central Zionist Archive ('CZA').

[4] Emphasis in original; 'Introduction' (n 1) v.

[5] Luís Duarte d'Almeida, John Gardner, and Leslie Green (eds), *Kelsen Revisited: New Essays on the Pure Theory of Law* (Hart 2013) 1 ('the twentieth century's foremost jurist and legal philosopher'); Philippe Sands, 'My Legal Hero: Hersch Lauterpacht' *The Guardian* (10 November 2010) http://www.

Jews, Sovereignty, and International Law. Rotem Giladi, Oxford University Press. © Rotem Giladi 2021.
DOI: 10.1093/oso/9780198857396.003.0001

of California, wrote on 'Collective and Individual Responsibility for Acts of State in International Law'. The student, Hersch Lauterpacht—the Cambridge Whewell Professor of International Law—authored 'The Nationality of Denationalized Persons'.[6]

Other essays dealt with issues whose Jewish aspect was more manifest—or more openly stated. They were written by persons who had earned PhDs from Vienna, Rome, and Paris; LLDs from London; and SJDs from Harvard. They were scholars, barristers, and leaders of Jewish legal advocacy—including two professors at the Hague Academy of International Law, as the table of contents presented those invited to deliver courses at the prestigious institution. Of the others, several would be so invited in later years.[7]

Nathan Feinberg, 'Associate Professor of International Law and Relations at the Hebrew University at Jerusalem'—one of the *Yearbook's* editors—discussed 'The Recognition of the Jewish People in International Law'.[8] Jacob Stoyanovsky, the other editor, had made a name as an expert on the mandate system. His contribution addressed 'Law and Policy Under the Palestine Mandate'.[9] Ernst Frankenstein, one of the Hague Academy Professors, explored 'The Meaning of the Term "National Home for the Jewish People"'.[10] Benjamin Akzin, who boasted three doctoral degrees and had served, in the late 1930s, as personal secretary to Vladimir Jabotinsky—leader of revisionist Zionism—commented on 'The United Nations and Palestine'.[11]

Others approached Jewish questions in broader normative contexts. Dr Jacob Robinson, 'Director, Institute of Jewish Affairs' ('IJA') in New York, marked the transition 'From Protection of Minorities to Promotion of Human Rights'.[12] His brother Nehemiah, the head of the Indemnification Office at the World Jewish Congress ('WJC'), discussed 'Reparation and Restitution in International Law as Affecting Jews'.[13] Norman Bentwich—a second-generation Zionist lawyer, former Attorney-General of mandatory Palestine, and, since 1932, the Weizmann Chair of

theguardian.com/law/2010/nov/10/my-legal-hero-hersch-lauterpacht ('stands out as the great international jurist of the 20th century') accessed 20 January 2020; Philippe Sands, *East West Street: On the Origins of Genocide and Crimes against Humanity* (Knopf 2016); Hans Kelsen, 'Tribute to Sir Hersch Lauterpacht' (1961) 10 ICLQ 1, 2–3.

[6] Hans Kelsen, 'Collective and Individual Responsibility for Acts of State in International Law' (1948) 1 Jewish YB Intl L 226; Hersch Lauterpacht, 'The Nationality of Denationalized Persons' (1948) 1 Jewish YB Intl L 164.

[7] 'Contents' (1948) 1 Jewish YB Intl L vii–viii.

[8] (1948) 1 Jewish YB Intl L 1.

[9] ibid, 42.

[10] ibid, 27.

[11] ibid, 87.

[12] ibid, 115.

[13] ibid, 186.

International Peace at the Hebrew University[14]—commented on the 'International Refugee Office of the United Nations'.[15] Anatole Goldstein, an IJA researcher, wrote on 'Crimes Against Humanity—Some Jewish Aspects'.[16]

Other contributors, mostly of lesser renown, added shorter 'Notes' on matters that tended towards the parochial. One dealt with '*Habeas Corpus* in Palestine';[17] another with 'Immigrant Ships before the Palestine Courts'.[18] A third discussed 'The Boycott of "Zionist Goods" by the Arab League'.[19] The penultimate note, penned by Sefton WD Rowson, dealt with 'The Abolition of Nazi and Fascist Anti-Jewish Legislation by British Military Administrations of the Second World War'.[20] Marc M Vishniak, the other Hague Academy Professor, wrote the last note on 'Post-War Legislation against Racial Hatred'.[21]

The contributors were all men. All were born Jewish.[22] Many were Zionist or at least harboured sympathy to the Jewish national revival project in Palestine.[23] All had law degrees. Many were versed in Jewish affairs, old hands of Jewish politics, advocacy, and diplomacy. None was now living in the country of his birth.

The *Jewish Yearbook* was a polyglot affair. Correspondence was conducted in Hebrew, *Yiddish*, English, German, French, Russian, and Polish. It was, equally, a cosmopolitan affair, even if that correspondence passed over sites now erased from the map of Jewish demography: Berlin, Vienna, Warsaw, Lvov. The collective work of the contributors was a testimony to Jewish intellectual achievement, their biographies a monument to Jewish persecution, displacement, and annihilation. Together, their essays and itineraries sketched an inventory of international law's engagement with the Jewish Question—and of the Jewish engagement with international law—since the nineteenth century.

[14] Norman Bentwich, *My 77 Years: An Account of my Life and Times 1883–1960* (Jewish Publication Society of America 1962) 97–8. Chaim Weizmann, the elderly Zionist leader, was appointed Israel's first President in February 1949.

[15] (1948) 1 Jewish YB Intl L 152.

[16] ibid, 206.

[17] Edward David Goitein, '*Habeas Corpus* in Palestine' (1948) 1 Jewish YB Intl L 240.

[18] Arnold M Apelbom, 'Immigrant Ships before the Palestine Courts' (1948) 1 Jewish YB Intl L 247.

[19] Edoardo Vitta, 'The Boycott of "Zionist Goods" by the Arab League' (1948) 1 Jewish YB Intl L 253.

[20] (1948) 1 Jewish YB Intl L 261.

[21] ibid, 268.

[22] Kelsen converted to Catholicism in 1905, and became a Lutheran in 1912, but reportedly retained or regained a Jewish identity: Reut Yael Paz, *A Gateway between a Distant God and a Cruel World: The Contribution of Jewish German-Speaking Scholars to International Law* (Brill 2012) 116; Feinberg, *Reminiscences* (n 1) 91 (Kelsen regretting assimilation in 1932); Nathan Feinberg, 'The Judaism of Hans Kelsen' in Nathan Feinberg, *Essays on Jewish Issues of Our Times* (Dvir 1980) (Hebrew) 235, 236 ('very sympathetic to Jewish people's revival movement and supported renewal of its political life in its homeland'); cf Eliav Lieblich, 'Assimilation Through Law: Hans Kelsen and the Jewish Experience' in James Loeffler and Moria Paz (eds), *The Law of Strangers: Jewish Lawyers and International Law in the Twentieth Century* (CUP 2019) 51.

[23] Chs 2–3 discuss Lauterpacht's Zionism; Eliav Leiblich and Yoram Shachar, 'Cosmopolitanism at a Crossroads: Hersch Lauterpacht and the Israeli Declaration of Independence' (2014) 84 Brit YB Intl L 1; James Loeffler, 'The "Natural Right of the Jewish People": Zionism, International Law, and the Paradox of Hersch Zvi Lauterpacht' in Loeffler and Paz (n 22) 23.

Taking stock was a deliberate choice. The editors elected to characterize the volume as:

> [A]n attempt ... to *sum up* the unique position of the Jewish people in a series of articles, notes and documents, some of which deal with various questions arising out of the Palestine Mandate, while others relate to more general questions which present certain specifically Jewish aspects or in which the Jewish people as a whole has a particular interest.[24]

The 'plan of this volume has been conceived', they confided, 'with an eye to the past rather than to the future'. The issues addressed by the various contributors sought to capture, or 'sum up', the past.[25] One reviewer was blunt: the establishment of the State of Israel, wrote Francis A Mann, another Jewish jurist-refugee, 'resulted in depriving many of the articles included in this volume of their topical character so that they have now an historical interest only'.[26] Change had come.

Publishing a *Jewish* yearbook of international law, however, was a sign of time present.[27] The past portrayed by the editors' *Introduction* was one that clearly culminated in the present. Documents of import, reproduced at the end of the volume, included, first, the 1947 Partition Resolution of the United Nations ('UN') General Assembly;[28] it was followed by the texts (and annexes) of the Assembly Resolutions adopting the Universal Declaration of Human Rights and the Genocide Convention of 10 and 9 December 1948, respectively.[29] Another document the editors deemed too significant for an annex. They placed Israel's Declaration of Independence immediately after their introduction of the volume, at the end of a four-page essay they authored.[30]

The volume sought to set past and present apart. The *Introduction* explicitly marked the transition of the Jewish people. In the past, the editors observed, 'they were merely the *object*, never the subject, of international law'. They were, the editors emphasized, the '*object* of discriminatory legislative and administrative measures which went beyond the bounds of domestic jurisdiction'. They were, the

[24] Emphasis added; 'Introduction' (n 1) v.
[25] ibid.
[26] Francis A Mann, 'Book Review' (1950) 3 ICLQ 608, 609. Lawrence Collins, 'F. A. Mann (1907–1991)' in Jack Beatson and Reinhard Zimmermann (eds), *Jurists Uprooted: German-Speaking Emigré Lawyers in Twentieth Century Britain* (OUP 2004).
[27] '[S]uch a book, the first of its kind in the State of Israel, with the participation of the greatest of scientists of the world ... has also a great propaganda [value] to the Hebrew University—at a time when the country was absorbed by life-or-death war the men of science ... including the ... editor, did not stop dealing with matters of the highest import to the scientific world': Rubin Mass Publishing to Hebrew University Management, 14 June 1949, Feinberg-Personal File 1945–55 vol 2, Hebrew University Archive ('HUA').
[28] 1 Jewish YB Intl L 273.
[29] ibid, 293, 300.
[30] 'Israel's Declaration of Independence' (1948) 1 Jewish YB Intl L xi.

editors recalled, no more than 'the *object* of international conferences, of diplomatic notes, of humanitarian interventions, and more recently, of judicial cognizance by the International Military Tribunal at Nuremberg'. They were an '*object* of the international system of the protection of minorities and of the internationally secured national home in Palestine'. The essence of the Jewish past could thus be captured by a simple international law distinction that was, nonetheless, pregnant with significance: 'At all the times they were merely the *object*, never the *subject*, of international law.'[31]

The present, however, brought a radical transformation.[32] All that was in the past: the Jewish people could not 'have been anything else *before*', the editors reported, 'the establishment of the State of Israel'.[33] The volume may have dealt with the past, but it was conceived and prepared out of an acute, pervasive sense of the present that sought to note, mark, and seal off the past. In a sense, the first volume of the *Jewish Yearbook* aimed to render obsolete Jewish objecthood, the very object of its inquiry.

The present was paramount. The editors' essay on Israel's Declaration of Independence spoke of 'the centuries of world wide dispersion', of past 'moral and physical oppression ... repeated persecutions and pogroms' culminating 'in the Nazi atrocities which resulted in the massacre of six millions' Jews.[34] But much of what they wrote pertained to the circumstances of Israel's birth, stressed its legal foundation in 'positive international law', and decried the UN's failure 'to prevent that war or even to name the aggressor'.[35] Discussing, last, Israel's impending UN admission, the editors recorded the formalities of transition. Quoting the opening paragraph of the 1776 United States Declaration of Independence, deliberately referenced by Israel's own constituent document,[36] the editors proceeded to proclaim:

> On joining the family of nations the Jewish State will have assumed 'among the powers of the earth the separate and equal station' of which the Jewish people was deprived for centuries.
>
> In law and in fact Israel has come to stay.[37]

[31] Emphases added; 'Introduction' (n 1) v. Feinberg's contribution (n 8) systematically delved into these themes.

[32] Uri Yadin, 'The Jewish Question in the Eyes of International Law' (1949) 7 BeTerem: A Quarterly for Policy, Social Affairs and Critique 63 (Hebrew) ('no rung in a ladder, no "another step forward", but a total, fundamental revolution ... From people-no people, an entirely exceptional creature, we have turned into a nation like all others').

[33] Emphasis added; 'Introduction' (n 1) v.

[34] 'Israel's Declaration' (n 30) xi.

[35] ibid, x.

[36] '[T]he necessity of solving the problem of the homelessness and lack of independence of the Jewish people by re-establishing the Jewish State which ... would endow the Jewish people with equality of status within the family of nations': 'Israel's Declaration' (n 30) xiii. See Yoram Shachar, 'Jefferson goes East: the American Origins of the Israeli Declaration of Independence' (2009) 10 Theoretical Inquiries in Law 589.

[37] 'Israel's Declaration' (n 30) x.

Still subscribing, evidently, to a view of international law that withheld sovereign capacity from those who had no knowledge of its rules,[38] the very publication of the *Jewish Yearbook* signified a sovereign claim.[39] With its appearance, the non-sovereign Jewish past was put to rest.

Yet the 1948 volume of the *Yearbook* also contained signs of things to come. In the *Introduction*, the editors refused to prophesize any future 'different approach' to international law, 'the exact implications of which the editors cannot now foresee and in respect of which they cannot now commit themselves'.[40] 'Time alone', yet unknown to them, would 'determine the nature and scope of the future volumes of the *Yearbook* or of any other international law periodical which may be published in Israel'.[41] They would not predict the nature of future Jewish engagement with international law. Yet for all their circumspection, they had no doubt that the present and future, not the past, were to be the real focus of attention henceforth. 'In the meantime', they wrote, we 'trust that some useful purpose will have been served by the publication of the present volume'[42] dedicated, after all, to the past. For all its potential usefulness, this volume was to be a record of a past now dead.

There were other signs of the future, many yet unknown to the editors. Stoyanovsky would dedicate himself to private practice. Feinberg would soon be appointed the first Dean of the Law Faculty of the Hebrew University.[43] Akzin would follow him in that position, for three different terms.[44] The author of one note, Edward David Goitein, would soon become Israel's first envoy to South Africa. Appointed to Israel's Supreme Court in 1953, he would later serve as an *ad hoc* judge in Israel's claim against Bulgaria at the International Court of Justice.[45] Arnold Apelbom, the author of another note, would be the first executive editor of the *Israel Law Review*, founded by the Hebrew University Law Faculty in 1966.[46] While his academic pursuits were secondary, he also left strong impressions on students of international law and English law as 'Visiting teacher at the Hebrew University, Tel Aviv branch' (later, the Tel Aviv University).[47]

[38] Martti Koskenniemi, *The Gentle Civilizer of Nations: The Rise and Fall of International Law 1870–1960* (CUP 2001).

[39] Captured by Yadin (n 32) 63 ('from the object of problems we have turned into a contributing member to that noble creation called international law').

[40] 'Introduction' (n 1) v.

[41] ibid.

[42] ibid.

[43] Assaf Likhovski, 'Law Studies at the Hebrew University during the British Mandate Period' in Hagit Lavsky (ed), *The History of the Hebrew University of Jerusalem: A Period of Consolidation and Growth* (Magnes 2005) 543 (Hebrew); Rotem Giladi, 'At the Sovereign Turn: International Law at the Hebrew University Law Faculty Early Years' in Yfaat Weiss and Uzi Rebhun (eds), *The History of the Hebrew University in Jerusalem*, vol 5 (forthcoming Magnes 2021) (Hebrew).

[44] Later, he founded the Hebrew University's Political Science Department and became Haifa University's first rector.

[45] Case Concerning the Aerial Incident of 27 July 1955 *(Israel v Bulgaria)* (Preliminary Objections, Judgment) [1959] ICJ Rep 127; Dissenting Opinion of Judge Goitein 195.

[46] (1966) 1 Isr L Rev; Kelsen, Bentwich, and Apelbom wrote for the first volume.

[47] Aviezer Chelouche, *Who Was That Apfelbaum* (Rahel Publishing 1999) 326–39 (Hebrew); Editorial Board, 'Arnold M. Apelbom—In Memoriam' (1969) 4 Isr L Rev 173; email from Prof Yoram

Some of the contributors fast became members of Israel's academic, judicial, and diplomatic elite.

For two of the contributors, the path for the future was already largely determined by the time the *Yearbook* was published. Lithuania-born Jacob Robinson (1889–1977) was a veteran of Jewish politics and international law advocacy.[48] Years later, Hannah Arendt would mock his credentials as an 'eminent authority on international law' in the polemic that followed the trial of Adolf Eichmann. She was likely correct in questioning Robinson's eminence; but this largely forgotten jurist was, without a doubt, an international law authority.[49] In 1947, his expertise and experience proved indispensable for the cause of the Jewish state. Though presented in the *Yearbook* as the Director of the New York-based IJA, that year he was loaned to the Jewish Agency's UN mission, joining a small band of would-be diplomats—otherwise bereft of any experience in multilateral diplomacy or international institutions—campaigning for the establishment of a Jewish state.[50] Following Israel's independence, at age 59, he was appointed legal adviser to Israel's UN mission. He would remain in that post until his retirement, in 1957. In the years it took to birth the *Yearbook* he had served, effectively, as a one-man editorial board.

Another contributor who, by 1949, was set in his future career path was the author of the penultimate note. Probably the youngest of the authors, in 1949 he could boast rather modest credentials. 'S.W.D. Rowson LL.B.', as he was introduced in the *Yearbook*, was born in London three weeks before the Balfour Declaration proclaiming His Majesty's sympathy to the Jewish 'National Home' policy in Palestine. At the end of 1947 he immigrated to Palestine to work for the Jewish Agency. Following independence, he was appointed the first legal adviser to Israel's Ministry of Foreign Affairs ('MFA'), a post he held until 1967. Under a new name, he would gain renown, in years to come, as an international law scholar and an expert on, among other matters, the International Court of Justice: Sefton Wilfred David Rowson became Shabtai Rosenne (1917–2010).[51] Together, Robinson and Rosenne would play a central role in conceiving, debating, shaping, and putting into effect the new state's outlook on and practice of international law in the decade that would follow and beyond. They were the main protagonists of the future that the editors would not foresee.

Sachar to author (29 June 2014); Uri Kesari, 'The Kfar Shmaryahu Gentleman' *Ha'aretz* (11 April 1969) (Hebrew).

[48] Ch 5 delves into Robinson's background.

[49] cf Hanna Arendt, 'The Formidable Dr. Robinson: A Reply' *New York Review of Books* (20 January 1966).

[50] Shabtai Rosenne, 'Jacob Robinson—In Memoriam' (1978) 8 Isr L Rev 287; Moshe Sharett, *At the Threshold of Statehood: 1946–1949* (Am Oved 1958) (Hebrew).

[51] Ch 1 provides more background on Rosenne; Rotem Giladi, 'Shabtai Rosenne: The Transformation of Sefton Rowson' in Loeffler and Paz (n 22) 221.

One portent of things to come could be read in the fate of the *Jewish Yearbook* itself. The editors' optimism with regard to 'future volumes' proved unwarranted. There were, even prior to publication, words of encouragement. Reception was, on the whole, favourable:[52] 'the appearance of The Jewish Yearbook of International Law', reported a member of the *Yale Law Journal* editorial board, was 'an important service' to the 'advancement of legal scholarship', and a 'significant event'.[53] If reviewers noted that some of the materials were not original, or that legislative and institutional developments at the UN rendered some of the contributions a tad outdated, they did not hold it against the editors.[54] One regretted that Lauterpacht's contribution was included in 'a publication to which the general reader will not have ready access'.[55] Another, however, considered the *Yearbook* 'evidence that Israel can now cast its lot with formalized law'; that its 'outlook is international'; and that its '[e]mphasis on international law' demonstrated 'the solicitude for international law typical of the infant State'.[56] In Israel, the volume's value for lawyers and diplomats, as well as 'wider audiences, Jewish and non-Jewish alike, in and outside the country' was noted.[57] A year after the *Yearbook* was published, Rosenne wrote to Moshe Sharett, Israel's first Minister of Foreign Affairs, that the *Yearbook* 'acquired reputation in the greater legal world and undoubtedly raised the prestige of Jewish Science in this area'.[58]

'A few days' after *Yearbook* was published, Rosenne sought to secure MFA support for the project, on the assumption that it would continue.[59] Feinberg and Stoyanovsky, however, refused to commit themselves.[60] Neither was enthused, apparently, by their collaboration; there were hints of disagreements over the role of an editor.[61] They were exhausted with deferrals, rejections, and other aggravations of editorial life. Feinberg's attention, besides, was turning to more pressing projects.[62]

[52] 'Enthusiastic', in Feinberg, *Reminiscences* (n 1) 151; encouragements or congratulatory letters received from international law luminaries including eg Manley O Hudson, Hersch Lauterpacht, Georges Scelle, Georg Schwarzenberger, Maurice Bourquin, Arthur Goodhart, Arnold McNair, JHW Verzijl, William Rappard; Feinberg and Stoyanovsky, Jewish Yearbook of International Law, December 1946, A/306/6, CZA. Stoyanovsky, however, was dismayed that the *Yearbook* 'was received with seeming aloofness and did not evoke the response hoped for': Stoyanovsky to Rosenne, 29 October 1951, FM-1816/1, Israel State Archive ('ISA').

[53] Arthur M Michaelson, 'Book Review' (1950) 59 Yale LJ 389.

[54] Mann (n 26) 609–10; Lawrence Preuss, 'Book Review' (1951) 45 AJIL 619 ('Forthcoming issues ... will undoubtedly have a more general content; the present volume has exceptional value in collecting a wide range of material upon some of the most interesting legal problems of our time').

[55] Mann (n 26) 609.

[56] Michaelson (n 53) 389, 391. Arthur Goodhart, 'International Law' *Jewish Chronicle* (25 November 1949) 12–13.

[57] Yadin (n 32) 63, who 'later served as chief codifier of the law of Israel': Leiblich and Shachar (n 23) 10.

[58] Rosenne to Sharett, 14 June 1950, FM-1816/1, ISA.

[59] Rosenne to Sharett, 27 April 1949, FM-1816/1, ISA.

[60] Feinberg, *Reminiscences* (n 1) 151–2; Stoyanovsky to Rosenne, 29 October 1951 (n 52).

[61] Feinberg, *Reminiscences* (n 1) 150, who nonetheless admired Stoyanovsky's skills: see also Nathan Feinberg, 'In Memoriam—Dr. Jacob Stoyanovsky' in *Essays on Jewish Issues of Our Times* (Dvir 1980) 239, 240 (Hebrew).

[62] Rosenne to Robinson, 10 December 1950, FM-1816/1, ISA.

'[O]ne thing was clear', Robinson confirmed: 'Feinberg-Stoyanovsky ... are not going to continue'.[63] He counselled that 'there is only one more factor which can take over—the Foreign Office'.[64]

Rosenne moved to do precisely that. Having first consulted Lauterpacht—the editor of the *British Yearbook of International Law*—he proceeded to report the latter's concerns with the *Yearbook's* discontinuation to Sharett. He proposed a government takeover, with himself installed as general editor.[65] Sharett was accommodating.[66] Plans were drawn and revised, prospective contributors identified and approached. Dilemmas about language,[67] authorship, readership, 'scientific objectivity', and scope were debated and rehashed. Difficulties emerged: resources were limited; paper was scarce; prospective contributors declined or evaded Rosenne's overtures.[68] He became 'despaired with the university people', their divisions and intrigues, and their resistance to government involvement: the cooperation of the original editors was not forthcoming. Mutual recriminations followed.[69] 'I see that the entirety of our beautiful plan goes down the drain', Rosenne lamented to Robinson;[70] he admitted to Stoyanovsky: 'the efforts we have exerted ... came to naught'.[71] By the end of 1951, Rosenne became resigned.[72] The *Yearbook* faltered, stalled, and was abandoned. Rosenne would, every now and then, attempt to revive it, without success.[73]

Two matters, nonetheless, were clear all along. If it were to continue, the *Jewish Yearbook* would have to be renamed. Rosenne proposed to Feinberg 'to change the name of the book to "Israeli Yearbook"' of international law.[74] Implicit in the change of name was a change of outlook. Echoing the editors' own sense that Jewish perspectives on international law were now bound to change, Sharett's scribbled response to Rosenne was that 'the change of name should be reflected in the transformation of the content's center of gravity'.[75] Robinson, while taking the position that the *Israeli* yearbook should serve 'Israel and Diaspora Jewry' both, considered

63 Robinson to Rosenne, 31 May 1950, FM-1816/1, ISA.

64 ibid.

65 Rosenne to Sharett, 14 June 1950 (n 58); Rosenne, Israel Yearbook of International Law: Plan, 6 August 1950, FM-1816/1, ISA.

66 Eytan to Sharett, 15 June 1950, FM-1816/1, ISA with Sharett's handwritten notes.

67 The exclusion of Hebrew brought censure from the leadership of the 'national institutions': Feinberg, *Reminiscences* (n 1) 150.

68 Rosenne to Robinson, 28 February 1951, FM-1816/1, ISA.

69 Rosenne to Robinson, 22 November 1950; Rosenne to Robinson, 20 March 1957, FM-1816/1, ISA ('the thing will have to be dropped again until the Hebrew University has a professor of international law who is capable of some constructive work').

70 Rosenne to Robinson, 9 October 1951, FM-1816/1, ISA.

71 Rosenne to Stoyanovsky, 11 October 1951, FM-1816/1, ISA.

72 Rosenne to Robinson, 22 November 1951, FM-1816/1, ISA.

73 1957 saw his last recorded attempt: Rosenne to Feinberg, 22 February 1957, FM-1816/1, ISA.

74 Rosenne to Sharett, 27 April 1949 (n 59); Rosenne to Sharett, 14 June 1950 (n 58); Rosenne, 'Plan', 6 August 1950 (n 65). This change was also proposed by Yadin (n 32) 64.

75 Rosenne to Sharett, 27 April 1949 (n 59) with Sharett's handwritten notes, 28 April 1949, 1 May 1949, FM-1816/1, ISA.

nonetheless that 'matters of particular interest to Jewry as such', which could fall within the *Yearbook's* purview, were 'mostly of marginal nature'.[76] The task of the *Israeli* yearbook of international law, Rosenne wrote, would be to 'emphasize for future generations [the part of] Israeli science in this area among all those who deal with international law'.[77]

At the end of things, there was no demand for a *Jewish* yearbook of international law in the Jewish state. Revival of Jewish sovereignty spelled a departure from the past. In the state of Israel, as the editors implied, breaking away from *Jewish* engagement with international law was imperative. After 1948, the justification for a *Jewish Yearbook of International Law* contained the seed of its own negation. It was an epilogue, not a prologue, required to pave the way for a different future yet unseen. '[I]nasmuch as it is dedicated to the study of the Jewish Question', declared the director of legislation of Israel's Ministry of Justice, the *Yearbook* was 'no beginning but an end'.[78] Feinberg would later write chapters of the history of the Jewish engagement with international law;[79] Rosenne and Robinson would now tread a different path. The first volume of the *Jewish Yearbook of International Law* would also be its last.

[76] Robinson to Rosenne, 31 May 1950 (n 63); Yadin (n 32) 63: ('to our joy, the need for periodical publications to clarify the Jewish Question from the perspective of international law has now lapsed').

[77] Rosenne to Sharett, 27 April 1949 (n 59).

[78] Yadin (n 32) 64.

[79] Giladi, 'Sovereign Turn' (n 43) appraises Feinberg's *œuvre*.

Introduction

A Radical Transformation?

International Law and the Sovereign Turn in Jewish History

1. Continuity and Change: From Jewish to Israeli Engagement with International Law

This book explores the future that the editors of the *Jewish Yearbook of International Law* would not, in the spring of 1949, prophesize.[1] The question is *not* how international law approached the 'Jewish Question' at the age of Jewish legal-political sovereignty. Rather, it is how the Jewish state now approached international law. After all, the editors' sense of time revealed an acute awareness that the transformation in the political and legal status of the Jewish people, affected by the establishment of the state of Israel in May 1948, would likely produce changes in the terms of Jewish engagement with international law.[2] The book charts, then, the *sovereign turn* in Jewish history—from 'object' to 'subject' of international law, in the words of the *Yearbook*'s editors[3]—and its effect on Israel's attitude towards international law; it seeks to recover, that is, the *terms* of the Jewish state's early engagement with international law.

This is, then, a question of continuity and change. In the past few decades, Jewish pre-sovereign engagements with international law and diplomacy have attracted the attention of scholars of international legal and Jewish history alike.[4] Works in this vein, however, tend to come to a halt in 1948 so that any *longue durée* perspective on Jewish international law engagement and legal diplomacy recedes to the non-sovereign background: Jewish engagement with international law has so far been imagined largely as the experience of the stateless; the terms of the international law engagement of the sovereign Jewish state has hitherto received only scant attention. Still, existing inquiries into the twentieth century lives and work of Jewish international law scholars—or of Jewish institutions with significant international law investment—point to pertinent questions: was the Jewish state's attitude to international law rooted in pre-sovereign Jewish

[1] 'Introduction' (1948) 1 Jewish YB Intl L v, discussed in the Prologue.
[2] ibid.
[3] ibid.
[4] These works are cited throughout the book.

Jews, Sovereignty, and International Law. Rotem Giladi, Oxford University Press. © Rotem Giladi 2021.
DOI: 10.1093/oso/9780198857396.003.0002

sensibilities—cosmopolitan[5] or otherwise—and experience? Or was it driven by an entirely novel, and particularistic—sovereign perspective determined principally by geopolitical circumstance and the exigencies of the Middle East conflict?

In this book, I make the case that the Jewish state approached international law with *ambivalence*. Though there were instances where Israel acknowledged its interest in the strength, goals, and promotion of post-war international law, its attitude towards international law for the most part ranged from indifference to hostility. I argue, further, that this ambivalent attitude stemmed directly from pre-sovereign sensibilities and experience that were only exacerbated by a newly acquired sovereign perspective. That is, Israel's ambivalence towards international law demonstrates *both* continuity and change: it expressed sovereign sensibilities—but these preceded the sovereign turn and were rooted in the terms of pre-state Jewish engagements with international law preceding Israel's establishment. The acquisition of sovereign status, at the same time, heightened these sensibilities and, often, brought them to the fore and made them explicit. Furthermore, I also argue that these sensibilities—and Israel's resulting ambivalence towards international law—were rooted in *identity*, *ideology*, and *political experience*: that is, in Israel's Jewish identity—and in the ideology and political experience of the Jewish national movement that sought to establish a Jewish state in Palestine: Zionism.

2. Arenas, Institutions, Protagonists

This is the argument in a nutshell. Its amplification requires the elaboration of meaning, context, and the choices made in the design of this study of Israel's attitude towards international law: this is the task of this introduction. It also requires an examination of pre-sovereign Zionist and other Jewish engagements with international law; that is the task, largely, of chapter 1.

Thus, when referring to that international law *attitude*, I am referring first and foremost to the opinions, positions, and policies of Israel's Ministry of Foreign Affairs ('MFA'). The *arena* examined in this book is the foreign policy arena; the book, in that sense, narrates diplomatic history as much as it does a history of international law—or, indeed, Jewish history. Other branches of government and other departments of the executive make occasional appearances in the episodes examined here; still, Israel's MFA remains the main object of analysis. Accordingly, much of the evidence I cite on Israel's attitude towards international law comes from MFA files deposited in Israel's State Archive in Jerusalem ('ISA').

Within the MFA, the principal *protagonists* whose actions, positions, and thoughts serve to gauge Israel's attitude to concrete international law regimes

[5] James Loeffler, *Rooted Cosmopolitans: Jews and Human Rights in the Twentieth Century* (Yale UP 2018).

are two legal advisers. Both, fittingly, had contributed to the *Jewish Yearbook of International Law*. The older, Jacob Robinson (1889–1977), was loaned to the Jewish Agency's ('JA') mission to the United Nations ('UN') in 1947. After Israel's establishment, he left the New York Institute of Jewish Affairs ('IJA') for good to now serve as legal adviser to Israel's UN mission. The younger was Shabtai Rosenne (1917–2010), formerly known as Sefton Rowson. Twenty-eight years Robinson's junior, he had worked for the JA's London office since the spring of 1946. At the end of 1947, he immigrated to Mandatory Palestine to work in the JA's Political Department under Moshe Shertok. In the summer of 1948, now Israel's first Foreign Minister, Shertok appointed Rosenne to serve as the MFA's first legal adviser.[6] Robinson would remain in his post until his 1957 retirement; Rosenne would hold his position until 1967, but remain in Ministry service for some years after. Israel's early attitude towards international law was, to a remarkable degree, the product of these two jurist-diplomats. Their outlook had a cardinal effect on how MFA and, in turn, Israel would approach international law in the external as well as the domestic arena. Israel's early ambivalence to international law can most patently be discerned in their actions—and in the voluminous correspondence exchanged between the two.

Other, more or less familiar names make occasional appearances in the tale about to unfold. They include MFA colleagues, such as Israel's first Foreign Minister, who soon would change his name to Sharett; Abba (Aubrey) Eban, who headed Israel's UN mission at the period examined here; Walter Eytan (Ettinghausen), the MFA's Director-General; and Ezekiel Gordon, a former—and future—official at the UN Secretariat who had served, for a brief but important period, as director of the MFA's International Organizations Division ('IOD'). Haim (Herman) Cohn and Pinchas (Felix) Rosen (Rosenblüth)—Israel's Attorney-General and Justice Minister, respectively—also play a role in the episodes recounted here. Outside government circles, the *dramatis personae* include scholars and practitioners of international law. Of these, several had been involved in the *Jewish Yearbook* project: they include, among others, Hersch Lauterpacht of Cambridge University; Nathan Feinberg, one of the *Yearbook*'s editors and, soon after its publication, the founding dean of the Hebrew University Law Faculty;[7] Norman Bentwich, who

[6] Very little information on Rosenne's appointment can be found in the relevant files. By January 1948 his name was already coming up as a good candidate 'for the Legal Division' of the future foreign office; it was also 'tentatively' agreed that Robinson would head the UN Division 'if he'll come to Palestine': Eytan to Sharett, 19 January 1948, FM-126/9, ISA. Robinson did not come to Palestine; Rosenne's appointment was publicly announced in late July: 'Foreign Ministry Structure Complete' *HaMashkif* (21 July 1948) (Hebrew). The 'In Memoria' section of the MFA's website reports he was hired on 16 May 1948, two days after Israel's establishment: https://mfa.gov.il/memorial/Perpetuated/Pages/Shabtai-Rosenne.aspx accessed 30 July 2020 (Hebrew).

[7] On Feinberg, see Rotem Giladi, 'At the Sovereign Turn: International Law at the Hebrew University Law Faculty Early Years' in Yfaat Weiss and Uzi Rebhun (eds), *The History of the Hebrew University in Jerusalem*, vol 5 (forthcoming Magnes 2021) (Hebrew). Feinberg's international law engagement is the subject of a research project I am currently working on.

had held the Weizmann Chair of International Peace at the Hebrew University since 1932; as well as Raphael Lemkin, 'father and midwife'[8] of the Genocide Convention, conspicuously absent from the list of *Yearbook* contributors.[9] Past and present officers of Jewish non-governmental organizations, such as Paul Weis, now at the Office of the UN High Commissioner for Refugees ('UNHCR'), or Maurice Perlzweig of the World Jewish Congress ('WJC'), also took some part in the drama. All these and others had a role to play: superiors and subordinates, colleagues and collaborators, interlocutors and fellow-travellers, and, sometimes, rivals and antagonists. Whatever role they had played, it was secondary to that of Robinson and Rosenne; they come into the limelight only to help identify and measure our two main protagonists' attitude, and ambivalence, towards international law.

3. Framing Time: The Sovereign Turn

This book does not set out to identify any *longue durée* perspective on Israel's international law engagement. Rather, I seek to recover Israel's attitude towards international law in the first few years of independence. The foregoing chapters demonstrate amply that it was in those few first years that the sovereign sensibilities of the Jewish state—more on these to come—were *openly* reflected on and elaborated by the makers of its legal foreign policy, Robinson and Rosenne in particular. In later years, these sensibilities would become submerged by diplomatic habit, established vernaculars, and entrenched policies. Change and continuity would become harder to discern. Supervening circumstances—in Israel's global orientation between East and West, in its circumstances in the Middle East, in its relationship with world Jewry, and in its domestic arena—would also play a role in blurring cause and effect, reason and habit, *weltanschauung* and circumstance. That limited scope of inquiry into change and continuity—roughly, the period between 1949 and 1954—is not meant to consecrate any 'original' moment as such but rather to take a snapshot at a time when evidence of continuity and change was still conspicuous. How to relate any findings of ambivalence to the present—indeed, why relate my findings to the present at all—is a dilemma I turn to only in the concluding pages of the book.

Still, the recovery of early or even 'original' attitudes may well have some merit. Commentators on Israeli politics, society, and history often speak of the first, formative decade of Israel's existence for a reason.[10] There are good reasons to consider, in the same vein, the years leading up to the 1956 Suez Crisis as the formative

[8] William Korey, *An Epitaph for Raphael Lemkin* (American Jewish Committee 2001) iii.

[9] Ch 5 discusses Lemkin's absence.

[10] Zvi Zameret and Hanna Yablonka (eds), *The First Decade, 1948–1958* (Yad Ben-Zvi 1997) (Hebrew).

period of Israel's foreign policy.[11] There are, likewise, good reasons to study the formation of Israel's legal system and institutions in the 'first decade'.[12] Moreover, the post-war reform of international law itself points to numerous episodes of law-making and normative contestation where states' attitudes—including that of the Jewish state—towards multiple international law projects and developments can be easily discerned. When Israel appeared on the world stage, many items on the UN agenda still involved the making of a new legal world order. Not a few of these were considered by those involved to be responses to the interwar Jewish crisis and the ensuing Holocaust and were, for that very reason, the subject of Jewish advocacy efforts. Such 'Jewish' agenda items furnish ample opportunities to gauge and reflect on Israel's attitude towards international law and, so, to consider (dis)continuities in the terms of the Jewish engagement with international law. That these and other agenda items and legal reforms could be, and at times were, invoked in connection to the bitter conflict over Palestine provides additional vantage points on Israel's international legal outlook.

In this book I explore, then, Israel's *early* attitude towards international law. My point of departure is not, however, Israel's establishment on 14 May 1948 but a year later. On 11 May 1949, Israel's second bid for UN admission was successful.[13] To Moshe Sharett, Israel's Foreign Minister, that event marked the completion of a transformation in the legal status of the Jewish people—and, necessarily, a new phase in Jewish political history. Israel's admission to 'world councils',[14] he told the General Assembly ('GA') after the vote was conducted and result announced, 'was *the consummation of a people's transition* ... from exclusion to membership in the family of nations'.[15] It was, in other words, the final scene in the sovereign turn in Jewish history. Sharett's maiden speech—the first delivered as a representative of a member state—captures in highly concise form the terms of that turn and its significance. It also encapsulates, in brief code, many of the ideological readings that drove Israel's ambivalence towards international law. In the chapters that follow, I revisit Sharett's speech time and again to decipher the sovereign sensibilities of our two protagonists and identify the source of their ambivalence towards international law. For now, however, I only cite that speech to demarcate this book's

[11] Uri Bialer, 'Top Hat, Tuxedo and Cannons: Israeli Foreign Policy from 1948 to 1956 as a Field of Study' (2002) 7 Israel Stud 1.

[12] Pnina Lahav, 'The Formative Years of Israel's Supreme Court 1948–1955' (1989) 14 Iyunei Mishpat 479 (Hebrew); Ron Harris, 'Israeli Law' in Zameret and Yablonka (n 10) 244; cf Yoram Shachar, 'History and Sources of Israeli Law' in Amos Shapira and Keren C DeWitt-Arar (eds), *Introduction to the Law of Israel* (Kluwer 1995) 4. For a reassessment of legal continuity and change after 1948 see Assaf Likhovski, 'Between "Mandate" and "State": Re-Thinking the Periodization of Israeli Legal History' (1998) 18 J of Israeli Hist 39.

[13] UNGA Res.273(III) (11 May 1949).

[14] Speech to the General Assembly by Foreign Minister Sharett, 11 May 1949 in Meron Medzini (ed), *Israel's Foreign Relations: Selected Documents, 1947–1974* (MFA 1976) 119; GAOR, Plenary (11 May 1949) 332.

[15] Emphasis added; GAOR, Plenary (11 May 1949) 332.

point of departure: the onset of a sovereign foreign policy and international law outlook.

Nonetheless, where relevant, I examine earlier evidence on Israel's attitude (or, at times, that of the JA) towards the three post-war international law projects this book examines; more on these case studies below. One recurring theme emerges from that evidence: prior to Israel's UN admission, its foreign policy leaders and budding diplomatic service had little resources to expend on and little interest in matters on the UN agenda that did not directly concern partition, conflict, independence, and admission. What, if any, shift had followed Israel's UN admission remains the object of my inquiry.

The period studied here ends, roughly, in 1954, at a time when the relevant aspects of the three legal projects serving as my case studies no longer commanded much of Rosenne and Robinson's attention. Where pertinent, however, I also note subsequent evidence that helps illuminate their perspectives. I invite the reader who remains unconvinced that five years form an appropriate sample size to consider this question again at the book's conclusion: the intensity of these formative years and the resulting volume of legal and diplomatic practice should, I believe, allay any lingering doubts.

Crucially, the book also turns, frequently, to the non-sovereign past; that is, to the years preceding 1948. Assessing Israel's early international law engagement requires, necessarily, canvassing Jewish engagements predating its establishment and UN admission. To that end, chapter 1 provides a brief primer on the place of international law in what may loosely be termed Jewish political thought and diplomatic praxis since the late nineteenth century. Each of the three case studies, however, also delves into concrete sites of Jewish pre-sovereign international law engagement in order to trace the sensibilities of our protagonists and highlight issues of continuity and change. These case studies concern the question, in the early work on the Human Rights Covenant, of the right of petition to international organizations; the 1948 Genocide Convention;[16] and the 1951 Refugee Convention.[17] One common denominator of these three projects is that each touched—in ways to be discussed—on Jewish questions that long preceded Israel's establishment. For that very reason, each had attracted some pre-sovereign Jewish international law engagement. Jewish scholars, practitioners, and organizations reflected on and invoked the right to petition the League of Nations long before the 1948 Universal Declaration on Human Rights or the early UN attempts to draft a Human Rights Covenant;[18] the model of protection on which the 1948 Genocide Convention was predicated drew on Jewish political thought and experience in the

[16] Convention on the Prevention and Punishment of the Crime of Genocide (9 December 1948) 78 UNTS 277.

[17] Convention Relating to the Status of Refugees (28 July 1951) 189 UNTS 137.

[18] Chs 2–3 discuss the right of petition.

decades before Raphael Lemkin had coined the term;[19] and Jewish refugeehood, in particular in the interwar years, gave rise to extensive Jewish international law and diplomatic investment.[20] Turning to the pre-sovereign past entails, therefore, inquiries into the policy, practice, and perspective of Jewish diplomacy and advocacy on Jewish questions that would, after 1945 or 1948, be addressed by these three projects of legal reform. This involves canvassing the attitudes of the Zionist movement, Zionist leaders and thinkers, the Jewish Agency for Palestine, *Yishuv* leadership—that is, the pre-independence Jewish community in Palestine—and a range of Zionist and non-Zionist Jewish organizations, scholars, and public activists. Whenever pertinent, these forays into pre-sovereign engagements with international law pay particular attention to the pre-1948 involvement and perspectives of our two protagonists.

4. Ambivalence and Identity

Examining Israel's early attitude towards international law could entail a comprehensive survey of its practice in multiple subject-areas governed by international law. Yet my concern is not with Israel's law and policy on matters such as diplomatic relations, the law of treaties, or the law of the sea. Instead, I examine Israel's engagement with international law projects directly touching on Jewish questions: international law projects, that is, seen by contemporaries as involving Jewish concerns or affecting Jewish interests. In part, this choice stems from the terms of the pre-sovereign Jewish engagement with international law itself. Prior to sovereignty, Jews required and tended on the whole to make little investment eg in the law of diplomatic relations, the law of treaties, or the law of the sea. These areas of international law had little to do with Jewish concerns and interests—in short, with the Jewish Question. In such areas, therefore, the search for (dis)continuity would have little meaning; it may be—as noted below, I have some doubts on that account—that, in such areas, the sovereign turn allowed Israel's foreign policy makers to approach international law anew, largely unencumbered by preexisting sensibilities and previously acquired experience. In such areas, it may be assumed, in the absence of further evidence, that interests alone drove how Israel approached discrete international law questions.[21] Israel's early ambivalence to international law, however, reveals itself most patently in areas where international law touched on Jewish questions directly; here, its ambivalent attitude was largely driven by *identity*, *ideology*, and *political experience*.

[19] Chs 4–5 discuss the Genocide Convention.
[20] Chs 6–7 discuss the Refugee Convention.
[21] I offer one reservation below, when discussing the choice of case studies.

To argue that *identity* was relevant to Israel's international law engagement may seem a trite extension of the view that that identity had always been relevant to its external outlook. When it comes to identity—or self-understanding—my argument here *appears* to cohere with traditional understandings of Israel's foreign policy. Commentators have long underscored the centrality of the 'Jewish aspect' of Israel's diplomacy.[22] In this now-traditional reading, Israel's self-perception as the Jewish state, accompanied by a strong Jewish historical awareness, is essential to understanding not only its domestic but its external policy as well. Proponents of this reading identify a variety of ways in which Jewish concerns affected Israel's foreign policy. Such Jewish concerns, they argue, often clashed with and at times may even have prevailed over Israel's preferences, interests, and *raison d'état*. In such accounts, commitment to the Jewish people in the Diaspora constrains Israel's foreign policy choices and entails diplomatic and strategic costs.[23] Some commentators go further to discern a moral component innate in the Jewish aspect of Israel's foreign policy, captured by notions such as 'light unto the nations'.[24] They point to a conviction, patent in the writings and pronouncements of Israel's early leaders, that Israel's Jewish identity—driven by the lessons of Jewish history—makes or ought to make the Jewish state serve as a spiritual, cultural, or moral universal role model.[25] This reading, incidentally, resonates with the view held by scholars of international law and Jewish history who consider the international law engagement of Jewish scholars in terms of a cosmopolitan commitment[26]—one that, for some, had lamentably to yield to harsh geopolitical necessities.

Later, more critical commentators question however the actual weight assigned to the Jewish factor in Israel's foreign policy decisions. They point to the need to distinguish abstract declarations or ruminations from actual diplomatic practice,[27] and argue that Israel's foreign policy had been driven, predominantly, by *raison d'état* and state interests, often at the expense of Jewish concerns. Neither camp, notably, assesses the Jewish aspect of Israel's foreign relation in the legal sphere or

[22] Michael Brecher, *The Foreign Policy System of Israel: Setting, Images, Process* (New Haven 1972); Aaron Klieman, *Israel and the World After 40 Years* (Pergamon-Brassey's 1990); Moshe Zack, 'Jewish Motifs in Israel's Foreign Policy' (1984) 30 Gesher 32 (Hebrew); Shmuel Sandier, 'Is There a Jewish Foreign Policy?' (1987) 29 Jewish J of Sociology 115; Shabtai Rosenne, 'Basic Elements of Israel's Foreign Policy' (1961) 17 India Quarterly 328.

[23] Brecher (n 22) 229–44; Shlomo Avineri, 'Ideology and Israel's Foreign Policy' (1986) 37 Jerusalem Quarterly 3.

[24] Brecher (n 22) 242–4; Charles Liebman, 'The Idea of Or Lagoyim in the Israeli Reality' (1974) 20 Gesher 88 (Hebrew).

[25] The tension between such notions and legal and political realities, notably, is hardly explored. For a critical reading of the role Israel's Jewish identity had played in shaping its early foreign policy see Rotem Giladi, 'Negotiating Identity: Israel, Apartheid, and the United Nations 1949–1952' (2017) 132 (No. 559) English Hist Rev 1440.

[26] Loeffler, *Cosmopolitans* (n 5); James Loeffler and Moria Paz (eds), *The Law of Strangers: Jewish Lawyers and International Law in the Twentieth Century* (CUP 2019). Chs 2–3 address the cosmopolitan interpretation.

[27] Efraim Inbar, 'Jews, Jewishness and Israel's Foreign Policy' (1990) 2 Jewish Pol Stud Rev 165; Raymond Cohen, 'Israel's Starry-Eyed Foreign Policy' (1994) 1 Middle East Quarterly 28.

multilateral arena;[28] studies on the Jewish factor in Israel's foreign policy tend to focus on Israel's relations with particular states or specific Diaspora communities.[29]

The evidence presented in this book does not challenge the view that identity mattered. Robinson and Rosenne, when weighing on the implementation of human rights, the criminalization of genocide, or the protection of refugees did approach these legal projects as Jewish concerns. They approached policy choices presented by these legal projects, moreover, as self-conscious agents of the Jewish state. And yet, their cognizance of the Jewish aspect of this or that international law project, or their self-conscious Jewish agency, does little to explain in and of itself the ambivalent attitudes they expressed or came to adopt towards these projects. Identity, alone, offers no explanation as to *why* Robinson and Rosenne would reveal a marked disinterest in, display aversion towards, or express outright hostility to the right of individual petition to international organizations, the Genocide Convention and its progenitor, or the Refugee Convention and the status and protection it promised those displaced and uprooted. Nor does identity, alone, offer much instruction on the question of the weight our protagonists were willing to assign to the 'Jewish aspect' of these international law reforms in the calculus of Israel's foreign policy preferences. By itself, identity does not shed light on why they tended to treat the relevant UN agenda items enacting these projects as—in Robinson's words—'marginal' matters while, at times, investing inordinate amounts of their time and energy in these very agenda items. Identity, therefore, is a necessary yet insufficient explanation for our protagonists' ambivalence towards international law.

5. Ambivalence, Ideology, and Political Experience

Ambivalence was driven, rather, by *ideology*—reinforced, in turn, by *political experience*. Rosenne and Robinson were ambivalent towards the right of petition, the Genocide Convention, and the Refugee Convention precisely *because* of—not despite—the Jewish aspect of each of these international law projects. Their outlook on these projects, and on international law and institutions writ large, was determined by ideology: it was ideology that imbued their Jewish self-perception with significance. The prism through which they approached these projects and the policy choices each placed before the Jewish state was furnished by a particular strand of Zionism that, in 1948, became Israel's foundational ideology. For them, the yardstick for measuring international law and its effect on Jewish interests and concerns—indeed, for defining what *were* in fact Jewish interests and concerns—had been the creed of the Jewish national movement and its pre-sovereign political

[28] Cf Giladi, 'Negotiating Identity' (n 25).
[29] Yossi Shain and Aharon Barth, 'Diasporas and International Relations' (2003) 57 Intl Org 449.

experience. That was how they approached the right of petition, the Genocide Convention, and the Refugee Convention. In their ideological reading of these post-war projects, that yardstick decreed a gamut of attitudes: indifference, disinterest, and, sometimes, instrumental interest—but also suspicion, aversion, and plain hostility. In short, ideology decreed ambivalence. Yet to fathom why the creed of Jewish national liberation would impel such a range of conflicting attitudes requires some reflection on the meeting point between modern Jewish history and modern international law.

That is, essentially, the task of the first chapter. It serves, as already noted, as a primer on the place of international law in Jewish political thought and political-diplomatic praxis since the late nineteenth century. Specifically, it sets out to explore the terms of pre-sovereign Jewish engagements with international law. There, I first reflect on the terms of late nineteenth century Jewish turn to international law to argue that international law engagements by Jewish political thinkers, legal scholars and practitioners, or organizations can and should be considered as responses to the 'Jewish Question'. Jewish engagements with international law, that is, either sought to promote or at least embodied a choice among *competing* models of Jewish *emancipation* prescribing different solutions to the challenge of modernity. Diverse Jewish engagements with international law represented, then, investments in different visions of Jewish emancipation; they were, in other words, *ideologically* coded.[30]

The chapter proceeds to explore three such models of Jewish emancipation and the terms of their respective international law engagements: Assimilation—invested in the civic emancipation of Jews as individuals through acculturation and integration with their surrounding European society; Zionism—that sought a collective, national emancipation through the establishment of a territorial polity or centre in Palestine; and Diaspora Nationalism—prescribing national emancipation with no territorial component through the practice of Jewish autonomy in the Diaspora. Some of the sensibilities that would, after 1949, drive Rosenne and Robinson's ambivalence will become patent here. This survey of Jewish ideological attitudes also provides an essential conceptual framing of my main argument about the ideological roots of Israel's ambivalence towards international law and allows me to refine that argument by pointing to three sites where Zionist ideological sensibilities produced and expressed ambivalence towards international law.

First, ambivalence towards international law *inhered* in Zionist ideology. To the 'fathers' of that ideology of national liberation—Theodor Herzl, LL.D. in particular—who sought the recognition of Jews as a *nation* entitled to sovereignty,

[30] Readers interested in clarification of what I mean by 'ideology' are up for a disappointment: engagement with the theoretical debates surrounding this term is not required by the essentially historical argument I make here. I assume that presenting some of the components of particular ideologies, in ch 1, is sufficient for present purposes. For more, the standard reference is to Terry Eagleton, *Ideology: An Introduction* (Verso 1991).

international law offered a vehicle for transforming the legal and political status of the Jewish people. Yet, at the same time, international law also placed an obstacle on the path of emancipation. At the late nineteenth century, international law doctrine insisted on the exclusive legal capacity, personality, and subjecthood of the state in international law. This sovereign exclusion rendered the Jewish *people* (Zionism, after all, argued from its outset that Jews were a 'people') no more than an *object* of international law—not a recognized *subject* equipped with sovereign capacity. Zionism, even before Herzl's 1896 *Der Judenstaat*,[31] involved an investment in and, at the same time, harboured a measure of resentment towards international law on that account.

Second, the subsequent *political experience* of the Zionist movement served to entrench ambivalence towards international law inhering in Zionist ideology. Chapter 1 also demonstrates that international law investment, together with aversion and hostility, cohabited Zionist praxis. The episodes it recounts briefly concern, in particular, the Palestine Mandate: the legal instrument and its legal framework—Article 22 of the League of Nations Covenant—as well the British administration and League supervision of the institution. While I cannot offer here a history of the Palestine Mandate or of the Zionist engagement with international law, that brief excursus into practice furnishes sufficient evidence on how embedded had ambivalence become in the ideological sensibilities and political culture of the Zionist movement. The case for continuity rests, to a considerable extent, on this embeddedness.

Third, the legacy of ambivalence that the Jewish state inherited from Zionist ideology and praxis was in no small measure rooted also in the contestation between Zionism on the one hand and Assimilation and Diaspora Nationalism on the other. The ideological tensions between Zionism and these competing models of Jewish emancipation did not remain in the realm of dogmatic abstraction. Each of these ideological responses to the Jewish Question turned to international law for legitimation; each approached international law with certain assumptions on modernity and the Jewish condition; each, through its own institutions, developed its own *modus operandi*; and each pursued discrete international law programmes giving effect to its vision of Jewish emancipation. Chapter 1 also notes these differences, with particular reference to how they shaped Zionist sensibilities in the pre-sovereign period.

Each of the three case studies presented in parts II–IV corresponds to a theme: a core sensibility (or related sensibilities) driving first Zionist, then Israeli, ambivalence towards international law—inherent, acquired, or produced by contestation. The first theme concerns *voice*, the sum of ideological sensibilities on questions of Jewish legal status, standing, and representation (part II). Shaped by pre-sovereign

[31] Theodor Herzl, *Der Judenstaat: Versuch einer modernen Lösung der Judenfrage* (M Breitenstein's Verlags-Buchhandlung 1896).

preoccupation with Jewish legal objecthood,[32] these sensibilities were often shared by Rosenne and Robinson and affected their attitude—and ambivalence—towards all three projects examined in the case studies. It was, however, the question of the individual right of petition, debated in the UN in the context of consideration of means of implementing the proposed Human Rights Covenant, that provoked their voice sensibilities most directly. Bolstered by past and present experience with Jewish representation politics, these sensibilities drove their hostility towards the prospect of individual Jewish *locus standi* at UN institutions.

To expose these sensibilities on *voice*, and the ambivalence they gave rise to, chapter 2 reconstructs Hersch Lauterpacht's 1950 intervention made in Jerusalem, on the occasion of the Hebrew University's semi-jubilee, in favour of the individual right of petition. Lauterpacht's 'reproach' of Israel's policy is assessed against the backdrop of his own investment in Zionism and human rights and in light of interwar Jewish investment in the right to petition international organizations. Chapter 3 proceeds to recount Rosenne's response that castigated Lauterpacht's intervention, and the right of individual petition, on explicitly ideological grounds: for Rosenne, both expressed assimilationist sensibilities and an 'extreme non-Zionist, apolitical concept of Jewish public life and the Jewish place on the international scene'. For him, the right of petition—and, by extension, the proposed Human Rights Covenant—was essentially an assimilationist project. Premised on individual, not collective, Jewish subjecthood the right of petition and the human rights project were antithetical to the way Zionist ideology constructed the political status of Jews. The right of petition also challenged Zionism's identification of the Diaspora as the root cause of the modern Jewish predicament. Moreover, by investing individual Jews with individual legal capacity to make their case before UN institutions, the right of petition threatened to undermine the Jewish state's claim, as a full-fledged *subject* of international law, to paramount Jewish voice speaking for Jewish interests in the world arena.

The sovereign sensibilities animating Robinson and Rosenne's attitude on the right of petition stemmed directly from their own pre-sovereign grappling with Jewish legal objecthood and political exclusion; in that sense, the case of the right of petition was an extension of Jewish representation politics where Jewish institutions, long before 1948, vied with each other in the international arena over access, standing, and voice. Lauterpacht's public reproach of Israel's position challenged the sovereign status of Rosenne and Robinson as official, duly accredited representatives of the Jewish state equipped with the legal capacity to speak for Jewish interests with authority. This explains the harsh terms of Rosenne's retort: he challenged Lauterpacht's own capacity, standing, and *ideological* credentials.

[32] By no means an exclusively Jewish preoccupation: Natasha Wheatley, 'New Subjects in International Law and Order' in Patricia Clavin and Glenda Sluga (eds), *Internationalisms: A Twentieth-Century History* (CUP 2017) 265.

And yet, alongside hostility, the Jewish state's practice revealed a measure of investment in the right of petition. That right, and the proposed Human Rights Covenant, did promise a measure of protection—albeit ideologically flawed—to Jews in the Diaspora; participation in UN work did furnish the Jewish state, furthermore, with the opportunity to display an active contribution towards the realization of UN goals. These factors, and others noted in chapter 3, also drove a half-hearted Israeli investment in the human rights project. Even prior to Lauterpacht's intervention, and notwithstanding their aversion to competing Jewish voices or their objections to the ideological premises of the right of petition, Rosenne and Robinson reluctantly accepted the possibility that some Jewish organizations could be allowed to bring petitions before UN organs. Though largely averse to the right of petition and Jewish investment in the human rights project, the sum of their attitude registered ambivalence.

The right of petition was not the only post-war project predicted on a competing model of Jewish emancipation. The second theme concerns *protection* (part III)—the question of the nature and *locus* of Jewish national emancipation. Chapter 4 records the gamut of conflicting attitudes displayed by Robinson and Rosenne towards the Genocide Convention during its drafting, with regard to and following its ratification, and at the International Court of Justice ('ICJ') advisory proceedings on the question of Reservations to the Genocide Convention.[33] Chapter 5 proceeds to explore the origins of that range of attitudes—disinterest and indifference, acknowledgement and appropriation, derision and instrumentalism, aversion and hostility—towards the Convention and its progenitor. Here, too, it was the Convention's Jewish aspect that attracted their largely negative attitude. While Lemkin's unofficial status and private style of advocacy certainly offended their sovereign *voice* sensibilities, the root cause of their reserve was a reading of the Genocide Convention as an extension of interwar protection of minority rights—in essence, as a programme of Diaspora Nationalism.

At stake here were core Zionist assumptions about the Jewish condition and Zionism's very solution to the 'Jewish Question'. The Genocide Convention, adopted by the GA on 9 December 1948, was premised on a model of protection of Jewish rights, existence, and survival that identified the Diaspora—not Palestine—as the proper *locus* for Jewish national revival. From an ideological standpoint, the solution to the Jewish Question that the Convention was predicated on had already proven false with the failure of the League of Nations minorities system and, in particular, the Holocaust. For some Zionists—though not for our protagonists—it had been false all along. Read ideologically, the Genocide Convention not only challenged a cardinal Zionist principle that identified the Diaspora as the source of

[33] ICJ, *Reports* (1951) 15. Chs 4–5 develop and carry further the argument I first made in Rotem Giladi, 'Not Our Salvation: Israel, the Genocide Convention, and the World Court 1950–1951' (2015) 26 Diplomacy & Statecraft 473.

Jewish political inferiority and vulnerability; it also challenged Zionism's success[34] in achieving majority status in Palestine in the war of 1948—and negated the need for a Jewish state to guarantee the protection of Jews.

It is here that a biographical aspect comes into play. Much of our protagonists' ambivalence towards the Genocide Convention and Raphael Lemkin was driven by their past ideological engagements. To varying degrees, both Robinson and Rosenne had prior investments in Diaspora Nationalism. Political experience—driven by interwar crises, the Holocaust, and Israel's establishment—caused their disenchantment with its promise and brought both to profess, instead, the Zionist creed. Each would now approach the Genocide Convention with something of the zeal—and uncertainty—of the convert. In order to chart and decipher their past and sovereign sensibilities brought into play by the Genocide Convention, chapter 5 also traces Rosenne and Robinson's career trajectories, professional-political experience, and ideological transformations. It also demonstrates that, for all their aversion to Lemkin and hostility towards the Convention, they were at times willing to admit, reluctantly, the need for some Israeli investment in the Convention.

The third, last theme (part IV) concerns *refuge*. Here, our protagonists' ambivalence towards the Refugee Convention did not stem from their ideological objections to another solution to the Jewish Question, a competing model of Jewish emancipation. It was, rather, that the Refugee Convention *both* confirmed and challenged a cardinal Zionist principle. Read ideologically, the Convention on the one hand affirmed Israel's character as the Jewish state and, as such, that it was the Jewish people's state of asylum. It validated the Zionist principle of 'Return' and Israel's policy of the 'in-gathering of exiles' giving effect to it. At the same time, the Convention was superfluous: while it promised refugee status and treatment to displaced Jews, Zionism had already offered Jewish refugees a 'radical solution' and 'a better remedy' in the form of 'Return'[35] to the Jewish state. On the other hand, however, the Refugee Convention threatened to subvert the Jewish state's very *raison d'être* as a remedy to the Jewish Diasporic condition: a permanent political solution not only to the plight of individual Jewish refugees *but to Jewish statelessness itself.* In this reading, international protection was a marker of deficient, inferior, non-sovereign status; ideologically, Israel's establishment obviated Jewish recourse to such international protection. The persistence of such protection challenged the need for the Jewish state.[36]

Chapters 6 and 7 explore our protagonists' ambivalence towards the Refugee Convention; the first assesses Robinson's involvement in its drafting; in particular,

[34] From that ideological viewpoint, that a Palestinian tragedy ensued did not affect the assessment of that success.

[35] Law of Return—1950, 51 *Sefer HaHukim* (Laws) (5 July 1950) 159 (Hebrew).

[36] Chs 6–7 expand the argument I first made in Rotem Giladi, 'A "Historical Commitment"? Identity and Ideology in Israel's Attitude to the Refugee Convention 1951–4' (2014) 37 Intl Hist Rev 745.

it offers a critical reading of the degree to which Robinson was in fact representing the position of the Jewish state in this legislative process. Chapter 7 traces the various sensibilities that had brought Robinson and Rosenne to clash over the question of the Convention's ratification. Unlike the case of the right of petition or the Genocide Convention, here they divided. Past experience and pre-sovereign sensibilities drove them to adopt divergent ideological readings of the Jewish aspects of the Refugee Convention—and of the place of the Diaspora in Jewish life at the age of Jewish sovereignty. In the case of Robinson, his reading marked an ideological deviation—that was accentuated by Rosenne's actions and reading of the Convention.

Before I return to the matter of Robinson's deviation—or rather, to what it signifies—there is the question of my choice to leave out of the scope of this book other post-war international law projects involving Jewish questions. This concerns, in particular, the revision of the laws of war in the 1949 Geneva Conventions and the post-Nuremberg UN work on what we now call international criminal law. Both could constitute appropriate additional case studies for my argument about ambivalence and its roots. The temptation to look at the Geneva Conventions was great: much of my research to date concerns the history of the laws of war. Two factors informed my resistance to including the laws of war in this book. One is the sheer volume of general, Jewish, and Israeli practice on this post-war project; the other, related, is the existence of multiple 'background noises'—additional factors that would have rendered the reading of Israel's attitude to the Geneva Conventions too complex to do it justice within the confines of this book. Such factors include eg the relationships between Jewish organizations and the International Committee of the Red Cross ('ICRC')—in particular during the Holocaust;[37] the ICRC's relationship with the *Yishuv* and the newly established Jewish state—and its involvement in the Palestine conflict;[38] that war itself—and the role of the laws of war in signifying sovereign capacity and 'civilisation'.[39]

My choice not to examine Israel's attitude towards international criminal law, in turn, was informed by the apparent dearth of material and lack of persisting Israeli investment in that short-lived—in its post-war phase—project. Still, in the course of the research I encountered enough anecdotal evidence to suggest that ambivalence was at play in these two cases—and for similar reasons. The same can be said—again, by dint of anecdotal evidence—about Israel's attitude towards international law, and organization, in general; some blend of investment and aversion drawing on the same sensibilities recorded here can be found, to some extent, in Israel's early attitude towards the ICJ, the UN at large, and spheres of international

[37] Eg Jean-Claude Favez, *The Red Cross and the Holocaust* (CUP 1999).

[38] Eg Dominique-D Junod, *The Imperiled Red Cross and the Palestine-Eretz-Yisrael Conflict, 1945–1952: The Influence of Institutional Concerns on a Humanitarian Operation* (K Paul International 1996).

[39] Eg Rotem Giladi, 'The Phoenix of Colonial War: Race, the Laws of War, and the "Horror on the Rhine"' (2017) 30 Leiden JIL 847.

regulation with no patent Jewish aspect. Nonetheless, there is certainly room for further research on these questions. I can only hope that this book—and, in particular, the conceptual framework driving the argument on ambivalence and its roots—helps future researchers interested in the meeting points between Jewish history, Israeli diplomacy, and international law.

6. Protagonists and Ideology

Robinson's ideological deviation points to another recurring theme. All three case studies reveal how our protagonists—legal advisers in the service of the Jewish state—time and again elected to express or act on the requirements of the Zionist creed. In all cases, they were the ones—more than any of their MFA colleagues—to test the adherence of this or that international law project with that creed. They elected to interpret the implications of the sovereign turn: that is, when expressing or seeking to give effect to sovereign sensibilities, they chose to serve as ideological torchbearers.

The Zionist creed, like any other ideology, made demands of its adherents. Its answer to the Jewish Question presented external demands upon the world: the transformation of Jewish objecthood into legally recognized subjecthood was one such demand. It also required Jews to internalize modern subjecthood: abandon the ways of the Diaspora and transform themselves, physically,[40] mentally, and in a host of other manners in order to become, in short, 'New Jews'.[41] The appearance of a Jewish national movement, as Anita Shapira noted, was accompanied by 'a secular, revolutionary ethos predicated on a new value system, on a nexus between the Jew and his historical homeland, on new norms of conduct among Jews and between Jews and non-Jews'.[42] Testing international law for its adherence to Zionism's creed was, for Rosenne and Robinson, the act of revolutionaries who had observed, participated in, and experienced the Jewish sovereign turn; yet that very revolution also put them to the test. At stake was their own adherence to the demands of Zionism's creed, their own transformation into new, sovereign Jews. The Epilogue reflects on that test—and on the way each of them, in a manner, had failed to pass it.

In a sense, the story this book narrates concerns Robinson and Rosenne's investment in Zionism. I assume neither that investment nor its constancy[43] or continuity: their ideological investments, and sensibilities, were shaped by

[40] George L Mosse, 'Max Nordau, Liberalism and the New Jew' (1992) 27 J of Contemporary History 565.

[41] Anita Shapira, *New Jews, Old Jews* (Am Oved 1997) (Hebrew).

[42] ibid, 11. Consider also Anita Shapira, 'Anti-Semitism and Zionism' (1995) 15 Modern Judaism 215, 230 ('The utopian project of such Zionists aimed at a profound revolution in Jewish patterns of life, attitudes toward reality and the accepted norms guiding the relations between individual and society').

[43] Nor do I assume the constancy of Zionist ideology, a matter discussed in ch 1.

political-professional experience. Rather than point, *a priori*, to the origins and nature of their respective Zionist investments, I largely let their ideological sensibilities reveal themselves. Instead of offering preliminary biographical sketches,[44] the book draws attention to their career paths, politics, and ideological investments where these are relevant for deciphering their actions and interpreting their sensibilities in the context of the three case studies. The resulting scattered fragments of biographies, together, tell of ideological transformation: a process by which our two second- or third-row protagonists came to espouse the Zionist creed, express it, and use it to read and test international law—and, in turn, be tested by it.

As already noted, part V—comprising the Epilogue—reflects on lawyers, revolution, and the ideological test of our protagonists. It first sketches the principal findings and raises the question of long-term continuity, or the legacy of the past—of Israel's early ambivalence towards international law—today. The Epilogue, however, also revisits another question concerning the boundaries of this book to which I now turn.

7. Absence and Presence: Jews, Israelis, Palestinians

Last, this book is *not* about the Israeli–Palestinian conflict. In part, the reason has to do with my own career path; for nearly two decades, I have studied—and practiced, and taught—international law as it pertains to the tragedy and hope of the portion of the world where I was born and where I live. While tragedy persists and hope is on the wane, I have moved on to invest in other pursuits. The absence of the conflict, however, stems in large part from the nature of the questions I ask in this book: as pervasive as the conflict is to my own everyday life and politics, it is not the only prism through which I can reflect on my world and the meanings that structure it. The source material confirms the salience of other questions. Surely we ought to reflect on the significance of the patent detachment of the editors of the *Jewish Yearbook* who could reflect on past, stateless Jewish engagements with

[44] Ch 1, nonetheless, offers some detail on their respective backgrounds. For my attempt at an early—up to 1948—biographical sketch of Rosenne: Rotem Giladi, 'Shabtai Rosenne: The Transformation of Sefton Rowson' in Loeffler and Paz (n 26) 221. On Robinson, consider Shabtai Rosenne, 'Jacob Robinson—In Memoriam' (1978) 13 Isr L Rev 287; Abraham Tory, 'Jacob Robinson—In Memoriam' (1978–1979) 32 HaPraklit 125 (Hebrew). While various aspects and chapters of Robinson's life and career attracted the attention of scholars in recent years, a comprehensive biographical account is yet to be written. Notably, the MFA chapter of Robinson's career has hardly been addressed by the recent scholarship on his life and work. Consider Loeffler, *Cosmopolitans* (n 5); Giladi, 'Commitment' (n 36); Eglé Bendikaité and Dirk Roland Haupt (eds), *The Life, Times and Work of Jokubas Robinzonas—Jacob Robinson* (Akademia Verlag 2015) 39; Boaz Cohen, 'Dr. Jacob Robinson, the Institute of Jewish Affairs and the Elusive Jewish Voice in Nuremberg' in David Bankier and Dan Michman (eds), *Holocaust and Justice: Representation and Historiography of the Holocaust in Post-War Trials* (Yad Vashem/Berghahn 2010) 81; Omry Kaplan-Feuereisen, 'At the Service of the Jewish Nation: Jacob Robinson and International Law' (2008) 8–10 OstEuropa 157; Michael R Marrus, 'A Jewish Lobby at Nuremberg: Jacob Robinson and the Institute of Jewish Affairs, 1945–1946' (2006) 27 Cardozo L Rev 1651.

international law, in besieged Jerusalem, in 1948, without them pausing to consider the human suffering brought about by the war that surrounded them and the mass displacement of Palestinians it generated. The evidence discussed in the three case studies points to the merits of examining Israel's early attitude to international law from the vantage point of Jewish history and politics, not only the prism of the conflict. While the Epilogue reflects on these vantage points, three preliminary observations are in order here.

First, the conflict, its history, and its legal aspects have been thoroughly explored to date. The resulting literature—irrespective of the degree of partisanship it may or may not display—takes little account of the role of ideology in shaping Israel's legal outlook and practice. In this sense, this book offers to rectify an omission. *Second*, the consideration of ideology and the pre-sovereign Jewish outlook on international law in fact furnishes powerful insights on conflict-related Israeli legal practice. To supply one example discussed in the Epilogue, it serves to undercut a widely held belief, in Israel and outside it, in a liberal golden age of Israeli investment in international law and human rights that was undone by the Israeli occupation in the 1967 War. The evidence furnished here of Israel's early ambivalence towards international law, its origins, ubiquity, and power belies claims—or unstated assumptions—that such a golden age had ever existed.[45] This finding is particularly pertinent for highlighting the largely unexplored interplay of Jewish and Palestinian refugeehood in the making of the international refugee regime.[46]

Third and most importantly, the fact that this book is not *about* the conflict does not mean that it is quite absent. I follow, report, and analyse the paper trail left by Rosenne and Robinson. In that sense, the presence of the conflict in the book corresponds to its presence in what they wrote—and, at times, in what they did not. In another sense, the conflict is, in fact, both present and absent from how they came to consider the right of petition, the Genocide Convention, or the Refugee Convention. The chapters that follow record and note, therefore, both absence and presence. They point to a curious dialectical dynamic—an interplay between nearly implicit core concerns and explicit marginalia—that was one of the defining features of how the protagonists approached international law at the dawn of the age of Jewish sovereignty. The Epilogue reflects on this dialectic, the tensions it embodies, and the instruction these hold for understanding the intricate makeup of Rosenne and Robinsons' Jewish and conflict-related preoccupations, sensibilities, *weltanschauung*, and actions. It reflects, in short, on change and continuity—and on the relevance of considering critically the international law and foreign policy praxis of the Jewish state through the prism of Jewish ideology, politics, and history—now strained through the sieve of sovereign status, sensibilities, and exigencies.

[45] Giladi, 'Commitment' (n 36) critically examines the 'golden age' discourses.
[46] Chs 6 and 7 offer some insight into this interplay.

1

Terms of Engagement

International Law, the Jewish Question, Ideology, and Ambivalence

1. The Jewish Turn to International Law

At the core of this book is the argument that, immediately following the sovereign turn, the Jewish state approached international law with ambivalence—and that Israel's early ambivalence towards international law was rooted in inherent ideological sensibilities and acquired political experience. This argument forms part of a broader claim about the intersection between international law and Jewish history that proposes to consider international law, from the late nineteenth century onwards, *as a field of contestation* among competing approaches to the Jewish Question and competing visions for its solution—that is, among competing ideologies of Jewish emancipation.[1] Without considering ideological contestation, Israel's ambivalent early legal-diplomatic practice makes little sense.

This claim considers the international legal sphere as more than the source of modern political imagination or modern political vocabularies to inspire (and in turn be shaped by) Jews grappling with the challenges to Jewish existence presented by modernity. It also considers the modern international legal arena as more than a platform of fora where Jewish emancipatory claims could be formulated, advanced, negotiated, and translated into programmatic action by Jews themselves.[2]

[1] That 'international law, before or after 1948, must itself be considered as a field of political Jewish contestation' was one conclusion emerging from a study of Rosenne's early career: Rotem Giladi, 'Shabtai Rosenne: The Transformation of Sefton Rowson' in James Loeffler and Moria Paz (eds), *The Law of Strangers: Jewish Lawyers and International Law in the Twentieth Century* (CUP 2019) 221, 248.

[2] As the chapters that follow demonstrate, from the late nineteenth century international law would furnish the imagination, vocabularies, and platforms for the invocation and exercise of Jewish political and legal *agency*—and, in turn, serve as an arena for intra-Jewish contestation over 'ownership' of that agency in the forms of representation politics. Thus, in his contribution to the *Jewish Yearbook*, Feinberg noted a 'very long' 'record of humanitarian interventions on behalf of the Jews' by others, where 'the Jews were merely the subject of negotiations': Nathan Feinberg, 'The Recognition of the Jewish People in International Law' (1948) 1 Jewish YB Intl L 1, 2, 5. As I discuss below, the nexus between Jewish agency and international law was particularly complex. For the history of Great Power interventions on behalf of Jews, consider eg Carole Fink, *Defending the Rights of Others: The Great Powers, the Jews, and International Minority Protection, 1878–1938* (CUP 2004); Abigail Green, 'The Limits of Intervention: Coercive Diplomacy and the Jewish Question in the Nineteenth Century' (2014) 36 The Intl Hist Rev 473; Abigail Green, 'The British Empire and the Jews: An Imperialism of Human Rights?' (2008) 199 Past & Present 175; Abigail Green, 'Intervening in the Jewish Question, 1840–1878' in Brendan Simms and David JB Trim (eds), *Humanitarian Intervention: A History* (CUP 2011) 139.

Jews, Sovereignty, and International Law. Rotem Giladi, Oxford University Press. © Rotem Giladi 2021.
DOI: 10.1093/oso/9780198857396.003.0003

International law was all that but, at the same time, it was more. The claim here is that precisely because international law could inspire the adherents of diverse approaches to the Jewish Question and equip each with the vocabularies needed to formulate and pursue diverse emancipatory visions through concrete programmes, international law was an arena of Jewish ideological contestation, an extension of Jewish politics. This book, then, in addition to narrating international legal history and Israel's diplomatic history, equally concerns modern Jewish history.

By and large, then, individual and collective Jewish engagements with international law were intimately linked, in a myriad of ways, to the Jewish Question.[3] The claim here is that the late nineteenth century turn to international law by Jewish political thinkers and legal scholars and practitioners, as well as Jewish organizations, either deliberately sought to advance or, in the very least, embodied a choice among competing models of Jewish emancipation[4] prescribing different solutions to the challenge of modernity.[5] Diverse Jewish engagements with international law were, in other words, *ideologically* coded; they expressed discrete preferences for the answer to a question that was quintessentially formulated by Marx in his 1844 retort to Bruno Bauer, *Zur Judenfrage*: 'what *sort of emancipation is at issue*?'[6] The answer to that question—the preferred model of emancipation—would determine the terms of concrete Jewish engagements with international law. After 1949, these terms would in turn condition the Jewish state's attitude towards international law. That is, pre-sovereign ideological sensibilities would condition sovereign ambivalence.

[3] This resonates with Pnina Lahav's reflection on the Jewish turn to international law. Her point of departure is 'the emancipation of the Jews on the heels of the French Revolution' and its failures; she proceeds to observe: 'in the "age of reason", the promise of international law touched a deep cord in the heart of Jewish scholars. The ideal of a law of nations, a government of nations, external and superior to the nation-state, had a very powerful appeal to the recently emancipated Jews': Pnina Lahav, 'The Jewish Perspective in International Law' (1993) 87 ASIL Proc 331, 332.

[4] I am not proposing a reading of eg Tobias MC Asser, Lassa Oppenheim, Hans Kelsen, Hersch Lauterpacht, and many others that reduces them to their Jewish descent, nor an essentialist account of a role played by their respective Jewish self-perceptions—if any—in their international law *oeuvre* or *weltanschauung*. The claim is rather that their respective international law engagements can be located along an ideological axis, described below, comprising discrete models of Jewish emancipation and that such choices, whatever their causes in individual cases, can be ascribed with meaning by that political-ideological geometry. James Loeffler and Moria Paz, 'Introduction' in Loeffler and Paz (n 1) 1 survey some of the pitfalls of reduction and essentialism attending the consideration of Jewish history applied to the study of Jewish history of international law. For a reflective account of the study of Jewish intellectuals: Paul Mendes-Flohr, 'The Study of the Jewish Intellectual: A Methodological Prolegomenon' in Paul Mendes-Flohr, *Divided Passions: Jewish Intellectuals and the Experience of Modernity* (Wayne State UP 1991) 23.

[5] The literature on Jews and modernity is vast and multifaced. For a succinct primer see Jacob Katz (ed), *Toward Modernity: The European Jewish Model* (Transaction 1987).

[6] Emphasis in the original; Karl Marx, 'On the Jewish Question' in Joseph J O'Malley (ed) *Marx: Early Political Writings* (CUP 1994) 28, 31; Bruno Bauer, *Die Judenfrage* (Braunschweig 1843). For background: Shlomo Avineri, 'Marx and Jewish Emancipation' (1964) 25 J of the Hist of Ideas 445; for international law implications: Martti Koskenniemi, 'What Should International Lawyers Learn from Karl Marx?' (2004) 17 Leiden JIL 229.

Before proceeding to examine these competing models of Jewish emancipation, retrace the ideological creeds each had prescribed, and chart the terms of international law engagement entailed by each, we need to pause to reflect, however briefly, on the meeting point between Jewish history and international law; we need, that is, to historicize the Jewish turn to international law and consider its origins and disciplinary and Jewish contexts. Notwithstanding the growth of interest, in recent decades, in the international law engagement of Jewish scholars and institutions, no study has hitherto examined closely the *inception* of the Jewish turn to international law and its socio-politics.[7] Still, various insights produced by studies of modern Jewish history and the history of international law[8] help reconstruct some of the general contours of the time, place, and context of the Jewish turn to international law.

One obstacle to surmount in this respect is the hold of the interwar years and the twentieth century on existing explorations of Jewish presence and prominence in international law; these have served to somewhat occlude the origins of the Jewish turn to international law. Two factors, however, point to the two penultimate decades of the nineteenth century as the salient moment. The first concerns the birth of modern international law itself, described by Martti Koskenniemi as a 'radical . . . break that took place in the field [of international law] between the first half of the 19th century and the emergence of a new professional self-awareness and enthusiasm'.[9] If the 'Men of Ghent' who founded 'the *Institut de droit international* in 1873' were 'the first modern international lawyers',[10] any Jewish turn to international law—itself the result of a 'radical transformation of Jewish life' engendered by modernity[11]—could not precede the birth of the discipline.[12] This resonates with prosopographic evidence: whomever we might elect to include in the first cohort of modern Jewish international lawyers—Tobias Asser (born 1838),

[7] Works on individual Jewish scholars, institutions and, in particular, prosopographies or collective biographies furnish important yet incomplete insights in this respect: Reut Yael Paz, *A Gateway between a Distant God and a Cruel World: The Contribution of Jewish German-Speaking Scholars to International Law* (Nijhoff 2013); Jack Beatson and Reinhard Zimmermann (eds), *Jurists Uprooted: German-Speaking Emigré Lawyers in Twentieth Century Britain* (OUP 2004); Mónica García-Salmones Rovira, *The Project of Positivism in International Law* (OUP 2013); Moria Paz, 'A Non-Territorial Ethnic Network and the Making of Human Rights Law: The Case of the Alliance Israelite Universelle' (2009) 4 Interdisc J Hum Rights L 1; and Loeffler and Paz (n 1) whose introduction offers a useful discussion of approaches to, methodologies for, and epistemologies of the study of the Jewish presence in international law.

[8] In addition to the sources cited in n 7: Martti Koskenniemi, *The Gentle Civilizer of Nations: The Rise and Fall of International Law 1870–1960* (CUP 2001).

[9] ibid, 3–4.

[10] ibid, 3.

[11] Paul R Mendes-Flohr and Jehuda Reinharz (eds), *The Jew in the Modern World: A Documentary History* (3rd edn, OUP 2011) 4.

[12] Of the *Institut*'s founders, Tobias MC Asser was born Jewish but converted to Christianity around 1890. He came from a family of Dutch lawyers that both invested in and epitomized one of the models of Jewish emancipation discussed below; his great-grandfather, Moses Solomon Asser (1754–1826) was a key figure in the promotion of the civic emancipation of Jews in the Netherlands following the establishment of the pro-French Batavian Republic in 1795; Jewish emancipation was proclaimed the following year. Arthur Eyffinger, *T.M.C. Asser (1838–1913): In Quest of Liberty, Justice, and Peace* (Brill 2019).

Georg Jellinek (1851), Lassa Oppenheim (1858), or others—the international law component of the career path of individual members either links to Ghent (as in the case of Asser) or emerges in the two decades that followed the foundation of the modern discipline.

The second factor concerns the Jewish condition and points to various indicia of the progress and regression of emancipation—and their intersections with the new disciplinary sensibilities pronounced at Ghent: the opening of law faculties to Jewish students, of the legal profession to Jewish graduates, of public service to Jewish lawyers, and of the legal academia to Jewish scholars. This is not the place to map such processes in detail, nor to track the removal and reinstatements of formal and informal barriers in various jurisdictions. Still, the ebbs and flows of emancipation and, in particular, of Jewish access to modern legal education, practice, and public service (often including both judicial bench and professorial chairs)[13] suggest such factors likely played a cardinal role in the tracking[14] of Jewish students and young professionals towards international law no less than disillusionment with emancipation and xenophobic-nationalist reactions thereto. Part of the appeal of the new discipline had been that international law, like law in general, promised to serve as a marker of modernity (and, thus, a vehicle of individual social mobility) that could be acquired through *Bildung*.[15] The making of an *academic* international law career was propelled by structural, practical, as well as ideological reasons.

Locating the Jewish turn to international law first appears a far more facile task: all evidence, whether pertaining to the discipline itself or to the factors of Jewish history, points to Europe. The Jewish turn to international law had been, like international law itself, a Eurocentric affair.[16] While, as I note below, the construction of 'East' and 'West' does matter in the mapping of discrete models of Jewish emancipation,[17] it is not necessary for present purposes to narrow down

[13] Eg Kenneth Ledford, 'Jews in the German Legal Professions: Emancipation, Assimilation, Exclusion' in Ari Mermelstein , Victoria Saker Woeste , Ethan Zadoff , and Marc Galanter (eds), *Jews and the Law* (Quid Pro 2014).

[14] Here I borrow—admittedly, quite loosely—Bourdieu's notion of bureaucratic tracking and its relation to the acquisition of cultural capital: Pierre Bourdieu, 'Intellectual Field and Creative Knowledge' in Michael FD Young (ed), *Knowledge and Control: New Directions for the Sociology of Education* (Macmillan 1971). Paz, *Gateway* (n 7) 85–127 maps Jewish access to German legal education but not structural factors directing Jews towards international law.

[15] Koskenniemi, *Gentle Civilizer* (n 8) 76–85.

[16] On international law's Eurocentrism, consider eg Yasuaki Onuma, 'When was the Law of International Society Born?' (2000) 2 J Hist Intl L 1; Martti Koskenniemi 'Histories of International Law: Dealing with Eurocentrism' (2011) 19 Rechtsgeschichte—Legal History 152; James Thuo Gathii, 'International Law and Eurocentricity' (1998) 9 EJIL 184; Arnulf Becker Lorca, 'Eurocentrism in the History of International Law' in Bardo Fassbender and Anne Peters (eds), *The Oxford Handbook of the History of International Law* (OUP 2012).

[17] As discussed below, the ideologically coded models of Jewish emancipation were also geographically coded in an East–West division: Yfaat Weiss, *Ethnicity and Citizenship, German and Polish Jews 1933-1940* (Magnes 2000) (Hebrew); Dan Diner, 'Zweierlei Emanzipation—Westliche Juden Und Ostjiden gegenübergestellt' in Dan Diner, *Gedächtniszeiten: Über jüdische und andere Geschichte* (CH Beck 2003) 125.

the *locus* of the Jewish turn to international law or select among Western Europe, Eastern Europe (home to the vast majority of European Jews), or the *deutscher Kulturbereich* in Central Europe. If the turn to international law maps unto shifts in Jewish emancipation, one may venture to hypothesize that each *locus* had produced its own version, or versions, of the gravitation of Jews to international law. What matters, nonetheless, is that the 'Europe' in question had been a cultural, not geographical, space. It is the same Europe of the 'Family of Nations' that produced international law and to whom it applied, according to a core sensibility shared by the founders of the new, modern discipline.[18]

This is precisely where questions on the *location* of the Jewish turn to international law give way to ontological inquiries and where the Jewish *encounter*—I use this term deliberately—with international law ought to be theorized, not merely historicized. The key question here may be conveniently put in the following terms: on what civilizational—and, therefore, political and legal—footing could Jews engage with international law? If modern 'public international law in its historical evolution' had been, as Rosenne himself would readily concede,[19] 'essentially the product of European Christian civilization';[20] and if international law, moreover, had been exclusive in its application to members of the family of *civilized* nations, than we must consider any Jewish turn to international law and any Jewish international law engagement as embodying, explicitly or implicitly, *some* civilizational premise or claim.[21] That is not to say that international law scholars, Jewish or non-Jewish, raised *explicitly* the question of which of the cultural-political categories comprising international law's 'standard of civilization'—'civilized' nations, 'semi-civilized' nations, and 'savages'[22]—had applied to Jews; curiously, they did not. International law treatises, even when delving into Jewish matters, did not directly address the question of whether the Jews were 'civilized'.[23] Yet there was no escaping the *implications* of the answer. If the study or

[18] Koskenniemi, *Gentle Civilizer* (n 8).

[19] Shabtai Rosenne, 'The Influence of Judaism on International Law: A Research Program' (1957) 14 HaPraklit 3, 4 (Hebrew); subsequent, slightly differently titled versions appeared in (1958) 5 Netherlands Intl L Rev 119; Shabtai Rosenne, *An International Law Miscellany* (Martinus Nijhoff 1993) 509; and Mark W Janis (ed), *The Influence of Religion on the Development of International Law* (Springer 1991) 63.

[20] Earlier Jewish commentators on international law were acutely aware of this claim of international law's origins: Rosenne in fact borrowed, uncredited, that language from Oppenheim's first edition, for whom international law was famously 'in its origin essentially a product of Christian civilisation': Lassa Oppenheim: *International Law: A Treatise*, vol 1 (1st edn Longmans, Green & Co 1905) 3–4.

[21] Such a claim thus underscored Rosenne's highlighting of a Hebraist tradition in early international law scholarship: Rosenne, 'Judaism' (n 19).

[22] Gerrit W Gong, *The Standard of 'Civilization' in International Society* (Clarendon 1984); Koskenniemi, *Gentle Civilizer* (n 8) 98–178; Antony Anghie, *Imperialism, Sovereignty and the Making of International Law* (CUP 2005).

[23] Paz, *Gateway* (n 7) 6 thus speaks of 'an attempt to civilize (Christianize) the Jew in Europe', observing that an 'extensive treatment of this colonization is still missing from the historical records of the discipline'. She proposes to 'characterize the role international law played in the colonization of the Jew but also how the colonized Jew reacted, resisted, and therefore also contributed to international law' ibid, 11.

practice of international law, within or without Europe, necessarily encapsulated a civilizational claim,[24] than to invoke or utilize international law in the promotion of this or that model of Jewish emancipation involved, necessarily, making a claim about the civilizational 'level' of Jews. To engage international law in the furtherance of any model of Jewish emancipation was to face the dilemma of what some postcolonial theorists of modern Jewish history described as the elusiveness not merely of modern Jewish identity,[25] but of modern Jewish 'otherness' itself.[26] Modernity, to borrow a phrase from Jonathan Boyarin, had rendered Jews both 'others within' *and* 'others without'.[27] European Jews, in other words, were placed concurrently at international law's centre *and* at its periphery,[28] whether in the 'West' or 'East' of Europe.

This insight on the elusive, indeterminate Jewish otherness furnishes crucial analytical prisms for reflection on the Jewish turn to international law, its terms, and its conundra. If knowledge of international law was by itself a marker of civilization and, therefore, of inclusion and entitlement, Jews could by the very early nineteen hundreds display patent proficiency in its doctrines and theories: unlike other 'others', European Jews who turned to international law had no need to *translate* the seminal treatises of international law.[29] At the same time, how could Europe's perennial others be included in international law's political-cultural community that was defined in terms of religion and, increasingly, race? How could dispersed Jews, besides, be included in a family of *nations* and be entitled to the *status* such inclusion implied? Reading the Jewish turn to international law and its terms requires attention to the particular forms of the tensions underlying the question of Jewish exclusion-inclusion.[30] These did not always reflect civilizational sensibilities in explicit terms, yet such sensibilities were present, if implicit and muted, in

[24] Arnulf Becker Lorca, *Mestizo International Law: A Global Intellectual History 1842–1933* (CUP 2015).

[25] Paul Mendes-Flohr, *German Jews: A Dual Identity* (Yale UP 1999).

[26] Amir R Mufti, *Enlightenment in the Colony: The Jewish Question and the Crisis of Postcolonial Culture* (Princeton UP 2007) 7 considers, in the context of India's partition, the European 'Jewish Question' to be 'an early, and exemplary, instance of the crisis of minority' exported to colonial settings so that coding 'the other' in colonial society as a 'Jewish other' paved the way, he argues, to excluding that minority. Anne Orford (ed), *International Law and its Others* (CUP 2006) examines 'otherness' in international law.

[27] Jonathan Boyarin, *Storm from Paradise: The Politics of Jewish Memory* (University of Minnesota Press 1992) 77–98; Jonathan Boyarin, *The Unconverted Self: Jews, Indians, and the Identity of Christian Europe* (University of Chicago Press 2009). That is not to suggest that the position of international law's 'others' had not been marked by elusiveness: Rotem Giladi, 'The Phoenix of Colonial War: Race, the Laws of War, and the "Horror on the Rhine"' (2017) 30 Leiden JIL 847.

[28] Anghie (n 22) 32–114.

[29] Cf Zhiguang Yin, 'Heavenly Principles? The Translation of International Law in 19th-Century China and the Constitution of Universality' (2017) 27 EJIL 1005; Elisabetta Fiocchi Malaspina and Nina Keller-Kemmerer, 'International Law and Translation in the 19th Century' (2014) 22 Rechtsgeschichte—Legal History 214.

[30] On international law's 'logic of exclusion—inclusion': Koskenniemi, *Gentle Civilizer* (n 8) 127.

attempts to describe or prescribe a place for Jews—individually *or* collectively—in the international legal system.

Such civilizational sensibilities did not disappear with the acquisition of sovereignty or upon admission to the United Nations ('UN')—the formal resolution of the question of Jewish inclusion in the international law community. Indeed, these events too had a role in affecting a persisting ambivalence towards international law among Israeli diplomats. As I demonstrated elsewhere, in relation to early UN debates on the question of *apartheid*, a postcolonial—or decolonized—outlook was an important component in the self-understanding of the Jewish state's early diplomats and of how they approached items on the General Assembly's agenda such as 'The Treatment of People of Indian Origin in the Union of South Africa'.[31] That is not to say that the reader should expect to find in this book a structured study of Jewish otherness[32] or a sustained application of postcolonial theory to any Jewish or early Israeli engagement with international law. Nonetheless, it is important to note early that ambivalence, even after 1949, also emanated from pre-sovereign cultural sensibilities and was often couched in civilizational terms.

2. Emancipation, Ideology, Ambivalence

The Jewish quest for emancipation could find in international law a source of modern political imagination, modern vocabularies of emancipation and, with the establishment of the League of Nations in the wake of the Great War, an institutional platform to pursue emancipatory visions. That is not to say that all answers to the Jewish Question—all imagined models of emancipation—could find in international law inspiration, validation, or the institutional platforms where particular programmes could be advanced. Religious Orthodoxy—itself a response to modernity—had its own self-validating source of authority and its own prescriptions marking the path to salvation.[33] So did, for that matter, Marxism. Jewish Marxists preoccupied with the Jewish Question followed the doctrine that class struggle and the version of internationalism it gave rise to would see the Jewish Question vanish. They had no need for engagement with legal internationalism of

[31] Rotem Giladi, 'Negotiating Identity: Israel, Apartheid, and the United Nations 1949–1952' (2017) 132 (No.559) English Hist Rev 1440.

[32] Ivan Davidson Kalmar and Derek Jonathan Penslar (eds), *Orientalism and the Jews* (Brandeis UP 2005); Ethan B Katz, Lisa Moses Leff, and Maud S Mandel (eds), *Colonialism and the Jews* (Indiana UP 2017).

[33] A handful of pre-sovereign Orthodox thinkers did engage international law, but such engagements were peripheral to Orthodox doctrine: Amos Yisrael-Flishauer, *The Attitudes of Jewish Law Towards International Law: Analyses of Legal Materials and Processes* (PhD dissertation, Tel Aviv University 2011) (Hebrew); Michael Broyde, 'Public and Private International Law from the Perspective of Jewish Law' in Aaron Levine (ed), *The Oxford Handbook of Judaism and Economics* (OUP 2010) 365; Alexander Kaye, *The Legal Philosophies of Religious Zionism, 1937–1967* (PhD dissertation, Columbia University 2012). Similarly, the international advocacy of the ultra-Orthodox *Agudas Israel* appears sporadic.

the liberal kind: '[t]here was one cure for all the ills of the world—socialism. That was the fundamental law of laws for us', wrote a Jewish student in Kiev after the 1881 pogroms.[34] For Karl Marx, besides, 'notions such as ... "international law"—had he given it a second's thought, which he never did—were part of the problem, not of its resolution'.[35]

Other approaches to the Jewish Question, however, sought to tap international law's emancipatory potential. It is among adherents of assimilation, Diaspora Nationalism (or Autonomism), and Zionism[36] that a significant and consistent engagement with international law can be traced. And it is in the contestation among these three models of Jewish emancipation that early Israeli ambivalence towards international law—given voice by Rosenne and Robinson—was rooted.

2.1 Assimilation

Assimilation, the first model of emancipation to which my argument pertains, endorsed acculturation:[37] Jewish embrace of modernity through cultural integration with the surrounding European society. It drew directly on the tradition of European Enlightenment and placed faith in the promise of Emancipation—as a concrete historical event—first made by revolutionary France to treat 'individuals of the Jewish persuasion'[38] as equal citizens.[39] Liberal, 'civic' emancipation 'spoke of civic status, naturalization, national equality, and the granting of equal political rights'.[40] It promised to treat Jews as equal citizens within the national body

[34] Quoted in Jonathan Frankel, *Prophecy and Politics: Socialism, Nationalism, and the Russian Jews, 1862–1917* (CUP 1981) 52. No allusion whatsoever to international law is made in Abram Leon, *The Jewish Question: A Marxist Interpretation* (Pathfinder 1970). Warsaw-born Leon (1918) was a Zionist who first immigrated to Palestine, turned to Stalinism and later, in Belgium, to Trotskyism. He died in Auschwitz in 1944: John Rose, 'Karl Marx, Abram Leon and the Jewish Question: A Reappraisal' (2008) 119 Int'l Socialism <http://isj.org.uk/karl-marx-abram-leon-and-the-jewish-question-a-reappraisal/>. Studies of the Bund (The General Jewish Labor Union in Russia and Poland—*Algemeyner Yidisher Arbeter Bund in Lite, Poyln un Rusland*), established in 1897, do not furnish evidence of international law engagement—or, for that matter, raise the question.

[35] Koskenniemi, 'Marx' (n 6) 230.

[36] I disregard here Jewish territorialism associated with Israel Zangwill (1864–1926) and treat it essentially as a short-lived (1905–1925) offshoot of Zionism. Territorialists considered themselves true heirs to Theodor Herzl, founder of Political Zionism. Ideologically, their withdrawal from the Zionist Organisation was driven by the claim that a territorial, national solution to the plight of Jews could be achieved—at least temporarily—anywhere, not merely in Zion/Palestine. All evidence suggests that territorialists retained Herzl's diplomatic *modus operandi* based on his view that international guarantees needed to precede Jewish settlement, discussed below: Israel Zangwill, *Jewish Territorial Association: Manifesto and Correspondence* (London 1905) 4; Gur Alroey, *Zionism Without Zion: The Jewish Territorial Organization and Its Conflict with the Zionist Organization* (Wayne State UP 2016).

[37] Mendes-Flohr (n 25) 3.

[38] The French National Assembly (28 September 1791) 'The Emancipation of the Jews of France' in Mendes-Flohr and Reinharz (n 11) 127.

[39] Jacob Katz, 'The Term "Jewish Emancipation", Its Origin and Historical Impact' in Alexander Altman (ed), *Studies in Nineteenth-Century Jewish Intellectual History* (Harvard UP 1964) 1.

[40] Pierre Birnbaum and Ira Katznelson, 'Emancipation and the Liberal Offer' in Pierre Birnbaum and Ira Katznelson (eds), *Paths of Emancipation: Jews, States, and Citizenship* (Princeton UP 1995) 3.

politic; Jewish difference was reduced to faith, or religious 'persuasion'. Some, like Bruno Bauer, would nonetheless attach a condition, arguing that to be truly emancipated, Jews needed relinquish their faith.[41] Conversion ever remained at the end of the spectrum of assimilatory practices, whether as a mimetic strategy[42] or as a career choice deemed necessary for professional advancement—including in international law. The study of law, and international law all the more so, was itself an assimilationist strategy, a response to the challenge to modernize, and a ticket of admittance into the modern political order of civilized, European society.[43] Pursuit of the profession, like other forms of acculturation, was often not enough: consider Tobias Asser, who converted around 1890;[44] or Hans Kelsen, who converted, then changed denomination.[45]

Adherents (and practitioners) of assimilation constructed Jews as *individuals* deserving the status and treatment prescribed by liberal thought. Assimilationists proposed to resolve Jewish otherness and the conundrum presented by the standard of civilization by insisting that Jews belonged to the sphere of civilization not as a nation, but rather by dint of their affiliation to members of the family of civilized nations: Germany, France, Britain, and so forth. Dispersion was no bar to inclusion; as individuals, Jews could be as civilized as their compatriots.

To each other, within or without the national body politic, assimilationist Jews were 'co-religionists'. This self-perception not only inhered in Enlightenment thought; it was demanded by the terms of Emancipation itself. In December 1789, a few months after its establishment, the National Assembly held a long debate on 'Religious Minorities and Questionable Professions'—actors and executioners—all of whom had suffered from various legal disabilities and exclusions before the Revolution. Earlier, in August, the Assembly had adopted the *Declaration of the Rights of Men and Citizens*. The question now was to whom it applied: who were 'men and citizens'? When one Deputy proposed a law to cover non-Catholics, another wondered if this included the Jews. The Revolution had already abolished corporate forms of social organization and, with them, the semi-autonomous Jewish *Kehila* (community). During the debate, a liberal Deputy presented an interpretation of the modern status of Jews under the new regime, the *Declaration*, and the Republic. Answering the charge that 'the Jews have their own judges and laws', Count Stanislas Marie Adélaide de Clermont

[41] Bauer (n 6).

[42] Advising Rosenne, in 1950, on the renewal of the *Jewish Yearbook of International Law* and of potential contributors, Robinson described Joseph Kunz as a 'crypto-Jew': Robinson to Rosenne, 31 May 1950, FM—1816/1, Israel State Archive ('ISA').

[43] Ledford (n 13).

[44] See information and sources cited above (n 12).

[45] Eliav Lieblich, 'Assimilation through Law: Hans Kelsen and the Jewish Experience' in Loeffler and Paz (n 1) 51 offers a nuanced, insightful account of Kelsen's assimilationist politics.

Tonnerre placed blame upon the Old Regime for allowing it, and proceeded to spell out the terms of Emancipation:

> We must refuse everything to the Jews as a nation and accord everything to Jews as individuals. We must withdraw recognition from their judges; they should only have our judges. We must refuse legal protection to the maintenance of the so-called laws of their Judaic organization; they should not be allowed to form in the state either a political body or an order. They must be citizens individually ... If they do not want to be citizens, they should say so, and then, we should banish them. It is repugnant to have in the state an association of non-citizens, and a nation within the nation.[46]

Later, the rise of European nationalism would only increase the pressures on the loyalty of Jews and exacerbate the dilemma of assimilated Jews. On the one hand, their claim for inclusion in the nation drew on universal values; on the other, the very act of *national* Jewish organization to defend equality hinted at loyalties that traversed national boundaries. Espousing any *global* mission of Jewish solidarity—advocacy or philanthropy on behalf of Jewish communities suffering discrimination or persecution in Europe and beyond—rendered the loyalties of Jews even more suspect. Yet, paradoxically, so could the pursuit of organized Jewish politics *within* the nation.

That dilemma was shared by the various Jewish organizations that institutionalized assimilationist credo and politics: the French *Alliance Israélite Universelle* ('AIU'), the first of its generation, was founded in 1860 in the wake of French-Jewish intercessions in the 1840 Damascus Affair.[47] Its establishment, seven decades after Emancipation,[48] attested to security in its achievement; from the outset, the AIU espoused a mission that was universal.[49] Its founders' point of departure was the need to represent and protect those bereft of any government with 'a special interest and an official duty to represent and speak for them'.[50] This did not extend to emancipated Jews in France or elsewhere.[51] Underpinning the AIU's universal mission—and its civilizing mission

[46] Lynn Hunt, *The French Revolution and Human Rights: A Brief Documentary History* (Macmillan 1996) 86–8.

[47] André Kaspi, *Histoire de l'Alliance Israélite Universelle de 1860 à Nos Jours* (A Colin 2010); Paz, 'Network' (n 7). On the Damascus blood libel: Jonathan Frankel, *The Damascus Affair: 'Ritual Murder', Politics, and the Jews in 1840* (CUP 1997).

[48] Michael Graetz, *The Jews in Nineteenth Century France: From The French Revolution to the Alliance Israelite Universelle* (Stanford UP 1996).

[49] Kaspi (n 47); Paz, 'Network' (n 7).

[50] Quoted in David Vital, *A People Apart: A Political History of the Jews in Europe 1789–1939* (OUP 2001) 485–6.

[51] This security in the achievement of emancipation accounts for what has been described as the AIU's surprise and passivity in response to the Dreyfus Affair: Paula E Hyman, *The Jews of Modern France* (University of California Press 1998). On the position of Jews in France at the time: Michael R Marrus, *The Politics of Assimilation: A Study of the French Jewish Community at the Time of the Dreyfus Affair* (Clarendon 1971).

among Jews outside Europe[52]—was Jewish 'solidarity' that was religious, not ethnic.[53]

Other assimilationist organizations followed: in 1871, the Anglo-Jewish Association; the year after, the *Israelitischer Allianz zu Wien*; in Germany, the *Centralverein deutscher Staatsbürger jüdischen Glaubens* ('CV') was established in 1893 and the *Hilfsverein der deutschen Juden* in 1901; across the Atlantic, the American Jewish Committee ('AJC') was founded in 1906.[54] In contradistinction to the AIU, the CV long limited its effort to Germany alone, investing in politics and parliamentary struggle against anti-Semitism and eschewing any universal mission.[55] All these bodies faced the same tension between Jewish cosmopolitan solidarity and loyalty to the nation; each devised its own manner of negotiating the dilemma.

Assimilationist organizations tended, nonetheless, to share important characteristics. They all hailed from countries where the liberal emancipation of Jews-as-individuals was formally assured by law; that is, they operated in the 'West'. The philanthropic and advocacy activities of most were largely directed at unemancipated Jews of the 'East': the Yiddish-speaking *Ostjuden* of Eastern Europe and, in the case of the AIU, the Jews of the Orient. Jewish universal solidarity had its own 'others': coding civilizational sensibilities, it could serve to reaffirm the espousal of modernity of emancipated, Occidental Jews.[56]

Although some had mass membership—the CV comes to mind—these organs of Western emancipation tended to be elitist, 'oligarchic' affairs.[57] Their members

[52] Aron Rodrigue, *French Jews, Turkish Jews: The Alliance Israélite Universelle and the Politics of Jewish Schooling in Turkey, 1860–1925* (1990); Eli Bar-Chen, *Weder Asiaten noch Orientalen: Internationale jüdische Organisationen und die Europäisierung 'rückständiger' Juden* (Ergon Verlag 2005); Lisa Moses Leff, 'Jews, Liberals and the Civilizing Mission in Nineteenth-Century France' (2006) 32 Historical Reflections 105; Lisa Moses Leff, *Sacred Bonds of Solidarity: The Rise of Jewish Internationalism in Nineteenth Century France* (Stanford UP 2006).

[53] Leff (n 53).

[54] Abigail Green, 'Religious Internationalisms' in Glenda Sluga and Patricia Clavin, *Internationalisms: A Twentieth-Century History* (CUP 2017) 17. I leave aside the complex ways these bodies related to earlier representative institutions; for present purposes, it is sufficient to note that by the late nineteenth century organizations such as the British Board of Jewish Deputies (1760) espoused similar assimilationist worldviews.

[55] Sophie Schönherr, *Identitätsbildende Prozesse im Centralverein deutscher Staatsbürger jüdischen Glaubens zur Zeit des Wilhelminischen Deutschlands* (Grin 2019); Avraham Barkai, '"*Wehr dich!' Der Centralverein deutscher Staatsbürger jüdischen Glaubens (C.V.) 1893–1938* (CH Beck 2002). But compare to the *Hilfsverein*: Eli Bar-Chen, 'Two Communities with a Sense of Mission: The Alliance Israélite Universelle and the Hilfsverein der deutschen Juden' in Michael Brenner, Vicki Caron, and Uri R Kaufmann (eds), *Jewish Emancipation Reconsidered: The French and German Models* (66 Schriftenreihe wissenschaftlicher Abhandlungen des Leo Baeck Instituts, Mohr Siebeck 2003) 111.

[56] While safeguarding the privileged position of emancipated Jews in the West against anti-Semitic responses to the presence of newly arrived Ostjuden: Weiss (n 17); Matthew M Silver, *In the Service of the West: A New Look at Modern Jewish History* (HaKibbutz HaMeuchad 2014) (Hebrew); Kalmar and Penslar (n 32).

[57] Discussing Britain, Abigail Green describes 'a small and wealthy "cousinhood" of elite, interrelated families' who 'proved well able to defend its oligarchic position even after the onset of mass migration from eastern Europe in the 1880s and 1890s': Abigail Green, 'The West and the Rest: Jewish Philanthropy and Globalization to c. 1880' in Rebecca Korbin and Adam Teller (eds), *Purchasing Power: The Economics of Modern Jewish History* (Pennsylvania UP 2015) 168.

were affluent, socially accepted, and politically connected Jews of status (in Europe, sometimes ennobled) described by their opponents, who decried such institutions as undemocratic, as self-appointed 'Patricians'.[58] There was more than a grain of truth in this: when the question of *electing* members came up for discussion at the AJC's establishment, one participant shot down the propriety of democratic representation. 'Is it necessary that this Committee represent the riff raff and everybody? If this Committee represents the representative and high class Jews of America, that is enough.'[59] Notwithstanding recourse to philanthropic, humanitarian activities that by nature were visible, the preferred *modus operandi* of advocacy by these Western institutions shunned publicity and relied, instead, on personal ties and behind the scenes exertions of influence by member notables. This intercessional style, like the aversion to 'mass' movements, was also driven by fears of creating an appearance of worldwide Jewish influence—and the charge of dual loyalty.

Whereas individual engagement with international law by Jewish scholars signalled a *private* preference for this model of emancipation, assimilationist institutions—and Jewish notables—were first invested in promoting the religious and civic equality of other, unemancipated Jews through intercessional diplomacy that only on occasion sought to produce public *norms* at the national or international level. An early example of such *ad hoc* investment was the demand presented at the 1878 Berlin Congress 'that civil and political rights be granted to the Jews of Bulgaria, Serbia, Montenegro and Roumania'[60] in the wake of the Russo-Turkish War and the rather ambiguous language of Article 44 of the resulting Treaty of Berlin.[61] The 1919 Versailles Conference and establishment of the League of Nations would signal a shift towards a more regular assimilationist investment in international law and institutions.[62] By the mid-1940s, much of that investment would take the form of promoting the project of universal human rights.[63] Throughout those years of Jewish crises, the core ideological outlook, attendant sensibilities, and preferred *modus operandi* of these Western Jewish institutions would persist in spite of—and often because of—the challenges presented

[58] Peter Y Medding, 'Patterns of Political Organization and Leadership in Contemporary Communities' in Daniel Judah Elazar (ed), *Kinship and Consent: The Jewish Political Tradition and Its Contemporary Uses* (UP of America 1983) 261.

[59] Quoted in Nathan Schachner, *The Price of Liberty: A History of the American Jewish Committee* (AJC 1943) 28.

[60] Nahum M Gelber, 'The Intervention of German Jews at the Berlin Congress 1878' (1960) 5 Leo Baeck Inst YB 221 notes institutional involvement. Feinberg, 'Recognition' (n 2); tellingly, Lithuanian-born Feinberg—an *Ostjude*—did not account for Jewish involvement; ch 2 reproduces some of his critique of the assumptions and *modus operandi* of assimilationist institutions.

[61] Treaty between Great Britain, Germany, Austria, France, Italy, Russia, and Turkey for the Settlement of Affairs in the East (Berlin, 13 July 1878) (1908) 2 AJIL Suppl 401, 419 discussed by Fink (n 2) 3–38.

[62] Nathan Feinberg, *La Question Des Minorités à la Conférence de la Paix De 1919–1920 et l'action Juive en faveur de la Protection Internationale Des Minorités* (Rousseau & Cie 1929); Mark Levene, *War, Jews, and the New Europe: The Diplomacy of Lucien Wolf, 1914–1919* (OUP 1992).

[63] Chs 2–3 explore competing Jewish perspectives on the human rights project.

by proponents of other solutions to the Jewish Question. The emergence, towards the end of the nineteenth century, of ideologies of Jewish nationalism revealed another sensibility shared by the institutes of assimilation: all would reject any doctrine that constructed Jews in collective, group terms and deny, often vociferously, that Jews were a 'nation'. All would, in particular, for a long time to come disavow Zionism on ideological grounds.

The dilemma of assimilated Jews, torn between the liberal promise and the lived experience of exclusionary social reality, was exacerbated by the rise, at turn of the century, of modern popular and 'scientific' anti-Semitism. That dilemma was depicted in what some saw as the best literary output[64] of a less-than-successful playwright who had studied law at Vienna and made a living as a journalist for the *Neue Freie Presse*. Born in Budapest to a German-speaking secular, assimilated family, the author of the 1894 *Das Neue Ghetto*—'The New Ghetto'—described the uncertain position of emancipated, upper middle class Jews who would not be treated equally or accepted by Christian Viennese society despite fully adopting a modern, liberal, Western lifestyle and worldview. In the play, the protagonist—a lawyer by profession—meets his fate in a duel with an anti-Semitic nobleman.[65] By the time the controversial play premiered in Vienna's *Carltheater*, the author had already abandoned the pseudonym Albert Schnabel and came to prescribe another solution to the Jewish Question—one that rejected the promise of *individual* emancipation and offered an alternative reading of assimilation.

2.2 Zionism

Whether it was in Vienna, where Theodor Herzl had experienced first-hand the limits of assimilation and came to witness, in the mayoral elections of 1895,[66] the political purchase of modern anti-Semitism; or in Paris, whence he reported of the virulent sentiments unleashed by the accusation, court martial, and ceremonial *dégradation* of Alfred Dreyfus at the courtyard of the *École militaire*; it

[64] Amos Elon, *Herzl* (Holt, Rinehart & Winston 1975) 123; cf Shlomo Avineri, *Herzl's Vision: Theodor Herzl and the Foundation of the Jewish State* (Bluebridge 2014) 78. For analysis: Derek Penslar, *Theodor Herzl: The Charismatic Leader* (Yale UP 2020) 64–70, to whom I am grateful for sharing with me an advance copy of the book; Jacques Kornberg, *Theodor Herzl: From Assimilation to Zionism* (Indiana UP 1993) 103 et seq; Ritchie Robertson, 'The *New Ghetto* and the Perplexities of Assimilation' in Gideon Shimoni and Robert Wistrich (eds), *Theodor Herzl: Visionary of the Jewish State* (Magnes 1999) 39.

[65] Theodor Herzl's biographers noted the autobiographical resonance of the duel—another form of acculturation: eg Avineri (n 64) 95–6; Penslar (n 64) 25–6, 64–5, 138. For a gendered reading of the duel in Herzl's writing: Michael Gluzman, 'The Zionist Body: Nationalism and Sexuality in Herzl's *Altneuland*' in Harry Brod and Shawn Israel Zevit (eds), *Brother Keepers: New Perspectives on Jewish Masculinity* (Men's Studies Press 2010) 89; Daniel Boyarin, 'The Colonial Drag: Zionism, Gender, and Mimicry' in Fawzia Afzal-Khan and Kalpana Seshadri-Crooks (eds), *The Pre-Occupation of Post-Colonial Studies* (Duke University Press 2000) 234.

[66] Avineri (n 64) 91–3.

was disillusionment with Emancipation that led him to prescribe a *national* solution to the Jewish Question.[67] Early in 1896, he authored a pamphlet in hope of enlisting the support of the Rothschilds, the Jewish banking family, to the cause of his 'Modern Solution for the Jewish Question'. The title page of *Der Judenstaat* reported his credentials: *Doctor der Rechte*.[68] It was his reading of modern anti-Semitism that led Herzl to reject the emancipation of Jews-as-individuals: assimilation, he wrote, would amount to 'annihilation'.[69]

The introduction to *Der Judenstaat* observed that 'civilized nations do not even yet seem able to shake off, try as they will', the 'Jewish question'—that is, modern anti-Semitism.[70] It may have been 'a remnant of the Middle Ages',[71] but there was no denying its persistence in modern times. Rather than resolved by modernity, modernity facilitated its toxic circulation. Anti-Semitism was, for Herzl, a companion of modern Jewish existence:

> The Jewish question exists wherever Jews live in perceptible numbers. Where it does not exist, it is carried by Jews in the course of their migrations. We naturally move to those places where we are not persecuted, and there our presence produces persecution. This is the case in every country, and will remain so, even in those most highly civilised—France itself being no exception—till the Jewish question finds a solution on a political basis. The unfortunate Jews are now carrying Anti-Semitism into England; they have already introduced it into America.[72]

Herzl proceeded to characterize the Jewish Question as a *national* question requiring an *international* solution: '[i]t is a *national* question, which can only be solved by making it a *political world-question* to be discussed and controlled by the *civilized nations of the world in council*'.[73]

Herzl's analysis and the solution he prescribed embodied both a critique of and a reinvestment in modernity. The anti-Semitism Herzl professed to 'understand ... without fear or hatred', though modern, could not be 'subdued by reasonable arguments'.[74] The subtitle of *Der Judenstaat* spoke of an 'attempt' (in other

[67] Herzl's turning point is the subject of an ongoing debate among his biographers. The Dreyfus affair (1894–1906) involved the false conviction for treason of an Alsatian artillery officer of Jewish descent; Dreyfus was exonerated and reinstated in 1906.

[68] Theodor Herzl, *Der Judenstaat: Versuch einer modernen Lösung der Judenfrage* (M Breitenstein's Verlags-Buchhandlung 1896).

[69] All references are to Theodor Herzl, *The Jewish State: An Attempt at a Modern Solution for the Jewish Question* (Maccabæan 1904) 24. The pamphlet also offered careful but systematic refutations of prospective objections by assimilationists.

[70] ibid, 4.

[71] ibid.

[72] ibid.

[73] Emphases added; ibid, 4–5.

[74] ibid, 4, 93.

translations, a 'proposal') at a 'modern solution'. Its pages offer ample testimony of Herzl's modernist sensibilities: they alluded to the 'ingenious invention of a modern mind',[75] used metaphors of 'steam-power' and 'large engine',[76] and expressed faith in 'technical' and other manifestations of 'progress',[77] 'scientific improvements',[78] and 'scientific principles'.[79] Herzl's *Der Judentaadt* sang the praise of *Bildung*, marked levels of civilization, and was premised on the gradual, yet assured, 'ascent of man to higher and yet higher grades of civilisation'.[80]

If assimilation mandated Jewish mimicry on an individual level, Herzl's solution to the Jewish Question, revealed in the title, involved mimicry on a grand, collective scale. In characterizing it as a 'national question', soluble only by making it an international and 'political' question, Herzl's solution constructed Jews, dispersion notwithstanding, as a nation. Having politicized the Jewish Question—a 'world-question to be discussed and controlled by the civilized nations of the world in council'—Herzl proceeded to pronounce Jewish national consciousness: 'We are a people—One people'.[81] Herzl's Jewish nationalism, however, was ambivalent at its core: it was predicated on the *rejection* of European nationalism—a mirror of the rejection of Jews by European nationalism—yet, at the same time, sought to *emulate* it.[82] Having eschewed assimilation, the model of emancipation Herzl now prescribed—his 'attempt to solve the Jewish Question'—decreed 'the restoration of the Jewish State'.[83] By leaving the Diaspora—for Herzl and those who will follow him, the root cause of the Jewish predicament—and 'acquiring the sovereignty over a strip of territory',[84] Jews would return to history through another mimetic act;[85] like any other nation,[86] they would have 'sovereignty over a ... piece of land'.[87]

[75] ibid, xvii.
[76] ibid, xviii.
[77] ibid, 1.
[78] ibid, 55.
[79] ibid, 83.
[80] ibid, 3; Jehuda Reinharz and Yaacov Shavit, *Glorious, Accursed Europe: An Essay on Jewish Ambivalence* (Brandeis UP 2010) 34.
[81] Herzl, *The Jewish State* (n 69) 5.
[82] Gideon Shimoni and Robert Wistrich, 'Introduction' in Shimoni and Wistrich (n 64) xviii; Hedva Ben-Israel, 'Zionism and European Nationalisms: Comparative Aspects' (2003) 8 Isr Stud 91, 94.
[83] Herzl, *The Jewish State* (n 69) xvi.
[84] ibid, 68.
[85] The notion of 'return to history', 'stressing the Jews' capacity to re-enter the historical arena as autonomous agents, constituted the core of the revolutionary dimension of Zionism'; it prescribed return 'as a politically active collectivity, in contrast to their political passivity throughout the Exile': Shmuel Noah Eisenstadt, 'Did Zionism Bring Back the Jews to History?' (1997) 38 Jewish Stud 9, 13.
[86] 'The fathers of Zionism—and certainly Herzl among them—believed that the Jewish people could follow the example of the European nations and arrive at the territorial concentration and political independence of a progressive society guided by the principles of the European Enlightenment ... Herzl always emphasized the like-other-nations motif': Gideon Shimoni and Robert Wistrich, 'Introduction' in Shimoni and Wistrich (n 64) xvii.
[87] Herzl, *The Jewish State* (n 69) 27. *Der Judenstaat* still considered Argentina, the object of Jewish colonization projects funded by philanthropist Baron Maurice de Hirsch, as a possible alternative to Palestine.

Predicated on both the rejection and mimicry of modernity, emancipation, and European nationalism, the depth of ambivalence underscoring Herzl's version of Jewish nationalism could be fathomed by his reinvestment in European modernity. For Herzl did more than propose to take the Jews outside Europe or even envision the Jewish state as an extension and emissary of European culture[88]—no less than a 'rampart of Europe against Asia, an outpost of civilisation as opposed to barbarism'.[89] Rather, the Jewish state that took hold of his imagination was to be 'a land of experiments and a model State'.[90] Some of the features that would make the Jewish state exemplary were already alluded to in *Der Judenstaat*. In 1902, the *dramatiker* would turn to other literary genres to portray an imagery of the Jewish state in Palestine that he now called 'The New Society'. *Altneuland*—as much a work of alternate history as a social-political utopia—laid bare just how liberal, progressive, modernist, European, and international Herzl's sensibilities remained.[91] The Jewish state was to be a particularist solution to the Jewish Question; but, though cast in a European mould, it also was to have a universal mission. The Jewish state, Herzl wrote 'is essential to the world'.[92]

Herzl's universal mission itself gave voice to ambivalence that only compounded one of the paradoxes facing theorists of nationalism: formal universalism manifest in assertions of unique particularities.[93] On the one hand, the universal mission of the Jewish state reaffirmed European civilization: it expressed universal sensibilities that bolstered Jewish civilizational claims and promised a Jewish contribution to European civilization. On the other, Herzl's assertation that the Jewish state was 'essential to the world'[94] ('*ein Weltbedürfniss*') was predicated on a severe critique of Europe. Herzl's Zionism was driven by a catastrophic prognosis of what European nationalism holds in store for the Jews. From this perspective, anti-Semitism and Jewish suffering were not Jewish but European, Gentile problems: they were blots on European civilization. Herzl's Zionism thus provided civilized states with an opportunity 'to chase away the spectres of their own past'.[95] From this perspective, mending the Jewish situation was, really, an opportunity for Europe to mend and redeem itself.

[88] Herzl's Zionism 'would remove Jews from Europe in order to reintegrate them as Europeans on a new basis': Jacques Kornberg, 'The Construction of an Identity' in Shimoni and Wistrich (n 64) 15, 25.

[89] Herzl, *The Jewish State* (n 69) 29.

[90] ibid, 96, 24.

[91] Theodor Herzl, *Altneuland: Roman* (Hermann Seemann Nachfolger 1902); all references are to Theodor Herzl, *Old-New Land* (Bloch 1941).

[92] Herzl, *The Jewish State* (n 69) xix.

[93] That is, the 'formal universality of nationality as a socio-cultural concept ... vs. the irremediable particularity of its concrete manifestations, such that, by definition, "Greek" nationality is sui generis': Benedict Anderson, *Imagined Communities: Reflections on the Origins and Spread of Nationalism* (rev edn, Verso 2006) 5.

[94] Herzl, *The Jewish State* (n 69) xix.

[95] ibid, 90.

For Herzl, the Jewish Question required an international solution.[96] Though his many biographers tend to gloss over his investment in international law,[97] it had a central role to play in this vision of national Jewish emancipation. The extent of that role can be measured by international law's hold on his political imagination.[98] It is not just that international law vernaculars of the late nineteenth century—protectorates, charters, guarantees, cessions, and other familiar terms of the discipline—laced Herzl's writing, speeches, and journal entries. And it is not merely that international legal sensibilities shaped Herzl's political *modus operandi*. Rather, Herzl's Political Zionism made an ideological investment in international legalism. It considered international law no less than a path—*the* path—to Jewish emancipation. Herzl opposed the trickle, by private initiative, of Eastern Jews to Palestine following the pogroms in the early 1880s. This was, for him, 'infiltration'[99] that followed the old pattern of Jewish immigration that carried with it the seeds of anti-Semitism. In 1897, at the first Zionist Congress in Basle, he denounced any who believed that 'the Jews can as it were smuggle themselves into the land of their forefathers' as one who 'deceives himself or is deceiving others'.[100] His position expressed pragmatic prudence that was grounded, however, in principle. From the outset of his turn to Jewish nationalism, Herzl imagined a planned, mass restoration of the Jews *sanctioned by international law*: '[o]ur first object is', he wrote in *Der Judenstaat*, 'as I said before, supremacy, assured to us by international law, over a portion of the globe sufficiently large to satisfy our just requirements'.[101] The pamphlet—though 'not intended for lawyers'[102]—signalled that national emancipation would follow the path of international legality: Jews would immigrate to Palestine 'with *absolute conformity to law*, openly and by light of day, under the eyes of the authorities and the control of *public opinion*'.[103] When Jews would leave Europe, he wrote,

[96] ibid, 4–5; consider also his first address to the Basle Congress: Michael J Reimer, *The First Zionist Congress: An Annotated Translation of the Proceedings* (SUNY Press 2019) 92–4.

[97] And, avoid, curiously, a systematic exploration of the formative role of his legal education: although his brief brush with Roman law in *Der Judenstaat* attracted some attention, most of his biographers tend to focus Herzl's student-days *Burschenschaften* engagements and the choice of law as indices of assimilation: eg Ernst Pawel, *The Labyrinth of Exile: A Life of Theodor Herzl* (Farrar, Straus & Giroux 1992) 34–5, 49.

[98] Compare Herzl's portrayal of the 'Peace Palace', in Jerusalem in 1902, to the way it was described by Andrew Dickson White, the senior American diplomat in the 1899 Hague Conference, when seeking to secure Andrew Carnegie's donation that same year: Herzl, *Old-New Land* (n 91) 247 et seq; Arthur Eyffinger, *The Peace Palace: Residence for Justice, Domicile of Learning* (Carnegie 1988) 49. Herzl's connections to the peace movement are well-recorded: Alan T Levenson, 'Theodor Herzl and Bertha von Suttner: Criticism, Collaboration and Utopianism' (1994) 15 J of Isr Hist 213.

[99] Herzl, *The Jewish State* (n 69) 28 ('An infiltration is bound to end in disaster ... Immigration is consequently futile unless based on an assured supremacy').

[100] Reimer (n 96) 95.

[101] Herzl, *The Jewish State* (n 69) 83.

[102] ibid, 77.

[103] Emphases added; ibid, 94. For the professional and ideological sensibilities captured by the phrase 'public opinion': Koskenniemi, *Gentle Civilizer* (n 8) 11–19.

> Their exodus will have no resemblance to a flight, for it will be a well-regulated expedition under control of public opinion. The movement will not only be inaugurated with absolute conformity to law, but it cannot even be carried out without the friendly intervention of interested Governments, who would derive considerable benefits from it.[104]

Herzl international legal sensibilities determined the *modus operandi* of his 'Political'—as opposed to on-the-ground 'Practical'—Zionism.[105] Instead of meagre *avant-garde* colonization efforts, Herzl turned to high diplomacy aimed at securing from Europe's rulers legal guarantees, a legal 'charter', and legal recognition of the Zionist project.[106] The plan envisioned the establishment of a corporation[107]—another evidence of the font of Herzl's political imagination—to promote and manage the plan; it was to 'secure by international law' the land; though the land was to 'be privately acquired',[108] what Herzl sought was no less than 'sovereignty . . . over a portion of the globe large enough to satisfy the reasonable requirements of a nation; the rest we shall manage for ourselves'.[109]

Translating the vision into a political programme required, however, the introduction of some ambiguity. The first Zionist Congress convened in 1897 placed international law at the centre of the Zionist credo but, at the same time, sacrificed it to diplomatic exigencies. The Basle Programme adopted by the Congress proclaimed the overarching end of the movement: 'Zionism strives to create a *homeland* in Palestine for the Jewish people, *secured under public law*'.[110] '*Judenstaat*' turned to '*Heimstätte*'—homeland—for the 'Jewish people'; 'international law' was replaced by 'public law'; and while the Programme spoke of the need to secure the agreement of governments, it was silent on any 'guarantee' by Europe's Great Powers. In all cases, ambiguity sought to avoid offence to the Sublime Porte—Palestine's sovereign—that Herzl was courting.[111] Yet it was clear to all that what was meant by 'public law'—*öffentlich-rechtlich* in the original German—was, precisely, international law: there was ambiguity but no ambivalence there. The demand to add 'international' before 'law'[112]—thus read the original draft[113]—was the only point debated by the Congress plenary. In the end, Herzl's Presidential motion

[104] Herzl, *The Jewish State* (n 69) 13.
[105] On Practical Zionism, see eg Gideon Shimoni, *The Zionist Ideology* (Brandeis UP 1995) 86, 102, 113.
[106] Isaiah Friedman, 'Theodor Herzl: Political Activity and Achievements' (2004) 9 Israel Stud 46 offers a concise assessment of Herzlian diplomatic efforts.
[107] Herzl, *The Jewish State* (n 69) 31.
[108] ibid, 33.
[109] ibid, 25, 68 ('acquiring the sovereignty over a strip of territory', assisted by the 'Powers').
[110] Emphases added; Reimer (n 96) 215.
[111] Nathan Feinberg, 'Legal Significance of the Basle Program' in Nathan Feinberg, *Palestine Under the Mandate and the State of Israel* (Magnes 1963) 3, 5–6 (Hebrew).
[112] Reimer (n 96) 210–15.
[113] ibid, 219.

to have the word 'public' inserted before 'law' was carried, and the Programme was adopted by acclamation.[114]

For all his investment in international law, Herzl harboured a measure of reserve. Though appreciative of the support of the peace activist, his diary notes the 'futility of efforts to "combat anti-Semitism"' with 'paper declamations' and philanthropic 'relief committees'. 'The noble Bertha von Suttner', he recorded, 'is in error ... when she thinks that such a committee can be of help'.[115] Herzl eschewed philanthropy:[116] *first*, the philanthropic solution of 'assimilated' Jews to instances of Jewish persecution elsewhere.[117] *Second*, colonization projects by Jewish philanthropies.[118] And *third*, the benevolence underscoring Great Power intervention on behalf of Jews. What he sought to obtain from Europe's 'civilized nations' was legal right, not *charity*. At Basle, addressing the matter of prospective negotiations with governments 'over the settlement of the Jewish popular masses on large scale', Herzl told the delegates:

> It would be an idle business to spend much time talking about what sort of legal form the agreement will ultimately take. But one thing ought to be maintained as an inviolable principle: its basis *must be a condition of legal right and not tolerance.* We have had by now quite enough of tolerance and living as Jews under the [revocable] 'protection' of the state.[119]

Or, one may add, under the protection of international law that had hitherto offered Jews such 'paper declamations' and 'tolerance' in the form of humanitarian and diplomatic interventions.[120] Herzl's aversion to 'tolerance' and 'paper declamations' would become part of Zionism's *weltanschauung*—and in time, as we shall see, part of Israel's ambivalent attitude towards international law.

What Herzl sought—to borrow a phrase from the editors of the *Jewish Yearbook of International Law*—was to turn the Jews from an 'object' to a 'subject' of international law.[121] Jewish legal objecthood, however, rendered international law both a platform for and, at the same time, an *obstacle* to Jewish national emancipation. The very international law investment Herzl bequeathed to adherents of Zionism—the grant of sovereignty secured by international law—confirmed their legal incapacity to claim, negotiate, and receive such a grant. Herzl's insistence on

[114] ibid, 215.

[115] Theodor Herzl, *Theodor Herzl: Excerpts from His Diaries* (Scopus 1941) 3.

[116] Herzl, *The Jewish State* (n 69) xvi.

[117] ibid, 11 ('these charitable institutions are created not for, but against, persecuted Jews—are created to despatch these poor creatures just as fast and as far as possible').

[118] ibid, xvi; here, too, his entreaties with Jewish philanthropists bred a measure of ambiguity.

[119] Emphasis added; Reimer (n 96) 94.

[120] Herzl, *The Jewish State* (n 69) 90; for humanitarian and diplomatic interventions on behalf of Jewish communities, consider the sources cited above (n 2).

[121] 'Introduction' (1948) 1 Jewish YB Intl L v discussed in the Prologue ('At all the times they were merely the *object*, never the *subject*, of international law').

international legalism presented a conundrum that would drive Zionist ambivalence towards international law.

International law at the end of the nineteenth century not only limited sovereignty to 'civilized' nations alone, excluding Europe's others from the 'gift of civilization'.[122] Prevailing positivist international law doctrine, articulated at Herzl's Vienna Law Faculty and elsewhere, also asserted the *exclusive* legal personality, subjecthood, and capacity of the state in international law. As Lassa Oppenheim wrote in 1905, a year after Herzl's death:

> States solely and exclusively are the subjects of International Law. This means that the Law of Nations is a law for the international conduct of States, and not of their citizens. Subjects of the rights and duties arising from the Law of Nations are States solely and exclusively ... This is a consequence of their sovereignty and of the fact that the Law of Nations is a law between, not above, the States.[123]

This meant that only states could have legal status, legal rights, and legal obligations under international law: only states could enter legal relations and entreat with other subjects—that is, other states—of international law. For a Jewish state to come into existence, it had to be 'admitted into the Family of Nations'[124] by members of that 'Family'—the so-called 'civilized' states.[125] International law decreed that Jews—even if organized in the manner proposed by Herzl—lacked any legal capacity to negotiate or become a party to any legal instrument securing the creation of a Jewish state. This compelled both investment in *and* protest against international law that deprived Jews of capacity and standing and rendered them, in law, voiceless.

International law may have been an indispensable vehicle for Jewish political revival; alas, it was also an obstacle to achieving it. Not possessing a state, the Jewish people did not constitute, legally speaking, a 'nation'; and in the absence of 'nationhood', they could not possess their own state. Subjecthood, as Rosenne would come to observe in 1947, was a vicious circle for those located outside it.[126] For individual Jews, or individual Jewish communities, international law could have been an instrument of amelioration; for Jews collectively, as for many non-European 'others', international law was an instrument of exclusion, a marker of political inferiority and legal incapacity.

Ambivalence towards international law inhered in Herzl's outlook, even if his critique of the sovereign exclusion of Jews produced by international law had

[122] Koskenniemi, *Gentle Civilizer* (n 8) 98–178.
[123] Oppenheim (n 20) 18–20.
[124] ibid, 17.
[125] Anghie (n 22).
[126] Shabtai Rowson, 'International Law and the Jewish People' (1947) 11 Tarbut 4 (Hebrew) discussed in ch 5.

been only implicit in his quest for international legal *right*. That critique, in fact, preceded his preoccupation with the Jewish Question. That is, it was inherent in modern Jewish national thought preceding Herzl. Leon Pinsker's influential 1882 *Auto-Emancipation*,[127] with which Herzl was not familiar when he wrote *Der Judenstaat*,[128] had already expressed the disillusionment with emancipation, censure of assimilation, and the investment in *and* critique of international law to be later found in Herzl's thought.[129] Pinsker argued that '[o]nly ... when the equality of the Jews and the other nations becomes a fact', based on mutual respect that is 'generally regulated and secured by international law or by treaties' will 'the problem presented by the Jewish Question be considered solved'.[130] At the same time, Jewish statelessness, and objecthood, were also bars to achieving that very equality:

> Unfortunately ... under present conditions ... the admission of the Jewish people into the ranks of the other nations seems illusory. They lack most of those attributes which are the hall-mark of a nation. They lack that characteristic national life which is inconceivable without ... a common land. The Jewish people have no fatherland of their own ... they have no rallying point, no centre of gravity, no accredited representatives.[131]

For Herzl and Pinsker alike, ambivalence inhered in the conundrum of objecthood and the lack of Jewish *locus standi* it entailed. Their diagnosis of the obstacle of legal standing foregrounded a ceaseless preoccupation with questions of *standing* and *representation* that would underscore the international law engagement of Zionist international lawyers[132] and drive the contentious politics of Jewish representation between Zionists and their ideological rivals.[133] Lawyers invested in the Zionist cause, that is, were ideologically predisposed to invest in overcoming the obstacle of objecthood and embroil in intra-Jewish competition over the question of authority to speak for the Jews—a struggle for and over the Jewish *voice*. In 1949, these sensibilities became the

[127] Leon Pinsker, *Autoemancipation!: Mahnruf an seine Stammesgenossen von einem russischen Juden* (W Issleib 1882); all references are to Aubrey S Eban (ed), *Auto-Emancipation by Leo Pinsker* (Federation of Zionist Youth 1939) 15.

[128] 'A pity that I had not read it before my own pamphlet was printed': Marvin Lowenthal (ed), *The Diaries of Theodor Herzl* (Dial Press 1956) 96; Dimitry Shumsky, 'Leon Pinsker and "Autoemancipation!": A Reevaluation' (2011) 18 Jewish Social Stud 33.

[129] Pinsker (n 127) 15–18.

[130] ibid, 16.

[131] ibid; '*Vertretung*'—the German original read '*est hat Kein Zentrum, keinen Schwerpunkt, keine eigne regierung, keine Vertretung*'—should translate 'representation'; the translation, nonetheless, accurately reflects a core Zionist sensibility with regard to formal standing.

[132] Rotem Giladi, 'At the Sovereign Turn: International Law at the Hebrew University Law Faculty Early Years' in Yfaat Weiss and Uzi Rebhun (eds), *The History of the Hebrew University in Jerusalem*, vol 5 (forthcoming Magnes 2021) (Hebrew).

[133] This is a recurring theme in all case studies examined in this book, but is particularly patent in chs 2–3.

markers of sovereign transition; Sharett's maiden speech to the GA emphasized, accordingly, that UN admission consummated the 'transition' of the Jewish people 'from political anonymity to clear identity, from inferiority to equal status, from mere passive protest to active responsibility, from exclusion to membership in the family of nations'.[134] Such sensibilities would play a crucial role in how Robinson, Rosenne, and their peers approached international law after May 1949.

It is perhaps telling that in 1896, to overcome sovereign exclusion and legal incapacity, Herzl had to find a solution outside the corpus of international law. Instead, he had to turn to Roman law to advance what he described as 'my theory of the legal basis of a State'.[135] Though ostensibly dealing with 'a question which has seriously occupied doctors of jurisprudence in every age',[136] his answer really sought to resolve the question of the legal incapacity of the Jewish people to entreat with Europe's sovereigns. Having 'cursorily' refuted Rousseau's social contract and other state theories, Herzl proceeded to argue that the legal foundation of the state is captured by the Roman law notion of *negotiurum gestio*[137] under which the *gestor* manages the affairs of others not by dint of authorization ('human warrant') but by superior necessity: 'higher obligations authorise him to act' to safeguard the endangered 'property of an oppressed person'.[138] For Herzl, the Jewish 'dominus—the people',[139] required a *gestor* to manage its political affairs precisely because, dispersed, it was incapable of managing its own affairs:

> The Jewish people are at present prevented by the diaspora from undertaking the management of their business for themselves. At the present time they are in a condition of more or less severe distress in many parts of the world. They need, above all things, a gestor.
>
> This gestor cannot, of course, be a single individual. Such a one would either make himself ridiculous, or—seeing that he would appear to be working for his own interests—contemptible.
>
> The gestor of the Jews must therefore be a body corporate.
>
> And that is the Society of Jews.[140]

[134] Speech to the General Assembly by Foreign Minister Sharett, 11 May 1949 in Meron Medzini (ed), *Israel's Foreign Relations: Selected Documents, 1947–1974* (MFA 1976) 119; GAOR, Plenary (11 May 1949) 332.

[135] Herzl, *The Jewish State* (n 69) 77.

[136] ibid, 79.

[137] ibid ('I believe it is to be found in the "negotiorum gestio", wherein the body of citizens represent the dominus negotiorum, and the government represents the gestor').

[138] ibid.

[139] ibid, 80.

[140] ibid, 81; elsewhere, Herzl made it clear that the Society, a body corporate with legal personality, will 'be authorised to confer or treat with Governments in the name of the people' and negotiate 'with the present masters of the land, putting itself under the protectorate of the European Powers'. Theodor Herzl, 'A "Solution to the Jewish Problem"' *The Jewish Chronicle* (17 January 1896) 12, 13.

And yet, the very convening of the Basle Congress and the establishment of the Zionist Organisation sought to demonstrate that the Jewish people were capable of managing their own affairs, dispersion notwithstanding. In law, the root cause of incapacity was not the Jewish Diasporic condition but the sovereign exclusion affected by international law itself: the insistence that only states could enjoy legal personality, enjoy rights, and assume obligations. Herzl's *gestor* was to have a measure of legal personality to constitute a state in the making, *in statu nascendi*. Although it would not be able to 'exercise sovereign power',[141] it would seek recognition as a 'State-forming power'.[142]

Investment and resentment—that would be the Herzl's legacy of ambivalence to Zionist engagements with international law. His resentment might have been implicit: he did not expound on the obstacle of objecthood, likely for tactical reasons. Instead, he had sought ways to overcome it. In the years that followed his death, that resentment—and investment in attempts to resolve the conundrum of objecthood—would become more patent among adherents of Zionism. It would certainly not remain the province of Zionist international lawyers. Zionist leaders would be equally preoccupied with Jewish legal standing, incapacity, and voicelessness; they, too, would reveal resentment towards international law and invest in overcoming the deficiency it deemed Jews, as a nation, to suffer. Often, in their attempts to surmount it, they would point to the establishment of the Zionist Organisation as the expression of popular will—and later, to the Palestine Mandate—as overcoming Jewish objecthood and obtaining legal status; even then, resentment would persist.

So would ambivalence. Consider, in this regard, one speech delivered on 29 September 1930, in Berlin, by David Ben-Gurion—not yet a member of the Zionist Executive. In the Diaspora, he argued, 'the Jewish people was not a subject of political possibilities or political will'. The advent of the Zionist movement, however, refuted the claim that 'a stateless people cannot constitute a political actor or a subject of the law of nations'. The law of nations came to validate 'Jewish right over *Eretz-Israel*', and the Zionist Organisation became 'an official international agency of the Jewish people as regards' Palestine. Ben-Gurion, however, proceeded to deride international law's pedigree and recall a historical grievance: 'within the existing law of nations the Jewish people has for generations been denied of law, deprived of right, lacking the capacity to express its will and wishes in a manner permissible and recognised'. Ben-Gurion next described how Zionism—'a new force added to international politics, a new partner in the law of nations'—overcame objecthood and attained 'international rights over *Eretz-Israel*'. The import of 'achievement',

[141] Herzl, *The Jewish State* (n 69) 31.

[142] ibid, 83 ('Externally, the Society will attempt ... to be acknowledged as a State-forming power. The free assent of many Jews will confer on it the requisite authority in its relations with Governments' aimed at obtaining 'supremacy, assured to us by international law, over a portion of the globe').

nonetheless, was neither to be considered lightly nor, however, to be 'exaggerated'. Ben-Gurion's ambivalence was directed, equally, at international organization: 'we have the right to demand that our voice be heard in the mandate government and in the League of Nations. Flawed with sin as these institutions may be, they are still the only institutions with authority and power over the country's destiny'.[143] National consciousness and organization, even when sanctioned by international law, could not quite overcome Jewish objecthood, inferior legal status, and all that it implied. The chapters that follow reveal that these sensibilities, and the ambivalence they expressed, would not disappear with the establishment of the Jewish state or its UN admission.

Before proceeding to present the third model of emancipation that drove Jewish international law investment, two clarifications ought to be made. *First*, I cannot offer here a history of the Zionist ideology or a chronology of events and forces that shaped and reshaped it.[144] I touch on a few of these below, *apropos* the discussion of how ambivalence became embedded in the political experience of Zionism, but otherwise assume that the reader—whether an international lawyer, a student of Israeli history or politics, or a Jewish history scholar—has some knowledge of key political developments and legal instruments. Otherwise, I gloss over such events and forces as well as subtle or patent shifts in Zionist ideology and provide background information only where necessary for and to the extent that it is pertinent to the argument: the so-called 'Uganda Controversy' of 1903–1905 over the prospect of establishing a Jewish homeland, under British protection, in Eastern Africa (present day Kenya);[145] Herzl's 1904 death; or the 1906 Helsingfors synthesis between 'Political' and 'Practical' Zionism[146]—one invested in law and diplomacy, the other in immigration to and colonization in Palestine from below.

Second, I offer here no chart mapping the various strands of Zionist thought. This concerns my rather loose use of the term 'Zionism', sometimes with but often without qualifiers: 'Political', 'Practical', 'Spiritual', 'General', etc. As the late Amos Oz once observed, 'from its foundation and outset, Zionism had been a family name, not a first name'.[147] My argument, however, does not often require introduction to members of the extended family; where a qualifier is warranted, introductions follow to the necessary extent. Other than (sometimes) in this chapter, Zionism, unqualified, refers to a range of *consensus* ideological assumptions, positions, and sensibilities shared by most or all Zionist political parties in the *Yishuv*.

[143] David Ben-Gurion, 'The External Policy of the Jewish People' in David Ben-Gurion, *From Class to People* (Ayanot 1955) 102 (Hebrew).

[144] Shimoni (n 105).

[145] David Vital, *Zionism: the Formative Years* (Clarendon 1982); Adam Rovner, *In the Shadow of Zion: Promised Lands Before Israel* (NYU Press 2014); Eitan Bar-Yosef, 'Spying Out the Land: The Zionist Expedition to East Africa, 1905' in Eitan Bar-Yosef and Nadia Valman (eds), *'The Jew' in Late-Victorian and Edwardian Culture: Between the East End and East Africa* (Palgrave-Macmillan 2009).

[146] Shimoni (n 105) 114–15.

[147] Amos Oz, *All Our Hopes* (Keter 1998) 11 (Hebrew).

This range, itself, was by no means static; the final years of the British mandate and, in particular, the sovereign turn saw that consensus refined, reinterpreted, and crystallized to form Israel's foundational ideology.[148] It was through the prism of this version of Zionism that Rosenne and Robinson would now approach international law.

2.3 Diaspora Nationalism

Diaspora Nationalism shared one point of departure with Zionism but challenged another. Both creeds considered Jews to be a nation, and both asserted that the promise of emancipation could only be fulfilled politically and collectively—not individually—through national political organization. Yet instead of prescribing collective emancipation and the acquisition of political subjecthood by following the example of the European nation-state, Diaspora Nationalism decreed the pursuit of national life *in the Diaspora*. In that, it contested Zionism's identification of the Diaspora as the root cause of the modern Jewish condition—and the Zionist principled 'Negation of the Diaspora'.[149] In diametrical opposition to Herzlian Zionism, Diaspora Nationalism required neither a territorial base nor international law's guarantee of sovereignty over it.

Diaspora Nationalism came to be identified with the scholarship and teaching of Russian-born historian Simon Dubnow (1860–1941); often, it is referred to as 'Dubnowism'. His version of Jewish nationalism was unveiled[150] as a response to—and critique of—Herzlian Zionism in 1897, the year of the Basle Congress. In a series of press articles, later collected and published as *Letters on Old and New Judaism*, Dubnow denounced 'Political Zionism' as 'merely a renewed form of messianism' that 'blurs the lines between reality and fantasy'.[151] Dubnow also dismissed the Zionist investment in a far-off future in Palestine; instead of 'work of the future', he called for *Gegenwartsarbeit*—'work of the present'.[152] *Gegenwartsarbeit*

[148] Gideon Shimoni, 'The Ideological Debate in World Zionism Since the Establishment of Israel' in Mordechai Bar-On, *The Challenge of Independence: Ideological and Cultural aspects of Israel's First Decade* (Yad Ben-Zvi 1999) 104 (Hebrew).

[149] Eliezer Schweid, 'The Rejection of the Diaspora in Zionist Thought: Two Approaches' (1984) 5 Stud in Zionism 43.

[150] Marcos Silber, 'The Metamorphosis of Pre-Dubnovian Autonomism into Diaspora Jewish-Nationalism' in Minna Rozen (ed), *Homelands and Diasporas: Greeks, Jews and their Migrations* (Taurus 2008) 235, 236.

[151] Simon Dubnow, *Nationalism and History: Essays on Old and New Judaism* (Jewish Publication Society of America 1961) 157.

[152] Dmitry Shumsky, 'Gegenwartsarbeit' in Dan Diner (ed), *Enzyklopädie Jüdischer Geschichte und Kultur*, vol 2 (Metzler 2012) 402; Israel Bartal, *Cossack and Bedouin: Land and People in Jewish Nationalism* (Am Oved 2007) (Hebrew); Matityahu Mintz, '"Work for the Land of Israel" and "Work in the Present": A Concept of Unity, A Reality of Contradiction' in Jehuda Reinharz and Anita Shapira (eds), *Essential Papers on Zionism* (Cassell 1996) 161.

decreed the full exercise of *national* life—in politics and culture—in the Diaspora.[153] Formulated against the backdrop of rising nationalism within the multi-ethnic empires of Eastern and Central Europe—and, after the Great War, the new states born at Versailles—this 'Eastern' model of Jewish emancipation prescribed *national* Jewish autonomy—'[s]triving for national rights or cultural autonomy in the Diaspora'.[154] Diaspora Nationalism, or Dubnowism, is often referred to as 'Autonomism'.

That is not to say that Diaspora Nationalism had no international law investment. Instead of territory, Dubnow sought the guarantee of 'public law'[155] for minority rights. First invested in domestic politics, the post-war settlement furnished the vocabularies and institutional arenas where autonomous claims could be formulated and pursued. Dubnow's ideas drove Jewish engagement with minorities politics, law, and advocacy at the national level and, at and after Versailles, internationally.[156]

The international law investment and ideological outlook of Diaspora Nationalism are accounted for in greater detail in chapter 5. In both respects, Diaspora Nationalism shared much with Zionism. The common ground of these two theories of Jewish nationalism, under the pressure of external circumstances and internal politics, wrought another synthesis formulated at Helsingfors: a new programme, calling for investment both in Diaspora work—*Gegenwartsarbeit*—and in Palestine. Dubnow, for his part, had tempered some of his early critique of Zionism.[157] The dual investment announced in the Helsingfors formula, writes Dmitry Shumsky,

> became the fundamental comprehensive framework of Zionist political consciousness in the post-Herzlian era. Since the Uganda crisis, and at least until the middle of the interwar years, the Zionist movement—especially that originating in Eastern and East-Central Europe—stood on two rails: striving to obtain maximal territorial self-rule in *Eretz Israel* on the one hand, and striving to obtain maximal extraterritorial self-rule in the multinational Diaspora countries on the other.[158]

[153] Simon Rabinovitch (ed), *Jews and Diaspora Nationalism: Writings on Jewish Peoplehood in Europe and the United States* (Waltham 2012); Simon Rabinovitch, *Jewish Rights, National Rites: Nationalism and Autonomy in Late Imperial and Revolutionary Russia* (Stanford UP 2014).

[154] Dubnow (n 151) 86.

[155] ibid, 179.

[156] Oscar Janowsky, *The Jews and Minority Rights, 1898–1919* (Columbia UP 1933); Fink (n 2) 193–235; Levene, *Diplomacy* (n 62); Mark Levene, 'Nationalism and its Alternatives in the International Arena: The Jewish Question at Paris, 1919' (1993) 28 J of Contemp Hist 511; Stanislaw Sierpowski, 'Minorities in the System of the League of Nations' in Paul Smith (ed), *Ethnic Groups in International Relations* (NYU Press 1991) 13.

[157] Dmitry Shumsky, 'Zionism in Quotations Marks, or To What Extent Was Dubnow a Non-Zionist' (2012) 77 Zion 369 (Hebrew).

[158] ibid, 379.

When it was time to formulate a post-war agenda, the Zionist wartime office in Copenhagen could issue a manifesto titled 'The Demands of the Jewish People'. The inclusive formula contained in the Copenhagen Manifesto of 25 October 1918 presented a trifecta of demands that appeared to reconcile, in one programme, the tenets of assimilationism, Zionism, and Diaspora Nationalism:[159] the 'establishment of Palestine ... as the Jewish national home'; '[f]ull and actual equality for the rights of Jews of all countries'; and '[n]ational autonomy, cultural, social and political, for the Jewish population of countries largely settled by Jews, as well as of all other countries whose Jewish population demands it'.[160] The long-drawn wartime jockeying between Zionists and assimilationists for the attention of the architects of the future post-war settlement, just like the ensuing intra-Jewish contestation at Versailles, made it clear that the ideological divides separating Jewish nationalism and assimilationism remained as potent as ever.[161] The expansive Zionist formula was driven less by a change of fundamental doctrine and more by Zionist self-perception as a representative national movement claiming to speak for all Jews; Jewish politics—in particular, Jewish representation politics—underscored the expansive formula.[162] Already in 1917, the Balfour Declaration—expressing the British government's favourable attitude towards 'the establishment in Palestine of a national home for the Jewish people'[163]—had drawn the ire of assimilationist Jews in Britain and elsewhere notwithstanding a proviso stating that 'nothing shall be done which may prejudice ... the rights and political status enjoyed by Jews in any other country'. This was not, like other parts of the brief text, a phrase of Chaim Weizmann's choosing but a British cabinet attempt to appease assimilationist Jews,

[159] James Loeffler, '"The Famous Trinity of 1917": Zionist Internationalism in Historical Perspective' (2016) 15 Simon Dubnow Institute YB 211, 228–9.

[160] [Victor Jacobson], *Report of the Work of the Copenhagen Office of the Zionist Organization: February 1915–December 1919* (Rasmussen & Rughs [n.d.]) 23. For background: Nahum Goldmann, *Die drei Forderungen des jüdischen Volkes* (Jüdischer Verlag 1919); Janowsky (n 156) 272–3.

[161] Compare eg the accounts of Jewish diplomacy at Versailles offered by Feinberg, *La Question* (n 62); and Levene, *Diplomacy* (n 62), Levene, 'Nationalism' (n 156).

[162] In the introduction of an essay collection published by members of Weizmann's circle in the wake of the Balfour Declaration, he wrote: 'In the settlement which will follow the War ... Jews will ask ... for equal treatment in countries where hitherto they have been denied the rights of men and citizens—and this time *perhaps* not in vain. *But even more urgent than the claim of the individual Jew to human rights will be the claim of the Jewish people to that equality of opportunity which it can achieve only by becoming once more master of its own destinies.*' He also claimed that 'Mr. Balfour's letter *puts a summary end to all these stock objections of the anti-Nationalists*'—that is, assimilationists—to Zionism. He called all Jews to rally behind the Zionist cause: the Declaration made 'the question of Palestine ... no longer a party matter'; it created 'for Jewry a new era upon a higher plane, far above all our comparatively petty strivings and puny struggles ... The invitation to us is to enter into the family of the Nations of the Earth endowed with the franchise of Nationhood, to become emancipated, not as individuals or sectionally, but as a whole people': Chaim Weizmann, 'Introduction: Zionism and the Jewish Problem' in Harry Sacher, *Zionism and the Jewish Future* (Murray 1917) 1, 8–10; emphases added. The wartime struggle between Zionists and assimilationists—between Weizmann and Lucien Wolf—over Britain's Jewish policy is told in detail in Jonathan Schneer, *The Balfour Declaration* (Random House 2010).

[163] The text is reproduced in Mendes-Flohr and Reinharz (n 11) 660; for background, see James Renton, *The Zionist Masquerade: The Birth of the Anglo-Zionist Alliance, 1914–1918* (Palgrave MacMillan 2007); Schneer (n 162).

including one of its members.[164] For Weizmann, whose role in securing Britain's favour for the Zionist cause against the efforts of the institutions of assimilated British Jewry would catapult him to leadership of the Zionist movement, the subsequent post-war expansive formula put forward by Zionists was a similar compromise driven by political and ideological sensibilities alike. His misgivings with the Helsingfors formula and his reserve towards the Copenhagen Manifesto are noted by his biographer; he was not involved in the latter out of concern that any demand for Jewish rights in the Diaspora might undermine the Zionist effort with regard to Palestine; for him, campaigning for such rights fell outside the goals of the Zionist Organisation.[165]

Derision of the assimilationist solution to the Jewish Question[166] and resentment of Western assimilationist institutions, their privileged access to power, their elitist *modus operandi*, and their philanthropic-paternalistic approach to the plight of other Jewish communities persisted, expressing sensibilities that would be shared by the two strands of Jewish nationalism throughout the interwar years.[167] The synthesis between the two national visions of emancipation generated another common ground. International Jewish investment in minority rights—at the League of Nations or the Congress of National Minorities[168]—was institutionalized. The institutional common ground was embodied in the *Comité des Délégations Juives auprès de la Conference de la Paix* ('CDJ'), a vestige of a collaborative platform for some, not all, Jewish representations sent to Paris in 1919. It was in the name of the CDJ that, until the mid-1930s, international lawyers like Jacob Robinson and Nathan Feinberg could undertake legal advocacy *as pursuit of Diaspora work* that claimed, at the very same time, Zionist credentials. Although established by the Zionist Organisation, the CDJ ever remained underfunded, always on the brink of becoming defunct. It was far more a voluntary, nearly *ad hoc* network of individuals than a permanent organ of Zionist diplomacy. The centre of gravity of Zionist diplomacy remained in the hands of Chaim Weizmann and, from the 1930s, of his *Yishuv* disciples and successors; Palestine remained its focus. The work of the *Comité* did not attract their interest; conversely, Palestine was not an item on the *Comité*'s agenda. Were one unkind, one might say that the *Comité* was the institutional arrangement that allowed Weizmann to keep Leo Motzkin,

[164] Schneer (n 162) 341; Feinberg, *La Question* (n 62) 39 ('*or, le gouvernement britannique ... n'avait admis cette disposition dans le texte définitif gue pour donner ainsi des apaisements à certains milieux juifs assimilés de l'Europe occidentale, qui appréhendaient beaucoup qu'à la suite de la Déclaration leurs droits ne fussent diminués*').

[165] Jehuda Reinharz, *Chaim Weizmann: The Making of a Stateman* (OUP 1993) 267, 276; Jehuda Reinharz, *Chaim Weizmann: The Making of a Zionist Leader* (OUP 1985) 297–8.

[166] Goldmann (n 160) 15.

[167] See in particular chs 2, 5, 7.

[168] Sabine Bamberger-Stemmann, *Der Europäische Nationalitätenkongreß 1925 bis 1938: Nationale Minderheiten zwischen Lobbyistentum und Großmachtinteressen* (Verlag Herder-Institut 2001).

the *Comité*'s President, busy and out of his hair.[169] The *Comité*'s Zionist self-identification, at the same time, served the appearance of unity and popularity of the Zionist cause.

While the Zionist movement, like other Jewish political parties in Eastern Europe, came to espouse a *Gegenwartsarbeit* programme, the ideological tension between autonomism and work for Palestine persisted: the former stood for inclusive Jewish nationalism that was willing to admit national work in the Diaspora as means or prioritize it as an end; the latter saw the building of the National Home as the primary, if not exclusive, imperative of Jewish nationalism. At times, that tension could appear to be largely latent or seem limited to radical individuals and factions that opposed the Helsingfors formula, continued to subscribe to a narrow reading of Zionism's base assumptions, and rejected outright the Diasporic condition.[170] Political pragmatism often obscured the persistence of tension. On occasions, still, that tension would be given voice by Zionist and *Yishuv* leadership. Whether autonomy and minority status could overcome Jewish objecthood or, instead, only served to entrench it remained an unresolved preposition. The question did not stay in the realm of theoretical speculation. A series of events—in Eastern Europe, Geneva, Whitehall, and Palestine—would all in time come to test the premises of Jewish engagement in minority rights. By the mid-1930s, as chapter 5 recounts, aversion to minority status and protection—in Eastern Europe and in Palestine—revealed the power and persistence of the ideological divides; that aversion became once again, overtly, a core sensibility of Zionism that was growing increasingly Palestinocentric, according primacy to *Yishuv* interests over any Diasporic concern. The interwar years, the Holocaust,[171] and Israel's establishment would furnish for many the ultimate proof that Dubnow's theories, and the international law engagement they required, had failed; the Jewish state's foundational ideology would see aversion to minority rights, autonomy, and Dubnowism turn into open antagonism: Dubnow's teachings would now be openly treated as an apostasy.

None illustrates more vividly the limits and transience of the synthesis between Diaspora Nationalism and Zionism—and the potency of the fundamental divergence inhering in how each constructed the Jewish condition and the path for overcoming Jewish objecthood—than Jacob Robinson. His journey from Dubnow's teaching and investment in Jewish Autonomism was slow and gradual; his disenchantment with minority rights, though rarely expressed publicly, did not

[169] It is telling that Weizmann's autobiography, while deprecating Motzkin's investment in minor matters as a waste of a great talent, makes no mention whatsoever of the *Comité*: Chaim Weizmann, *Trial and Error: The Autobiography of Chaim Weizmann* (Harper 1949) 60–1.

[170] Joseph Goldstein, *Menachem Ussishkin—A Biography*, vol 1 (Magness 1999) (Hebrew).

[171] Joshua M Karlip, *The Tragedy of a Generation: The Rise and Fall of Jewish Nationalism in Eastern Europe* (Harvard UP 2013); Joshua Karlip, 'In the Days of Haman: Simon Dubnow and His Disciples at the Eve of WWII' (2005) 4 Simon Dubnow Institute YB 531.

start in New York, in the early 1940s, with the news coming from Nazi-occupied Europe.[172] This was only the most dramatic, urgent, and profound in a series of crises that began, at the latest, with the withdrawal of the Jewish autonomy in Lithuania in the 1920s. Chapter 5 follows the path of Robinson's disillusionment and his gravitation towards a narrow, radical reading of Zionist ideology. Chapter 7 and the Epilogue illustrate, nonetheless, that his ideological transformation—like that of Rosenne—was never made complete.

3. Ambivalence and Political Experience

If ambivalence towards international law inhered in Zionist ideology, the political experience of the Zionist movement confirmed the sensibilities that produced and expressed that ambivalence. Such sensibilities became entrenched in the terms of Zionist engagement with international law; in time, they would come to shape Israel's international law outlook.

As the case studies demonstrate, the sites where the political experience of the Zionist movement was accrued were many. So were the forms of ambivalence generated or entrenched by that experience. Mapping these sites and forms—writing, that is, a history of Zionist engagements with international law—would require another book altogether. Instead, this section offers a brief excursus on Zionist political experience in connection with the Palestine Mandate, aimed at illustrating how embedded had ambivalence become in the ideological sensibilities and habitus of the Zionist movement; its persistence past the sovereign turn is demonstrated by the case studies.

The praxis of Zionist diplomacy with regard to the Palestine Mandate represents, on the one hand, investment in international law and organization alongside disenchantment, disillusionment, and resentment. Investment survived the 'Uganda' controversy, Herzl's death, and the synthesis between Political Zionism—emphasizing diplomatic action and legal (and lawful) means—and Practical Zionism and the priority it gave to nation-building from below. The 1917 Balfour Declaration, and the approval of the Palestine Mandate by the League Council in July 1922, impelled renewed investment. The Versailles Settlement applied the principle of national self-determination to Central and Eastern European territories where Jews, and Zionists in particular, could witness first-hand the 'principle of nationalities' given effect by international fiat; the mandate system, framed in Article 22 of the League of Nations Covenant, sketched pathways to national liberation elsewhere; the mandate instrument denoted Jewish standing, capacity, and recognized rights—in short, Jewish subjecthood. Adherents of Zionism could

[172] Ch 5; cf Gil Rubin, 'The End of Minority Rights: Jacob Robinson and the Jewish Question in World War II' (2012) 11 Simon Dubnow Institute YB 55.

well read it as giving effect to the Basle formula—or, at least, consider that its realization was at hand. The promise of this new world order could not but attract a renewed Zionist investment in world politics and world law that had waned after Herzl's death.

Alongside promise and investment, there was resentment. The Zionist achievement 'during the great territorial transformations that followed' the Great War was, for Ben-Gurion, 'not at all like the achievements won by the Poles in Poland and the Czechs in Czechoslovakia'.[173] The Balfour Declaration revealed the continuity of Jewish dependence on imperial benevolence.[174] The endgame of the mandate system was at best vague; if it promised independence to the peoples of the empires, now placed under mandatory 'tutelage' under League supervision, that promise was deferred and independence was to be subordinate.[175] Besides, the mandate system, and the Palestine Mandate, were predicated on and served to confirm the political and legal inferiority of its subjects.[176] Classified as an 'A' mandate, Palestine was treated as a territory characterized by a relatively high 'stage of the development'.[177] But this civilizational advantage was relative, and limited; while acknowledging that the peoples of 'A' mandates 'have reached a stage of development where their existence as independent nations can be provisionally recognized', Article 22 still made that provisional recognition 'subject to the rendering of administrative advice and assistance by a Mandatory until such time as they are able to stand alone'.[178] The Palestine Mandate, read in light of Article 22, attested to the persistence of Jewish otherhood—and entrenched Jewish objecthood. It codified the standard of civilization and institutionalized sovereign exclusion: it treated Jews as 'peoples not yet able to stand by themselves under the strenuous conditions of the modern world' and proceeded to apply to them 'the principle that the well-being and development of such peoples form a sacred trust of civilization and that securities for the performance of this trust should be embodied in this Covenant'.[179]

Resentment, at times, stemmed from the civilizational—and racial—assumptions and implications surrounding the Jewish position under the League mandate system. In May 1926, Haim Arlosoroff—Shertok's predecessor as the head

[173] Ben-Gurion, 'External Policy' (n 143) 103.

[174] Arie M Dubnov, 'On Vertical Alliances, Informal Imperialism, and "Perfidious Albion": Reflections on the Balfour Declaration Centennial' (2017) 49 Theory & Criticism 177 (Hebrew); Derek J Penslar, 'Declarations of (In)Dependence: Tensions within Zionist Statecraft, 1896–1948' (2018) 8 J of Levantine Stud 13.

[175] Mark Mazower, *No Enchanted Palace: The End of Empire and the Ideological Origins of the United Nations* (Princeton UP 2009).

[176] Antony Anghie, 'Colonialism and the Birth of International Institutions: Sovereignty, Economy, and the Mandate System of the League of Nations' (2002) 34 NYU J Int'l L & Pol 513; Anghie (n 22) 119–95.

[177] Article 22, League of Nations Covenant.

[178] ibid.

[179] ibid.

of the Jewish Agency's ('JA') Political Department—left Palestine to attend a session of the League's Permanent Mandates Commission ('PMC'). The 'Geneva Diary' he had written during his journey both replicated and challenged the civilizational sub-categories underscoring Article 22 and the mandate system it had established. Here he had ruminated on Jewish objecthood:

> A strange fate has caused this state of affairs that we, a people of sixteen million, became an object of the mandate system, this new invention! Together with the Papuas in New Guinea, the Druz in Syria and the Ashanti in Africa—we stand under the supreme supervision of the [Permanent Mandates] Commission. A nation of sixteen million, that even now belong to it in their blood and essence ten people like Einstein and Freud, like Bergson, Libermann, Luzzatti, Trotsky, Herbert Samuel, Weizmann, Bialik and Lord Reading, for example,—and it stands under such mandatory management! I am not referring here, of course, to legal precision. In the precise legal sense it is only the 'National Home' in *Eretz Israel* so managed, and in the precise legal sense neither Trotsky nor Reading or others would desire to acknowledge their nexus to that nation. But the political and psychological fact exists, and in this respect we must not forget that for the men of the Mandate Commission the question of our 'National Home' is but one of many different questions 'in the matter of natives', one of the most complex and troubling such problems.[180]

Such open acknowledgements—even if recorded in the privacy of a personal journal—of elusive Jewish otherness may not have been so common; it was not only international law treatises that did not directly address the question of the civilizational grade of Jews.[181] The sensibilities at play, however, and the resentment they betrayed, were inescapably entrenched in the ambiguous Jewish position and Zionist experience under the mandate system: they were strong enough to survive, as already noted, past Israel's establishment and its admission to the 'family of nations'.[182]

Investment and resentment cohabited Zionist practice. Ambivalence towards the Balfour Declaration,[183] Great Britain, the Palestine Mandate and its British administration,[184]

[180] Haim Arlosoroff, 'Geneva Diary' (30 May 1926) in Jacob Steinberg (ed), *Kitvei Haim Arlosoroff* [The Works of Haim Arlosoroff]: *A Glass Wall*, vol 1 (Stybel 1934) 45, 46 (Hebrew). That year he wrote: 'To this day we are a special element of colonial settlers with white skin, and on top of that an element with a developed mind possessing education, possessing political demands, in short—an element that is considered an interruption and a nuisance for the administration': Haim Arlosoroff, 'A Glass Wall', in ibid, 29, 30.

[181] Discussed at text to n 23.

[182] Giladi, 'Negotiating Identity' (n 31).

[183] Dubnov (n 174); Renton (n 163); Schneer (n 162). Yaacov Shavit and Barbara Harshav, 'Cyrus King of Persia and the Return to Zion: A Case of Neglected Memory' (1990) 2 History & Memory 51.

[184] Haim Arlosoroff, 'The British Administration and the National Home' (1928) in Steinberg (n 180) 71. Elsewhere he wrote of the administration's lack of goodwill towards the National Home rooted

the mandate system, the PMC,[185] and the League itself was a recurring theme—or, rather, a permanent condition—of the Zionist mandatory experience. What appeared as political pragmatism often stemmed from conflicting impulses. Thus, Zionist critique of Jewish legal objecthood under the mandate tended to be subtle and less explicit. To point at Jewish objecthood would undermine the case for Jewish recognition, however provisional or imperfect, and the assertion of Jewish subjecthood and Jewish claims to Palestine. On occasion, however, such ambivalence was given voice in direct, explicit terms. One example can be found in Ben-Gurion's 1930 speech at a Berlin Zionist Labour Congress. In that speech, titled *The External Policy of the Jewish People*, Ben-Gurion carefully navigated conflicting readings of Jewish objecthood and subjecthood, exclusion and inclusion, investment and disenchantment; the text records conflicting impulses, articulates ambivalence, and demonstrates how these drove pragmatic sensibilities.[186]

In that speech, Ben-Gurion first raised the question whether a 'people in exile, dispersed and separated by the four corners of the earth, could have a foreign policy'.[187] This pointed to the centrality of Zionist preoccupation with Jewish objecthood and subjecthood. His answer refuted the view—he attributed it to early detractors of Zionism—that asserted that 'a stateless people cannot constitute a political actor or a subject of the law of nations'.[188] Ben-Gurion acknowledged that that had been the previous state of affairs: in the Diaspora, he argued, 'the Jewish people had not been a subject of political possibilities or political will'.[189] He went further to decry past Jewish exclusion and voice a historical grievance with international law: none could take lightly the fact that 'within the existing law of nations the Jewish people has for generations been denied of law, deprived of right, lacking the capacity to express its will and wishes in a permissible and recognised manner'.[190]

Things, however, had changed: that was no longer the legal position of the Jewish people. For Ben-Gurion, notably, transition was obtained first and foremost by dint of an act of self-emancipation, not external recognition. For him, it was the establishment of the Zionist movement, giving rise to 'Jewish policy

in colonial habit as an insurmountable 'very tall high wall: beyond that was, under the bright sunshine, as paradise locked, lies the actual realization of the mandate. Yet this wall cannot be shattered. And it is very hard to pass it': Haim Arlosoroff, 'A Glass Wall' in Steinberg (n 180) 31.

[185] Arlosoroff would observe that the first PMC report on Palestine was 'a Zionist defeat'; he lambasted its members for ignoring key pertinent questions, ignorance of conditions in Palestine, and a fundamental misunderstanding of the nature of the Zionist project in Palestine—and for relinquishing their supervisory authority in favour of the 'doctrine of absolute state sovereignty' of the mandatories. Still, he concluded with the need to re-engage with the PMC: 'we are not permitted', he wrote, not to tell PMC members of their errors: Haim Arlosoroff, 'The Mandates Commission and Zionism' (1925) in Steinberg (n 180) 15, 25.

[186] Ben-Gurion, 'External Policy' (n 143).

[187] ibid, 102.

[188] ibid.

[189] ibid.

[190] ibid, 102–3.

as the expression of the collective will of the Jewish people',[191] that gave birth to Jewish subjecthood. At the same time, self-declared subjecthood had been accorded legal recognition:

> the historical connection between the people of Israel and *Eretz-Israel* was upheld and accepted by the law of nations. The Jewish people was recognised as the owner of right over *Eretz-Israel.* The Zionist Organisation became from a voluntary organisation of 'popular volunteers' to an official international agency of the Jewish people as regards its homeland.[192]

International law may have had the power to uphold Jewish subjecthood and accept Jewish claims; Ben-Gurion, nonetheless, proceeded to cast doubt as to international law's vitality (or pedigree: the language he used here is ambiguous). He also warned his audience that the import of the Zionist 'achievement' in the international legal arena was not to be considered lightly; but warned next that neither was it to be 'exaggerated'. Ben-Gurion's ambivalence was directed, equally, at international organization: 'we have the right to demand that our voice be heard in the mandate government and in the League of Nations. Flawed with sin as these institutions may be, they are still the only institutions with authority and power over the country's destiny'.[193] Pragmatism compelled investment—but gave voice to acute disenchantment.

This last sentence by Ben-Gurion draws attention to another sort of resentment—one driven by Zionist disillusionment. Ben-Gurion's speech preceded by two days the formal announcement of a change in British policy in Palestine. Under the Passfield White Paper, Jewish immigration and land acquisition were to be restricted; a Legislative Council was to be formed with equal representation to Arab majority and Jewish minority. The Zionist movement denounced the White Paper as a British withdrawal from the 'National Home' principle; it ran counter to its interpretation of the Mandate under which that principle constituted the chief, if not exclusive, goal of the British mandate—a trust in favour not of the inhabitants of the territory but of Jews yet to immigrate there. In the end, the Zionist campaign—that also involved turning to the League's PMC—proved successful; the White Paper was effectively, albeit not formally, withdrawn.[194]

Not all Zionist attempts to have British policy reversed proved successful; disillusionment with Great Britain—and with League supervision—attended Zionist

[191] ibid, 102.
[192] ibid.
[193] ibid, 103.
[194] Carly Beckerman-Boys, 'The Reversal of the Passfield White Paper, 1930–1: A Reassessment' (2016) 51 J of Contemporary Hist 213; Gabriel Sheffer, 'Intentions and Results of British Policy in Palestine: Passfield's White Paper' (1973) 9 Middle Eastern Stud 43.

experience following the 1922 White Paper;[195] the separation of Transjordan from the Palestine Mandate; the first PMC report on Palestine; and a succession of events culminating in the White Paper of 1939 that marked, for some historians, 'the end of the alliance between the Zionist movement and Britain'.[196] The League's slow demise, in the second half of the 1930s, signalled that Geneva would not be where British policies could be *effectively* opposed and reversed.[197]

Back in 1930, Ben-Gurion nonetheless assured his Berlin audience that the Zionist movement remained invested in the Mandate and in League supervision. If given the power, he said, to make 'England leave *Eretz-Israel*, and the League of Nations to withdraw all supervision over it', he would refuse to exercise it.[198] For him, 'the existence of a supreme rule in the land to protect the rights of the Jewish people and the concerns of the Arab [community] in *Eretz-Israel*... in the name of organised humanity' remained a necessity.[199] At the very same time, the 'trustee" was not 'worthy of its role' and 'the international institution that appointed it' was not 'faithful'.[200]

In time, late *Yishuv* and Israeli political memory would produce narratives, and historiographies, that would tell of broken promises,[201] denounce 'perfidious Albion',[202] and decry institutional weakness and failed supervision. These accounts would efface partnership and investment.[203] There was no need, however, to invent disillusionment; it had been present in Zionist diplomacy all along. My concern here, at any rate, is not with passing the verdict of history on the British mandate and the PMC, but with tracking Zionist perceptions and political memory. At stake is not Susan Pedersen's observations that in Palestine alone the PMC 'came down on the side of one party to the debate' and that 'not all members of the PMC came to support the Zionist cause, but over time a majority did so'.[204] Rather, at stake are Zionist perceptions and their entrenchment. On that account, what matters is not the Palestine record of the PMC but the sentiment expressed by Arlosoroff

195 For background and analysis: Bernard Wasserstein, *The British in Palestine: The Mandatory Government and the Arab-Jewish Conflict 1917–1929* (2nd edn, Basil Blackwell 1991) 109–39.

196 Anita Shapira, *Israel: A History* (Brandeis UP 2012) 75.

197 The Zionist campaign against the 1939 White Paper—and the unfinished PMC deliberations of the change in British policy—could only confirm that conclusion: Nathan Feinberg, 'The Attitude of Members of the Mandates Commission to the Palestine Mandate' in Nathan Feinberg, *Essays on Jewish Issues of Our Time* (Dvir 1980) 156; Susan Pedersen, *The Guardians: The League of Nations and the Crisis of Empire* (OUP 2015) 385–391.

198 Ben-Gurion, 'External Policy' (n 143) 109.

199 ibid, 112.

200 ibid.

201 Chaim Shenhav, *The British Mandate: A Shattered Dream* (Am Oved 2007) (Hebrew).

202 Dubnov (n 174).

203 ibid; Eitan Bar-Yosef, 'Bonding with the British: Colonial Nostalgia and the Idealization of Mandatory Palestine in Israeli Literature and Culture after 1967' (2017) 22 Jewish Soc Stud 1; Motti Golani, *The End of the British Mandate for Palestine, 1948: The Diary of Sir Henry Gurney* (Palgrave MacMillan 2009); Motti Golani, 'Palestine, 1945–1948: A view from the High Commissioner's Office' in Rory Miller (ed), *Britain, Palestine and Empire: The Mandate Years* (Ashgate 2010) 177.

204 Pedersen (n 197) 95.

when he wrote in the summer of 1932 to Weizmann of a pending 'new international armed conflict . . . in which the British Empire would be involved . . . we are heading for a new great war'. 'On the day of the declaration of war', he wrote to his mentor, 'the Mandates system will collapse and the League of Nations adjourn for a summer vacation'.[205] It is that sentiment that has the power to explain why, two years after the war, and at the same time Jacob Robinson was preparing to overcome Jewish objecthood in the impending UN debate on the Palestine Question, Shabtai Rosenne could assert the futility of Jewish, and Zionist, reliance on international law.[206]

Before returning to our protagonists, another manifestation of ambivalence deserves mention. This concerns the limits of the Zionist international law investment. Histories of the JA's Political Department—the foreign office of the state-to-be—have little to naught to say on its international law investment.[207] This is more than mere oversight; that investment was largely secondary. That is not to say that the JA, or the Zionist Organisation, made no recourse to international law arguments or no use of international law vocabularies. For interwar Zionist diplomacy concerned with the 'National Home' in Palestine, however, international law existed at the margin of empire.[208] Whitehall, not Geneva, was the first—and often, last—port of call for Zionist leaders and the destination of Zionist memoranda: Zionist diplomacy, Arlosoroff knew, was bound to remain 'tied . . . to England more than to Geneva'.[209] Ties with members of the League's PMC were certainly cultivated by Zionist leaders;[210] these relations cannot, however, be compared with the Zionist investment—especially under Weizmann—in the politics of the British Empire. There had certainly been bouts of Zionist activity directed at Geneva;[211] Zionist appeals to PMC's supervision were made when it had been deemed that the British government's commitment to the 'National Home' policy—or its acceptance of the Zionist interpretation of the mandate instrument—was on the wane; such bouts

[205] Arlosoroff to Weizmann, 30 June 1932, in Eran Kaplan and Derek J Penslar (eds), *The Origins of Israel 1882–1948: A Documentary History* (University of Wisconsin Press 2011) 229, 233.

[206] Rowson (n 126) discussed in chs 3, 5; Giladi, 'Transformation' (n 1) 241–4.

[207] Moshe Yegar, *The History of the Political Department of the Jewish Agency* (The Zionist Library 2011) (Hebrew).

[208] Arie M Dubnov, 'Jewish Nationalism in the Wake of World War I: A "State-in-the-Making" or The Empire Strikes Back?' (2016) 24 Israel: Studies in Zionism and the State of Israel 5 (Hebrew); Dubnov (n 174); Yehouda Shenhav, 'Introduction' in Yehouda Shenhav (ed), *Zionism and Empires* (Van Leer 2015) 7 (Hebrew).

[209] The *Yishuv*'s 'political struggle for the realisation of the mandate' was thus to be conducted in London: 'the address cannot be Geneva . . . the point of greatest resistance and most doubtful utility'. The *Yishuv* ought only to turn to Geneva as a 'last measure' and keep such action as a 'political reserve': Arlosoroff, 'A Glass Wall' (n 184) 36–7.

[210] Eg Weizmann to Rappard, 15 November 1924, LNA-R17, 1/40556/2413, discussed in Natasha Wheatley, 'Mandatory Interpretation: Legal Hermeneutics and the New International Order in Arab and Jewish Petitions to the League of Nations' (2015) 227 Past & Present 205; I am grateful to Dr Wheatley for providing me with a copy of the document. See also Pedersen (n 197) 100; Feinberg (n 197).

[211] In 1925, a small Geneva office was established by the Zionist Organisation: Wheatley (n 210) 218.

and appeals, nonetheless, were meant to affect British policy, not supplant British authority.[212]

Recourse to international law was little grounded in Zionist diplomacy's *institutional* culture. It is evident that Weizmann, instead, would call on the services of members of his inner circle—jurists, but not necessarily international law experts—whenever legal skill was required. On other occasions, in particular after the Zionist movement's centre of gravity moved to Palestine in the 1930s, the JA would turn, *ad hoc*, to the services of *Yishuv* practitioners.[213] It is highly instructive that multiple proposals to establish a legal department 'in the field of international law'[214] to support the work of the JA's Political Department were made only in early 1947—at the precise moment Great Britain resolved to turn the question of the 'Future of Palestine' over to the UN.[215] We can treat such proposals, coming from jurists in and outside Palestine, as marking a departure from empire as the principal field of Zionist diplomatic investment; and the harbinger of institutionalized Zionist investment in international law and organization.[216] It is telling that, to avail the Zionist campaign for Jewish statehood at the UN with the requisite international law knowledge, Sharett had to look outside the circles of Zionist legal-diplomatic experience. Like Weizmann, when faced with the need to prepare a 'Jewish' testimony for Nuremberg, Sharett turned instead to the expertise of Jewish legal diplomacy—that is, to Jacob Robinson.[217]

One final anecdote illustrates the secondary role of international law in Zionist *praxis*. A month after arriving in Palestine, Rosenne reported to Hersch Lauterpacht his concerns with 'the legal side of the library for our [future] foreign office'.[218] Rosenne and Robinson would exert great effort to collect, purchase, and beg international law books, paralleling Nathan Feinberg's efforts at the Hebrew

[212] As Ben-Gurion, 'External Policy' (n 143) makes abundantly clear; Wheatley (n 210); Pedersen (n 197).

[213] Feinberg narrated how the Zionist Executive, on the advice of Lord McNair and Professors Brierly and Laski, turned to Stoyanovsky—later, the co-editor of the *Jewish Yearbook*—to prepare a refutation of the British White Paper of October 1930: Nathan Feinberg, 'In Memoriam—Dr. Jacob Stoyanovsky' (1977) 31 HaPraklit 239 (Hebrew).

[214] Vitta, 'Proposal to Establish a Legal Department of the Jewish Agency', 22 June 1947, S25\8995-4/5, Central Zionist Archive ('CZA').

[215] ibid; Brodetsky to JA Executive, 12 February 1947, S25\8995-8, CZA; Tadesci to Levavi, 19 February 1947, S25\8995-10, CZA; Anon., [n.d.], S25\8995-3, CZA.

[216] A legal adviser was only appointed in early January 1948, a few weeks after the GA resolved to partition Palestine. Dov Yosef's appointment—barrister by training, a Labour Party functionary, and no international law expert—was precipitated by the legal transition decreed by the Partition Resolution: Ben-Gurion to Yosef, 4 January 1948, S25\9697-4, CZA. This was, at best, a part-time job: he was soon also appointed as the civil governor of Jerusalem's Jewish sector.

[217] Robinson's recruitment is discussed below and in ch 5. For Weizmann's request see WJC-C14/21 (World Jewish Congress Records, MS-361), American Jewish Archives ('AJA'); Boaz Cohen, 'Dr. Jacob Robinson, the Institute of Jewish Affairs and the Elusive Jewish Voice in Nuremberg' in David Bankier and Dan Michman (eds), *Holocaust and Justice: Representation and Historiography of the Holocaust in Post-War Trials* (Yad Vashem/Berghahn 2010) 81, 90.

[218] Rowson to Lauterpacht, 28 January 1948, S25/1189, CZA; [Shabtai Rowson], Draft Book-List for the Proposed Foreign Office Library of the Jewish State, 31 January 1948, G-112/9, ISA.

University.[219] Their efforts speak volumes on the limited scope of the JA's *institutional* investment in international law. The Zionist international law habitus was little embedded in institutions that in 1948 would become the foundations of Israel's foreign ministry.

4. Protagonists and Engagement

'[W]e will certainly have a great deal of things to work together', wrote Jacob Robinson, from New York, in early July 1948 to congratulate Shabtai Rosenne on his appointment as the Ministry of Foreign Affairs ('MFA') legal adviser.[220] Thus began a close, at times fraught, relationship that would end with Rosenne's eulogizing Robinson as the '[t]he Great Advocate of the Jewish People'.[221] More than four decade later, Rosenne would reminisce:

> I was on very close personal relations with a man who was the legal advisor of the delegation in New York ... he ... had had a great deal of experience with the League of Nations in the minorities question. He had at one time been legal advisor to the government of Lithuania ... That is how we were able to handle the UN quite early in our existence with a great deal of professionalism ... I got into the habit of writing personal letters to him on a first name basis.[222]

Robinson came to Israel's foreign service as a veteran of Jewish politics and diplomacy, a veritable expert—notwithstanding Hannah Arendt's disparagement[223]—of international law as it pertained to Jewish matters in the interwar period. His earlier career has now attracted some scholarly attention: the interwar investment in Jewish-Lithuanian politics and the European minority movement, wartime research and advocacy at the New York Institute of Jewish Affairs, and post-war involvement in the Nuremberg trials. So did, for this matter, Robinson's polemic with Arendt in the wake of the Eichmann trial where he served on the prosecutor's team.[224] The sovereign chapter of his career and its implications for the study of Jewish international law engagements in the twentieth century, curiously, have hardly been explored. Robinson had not only contributed much, before and after May 1948, to the planning, establishment, and organization of what would become

[219] Giladi, 'Sovereign Turn' (n 132); Yegar (n 207) 364.
[220] Robinson to Rosenne, 8 July 1948, FM-74/3, ISA.
[221] This is the literal translation of the title of the obituary: Shabtai Rosenne, 'Jacob Robinson—In Memoriam' (1978) 24 Gesher 91 (Hebrew).
[222] Interview with Shabtai Rosenne, UN Oral History Project, ST/DPI/Oral History (02)/R673 (12 June 1990) 52.
[223] In the context of their polemic concerning the Eichmann trial: Hannah Arendt, '"The Formidable Dr. Robinson": A Reply' *NY Rev of Books* (20 January 1966).
[224] The literature on Robinson is cited throughout the book.

Israel's MFA;[225] his legal erudition and knowledge of the ways of international organizations placed him in a unique mentoring position for the JA team working on partition, which in 1949 became Israel's Permanent Mission to the UN. Sharett would recall that an

> invaluable aid to the novice Jewish delegation, and since then until his recent retirement, was then Dr. Jacob Robinson—a veteran Zionist, Hebrew *Maskil* and a distinguished expert of international law—who already then had intimate knowledge of the UN Charter and vast erudition in the rules of procedure and the internal logic of the ways of operation of the new international organisation.[226]

Robinson's investment in Zionism, by his own admission, was for a long time no more than nominal. Born in 1889 in a small town on the outskirts of Czarist Russia—today, southern Lithuania—he was a participant-witness in the short-lived Jewish autonomy in Lithuania and an old hand of European minorities politics. Until the early 1940s, his investment in Jewish nationalism—in 'Eastern' models of Jewish emancipation—aligned with the teachings of Simon Dubnow; the two collaborated on several occasions. How he came to abandon that investment forms an inseparable part of this book;[227] it is a story of a long-drawn ideological transformation. The point, for now, is that by the time he had placed himself at the exclusive service of the Zionist cause, Robinson had several decades of experience in Jewish politics and international law knowledge acquired through advocacy, diplomacy, and scholarship.

In 1948, Rosenne could boast far fewer credentials—and little political experience. His contributions to legal scholarship were well published;[228] with one important 1947 exception, published in an obscure Zionist periodical in Hebrew, none addressed Jewish concerns.[229] Sefton Rowson was born in 1917 to a well-to-do assimilated London family of film industry pioneers. By his own account, he had found Zionism at the age of sixteen; like Hebrew, the language of national revival, it was not taught at the Rowson home.[230] His early investment in Zionism was manifest in activity in Zionist Youth and student organizations as in prolific

[225] Eg Robinson to Eytan, Organization of the Foreign Office, 29 June 1948, FM–74/3, ISA.

[226] Moshe Sharett, *At the Threshold of Statehood: 1946–1949* (Am Oved 1958) 63 (Hebrew); Eytan to Robinson, 2 August 1957, FM–5849/7, ISA. *Haskalah* was an eighteenth- and nineteenth-century intellectual movement of Jewish Enlightenment; *Maskil* remained a term denoting intellectual erudition, scholarship, and education.

[227] Chs 4–5 especially.

[228] Before 1947, Rowson published in the *Law Times*, *Law Quarterly Review*, *British Yearbook of International Law*, and *Modern Law Review*: Giladi, 'Transformation' (n 1) 223–4.

[229] Rowson (n 126); Giladi, 'Transformation' (n 1).

[230] [Shabtai Rowson,] Youth and Reconstruction: Speech Delivered at Hendon Young Zionist Society (18 October 1943) ('Rosenne Papers'). Mr Daniel Rosenne kindly made available all documents from this collection, all on file with the author. In 1935, Rowson took to learning Hebrew: Yaacov Morris, 'Britons in Israel: Shabtai Rosenne' *Jewish Vanguard* (11 September 1953).

writings in the English Zionist press. It hardly revealed itself, however, in Rowson's early international law engagement.[231] In that, he may have emulated the example of Hersch Lauterpacht, whom he came to consider as a mentor.[232] Keeping apart his two engagements hinted at assimilationist sensibilities—whether ideological, professional, or pragmatic. Indeed, alongside Zionism, Rowson had been involved with the assimilationist Anglo-Jewish Association until he resigned from its Council—not quietly—in protest of its 'Anti-Zionist Stance'.[233] Now he took care to publicly distance himself from assimilationist organizations and views: in one book review, he chided the author that he had 'insufficiently treated' the 'activities of the Jewish delegations' at Versailles, 'especially the obstructionists from the West'.[234]

In the late years of the Second World War, he also flirted with Dubnow's writings on Diaspora Nationalism. If for Robinson 'the old controversy concerning the possibility of Jewish national survival in the Diaspora'[235] had represented lived experience, Rowson's investment in Diaspora Nationalism took the form of intellectual reflection—and was short-lived: he soon abandoned the book he was writing on Dubnow's theories as well as any desire to 'reconstruct' the Diaspora.[236] His wartime Royal Air Force service furnished opportunities to visit Palestine.[237] The war, his sister recalled, 'just made him more sure of his Zionism'; disillusionment with the British government's anti-immigration policies in Palestine made him 'quite anti-British'.[238] Rosenne's own ideological transformation—accelerated and less dramatic than Robinson's, albeit more radical in its outcome—is also part of the story told in this book.

Rowson was demobilized on 1 April 1946; he went immediately to serve as a 'clerk' at 'the Political Department of the London office of the Jewish Agency for Palestine'.[239] There, he launched a campaign to be transferred to Palestine; after assurances, delays, and disappointments, he finally arrived in Jerusalem, *en famile*, at

[231] Giladi, 'Transformation' (n 1).

[232] 'Acceptance Speech by Professor Shabtai Rosenne' (2004) 51 Netherlands YB Intl L 475. Lauterpacht's assimilation strategies are discussed by Koskenniemi, *Gentle Civilizer* (n 8) 371–4; and in chs 2–3.

[233] *The Jewish Chronicle* (28 January 1944), (15, 22 December 1944) and (19 January 1945); SWD Rowson, Memorandum on the Anti-Zionist Stance of the Anglo-Jewish Association, [n.d.], F13\77, CZA; Stephan EC Wendehorst, *British Jewry, Zionism, and the Jewish State, 1936–1956* (OUP 2012).

[234] Shabtai Rowson, 'A Century of Jewish History' *Zionist Review* (28 August 1944); reviewing an AJC study on 'Jewish Post-War Problems', Rowson commended the authors for their objectivity, 'excellent' sources, and the 'invaluable service' rendered by the study. He took care, nonetheless, to emphasise his ideological aversion: 'Most Zionists—the present reviewer included—disapprove of the policy of the American Jewish Committee not only in regard to Palestine but also in regard to the Diaspora.': Shabtai Rowson, 'Preparing the Peace' *Zionist Review* (11 August 1944).

[235] SWD Rowson, 'Epilogue: Jewish Nationalism Today' (1944) 99/242, Rosenne Papers.

[236] Ch 5.

[237] Shabtai Rowson, 'What Is It Like in Eretz Israel' *Zionist Review* (1 March 1946).

[238] Interview with Janet Davis (UK) (25 October 2014); I am grateful to Mrs Davis for her time and goodwill and her son, Mr Adam Davis, for conducting the interview on my behalf.

[239] Rosenne to Robinson, 6 August 1957, FM–5849/7, ISA; Rosenne UN Interview (n 222) 1, 2.

the end of December 1947.[240] As an employee of the JA's Political Department, he was 'temporarily assigned' to the legal secretariat of the Preparatory Commission tasked 'to prepare for the independence of the Jewish state'[241] envisioned by the Partition Resolution. Although this gave Rosenne the opportunity to acquaint himself with Israel's future legal and judicial elites, working for the Preparatory Commission in besieged Jerusalem kept him away from the centre of decision-making in Tel Aviv. His work for the Preparatory Commission, by and large, was technical, dealt with mundane legal matters[242] and, like that of the Commission as a whole, had little impact on events. His appointment as the MFA legal adviser was a major career leap; Robinson's departure from the directorship of the New York Institute of Jewish Affairs, by contrast, was a step down.

In the years to come, Rosenne and Robinson would collaborate closely, and intimately, consulting each other on matters minor and major. Often, they shared the same sensibilities and the same basic perspective on questions arising from Israel's UN involvement; coming to a common position had been the usual manner of things. How they divided responsibility reflected both their respective locations and MFA institutional structures; yet it was also natural that Robinson would be the one to take the lead on 'Jewish' items on the UN agenda and that Rosenne would be the point man in matters involving other government departments. Robinson treated Rosenne as an equal and respected his position as the MFA legal adviser; he had willingly placed his knowledge, experience, and counsel at Rosenne's disposal. Rosenne, in time, would name Robinson his mentor—alongside Lauterpacht.[243] With Robinson's retirement, Rosenne had lost 'a faithful friend, teacher and master . . . a role model of Jewish and Zionist jurist'.[244]

At the same time, Robinson's vast experience was a source of some anxiety for his younger colleague.[245] A few months after Rosenne's appointment, the MFA came to consider the prospects of employing Ezekiel Gordon—a lawyer with intimate knowledge of the UN Secretariat—in Rosenne's legal department. Rosenne wrote 'discretely' to another veteran of the JA's London Office, now posted in New York: '[a]s you know I am really too young for my job and a man who is much older might feel reluctant to be placed under me'.[246] Arthur Lourie allayed Rosenne's concerns by addressing their source: 'I believe strongly that you should

[240] Giladi, 'Transformation' (n 1).

[241] Even-Tov to Kaplan, 29 January 1948, G–110/40, ISA; Rosenne UN Interview (n 222) 14–15; Yehudit Karp, 'The Legal Council: The Story of Early Legislation' in Aharon Barak and Tana Spanic (eds), *In Memoriam: Uri Yadin*, vol 2 (Bursi 1990) 209.

[242] Rowson to Joseph, 4 February 1948, G–119/14; Joseph to Cohn, 30 January 1948, G–110/40. He had an opportunity, nonetheless, to comment on the plans for the MFA's establishment: Rowson to Eytan, Outline Plan for Foreign Office, [n.d.], G–7345/38, ISA.

[243] 'Acceptance Speech' (n 232).

[244] Rosenne to Robinson, 6 August 1957 (n 239).

[245] As was Nathan Feinberg's academic position at the Hebrew University: Giladi, 'Sovereign Turn' (n 132).

[246] Rosenne to Lourie, 9 September 1948, FM–67/5, ISA.

have no solicitude on this score'. He was also 'inclined to think that he would not raise difficulties. I should like to make it clear that while quite possibly a competent person, *he is not by any means a second Robinson* in either erudition or personality'.[247] Neither Rosenne nor Robinson had ever raised, as far as I can ascertain, the question of institutional seniority.[248]

Together and apart, Rosenne and Robinson sought to interpret Jewish sovereignty in light of Zionist ideology and give effect to Jewish subjecthood. At times, their relationship would become strained. Rosenne's preoccupation with his professional credentials played some role in such episodes; his interest in the International Court of Justice and frantic efforts to appear before the World Court at The Hague became, for a while, the source of some tension between the two.[249] Ideological sensibilities would also play a role in generating friction; while their common ambivalence towards the right of petition to UN bodies and the Genocide Convention was driven by shared sensibilities, in the matter of Jewish refugeehood they diverged radically on what the Zionist creed had demanded and how to give it effect. This matter became, inevitably, a test of their adherence to the Zionist creed; at stake was their own Jewish subjecthood, their own credentials as sovereign Jews. These were the same credentials they came to assert when faulting the deficient, non-sovereign standing of Hersch Lauterpacht to represent Jewish interests in the matter of the right of petition, the subject of the next two chapters.

247 Emphasis added; Lourie to Rosenne, 23 September 1948, FM–67/5, ISA.

248 Rosenne, on the other hand, did not shy away from asserting his professional seniority vis-à-vis others; he had argued in blunt terms that in matters of international law he, not the Attorney-General, was the final arbiter: ch 4.

249 Ch 4.

PART II
VOICE

2

Lauterpacht in Jerusalem

Individual Petition and the Politics of Jewish Representation

1. A Jubilee

For the new law faculty at the Hebrew University in Jerusalem, founded less than a year before, 8 May 1950 was a special day. For the past several days, the university—founded in 1925 to serve as 'a temple of science for all nations'[1] but also to form 'an integral part of the Jewish national renascence ... a factor of the first importance in the intellectual and spiritual life of the Jewish people'[2]—had been celebrating its semi-jubilee. The programme included the 'unavoidable curse of long and many speeches',[3] a tea party and a ball, an exhibition and dance show, a concert conducted by Leonard Bernstein, a public prayer, and a reception by the state President, Chaim Weizmann. Stamps were issued, journalists were briefed, and commemorative books were published; congratulatory messages arrived from five continents. The academic programme comprised of public lectures delivered by local faculty and overseas guests—'distinguished representatives of learned institutions in many parts of the world'.[4] On 7 May, one such luminary addressed, in Hebrew, 'State Sovereignty and Human Rights'. The following day, the law faculty hosted him for an additional lecture, in English, on 'International Law After the Second World War'.[5]

[1] Menachem Ussishkin, a Zionist leader involved in the university's founding, used the phrase when introducing the 'first academic lecture', delivered on 7 February 1923 by Albert Einstein: Yair Paz, 'The Hebrew University on Mount Scopus as a Secular Temple' in Shaul Katz and Michael Heyd (eds), *The History of the Hebrew University of Jerusalem: Origins and Beginnings* (Magnes 1997) 281, 286–7 (Hebrew).

[2] Opening Ceremony, Semi-Jubilee Celebrations, 5 May 1950, Sir Leon Simon Address, Semi-Jubilee 91–1950 Speeches, Hebrew University Archive ('HUA').

[3] Urdang, Organizer's Report, 29 May 1950, Semi-Jubilee 91–1950 (May–), HUA.

[4] Simon Address (n 2). On the event and its significance in the construction of the University as the 'new priesthood of the nation': Uri Cohen, *The Mountain and the Hill: The Hebrew University of Jerusalem During Pre-Independence Period and Early Years of the State of Israel* (Am Oved 2006) 290–2 (Hebrew).

[5] Reports on the precise lecture titles, language, and dates vary: Elihu Lauterpacht (ed), *International Law, Being the Collected Papers of Hersch Lauterpacht*, vol 2 (CUP 1975) 159; and Elihu Lauterpacht (ed), *International Law, Being the Collected Papers of Hersch Lauterpacht*, vol 3 (CUP 1977) 416 ('CP'); and correspondence in Lauterpacht–92/1950, HUA. I rely on the invitation and programme: 'Semi-Jubilee Academic Lectures', [n.d.]; 'Program of Lectures', [n.d.], Lauterpacht–92/1950, HUA. See also Lauterpacht to Feinberg, 7 April 1950, 16 April 1950, Lauterpacht–92/1950, HUA; 'The Half-Jubilee Week Celebrations of the Hebrew University: A Program': Hed HaMizrach (5 May 1950) (Hebrew).

Jews, Sovereignty, and International Law. Rotem Giladi, Oxford University Press. © Rotem Giladi 2021.
DOI: 10.1093/oso/9780198857396.003.0004

That speaker was Hersch Zvi Lauterpacht (1897–1960), the Cambridge Whewell Professor of International Law.[6] Born in Zolkiew, near Lvov—then in Austrian Galicia, afterwards Poland, now Zhovkva in the Ukraine[7]—he would in 1955 be appointed to the International Court of Justice at The Hague ('ICJ'). This was neither his first, nor his last, involvement in the affairs of the Hebrew University. In 1925 he attended its 'opening ceremony'[8] as President of the World Federation of Jewish Students, which he co-founded.[9] During the Second World War, he allowed Norman Bentwich to persuade him to establish in Cambridge a branch of the Friends of the Hebrew University, 'out of a sense of duty and with little enthusiasm. He had no experience of raising money for good causes and did not find the task congenial'.[10] A few days after his death, the Law Faculty Council resolved to publish a Hebrew *Festschrift* in his honour.[11] In 1968, 'gifts made by numerous friends and former students all over the world' allowed the faculty to establish the *Hersch Lauterpacht Chair in International Law*.[12]

While representing Cambridge University,[13] Lauterpacht's participation in the semi-jubilee celebrations nonetheless expressed proclivities that were, ideologically and personally, rooted in his identity. His decision to deliver a lecture in a language he had not mastered—Nathan Feinberg, dean of the law faculty, had to commission a translation[14]—went beyond what was necessary[15] to show his support for the Hebrew University as a 'scientific endeavor'.[16] It also signified his support for the Hebrew University as part of the Jewish national revival project. That is, his participation reflected his Jewish and Zionist sensibilities.

[6] Hans Kelsen was also to be invited: Report of Meeting of Academic Committee, 17 January 1950, Semi-Jubilee 91–1950, HUA.

[7] For Lauterpacht's background: Philippe Sands, *East West Street: On the Origins of Genocide and Crimes against Humanity* (Knopf 2016).

[8] CP (n 5) 159.

[9] Albert Einstein served as the honorary President in Berlin: Arnold McNair, [Tribute to Sir Hersch Lauterpacht] (1961) 10 ICLQ 3, 4; Martti Koskenniemi, *The Gentle Civilizer of Nations: The Rise and Fall of International Law 1870–1960* (CUP 2001) 369–70.

[10] Elihu Lauterpacht, *The Life of Hersch Lauterpacht* (CUP 2010) 201.

[11] Nathan Feinberg (ed), *Studies in Public International Law in Memory of Sir Hersch Lauterpacht* (Magnes 1961) (Hebrew); Nathan Feinberg, *Essays on Jewish Issues of Our Time* (Dvir 1980) 227 (Hebrew).

[12] CP ii (n 5) 159.

[13] Lauterpacht to Feinberg, 2 March 1950, Lauterpacht–92/1950, HUA; CP ii (n 5) 159; Lauterpacht, *Life* (n 10) 339.

[14] Lauterpacht to Feinberg, 2 March 1950, 11 April 1950, Feinberg to Lauterpacht, 20 April 1950, Lauterpacht–92/1950, HUA.

[15] Just like his contribution, discussed in the Prologue, to the *Jewish Yearbook of International Law*.

[16] CP ii (n 5) 159.

2. A Zionist Engagement

Lauterpacht's Judaism and, in particular, his Zionism have in recent years attracted the interest of international law scholars.[17] The debate starts with an attempt to decipher the significance of Lauterpacht's Jewish identity in his scholarship,[18] but proceeds with accounting for the tensions underlying his evident cosmopolitanism *and* particularist investment in Jewish nationalism. For some, reconciliation of these two attachments can be achieved through a diachronic distinction. His earlier Zionism,[19] they suggest, receded to the background once he had immigrated to Britain, giving way to cosmopolitanism. 'Not much of his early Zionist politics is visible in later years', writes Martti Koskenniemi, and 'soon he allowed his Zionism to lapse and fall back on the more traditional Jewish association with liberal rationalism and individualist—hence cosmopolitan—ethics'.[20] 'From now on, he assimilated with post-war liberal internationalism, letting his Jewish background resurface only incidentally'.[21] Lauterpacht's very cosmopolitanism, Koskenniemi proposes, 'can also be understood as an *assimilative strategy*' in Britain's academic milieu.[22]

Others, however, take heed of the persistence of the tension between Lauterpacht's cosmopolitanism and Jewish nationalism.[23] His draft of Israel's Declaration of Independence has led Eliav Lieblich and Yoram Shachar to argue that 'by participating in a national project, Lauterpacht's cosmopolitanism was compromised'.[24] They argue, further, that 'his attempt to reconcile, in the Draft, between cosmopolitanism and national sovereignty'[25] had distorted the historiography of his legacy. That episode, they note, 'was downplayed, over the years, by those associated with Lauterpacht'[26] and those who 'have reconstructed Lauterpacht's cosmopolitan legacy'[27] in order 'to maintain the credibility of

[17] Eliav Lieblich and Yoram Shachar, 'Cosmopolitanism at a Crossroads: Hersch Lauterpacht and the Israeli Declaration of Independence' (2014) 84 Brit YB Intl L 1 conveniently survey the debate. In particular, Koskenniemi (n 9); Martti Koskenniemi, 'Hersch Lauterpacht (1897–1960)' in Jack Beatson and Reinhard Zimmermann (eds), *Jurists Uprooted: German-Speaking Emigré Lawyers in Twentieth Century Britain* (OUP 2004) 601; Reut Yael Paz, *A Gateway between a Distant God and a Cruel World: The Contribution of Jewish German-Speaking Scholars to International Law* (Nijhoff 2013); James Loeffler, 'The "Natural Right of the Jewish People": Zionism, International Law, and the Paradox of Hersch Zvi Lauterpacht' in James Loeffler and Moria Paz (eds), *The Law of Strangers: Jewish Lawyers and International Law in the Twentieth Century* (CUP 2019) 23.

[18] Paz (n 17).

[19] Manifest in his 1922 Vienna dissertation, 'The Mandate under International Law in the Covenant of the League of Nations', reprinted in CP iii (n 5) 29, 40.

[20] Koskenniemi (n 9) 371.

[21] ibid.

[22] Emphasis added; ibid, 373–4.

[23] For Paz (n 17) 184, part of Lauterpacht's constant 'opposing exigencies'.

[24] Lieblich and Shachar (n 17) 1; Paz (n 17) 288 ('put his legal objectivity at stake').

[25] Lieblich and Shachar (n 17) 1.

[26] ibid, 13.

[27] ibid, 1.

Lauterpacht's influential body of cosmopolitan jurisprudence'.[28] His son-biographer, to do away the tension, submitted that 'it could not then be foreseen that the fulfilment of this ideal would in due course lead to the sad contentions' prevailing in the Mid-East since. This allows Lauterpacht's Zionism to be depoliticized: 'Hersch's Zionism was a pure ideal to be pursued on the basis of historical knowledge, education and restraint'.[29] A third strand of thought, first presented by Reut Yael Paz, argues, however, that Lauterpacht's cosmopolitanism inhered in his Zionism[30] or considers Lauterpacht's legal cosmopolitanism and Zionist commitment as 'co-constitutive historical phenomena'. In this vein, James Loeffler has recently argued using new, early evidence that in 'Lauterpacht's mind, the twin projects of Jewish state-building and modern international law not only coincided temporally; they also informed one another directly'.[31]

Archival evidence suggests that Lauterpacht's Zionism did persist, in both professional and personal spheres. Professionally, it was often low-key and hedged by discretion and confidentiality. But he had frequently rendered behind-the-scenes advice whenever it was sought: pre-independence, by the Jewish Agency; post-independence, by the Jewish state and its agents.[32] His counsel covered diverse issues such as the interpretation of mandate provisions;[33] General Assembly competence and majority requirements during the partition debate;[34] Jewish and Arab rights under the United Nations ('UN') Partition Plan;[35] Israel's Declaration of Independence;[36] the publication and continuation of the *Jewish Yearbook*; the question of granting *post mortem* Israeli nationality to Jews who perished in the Holocaust;[37] and Israel's attitude to the World Court and prospective adjudication

[28] ibid, 13. Yael Reut Paz, 'Between the "Public" and the "Private"' (2011) 22 EJIL 863, 866 notes Elihu's unease 'with his father's Zionist political convictions and feels compelled to distance his father's politics from contemporary Zionism'.

[29] Lauterpacht, *Life* (n 10) 423.

[30] Paz (n 17) 187.

[31] Loeffler (n 17) 25, 30 urging the need 'to reconsider the larger intertwined histories of Zionism and international law'; James Loeffler, *Rooted Cosmopolitans: Jews and Human Rights in the Twentieth Century* (Yale UP 2018).

[32] Shabtai Rosenne, 'In Memoriam: Sir Hersch Lauterpacht' *Jerusalem Post* (12 May 1960): 'More than once, both before and after the War, he was able to assist the Jewish Agency with his well considered legal advice and I myself, as well as other colleagues, were aided by him on various occasions'.

[33] 'Article 18 of the Mandate for Palestine and the Dissolution of the League of Nations' in CP iii (n 5) 101; H Lauterpacht, The Interpretation of Article 18 of the Mandate for Palestine and on The Question of the Participation of Palestine in Imperial Preference, [n.d., 1939], Confidential, K14\89, Central Zionist Archive ('CZA'), deposited by Rosenne in 1971.

[34] Eg an untitled twelve-page memorandum on General Assembly voting and competence: [Lauterpacht's Opinion], [n.d.], FM–2267/23, Israel State Archive ('ISA').

[35] Eliahu Eilath, *The Struggle for Statehood: Washington 1945–1948* (Am Oved 1982) 691–2 (Hebrew) recalls a 'secret memorandum' authored by Lauterpacht for use by the Jewish Agency during the 1947 UN partition debate, as well as a 1948 ten-page brief negating Arab claims for statehood in the entirety of *Eretz-Israel*/Palestine west of the Jordan titled 'Jamal Husseini's Thesis: The Legal Basis for the Establishment of an Arab Dominated State in the Whole of Western Palestine'.

[36] Lieblich and Shachar (n 17).

[37] Nathan Feinberg, *Reminiscences* (Keter 1985) 166 (Hebrew).

before it.[38] Rosenne, in particular, fostered the relationship, effectively treating Lauterpacht as his mentor.[39] Following Lauterpacht's passing on 8 May 1960, Rosenne eulogized him in the *Jerusalem Post* as the 'Defender of Rights of Man'.[40] Their relations stretched back to Rosenne-Rowson's British days.[41] Once in Palestine, Rosenne made it a habit to frequently report to Lauterpacht, seek legal (and career) advice—and, at times, invoke the weight of Lauterpacht's opinion for support in the Ministry of Foreign Affairs' ('MFA') internal decision-making processes.[42]

In the personal sphere, Lauterpacht had various ties to Israel. He met Rachel Steinberg, a music student, in Vienna; they were engaged in Berlin and married, again in Vienna, in 1923, soon to leave for England. 'I had lunch with Mrs Lauterpacht, the evacuated wife of the Cambridge professor of law', wrote Isaiah Berlin during the war years: 'very nice, very Palestinian'—as opposed to her 'dull husband'.[43] Her father immigrated to Palestine from Czarist Russia in 1884, part of the first wave of ideology-driven Jewish immigration there. He took part in the founding of several Palestine colonies, expatriated to South Africa, and finally settled in Motza, a small village on the road to Jerusalem where he founded a brick and tile factory.[44] Through the pedigree of this marriage, Lauterpacht would acquire relation to Israel's political, diplomatic, and military elites.[45] Old friends from Lauterpacht's Zionist youth in Galicia immigrated to Palestine; one, David Horowitz, was now the Director-General of Israel's Finance Ministry and later, first Governor of the Bank of Israel.[46] Attending the Hebrew University opening ceremony in 1925, Lauterpacht had sought a job with the fledging institution;[47] when, in October 1959, he was 'taken ill and had to leave the Bench in the middle of a major case, he came to Israel to convalesce'.[48]

[38] In 1948 Lauterpacht was already advising Israel on the ICJ, in connection with a Syrian initiative to refer the question of Israel's statehood to the ICJ: Robinson to Lauterpacht, 21 July 1948, FM–129/6, ISA.

[39] 'Acceptance Speech by Professor Shabtai Rosenne' (2004) 51 Netherlands YB Intl L 475.

[40] Rosenne (n 32).

[41] Rowson to Lauterpacht, 28 January 1948, S25\1189, CZA.

[42] '[W]hen Prof Lauterpacht was here he proposed to charge me with taking over the editorship' of the *Jewish Yearbook*: Rosenne to Eytan, Short Report on Consultations with Dr. J. Robinson, [n.d., *circa* July 1950], FM–5850/2, ISA.

[43] Isaiah Berlin, *Flourishing: Letters 1928–1946* (Chatto & Windus 2004) 370, 411.

[44] David Tidhar, 'Yehiel Michael Steinberg', *Encyclopedia of the Founders and Builders of Israel*, vol 2 (Sifriyat Rishonim 1947) 576 (Hebrew).

[45] Rachel's niece Suzy married Abba Eban, Israel's first UN Permanent Representative and later ambassador to the US and Foreign Minister. Her sister Ora married Chaim Herzog, Israel's military Chief of Intelligence and, later, Israel's UN Permanent Representative and State President: Chaim Herzog, 'Sir Hersch Lauterpacht: An Appraisal' (1997) 2 EJIL 299. Both were Cambridge educated, both became *Knesset* members; Suzy Eban, *A Sense of Purpose: Recollections* (Halban 2008) 35, 311.

[46] David Horowitz, *HaEtmol Sheli* (Schocken 1970) 69 (Hebrew).

[47] Lauterpacht, *Life* (n 10) 39; Norman Bentwich, 'Sir Hersch Lauterpacht' in Feinberg, *Studies* (n 11) 68–9.

[48] Rosenne (n 32).

He stayed for four months or so[49] and contemplated, reportedly, settling in Israel.[50]

3. International Law 'in the City of Prophets'

Jewish identity and Zionist sensibilities were patent in Lauterpacht's two 1950 interventions. On 8 May, at the law faculty—to an audience versed in the discipline—he reflected, in English, on 'International Law After the Second World War'. This opened with a courtesy alluding to the 'profound significance' of the 'fact that international law, under the distinguished leadership' of Dean Feinberg, 'has been assigned a distinct and important place in this University'. 'What can be more proper', he asked, 'than that the discipline of the rule of law among nations should be taught in the City of the Prophets who first proclaimed . . . the ideals of international peace and brotherhood among the nations of the earth?'[51] A similar 'personal note' concluded that talk. Apologizing for 'marring a festive occasion' with gloomy reflections on the legality and criminality of recourse to 'atomic warfare', Lauterpacht averred that it was nonetheless 'fit that this call should come, at this time, from Jerusalem':

> There is a future of promise and deep meaning for the science of international law—and for other sciences—in the City in which Isaiah proclaimed the message of eternal peace and of transformation of weapons of death into implements of creative effort.[52]

Still, the substance of this general exposé of achievement and challenge facing international law was largely devoid of particular Jewish or Israeli salience. It could well have been delivered at Cambridge, Geneva, New York, or anywhere else.

The day before, to a lay audience consisting of the Jewish state's elites, he spoke the language of national revival to address 'State Sovereignty and Human Rights'. Clearly, Lauterpacht considered this a matter of Jewish significance—conceiving of human rights as a Jewish problem and, perhaps, a Jewish solution. He started this lecture by making this very point:

> It is fitting that the . . . lecture in the field of international law which I have the honour to give in the Hebrew University on this auspicious occasion should be devoted to some aspects of the question of the international recognition and protection of the fundamental rights of man. There is not—and never has been—a nation which has suffered more frequently and more cruelly from a denial of

49 Lauterpacht, *Life* (n 10) 418.
50 Feinberg, *Studies* (n 11) 5.
51 CP ii (n 5) 159.
52 ibid, 170.

these rights than the Jewish people. These inalienable human rights have now been recognized—and the way opened for the international supervision of their observance—largely as a reaction against the perversion and the magnitude of the contempt shown for them at the hands of the persecutors of the people of Israel. And Jews—individually and collectively—have played a leading rôle in making the natural rights of man part of the positive Law of Nations.[53]

4. A Jewish Engagement

That Lauterpacht would speak on human rights could not come as a surprise to any familiar with his work. He had written and spoken about this extensively since 1942.[54] *Openly* framing human rights as a Jewish affair was, however, new. But it had Jewish roots all along; when commissioned, that year, to prepare what was to become in 1945 *An International Bill of the Rights of Man*,[55] he confided to his wife that 'the book for the [American] Jewish Committee' was to be 'on the International Bill of Rights of the Individual (or something like that) with special application to the Jewish Question'.[56] The penultimate paragraph of the book's preface did acknowledge the assistance of the American Jewish Committee ('AJC'). It spoke of a Jewish agency in human rights work. It hinted that the AJC was in fact acting in this matter as the representative of the Jewish people, and recognized the pedigree of its human rights work:

> It is fitting, for many reasons, that the Committee should have actively interested themselves in the problem of an International Bill of the Rights of Man. No other people in history has suffered more cruelly from a denial of elementary human rights. At the end of the first World War representatives of Jewish organizations, from the United States and elsewhere, played a prominent part in securing the Minorities Treaties—a significant step in the direction of the general international protection of the rights of man.[57]

Nonetheless, the text of the monograph, extending over more than 200 pages, did not contain *any*, let alone 'special application to the Jewish Question'.[58] 'Jews', 'Jewish', 'anti-Semitism', etc did not merit index entries.[59] The book read as a universal argument for making human rights part of positive international law.

[53] ibid, 416.
[54] Lauterpacht's human rights works are listed in CP iii (n 5) 407.
[55] Hersch Lauterpacht, *An International Bill of the Rights of Man* (Columbia UP 1945).
[56] Lauterpacht, *Life* (n 10) 199.
[57] Lauterpacht, *International Bill* (n 55) vii.
[58] ibid, 86 contained a passing reference to the World Jewish Congress concerning 'phraseology'.
[59] ibid, 225, 227. If the monograph betrayed any particularistic identification, it was British: eg 54–65; Paz (n 17) 238.

Lauterpacht's Jewish investment in human rights was also terribly personal.[60] In the spring of 1942, around the time that the AJC first contacted him, though unbeknown to him, the first deportations from Lvov to the extermination camps were taking place.[61] Later that year, he wrote of the book: 'I have not started yet! But I must do it—one reason being that I want to keep my mind off the news about extermination in [the] occupied territories'.[62] Save for one niece, his entire family perished at the hands of the Nazis.[63] In Jerusalem, in Hebrew, in 1950, Lauterpacht could openly assert the Jewish salience, provenance,[64] and agency of his human rights project.[65] He now hinted that the mantle of representation had passed from 'Jewish organizations' such as the AJC to the Jewish state. And the last sentence of his lecture, where he tied the promise of human rights protection to his vision for world society, assigned the Jewish state a vocation; it spoke of

> a more complete integration of international society . . . the consummation of the organized *civitas maxima* with the individual human being in the very centre of the constitution of the world. To that development—it is to be hoped confidently and fervently—the State of Israel will contribute its proper and appointed share.[66]

Otherwise, Lauterpacht's human rights lecture followed familiar trajectories. As elsewhere, he offered a generous reading of the human rights provisions of the UN Charter.[67] As elsewhere, his ambivalence towards the Universal Declaration adopted by the UN General Assembly on 10 December 1948 was evident.[68] Careful to credit its Jewish promoters, he nonetheless expressed his discontent with its nonbinding character and the absence of any means of enforcement attending it. Effective enforcement—ever a persistent theme in his human rights scholarship—also drove the thrust of his Jerusalem lecture; at its heart was the right of petition:

60 Koskenniemi (n 9) 388.

61 Lauterpacht, *Life* (n 10) 100–1; Sands (n 7) 243.

62 Lauterpacht, *Life* (n 10) 219.

63 ibid, 11, 101.

64 Crediting 'the efforts of Jewish organizations' in Paris 1919 and San Francisco 1945 CP iii (n 5) 416.

65 Stoyanovsky, who knew Lauterpacht from the 'Fry Library and . . . our Research Class at the LSE', asked for his *Jewish Yearbook* contribution to deal 'with the Rights of Man—a question which you have treated in a recent work of yours'; Lauterpacht declined: Stoyanovsky to Lauterpacht, 5 April 1946, Lauterpacht to Stoyanovsky, 24 April 1946, A306\6, CZA. Lauterpacht accepted the invitation to attend the semi-jubilee on condition that his lectures would not be published: Feinberg to Cherrick, 2 July 1950, Semi-Jubilee 91–1950 (May–), HUA.

66 CP iii (n 5) 430. For Lauterpacht's Kantian federalism: Koskenniemi (n 9) 354–8.

67 Lauterpacht, *International Bill* (n 55).

68 Samuel Moyn, *Human Rights and the Uses of History* (Verso 2014) 163–4 (Lauterpacht 'denounced the Universal Declaration as a shameful defeat of the ideals it grandly proclaimed'); Lauterpacht, *Life* (n 10) 259–63; Jewish Telegraphic Agency, 'International Legal Expert Voices Criticism of Declaration of Human Rights' (7 August 1947); Hersch Lauterpacht, 'The Universal Declaration of Human Rights' (1948) 25 Brit YB Intl L 354.

> the right of petition is one of the central problems of the international protection of human rights. To that problem of the right of petition under the Charter and in connection with the proposed International Bill of Human Rights I propose to devote to a large extent this lecture on 'State Sovereignty and Human Rights'. For few matters shed so much instructive light on the relation of State Sovereignty to human rights as the question of the effective right of international petition.[69]

5. 'Legal *Locus Standi*'

For Lauterpacht, few matters were as crucial to the development of human rights as the question of enforcement. In 1943, his first published text on human rights already asserted that '[i]f the enthronement of the rights of man is to become a reality, then they must become part of the positive law of nations suitably guaranteed and enforced'.[70] And few matters were as crucial for human rights enforcement as the right of petition: the right of individuals and organizations to bring grievances, arising from human rights violations, before international bodies. In the 1945 monograph for the AJC, he warned against the prospect of the 'rights of man' turning into 'another example of the evasion and the concealment typical of international intercourse'.[71] 'Enforceability', he wrote, 'is of the essence of any rule of law'.[72]

Realizing 'the purpose of the Bill of Rights', Lauterpacht observed, required the 'conferment on the individual of ... [some] form of international procedural capacity'. This meant, predominantly, 'the right of petition, which must be safeguarded as a special right enshrined in the International Bill of the Rights of Man'.[73] The 'Bill of Rights', he insisted, 'must establish the right of petition as a legal right of the individual in the international sphere'.[74] Accordingly, Article 19 of Lauterpacht's proposed Bill pronounced the right of individual and organizational petition.[75] What was 'radical' with this 'innovation' was 'the fact that the protection of the rights of the individual is declared to be the task of the Law of Nations'.[76] Unlike the practice of the League of Nations minorities protection system, under Lauterpacht's Bill individuals would have 'legal *locus standi* in the matter'.[77] Emanating from an international 'legal right of the individual', and expressing the character of individuals

[69] CP iii (n 5) 416–17.
[70] Hersch Lauterpacht, 'The Law of Nations, the Law of Nature and the Rights of Man' (1943) 29 Trans Grot Soc 1, 31.
[71] Lauterpacht, *International Bill* (n 55) 76.
[72] ibid, 78.
[73] ibid.
[74] ibid, 201.
[75] ibid, 74 ('The right of individuals and organizations to petition the High Commission in the matter of the observance of this Bill of Rights shall not be denied or impaired').
[76] ibid, 195.
[77] ibid, 217.

as subjects of international law, their petitions would now be more than a mere communication of information to an international organization.[78]

Lauterpacht's plan to publish an expanded treatment of human rights[79] bore fruit in 1950. *International Law and Human Rights* appeared in May, the same month he travelled to Jerusalem to address the right of petition.[80] Naturally, it contained an expanded treatment of the right of petition as a principal method for human rights enforcement. It also took account—and a dim view—of emerging UN practice that had, in Lauterpacht's opinion, amounted to 'a denial of the effective right of petition and to an abdication of the crucial function of the United Nations in this respect'.[81] This concerned the Economic and Social Council ('ECOSOC') approving a February 1947 statement by the Human Rights Commission; there the Commission 'recognise[d] that it had no power to take any action in regard to any complaints concerning human rights'.[82] Lauterpacht's critique was, in his own words, 'highly controversial and very much outspoken ... it will be certainly frowned upon by the Commission on Human Rights and by the Human Rights Division' of the UN Secretariat. This led him, in December 1949, to suggest to the AJC (who commissioned that work, too) to abandon publication lest the organization is 'held responsible', has its 'relations with the organs of the United Nations' hampered, and has its future work jeopardized.[83]

The book was published. Lauterpacht's revised *Draft of the International Bill of the Rights of Man* now included a direct and explicit provision stating 'the full freedom of petition to the national authorities and to the United Nations'; the proposed 'Human Rights Council' was to base itself on the recognition of 'the right of petition of any State, organization, body, or individual'.[84] This now became 'the most essential feature of the scheme'.[85] The 'principle of effective petition' was of 'paramount importance'.[86] He railed against the UN position: '[t]here is no legal justification for that statement'. 'These bodies, and, in particular, the Commission

[78] ibid, 201.
[79] ibid, vii.
[80] Hersch Lauterpacht, *International Law and Human Rights* (Stevens & sons 1950). This, too, was under contract with the AJC, though no such credit was included: Lauterpacht, *Life* (n 10) 263; even this expanded *tome* harboured no application to the 'Jewish Question'; a single footnote, and an accompanying index entry, dealt with two examples of nineteenth-century intercessions in favour of Jews in Russia and Germany: Lauterpacht, *Human Rights*, 33ff, 471.
[81] ibid, 225–6.
[82] ECOSOC Res.75(V) (5 August 1947); UN Doc. E/259, Report to the Economic and Social Council on the First Session of the Commission in ECOSOC Official Records, Suppl.3 (1947) 6; John P Humphrey, *Human Rights and the United Nations: A Great Adventure* (Transnational 1984) 82; Roger Normand and Sarah Zaidi, *Human Rights at the UN: The Political History of Universal Justice* (Indiana UP 2008) 140, 145, 157–66; Ton JM Zuijdwijk, *Petitioning the United Nations: A Study in Human Rights* (St. Martin's 1982); Jakob T Möller, 'Petitioning the United Nations' (1979) 1 Universal Human Rights 57.
[83] Lauterpacht, *Life* (n 10) 263.
[84] Lauterpacht, *Human Rights* (n 80) 315, 318.
[85] ibid, 379.
[86] ibid, 241.

on Human Rights, are not only entitled to take such action. By the terms of the Charter they are bound to do so'. In his reading, the Human Rights Commission was, by dint of the Charter, under a 'duty to receive petition alleging violations of human rights, to examine them, and ... to take all requisite action short of intervention'.[87] What transpired instead, Lauterpacht protested, was a 'renunciation by these bodies of a power and obligation grounded in the Charter ... a denial of the effective right of petition inherent in the Charter'.[88] He denounced 'the extraordinary degree of abdication, on the part of the United Nations, of its function'.[89] He warned that '[t]he United Nations will fail in a crucial—perhaps *the* crucial—aspect of its purpose' if it followed such a restrictive view.[90] Long tracts offered diverse refutations of the Commission's position. '[R]udimentary to the point of being nominal';[91] 'evasive';[92] 'shrouded in secrecy';[93] 'no guarantee';[94] '*non sequitur*';[95] 'self-imposed limitation';[96] 'danger ... imaginary';[97] 'self-effacing abdication';[98] these were just a few of the terms Lauterpacht employed in critique of the procedure adopted by the Human Rights Commission for dealing with petitions it had received. The book also offered extensive answers to 'objections to the exclusion of the right of individuals to initiate proceedings before international organs'.[99] All this was meant to contest 'the negative attitude of Governments to the question of the right of petition by individuals'.[100]

And so, when Lauterpacht devoted his Jerusalem lecture to 'the question of the effective right of international petition',[101] he was not merely propounding his recent scholarship; he was championing a cause. This was one more battle waged in a campaign he was already losing, in part owing to his Jewish background.[102] Invoking, in Jerusalem, the Jewish salience and provenance[103] of human rights and

[87] ibid, 230.
[88] ibid, 235.
[89] ibid, 236.
[90] ibid, 231; emphasis in the original.
[91] ibid, 237.
[92] ibid.
[93] ibid.
[94] ibid, 238.
[95] ibid.
[96] ibid, 240.
[97] ibid, 242.
[98] ibid, 247.
[99] ibid, 289.
[100] ibid, 290.
[101] CP iii (n 5) 416–17.
[102] Lauterpacht's contribution to the Human Rights Commission's work was thwarted by the Foreign Office legal adviser, Beckett: 'Lauterpacht would be a very bad candidate ... It would be disastrous, I think, to make him the delegate ... [He,] though a distinguished and industrious international lawyer, is, when all is said and done, a Jew recently come from Vienna. Emphatically, I think that the representative of HMG on human rights must be a very English Englishman imbued throughout his life and hereditary': Alfred WB Simpson, *Human Rights and the End of Empire: Britain and the Genesis of the European Convention* (OUP 2001) 350.
[103] See n 64.

concluding his lecture by alluding to Israel's 'proper and appointed share' in realizing the human rights ideal, Lauterpacht was attempting—'confidently and fervently',[104] yet also desperately—to enlist the Jewish state to the cause of the right of individual petition.

6. Tradition Invoked: Nathan Feinberg and the Right of Petition

Lauterpacht's human rights lecture in Jerusalem could, and did, invoke a Jewish tradition of investment not merely in human rights but, specifically, in the right of petition. The recognition of human rights and the possibility of 'the international supervision of their observance' was, his lecture's opening paragraph asserted, 'largely as a reaction against' the persecution of Jews.[105] That paragraph noted the 'individual efforts of Jewish lawyers' who played a 'leading rôle in making the natural rights of man part of the positive Law of Nations'.[106] It paid, first, tribute to René Cassin.[107] Second, felicitously, it could proceed to take the form of an homage to Lauterpacht's host:

> One of the most valuable scientific productions of Professor Feinberg, the present occupant of the Chair of International Law at the Hebrew University, has been his course of lectures, delivered at the Hague Academy of International Law, on the right of petition in international law. I am mentioning this not merely because it affords a welcome opportunity of paying a well-deserved tribute to Professor Feinberg's scholarship but also because the right of petition is one of the central problems of the international protection of human rights.[108]

This homage provided Lauterpacht with the occasion to announce that that lecture on 'State Sovereignty and Human Rights' would be devoted to 'that problem of the right of petition'. This eloquent blend of courtesy and oratory device, however, also served to remind the audience, and Feinberg, that the right of petition was, and remained, a Jewish concern.[109]

[104] CP iii (n 5) 430.
[105] ibid, 416.
[106] ibid, 416.
[107] Whom Feinberg proposed to invite, but had to decline: '*a Lake Success pour commission droit de l'homme*': Cassin to Senateur, 20 February 1950, Semi-Jubilee, 91–1950, HUA. See Jay Winter and Antoine Prost, *René Cassin and Human Rights: From the Great War to the Universal Declaration* (CUP 2013).
[108] CP iii (n 5) 416.
[109] Thirty-five years later, a still-grateful Feinberg recorded the accolade in his memoires: Feinberg, *Reminiscences* (n 37) 72.

In 1932, Nathan Feinberg (1895–1988) was based in Switzerland holding the title of Privat-docent—with no regular appointment or salary—at the University of Geneva.[110] His persisting efforts to secure a position at the Hebrew University produced, the following year, proposals to extend 'juridical studies' at that institute. These included 'studies of questions pertinent to the legal position of the Jews'.[111] '[T]here is a wide'—but 'neglected'—'field of international law, that concerns directly the [Jewish] people', Feinberg wrote.[112] Norman Bentwich—Professor of International Relations and holder of the *Chaim Weizmann Chair of International Law of Peace* at the Hebrew University—considered him 'a sound but not inspiring jurist',[113] a 'painstakingly legal scholar of international affairs in a rather limited field'. Feinberg, he wrote, had 'in excess just those qualities to which our students are too prone already: a legalistic and narrowly Jewish approach to the subject'.[114] The subject of research proposed by Feinberg's 1933 memorandum, alas, was 'rather narrow'.[115] Still, Feinberg's familiarity with what he called 'Jewish public law'[116] worked somewhat in his favour at times when Bentwich's engagement in public affairs[117] raised the prospect of hiring a temporary lecturer to second for Bentwich.[118] His 1932 Hague Academy course commended by Lauterpacht in 1950—*La pétition en droit international*, conceived with evident, if implicit, Jewish concerns[119]—was likely his most significant academic achievement at that point. In 1945, Feinberg finally obtained a Hebrew University lectureship, following favourable opinions from William Rappard and Lauterpacht.[120] Much of his future

[110] *Curriculum Vitae* and Publications of Dr Nathan Feinberg, 29 December 1944, Feinberg 1929–1944, HUA; Feinberg, *Reminiscences* (n 37) 71; Rotem Giladi, 'At the Sovereign Turn: International Law at the Hebrew University Law Faculty Early Years' in Yfaat Weiss and Uzi Rebhun (eds), *The History of the Hebrew University in Jerusalem*, vol 5 (forthcoming Magnes 2021) (Hebrew); I am currently working on a project focused on Feinberg.

[111] Nathan Feinberg, The Extension of Juridical Studies at the Hebrew University of Jerusalem, August 1933, A306\151, CZA, and Feinberg 1929–1944, HUA. Assaf Likhovski, 'Law Studies at the Hebrew University during the Period of the Mandate' in Hagit Lavsky (ed), *The History of the Hebrew University of Jerusalem: A Period of Consolidation and Growth* (Magnes 2005) 543 (Hebrew).

[112] Feinberg, Juridical Studies (n 111).

[113] Bentwich to Senator, 2 January 1938, Bentwich Personal File I: 1924–1947, HUA ('the University need not go out of its way to create a place for him ... he might be a deputy for me when I have to be away. For that part he is of course well fitted; though if Stoyanovsky ... is still in Palestine, his claims seem to me as strong').

[114] Bentwich to Senator, 11 May 1942, Bentwich Personal File I: 1924–1947, HUA.

[115] Bentwich to Ginzberg, 1 February 1934, Bentwich Personal File I: 1924–1947, HUA.

[116] Feinberg, Juridical Studies (n 111).

[117] Eg serving as assistant to James G McDonald, High Commission for Refugees from Germany.

[118] Bentwich to Senator, 2 January 1938 (Feinberg 'suitable', and if 'specified research on the juridical status of the Jewish people, F[einberg] would have the stronger qualifications'); Bentwich to Magnes, 19 November 1933 (Feinberg 'specially qualified' to 'give a course of lectures on some subject like "Minority Rights"'); and Bentwich to Senator, 11 May 1942, Bentwich Personal File I: 1924–1947, HUA ('adequate lecturer' but not 'the right choice for the Chair'). Feinberg, at any rate, insisted on a full, regular appointment.

[119] Nathan Feinberg, 'La pétition en droit international' (1932) 40 RdC 525.

[120] Report on the Appointment of a Teacher in International Relations, 17 January 1945, Feinberg, Personal File 1945–1955, HUA.

scholarship would chronicle episodes in the history of the Jewish engagement with international law, and international law's engagement with the Jewish Question.[121]

These interests were not purely scholarly; they also reflected Feinberg's own involvement in the *praxis* of interwar Jewish advocacy. Born in Kaunas in 1895—then in Czarist Russia—Feinberg received general (that is, non-Jewish) education at a government gymnasium against the odds of the *numerus clausus*,[122] complemented by private education reflecting his parents' Jewish faith and Zionist leanings.[123] Stranded in Germany at the outbreak of WWI, he made his way to Zurich, where in 1918 he was awarded the degree of *doctor juris utriusque (magna cum laude)*.[124]

For the next decade and a half, Feinberg would alternate between Europe and Palestine, oscillating between minorities advocacy,[125] private practice, and the pursuit of Zionism. He first returned to independent Lithuania to work for the Ministry for Jewish Affairs, putting to practice this 'experiment' in Jewish autonomy.[126] In 1922–1924 he was in Paris, serving as the Secretary of the *Comité des Délégations Juives auprès de la Conference de la Paix*[127]—an organization comprising representatives of the different Jewish delegations to the Paris peace conference, established in 1919 by the World Zionist Organisation *vouée à la défense de la cause juive.*[128] The *Comité* represented the interests of Jewish minorities at the League of Nations and was succeeded, after 1936, by the World Jewish Congress ('WJC').[129] In 1924 Feinberg immigrated to Palestine to practice law in Tel Aviv. He returned to Europe in 1928, at the invitation of Leo Motzkin, a prominent Zionist leader and President of the *Comité des Délégations Juives*, to work again for that body; the promised position, however, never materialized.[130] In Geneva, Feinberg obtained a *diploma* in

[121] Giladi (n 110); Feinberg's 'Principal Publications' are compiled in (1985) 20 Isr L Rev 116–22; of note is Nathan Feinberg, 'The International Protection of Human Rights and the Jewish Question: A Historical Survey' (1968) 3 Isr L Rev 487.

[122] Feinberg, *Reminiscences* (n 37) 12–15.

[123] Ruth Lapidoth, 'Nathan Feinberg: A Tribute' (1985) 20 Isr L Rev 113.

[124] Feinberg, *Reminiscences* (n 37) 26–9. His thesis dealt with high treason under the Swiss Criminal Code: Nathan Feinberg, *Das Vergehen des Hochverrates nach dem geltenden und zukünftigen schweizerischen Strafrechte (Vorentwurf 1916) mit Berücksichtigung der deutschen und österreichischen Entwürfe* (Funk 1920).

[125] Giladi (n 110). Chs 4, 5 discuss Jewish engagements with minority rights.

[126] Feinberg, *Reminiscences* (n 37) 41–8; Nathan Feinberg, 'The Jewish Autonomy in Lithuania (Reminiscences)' (1973) 19 Gesher 40 (Hebrew); Nathan Feinberg, *Tautiniu Mazumu Problema* [*The Problem of National Minorities*] (Bako 1922)(Lithuanian); Nathan Feinberg, 'The Lithuanian Constitution and the Jewish National Autonomy' *The Morgen-Journal* (21 September 1922) (Yiddish); Šarūnas Liekis, *A State Within a State?: Jewish Autonomy in Lithuania 1918–1925* (Versus Aureus 2003).

[127] Feinberg, *Reminiscences* (n 37) 53–9.

[128] *Comité des Délégations Juives, Dix-Sept Ans D'activté* (Paris/Genève 1936).

[129] Feinberg, *Essays* (n 11) 72; A Leon Kubowitzki, *Unity in Dispersion: A History of the World Jewish Congress* (WJC 1948); Zohar Segev, *The World Jewish Congress during the Holocaust: Between Activism and Restraint* (de Gruyter 2014); Menachem Z Rosensaft (ed), *Voice of a People: The World Jewish Congress, 1936–2016* (WJC 2017); *Comité des Délégations Juives, Dix-Sept Ans* (n 128).

[130] Feinberg, *Reminiscences* (n 37) 66; he nonetheless composed, for the *Comité*, Nathan Feinberg, *La Question Des Minorités à la Conférence de la Paix De 1919–1920 et l'action Juive en faveur de la Protection Internationale Des Minorités* (Rousseau & Cie 1929).

international law from the *Graduate Institute of International Studies*,[131] founded the year before by William Rappard and Paul Mantoux, scholar-diplomats at the League of Nations Secretariat.[132] The *travail d'habilitation* that earned him the Privat-docentship, and paved the way for his Hague Academy lectures on the right of petition, dealt with enforcement of the minorities treaties.[133] Feinberg would return to Palestine at the end of 1933; before he did, he became involved, on behalf of the *Comité*, with the Bernheim petition.[134]

In 1957, Feinberg would publish a Hebrew monograph on the Bernheim petition. The telling subtitle, translated, was *The Jewish Struggle Against Hitler in the League of Nations*.[135] The monograph drew not only on League of Nations records, but also on Feinberg's own document collection—and recollection—of the episode. It detailed its unfolding—and Feinberg's own role in the affair as the 'coordinator of the political action on behalf' of the *Comité des Délégations Juives*. Based in Geneva, he came to possess an 'unmediated familiarity of the facts'.[136]

By the spring of 1933, shortly after Adolf Hitler became *Reichskanzler*, the *Comité* had been searching for a suitable petitioner for some time—one whose case could be used to address German discriminatory racial legislation before the League. At Versailles, Germany was exempt from minority obligations.[137] Thus, no recourse could be made to the normal League protection of minorities procedures to address Germany's treatment of its Jews. The sole exception was Upper Silesia, a 'plebiscite territory'[138] governed by a 1922 German-Polish treaty. The Geneva Convention spelled out minorities obligations and established various recourse avenues, thus offering diverse platforms for advocacy and publicity. Unlike the normal League procedure, it promised individual petitioners from Upper Silesia

[131] Feinberg, *Reminiscences* (n 37) 70–1; his studies produced Nathan Feinberg, *La Juridiction de la Cour Permanente de Justice Internationale dans le Systeme des Mandats* (Rousseau & Cie 1930).

[132] Feinberg, *Reminiscences* (n 37) 66. Both were invited to attend the semi jubilee: both regretted to decline: Semi-Jubilee 91–1950 (January–March 1950: Congratulatory Letters and Cables), HUA.

[133] Nathan Feinberg, *La juridiction de la Cour Permanente de Justice dans le systeme de la protection internationale des minorites* (Rousseau & Cie 1931). In 1937 he lectured again at The Hague Academy on these topics: Nathan Feinberg, 'La juridiction et la jurisprudence de la Cour Permanente de Justice Internationale en matire de mandats et de Minorités' (1937) 59 RdC 591. See Feinberg to Senator, 16 July 1944, Feinberg 1929–1944, HUA.

[134] Feinberg, *Reminiscences* (n 37) 8 ('central role'), and 78–85.

[135] Nathan Feinberg, *HaMa'arakhah HaYehudit Neged Hitler Al Bimat Hever HaLeummim (HaPetitzia Shel Bernheim)* (Bialik Institute 1957) (Hebrew) [*Jewish Struggle*]; chapter 3 translated as Nathan Feinberg, 'The Activities of Central Jewish Organizations Following Hitler's Rise to Power' (1957) 1 Yad VaShem Studies 67.

[136] Feinberg, *Jewish Struggle* (n 135) [book jacket] 8; Feinberg, *Reminiscences* (n 37) 78–84.

[137] Feinberg, *Jewish Struggle* (n 135) 18–19. On the Bernheim petition, Philipp Graf, *Die Bernheim-Petition 1933: Jüdische Politik in der Zwischenkriegszeit* (Vandenhoeck & Ruprecht 2008); Philipp Graf, 'The Bernheim Petition 1933: Probing the Limits of Jewish Diplomacy in the Interwar Period' (2016) 15 Simon Dubnow Institute YB 167; I am indebted to Dr Graf for generously placing at my disposal an early copy of this manuscript and various documents cited here.

[138] Article 88, Treaty of Peace between the Allied and Associated Powers and Germany (28 June 1919) [1919] 225 CTS 188; Georges Kaeckenbeck, *International Experiment in Upper Silesia* (OUP 1942).

direct access to the League Council.[139] Franz Bernheim fitted the bill: he was an Austrian-born Wurttemberg Jew of German nationality who had lost his employment as a clerk in a Gleiwitz department store; he was also safely outside Germany.

Feinberg credited Motzkin with leading the campaign—he would dedicate *The Jewish Struggle* to 'that doughty fighter for Jewish rights',[140] who died later in 1933. Credit for drafting Bernheim's petition went to Emil Margulies—a Czechoslovak Jewish lawyer active in Jewish, Zionist, and minorities advocacy, long associated with the *Comité*.[141] The legal strategy for approaching the League was drawn in exchanges between Margulies in Leitmeritz, Jacob Robinson in Kaunas, and Feinberg himself. Feinberg, nonetheless, was the lawyer on the spot in Geneva[142]—and had already dealt with the Silesian Convention in his Hague lectures.[143] With Motzkin, in Paris, frequently unresponsive, Feinberg's role extended to urging the more senior Robinson—who had just published, in Kaunas, a favourable *Yiddish* review of Feinberg's Hague lectures on the right of petition[144]—to 'write to Motzkin again ... and push him to discuss the question seriously', for 'nothing serious is being done in this direction'.[145]

The petition was submitted to the League of Nations on 17 May 1933.[146] Conditions were favourable. The day after, the Secretary-General did deem it 'urgent', meriting its direct referral to the Council; this allowed, as was hoped, the matter to be discussed in the first Council session after the Nazis' rise to power.[147] The Council did debate the petition in public meetings. Germany's objections to having the item included in the agenda were overcome. The *Rapporteur* did issue a favourable report. Germany's objections—that Bernheim was entitled to neither 'submit a petition' nor 'raise a general question'[148]—were referred to a Committee of Jurists,[149] to be unanimously rejected.[150] The Council did adopt the *Rapporteur's* final report: 'the mere perusal' of German laws and administrative orders did 'show

[139] Article 147, Convention Concerning Upper Silesia, signed at Geneva 15 May 1922; the relevant provisions were annexed to the *Rights of Minorities in Upper Silesia (Minority Schools)* (Judgment 26 April 1928), PCIJ (Ser. A) No.15, 75, 85; Feinberg, *Jewish Struggle* (n 135) 24–25.

[140] Feinberg, *Central Organizations* (n 135) 69.

[141] Feinberg, *Jewish Struggle* (n 135) 53.

[142] ibid; Feinberg, *Central Organizations* (n 135) 78. Early on, Robinson seems to have advocated using the individual petition path: Robinson to Feinberg, 20 April 1933, A126\616, CZA (Robinson 'raised the question of petition and its legal aspect' in late March or early April'); Philipp Graf, 'The Bernheim Petition 1933: Jacob Robinson's Contribution to Jewish Minority Diplomacy in the Interwar Years' in Eglé Bendikaitė and Dirk Roland Haupt (eds), *The Life, Times and Work of Jokubas Robinzonas—Jacob Robinson* (Akademia Verlag 2015) 179.

[143] Feinberg, '*La pétition*' (n 119) 610–12, 637.

[144] Yacob Rabinzon, 'Di Petitia in Valkerrecht' *Di Idishe Shtime* No.89 (21 April 1933) 9 (Yiddish).

[145] Feinberg to Robinson, 26 April 1933, Feinberg to Motzkin, 11 May 1933, A306\71, CZA.

[146] The petition and League documents are reproduced in 'Review of the Year', (1933/1934) 35 American Jewish Year Book 74–101; Feinberg, *Jewish Struggle* (n 135) 56.

[147] ibid, 59, 48.

[148] 'Review' (n 146) 83.

[149] Comprising Huber, Bourquin, and Pedroso.

[150] 'Review' (n 146) 99.

that' they could not apply to Upper Silesia 'without conflicting' with Germany's treaty obligations.[151] Germany was embarrassed, not least by having to admit that its domestic legislation had to give way to international obligations.[152] And, as the petition's architects had hoped, other Council representatives did not limit their censure of Germany to the situation in Upper Silesia; instead, they addressed the 'more general and more moving problem' of the 'the rights of a race scattered throughout all countries'.[153] And the report did generate follow-up activities by the *Comité* with regard to Upper Silesia but also elsewhere.[154] Feinberg's 1957 monograph and other writings could, therefore, pronounce the enterprise a success.[155]

Reflecting on the affair in 1957, Feinberg was also compelled to ponder futility. Robinson, for one, was convinced in 1933 that 'the petition must be submitted, and soon'; but he also acknowledged that 'we are aspiring, mostly, for a moral verdict' as 'no change for the better in the situation of Germany's Jews would come'. 'The purpose of the action', he wrote to Feinberg, 'should perhaps be mostly didactic'.[156] Feinberg, in 1957, conceded that the 'struggle against Hitler' at the League of Nations was but one 'political episode', with no 'practical results for the five hundred and fifty thousand German Jews'.[157] Notwithstanding Germany's withdrawal from the League in October 1933, and the Nuremberg Laws of 1935, no discriminatory law would apply to Upper Silesia Jews until 1937, when the Convention came to its scheduled expiry.[158] Feinberg, however, was acutely aware of the fact that the Jews of Upper Silesia did not escape the extermination that ensued.[159] The petition may have 'awakened human conscience',[160] and demonstrated the League's role in 'securing human rights and the moral principles of civilized nations';[161] but it offered Jews only 'small solace'.[162] In the end, Feinberg could claim no more than moral victory. His future scholarship would again and again revisit the Bernheim

151 ibid, 92.

152 In the vein hope of delaying debate: Johann W Bruegel, 'The Bernheim Petition: A Challenge to Nazi Germany in 1933' (1983) 17 Patterns of Prejudice 17.

153 'Review' (n 146) 84; Graf, 'Probing the Limits' (n 137) 170.

154 Nathan Feinberg, *The Jewish League of Nations Societies: A Chapter in the History of the Struggle of the Jews for Their Rights* (Magnes 1967) (Hebrew); Feinberg, *Jewish Struggle* (n 135) 7, 86–129; [Nathan Feinberg,] Remarks on Germany's Obligations to Repeal the Anti-Jewish Legislation So Far As It Applies to Upper Silesia, [20 September 1933], A126\616, CZA submitted to the League *Rapporteur*; Hebrew version reproduced in Feinberg, *Jewish Struggle* (n 135) 175.

155 Feinberg, *Jewish Struggle* (n 135) 8, 81–5; for historiographic assessment: Graf, 'Probing the Limits' (n 137) 169–73.

156 Robinson to Feinberg, 20 April 1933 (n 142).

157 Feinberg, *Jewish Struggle* (n 135) 8.

158 Brendan Karch, 'A Jewish "Nature Preserve": League of Nations Minority Protections in Nazi Upper Silesia, 1933–1937' (2013) 46 Central European History 124. Just before the Convention expired, Lauterpacht was approached by Paul Guggenheim, who had been counselling Upper Silesia Jews, for advice: Lauterpacht, *Life* (n 10) 80–1; he had little succour to offer.

159 Feinberg, *Jewish Struggle* (n 135) 8.

160 ibid.

161 ibid, 174 (Leo Motzkin's address on Radio Geneva, 31 May 1933).

162 ibid, 8.

petition, marking it as the apex of the Jewish struggle against Nazi Germany—but never quite answering lingering questions whether this was, or could be, enough.

Lauterpacht's 1950 invocation of Feinberg's Hague lectures in conjunction with 'individual efforts of Jewish lawyers' and the work of Jewish organizations effectively called on Feinberg not to forego his earlier *praxis*. But that homage was misplaced. Lauterpacht was likely unaware of—or possibly willing to ignore—the irony of calling on Feinberg to remain true to his past efforts for the right of individual petition. Though Franz Bernheim did become a 'symbol of the Jewish tragedy',[163] the petition was, for Feinberg, *individual* only in the narrowest technical sense—and *faute de mieux*.[164] He took care to note that outside of Margulies, none of those who espoused his cause had ever seen Bernheim.[165] The petition, except for the personal particulars, had been drafted before Franz Bernheim was identified as a suitable petitioner.[166] Feinberg begrudged the jurisdictional necessities that compelled the *Comité* to espouse Bernheim's *individual* case:

> things have so turned out that this person, of no name if one can so say, with no public past and with no status whatsoever in the Jewish and Zionist national movement, was the one to whom was appointed the mission of heavy responsibility at one of the direst moments in the life of the Jewish nation, only because formally he was entitled under the Geneva Convention to submit a complaint to the League of Nations.[167]

In his 1958 lecture course on *The Jewish Question from the Perspective of International Law*, Feinberg again lamented that the *Comité* 'had no choice but to rely' on the Geneva Convention rather than approach the League directly. 'As a result of these searches', Feinberg told his Hebrew University students:

> a former clerk was found ... by the name of Franz Bernheim. One could say about him that he was a nameless person who had emerged from the darkness of anonymity, and that his entire role in the episode was limited to signing the petition, planned and drafted by others.[168]

[163] ibid, 41.

[164] Bernheim 'only a supernumerary behind the complaint': Graf, 'Probing the Limits' (n 137) 169.

[165] Similarly, 'It should not be forgotten that Bernheim took no part in the case; all was done by the Committee of Jewish Delegations': Robinson to Smolar, 14 July 1944, WJC-C128/7 (World Jewish Congress Records, MS-361), American Jewish Archives ('AJA').

[166] 'It was decided to start searching without delay a Jew from among the inhabitants of the area, who has already left the place and will not fear the consequences of him signing the petition': Feinberg, *Jewish Struggle* (n 135) 41.

[167] ibid, 41–2.

[168] *The Jewish Question from the Perspective of International Law: Notes According to the Lectures of Prof. N. Feinberg in the Academic Year 1958* (edited by Yoram Dinstein, Hebrew University Student Association 1958) 100–1 (Hebrew); I am grateful to Ruth Lapidoth—Feinberg's student—for the copy of these 'absolutely internal' lecture notes.

Twin concerns animated Feinberg's grudges. One touched on the lack of *official status* besetting the *Comité*—and Jewish interwar diplomacy; unlike all other European minorities, Jews did not have a majority state to espouse their claims.[169] The other, closely related, concerned the Jewish *voice*: to whom should 'the mission' of speaking for Jewish interests be appointed? To these concerns—to the politics of Jewish representation—Feinberg dedicated an entire chapter of his 1957 monograph, titled 'The Position of the Central Jewish Institutions'.

Feinberg and the other architects of the Bernheim petition explored all possible paths for placing the situation of Germany's Jews on the agenda of the world organization including, for example, trying to mobilize other League members to raise the matter before the Council based on Article 11(2) of the Covenant. Their preferences were largely shaped by what was most likely, given jurisdictional and admissibility constraints in the prevailing political conditions, to yield denunciation of Germany by League members and organs. Yet the paper trail they left makes it clear that the path that led them to choose, eventually, an individual petition under Article 147 of the Geneva Convention was also marked by considerations pertaining to status and voice.

By the end of March 1933, it became clear that Great Britain was not keen to espouse the Jewish cause. Action under Article 11 would have followed, now in institutional settings, the tradition of nineteenth century humanitarian intervention—with all its advantages and disadvantages.[170] What led Robinson to point to the Geneva Convention as a source of access to the League was a House of Commons statement by the British Foreign Secretary that there was no legal basis in the Covenant for raising the question of Germany's Jewry before the Council.[171] This only accentuated the lack of official status on the part of Jewish diplomacy; Feinberg commented to Robinson: 'Again we find ourselves dependant on the charity of others'.[172] In his memoire, he would describe himself and his compatriots as 'the envoys of a persecuted, stateless people'.[173] What was needed to counter Nazi policies was 'a well-calculated and planned *political* action, and *official* intervention'.[174] In 1957, he would criticize the institutions of British Jewry—epitomized by a short paper read by Norman Bentwich before the London Grotius Society, whom he deemed 'not sufficiently familiar' with the Geneva Convention—for their narrow *modus operandi*:[175]

[169] Hannah Arendt, *The Origins of Totalitarianism* (Meridian 1961) 289.

[170] Carole Fink, *Defending the Rights of Others: The Great Powers, the Jews, and International Minority Protection, 1878–1938* (CUP 2004).

[171] Robinson to Motzkin, 1 April 1933, A306\126, CZA; Graf, 'Robinson's Contribution' (n 142) 182–3.

[172] Feinberg to Robinson, 26 April 1933 (n 145).

[173] Feinberg, *Reminiscences* (n 37) 80.

[174] Emphases added; Feinberg, *Jewish Struggle* (n 135) 17.

[175] ibid, 27–34, 39–40; Feinberg, *Central Organizations* (n 135) 69–77; Norman Bentwich, 'The League of Nations and Racial Persecution in Germany' (1933) 19 Trans Grot Soc 75.

> British Jewry concentrated entirely upon getting the League of Nations, through the initiative of the British Government, to act, on the basis of Article 11 of the Covenant. These efforts, however, proved of no avail ... Unlike the leaders of British Jewry, the Comité des Délégations Juives refused to regard Article 11 as the sole means of assisting German Jewry.[176]

Division in *modus operandi* also reflected tactical and 'principled' divisions separating 'philanthropy' by assimilationist Western Jewry and 'animated political actions' by Eastern Jewry:[177] the *Comité* posited its advocacy as professional, democratic, collectivist, *and* political—as opposed to patterns of *ad hoc* past intercessions by wealthy or renowned Western Jewish notables.[178] Such divisions were, in the first place, ideological. Feinberg noted that Jewish organizations were divided 'by dint of their diverse approaches and perceptions of the Jewish problem'.[179]

Ideology and representation were closely tied. For Feinberg, what ultimately set the *Comité* apart from British Jewry, or Bernheim's own profile, was the *national* character of its action—its 'public and national significance'.[180] The Bernheim petition was, for its authors, the perfect synthesis of autonomism and Zionism, a genuine practice of *Gegenwartsarbeit*.[181] Feinberg's recollections repeatedly noted the Zionist proclivities and associations of those involved.[182] In 1957, he would expand on the 'mental tendency' of the *Comité*:

> The fact that the leaders of the Comité des Délégations Juives were mainly concerned about invoking the Geneva Convention and ... the possibilities it allowed ... stemmed also from the basic principle inspiring all its efforts to protect Jewish rights—that its representations be made by Jews themselves, without fear and in the full light of day. Proposals such as getting the League of Nations to act upon the initiative of one of the members of the Council, under Article 11 ... were favoured by [Anglo-Jewish] bodies ... [who] preferred action by non-Jews in the international arena. In contrast, the Comité des Délégations Juives sought the

176 Feinberg, *Jewish Struggle* (n 135) 33–4; Feinberg, *Central Organizations* (n 135) 77–8.

177 Feinberg, *Jewish Struggle* (n 135) 85, 129; Feinberg, *Reminiscences* (n 37) 81. Such divisions in style of diplomacy resonate with divisions in political culture between Eastern and Western Jewry: Yfaat Weiss, *Ethnicity and Citizenship, German and Polish Jews 1933–1940* (Magnes 2000) (Hebrew).

178 Graf, 'Probing the Limits' (n 137) 172.

179 Feinberg, *Jewish Struggle* (n 135) 26; the text in Feinberg, *Central Organizations* (n 135) 68 diverges from the Hebrew original; at 34 (Anglo-Jewish 'hesitations whether it was advisable—ideologically speaking—to raise the question of denial of rights of Jews as a question of minority'); Robinson to Feinberg, 20 April 1933 (n 142) ('the only matter that separates us is the question of Jewish nationhood').

180 Feinberg, *Jewish Struggle* (n 135) 85; see also Arendt (n 169) 273.

181 Chs 1, 5 discuss this term and its ideological significance.

182 Motzkin's Radio Address thus alluded to League efforts to establish the Jewish National Home in Palestine; Feinberg, *Reminiscences* (n 37) 81 ('none of ... the non-Zionist, non-national' institutions 'rose to act').

> course of petitioning the League ... also because it regarded such a course as an act of self-defence to be undertaken by pride and resolution.[183]

From this perspective, it was clear that Bernheim's faulty credentials—'no public past' or 'status ... in the Jewish and Zionist national movement'—meant that an *individual* petition, alone, would not do. There was some risk that, owing to admissibility rules, multiple petitions could have adversely affected each other's prospects. Nonetheless the *Comité*, largely at Feinberg's urgings, simultaneously submitted to the League another, separate petition, 'in its own name',[184] under another provision of the Geneva Convention. Legally, that second petition was superfluous.[185] Its drafters knew well the prospects that it would be the one to be debated by the Council were slim. Its function, however, was to denote the public, thus *national*—rather than *individual*—character of the Jewish intercession.[186] Hence its collective nature: Feinberg urged Motzkin 'that the petition should be signed—if at all possible—by all Jewish organizations whose goal is protection of Jewish rights'.[187] Robinson, likewise, advocated that 'a petition signed by all great [Jewish] organizations would have an altogether different value'; the petition, he wrote, was to serves as a demonstration 'internally and externally both'.[188]

At the same time, Feinberg opposed the submission of more than a hundred petitions instigated by Margulies—petitions already written, signed, collected, and delivered to Geneva—a mass 'petitionist movement'.[189] Feinberg's reticence towards this *actio popularis* combined legal, tactical, and status concerns. In the end, the *Comité*'s public petition only referred to these other petitions at the end of a single-page annex listing nine (mostly lesser) organizations who added their names to the *Comité*'s, and noting '*de nombreuses autres organizations, communautés, etc. ainsi que de milliers de signatures individuels*'.[190] Individuals and communities were subsumed by the self-perceived globally representative[191] institution.[192] Though

[183] Feinberg, *Jewish Struggle* (n 135); Feinberg, *Central Organizations* (n 135) 82. A year later he averred: 'I belong to those who take an absolutely positive attitude towards the so-called "Diaspora work" and who are at the same time deeply convinced of the necessity for a central Jewish representative body which should be entitled to fight for Jewish rights': 'Dr. Feinberg Frowns on League Entry' *Jewish Daily Bulletin* (4 October 1934).

[184] Feinberg, *Central Organizations* (n 135) 81.

[185] ibid; Feinberg to Motzkin, 5 April 1933, A126\616, CZA.

[186] 'There is no room for each and every of these institutions to appear before the League of Nations separately. Only if the attempt to submit a collective petition should fail can the *Comite* discuss whether it should take that step. Alone': Feinberg to Robinson, 17 April 1933, A306\73, CZA.

[187] Feinberg to Motzkin, 27 April 1933, A306\71, CZA.

[188] Robinson to Feinberg, 20 April 1933 (n 142); he warned Feinberg it cannot appear 'too abstract': Robinson to Feinberg, 14 May 1933, A306\71, CZA.

[189] Feinberg, *Jewish Struggle* (n 135) 43–50.

[190] *Comité des Délégations Juives au Conseil de la Société des Nation*, [n.d.], A126\616, CZA.

[191] '*La Pétition Bernheim*' in *Dix-Sept Ans* (n 128) 10 ('*présenter au tribunal de Genève la cause des Juifs allemands et, par conséquent, celle de l'égalité des droits des Juifs dans le monde*').

[192] Neville Laski claimed the British organizations heard of the petition by the 'almost defunct comite' first 'from the newspapers': Neville Laski, Joint Foreign Committee, to Cyrus Adler, AJC, 22 May 1933, A126\616, CZA. Indeed, Feinberg reported that Motzkin was reticent to negotiate with other Jewish

Feinberg—like Robinson—considered that Jewish organizations were not ideologically divided over the situation of German Jews, thus allowing for united action notwithstanding the 'tradition of mutual reserve',[193] his recollection carefully noted just how ideological these divisions had been.[194] Lauterpacht's 1950 homage to Feinberg—an appeal in favour of individual petitions—was indeed framed in terms of a Jewish international law *habitus*; but it entirely misread Feinberg's collectivist, public, official, and national sensibilities—or how much Feinberg detested the need to make recourse to an *individual* petition. Whatever had been, in 1933, his perspective on the Bernheim petition,[195] by 1950 Lauterpacht came to espouse assimilationist sensibilities on status and voice. In 1950 he missed, in other words, just how much representation mattered to some organs of Jewish diplomacy—and how ideologically charged it could be.

7. 'Some Sacrifice of Sovereignty'

Feinberg's national sensibilities were not the only ones misread by Lauterpacht's Jerusalem lecture. Following introduction and homage, Lauterpacht returned to themes familiar from his writings. He insisted that there was more to the Charter human rights provisions that met the eye.[196] He urged that teleology and the principle of effectiveness in interpretation mandated that these provisions contained 'legally binding obligations' and that they 'must be given effect', even if the Charter failed to enumerate or define human rights or spell out how, precisely, they were to be implemented.[197] He reiterated that the Charter duty to 'promote respect for human rights includes the legal duty to respect them' as well as an obligation, incumbent on the UN 'as a whole to further the adoption of means and establishment of agencies for the effective international enforcement of these rights'.[198] He warned that if no 'effective right of petition is accepted', there would be 'no prospect of the fulfilment of the purpose of the Charter in the matter of human rights'.[199] Acknowledging that the 'Charter does not refer to the right of petition', he asserted

organizations, speculating that the *Comité*'s weakness was the possible reason: Feinberg to Robinson, 17 April 1933 (n 186).

[193] Feinberg, *Jewish Struggle* (n 135) 26.

[194] ibid, esp. 26–38, 81–5, 129; Feinberg, *Central Organizations* (n 135).

[195] There is no evidence of any involvement he had in the affair; but in June 1933 he informed Bentwich he could not 'continue to co-operate in the [Joint Foreign] Committee's work' given its decision to 'be confined to inducing the League to take action in the humanitarian field' in aid to departing German Jews; that, he wrote, would only validate persecution and invite other governments to follow Germany's example: Lauterpacht to Bentwich, 21 June 1933, A255\477, CZA.

[196] CP iii (n 5) 417.

[197] ibid, 418.

[198] ibid, 419.

[199] ibid, 421.

nonetheless that it 'must be held to be implied in the Charter as the very minimum of the means of its implementation'.[200] He lamented 'the emaciation of the right of petition at the hands of the Commission on Human Rights', again decrying the 'renunciation of one of the principal functions of the Commission ... a denial of the right of international petition'.[201] He recited familiar legal, political, and practical refutations of objections to the recognition and operation of the right of petition in matters of human rights. He offered methods—'reasonable ... just and ... practicable'[202]—to avoid pitfalls in admitting and administering it. These and other arguments, and the language they employed, were largely borrowed from his latest book; but the overall tone was even more urgent.

In Jerusalem, Lauterpacht's discussion of the *individual* right of petition concluded with a call to states, any and all, to sacrifice 'some attributes, both substantive and formal, of their sovereignty' if 'the Bill of Rights is not to be a mere gesture'.[203] States, he professed, needed to

> ensure an irreducible minimum standard of respect for fundamental human rights and of the requisite international guarantees ... [This] cannot be accomplished without some sacrifice of sovereignty not only in respect of the substance of the Bill but also of its enforcement. The essence of a Bill of the Rights of Man is that it implies a limitation upon the existing and the future powers of the State. There is no country so advanced or entitled to such absolute conviction of the excellence of its law and its institutions as not to be able to make a contribution to the common stock of a Bill of Rights by consenting to some change in its legal and constitutional system, or to the principle of international judicial or semi-judicial examination and review of its ... conduct—including such examination and review in pursuance of petitions by private individuals.[204]

'[S]kepticism about the power of the state';[205] constraining its sovereignty; stripping away, through law, its 'mystical sanctity';[206]—this was the very essence of Lauterpacht's human rights project, the very ambition of his overall international law scholarship.[207] His work first challenged international law doctrines that produced 'the State's ability to interpret for itself what its obligations are'.[208] This 'problem of self-judgment', wrote

200 ibid.
201 ibid, 420.
202 ibid, 424.
203 ibid, 426.
204 ibid.
205 Sands (n 7) 177.
206 Koskenniemi (n 9) 389.
207 Hersch Lauterpacht, *The Function of Law in the International Community* (Oxford 1933) 431 ('the sanctity and supremacy which metaphysical theories attach to the State must be rejected in any scientific conception of international law'), discussed by Koskenniemi (n 9) 365.
208 ibid, 358.

Martti Koskenniemi, was 'Lauterpacht's *mala malaficiorum*'.[209] With the 1945 *An International Bill of the Rights of Man*, Lauterpacht only changed his tactic, not the cause.[210] There he proclaimed that '[t]he renaissance of the law of nature'—of which he was a principal architect—only expressed

> the urge to find the spiritual counterpart to the growing power of the modern State … that power increasingly assumed the menacing shape of unbridled sovereignty of the State in the international sphere, it became the promoter of international anarchy and threatened, through the spectre of modern war, both the rights of man and the heritage of his civilization.[211]

Lauterpacht's choice to conclude the discussion of the right of petition by urging states to accept limitations on their sovereignty had addressed states at large. In Jerusalem, however, it was primarily meant to urge, through his Israeli audience, the Jewish state to follow suit—if not lead by example—and carry out, in his words, its 'proper and appointed' share in the promotion of human rights.

For all its careful devices, Lauterpacht's appeal was ill-timed and ill-placed. He delivered this appeal to celebrate an academic institution that had recently become a 'university in exile'[212]—'cut off from its home on Mt. Scopus'[213]—that had, as a result of strife and war, to scramble for makeshift accommodation in buildings scattered all across the western, Jewish sector of Jerusalem.[214] He delivered it in the divided, contested capital of a newly established Jewish state that had recently emerged from a bloody war of independence. The semi-jubilee celebration itself, taking place 'precisely at a juncture when the University is suffering exile', was held by its planners as an act of UN defiance—'a battle-ground on which the anti-internationalisation of Jerusalem is fought'.[215] That was neither the place

[209] ibid, 366.

[210] ibid, 391–2.

[211] Lauterpacht, *International Bill* (n 55) 40.

[212] *The Hebrew University of Jerusalem 1925–1950: Semi-Jubilee Volume* (Goldberg Press 1950) 62.

[213] Simon Address (n 2).

[214] '[E]xile' in '*ad hoc* laboratories, *ad hoc* libraries, *ad hoc* lecture rooms': Address of Professor Brodetsky, President of the Hebrew University, at the Opening Ceremony of the Semi-Jubilee Celebrations 5 May 1950, Semi Jubilee 91–1950 Speeches, HUA. Demilitarised in July 1948, Mount Scopus remained under Israeli control as an enclave surrounded by Jordanian-controlled areas until 1967. The 3 April 1949 Israel–Jordan Armistice recorded 'agreement in principle' on 'resumption of the normal functioning of the cultural and humanitarian institutions on Mount Scopus and free access thereto', but was never implemented: Yfaat Weiss, '"*Nicht durch Macht und nicht durch Kraft, sondern durch meinen Geist*": *Die Hebräische Universität in der Skopusberg-Enklave*' (2015) 14 Simon Dubnow Institute YB 59; Moshe Hirsch, Deborah Housen-Couriel, and Ruth Lapidoth, *Whither Jerusalem? Proposals and Positions Concerning the Future of Jerusalem* (Nijhoff 1995) 3, 153, 157.

[215] Urdang, Organizer's Report, 29 May 1950 (n 3). The same rationale was hinted in the University President's invitation to Jan Smuts to deliver the 'main address': 'since now temporarily unable use Mount Scopus University site and forced carryon under [unclear word] difficulties your attending and lecturing would be act unsurpassable friendship': [draft] cable, Brodetsky to Smuts, [n.d.], Semi-Jubilee 91–1950 (February 21–April 30), HUA. On internationalization, provided for in the 1947 General Assembly Partition resolution: Uri Bialer, 'The Road to the Capital: The Establishment of Jerusalem as the Official Seat of the Israeli Government in 1949' (1984) 5 Stud in Zionism 273.

nor the time to inspire charitable sentiment towards a 'sacrifice of sovereignty'. Lauterpacht's insensitivity to Feinberg's national sensibilities marked him as an outsider to Jewish representation politics; his failure to perceive the sensibilities of his Jerusalem audience suggests that his outsiderness was a persistent condition—a theme to which the following chapter returns.

What reactions did Lauterpacht's appeal attract? We have no record of the immediate reception, in Jerusalem,[216] of his human rights lecture. If questions were asked, answers furnished, or a debate ensued, no note was made or survived. Yet neither Feinberg nor the Hebrew University audience were the main targets of Lauterpacht's appeal. It was directed at Israel's diplomats; specifically, it was directed at Shabtai Rosenne, the thirty-three-year-old legal adviser of Israel's MFA. That appeal, as Lauterpacht would soon acknowledge, was meant to serve as a 'reproach'. This acknowledgement, and Rosenne's retort, would reveal the fate of Lauterpacht's appeal to the Jewish state to sacrifice its newly acquired sovereignty and assume the mantle of representation of Jewish interests by promoting the individual right of petition.

[216] In early July, Bentwich made the case for the individual right of petition in a short newspaper article that decried, 'the grave setback to the bright hopes of international assurance of the rights of man lies in the unwillingness of the democratic Powers to grant the individual the rights of petition, which they recognise as fundamental for liberties in their own State'. While the arguments, and language, closely followed Lauterpacht's, it sought to convince a British, not Israeli (or Jewish), audience: Norman Bentwich, 'Human Rights and the Right of Petition' *Manchester Guardian* (3 July 1950) in FM–1824/3, ISA. Consider also Norman Bentwich, 'The Limits of the Domestic Jurisdiction of the State' (1945) 31 Trans Grot Soc 59.

3

'The Extreme Non-Zionist, Apolitical Concept of Jewish Public Life'

Petitions, Human Rights, Standing, and Representation

1. Lauterpacht's 'Method of Reproach'

Following Hersch's Jerusalem lecture,[1] Rosenne accompanied the Lauterpachts on a tour of Israel.[2] There was occasion to discuss Lauterpacht's appeal; Rosenne, apparently, voiced his protests. Three weeks later, Lauterpacht commented on Rosenne's objections; clearly, he was not convinced. His letter confirmed that the lecture was, in fact, meant for Rosenne—and geared towards producing a change in Israel's policy. Lauterpacht's only 'regret' was 'that that method of reproach'—that is, a *public* censure of a position for which Rosenne was largely responsible—'should have come necessary':

> As to your contribution to the questionnaire on human rights—it is possible that it is dictated by the special circumstances of Israel and its own problems of minorities. For that reason I must not be critical of it, although I regret that that method of reproach should have come necessary. If these special circumstances did not exist—I do not know to what extent they do in fact exist—I would nor [sic] consider your contribution as either helpful or progressive. The right of petition by individuals is, in my view, of the essence of an international protection of human rights ... As I have said, there may be compelling reasons why you adopted that attitude. It is too easy to criticize it from a distance. But apart from these reasons I would have preferred the Israel approach to the subject to be more in accordance with Jewish ideals and with Jewish experience.[3]

Lauterpacht's letter delicately balanced latitude with fortitude. He was willing to admit the possibility of Israel's 'special circumstances', its 'own problems', and 'compelling reasons' justifying it taking *some* exception to the right of petition. He accepted, to an extent, his possible ignorance of facts and somewhat diminished

[1] Ch 2.
[2] Rosenne Journal, 3–9 May 1950, FM-5850/2, Israel State Archive ('ISA').
[3] Lauterpacht to Rosenne, 29 May 1950, FM-1824/3, ISA.

Jews, Sovereignty, and International Law. Rotem Giladi, Oxford University Press. © Rotem Giladi 2021.
DOI: 10.1093/oso/9780198857396.003.0005

standing in the matter: '[i]t is too easy to criticize it from a distance'. He nonetheless insisted on his view; that method of reproach *was* necessary; Israel's approach *was* neither helpful nor progressive; its actions *did* deviate from Jewish interests, 'ideals and experience'. Lauterpacht also hinted that Rosenne's invocation of 'special circumstances' may have been overstated. He regretted, after all, only that a public 'reproach' had proven necessary. What prompted this necessity was Israel's 'contribution' to a United Nations ('UN') 'questionnaire on human rights'.[4]

2. A Questionnaire

The fifth session of the Commission on Human Rights, convened at Lake Success in mid-1949, attracted the attention and attendance of numerous Jewish organizations.[5] The agenda included, among other items, the draft 'International Covenant on Human Rights and Measure of Implementation'. 'The Right of Petition' was important—or controversial—enough to merit inclusion as a separate item.[6] Various proposals on measures of implementation of the future Covenant were placed before the Commission. Some foresaw individuals exercising the right.[7] When this became the subject of some debate,[8] the Commission instructed the Secretary-General ('SG') to prepare a 'methodical questionnaire for the consideration of the Commission with a view to its submission to Governments for their comments'.[9] Chapter 2 of the Questionnaire began with '[q]uestions relating to the right of individuals, groups of individuals and of organizations to petition'. It asked whether 'the right of petition' should 'be open to ... individuals ... groups of individuals' and 'non-governmental organizations'. Other questions addressed the operation of the right.[10] The first day of 1950 was set as the deadline for responses. Comments on the '[d]raft Covenant' and '[d]raft Measures of Implementation' of human rights were also invited.[11]

The few governments responding to the Questionnaire elaborated on various aspects of the draft Covenant.[12] Israel, by contrast, preferred to limit its answers to the matter of measures of implementation, reserving the right to add at 'a later date ... comments and proposals'[13] on the Covenant itself. Israel's response consistently displayed the sovereign sensibilities a newly independent state could be

4 ibid.
5 UN Doc. E/L371 (23 June 1949) 3–4.
6 ibid, 6–7.
7 ibid, 14–15.
8 ibid, 15–16.
9 ibid, 16.
10 UN Doc. E/CN.4/327 (14 June 1949).
11 Secretary-General to Foreign Minister, 29 July 1949, FM–1824/3, ISA.
12 UN Doc. E/CN.4/353 (22 March 1950).
13 UN Doc. E/CN.4/365/Add.4 (23 January 1950), sent 19 December 1949. The Ministry of Justice failed to comment in time.

expected to, but many established states did, in fact, display.[14] It was not keen on the prospect of being subjected to international supervision.[15] It preferred enforcement to remain a province of states,[16] though it conceded that '*some* form of international implementation of human rights is necessary in addition to national implementation'.[17] What it had in mind was a weak form of international implementation, hedged by traditional purviews of sovereign discretion and constrained by traditional requirements of state consent.[18] Israel also proposed that such matters be dealt with by a new, separate '[s]pecialized Agency' rather than be 'entrusted' to the UN.[19]

Standing, at any rate, would *not* extend to individuals. Israel preferred that only states and a limited class of non-governmental organizations ('NGOs') would be able to access international enforcement: '[a]ction may be initiated on the basis of complaints of states or by petitions of non-governmental organizations *given the right of petition by the Agency*'.[20] This class was to be narrower than the list of NGOs enjoying consultative status with the Economic and Social Council ('ECOSOC').[21] And 'complaints' by states were to be privileged over the more limited 'petitions' by recognized NGOs; substantial differences distinguished the two procedures.[22] Israel, evidently, did not share Lauterpacht's suspicion of the state. Its Questionnaire response envisioned a weak, and rather technical, international implementation[23]—not quite 'the cornerstone of a future international legal order',

[14] Lauterpacht's Great Britain generally opposed the right of petition: Alfred WB Simpson, *Human Rights and the End of Empire: Britain and the Genesis of the European Convention* (OUP 2001) 354–7.

[15] Eg insisting that investigations by the implementing body could take place 'within the jurisdiction of a State only with the consent of the State concerned': UN Doc. E/CN.4/365/Add.4 (n 13) 14.

[16] ibid, 1; at the same time, Israel was averse to the proposal that each signatory set up in its territory a national 'body to promote respect for human rights and fundamental freedoms': ibid, 18.

[17] ibid, 1; emphasis added.

[18] ibid, 2, 18–19 (rejecting proposals for establishing 'a special Court of Human Rights' or 'a special chamber of the International Court of Justice' as redundant).

[19] ibid. Israel proposed attenuating the UN's human rights role—especially that of its Commission on Human Rights—by vesting responsibility for international implementation with a new, separate body, with its own treaty-based membership, assembly, and secretariat, to be brought into a relationship with the UN as a specialised agency under the Charter. The composition, designation, and election of members of that body was to be tightly controlled by 'the covenanting States': ibid, 1–2, 9, 15, 19–20. These proposals, too, attracted Lauterpacht's disapproval: Lauterpacht to Rosenne, 29 May 1950 (n 3).

[20] Emphasis added; UN Doc. E/CN.4/365/Add.4 (n 13) 2, 6; Gordon to Rosenne, 16 December 1949, FM–1824/3, ISA.

[21] UN Doc. E/CN.4/365/Add.4 (n 13) 12.

[22] Israel submitted that the right to initiate proceedings 'should be limited to Covenanting States only': ibid, 5. 'The right of petition', however, 'should be restricted to non-governmental organizations recognized for this purpose by the implementation body': ibid, 5–6. It favoured 'detailed regulations for such petitions concerning ... their receivability [and] ... their preliminary examination': ibid, 6. Additional conditions were to limit the right of petition to recognized NGOs: ibid, 7. Unlike 'hearings on complaints of States', which could 'be held in open meetings', 'hearings on petitions from [NGOs] should be conducted in private meetings only': ibid, 14.

[23] Israel's position would limit the procedures for human rights implementation to the 'form' of traditional interstate dispute resolution mechanisms. Such procedures would be elaborated in a separate 'instrument modelled on the General Act for the Pacific Settlement of Disputes of 26 September 1928': ibid, 2. That treaty 'does not offer any means for making this binding obligation enforceable' but only 'a "menu" of possible methods of peaceful settlement without giving priority to any of them'. Nor

as one World Jewish Congress ('WJC') lawyer would envision the future Covenant a few months later.[24]

3. 'A Large and Potentially Hostile Minority Population'

Israel's position drew on sovereign sensibilities. One related to its position, obtained in the course of its recent war of independence, as a Jewish majority state.[25] Recently, it has been suggested that Israel was averse to individuals being afforded the right to petition owing to the prospect that it would be called to account, to the UN, for how it treated its own Arab minority. Nathan Kurz, in a first treatment of the episode, argued that '[a] major concern was the particular problem of the "potentially hostile minority population" (e.g. the 150,000 Palestinian Arabs) that had been put under military rule in 1949'.[26] Kurz argues, further, that Israel's support for NGO petitions was, relatedly, rooted in power imbalances vis-à-vis the Arab states in the UN arena and sought to capitalize on the UN presence of multiple Jewish organizations:

> Limiting the right of petition to a few select NGOs would, in Israel's view . . . allow the 'the Jews of the Diaspora . . . adequate means to bring legitimate grievances' while preventing a restless Arab minority and its supporters abroad from doing the same. This policy sought to capitalize on the highly institutionalized structure of Western Jewry whose numerous international organizations could not be matched by the Palestinian Arab diaspora.[27]

does it provide 'any means to enforce the obligation to have recourse to peaceful means or the solution obtained, thus making the obligation of peaceful settlement a binding duty devoid of any sanction': Alain Pellet, 'Peaceful Settlement of International Disputes', *Max Planck Encyclopedia of Public International Law online* (August 2013 OUP) http://www.mpepil.com accessed 20 January 2020. Israel sought to preserve the freedom of states as to *which* implementation mechanisms to subscribe to—and *whether* to subscribe to any at all. Under its position, a 'State would be permitted to adhere to those sections of the instrument which it deems appropriate': UN Doc. E/CN.4/365/Add.4 (n 13) 2, 24. Similarly, Israel expressed preference for negotiations over compulsory settlement, ibid, 4; state consent would remain the controlling feature of the scheme: ibid, 23. Lauterpacht's 'self-judgment' *problem*—discussed in ch 2—was, for Israel, a fundamental aspect of the *solution*. Its proposed scheme of implementation was not quite a condition precedent for the adoption of the Covenant: ibid, 2.

[24] Bienenfeld, Report on the Seventh Session of the Human Rights Commission, May 1951, FM-1824/4, ISA.

[25] Benny Morris, *The Birth of the Palestinian Refugee Problem Revisited* (CUP 2004).

[26] Nathan A Kurz, 'Jewish Memory and the Human Right to Petition, 1933–1953' in Simon Jackson and Alanna O'Malley (eds), *The Institution of International Order: From the League of Nations to the United Nations* (Routledge 2018) 90, 103. I am grateful to Nathan Kurz for sharing an early version of the manuscript. James Loeffler, *Rooted Cosmopolitans: Jews and Human Rights in the Twentieth Century* (Yale UP 2018) 176–7 treats the episode briefly as evidence of a clash between Lauterpacht's 'idealistic vision of Jewish internationalism' and 'the tough-minded statecraft being practiced in Israel'.

[27] Kurz (n 26) 103; note omitted.

Materials in the Ministry of Foreign Affairs ('MFA') archives offer only some support for this reading. The prospect of Arab minority petitions was at times alluded to in the course of the preparation of Israel's Questionnaire response. The first draft response to the UN Questionnaire prepared by the International Organizations Division ('IOD') was silent on this matter,[28] but Rosenne first raised it in his comments on that draft, noting 'the fact that we have a large and potentially hostile minority population in Israel'. For Rosenne, this was not an independent concern; rather, he raised it as a factor to be weighed against 'the position of the Diaspora, and ... its needs'.[29]

It fell to the head of the UN Department at the IOD, Ezekiel Gordon, to furnish explanations for Israel's proposed response to the Questionnaire. He was intimately familiar with the issue: before his MFA appointment, Gordon had worked in the UN Secretariat's Human Rights Division, where he dealt with matters covered by the Questionnaire.[30] Requested by Rosenne to elaborate the reasoning underlying the IOD's proposal, Gordon noted that it was 'unquestionable to the interests of the State of Israel that each individual Arab could not bring his complaint against the State before the international forum'.[31] For Gordon, too, this was a counterpoint to Jewish Diaspora interests, not a standalone concern: 'From the point of view of the Jews in the Diaspora, it is essential that non-governmental organizations ... should have the right to petition on behalf of the local Jews.' He was willing to have the Jewish state accommodate such interests:

> As you probably know, five Jewish Organizations have been granted consultative status with the ECOSOC. We assume that the same organizations will be granted the right of petition. The Jews of the Diaspora will, therefore, have an adequate means to bring any ligitimite [sic] grievances to the attention of the implementation bodies ... I trust that the median line ... is in accordance with the interest of Israel and of the Jews in the Diaspora'.[32]

Yet exposure to petitions from Israel's Arab minority was only one cause driving Rosenne's aversion to individual petitions. Responding to Lauterpacht's letter, in late June 1950, Rosenne presented additional objections. These included, among

[28] [IOD], [Draft] Reply of the Government of Israel [n.d.], FM-1824/3, ISA with Rosenne's handwritten comments.

[29] Rosenne to Tzippori, 1 December 1949, FM-1824/3, ISA.

[30] Gordon to Robinson, 26 August 1949, FM-1824/3, ISA. Following a two-year stint with the MFA (1949–1951), he returned to UN service: Jewish Telegraphic Agency, 'Dr. Gordon, Israeli Officer in U.N. Secretariat, Dies; Was 57' (16 February 1962); Russian-born Gordon (1905–1962) joined the UN Secretariat in 1947; a few references to his work appear in John P Humphrey, *Human Rights & the United Nations: A Great Adventure* (Transnational 1984).

[31] Gordon to Rosenne, 8 December 1949, FM-1824/3, ISA with Rosenne's handwritten comments.

[32] ibid.

others, concerns that the 'quantity' of individual petitions would derail the eventual human rights machinery.[33] Rosenne also insisted that 'those who support' the individual right of petition—like Lauterpacht—'over-exaggerate its practical value'. He deemed it out of tune with 'international realities': 'a good many states are opposed to the right of individual petition'. 'I must confess', he added, 'that I do not find myself very much in favour of it'.[34] These objections gave voice to other sovereign sensibilities; specifically, to an aversion to individual standing rooted, as we shall see, in Jewish sensibilities.

Apprehensions about individual Arab petitions, then, were not quite a major concern underlying Rosenne's contribution to drafting Israel's position.[35] They did not carry enough weight, notably, to propel Israel to actively lobby against the individual right of petition. Rosenne and his MFA colleagues were content to record Israel's objection to individual petitions in response to a UN Questionnaire, without more; exposure to Arab petitions, while a cause of some concern, was not seen by them as an eminent or grave enough political threat.

Rosenne and Gordon's aversion to individual petition on 'Arab' grounds appears, moreover, to have been instinctive rather than the outcome of meticulous reflection. Their reasoning for the balance obtained between Jewish Diaspora interests, mandating NGO petitions, and Israeli interests, militating against individual petitions, was not very persuasive. Had Israel's main concern been averting any Arab claims, it would not have insisted on privileging state complaints over limited petitions by a limited class of NGOs.[36] UN membership at the time included six Arab states; arithmetical disparity, in other words, should have led Israel to object to *state* complaints of human rights violations or, in the very least, insist on equal status for NGO petitions. Moreover, of those six Arab members, four supported the USSR's position that any 'proposed measures of implementation' of human rights 'constituted an attempt to intervene in the domestic affairs of states'.[37] Seemingly, Arab UN members did not consider individual petitions an instrument for haranguing Israel for its treatment of its Arab minority.

[33] Rosenne to Lauterpacht, 26 June 1950, FM-1824/3; Robinson to Rosenne, 31 May 1950, FM-1816/1, ISA (the 'idea' of '2,500,000,000 potential petitioners is horrifying').

[34] Rosenne to Lauterpacht, 26 June 1950 (n 33).

[35] [IOD], [Draft] Reply, [n.d.] (n 28) with Rosenne's handwritten comments. Robinson's commentary on Israel's Questionnaire response did not mention this issue: Robinson to Rosenne, 31 May 1950 (n 33); nor did Gordon's advice on how to answer Lauterpacht's critique: Gordon to Rosenne, 5 June 1950, FM-1824/3, ISA.

[36] Gordon to Rosenne, 8 December 1949 (n 31). Rosenne agreed: 'The conditions for admitting petitions should be much more stringent than when the complaint is emanating from a State'.

[37] E/L371 (n 5) 16; UN Press Release GA/SHC/234 (15 November 1950), FM-1824/4, ISA; at the Third Committee, an Egyptian representative later expressed objections to the individual right of petition that were strikingly similar to Rosenne's objections: UN Press Release GA/SHC/221 (1 November 1950), FM-1824/4, ISA.

Rosenne was likely overstating Israel's apprehensions of individual Arab petitions when he intimated to Lauterpacht that Israel's answer to the Questionnaire was meant to shield it from 'political and quasi-legal interventions on the part of the Arabs and their supporters and other enemies of Israel'. In his June 1950 letter to Lauterpacht, Rosenne sought to justify Israel's response to the UN Questionnaire. Here he invoked Israel's position 'vis-a-vis the Arab world', 'vital security questions', and 'vital security reasons'.[38] Lauterpacht's misgivings with Rosenne's allusion to 'the special circumstances of Israel and its own problems of minorities'[39] were not entirely unwarranted. Rosenne assigned this factor greater weight in his polemic with Lauterpacht than when making his contribution to Israel's response to the UN Questionnaire.

Apprehensions of exposure to the grievances of its Arab citizens, in addition, would play little role in Israel's actual practice in the early 1950s. Its officialdom was certainly not enthused with the prospect of facing complaints concerning or originating from its minority Arab population. In reality, however, it did not consider these a serious threat raising 'vital security questions'. Receiving from the UN Secretariat anonymous 'communications' under the ignominious procedure adopted under ECOSOC Resolution 75,[40] officials in different government agencies were inclined to view the grievances driving such communications as frivolous or vexatious, or treat their authors as a persistent nuisance. They were keen neither to respond to nor to acknowledge receipt of such communications emanating from Jews, Arabs, and Christians alike. What reticence they recorded was bureaucratic in nature, not political.[41]

Additional considerations recommend a closer look at Rosenne's and Gordon's allusions to Diaspora interests. These suggest that Israel's willingness to see the right of petition extend to NGOs did not quite amount to a policy aimed at guaranteeing the effective protection of Diaspora Jews. Nor did it quite adopt the position of Jewish NGOs whose goal, as we shall see, was to secure an individual right of petition, to which Israel had objected. Gordon's allusion to Jewish Diaspora interests as justification for Israel's position on the NGO right of petition was not meant to indicate that Israel subscribed to a general Jewish position. He did observe that it was 'essential' that the right of petition should pertain to NGOs. This, however, was accompanied with a crucial proviso: '[f]rom the point of view of the Jews in the Diaspora'.[42] This was no

[38] Rosenne to Lauterpacht, 26 June 1950 (n 33).

[39] Lauterpacht to Rosenne, 29 May 1950 (n 3).

[40] The object of Lauterpacht's accusation that the Commission on Human Rights abdicated its responsibility, discussed in ch 2.

[41] Sidor to Tsur, 17 April 1955, FM-2006/8, and various examples in FM-2006/7, FM-2006/8, G-5758/1; [Statement by] H Cohn, Fourteenth Session of the Commission on Human Rights, [n.d., circa. 1958], FM-1825/4, ISA ('communications . . . waste of public money . . . fraud on the authors').

[42] Gordon to Rosenne, 8 December 1949 (n 31); when Minister Sharett asked whether Israel had any special interest in promoting the Covenant owing to Jewish interests, Gordon was noncommittal: 'on

Israeli effort to secure Diaspora interests. It was, rather, an exception to Israel's etatist preference for 'state complaints'.[43] Gordon was willing to accept the right of NGOs to petition the UN; he did not propose, however, that this was an Israeli interest—that by the right of NGO petition '[t]he Jews of the Diaspora will, therefore, have an adequate means'[44] to bring complaints to the UN therefore represented a *concession* on the part of the Jewish state. It was not, as Kurz suggests, the pursuit of a 'policy' that 'sought to capitalize on the highly institutionalized structure of Western Jewry'.[45] It indicated willingness to accommodate Diaspora interests on the part of Israeli officialdom, not active effort to secure them. It was a reluctant concession to these interests. Israel support for the right of NGO petition was, after all, limited.[46] Rosenne, responding to Lauterpacht, was adamant that although Jews were 'most directly concerned', there was no reason for the Jewish state to advance 'an idealistic and altruistic' position. The government, he insisted—for reasons discussed below—would not engage in any 'undue over-emphasis of the position of the Diaspora'.[47]

At the time—more on that later—there had been little contact on human rights issues between Israel and the Jewish NGOs engaged in human rights advocacy at the UN.[48] This, too, suggests that Israel's response to the UN Questionnaire was not meant to advance Diaspora interests. When Robinson proposed that the MFA, before responding to the UN Questionnaire, 'should secure the views of Jewish organizations working in the field' despite the 'stumbling block' of their divisions and 'jealousies',[49] he assumed a divide between Israel and Diaspora interests. Gordon took that divide for granted; he also took for granted that Israel's sovereign status entailed that any such interaction would resemble an audience, not consultations among equals:

> The Government will be able to take into consideration the proposals, only if they are common to all organizations ... The various Jewish organizations ... should come together and prepare a short memorandum on their proposals in connection

the whole, the articles seem to afford reasonable protection to the [Jewish] minorities': Gordon to Sharett, 8 September 1950, FM-2006/7. Robinson acknowledged that the right of petition 'is of great interests to Jewish communities abroad' but observed that Israel's perspective will likely differ 'from that of the Jewish communities': Robinson, Analysis of the Provisional Agenda, Fourth Regular Session of the General Assembly, [n.d.], FM-1972/2, ISA.

[43] Discussed above (nn 20, 22).

[44] Gordon to Rosenne, 8 December 1949 (n 31).

[45] Kurz (n 26) 103.

[46] Discussed above (nn 21–22 and accompanying text).

[47] Rosenne to Lauterpacht, 26 June 1950 (n 33).

[48] Robinson to Eytan, 9 March 1950, FM-1824/3 ('we have worked out no policy in regard to our co-operation with the Jewish organizations having consultative status'). Some of the smaller Jewish NGOs tried, later, to influence Israel's position on the right of petition or mobilise it to their goals, but with little success: Yapou to Rosenne, 11 May 1951, Goodman to Elath, 19 April 1951, FM-1824/4, ISA.

[49] Robinson to Gordon, 14 August 1949, FM-1824/3, ISA.

> with the Covenant and the measures of implementation ... the government will be able to take into consideration the proposals, only if they are common to all organizations. Contradictory proposals from various Jewish organizations would make our task only more difficult. This memorandum should reach us as soon as possible and not later than October 1st.[50]

Rosenne, for his part, was not entirely convinced of the need for this limited concession when he weighed Gordon's explanations. To Lauterpacht, he intimated that some in the MFA 'insisted upon no non-governmental position at all'; that, in other words, only governments would have standing to submit petitions. This, likely, only expressed his own preference. To Gordon, rather than balance, he emphasized his concern with 'a possible conflict of interests, between Israel and Diaspora.' This, he observed, had already 'occurred in the fourth session.'[51] He implied that Gordon's 'median line' between the interests of the Jewish Diaspora and those of the Jewish state could have been drawn closer to the latter; but he did not pursue the matter.

4. Rosenne's Retort: Sovereign Jewish Sensibilities

At its core, Rosenne's objection to the individual right of petition was principled; Israel's position on the right of petition was driven, predominantly, by sovereign sensibilities. It insisted on state consent; on national over international implementation; on weak international enforcement; and on paramount sovereign capacity to bring international claims. All these preferences displayed sovereign sensibility typical of a newly independent state. Yet they were scarcely linked, in the course of the drafting Israel's Questionnaire response, to the question of Israel's Arab minority. Rosenne's retort to Lauterpacht, in fact, openly alluded to *ideological* sensibilities driving Israel's position.[52] His letter to Lauterpacht explicitly professed that creed, not interest, was the key to Israel's position. The crux of his retort offered an ideological reading of the right of petition. That reading expressed Jewish concerns: Jewish status, standing, and representation; in short, Jewish *voice*. It was here that Rosenne expressed animosity to the individual right of petition and pointed to an ideological rift separating him from Lauterpacht.

[50] Gordon to Robinson, 26 August 1949 (n 30); Robinson to Gordon, 29 September 1949, FM–2006/7 (bringing five organizations together 'unrealistic'); UN Mission Meeting, 10 October 1949, FM–1972/2, ISA discussed below.

[51] Gordon to Rosenne, 8 December 1949 (n 31) with Rosenne's handwritten comments; it is unclear what conflict he was referring to.

[52] Rosenne to Lauterpacht, 26 June 1950 (n 33).

4.1 Palestinocentrism: 'Undue Over-emphasis of the Position of the Diaspora'

Rosenne did not appreciate Lauterpacht's censure. He reported to Robinson that Lauterpacht, 'in one of his Hebrew University lectures has dedicated much time to the problem of the individual right of petition'; Lauterpacht, he wrote, expressed 'a position so severe towards our approach'.[53] Gordon was not surprised of Lauterpacht's 'severe critique' given his known aversion to the Universal Declaration; Lauterpacht, he wrote, had espoused 'a radical position' on the question of individual petition.[54]

Equipped with his colleague's input, Rosenne proceeded to write a three-page letter addressed to 'Dear Professor Lauterpacht'. The letter was highly uncharacteristic: it displayed little of the deference abounding in his prolific correspondence with Lauterpacht. '[T]he strictures' of Lauterpacht's letter, he wrote, did 'merit a reply' on his part. Much of that letter considered the right of petition from a Jewish perspective. Even the matter of Israel's position 'vis-a-vis the Arab world' Rosenne approached through the prism of 'the position of the Jewish communities of the Diaspora'. These two considerations 'had to be balanced'. There was no question as to which interest prevailed. For Rosenne, there could be no equivalence between the interests of the Jewish state and those of the Jewish Diaspora. 'In more brute terms', Rosenne wrote, the 'Government could not' give 'undue over-emphasis' to 'the position of the Diaspora communities'.[55]

These 'brute terms' expressed a prevalent, Palestinocentric position. It held the interests of first the *Yishuv*, then the Jewish state, paramount to any Diasporic Jewish interest.[56] What justified such a hierarchal reading was the doctrine holding that the national project in Palestine was in the interests of all Jews, present and future, Zionist and non-Zionist alike. The 'National Home', and later the Jewish state, were considered a trust held in favour of future generations of the Jewish people; that trust could not be jeopardized by ephemeral Jewish requirements that did not promote, or could even risk, its preservation. '[T]he vital interests of Israel come first—because Israel is vital for world Jewry'.[57] What was formulated in the

[53] Rosenne to Robinson, 9 June 1950, FM–1824/3, ISA.

[54] Gordon to Rosenne, 5 June 1950 (n 35).

[55] Rosenne to Lauterpacht, 26 June 1950 (n 33).

[56] Efraim Inbar, 'Jews, Jewishness and Israel's Foreign Policy' (1990) 2 Jewish Pol Stud Rev 165, 167.

[57] Michael Brecher, *The Foreign Policy System of Israel: Setting, Images, Process* (New Haven 1972) 232 quoting David Ben-Gurion ('we have always to consider the *interests* of Diaspora Jewry—any Jewish community that was concerned. But … not what *they* think are their interests, but what *we* regarded as their interests. If it was a case vital for Israel, and the interests of the Jews concerned were different, the vital interests of Israel come first—because Israel is vital for world Jewry'; emphases in original). Rosenne observed, in 1960, that Israel's 'continued existence and its continued security and prosperity are … the condition of survival of the Jewish people'; 'Israel exists', he wrote, 'to meet the needs of the Jewish people as a whole'. Jewish sovereignty was 'the instrument for Jewish survival': Shabtai Rosenne, 'Basic Elements of Israel's Foreign Policy' (1961) 17 India Quarterly 328, 335, 339.

1930s and the 1940s in response to the pressures on Jewish existence in Europe and in light of Zionism's limited achievement, *Yishuv* helplessness, and limited resources[58] became, after 1948, part of Israel's etatist creed.[59] This was the ideological foundation of the attitude expressed by Rosenne and Gordon: the right of individual petition may have been a Jewish interest; pertaining to the Jewish Diaspora, however, meant that it was not, markedly, an Israeli interest.[60]

The Palestinocentric outlook did not necessarily entail Israeli aloofness to the fate of Jews in the Diaspora.[61] Putting Israel first, however, did entail that balancing Israel's interests against those of Diaspora communities was a task reserved for the Jewish state alone.[62] Rosenne's letter to Lauterpacht, accordingly, emphasized that it was the Jewish state that had the authority to determine the balance between competing Jewish interests. The question of human rights and petitions may have been a 'vital matter ... of direct concern to Jewry as a whole', he wrote. Yet he was adamant that Diaspora interests must give way to Israel's interests, and that this was the Jewish state's decision, alone, to make.[63]

4.2 'Only the Government': Lauterpacht's Deficient Standing

This ideological perspective allowed Rosenne to refute Lauterpacht's assessment of past Jewish experience, present Jewish interest, and what Jewish ideals entailed. Israel's position was justified 'in light of the not too satisfactory experience of the League of Nations', he wrote to Lauterpacht. Past Jewish investment in individual petitions, he implied, did not bear fruit; another, sovereign strategy for the

[58] Yechiam Weitz, *Aware But Helpless: Mapai and the Holocaust 1943–1945* (Yad Ben-Zvi 1994) 95–8 (Hebrew); Shabtai Beit-Zvi, *Post-Ugandan Zionism on Trial* (Beit-Zvi 1991); Tom Segev, *The Seventh Million: Israelis and the Holocaust* (Holt 2000); Dina Porat, *An Entangled Leadership: The 'Yishuv' and the Holocaust 1942–1945* (Am Oved 1986) (Hebrew).

[59] The 'Israeli political elite' took the position 'that Israel's well-being is the paramount interest of the Jewish people and all other considerations are to be subordinated to it. Actually, this feature was a continuation of the Palestinocentric approach to foreign policy of the Yishuv leadership': Inbar (n 56) 167. On Israeli etatism, Nir Keidar, *Mamlakhtiyut: David Ben-Gurion's Civic Thought* (Ben-Gurion UP 2009) (Hebrew).

[60] The ideological tension between protection of Diaspora Jews and *Yishuv* Zionism drew on both Zionism's foundational catastrophic outlook and the remedy it prescribed in the form of immigration to Palestine/Israel. In 1943, *Yishuv* activists reported that Jews in Rumania, Bulgaria, and Hungary sought 'to have equal status with the non-Jews, to be like non-Jews, to get rid of [discriminatory] laws and the yellow star of David, and of the prohibition to travel from one place to another'. One participant in the ensuing debate warned against the dangers of post-war equality in Poland and Yugoslavia, namely waning support for the Zionist cause: Weitz (n 58) 108–9. In 1949, with regard to human rights of Jews in these same countries, one MFA official wrote that 'matters of immigration at the moment override any preventative act for the protection of Jewish rights wherever they are': Walter, East Europe Division to IOD, 2 September 1949, FM–2016/6, ISA. On catastrophic Zionism: Anita Shapira, *Land and Power: The Zionist Resort to Force, 1881–1948* (Stanford UP 1992) 152–3, 321–3.

[61] Rosenne (n 57) 334.

[62] Brecher (n 57) 232; Inbar (n 56) 168 ('Ben-Gurion emphasized that he was willing to consider diaspora interests as he defined them and not as perceived by the diaspora Jews themselves').

[63] Rosenne to Lauterpacht, 26 June 1950 (n 33).

protection of Jewish rights was called for. He also challenged Lauterpacht's reading of what Jewish interests required 'in the year 1950'. In the present state of a world torn by the Cold War, and of a Jewish world torn by it, he asserted, Israel's compromise position was prudent—'a wise precaution and certainly not out of accord with Jewish ideals and with Jewish experience'.[64]

Rosenne, at the same time, also challenged the authority of Lauterpacht's voice: here, his retort turned defiant. Jewish experience with the League, Israel's exposure to Arab petitions, Diaspora interests and how these were to be balanced—all these, he wrote, were matters of which 'only the Government can be the judge'.[65] Lauterpacht, Rosenne implied, lacked the necessary standing to determine Jewish interests. This, equally, concerned Rosenne's own standing: 'only the Government'—that is, Rosenne, its duly appointed representative, not Lauterpacht, at best the unofficial representative of the Diaspora—could speak in such matters. The fault with Lauterpacht's criticism was his lack of official status, the defect in his credentials. It was the same fault that Feinberg had found in Franz Bernheim, now exacerbated by sovereign status and sensibilities.[66] Having faulted Lauterpacht's interpretation of Jewish past, reading of the Jewish present, claim to interpret Jewish 'ideals', and standing to judge in these matters, Rosenne proceeded to the 'merits of the issue'.[67] These, too, were ideological.

4.3 Political, Sovereign Jews: 'Two Diametrically Opposed Views . . . of Jewish Public Life and the Jewish Place on the International Scene'

'[Y]ou can imagine discussion on the merits was arduous', Rosenne averred to Lauterpacht. He intimated that an internal debate had taken place at the MFA between 'some of us who insisted upon individual right of petition' and 'others who insisted' that the right of petition pertained to governments alone. He implied that Israel's ultimate position involved, therefore, some compromise.[68]

No evidence of any, let alone an 'arduous', debate exists in the relevant MFA files.[69] Rosenne, in reality, rode roughshod over the process of drafting Israel's Questionnaire response and the IOD junior staff tasked with preparing its first version.[70] He was, in all likelihood, again overstating matters in order to demonstrate

64 ibid.
65 ibid.
66 Ch 2.
67 Rosenne to Lauterpacht, 26 June 1950 (n 33).
68 ibid.
69 Gordon to Robinson, 19 December 1949, FM-1824/3, ISA (suggesting that the only IOD disagreements with Rosenne concerned technical or drafting questions).
70 Rosenne to Tzippori, 1 December 1949 (n 29) ('a bad piece of work, ill thought and, inconsistent and to a large extent unintelligible').

to Lauterpacht that Israel's position was well considered and did in fact account for Diaspora interests.

All the same, Rosenne took care to clarify that Israel's aversion to the right of individual petition—and his disagreement with Lauterpacht—was rooted in ideological difference. To that end, he offered a mapping of competing Jewish readings of the right of petition as manifestations of different ideological positions:

> There were some of us who insisted upon individual right of petition. There were others who insisted upon no non-governmental petition at all. To a certain extent, therefore, our final answer is a compromise between these two diametrically opposed views. These views themselves represent, if I may say so, on the one hand the extreme non-Zionist, apolitical concept of Jewish public life and the Jewish place on the international scene, and the strict statist approach of the political Zionists and even non-Zionist Jewish nationalist on the other.[71]

This, too, faulted Lauterpacht. His advocacy for the individual right of petition gave effect to 'the extreme non-Zionist, apolitical concept of Jewish public life'. On the surface, this was a censure of Lauterpacht's claim to represent Jewish 'ideals', interests, and 'experience', and a challenge to his standing; substantively, however, this disparaged Lauterpacht's Zionism. Ideologically, Rosenne found the individual right of petition (and Lauterpacht's reproach) that offensive.

The two 'diametrically opposed views' described by Rosenne contrasted Jewish nationalism with Jewish assimilation. The right of petition touched, in his words, on the question of the correct model for 'Jewish public life and the Jewish place on the international scene'. It juxtaposed, that is, two models of Jewish emancipation, two competing answers to the Jewish Question.[72] For Rosenne, to invest a Jew with an individual right to petition an international authority was to depoliticize the Jew—to render the Jew, in his words, 'apolitical'. To grant standing to individual Jews was to deny any 'Jewish public life' and any 'Jewish place on the international scene'. This is what made Rosenne denounce Lauterpacht's position as expressing an 'extreme non-Zionist' view: it constructed individual Jews as bearers of *individual* rights that could be enforced by *individual* recourse to international mechanisms. This obviated, if not outright negated, the Jewish national project. If international law and organization could guarantee Jewish rights—League experience, he averred, was 'not too satisfactory' in this respect—there was no need for *national* protection of Jewish rights. For Rosenne, 'apolitical' meant a-national; from this ideological perspective, Jewish politics could only be *national* politics. Rosenne, who came to renounce his own assimilationist upbringing by practicing Zionism through immigration to Palestine, could no longer admit the possibility,

[71] Rosenne to Lauterpacht, 26 June 1950 (n 33).
[72] Ch 1 discusses these models.

or the ideological propriety, of Western-style Jewish emancipation.[73] An individual right of petition was, after all, the programmatic expression of the creed professed by assimilationist Jewish organizations such as the American Jewish Committee ('AJC'), the sponsor of Lauterpacht's human rights scholarship: a denial that Jews were a 'people' possessed of collective, *national* rights.[74]

By contrast, what Rosenne termed 'the strict statist approach of the political Zionists' prescribed protection of Jewish rights by and within the Jewish state. This was the Zionist solution to Jewish disenfranchisement and discrimination in the Diaspora: the establishment of, and mass immigration to, a Jewish state.[75] This guarantee of Jewish rights obviated the need for individual protection at the national or international level;[76] it also dictated a national, 'statist' approach to Jewish representation. That Jews would possess the right to represent their own, individual affairs, be granted individual legal standing, and speak with an individual voice was an anathema to the national, etatist principle of 'political Zionists'.[77] For those who subscribed to Political Zionism, official Jewish *voice* was precisely what the establishment of a Jewish state was meant to produce;[78] its absence was precisely the impediment that international law placed in their path to emancipation prior to 1948. From this ideological perspective, it was not individuals Jews who required, *à la* Lauterpacht, 'legal *locus standi*';[79] rather, it was the Jewish *people*, collectively, who required *national* legal standing.

Prior to independence, such sensibilities were tied to sovereign exclusion: the lack of official standing to represent the Zionist cause before the 'world councils'. In his maiden speech, Sharett told the General Assembly that Israel's UN admission represented 'the consummation of a people's transition from political anonymity to clear identity, from *inferiority* to equal *status*, from mere *passive* protest to *active* responsibility, from *exclusion* to *membership* in the family of nations'.[80] Voicelessness and objecthood, the markers of Jewish sovereign incapacity, were recurrent themes in the writings of Zionist and early Israeli diplomats, especially those involved in

[73] Ch 1 discusses Rosenne's background; Rotem Giladi, 'Shabtai Rosenne: The Transformation of Sefton Rowson' in James Loeffler and Moria Paz (eds), *The Law of Strangers: Jewish Lawyers and International Law in the Twentieth Century* (CUP 2019) 221.

[74] Ch 2.

[75] Discussed in chs 6, 7.

[76] In 1947, speaking in one of the UN committees, Sharett commented on the reference to human rights in the Charter's preamble: 'We believe that the dignity and worth of the of Jews as human persons cannot be fully materialised ... unless' the Jewish 'people ... are introduced on the basis of complete equality with all other people ... [and] their national existence is assured ... by independence': quoted in Moshe Sharett, *At the Threshold of Statehood: 1946–1949* (Am Oved 1958) 128 (Hebrew).

[77] Rosenne to Lauterpacht, 26 June 1950 (n 33).

[78] Patent in Feinberg's introduction to the *Jewish Yearbook of International Law* and his reading of the Bernheim petition: Prologue, ch 2.

[79] Hersch Lauterpacht, *An International Bill of the Rights of Man* (Columbia UP 1945) 217.

[80] Emphasis in original; Speech to the General Assembly by Foreign Minister Sharett, 11 May 1949 in Meron Medzini (ed), *Israel's Foreign Relations: Selected Documents, 1947–1974* (MFA 1976) 119; GAOR, Plenary (11 May 1949) 332.

the Palestine and, later, admission debates at the UN.[81] Robinson, in one of his first memoranda to the Jewish Agency, warned that 'the fact that the Jewish people has no general *locus standi* in international law' might preclude it from demanding the fulfilment of the 1917 Balfour Declaration should the mandate of Palestine terminate.[82] Rosenne, that same year, expressed the same sensibility:

> we do not even have the right to appear on any international stage to defend our demands even at a time of debate on an issue so important and sacred to us as our national existence in Eretz Israel. Before the UN Assembly in New York, the representatives of the Jewish people appeared as 'beggars' relying on the charity of the righteous nations of the world, seeking their benevolence in order to ensure the existence of our people.[83]

With independence, these sensibilities translated into an assumption that a single, centralized, and *sovereign* Jewish voice should speak for Jewish interests 'on the international scene'.[84] While intra-Jewish political reality denied the Jewish state that exclusive voice,[85] its envoys—like Gordon[86]—would continue to insist, in the very least, that the voice of the Jewish state should be paramount.[87]

[81] The UN Palestine debate aggravated concerns with lack of standing. Sharett observed that there were 'five UN member states who fight us. Everything they say has the weight of UN membership; they have the right to vote on matters that decide our fate at a time when we have no single voice': UN Mission Meeting, 18 October 1948, FM-131/18, ISA.

[82] Emphases in original; Robinson, Some Legal Aspect of the Palestine Problem Before the United Nations, 26 March 1947, P-1035/1, ISA. This was not a new concern: in 1943, he proposed the following post-war demand for the WJC: 'In view of the distinctiveness of the Jewish problem, the Jewish people demands the right to have its duly accredited representatives take part in the councils of the United Nations': Robinson, Jewish Post-War Program of the WJC, First Tentative Draft, 6 July 1943, WJC-C97/17 (World Jewish Congress Records, MS-361) American Jewish Archives ('AJA').

[83] Shabtai Rowson, 'International Law and the Jewish People' (1947) 11 Tarbut 4, 6 (Hebrew).

[84] Eban to Lie, 28 June 1948, FM-72/16; Lourie to Lie, 11 December 1947, FM-2274/45, ISA (requesting the SG to afford 'the Jewish Agency for Palestine, as representing the interests of the Jewish community in Palestine *and of the Jewish people generally in regard to Palestine*', 'the opportunity to be admitted and to be heard in any discussions ... in the Security Council regarding the Palestinian question'; emphasis added).

[85] Conflicts over Jewish representation led to a 1950 'clarification' between the AJC President, Jacob Blaustein, and Ben-Gurion, Israel's Prime Minister: 'Jews of the United States ... owe no political allegiance to Israel ... the State of Israel represents and speaks only on behalf of its own citizens and in no way presumes to represent or speak in the names of ... [Jewish] citizens of any other country'; in AJC, *In Vigilant Brotherhood* (AJC 1965) 53–8, 64–70. The exchange resolved ideological and political tensions at neither working nor leadership levels, evident in recurring AJC demands to 're-affirm' it. AJC officers reported in 1960 to have found 'Golda Meir and other Israel officials firm in the conviction that Israel is the sole authority to speak and act for Jews everywhere': quoted in Charles S Liebman, 'Diaspora Influence on Israel: The Ben Gurion-Blaustein "Exchange" and its Aftermath' (1974) 36 Jewish Soc Stud 271, 279; Zvi Ganin, *An Uneasy Relationship: American Jewish Leadership and Israel, 1948–1957* (Syracuse UP 2005); Ariel L Feldstein, *The Gordian Knot, David Ben Gurion, the Zionist Organization, and US Jewry* (Ben-Gurion Institute 2003) (Hebrew); Menahem Kaufman, *An Ambiguous Partnership: Non-Zionists and Zionists in America, 1939–1948* (Magnes 1991).

[86] Gordon to Robinson, 26 August 1949 (n 30) discussed above (nn 49–50).

[87] Brecher (n 57) 230 ('Israel as the voice, the representative, and the defender of Jews in distress anywhere ... a role which flows naturally from the "Jewish prism" ' of Israel's foreign policy).

4.4 'No Other Way of Securing Their Rights': Human Rights Aversion

Such ideological opposition to the individual right of petition attested to aversion for the human rights project itself. Rosenne had expressed such sentiments even prior to Israel's independence. In his first essay to ever deal with both Jewish affairs and international law, he lamented the inferior status to which international law condemned the Jewish people. Until a Jewish state was established, international law attested to an 'inherent defect' in their sovereign capacity and entrenched that inferior legal, and political, status. For Rosenne, writing on the occasion of the Palestine Special Session of the General Assembly, the only cure to that defect, and the only way to secure Jewish rights, was the establishment of a Jewish state—neither minority treaties nor 'humane rights':

> It is a vital necessity for the Jewish people that its international position is made equal to the legal position of all other 'recognized' nations. As long as this has not been achieved, all rights that will be granted to Jews and to our people, whether in *Eretz Israel* under a new trusteeship instrument or in the Diaspora under new minority treaties, would be hollow and lack any meaningful value. Under present conditions, the Jews cannot even be assured that they would benefit from the famous 'Four Freedoms' *or from the 'humane rights' that many now talk of.* For this reason, in the present state of international law the Jews have no other way of securing their rights and achieving their demands than the establishment of an independent Jewish state whose international status would be equal to that of all other states.[88]

Post-independence, this aversion took on sovereign form. The same sovereign sensibility Rosenne expressed with regard to the individual right of petition underlined his subsequent opposition to the idea that Israel sponsor the initiative of Moses Moskowitz, the Secretary of the Consultative Council of Jewish Organizations ('CCJO'), to establish an office of a UN Attorney-General for Human Rights.[89] But it could also be presented as a realist critique of the 'idealistic and utopian' nature of the human rights project.[90] Human rights were, for Rosenne, a low priority, 'sixth heaven' affair.[91] As such, rather than a Jewish shield, human rights

[88] Rowson (n 83) 6.

[89] Rosenne to Robinson, 28 December 1951, FM-1824/4, ISA ('uncomfortable'). The initiative, inspired by Cassin, sought to reintroduce the idea of individual petitions through other means: Michael Galchinsky, *Jews and Human Rights: Dancing at Three Weddings* (Rowman & Littlefield 2008) 42; Kurz (n 26) 100; Moses Moskowitz, *Human Rights and World Order: The Struggle for Human Rights in the United Nations* (Oceana 1958); Antoine Prost and Jay Winter, *René Cassin and Human Rights: From the Great War to the Universal Declaration* (CUP 2013).

[90] Rosenne to Robinson, 28 December 1951 (n 89).

[91] Rosenne to Attorney-General, 15 May 1957, FM-2006/9, ISA.

could be used as an Israeli sword. His successive contributions to the early issues of the *United Nations Yearbook of Human Rights* were neither advocacy efforts nor academic inquiries; he found the task 'irksome' and repeatedly tried to have other government departments shoulder the burden.[92] These contributions, Rosenne confided to Israel's Attorney-General Haim Cohn, he made 'for political reasons'; they were a 'platform of publicity',[93] a 'scientific propaganda'.[94] He generally preferred to leave work on human rights issues to the IOD and the UN mission.[95]

Robinson had his own aversions to the human rights project; they, too, were shaped by Jewish, and sovereign, sensibilities. Not having been consulted in advance with regard to the UN Questionnaire, he nonetheless supported the final product while, at the same time, considering Israel's proposals 'unrealisable'. That, for Rosenne, may well have been the point. Robinson shared Rosenne's aversion to the individual right of petition: 'I personally feel very strongly against the individual right of petition. In my view, the importance of this problem is unduly exaggerated'; its effect on implementation would be 'grave'.[96] Sovereign sensibilities led him to find the prospect of '2,500,000,000 potential petitioners' approaching the UN 'horrifying'. He estimated that the Jewish NGOs 'were all ready to settle for such a limited right of petition', but also that the ECOSOC experiment with NGO participation 'proved to be a complete flop'.[97]

Robinson's path to these sovereign sensibilities was different. Unlike Rosenne, he had previous involvement and intimate familiarity with the human rights project. And, unlike Rosenne, his misgivings with regard to the utility of individual petitions as instruments for protecting Jewish rights were rooted in experience, accrued in the course of work on the Bernheim petition.[98] Later, in the early 1940s, as director of the Institute of Jewish Affairs' ('IJA'), he would devise a research programme mandating studies devoted 'to the political and legal status of the Jews within the framework of the larger problems of government and protection *of individual and group rights*'.[99] He corresponded with Lauterpacht, who assured him that 'the idea of an International Bill of Rights should not be permitted to or used

[92] Rosenne to Robinson, 7 December 1953, Rosenne to Cohn, 16 July 1953, FM–1825/2, ISA; Shabtai Rosenne, 'Human Rights in Israel' [1949] UN YB on Hum Rts 122; Shabtai Rosenne, 'Human Rights in Israel' [1950] UN YB on Hum Rts 161; Shabtai Rosenne, 'Note on the Development of Human Rights' [1951] UN YB on Hum Rts 182; Shabtai Rosenne, 'Note on the Development of Human Rights' [1952] UN YB on Hum Rts 144; Shabtai Rosenne, 'Human Rights in Israel in 1953' [1953] UN YB on Hum Rts 147; Shabtai Rosenne, 'Israel' [1954] UN YB on Hum Rts 161. In 1955, Cohn assumed the responsibility and, in time, became invested in human rights.

[93] Rosenne to Cohn, 16 July 1953 (n 92).

[94] Rosenne to Attorney-General, 27 October 1955, Rosenne to Attorney-General, 15 April 1956, FM–1825/4, ISA.

[95] Legal to IOD, 27 May 1951, FM–1824/4, ISA.

[96] Robinson to Rosenne, 31 May 1950 (n 33).

[97] ibid.

[98] Robinson to Feinberg, 20 April 1933, A126\616, Central Zionist Archive ('CZA'); ch 2 discusses his involvement.

[99] IJA, *Institute of Jewish Affairs: Program* (American Jewish Congress/WJC 1941).

for the purpose or with the effect of whittling down the existing protection of Jewish rights or of preventing the necessary extension of that protection'.[100] This, however, did not allay his suspicion that the promise of human rights might encourage Jews to abandon what protection they had, before the war, under the minority system; and that human rights would achieve even less, in the end, than the *acquis* of minority protection.[101] In 1944, he observed that 'under an International Bill of Rights . . . Jewish organizations would have less of a *locus standi* in any international procedure than they had under the minorities system'.[102] During the Holocaust years, as he became disenchanted with minority rights,[103] he started approaching the human rights project even more cautiously.

Some of Robinson's human rights aversion reflected the competition among Jewish NGOs. The 1944 'Declaration of Human Rights' by the AJC,[104] he judged, 'represents a disservice to the Jewish cause'.[105] Some was strategic: he had 'fundamental objections to an international bill of rights on a universal basis'.[106] Some of his objections, however, were principled. They were rooted in his reading of the unique Jewish predicament and post-war needs: what these demanded lay beyond what human rights could satisfy.[107] Jewish 'real needs at this moment', he observed, were 'different from the abstract formula of human rights'.[108] The 'distinctiveness of the Jewish problem',[109] he thought, placed it beyond the promise of human rights. 'Not a single one of these problems can be solved by human rights and fundamental freedoms even when they are supervised and even when they are enforced'.[110] Interwar sensibilities persisted: human rights, he noted, could protect Jews who, living in liberal democracies of the West, had no need for them; they

[100] Lauterpacht to Robinson, 5 October 1944, WJC–C13/5; the two seem to have corresponded regularly: Robinson to Lauterpacht, 19 December 1946, WJC–C16/2, AJA.

[101] Robinson to Office Committee, 30 October 1944, WJC–B86/2, AJA ('under no circumstances should we give up existing legal titles for problematic new ones').

[102] Robinson to Smolar, 14 July 1944, WJC–C128/7, AJA.

[103] Gil Rubin, 'The End of Minority Rights: Jacob Robinson and the Jewish Question in World War II' (2012) 11 Simon Dubnow Institute YB 55; ch 5 explores this disenchantment.

[104] James Loeffler, '"The Conscience of America": Human Rights, Jewish Politics, and American Foreign Policy at the 1945 United Nations San Francisco Conference' (2013) 100 J Am Hist 401. Robinson thought the Declaration was a 'maneouvre' [sic] meant to block any initiative by the WJC: Robinson to Office Committee, 30 October 1944 (n 101).

[105] Robinson to Office Committee, 30 October 1944 (n 101). Robinson found it 'humiliating', a 'tremendous retrogression . . . in comparison with the detailed and concrete Jewish post-war program worked out by' the WJC; 'while dictated by the Jewish situation', he observed, 'the word Jew is never mentioned'; the AJC, he accused, 'camouflage[d]' 'Jewish demands under the mask of general ones'. He claimed WJC credit for already having come up with the human rights idea in 1941: WJC, Meeting of the Administrative Committee, 2 July 1945, WJC–C98/14, AJA.

[106] ibid.

[107] ibid. Robinson, Some Fundamental Problems of Jewish Post-War Planning, [n.d.], WJC–C118/8, AJA ('inadequate to meet the post-war Jewish emergency').

[108] WJC Meeting 2 July 1945 (n 105).

[109] ibid (such as punishing war criminals; 'reconstruction of the Jewry'; 'the problem of immigration'; and 'the possibility of a Jewish life in a hostile world').

[110] ibid.

could not protect Jews in Eastern Europe who had such need.[111] Once again, the *national* needs of Eastern European Jewry were different from those of *individual* Western Jews.

These attitudes, and the dilemma between minority and individual protection, were nonetheless only subsidiary to Robinson's fundamental outlook, radically transformed during the Holocaust years.[112] In early 1943, he came to the 'controversial'[113] conclusion that, in order to secure 'the right of the Jewish people to survival',[114] Jewish post-war demands must be based on the realization that 'the Jewish problem be considered a *national* problem for which there is only one solution—a *national* state'.[115] Though he subscribed to Zionism before, he had 'regarded Palestinian resettlement as secondary to the protection of Jewish life in the Diaspora'. The 'force of events', however, compelled him to adopt 'extreme Zionism'.[116] It was time, he urged, to choose between the *Yishuv* and the Diaspora:

> the time for 'both—and' has passe[d]. Today is the time for 'either—or.' The number of Jews left in Europe after the war ... will be so small that all of them will be needed for the upbuilding of either European Jewry or the Yishuv ... However, under the conditions which we will find in the European countries], the reestablishment of Jews would be a crime not only against those restored, but especially against their children.[117]

This, he warned, was 'an hour of decision' for the WJC. Rather than 'be confined to short-range individualistic solutions', the WJC must shift to 'a long-range collective solution': Palestine.[118]

This baffled his colleagues convened in the first meeting of the WJC *Peace Aims Planning Committee*: Nahum Goldmann, the chairperson, considered Robinson's idea 'quite revolutionary to us'.[119] In a memorandum preparatory to the meeting Robinson observed that '[i]nstead of concentrating all their efforts upon the national aim of establishing their national freedom' in the post-war arrangements,

[111] ibid (no 'court outside the Soviet Union can give the Jews protection when the Soviet Union refuses to give such protection').

[112] Rubin (n 103); ch 5.

[113] Robinson to Wise and Goldmann, 25 June 1943, WJC–C97/17, AJA.

[114] Robinson, An Elucidation of Preliminary Problems Concerning a Jewish Post-War Program, [n.d.], WJC–C118/8, AJA.

[115] Emphases added; Peace Planning Committee Meeting, 10 March [1943], WJC–C118/8, AJA; Robinson, Fundamental Problems [n.d.] (n 107) ('*our single demand* should be the establishment of a Jewish Commonwealth in Palestine' to solve 'the refugee and repatriation problems': emphasis in the original).

[116] Robinson to Wise and Goldmann, 25 June 1943 (n 113); ch 5 delves into Robinson's ideological investment.

[117] Robinson to Wise and Goldmann, 25 June 1943 (n 113).

[118] ibid; Robinson, Jewish Post-War Program, 6 July 1943 (n 82).

[119] Peace Planning Meeting, 10 March [1943] (n 115); other participants shared Goldmann's bafflement. Some of their objections can be found in WJC–C97/17, AJA.

Jews 'are greatly confused, and are producing a very long catalogue of demands'.[120] Essentially, what he proposed was for the WJC to limit its post-war demands to Palestine, and operate on the assumption that Diaspora interests would be secured, anyway, by the war aims and post-war settlement of the UN. This meant, in effect, that a bill of rights should not be a WJC 'peace demand'. The WJC should support it, but not actively invest in its attainment; it would not form part of a 'specific Jewish program'.[121]

Robinson's colleagues were correct to note that this was a proposal to do 'away with the specifically Jewish problems in the Galuth [Diaspora]'.[122] Ideologically, this amounted to 'the negation of the Galuth'; pragmatically, it spelled the abandonment of *Gegenwartsarbeit*.[123] 'Dr. Robinson thinks that the Jewish problem' outside Palestine, one participant noted, 'can be solved basically along lines of a bill of rights'.[124] For Robinson, Jewish post-war investment in rights, as a Diaspora interest, was to be secondary to the main Jewish demand; so was his dilemma as to the preferred 'form in which Jewish rights' in the Diaspora 'should be guaranteed, minority treaties ... [or] a Bill of Rights'.[125]

The WJC rejected Robinson's radical proposal.[126] Nonetheless, his IJA position entailed involvement in the early phases of the human rights project. He commented on the human rights implications of the Dumbarton Oaks proposals[127] and advised, while representing the WJC, three Jewish delegations attending the San Francisco Conference. He was not enthused with the UN Charter's human rights provisions, noting 'the very modest place San Francisco takes in Jewish life'.[128] On human rights, the Charter did not amount to much: 'no enactment of human rights, no supervision of human rights and no enforcement of human rights. No procedure, no Jurisdiction; all these things don't exist'.[129] He denounced the AJC for 'riding around the country and boasting of things which were not achieved'.[130] The Charter, he observed, speaks 'the words of human rights ... without any power'; it was an 'embryo which didn't yet develop'.[131] As elsewhere, Robinson's

[120] Robinson, Jewish Peace Aims, [n.d.], WJC–C118/8, AJA.
[121] ibid.
[122] Peace Planning Meeting, 10 March [1943] (n 115).
[123] For these terms and what they signify, see ch 1.
[124] Peace Planning Meeting, 10 March [1943] (n 115) (Laserson).
[125] Robinson, Elucidation [n.d.] (n 114); Robinson, The Atomistic and Collectivistic Approach to the Jewish Post-War Aims, [n.d.], WJC–C118/8, AJA.
[126] IJA, Planning a Post-War Program: Report, 28 February 1944, WJC–C97/17, AJA.
[127] Robinson to Office Committee, The Dumbarton Oaks Proposals and the Problem of Human Rights and Fundamental Freedom, 26 February 1945, WJC–B86/2; Robinson, Tentative Proposals, 11 September 1944, WJC–C97/17, AJA ('We should not become over enthusiastic at the use of such high-sounding phrases as' human rights).
[128] WJC Meeting 2 July 1945 (n 105). In the course of the conference, Robinson and Perlzweig 'came to the conclusion that it was no longer practical or feasible to deal with the question of human rights and ... the question of minorities': ibid.
[129] ibid.
[130] ibid.
[131] ibid.

critique remained confined to internal fora and correspondence; in public writing, he was careful not to appear as an opponent of human rights. His misgivings, nonetheless, can be read between the lines of even his May 1946 *Human Rights and Fundamental Freedoms in the Charter of the United Nations*[132]—often cited as evidence of his human rights investment.[133]

This commentary on the Charter's human rights provisions presented the 'interpretation of the Charter as it now stands'[134] through extensive use of the *travaux préparatoires.* The characteristic tedium of minutiae revealed Robinson's intimate familiarity with Lauterpacht's work, as with the human rights advocacy by Jewish NGOs.[135] The volume's goal was to dispel the 'great confusion' surrounding the 'human rights and fundamental freedoms' clause of the Charter, its scope, and its binding force;[136] and to 'reveal whether the enthusiasts, the moderates, or the pessimists are right'.[137] Robinson's conclusion gave voice to all three views;[138] it was far less charitable than Lauterpacht's.[139] Yet the Charter also contained 'numerous latent possibilities for positive developments'[140] and some promise: Article 2(7) 'effected the first breach on the formerly inaccessible citadel of domestic jurisdiction'.[141] Still, in the end, what he prescribed was investment in interstate order, not individual rights: the 'first duty of all friends of human rights', Robinson concluded, was 'to assist the United Nations as a whole'. Only 'from a strong, efficient and effective United Nations can we expect help in the promotion of human rights'.[142] In private, his aversion persisted. A month after the commentary was published, he wrote to the WJC President Stephen S Wise that 'from the Jewish viewpoint', the human rights 'activities' of the UN 'should not be exaggerated. Nor is it of paramount importance today, from the Jewish viewpoint, to have an international Bill of Rights'.[143]

132 Jacob Robinson, *Human Rights and Fundamental Freedoms in the Charter of the United Nations: A Commentary* (IJA 1946).

133 Omry Kaplan-Feuereisen, 'At the Service of the Jewish Nation: Jacob Robinson and International Law' (2008) 8–10 Osteuropa 157, 168; Johannes Morsink, 'The Universal Declaration and the Conscience of Humanity' in Rainer Huhle (ed), *Human Rights and History: A Challenge for Education* (Stiftung EVZ 2010) 25, 40.

134 Robinson, *Human Rights* (n 132) 6.

135 ibid, 14–15, 43.

136 ibid, 13.

137 ibid, 16 (footnotes omitted).

138 Jacob Robinson, 'From Protection of Minorities to Promotion of Human Rights' (1948) *1 Jewish YB Intl L* 115, 151, written before the Universal Declaration was adopted, concluded with similar prudence: 'current policy eludes moral evaluation. The resultant syncretism of methods and ideas casts a queer light on the state of confusion of our civilization after the war.'

139 Discussed in ch 2.

140 Robinson, *Human Rights* (n 132) 104.

141 ibid.

142 ibid, 105–6. Robinson, Summary Report on the San Francisco Conference, 2 July 1945, WJC–C98/14, AJA.

143 Robinson to Wise, 12 June 1946, WJC–C16/2, AJA.

In late 1946, Robinson accepted the invitation of the UN Secretariat to help with preparations for the first session of the Commission on Human Rights,[144] but not without some reserve.[145] With John P Humphrey, the director of the Human Rights Division, he engaged in 'drafting [the Commission's] plan of work in early 1947'; 'to my regret', he wrote a decade later, 'the Commission did not accept my proposal but followed the path of futile work'.[146] After his ten-week assignment with the UN concluded in mid-February, Robinson was asked to direct his efforts elsewhere: he agreed to lend his services to the Jewish Agency's UN mission.

Robinson's aversion to human rights, now fed by sovereign sensibilities, persisted. 'Problems of human rights', he reflected in 1955, 'have never been dealt with as much as in the period after the Second World War', yet 'never have the results been so nil as during that period'.[147] Upon his election to the Commission on Human Rights, he observed that that body could not claim much credit for its first decade of activity: its task was to 'promote', rather than guarantee, human rights. He harangued the 'failed policy' of 'wasting most of its time' on 'legislating a human rights convention while knowing with certainty that such convention has no prospect'.[148] And he shared much of Rosenne's ideological and political sensibilities. In 1955, he confirmed the existence of a 'dichotomy' between Israel's policy and the policy of Jewish organizations on the question of human rights.[149] That dichotomy continued to hinder the possibility of coordinating Israel's 'policy on human rights' with that of 'leading Jewish organizations'.[150]

5. 'In Contradiction to the Efforts of the Jewish' NGOs: Jewish Representation Politics After 1949

If Israel's response to the UN Questionnaire prompted Lauterpacht's 'reproach', another contemporary commentator found it baffling. Johann Wolfgang Bruegel (1905–1986), a Czech international lawyer who found refuge in Britain,[151] wrote in 1953 of the Jewish state's position:

144 Shabtai Rosenne, 'Jacob Robinson: In Memoriam' (1978) 13 Isr L Rev 287, 290, 293.

145 '[D]espite grave apprehensions ... we could not refuse': IJA, Minutes of Meeting, 27 November 1946, WJC-C68/8, AJA. Zohar Segev, *The World Jewish Congress during the Holocaust: Between Activism and Restraint* (de Gruyter 2014) 206.

146 Robinson to Eytan, 26 July 1956, FM–2006/8, ISA; Robinson to Petegorsky, 4 March 1947, WJC–C16/5, AJA.

147 Robinson to Tsur, 18 April 1955, Rosenne to Tsur, 11 April 1955, FM–1825/4, ISA.

148 Robinson to Eytan, 26 July 1956 (n 146).

149 Robinson to Rosenne, 8 July 1955, FM–1825/4, ISA.

150 ibid.

151 Joseph P Stern, 'Defending the State Against the Nations: The Work of JW Bruegel' (1985) 28 The Historical J 1023.

> It was rather surprising to note that the Government of *Israel*, in contradiction to the efforts of the Jewish non-governmental organizations, had declared itself to be neither in favour of the individual's right to petition nor inclined to grant this right to groups of individuals.[152]

Others shared his bafflement. In July 1950, Abba Eban—Israel's Permanent Representative to the UN (and Lauterpacht's relation by marriage)—was asked by a French journalist 'why the Israel government, with respect to the Human Rights Covenant, rejects the right of petition of the individuals while all the Jewish organizations out at Lake Success are fighting for this right?'[153] Any response offered by Eban was not recorded.

The files of the WJC—by far, the Jewish NGO most active on human rights and the right of petition—do not record such surprise. They record, in fact, little on Israel's Questionnaire response.[154] Instead, they attest to a disconnect between Israel and the Jewish organizations, and an early WJC disillusionment. Following Israel's UN admission, the WJC had hoped for multiple-yet-coordinated Jewish advocacy.[155] Like other Jewish organizations, the WJC was 'eager to consult with the Israel Delegation' to the UN.[156] A mere three months after Israel's UN admission, its executive noted that despite WJC support for and assistance to Israel, its original assumption of 'mutual trust and collaboration' prevailing between 'the organisation which represents the interests of World Diaspora, as such' and the Jewish state 'have not fully materialised': 'the collaboration, taken all in all, remains one-sided'.[157]

When the WJC tried to communicate to Israel's UN mission 'its views on certain items of importance for the Jewish people', including the right of petition,[158] Israel's response was noncommittal. Eban wrote that the mission 'would be happy to consult with you from time to time'. What he had in mind was more of a courtesy call, less a collaborative process.[159] The WJC was Zionist, yet its primary beneficiary

[152] Emphasis in the original; Johann W Bruegel, 'The Right to Petition an International Authority' (1953) 2 ICLQ 542, 560.

[153] Goldstein to Marcus, 28 July 1950, WJC–B111/3, AJA.

[154] On one rare occasion, Perlzweig criticised the vagueness of Israel's Questionnaire answers: Perlzweig to Bienenfeld, 2 May 1950, WJC–B90/4, AJA. Israel's position, at times, hampered WJC efforts: Perlzweig to Riegner, 10 April 1950, WJC–B111/3. At others, it tried to put a positive spin on Israel's position: WJC, Observations Concerning the Draft First International Covenant on Human Rights, submitted to the 7th Session of the Human Rights Council, April 1951, WJC–B28/20, AJA.

[155] Eban's maiden speech at the GA's Political Committee, where Perlzweig spoke earlier, was 'the first occasion on which, at the same meeting two Jewish voices were heard, one representing a Non-Governmental Organization in the Diaspora and the other the newly admitted State of Israel': Perlzweig, Note, 13 May 1949, WJC–B28/13, AJA.

[156] Bienenfeld to N Robinson, 30 September 1949, WJC–B108/10, AJA.

[157] General Policy and Activities of the WJC [Draft], August 1949, WJC–B28/14, AJA.

[158] [Draft] WJC to Israel Delegation, 28 September 1949, WJC–B108/10, AJA.

[159] Eban to WJC, 30 September 1949, WJC–B80/12; Karbach to Marcus, 20 September 1950, WJC–B86/8, AJA; Robinson to Gordon, 14 August 1949 (n 49), Gordon to Robinson, 26 August 1949 (n 30) discussed (nn 49–50) above.

was the Jewish Diaspora; its mission was to 'represents the interests of World Diaspora, as such'.[160] Like Israel, it did not consider Jewish and Israeli interests as synonymous.[161] Its mission and self-perception necessarily challenged Israel's claim, as a full-fledged subject of international law, to paramount Jewish voice and representation in the world arena.[162]

The scant contact, on human rights questions, between Israel and Jewish NGOs suggests that although its response to the UN Questionnaire admitted a limited right of petition to NGOs, Israel's diplomats were on the whole disinterested in the substance of the human rights project.[163] Compared to the volume and quality of the WJC investment in the Covenant, and in the right of petition, Israel's overall attitude appears unconcerned.[164] What is surprising, therefore, is less that Israel's envoys were averse to the individual right of petition but, rather, that their sovereign sensibilities allowed them to accept that Jewish NGOs might have that right, however circumscribed: that acceptance effectively acknowledged the need for non-sovereign, organized, and competing Jewish voice, however limited.

Israel's early UN envoys were, nonetheless, averse to non-sovereign Jewish representation. MFA files recording Israel's participation in successive General Assembly sessions, and on agenda items touching on Jewish issues, are rife with uncharitable comments made by Israel's diplomats on Jewish NGOs and their representatives. Some, unfamiliar with pre-state Jewish advocacy, were curious to find other Jewish voices at the UN,[165] or that Jewish NGOs had official standing with the organization.[166] Others begrudged such competing Jewish

[160] General Policy, August 1949 (n 157); Miller, Memorandum [n.d., circa 1950], WJC–B7/9, AJA ('to represent the Jewish people before the United Nations and other governmental and international bodies in all such matters of a political, economic, social and cultural nature in which the Jewish people as such has a stake').

[161] 'While, obviously, we are a hundred per cent with and behind the State of Israel and Zionist aims generally, it is not our business to be an adjunct and gramophone record of either the State or Zionism': Easterman to Perlzweig, 3 February 1949, WJC–B2/5. When Israel's sovereign sensibilities led Robinson to take a 'leading' role in insisting that the exercise of jurisdiction by an international penal court would require the consent of the perpetrator's nationality state, the WJC representative on the spot was 'rather surprised'. The WJC sought to avoid drawing attention 'to the difference of opinion between Israel and the WJC', but was forced to protest that Israel's interests—and Robinson's statements—were 'not in harmony with the general interest of Jewry': Bienenfeld to Perlzweig, 8 August 1951, WJC–B90/4, AJA.

[162] When a Bolivian delegate assumed Israel spoke for all Jews, one WJC officer stressed that 'Jewry outside Israel is not represented by the Israeli Government but by the Jewish organizations admitted under Article 71 of the Charter to ECOSOC and especially by the [WJC]': Bienenfeld to Perlzweig, 6 May 1949, WJC–B90/4, AJA.

[163] This contests Kurz's reading of an Israeli policy seeking to protect Diaspora interests through coordination with Jewish NGOs: Kurz (n 26) 103. As noted below, only in late 1952 did Israel's UN mission see a need for regular contact with, and control of, Jewish NGOs.

[164] Karbach to Marcus, 20 September 1950 (n 159) ('Minister Sharett ... is not so familiar with the problems' of interest to Jewish NGOs).

[165] Katzanelson to Sharett, 26 October 1949, FM–2384/21 ISA (Perlzweig's 'very appearance in the presence of Israel's representation made a strange impression ... while our representatives ... at the committee had to remain silent').

[166] Locker to Rosenne, 2 September 1948 [with extract from Kahany's Memo No.14 of 6 August 1948], FM–1823/7, ISA where Israel's (and formerly the Jewish Agency's) representative in Geneva was

representation[167] and, at times, their familiarity with UN issues, structures, and procedures. Many tended to deride the divisions, 'jealousies', 'anarchy'[168] and petty rivalries of the Jewish organizations[169] or dismiss their competence and Diasporic concerns.[170]

Underpinning these gripes was a claim to paramount, sovereign Jewish voice.[171] A late 1949 'embarrassing' appearance of a WJC representative before a UN Committee drew the ire of Israel's UN mission: Eban reported that Maurice Perlzweig—Robinson's co-delegate to the San Francisco Conference—resorted to 'demands, shouts, and abstractions' that jeopardized Israel's 'interests and position'. Another mission member dubbed Perlzweig's appearance 'irresponsible', and expressed the general sentiment that 'the World Congress has *no authority* to appear before an international committee *in the presence of Israel's representatives* without consulting them and proper preparations'.[172] Sharett, informed of the 'problem of the World Jewish Congress', 'entirely agree[d] that the appearances of Congress representatives in bodies we attend must be stopped'.[173] An Israeli diplomat participating in the Assembly's Third Committee meetings in late 1951 complained that the 'activity' of Jewish NGOs 'embarrassed us in so far as many [Jewish] delegates did not distinguish between their views and ours, *as representing the views of the State*. They were especially troublesome on Human Rights'.[174] These

puzzled by the 'great number of Jewish International non-governmental organizations "enjoying" the consultative status category "B" with the ECOSOC', observing that '[t]hese are so to speak official Jewish observers; in addition to it some other less official or less "international" but still lobbying "Jewish observers" are also appearing from time to time'.

[167] Sharett to Posner, 26 August 1948, FM–67/5, ISA. Kahany reported from Geneva that the WJC attempt to upgrade its ECOSOC status 'is of course not a very happy coincidence' in 'view of our request for a hearing'. This 'move of the WJC' 'results in a great deal of confusion among the delegates, the Secretariat, the press, etc.': Locker to Rosenne, 2 September 1948 (n 166).

[168] Summary of Meeting in Minister's House, 9 June 1951, FM–2417/8, ISA.

[169] Robinson to Gordon, 14 August 1949 (n 49), Gordon to Robinson, 26 August 1949 (n 30), Robinson to Eytan, 9 March 1950 (n 48) ('unwise ... in view of the competitive spirit predominant among these organizations to favour one ... against another'); Locker to Rosenne, 2 September 1948 (n 166) (berating the absence of 'effective coordination' among the Jewish NGOs, creating 'confusion and bewilderment' among ECOSOC officials; Locker added: 'A final proof that the Jewish people is not united and is almost incapable of unified appearance'). Kahany to MFA, 17 July 1948, FM–371/25, ISA (no 'united front of Jewish organizations').

[170] Rosenne to Robinson, 28 December 1951 (n 89) (CCJO proposal for human rights Attorney-General 'must be' rejected and Jewish NGO should be told now to avoid 'embarrassing situations'). When the representative of an ultra-orthodox Jewish NGO sought to mobilise Israel and have the Commission on Human Rights discuss the question of Jewish children in Catholic custody, Robinson was not content to dismiss the matter, as other Jewish NGOs did, as negligent in scope; for Israel to lobby on the question, he wrote, 'would, in fact, be a continuation' of a pre-state 'mentality of which we have to get rid'; Robinson to Eytan, 9 March 1950 (n 48).

[171] The MFA Director-General, Eytan, could not see how 'Israel, as a sovereign state, appear in a conference of Jewish organizations' to deal with German reparations: Summary of Meeting, 9 June 1951 (n 168).

[172] Emphases added; UN Mission Meeting, 10 October 1949 (n 50).

[173] Sharett to Katzanelson, 4 November 1949, FM–375/4, ISA.

[174] 'At Dr. Robinson's suggestion', she reported, 'we convened a meeting for *these people* ... to acquaint them with *our standpoint* and to ask them to do nothing which might be detrimental to *our* position.

aversions, too, were ideological: they gave voice to the sensibilities of sovereign 'New Jews' free from the complexes besetting Diasporic 'Old Jews'.[175] Often, Israel's envoys preferred to act first and consult the NGOs only later.[176]

Robinson was more conflicted. He was intimately familiar with the Jewish NGO scene at the UN. His brother, Nehemiah, succeeded him as IJA Director.[177] The division of labour he and Rosenne had agreed on tasked him with providing legal advice on Jewish UN issues. Robinson was both prone to express sovereign sensibilities on Jewish voice and at pains to adapt to what imperatives they demanded. At times, his pre-state sensibilities would resurface. On the UN human rights Questionnaire, he had hoped—like he had when dealing with the Bernheim petition in 1933[178]—that 'some sort of unity among them' can be achieved despite the 'difference in emphasis and general philosophy' among the Jewish NGOs.[179] On other occasions, he complained that 'the Jewish organizations ... continue their old memorandomania as if nothing changed'.[180] By mid-1947, he was already recounting to Rosenne, still in London, in connection with his work on the Human Rights Commission, 'how unimportant became now the so-called private international organizations'.[181] His work at Israel's UN mission saw him grappling, time and again, with the ideological propriety of sovereign choices and trying to exorcise the pre-state 'mentality of which we have to get rid'.[182] At times, he kept himself at an arm's length from the Jewish organizations and their work.[183]

It even became necessary for us to explain to some delegates that the interests of certain world Jewish organizations did not always coincide precisely with the interests of the *sovereign State of Israel* ... impression of dissention among Jews ... could only have the effect of weakening *our* stand'; Z Harman to Kidron, 13 March 1952, FM-1972/6 (all emphases added). This led to attempts to structure collaboration with—and control of—Jewish organizations: UN Mission Meeting, 14 August 1952, FM-1973/6; UN Seventh Session, Minutes of Mission Meeting, 15 September 1952, FM-116/8, ISA.

[175] Anita Shapira, *New Jews Old Jews* (Am Oved 1997) 122–74 (Hebrew).

[176] Sharett observed on the question of German reparations: 'Had we consulted with the Jewish organization before drafting our note, either it would have never been written at all, or it would have been written and submitted out of strife with them. By making them face the fact ... we have brought them to a situation where they must identify with us': Summary of Meeting, 9 June 1951 (n 168).

[177] Nehemiah would write on the WJC UN work and a commentary on the Universal Declaration: Nehemiah Robinson, *The United Nations and the World Jewish Congress* (IJA/WJC 1956); Nehemiah Robinson, *The Universal Declaration of Human Rights: Its Origin, Significance, Application, and Interpretation* (IJA/WJC 1958).

[178] Ch 2.

[179] Robinson to Gordon, 14 August 1949 (n 49).

[180] Robinson to Rosenne, 6 February 1951, FM-1830/8, ISA; pre-1948, that had been his *modus operandi*.

[181] Robinson to Rowson, 15 July 1947, FM-2274/21, ISA.

[182] Robinson to Eytan, 9 March 1950 (n 48) on another occasion, reflecting on Israel's defeat in a Sixth Committee vote, he wrote: 'The very fact of raising this question is evidence of our difficulty in ridding ourselves of the discrimination and inferiority complex. We continue to think in terms of a minority looking for protection against discrimination and transfer the same mentality into the United Nations': Robinson, Convocation of International Conferences by the Economic and Social Council, 8 December 1949, FM-1823/7, ISA.

[183] Reportedly, on the matter of Jewish children in Catholic custody (n 170) Robinson responded that Israel could do little because 'now we are a government': Levin to Sharett, 1 July 1949, FM-1824/

Ideological perspectives controlled how the Jewish organizations themselves approached the questions of petitions and human rights—as well as their ensuing rivalries. The WJC, even as it was promoting human rights, was still often thinking in terms of minority protection. It inherited many of the sensibilities of its predecessor, the *Comité des Délégations*.[184] WJC advocacy often drew on the Bernheim affair as an example of 'effective use of the right of petition' when advocating for reading such a right into the Charter or incorporating it in the draft Covenant.[185] Yet, unlike the *Comité* in 1933, it was now highly invested in securing the *individual* right of petition in addition to NGO standing. After the Holocaust, any protection for Jewish existence would do; the precarious position of Jewry in a world divided by the Cold War facilitated the shift to individual protection. Location and personnel, however, also contributed to the change in perspective. Unlike the *Comité*, the WJC was based in New York and London. The *Comité*'s Eastern European disposition was waning, as the fate of the architects of the Bernheim petition reveals: Motzkin died in 1933; Feinberg returned to Palestine to pursue, eventually, an academic career; Margulies escaped the 1938 German occupation of the Sudeten, lived in Tel Aviv, and died in 1943; Robinson, though located in New York, espoused the cause of the Jewish state. WJC staffers, though often of Central or Eastern European origins, now hailed from Western liberal democracies.

WJC advocacy on the right of petition was led by Polish-born, Cambridge-educated Reform Rabbi Maurice L Perlzweig (1895–1985). Perlzweig 'hammered ... [the] view that without the Right of Petition any instrument designed to protect human rights was so greatly defective as to impair very obviously, if not to nullify, its value'.[186] Although the WJC had several key concerns with the draft Covenant—eg the principle of non-discrimination—it was the right of petition[187] for which it was willing to 'postpone action at this time rather than draft a Covenant which denies individuals and groups the right to directly petition the U.N.' for redress of grievances.[188] '[W]e regard', Perlzweig told members of the Human Rights

3; it was 'more appropriate' that 'humanitarian agencies lobby this not government': Eban to Sharett, 3 November 1949, FM-1824/3, ISA.

[184] Perlzweig, Note on the Right of Petition, 15 June 1949, WJC-B2/5; Congress Digest, 20 January 1950, WJC-B2/6; [Draft], 9 February 1950, WJC-B2/6 (right of petition 'a matter of the gravest urgency to minority populations and especially to certain Jewish communities'); Perlzweig to Goldmann, 4 August 1949, WJC-B23/14, AJA.

[185] WJC, Memorandum to the Commission on Human Rights Drafting Committee, 16 June 1947, WJC-B140/1; Perlzweig to Bernstein, 27 July 1949, WJC-B27/6; Perlzweig, Note on Petition, 15 June 1949 (n 184); Congress Digest, 20 January 1950 (n 184); Perlzweig to WJC Executive, Memorandum: Congress Policy and the Draft Covenant, 11 September 1950, WJC-B7/9; Perlzweig to Bienenfeld, 8 May 1950, WJC-B89/4, AJA.

[186] Perlzweig to Bienenfeld, 8 May 1950, WJC-B89/4, AJA.

[187] WJC, Observations Concerning the Draft First International Covenant on Human Rights, Submitted to the 11th Session of ECOSOC, 3 July 1950, WJC-B141/27, AJA.

[188] Perlzweig to UN Correspondents, 1 May 1950, WJC-B141/20, AJA.

Commission, 'the recognition of the Right of Petition, even if only in a modest form, as so fundamental in any scheme for the protection of human rights, that we should prefer delay rather than see the adoption of a Covenant without it.'[189]

WJC advocacy approached the right of petition in terms that echoed and at times were borrowed from Lauterpacht.[190] A day after he delivered his Jerusalem lecture, the WJC's organ, the *Congress Weekly*, ran a piece on *The Right of Petition*. It argued, echoing Lauterpacht, 'that the Covenant is scarcely worth having if it denies the fundamental right of petition and, with such denial, any effective remedy for those whose rights have been violated ... In the field of human rights ... the power of enforcement is everything'.[191] For the WJC, 'the value of the Covenant depends on the recognition of the Right of Petition'.[192] This was 'not a problem for juridical ingenuity but a matter of life and death'.[193] WJC investment in the individual right of petition, however, did nothing to blunt the old ideological rivalries between the WJC and organizations like the AJC, the *Alliance Israélite Universelle*, the Anglo-Jewish Association, or their UN front, the CCJO.[194] The question of petitions, if anything, exacerbated pre-existing sensibilities on Jewish voice, standing, and representation. A single, unified, Jewish voice at the international arena was the WJC's very *raison d'être*, the only way to justify the global aspiration of its mission.[195] From its perspective, official Jewish standing at the UN was the cure for Jewish voicelessness: Perlzweig told the Human Rights Commission that the Holocaust 'was facilitated' by 'then prevailing doctrine that what a government may do to its own nationals is a matter of domestic concern'. Protests failed, as their authors 'had to acknowledge *that their interventions had no formal legal basis*'.[196] In a 1947 press conference, he pointed out that the WJC 'had been granted consultative status' by ECOSOC, and was '*the only authorized voice to speak* in the interests

[189] The Right of Petition: Proposals by the WJC, 28 April 1950, WJC–B141/20, AJA.

[190] 'What is wrong', Perlzweig wrote, 'is the doctrine of the monopoly of governments. That system is bad in itself': Perlzweig to Bienenfeld, 8 May 1950 (n 185). Like Lauterpacht, Perlzweig considered ECOSOC Res.75(V), confirming that the Commission on Human Rights had no power to hear petitions, as 'the most unfortunate resolution passed so far in the matters of petitions': Bienenfeld to Perlzweig, 27 April 1949, WJC–B90/4, AJA; see ch 2.

[191] 'The Right of Petition' *Congress Weekly* 17(7) (8 May 1950) 4, 5; Perlzweig to Bienenfeld, 25 May 1950, WJC–B89/4; Untitled, 15 May 1950, WJC–B89/4 ('the Covenant, without the Right of Petition, would add nothing'); Marcus to Members of Third Committee, 20 October 1950, WJC–B86/8, AJA ('fundamental measure', 'indispensable').

[192] Untitled, 15 May 1950 (n 191).

[193] Perlzweig to Caplan, 15 July 1949, WJC–B90/2, AJA.

[194] Moskowitz to Proskaur, Memorandum on the Program of the CCJO, 4 April 1952, AJC–B8/27 (American Jewish Committee Records, MS–780), AJA.

[195] Like Robinson and Feinberg in the interwar period, Perlzweig decried the 'competition' inherent in the fact of 'several rival world Jewish representations': Perlzweig to Hayes, 28 June 1949, WJC–B89/3. In 1946, Robinson listed 'Representation of Non-Governmental Bodies' in ECOSOC as the first of the 'Matters of Jewish Interests' in the first session of the General Assembly: Robinson to Office Committee, 21 March 1946, WJC–B139/16, AJA.

[196] Emphasis added: Perlzweig, Note on Petition, 15 June 1949 (n 184).

of the political and human rights of hundreds of thousands of Jewish survivors of persecution'.[197] To mark itself apart from its rivals, the WJC drew on the pedigree and experience of its predecessor.[198] The WJC insisted that the right of petition should pertain at least to a 'small number of respectable organizations'; 'recognised representative international non-governmental organizations';[199] 'representative and authorised'.[200]

The WJC position was driven by concerns with standing, status, and the competition of Jewish representation politics no less than by its principled opposition to the 'monopoly of governments' over enforcement. Other Jewish organizations with ECOSOC consultative status—'our deadly rivals and competitors', wrote Perlzweig[201]—had their own Covenant agenda, and their own claims to Jewish representation. As in the interwar period, the differences were ideological-political, and involved turf and prestige. Like Feinberg in the 1930s, the WJC castigated the AJC for its 'old assimilationist view that rich communities have a philanthropic responsibility' to poorer Jewish communities and for remaining, in the words of the AJC president, 'unalterably opposed to any concept of world Jewish nationalism ... there is no question but that there can be no single spokesman for world Jewry, no matter who'.[202] The WJC Political Director declared that 'this ideology of the [American Jewish] Committee contradicts everything for which the [WJC] stands, including its concept of the unity of the Jewish people'. The AJC, he charged, lacks 'a moral or legal basis for participation in the affairs' of Jewry outside the US.[203] The WJC revelled in deprecating 'disastrous' UN interventions 'on the subject of petitions' by other Jewish organizations[204]—in terms strikingly similar to Israel's critique of the WJC's and its UN advocacy.[205]

[197] Emphasis added; WJC Press Release, 19 June 1947, WJC–B140/1. For the WJC's status, see WJC–B28/7, AJA.

[198] 'The Congress is the only international Jewish organization in the field of human rights which has had a long experience in these matters': Congress and the International Right of Petition [draft], 28 April 1950, WJC–B89/4, AJA.

[199] Perlzweig to Bienenfeld, 8 May 1950 (n 185); WJC, Observations, April 1951 (n 154).

[200] WJC, Observations, 3 July 1950 (n 187).

[201] Perlzweig to Baum, 9 May 1950, WJC–B2/6, AJA.

[202] Marcus to Dimant, 7 April 1950, WJC–B7/9, AJA; Brecher (n 57) 142 (AJC was 'anti-Zionist at the outset' and 'ambivalently non-Zionist' after the Holocaust).

[203] Marcus to Dimant, 7 April 1950 (n 202); he added that the AJC sought consultative status with ECOSOC only to 'compete with the World Jewish Congress', and was aligned with two 'like-minded groups ... known for their hostility to Zionism, the Anglo-Jewish Association and the Alliance Israelite Universelle'. Establishing the CCJO was 'a compromise between the necessity of appearing as an international group and the AJCommittee ideal of remaining a national U.S. body'. Perlzweig to Bienenfeld, 8 May 1950 (n 185); Perlzweig Memorandum, 25 May 1950, WJC–B89/4, AJA.

[204] Perlzweig to Goldmann, 26 July 1949, WJC–B23/14. Perlzweig to Bienenfeld, 20 May 1949, WJC–B89/3, AJA ('out of order ... in bad taste ... definitely harmful ... publicity stunt').

[205] See n 172 above.

6. Ambivalence and Appearances: A 'Sixth Heaven' Affair 'of Special Interest to Israel'

And yet, for all their ideological aversion to competing Jewish voices, Israel's envoys were willing to concede Jewish NGO standing, however circumscribed. Ideology dictated aversion to the NGO right of petition no less than to the individual right of petition. The right of NGO petition may not have undermined the collective reading of Jewish political status or obviated the principle of national representation; but it did challenge Israel's claim to sovereign primacy in Jewish representation. Israel's early diplomats, for all their sovereign sensibilities, were willing to concede a limited right of NGO petition—even if some, like Rosenne, were willing to do so more grudgingly than others. That willingness suggests that they approached the right of petition not only with aversion. Other sensibilities were at play. The sum of Israel's attitude was ambivalence.

One concerned Israel's own standing within the UN. The Mid-East Conflict and early Cold War orientation dilemmas[206] limited severely the number of issues on which Israel could make a contribution—or, sometimes, appear to make a contribution—to the UN and the furtherance of its goals.[207] Israel's envoys often found themselves abstaining in or absenting themselves from controversies debated at the UN;[208] in other cases, such as South Africa's racial discrimination policies, they elected to equivocate.[209] Such tactics, however, did not help Israel demonstrate good membership in the world organization, an important element of its early UN policy.[210] 'Marginal' agenda items—not of direct concern to Israel—like human rights furnished Israel's UN representatives with an opportunity to balance that picture.[211] This resulted in a tendency to ensure that when Israel's representatives made a contribution to UN work on such matters, that contribution would at least stand out in its quality.

[206] Uri Bialer, *Between East and West: Israel's Foreign Policy Orientation 1948–1956* (Cambridge 2008); Avi Shlaim, 'Israel Between East and West: Israel's Foreign Policy Orientation, 1948–1956' (2004) 66 Intl J of Middle East Stud 657.

[207] UN Mission Meeting, 19 September 1949, FM–89/1, ISA (Robinson).

[208] Israel abstained from taking sides on the question of the human right provisions of the peace treaties with Hungary, Bulgaria, and Hungary, even in the face of US pressure that alluded the Jewish provenance of these arrangements: Herlitz to Rosenne, 5 January 1950, FM–2016/6; Israel did not participate in the Assembly debate: Rosenne to Robinson, 20 November 1949, FM–2016/6; predominantly, Israel sought to avoid risking immigration from these countries: UN Mission Meeting, 19 September 1950, FM–89/1, ISA (Sharett).

[209] Rotem Giladi, 'Negotiating Identity: Israel, Apartheid, and the United Nations 1949–1952' (2017) 132 (No.559) English Hist Rev 1440.

[210] Nathan Feinberg, *Israel and the United Nations: Report of a Study Group Set Up By the Hebrew University of Jerusalem* (Manhattan 1956) 30–7; Sharett, *Divrei HaKnesset* (Parliamentary Record) (15 June 1949) 717–19 (Hebrew); Robinson to Rosenne, 14 March 1951, FM–1832/3, ISA.

[211] Robinson, in preparation for successive Assemblies, would distinguish between matters of direct concern to Israel and 'marginal' problems, including human rights and other 'Jewish' concerns: Robinson, Marginal Problems in the Third Session of the General Assembly: Observations, 4 September 1948, FM–131/22, ISA.

This policy, too, drew on ideological sensibilities. Zionism long held that Jewish national revival would not only rectify past grievances; it would also make a positive contribution to progress, civilization, and world affairs. The Jewish state was to have, that is, a universal vocation.[212] Israel's UN admission compelled its envoys to deliver on that promise.[213] Sharett's maiden UN speech asserted that Israel's admission signified the transformation in Jewish political status not only 'from exclusion to membership in the family of nations' but also 'from mere *passive* protest to *active* responsibility'.[214] Quality contribution to the drafting of the Covenant—or some concession with regard to its enforcement—were, too, signifiers of Jewish sovereignty.

Such notions, and such sensibilities, were ubiquitous in internal MFA correspondence concerning Israel's UN Questionnaire response and human rights more broadly. They explain Rosenne's extensive investment, qualitatively and quantitatively, in the drafting of Israel's Questionnaire response.[215] They equally explain his contributions to the *United Nations Yearbook of Human Rights*—despite his ideological reading of the right of petition, the low priority he accorded to human rights, and his view that they were a utopian, 'idealistic', 'sixth heaven' affair.[216] This was precisely what he professed to Lauterpacht: 'The Government', he wrote, 'felt that it could not put up a scheme entirely devoid of substance but that it should exert itself in the direction of proposing something which tries to overcome human frailties and realities by taking them into account'.[217] 'Our Ministry of Foreign Affairs', Rosenne wrote to Robinson in early 1951, in connection with one of Israel's first substantive comments on the draft Covenant, 'should maintain a high level in its contributions on this matter'. At the same time, Rosenne regretted he could not devote enough attention to that task.[218] Robinson, though feeling 'very strongly against the individual right of petition', lauded the quality of Israel's contribution even if Israel's 'excellent' proposal to trust human rights enforcement to a new agency was 'unrealisable'.[219] Earlier, he wrote to Gordon that it was 'obvious' that 'it is a moral duty of our Government to submit its views on the Covenant'.[220] This

[212] Ch 1.
[213] Eytan to Sharett, 5 September 1950, FM-2015/5, ISA; Eban, GAOR, Plenary (26 September 1949) 95.
[214] Emphases in original; Sharett (n 76) 119.
[215] Rosenne to Tzippori, 1 December 1949 (n 29).
[216] Rosenne to Lauterpacht, 26 June 1950 (n 33); Rosenne to Attorney-General, 15 May 1957 (n 91) (acknowledging that Israel's contribution to human rights debates could be improved).
[217] Rosenne to Lauterpacht, 26 June 1950 (n 33). This, apparently, worked: Humphrey was 'enthusiastic' with some of Israel's proposals: Robinson to Rosenne, 31 May 1950 (n 33).
[218] Rosenne to Robinson, 19 February 1951, FM-1824/4; Rosenne to IOD, 29 February 1952, FM-2006/7. On other occasions, he distanced himself from work on these issues: Rosenne to Gordon, 30 October 1950, FM-2006/7, ISA.
[219] Robinson to Rosenne, 31 May 1950 (n 33).
[220] Robinson to Gordon, 14 August 1949 (n 49).

concerned process and presence, not substance—which he did not comment on.[221] Appearances were important, vis-à-vis the UN membership and Secretariat as well as the Jewish organizations and their constituencies. When Sharett, in a meeting of Israel's UN mission, opposed a proposal that Israel assume human rights obligations 'that no other state committed itself to', Robinson noted that Israel should not openly eschew human rights 'lest we appear to the Jewish public as opponents of the Covenant'.[222]

Israel's envoys never denied that human rights were a Jewish concern. Rosenne did not refute Lauterpacht's assumption of a Jewish stake in human rights; he only gave priority to other Jewish interests. At times, Israel's diplomats even insisted that human rights were also an *Israeli* interest. This they did among themselves, in classified correspondence and internal meetings, not merely in public statements. Robinson, notwithstanding his aversion to human rights, asserted that 'human rights is a very important problem for us'.[223] And yet, in the summer of 1949, Israel's diplomats were not interested in membership of the Commission on Human Rights—notwithstanding Humphrey's support for the idea[224] and a general MFA preference of participating in the work of UN bodies when possible.[225] The Jewish aspect of human rights, ideologically interpreted, allowed Israel's envoys, in 1949–1950 and in later years, to invoke Israel's *Jewish* stake in human rights and, at the same time, resort to a selective, low-cost, low-risk engagement in the human rights project. An anonymous MFA official observed in the early 1950s that 'the problem of human rights is of special interest to Israel'. This meant that human rights were

> one of those [areas] in which Israel could give full expression to its spiritual values and aspirations, without particularly involving itself in political complications. These circumstances would seem to justify an approach *marked by* activity and initiative.[226]

221 Kurz (n 26) 102–3 argues that some MFA lawyers invoked a 'moral duty' to 'seek strong mechanisms for implementation of human rights'; the substance of Israel's response and Robinson's views cited here both refute this reading.

222 UN Mission Meeting, 5 November 1950, FM–89/1, ISA. On the question of Jewish children in Catholic custody, Eban proposed that when the draft Covenant came to ECOSOC or the Assembly, 'we can actually appear [to] fight for additions [and] amendments': Eban to Sharett, 3 November 1949 (n 183). See also Levin to Sharett, 1 July 1949 (n 183).

223 UN Mission Meeting, 6 October 1949, FM–1972/2, ISA.

224 Gordon to Kahany, 4 July 1949, FM–19/3; Kahany to MFA, 14 July 1949, FM–19/3; Gordon to Kahani, 21 July 1949, FM–2006/7; Gordon to Humphrey, 26 July 1949, FM–2006/7; Gordon to Kahany, [n.d.], FM–19/4; Kahany to Gordon, 1 August 1949, FM–19/4. Robinson and Eban feared membership in the 'subsidiary' Commission may harm Israel's prospects of being elected to ECOSOC, a 'principal organ' of the UN: Robinson to Gordon, 5 June 1950, FM–1823/7, ISA.

225 '*Diplomatie de présence*', identified early by Robinson as a guiding principle for Israel's UN diplomacy: Robinson to Foreign Office, 15 June 1948, FM–74/3, ISA; Robinson, Marginal Problems, 4 September 1948 (n 211).

226 Emphasis added; Anon., General Assembly Sixth Session, Draft International Covenant on Human Rights [n.d.], FM–1972/2, ISA.

The sum of all ideological imperatives, sovereign sensibilities, interwar experience, diplomacy preferences, and representation politics was ambivalence towards the right of petition, and towards human rights generally. Engagement and disinterest, aversion and assertion of import, investment in form and aloofness to content—all these marked how Rosenne, Robinson, and their MFA colleagues approached the right of petition and the emerging international human rights regime.

7. Afterword: The Outsider

In Jerusalem, in 1950, Lauterpacht felt comfortable enough to call on the Jewish state, in Hebrew, to espouse the individual right of petition, exercise 'some sacrifice of sovereignty', and 'contribute its proper and appointed share'[227] to the cause of human rights as a Jewish interest consonant with Jewish 'ideals and experience'. Lauterpacht's appeal was, as already noted, insensitive to the *national* sensibilities of Nathan Feinberg, his host, and of his Jerusalem audience. Yet Lauterpacht's appeal was equally insensitive to the sovereign sensibilities of Rosenne—the addressee of Lauterpacht's public reproach—and of his MFA colleagues, sovereign Jews equipped with official capacity, standing, and voice.

The very concerns that led Lauterpacht to make this appeal, during the semi-jubilee celebration of the Hebrew University in Jerusalem, produced its failure. Ideology drove his call, and ideology doomed any prospect of the Jewish state heeding it. Lauterpacht prescribed one vision of 'Jewish public life and the Jewish place on the international scene' at a time, and a place, where another vision had just triumphed. From his perspective, he had not abandoned the Zionism of his youth; but his Zionist sensibilities—not his cosmopolitanism—were precisely what marked him, in 1950, in a divided Jerusalem, as an outsider.

Unlike Robinson, Lauterpacht had not placed himself at the service of the Jewish state. Unlike Rosenne, he had not practiced Zionism's most fundamental demand of immigration to Zion. This deprived Lauterpacht of the requisite standing to pronounce, with an authorized Jewish voice, on what Jewish interests required. His deficient standing was only exacerbated by the content of his advocacy for the individual right of petition sponsored, after all, by the non-Zionist, assimilationist AJC. It drew on and expressed an ideological position that challenged Zionism's most fundamental postulate: that the Jews were a 'people' entitled to national rights, not a collection of individuals bereft of collective rights. In expressing such an 'extreme non-Zionist, apolitical concept' of Jewish political thought, Lauterpacht had placed himself, *by the very dint of his Zionist convictions*, outside the now-sovereign

[227] Elihu Lauterpacht (ed), *International Law, Being the Collected Papers of Hersch Lauterpacht*, vol 3 (1977) 430; ch 2.

Zionist camp.[228] His credentials were sufficient for him to render advice to the Jewish state;[229] they were deficient, alas, in ideological authority.

And yet, perhaps Lauterpacht's Zionism was deficient all along; he had been, perhaps, an outsider all along. When attending the London School of Economics, in the early 1920s, Moshe Shertok (Sharett) happened to lodge at the same house as the Lauterpachts. Hersch left a mixed impression on the future Israeli Minister of Foreign Affairs: 'a good lad, albeit a Galician'.[230] Politically, however, he found Lauterpacht lacking in 'class consciousness'. Ideologically, he was 'lukewarm material': neither here nor there. In particular, Shertok found fault in Hersch's Zionism: Lauterpacht, he wrote, did not have the 'courage even to be *Poalei Zion*'.[231] In Sharett's world outlook, Lauterpacht, affiliated to *Zeirei Zion*, was not sufficiently committed to either to socialism or Zionism.[232]

Dolek (David) Horowitz—first Director-General of the Ministry of Finance and, later, the first Governor of the Bank of Israel—knew Lauterpacht from their youth in Lvov. His memoire noted Lauterpacht's talent and education.[233] In later years, travel allowed the two to meet again and reminisce of the bygone world of their youth.[234] None of this blunted Horowitz's critique of Hersch's ideology. Lauterpacht, he reported, headed 'an academic Zionist organisation whose spirit was pretty conventional' and 'loyal' to the 'patterns of settled bourgeois Zionism'. '[W]e were foes and friends both', he wrote, 'in the Zionist youth movement in Lvov'.[235] Horowitz was 'among the leaders of the non-conformist *HaShomer Ha'tzair*'—a Zionist youth movement more active in its Zionism and more socialist in its programme than Lauterpacht's bourgeois *Herzlia*.[236] He, too, deemed Lauterpacht's ideological commitment, in both respects, lacking.

228 Rosenne would eventually absolve him, yet even his Lauterpacht *nécrologie* contained something of a backhanded compliment: 'Although his academic pursuits were later to lead him to the great Universities of England, he always remained faithful to his Zionist *background*'; emphasis added: Shabtai Rosenne, 'In Memoriam: Sir Hersch Lauterpacht' *Jerusalem Post* (12 May 1960).

229 At most; in 1957, Rosenne gave Eban 'a grave warning' against consulting Lauterpacht, now a judge at the ICJ, on prospective litigation against Egypt concerning passage through the Suez Canal: Rosenne to Eban, 6 June 1957, FM–5935/69, ISA; Rosenne was less concerned with impropriety, more with Lauterpacht's assimilationist sensitivities and qualifications.

230 Galician Jews were 'the ultimate "other" for German-speaking Jews, with whom they associated all the shortcomings of traditional Jewry': Rachel Manekin, 'Galitsianer', *The YIVO Encyclopedia of Jews in Eastern Europe* http://www.yivoencyclopedia.org/article.aspx/Galitsianer accessed 20 January 2020. Albert Lichtblau, '"Galitsianer" and the Mobility of Stereotypes' (2009) 11 Jewish Culture and Hist 84.

231 Moshe Sharett, *The London Days: Letters 1923–1925* (Moshe Sharett Heritage Society 2008) 58 (Hebrew).

232 Literally, 'Workers of Zion' and 'Youth of Zion'. See Ezra Mendelsohn, *Zionism in Poland: The Formative Years, 1915–1926* (Yale UP 1981).

233 Lauterpacht's 'penetrating eyes, the iron logic ... the irony and sarcasm ... his pragmatic rationalism—all these covered the dryness and coolness of his personality': David Horowitz, *HaEtmol Sheli* (Schocken 1970) 69 (Hebrew).

234 I thank Dr Neri Horowitz for sharing this information about his grandfather.

235 Horowitz (n 233) 69; Elihu Lauterpacht, *The Life of Hersch Lauterpacht* (CUP 2010) 23.

236 Literally, 'The Young Guard'. Horowitz immigrated to Palestine in 1920.

PART III
PROTECTION

4

From a 'Marginal Problem' to the 'Supreme International Jurisdiction'

Israel and the Genocide Convention

1. Defiance—and Contribution

On 26 December 1949, the *Knesset* reconvened in Jerusalem. The first substantive item on the agenda of Israel's parliament was a government bill implementing the Genocide Convention adopted by the United Nations ('UN') General Assembly ('GA') a year earlier.[1] It was, announced Justice Minister Pinchas (Felix) Rosen (Rosenblüth) (1887–1978), a 'most significant coincidence' that this should be the first item discussed by the *Knesset* in Jerusalem. Relocating the legislature was meant to signal defiance of the UN, where developments that 'seriously harmed the interests of the state of Israel' had taken place earlier that month.[2] Yet the Genocide Convention also presented the Jewish state with an opportunity, Rosen noted, to signify 'our fundamental desire to cooperate' with the UN and, as a member of the organization, 'to make our contribution' towards the achievement of its 'lofty, exalted goals'. In introducing the bill, Rosen marked other precedents: the Genocide Convention was the first treaty prepared by the UN 'as a general treaty open to all nations of the world for signature and ratification'; the Convention was also the first to be 'brought before the *Knesset* as a result of our participation in the international organisation of nations as a member of equal rights'; the bill itself was the first placed before the *Knesset* seeking to 'implement a general international treaty'.[3]

The UN was not the only object of Rosen's ambivalence; so was the Convention he was presenting to Israel's lawmakers. He offered a concise but well-informed account of the legal and political obstacles besetting the making

[1] Convention on the Prevention and Punishment of the Crime of Genocide (9 December 1948) 78 UNTS 277.

[2] Rosen, *Divrei HaKnesset* (Parliamentary Record) (26 December 1949) 313 (Hebrew). The move, announced on 11 December 1949, was triggered by renewed initiatives to affect Jerusalem's internationalization: UNGA Res.303(IV) (9 December 1949); Uri Bialer, 'The Road to the Capital: The Establishment of Jerusalem as the Official Seat of the Israeli Government in 1949' (1984) 5 Stud in Zionism 273; Motti Golani, 'Zionism without Zion: The Jerusalem Question 1947–1949' (1995) 16 J of Israeli Hist 39.

[3] Rosen (n 2) 313.

Jews, Sovereignty, and International Law. Rotem Giladi, Oxford University Press. © Rotem Giladi 2021.
DOI: 10.1093/oso/9780198857396.003.0006

of the Convention. He marked the role of the Holocaust in both inspiring the Convention and in surmounting these obstacles. He noted the work of Jewish organizations and credited Raphael Lemkin, a Polish Jewish lawyer, for coining the term 'Genocide'. This Jewish aspect was salient: Rosen asserted that as 'a first general instrument for the protection of national, religious and racial minorities ... we, as the state of the Jewish people, are particularly interested in' the Convention. He was presenting the Convention for *Knesset* consideration, he concluded, 'with a sentiment of dual responsibility towards the Jewish people that has a vital interest in this Convention and towards the international institution'.[4] Yet at the very same time, Rosen also observed that 'the decisive practical power of the Convention may be doubted'. The Convention, he recorded, 'has no power to return our victims to us'. Most crucially, he declared that the Convention was no solution to the Jewish problem:

> This Convention presents no solution for our dispersed people in the Diaspora. The radical solution is known to us, it was what had brought us to a state and it was what had allowed us to take part in the ratification of the treaty and in laying this law today before the *Knesset*.[5]

The next chapter returns to Rosen's 'radical solution'. For now, it is important to record Rosen's ambivalence to the Genocide Convention and its echoes in the *Knesset* debate that followed. Some members thought that the Convention was not sufficient. Others considered it redundant. A few speakers expressed both sentiments. More than a few used the occasion to recite their ideological reading of past and present and to censure, accordingly, political and ideological rivals. All approached the Convention as a Jewish concern, a lesson of the recent genocide perpetrated against the Jewish people. By-and-by, the drama that unfolded at the *Knesset* on that day—and in the months to come—turned from the merit of the Convention to the constitutional question of who possessed the power to ratify it.[6] In the ensuing contestation between the executive and the legislature, Shabtai Rosenne, the Ministry of Foreign Affairs ('MFA') legal adviser, would play a major role. He, too, was ambivalent about the Convention. So was, for that matter, Jacob Robinson, his counterpart at Israel's UN mission. Yet unlike the Justice Minister, or the *Knesset* Members taking the floor that day, Rosenne and Robinson's initial attitude to the Genocide Convention revealed disinterest.

[4] ibid, 314–16.
[5] ibid, 314.
[6] ibid.

2. Two Campaigns

On 11 December 1946, the UNGA pronounced genocide a 'crime under international law' and requested the Economic and Social Council ('ECOSOC') 'to undertake the necessary studies, with a view to drawing up a draft convention on the crime of genocide'.[7] Four months later, the UK requested the UN to place the Palestine question on its agenda.[8] On 29 November 1947, the Assembly adopted the majority report of the Special Committee on Palestine ('UNSCOP'), recommending the partition of Palestine into an Arab and a Jewish state; Jerusalem was to be, as a *corpus separatum*, internationalized.[9] Six more months passed before the mandate of Palestine terminated; the state of Israel was declared on 14 May 1948. On 9 December, the Assembly adopted the Genocide Convention.[10] After six more months, Israel's second UN membership bid succeeded.[11] This chronology is well known. So is the involvement of Jewish individuals—first and foremost, Raphael Lemkin—and organizations in the campaign for the Genocide Convention.[12] What often escapes notice is the fact that at the same time, at the same institutional arena, and often involving the same agents, two Jewish campaigns were taking place.

For two years, the preparation of the Genocide Convention followed a winding, rocky, and uncertain path within the new world organization. This included stops at and within: the UN Secretariat, extending also to consultations with a committee of three experts;[13] the Assembly's Committee on the Progressive Development of International Law and its Codification;[14] and ECOSOC. There were two rounds of invitations to governments of UN member states to comment on the draft.[15] The draft was considered by the General Assembly's Sixth (legal) Committee, its sub-committee, then the Assembly's plenary;[16] it was discussed by ECOSOC, again, and by an *ad hoc* committee it established (that appointed, in turn, a sub-committee).[17]

[7] UNGA Res.96(I) (11 December 1946); John Cooper, *Raphael Lemkin and the Struggle for the Genocide Convention* (Palgrave-Macmillan 2008) 76–87.

[8] GAOR, Second Session, Supp 11.

[9] UNGA Res.181(II) (29 November 1947).

[10] UNGA Res.260(III) (9 December 1948).

[11] UNGA Res.273(III) (11 May 1949); Marte Heian-Engdal, Jørgen Jensehaugen, and Hilde Henriksen Waage, '"Finishing the Enterprise": Israel's Admission to the United Nations' (2013) 35 Intl Hist Rev 465.

[12] Cooper (n 7) 88, 96; William Korey, *An Epitaph for Raphael Lemkin* (American Jewish Committee 2001). This is not to suggest that the campaign for the Genocide Convention was exclusively or even predominantly Jewish; many other actors and groups were involved. Lemkin, in particular, had his own reasons to sometimes frame it in universal terms. Jewish organizations taking part in the campaign had no doubt it was a Jewish cause they were advancing.

[13] William A Schabas, *Genocide in International Law: The Crimes of Crimes* (2nd edn, CUP 2009) 59–60. Hirad Abtahi and Philippa Webb, *The Genocide Convention: The Travaux Préparatoires* (Martinus Nijhoff 2008).

[14] Schabas (n 13) 63.

[15] ibid, 64, 66; of the four NGOs submitting observations, two were Jewish.

[16] ibid, 66–9.

[17] ibid, 69–70.

It was considered by the Commission on Human Rights, both at a sub-committee and the plenary;[18] the Commission on Narcotic Drugs;[19] and, again, ECOSOC, which returned the emerging draft to the Assembly. There, it was considered again by the Sixth Committee, including referral to a drafting committee.[20] At various stages, alternative drafts were prepared by different governments;[21] referral to other UN bodies, some yet unformed, was proposed or considered on multiple occasions.

The UN mission of the Jewish Agency—set up to carry out the campaign for partition and, later, Israel's admission (becoming, after May 1948, Israel's UN mission)—was involved in no way whatsoever at any stage of the campaign for the Genocide Convention. This was not the result of deficient standing, as Rosenne would claim six decades later.[22] It could, as had Jewish non-governmental organizations ('NGOs'), seek consultative status or a right to be heard in order to affect, if only to a limited extent, the fate of the Convention. It certainly sought access and standing when it wished to have its voice heard on other agenda items. The diplomatic apparatus of the nascent state, however, was not interested in the Genocide Convention. *Yishuv* diplomacy was primed on a single target and its derivatives—the establishment of a Jewish state in Palestine—to the exclusion of all others.

Such disinterest in the Genocide Convention was patent, for example, during the proceedings of the seventh ECOSOC session in Geneva. For the Genocide Convention, this was a crucial juncture. It was at that session that the spectre of death by committee—'committee-cide', in the words of one of Lemkin's Jewish collaborators[23]—was averted for the last time before the draft Convention finally was referred to the General Assembly for adoption. That result was achieved on 26 August 1948, following much manoeuvring. Success obtained thanks in no small measure to the support of Herbert V Evatt, the Australian Foreign Minister.[24] Evatt also chaired the UN *Ad Hoc* Committee on Palestine and rendered 'invaluable

[18] ibid, 76.
[19] ibid, 77.
[20] ibid, 77–9.
[21] ibid, 71–2.
[22] Shabtai Rosenne, 'Book Review' (2009) 39 Isr YB Hum Rts 379 published the year before his death, on Abtahi and Webb's compilation of the Convention's preparatory work (n 13). In a footnote, Rosenne claimed that the Jewish Agency's and Israel's early disinterest in the Genocide Convention was forced by constraints of standing, and implied that these constraints were overcome by Israeli collaboration with Jewish NGOs: 'Israel was not a member of the United Nations throughout the whole period covered by these two volumes. However, the Political Department of the Jewish Agency for Palestine maintained observer delegations to the United Nations ... and where necessary these worked in close cooperation with corresponding offices of the World Jewish Congress. In the General Assembly these delegations could only participate in the debate on questions relating to Palestine ... In the third session of the General Assembly ... [Israel's UN mission] had observer status limited to the question of Palestine. Nevertheless, it closely followed discussions on the Genocide Convention'. The evidence that follows contradicts these claims.
[23] Cooper (n 7) 104.
[24] ECOSOC Res.153(VII) (26 August 1948); Schabas (n 13) 77; Cooper (n 7) 127–42 describes that drama and its protagonists.

assistance' to the cause of Israel's establishment and admission.[25] No echo of that ECOSOC drama, however, made its way into the record of MFA reports and deliberations.

Israel did follow the proceedings of that ECOSOC session. Robinson, as would become his usual *modus operandi*, perused the provisional agenda in advance of the session, a few weeks after independence, almost a year before UN admission. He drew his colleague's attention to several agenda items, including no 19, but did not refer to 'genocide' by name or add any observation on that item.[26] His MFA colleagues shared his disinterest in that agenda item, notwithstanding their interest in what transpired at ECOSOC discussions.[27] One 'Preliminary Note' on the forthcoming session discussed 'the problems arising from the desirability of Israel's participation' as a non-member state. There were opportunities: this would be 'the first official appearance of the State of Israel on the international scene of Western Europe'; ECOSOC was, after all, 'one of the Principal Organs of the U.N.'; Israel's participation, the author observed, 'might serve as a useful first step towards' the forthcoming GA session in Paris and help prevent 'complete Arab control of a U.N. body'. Israel's main concern was the proposed Economic Commission for the Middle East; this warranted participation in whatever capacity, even if the question of non-member participation was far from clear.[28] Israel asked the UN for 'tickets of admission'; the right to observe proceedings touching on its interests;[29] and a hearing on a few agenda items. These efforts were not geared towards the question of genocide. It was referred to in neither MFA correspondence pertaining to the preparation of that ECOSOC session[30] nor reports on how it unfolded.[31]

The ubiquitous presence of Jewish NGOs in that ECOSOC session could not escape the notice of Israel's diplomats. At some stage, the head of the Israeli mission to Geneva noted that 'members of Jewish Consultative Bodies are beginning to arrive': but his account of Jewish interests in ECOSOC's work did not include any mention of the Genocide Convention. What they were after, Eliash reported, was influencing the work on 'refugees, the Appeal for children, the report on legal difficulties connected with presumption of death, etc'. Next, he lamented that being instructed to watch the session develop meant that 'a good deal of time may be

[25] Eban to Weizmann, 10 May 1949, FM-67/6, Israel State Archive ('ISA'); Moshe Sharett, *At the Threshold of Statehood: 1946–1949* (Am Oved 1958) 146 (Hebrew); William Louis, *The British Empire in the Middle East, 1945–1951: Arab Nationalism, the United States, and Postwar Imperialism* (1984) 490.

[26] Robinson to Foreign Ministry, 24 June 1948, FM-1823/7, ISA; UN Doc.E/830 (23 June 1948).

[27] Eban to Shertok, 18 June 1948, FM-2337/6, ISA, also in Yehoushua Freundlich (ed), *Documents on the Foreign Policy of Israel*, vol 1 (ISA 1981) 187–8.

[28] Locker, Preliminary Note on the Forthcoming Session of [ECOSOC], 1 July 1948, FM-1823/7, ISA.

[29] Kahany to Yates, 12 July 1948; Kahany to MFA, 17 July 1948, FM-371/25, ISA.

[30] Robinson to Foreign Office, 29 June 1948, Kahany to Robinson, 5 July 1948, Locker to Kahany, 6 August 1948, FM-1823/7, ISA.

[31] Eliash to Sharett, 20 July, 21 July, and 12 August 1948; Eliash to MFA, 10 August 1948, FM-1975/9; Locker to Kahany, 24 August 1948, FM-19/1, ISA.

wasted in doing nothing . . . If I see that I have nothing to do . . . I may take off some days for a short vacation'.[32]

Jewish presence in Geneva did raise, nonetheless, questions of Jewish standing, status, and representation. Israel's diplomats both complained and gloated on the absence of 'effective coordination' among the Jewish NGOs and the ensuing 'confusion and bewilderment' among officials.[33] This was one occasion for them to display their sovereign sensibilities and express aversion to competing Jewish voices.[34] The World Jewish Congress' ('WJC') attempt to upgrade its ECOSOC status, one observed, 'is of course not a very happy coincidence' in 'view of our request for a hearing'.[35] Jewish politics were interesting enough for Israel's diplomats to seek 'using the Jewish consultative bodies' to the ends of 'our problem'.[36] The reverse, however, was not contemplated: there was little or no Israeli interest in the problems preoccupying the Jewish organizations. All this was part of a larger, and earlier, trend; the Jewish Agency, before May 1948, had in effect surrendered advocacy on 'most of the problems discussed by ECOSOC to the Jewish non-governmental organizations'.[37] Criminalizing genocide had not been an Israeli concern. Disinterest in the Genocide Convention—or ignorance thereof, for some of Israel's UN representatives[38]—dovetailed with the apprehension of proponents of the Convention that its fate might become entangled in the vagaries of Israeli-Arab conflict.[39]

Israel's disinterest in the Genocide Convention did not change with statehood.[40] Its attention was still drawn elsewhere. Between Israel's establishment and the adoption of the Convention, and for some time after, Israel was engaged in war with its neighbours; multilateral diplomacy and new international law norms did not rate high on the list of priorities of its new foreign service. At the UN, Israel's only concern remained different manifestations of the 'Question of Palestine', including admission.[41]

[32] Eliash to Sharett, 21 July 1948 (n 31); a rare reference to the 'convention on the crime of genocide' as one agenda item of interest for the Jewish organizations is included in Kahany to MFA, 17 July 1948 (n 29). By contrast, Kahany noted two agenda items 'of interest to us as the Government of Israel'.

[33] Locker to Rosenne, 2 September 1948 [with extract from Kahany's Memo No.14 of 6 August 1948], FM-1823/7, ISA; Kahany to MFA, 17 July 1948 (n 29) (noting the absence of 'a united front of Jewish organizations').

[34] Ch 3.

[35] Locker to Rosenne, 2 September 1948 (n 33); this 'move of the WJC', he reported, 'results in a great deal of confusion among the delegates, the Secretariat, the press, etc'.

[36] Eliash to Sharett, 12 August 1948 (n 31) (Arab refugees and Jewish DPs).

[37] Kahany to MFA, 17 July 1948 (n 29).

[38] One Washington diplomat involved in the work of the UN mission confessed as late as January 1951 that 'this is the first time I ever heard about this problem': Herlitz to Eban, 9 January 1951, FM-1840/2, ISA.

[39] Considered further in ch 5.

[40] The instructions for Israeli delegation to the Paris GA session did not include any reference to the Genocide Convention or any other 'general question'; nor did the delegation's opening meeting discuss it: Shertok to Government Members, 10 September 1948, FM-2384/21, ISA; also Freundlich (n 27) 584–6.

[41] Freundlich (n 27) 584–6; Robinson's various memoranda, FM-74/23, ISA.

Independence, however, required Israel's envoys to reflect on this approach. In anticipation of the third GA session in Paris (which was to adopt the Convention), Robinson drafted an eleven-page report on 'Marginal Problems' to be discussed there. 'Our main interest during this session of the General Assembly', he wrote, should be focus on 'our own problems'. To that end, he advised, 'we certainly have to mobilise and concentrate all our energies in order to obtain favorable solutions to our problems'.[42] This did not obviate, however, the need for familiarity with other, 'marginal' agenda items that could be harnessed to the ends of Israel's goals. 'Our problems', he wrote, 'cannot be wholly separated from many other problems of a general nature which will in one way or another influence the debates and decisions on our own problems'.[43] '[W]e shall not neglect at least a certain number of marginal problems', he added: 'there may not be very much we can do about them, but it is at least important to know that such problems exist and should be taken into consideration when mapping our grand strategy'.[44] Interest in 'marginal problems' could be, at most, instrumental.

Robinson moved to enumerate and discuss several such 'marginal problems' that 'should be of interest to us'. 'Genocide' was one. It presented opportunities: '[t]he discussion on genocide may offer an excellent occasion to take up the treatment of Jews in oriental [viz Eastern bloc] countries'.[45] Equally, 'a case may be made against the practice in the Arab countries vis-à-vis the Jewish communities'[46] to counter to Arab claims against Israel. If it occurred to Robinson that such use of the issue by the Jewish state might embroil the Genocide Convention in the Israeli-Arab conflict and jeopardize the prospect of its adoption, he was evidently aloof to such consequence. The apprehensions of the Convention's supporters have been justified.

It speaks volumes that this position was expressed by the one member of Israel's mission most familiar with not only Jewish issues on the UN agenda but also Lemkin and his work on genocide. A few years earlier, while still the Director of the Institute of Jewish Affairs ('IJA'), Robinson had corresponded with Lemkin. Lemkin's 1944 *Axis Rule in Occupied Europe*, where he coined the term 'genocide' and accounted for its criminality,[47] was one of a score of books Robinson had taken

[42] Robinson, Marginal Problems in the Third Regular Session of the General Assembly: Observations, 4 September 1948, FM-131/22, ISA. Two months after the Assembly adopted the Genocide Convention Robinson observed, with regard to a forthcoming ECOSOC session: 'as long as we are not members of the UN we have no possibility of dealing with all the questions on the agenda of the session. Willingly or by coercion, we must be content with matters of direct concern to us ... For that reason we take no interest, and cannot take an interest, in general questions on the agendum ... we must contend with [dealing with] two agenda items, that is, the creation of the Middle East Economic Commission and the question of transportation in this region': Robinson to International Organizations Division ('IOD'), 14 February 1949, FM-1823/7, ISA.

[43] Robinson, Marginal Problems, 4 September 1948 (n 42).

[44] ibid.

[45] ibid.

[46] ibid.

[47] Raphael Lemkin, *Axis Rule in Occupied Europe* (Carnegie Endowment for International Peace 1944).

with him *en route* to Nuremberg.[48] Now, however, 'our problems' were for Robinson those of a state, not a people. And genocide was no longer 'our problem'—that is, an Israeli concern. What made it a marginal problem was, precisely, that it was a Jewish concern.[49]

In practice, Israel's diplomacy in connection with the third Assembly session was limited to various aspects of the Palestine question.[50] Seemingly, its representatives did not allude to the Genocide Convention or relate to it in any way. The adoption of the Genocide Convention on 9 December 1948 left no trace on the record of Israel's involvement in that session; MFA meetings, reports, and working papers make no mention of that project. Israel's UN admission, however, would change the calculus of its disinterest in the Genocide Convention.

3. 'A Cause . . . Close to Your Heart': Israel's Signature and Ratification

Two days after Israel's admission to the UN, its Permanent Representative, Aubrey (Abba) Eban (Even) (1915–2002), received a letter marked 'personal and confidential'. The author was Evatt, the Australian Foreign Minister elected to serve as the President of the third General Assembly.[51] A self-styled co-conspirator of Lemkin, Evatt had played a key role in the adoption of the Convention and later, in the efforts to have it widely ratified.[52] Evatt may have been acting on Lemkin's behest when he expressed, in his letter to Eban, the hope that 'your government will proceed, at the earliest possible date, with the signing and ratification of this Convention' so that the Convention would enter into force before the fourth session of the General Assembly due to convene in September 1949.[53]

A few days later, Eban was approached by Ivan Kerno, the UN Assistant Secretary-General and the organization's chief lawyer, 'with the request that Israel sign the Genocide Convention right now'.[54] Two weeks passed before the Secretary-General ('SG') wrote to Moshe Sharett, Israel's Foreign Minister. Trygve Lie—who later would express pride of his role in Israel's establishment

[48] Lemkin to Robinson, 28 August 1946; Materials to London, 19 September 1946, WJC-C14/21 (World Jewish Congress Records, MS-361), American Jewish Archives ('AJA'); ch 5 addresses this correspondence.

[49] After the conclusion of the GA fourth session, Robinson qualified 'matters of general Jewish interest' as 'including marginal matters': Robinson, Report by the Israel Delegation on the Fourth Session of the General Assembly: Outline and Comments, 8 December 1949, FM-75/14, ISA.

[50] Documents in FM-183/1, FM-131/18, FM-86/5, FM-130/5, FM-186/16, FM-1820/2, FM-70/17, FM-74/3, ISA.

[51] Evatt to Eban, 13 May 1949, FM-1840/1, ISA.

[52] Cooper (n 7) 136; Douglas Irvin-Erickson, *Raphaël Lemkin and the Concept of Genocide* (University of Pennsylvania Press 2016) 172–3, 176, 182, 187–8, 193.

[53] Evatt to Eban, 13 May 1949 (n 51).

[54] Robinson to Rosenne, 18 May 1949, FM-1840/1, ISA.

and admission[55]—drew Sharett's attention to the Assembly resolution adopting the Convention sixth months earlier. Having enclosed a certified true copy of the Convention, Lie proceeded to advise Sharett on the minute details of form: 'Should your Government intend to sign the Convention, I should be grateful if the necessary full powers could be provided to your Representative'.[56]

To the recently made-official representatives of the new UN member, this barrage of demarches seemed like a concerted appeal directed specifically at the Jewish state. Eban soon found out, however, that Evatt in fact addressed such letters to all UN members.[57] So, likely, did the SG. But the terms of Evatt's letter seemed designed to strike a Jewish chord. He was writing to Eban 'on behalf of a cause which I am sure is close to your heart'. Expressing the hope that Eban shared his own 'opinion that this Convention marks a milestone in the development of international law', Evatt emphasized the Convention's importance for the UN. He also intimated that 'general ratification' of the Genocide Convention would be 'easier to obtain ... now, before the systematic genocide perpetrated in the last war has faded from our memories'.[58] Evatt openly invoked Jewish sensibilities.

The matter was discussed in a mission meeting, with Sharett attending. Robinson was asked to 'prepare a memorandum on the subject and rush it to Tel Aviv'.[59] While I could find no record of that meeting, two matters seem clear. First, whatever had been Evatt, Kerno, and SG Lie's expectations of the Jewish state or its Jewish sensibilities, their appeal exposed just how much were members of Israel's UN mission innocent of knowledge of the Convention. Robinson had to ask his brother, Nehemiah—his successor as the IJA director—to put the manuscript of his 'extensive commentary of this Convention ... to the disposal of our authorities'.[60] Second, what first drew Israel's attention to the Genocide Convention were not Jewish but, rather, sovereign sensibilities triggered by appeals from UN officials. UN admission compelled Israel to ponder the Convention.

55 Heian-Engdal, Jensehaugen, and Waage (n 11) 469.

56 SG to Sharett, 27 May 1949, FM–1840/1, ISA.

57 Eban to Rosenne, 14 June 1949, FM–1840/1, ISA. Lemkin's ratification campaign strategy focused on small nations but also on new and prospective UN members who, 'kept out by the big powers, were frustrated in their international feelings and eager to prove their faith in the U.N. They could give no finer proof than by ratifying the convention, if given a chance'; Donna-Lee Frieze (ed), *Totally Unofficial: The Autobiography of Raphael Lemkin* (Yale UP 2013) 190, which does not mention Israel in this regard; Cooper (n 7) 173 et seq.

58 Evatt to Eban, 13 May 1949 (n 51).

59 Robinson to Rosenne, 18 May 1949 (n 54); Provisional Agenda of the Meeting of the UN Delegation, 19 May 1949, FM–70/8, ISA ('Our accession to International Conventions' was listed as one of 'Immediate Tasks in Connection with Our Admission').

60 A three-page brief was received by Rosenne in mid-June 1949: Nehemiah Robinson, The Three R's of the Genocide Convention, March 1949; Rosenne to Ministry of Justice, 28 July 1949, FM–1840/1, ISA. He would only a decade later publish Nehemiah Robinson, *The Genocide Convention: A Commentary* (IJA 1960).

3.1 'Can Israel Long Delay the Signature of a Convention Which Has Been Inspired Primarily by the Mass Slaughter of European Jewry?'

The various demarches set in motion a process of reflection on the Genocide Convention and on the advisability of Israel signing and ratifying it. The ensuing examination of the treaty marked some shift in Israel's attitude to the Convention. Israeli disinterest became instrumental—that is, geared towards 'our own problems'—along the lines advised by Robinson prior to admission.[61] Ambivalence, nonetheless, continued to characterize how Israel's envoys approached the Convention.

Robinson, from the start, was ambivalent with the prospect that Israel join the Genocide Convention. First, he wrote to Rosenne, it was necessary to identify 'exactly ... what are the duties Israel assumes under this Convention'.[62] Some factors militated against Israel's signing and ratifying the Convention. There was 'the duty to enact necessary legislation to give effect to the provisions of the Convention'. More importantly, Robinson noted, the Convention entailed 'a serious commitment' in the form of Article IX. That provision vested, in advance, jurisdiction over interstate disputes arising under the Convention to the International Court of Justice ('ICJ'). Israel had, however, already developed an aversion to the prospect of the Court's involvement in the Middle East conflict during the UN debate on the future of Palestine.[63] Joining the Convention would give other states a right to intervene in its domestic affairs. This, Robinson warned, would enable any state party to 'create a dispute with us on matters which did not happen' in its territory 'but in some other place. We may get into trouble.' He went on to hypothesize a state such as Denmark considering

> our legislation enacted under Article V of the Convention as insufficient to give penal protection to the Arab minority ... this convention ... [grants] signatories a certain, although limited, right of interference in the domestic case ... Denmark could be entitled to ... drag us into the Court. Such an interference may be considered morally very highly because it is disinterested. *Sapienti sat.*[64]

Robinson also informed Rosenne of the procedure for joining the Convention, which raised one more dilemma. The Convention was only open to signature until 1 January 1950; but to assume the obligations in the Convention, a signatory state

[61] Robinson, Marginal Problems, 4 September 1948 (n 42).
[62] Robinson to Rosenne, 18 May 1949 (n 54).
[63] List of Attempts to Introduce the [ICJ] into the Affairs of Israel, 30 October 1959, FM–499/18; UN Department to UN Mission, 17 January 1954, FM–2010/17, ISA. The terms of Israel's acceptance of ICJ compulsory jurisdiction, in September 1950, reflected this aversion: 108 UNTS 239.
[64] Emphasis in the original; Robinson to Rosenne, 18 May 1949 (n 54).

would also have to ratify it. After that date, however, a state wishing to join the treaty could only, in a single act, accede to the Convention.[65] The practical implication was that

> If we want to be among the original signatories of this Convention we want to do it before the end of this year. Of course, there is no difference between original and acceding membership. This problem is a deeper one involving certain moral issue. Can Israel long delay the signature of a Convention which has been inspired primarily by the mass slaughter of European Jewry?[66]

Robinson did not, notably, answer his own rhetorical question. He did point to a 'certain moral issue' impinging on the question of Israel's signatory status. The Genocide Convention was rooted in Jewish tragedy; Israel, as the Jewish state, could and perhaps should have displayed Jewish sensibilities by becoming one of its original signatories. This status, devoid of legal or practical meaning, would have a certain symbolic value. And yet, Robinson neither advocated ratification nor recommended, for that matter, that Israel should signs the Convention early—or at all.

For Robinson, and for others in the MFA, the Genocide Convention did touch on Jewish sensibilities; what action these compelled was, however, another matter. Ezekiel Gordon, the head of the MFA's UN Department at the IOD, was no less ambivalent towards the Convention than Robinson. He was familiar with the early stages of UN work on the Genocide Convention. As a UN officer,[67] he had served as the 'Assistant Secretary of the Ad Hoc Committee on Genocide' appointed by ECOSOC to produce the second draft of the Convention.[68] Gordon thought that 'the Convention as a whole does not involve undue liabilities for the State of Israel'. Accordingly, he answered Robinson's question negatively: 'Israel cannot for moral reasons delay the signature of the Convention'. He proceeded to advise Rosenne 'to sign the Convention as soon as possible'. But 'moral reasons' carried only so far. Accepting the ICJ's jurisdiction, he warned, was a 'serious liability for Israel'. This required a political, not legal, decision. He counselled 'to delay the ratification of it till the clarification of the situation in the Middle East', emphasizing—following Robinson—that this course of action would only be available if Israel signed the Convention by the end of 1949.[69] Israel's early signature on the Convention, for Gordon, was to serve a symbolic function.

[65] Article XI, Genocide Convention (n 1).
[66] Robinson to Rosenne, 18 May 1949 (n 54).
[67] Ch 3.
[68] Gordon to Rosenne, 14 June 1949, FM-2010/17, ISA; Abtahi and Webb (n 13) 1112.
[69] Gordon to Rosenne, 14 June 1949 (n 68).

Rosenne, frequently opposed to basing foreign policy decisions on sentiment, morality, or symbolism,[70] would have answered Robinson's rhetorical question differently. Unlike Gordon, he thought that Israel could delay not only ratification but also signature. Requesting the Justice Ministry's comments on Robinson's memorandum, he emphasized that the MFA 'has not yet taken a position on the problem'.[71] But he was operating within constraints. Eban, in New York, was pushing for progress: 'I earnestly hope that the necessary procedures and formalities can be accomplished before the forthcoming session of the General Assembly', he wrote to Rosenne, '[i]n view of our special relation to the genocide problem'. He asked Rosenne to confer with Robinson.[72]

Rosenne was fast becoming a minority of one. A consensus that Israel should at least sign the Convention was emerging between the New York mission (Eban and Robinson) and, at home, the IOD (Gordon) and the Ministry of Justice.[73] Most would avoid ratification, at least for some time. After being reminded by Gordon of the impending time limit,[74] and conferring with Eban, Rosenne reluctantly agreed to have the Convention signed. He preferred, still, not to make that recommendation himself. Instead, he proposed that Gordon 'recommend to the Foreign Minister that we sign the Convention at the earliest possible, but that our signature would be subject to ratification'.[75] He also reported that Eban agreed to that procedure.

Gordon, however, reminded Rosenne that under a recently distributed circular, 'it seems to me that preparing the Convention for signature is within the purview of your department'.[76] Rosenne relented; he reported to Sharett the agreement of 'Mr. Eban, Dr. Robinson, Dr. Gordon, and the Ministry of Justice' and proposed that the Minister 'issue instructions to Eban to sign the [Genocide] Convention at the earliest possible'—but subject to subsequent ratification. He left it for Sharett to decide whether he wanted to obtain a government decision before issuing such instructions. He did not elaborate on the reasons why Israel ought to sign the Convention.[77] Having been instructed by Sharett to submit the matter to the government, Rosenne informed the Cabinet Secretary that 'there will be no need to expedite *Knesset*' action.[78] Legislative action would only be required if the

[70] Discussing Israel's possible joining the International Refugee Organization, Rosenne declared that 'our policy matters must not be influenced by symbolic considerations': Report on Consultation with the Foreign Minister, 17 June 1949, FM-1976/9; Rosenne to Eytan, 10 August 1950, FM-5850/2; Rosenne to Robinson, 18 September 1950, FM-1820/6, ISA.

[71] Rosenne to Ministry of Justice, 9 June 1949, FM-1840/1, ISA.

[72] Eban to Rosenne, 14 June 1949 (n 57).

[73] Director to Rosenne, 10 July 1949, FM-1840/1, ISA (Justice Ministry will 'very much welcome' Israel joining the Convention).

[74] Gordon to Rosenne, 14 July 1949, FM-1840/1, ISA.

[75] Rosenne to Gordon, 17 July 1949, FM-1840/1, ISA.

[76] Gordon to Rosenne, 19 July 1949, FM-1840/1, ISA.

[77] Rosenne to Sharett, 25 July 1949, FM-1840/1, ISA.

[78] Rosenne to Cabinet Secretary, 4 August 1949, FM-1840/1, ISA.

government intended to ratify the Genocide Convention. At that point, there was no such intention.

3.2 'The Pressure on Our Representatives at the UN ... Is Great'

Israel's signature was meant to be symbolic. It was not meant to pave the way for ratification, by which Israel would assume the Convention's obligations. There was, at this stage, no decision to ratify the Convention. No serious discussion of the Convention's merit had yet taken place; both Robinson and Gordon, in fact, had already expressed misgivings at the prospects of Israeli ratification. Rosenne's misgivings, though inarticulate, were patent in his reluctance. If the 'moral issue'—that is, the Jewish aspect of the Convention—played a part in the decision to sign the Convention, it was sufficient, at most, to produce a symbolic gesture devoid of legal consequence. '[O]ur special relation to the genocide problem', in Eban's words, could be invoked to justify the recommended signature, but it was not what drove the decision to sign the Genocide Convention.

Instead, signing the Convention was meant to promote concrete, second-order interests. Rosenne alluded to these when referring the matter to the Cabinet Secretary. Here, he first acknowledged the Convention's Jewish aspect, origins, and paternity—only to conflate these with the 'Israeli and moral side'. Second, he revealed that what really was at stake was Israel's UN position:

> There is no need for me to specifically emphasize the global Jewish interest in the a/m Convention born not only out of the atrocities visited upon our people in the Second World War. But also out of intentional initiative of Jewish personae and bodies after the war. *In addition to that Israeli and moral side it is to be noted that the pressure on our representatives at the UN to take a positive step in this matter is great.*[79]

The pressure was, indeed, great. What Robinson had been remiss to mention when first informing Rosenne of the matter—but became evident in the meantime—was how important it was for Israel's UN mission to conform to the expectations of the UN apparatus. The envoys of the newly admitted member could not resist, let alone ignore, the combined appeals of Evatt, Kerno, and the SG. Long before independence and admission, mission members knew how important it was to have the good will of the UN Secretariat and influential delegates of member states. This did not change with statehood or admission. A few days after admission, Sharett warned his closest advisers that '[o]ur position [in the] UN [is] still

[79] ibid; emphasis added.

fraught [with] enormous difficulties'.[80] Israel's envoys were also acutely aware of their debt to the UN for sanctioning, in 1947, partition and the establishment of a Jewish state in Palestine. Six months before admission, Sharett reminded the members of Israel's UN mission that 'we are a child of the UN and we wish to remain loyal to our paternity. This for us is not only a moral duty but also a political consideration. In this conflicted world, the only way for us is to take the path of the UN'.[81] Similar sentiment led Walter Eytan (1910–2001), the MFA's Director-General, to observe in June 1950 that Israel's non-alignment policy stemmed from its Jewish identity and placed the Jewish state in a position to pursue a uniquely Jewish vocation: 'to do something great and energetic in the campaign for world peace' at the impending GA session[82] (concretely, what the Munich-born former Oxford don, who spent the war years at Bletchley Park, proposed was that Israel 'prepare the ground for the election of an Israeli to the position' of UN SG).[83]

In addition, the barrage of demands for action on the Genocide Convention strongly appealed to the newly acquired sovereign sensibilities of Israel's envoys. If the need for good will, prior to independence and admission, was a marker of deficient status,[84] being called upon to repay the debt marked transformation to full sovereign capacity. Israel's early diplomats to the UN felt, and were told by others, that as representatives of the Jewish state they were particularly expected to contribute to world affairs.[85] This was the transformation Sharett had proclaimed in his maiden UN speech: 'from exclusion to membership' and 'from mere *passive* protest to *active* responsibility'.[86] Ideology, sovereignty, and membership imposed on the Jewish state a duty of participation in and contribution to UN work.[87]

[80] Sharett to Kohn, Shiloah, 15 May 1949, FM–2329/6, ISA.

[81] Meeting of Israel's Mission to the UN, 25 November 1948, FM–131/18, ISA.

[82] Eytan to Sharett, 5 September 1950, FM–2015/5; Eytan to Sharett, 26 June 1950, FM–1820/6, ISA ('opportunity for Israel . . . as a member of the UN . . . to make a great contribution to the efforts of world peace'); Eytan to Shiloah, 11 August 1949 in Yemima Rosenthal (ed), *Documents on the Foreign Policy of Israel*, vol 4 (ISA 1986) 316–19 ('a first-class chance at the forthcoming General Assembly to strike a truly sensational blow for world peace . . . Israel can take a leading part in this').

[83] Sinclair McKay, *The Secret Life of Bletchley Park: The WWII Codebreaking Centre and the Men and Women Who Worked There* (Penguin 2012).

[84] Ch 3.

[85] Record of Government Meetings, 24 May 1949, ISA (Sharett); Eytan to Shiloah, 11 August 1949 (n 82) ('Jacob Robinson once told me that we had no idea how great were the expectations which many U.N. circles had of our membership of the U.N.'); Abba Eban, *Personal Witness: Israel Through My Eyes* (Jonathan Cape 1993) 196. This argument was used to promote admission: documents in FM–72/16, ISA.

[86] Emphases in original; Speech to the General Assembly by Foreign Minister Sharett, (11 May 1949) in Meron Medzini (ed), *Israel's Foreign Relations: Selected Documents, 1947–1974* (MFA 1976) 119; GAOR, Plenary (11 May 1949) 332.

[87] Robinson, Report Fourth Session (n 49) ('Having knocked energetically at the doors of the United Nations, we cannot but be an active member . . . This was, in fact, expected from us by numerous delegations . . . on our admission. It would be a disappointment to the world if we would confine ourselves exclusively to our own interests'; he proceeded, however, to circumscribe the scope of 'active participation').

Eban's memoires cite, as 'evidence of our new stature' following UN admission, various attempts to enlist Israel's support to causes debated at the UN.[88] They include, however, not a single mention of the Genocide Convention, which he ceremoniously signed on 17 August 1949.[89] Israel's signature of the Genocide Convention was meant to demonstrate its good membership and bolster its diplomatic standing in the UN.[90] The Genocide Convention remained a Jewish concern and, as such, only a 'marginal problem' for Israel; but as a Jewish concern, it could be appropriated to denote Israel's now-sovereign status.[91]

Within the MFA, the force driving Israeli signature and, later, ratification was the UN mission. Eban, the Permanent Representative to the UN (who in 1950 became also Israel's US ambassador), time and again demanded immediate action and results.[92] After signing the Genocide Convention, Eban proposed to proceed to have it ratified.[93] When Sharett or the Director-General sought to hasten matters, it was at Eban's behest or as a result of his pressure.[94] And that pressure, within the Ministry, focused on Rosenne, who had to repeatedly impress on the 'notoriously slow' Justice Ministry[95] that the MFA 'attaches much importance' to expediting the process.[96] When the *Knesset* first discussed the proposed bill, five days remained for Israel to become one of the original signatories. Even then, Eban tried to get the Attorney-General to expedite the *Knesset*'s work.[97]

3.3 Ratification 'As a Means of Propaganda'

Before Eban signed the Genocide Convention, Sharett brought the matter to the government. He opened 'with two formal matters'—a decision required on joining two 'UN Treaties': the 1946 Convention on the Privileges and Immunities of the UN[98]—and the Genocide Convention:

[88] Eban, *Witness* (n 85) 196 (the day after admission, '[i]nstead of haunting the halls and lounges of the General Assembly, seeking votes ... I suddenly found myself ... being solicited for votes in the service of other interests'); Abba Eban, *An Autobiography* (Random 1977) 144–5. Sharett made a similar report to the government: Record of Government Meetings, 24 May 1949 (n 85).

[89] Eban, *Witness* (n 85); Eban, *Autobiography* (n 88).

[90] Ch 3 discusses the ideological aspect of good UN membership.

[91] Radio Address by Arthur Lourie, 6 March 1950, FM–75/7, ISA.

[92] Eban to Rosenne, 14 June 1949 (n 57).

[93] Eban to Sharett, 26 August 1949, FM–1840/1, ISA.

[94] Sharett to Eytan and Rosenne, 2 December 1949, FM–2010/17 ('most important Knesset should immediately ratify genocide'); Eytan to Rosenne, 29 August 1949, 20 September 1949, FM–1840/1, ISA; ('please write to Mr. Eban and explain to him where things stand').

[95] Eytan to Rosenne, 12 September 1949, 29 August 1949, 8 September 1949; Rosenne to Eytan, 9 September 1949 ('there's no reason why it should not be done quickly'); Eytan to Rosenne, 19 September 1949, 20 September 1949; Rosenne to Eytan, [n.d.], FM–1840/1, ISA.

[96] Rosenne to Attorney-General, 18 September 1949, FM–1840/1, ISA.

[97] Subcommittee Protocol 5/2, 31 January 1950, K–26/6, ISA.

[98] 33 UNTS 261.

> First of all there is a treaty on something called 'genocide' – the destruction of a race. This is a direct outcome of the Jewish Holocaust in Europe, and it is an idea of a Jewish man, whose name is Lenkin [sic] who for the sake of Heaven ... obtained that it will be considered a crime if someone is exiled or deported for his belonging to some racial group. I assume we are joining this treaty.[99]

No further details were provided. No questions were asked. No discussion followed.[100] If members of the government took any interest, none was recorded. They proceeded to resolve, without ado, to 'join' the Genocide Convention. Next, Sharett empowered Eban to sign the Convention;[101] Eban did so on 17 August 1949.[102] A photograph was taken to record the occasion.[103] Israel became the twenty-eighth signatory.

Signature, however, was not enough for Eban. Soon he cabled Sharett: '[a]fter signature Genocide suggest *early* ratification'.[104] If Israel was to display good UN membership, swift action would be required—and a greater symbolic gesture than mere signature. Eytan, the Director-General, proceeded to instruct Rosenne 'to deal with the matter [of ratification] and expedite it'. Eytan also asked '[w]hether ratification must be given by the government or the *Knesset*'.[105] Rosenne had already asked himself—and others—the same question. Referring the matter to the Cabinet Secretary, he had proposed that the government decide to 'join' the Convention 'subject to [subsequent] approval by the *Knesset*'. He assumed that 'for Israel to join the treaty requires approval by the Knesset'.[106] Having been instructed by Eytan to affect ratification, he now wrote to the Attorney-General. Eban proposed, he wrote, ratification 'as soon as possible'. Rosenne reported, somewhat grudgingly, that 'this contradicts our previous decision ... that there will be no need to expedite the Knesset approval. It appears that circumstances changed and this is why the Ministry of Foreign Affairs is interested in finishing this affair soon.' He asked the Attorney-General to have the matter placed on the *Knesset*'s agenda after recess—assuming 'of course ... that you agree that the a/m Convention requires approval by the *Knesset* and not only by the government'.[107]

[99] Record of Government Meetings, 9 August 1949, ISA. Sharett did not elaborate whether 'joining' meant signature or ratification. At the time, there was no Hebrew term for ratification.

[100] ibid. Prime Minister Ben-Gurion raised one question on the UN immunities Convention. The discussion of the Genocide Convention covers less than half a page; it is the shortest item in the record of the entire meeting, covering nine agenda items in seventy-four pages.

[101] Sharett to Eban, 12 August 1949, FM–2416/12, ISA.

[102] UN Doc.C.N.101.1949. Treaties, 23 August 1949, FM–1840/1, ISA.

[103] PH–0028 P–03840 107, Abba Eban Archive, Harry S Truman Research Institute for the Advancement of Peace, Hebrew University of Jerusalem.

[104] Emphasis added; Eban to Sharett, 26 August 1949 (n 93).

[105] Eytan to Rosenne, 29 August 1949 (n 94).

[106] Rosenne to Cabinet Secretary, 4 August 1949 (n 78); Cabinet Secretary to Attorney-General, 16 August 1949, FM–1840/1, G–5576/4, ISA.

[107] Rosenne to Attorney-General, 30 August 1949, FM–1840/1, ISA.

It was Rosenne, then, who first proposed to involve the *Knesset*. What he meant by *Knesset* 'approval' was, however, limited to Israel's parliament adopting the legislation necessary to implement the Convention domestically before the government would assume its obligations internationally. Article V of the Convention required, as Robinson had already drawn Rosenne's attention to,[108] 'Contracting Parties' to pass 'the necessary legislation to give effect' to its provisions.[109] Under the dualist British constitutional position, international treaties had no domestic effect without internal implementing legislation; under British constitutional practice, the government abstained from assuming treaty obligations through ratification before securing the enactment of the necessary legislation in parliament. There had been, however, no Israeli precedent on these matters. Rosenne, trained in English law, assumed that the legal position in Israel would follow the English position.[110] When Eytan asked him '[w]hy does the Knesset need approve the Convention? Is government approval not sufficient?', Rosenne replied: 'I think not, since the Convention requires enactment of laws for its full execution'.[111]

That the *Knesset* should become involved had, for Rosenne, nothing to do with the subject-matter of the Genocide Convention or its Jewish aspect. It was, rather, a constitutional question of separation of powers. Rosenne was seeking to ensure that the executive branch did not make law and, even more so, that the legislature did not engage in the conduct of foreign relations. *Knesset* involvement was required only 'to implement [the Convention] internally'.[112] He had proposed that the government *first* decide to sign the Convention 'subject to approval by the *Knesset*' in the form of implementing legislation.[113] Thus, the government referred to the *Knesset* not a motion to ratify the Convention, but rather a bill for a first reading as per regular legislative procedure.[114] Justice Minister Rosen told the *Knesset*, accordingly, that the government will only ratify the Convention after the legislature passed the necessary law.[115]

Whatever were Rosenne's intentions, the *Knesset* had its own. The debate on the bill turned to the Genocide Convention itself, and then to the constitutional question of treaty powers. The drama that unfolded, Rosenne's radical reaction, and the imprint that both left on Israel's constitutional history, however, go beyond

[108] Robinson to Rosenne, 18 May 1949 (n 54).
[109] Genocide Convention (n 1) 280.
[110] Rosenne to Eban, 21 September 1949, FM–67/5, ISA.
[111] Eytan to Rosenne, 19 September 1949 (n 95); Rosenne to Eytan, [n.d.] (n 95).
[112] Rosenne to Cabinet Secretary, 4 August 1949 (n 78).
[113] Rosenne to Gordon, 17 July 1949 (n 75); Rosenne to Sharett, 25 July 1949 (n 77).
[114] Cabinet Secretary to Attorney-General, 16 August 1949 (n 106); Wilkenfeldt to Prime Minister Office, 6 December 1949; Cabinet Secretary to *Knesset* Speaker, 6 December 1949, G–5576/4, ISA; 27 Bills of the State of Israel 37 (14 December 1949) (Hebrew).
[115] Rosen (n 2) 315, 323; Tomer Broude and Gilad Noam, 'Parliamentary Involvement in Treaty-Making Processes: Understanding the Knesset's Past Record and Its Future Potential' (2008) 9 L & Business 175 (Hebrew).

the scope of this book. What transpired, in a nutshell, was that the government, to avoid delays, proposed a compromise formula that allowed the *Knesset* to claim that, in this case, it had been involved in the decision to ratify the Genocide Convention. The *Knesset* unanimously passed a resolution adopting that formula on 28 December 1949,[116] and proceeded to consider the bill at its leisure. It finally passed, three months later, 'The Crime of Genocide (Prevention and Punishment) Law'.[117]

Rosenne was incensed with what he considered *Knesset* encroachment on executive power. He protested to the Justice Minister that he had found it 'hard to agree with how the matter was handled'.[118] He pronounced the *Knesset* resolution devoid of legal effect: the 'Knesset', he admonished, 'better learn from this experience how to distinguish its legal powers and political powers'.[119] He denied that that resolution 'compels the government to ratify' the Genocide Convention,[120] and informed the Attorney-General that in future cases, he would act on his own interpretation of the constitutional position.[121] In the present instance, however, the MFA's priorities forced him to let the matter rest: 'I found out from New York and Washington that the deposit of our note of ratification is very important'.[122] In early 1951, however, he found the occasion to set the record straight. When the UN Secretariat requested information on 'national laws and practices in the matter of the conclusion of treaties', Rosenne seized the opportunity to respond in a manner that deprived the *Knesset* resolution of any precedential effect. He shrewdly placed on public record, in a UN document, his own interpretation of the constitutional position as a representation of the government's views.[123]

[116] Rosen (n 2) 345; the resolution declared that 'ratification shall be made ... and the instrument of ratification shall be deposited': Resolution, 28 December 1949, G-5660/26, ISA.

[117] (1949–1950) 4 Laws of the State of Israel 101 (29 March 1950).

[118] Rosenne to Justice Minister, 22 February 1950, G-5755/6, ISA.

[119] Rosenne to Attorney-General, 23 March 1950, 11 January 1950, G-5755/6, ISA.

[120] Attorney-General to Rosenne, 1, 19 March 1950, G-5755/6, ISA.

[121] Rosenne to Attorney-General, 23 March 1950 (n 119) ('I in any case need to direct my advice to the Ministry of Foreign Affairs according to how I perceive the law to be'). Rosenne's position vis-à-vis the Attorney-General had already been the cause of some contention: Rosenne to Sharett, 17 August 1948, FM-2379/1, Rosen to Sharett, 20 February 1950, Rosenne to Sharett, 1 March 1950, Sharett to Rosen, 5 March 1950, FM-2379/16, ISA. His claim to independence, as well as his attitude towards and critique of the Justice Ministry, drew the ire of Justice Minister Rosen, who protested to Sharett that despite Rosenne's expertise in a limited area of the law, he is 'willing to forgive his insolence provided it does not exceed certain limits. For he is young and when I was his age, I too exaggerated my own qualities and talents. He too will learn he is no genius and perhaps will understand after a while that as a jurist he can hardly hold a candle to [Attorney-General] Haim Cohn': quoted in Ruth Bondy, *Felix: Pinchas Rosen and His Time* (Zmora-Bitan 1990) 439 (Hebrew).

[122] Rosenne to Justice Minister, 22 February 1950 (n 118).

[123] 'Memorandum of 11 March 1951 from the Government of Israel' in *Laws and Practices Concerning the Conclusion of Treaties* (1953) UN Legislative Series iii, 67 (ST/LEG/SER.B/3 December 1952); this was preceded by Shabtai Rosenne, 'International Law and the Municipal Law of the State of Israel' (1950) 7 HaPraklit 258 (Hebrew) written while the implementing bill was being discussed at the *Knesset*.

Rosenne had not, however, entirely relented.[124] Israel's instrument of ratification, signed by Sharett, alluded to the *Knesset* decision 'that the Convention should be ratified', but declared that 'the government confirms and ratifies' the Convention.[125] This gave some credence to Rosenne's position that the *Knesset* lacked the power it purported to exercise. The instrument, at any rate, was deposited with the UN SG on 9 March 1950,[126] with the requisite accompanying public relations exercise: another ceremony was held, pictures were taken, UN press release issued, and Arthur Lourie delivered a radio address broadcast 'on the United Nations program'.[127]

From the MFA's perspective, then, Israel signed and ratified the Genocide Convention—and adopted the requisite legislation—in order to gain, first and foremost, in reputation. All this was meant 'to serve as a means of propaganda', as one Member of *Knesset*—formerly an IJA researcher under Robinson—observed in committee.[128] This goal compelled, in turn, that Israel's actions be seen. Rosenne asked the Justice Ministry to produce an urgent English translation of the law.[129] He would later circulate it to Israel's legations abroad and secured its publication by the UN.[130] The visibility exercise, apparently, was successful. A day after Israel's ratification was deposited, Lemkin wrote to Sharett to express his gratitude;[131] Robinson, later, sent Lemkin the translation of the law.[132] One Israeli representative spoke at a 'radio broadcast at the U.N. on the occasion of our ratification of the Convention'; Lemkin, who was mentioned, called to thank him.[133]

Ratification, however, seemed to have exhausted the MFA's interest—or, rather, instrumental disinterest—in the Genocide Convention. Its Jewish aspect could be invoked in order to bolster Israel's reputation vis-à-vis the UN, but it did not drive ratification, contrary to a commonly held belief.[134] If the Convention were to be

[124] Rosenne to Attorney-General, 11 January 1950 (n 119); Secretary to Justice Minister to Rosenne, 10 February 1950, G-5755/6, ISA.

[125] Instrument of Ratification, 16 February 1950, G-5755/6, ISA.

[126] Genocide Convention (n 1) 278; Tekoah to Ministry of Justice, 26 March 1950, G-5755/6, ISA.

[127] Lourie to Eytan, 10 March 1950; UN Press Release PM/1705, 9 March 1950, FM-2416/12, ISA

[128] Subcommittee Protocol 6/2, 15 February 1950, K-26/6, ISA ('when we send the law to our UN representatives, to serve as a means of propaganda'). On Zorach Warhaftig, see Assaf Likhovski, 'Peripheral Vision: Polish-Jewish Lawyers and Early Israeli Law' (2018) 36 Law & Hist Rev 235.

[129] Rosenne to Attorney-General, 31 March 1950, G-5755/6, ISA.

[130] Rosenne, Legal Brief No.13, 16 May 1950, FM-2416/12, ISA; Shabtai Rosenne, 'Human Rights in Israel' (1950) UN YB on Hum Rts 161, 2.

[131] Cooper (n 7) 184, quoting Lemkin to Sharett, 10 March 1950, Raphael Lemkin Papers (Manuscript Collection 60), A-1/15, AJA.

[132] Robinson to Lemkin, 5 June 1950, B1-F20, Raphael Lemkin papers, Manuscripts and Archives Division, The New York Public Library ('Lemkin Papers, NYPL').

[133] Lourie to Eytan, 22 March 1950, FM-2010/17, ISA.

[134] Eg Cooper (n 7) 183–5 ('Israel because of the annihilation of European Jewry during the War was one of the first states not only to ratify the Genocide Convention but to go a step further'). Cooper also argues that Lemkin's pressure on Israel, exerted through Jewish organizations, brought about Israel's ratification: all archival evidence points to the contrary. Michael Brecher, *The Foreign Policy System of Israel: Setting, Images, Process* (Yale UP 1972) 127; this seminal work on Israel's foreign policy mentions the Genocide Convention only in connection with the ratification constitutional debate, and suggests that a compromise was reached because of the 'special character' of that treaty; similarly, Broude and

noted in the memoires or biographies of those involved at all, it would be in connection with the *Knesset's* ratification imbroglio.[135] Following ratification, Israel took no further interest in the Convention itself. Nor did its envoys work on promoting its ratification by other states.[136] On the rare occasion that the possibility of Israel taking such a course of action was contemplated by an Israeli diplomat, Robinson and Rosenne recorded their vehement objection. In early 1951, Robinson wrote to Rosenne that 'I cannot see why we should become the lobbyist for the ratification of the Genocide Convention and why we should contact all these governments. We have sufficient troubles of our own.'[137] Later that month, Rosenne dismissed the notion that Israel's diplomats should 'do our best to get it ratified by the maximum number of countries'.[138] The Convention, for both, remained a Jewish matter and, as such, a 'marginal problem'; Israel's preparations for and work in future GA sessions maintained that attitude.[139]

4. The Reservations Case: Shabtai Rosenne Goes to The Hague

In November 1950, the GA requested the ICJ, the UN's 'principal judicial body', to render its advice on the validity of reservations to the Genocide Convention.[140] Framed in theoretical terms,[141] the question arose due to reservations entered mainly by Eastern bloc countries—and objections to such reservations expressed

Noam (n 115) 186ff. This, however, was not the quite the case. The (unsupportable) claim that Jewish concerns drove Israel's ratification was first made, albeit implicitly, public in a report by a Hebrew University 'study group', commissioned in 1952 by the Carnegie Endowment for International Peace, to look into public attitudes towards international organization. It was chaired by Nathan Feinberg; Rosenne was the rapportuer. Thus, the report continued his 'public relations' exercise: it asserted that Israel was 'especially concerned with the efficacy' of the Genocide Convention, as was 'stressed in the Knesseth debate on the ratification', owing to the Holocaust: Nathan Feinberg, *Israel and the United Nations: Report of a Study Group Set Up By the Hebrew University of Jerusalem* (Manhattan 1956) 174; it added that 'Israel ratified [the Genocide] Convention without reservation in 1950, and is one of the few states which has enacted domestic legislation in accordance therewith': ibid, 275. On the report and the decisive MFA role in determining its outlook: Rotem Giladi, 'At the Sovereign Turn: International Law at the Hebrew University Law Faculty Early Years' in Yfaat Weiss and Uzi Rebhun (eds), *The History of the Hebrew University in Jerusalem*, vol 5 (forthcoming Magnes 2021) (Hebrew).

[135] Eban, *Witness* (n 85); Eban, *Autobiography* (n 88); Bondy (n 121) (Rosen); Walter Eytan, *The First Ten Years: Diplomatic History of Israel* (Simon & Schuster 1958) do not mention the Genocide Convention; neither does Gabriel Sheffer, *Moshe Sharett: Biography of a Political Moderate* (Clarendon 1996); the only exception is Rosenne's 2009 Book Review: Rosenne (n 22).

[136] Feinberg, *Israel and the UN* (n 134) 174—drafted largely by Rosenne—asserts that 'opinion *in Israel* is disconcerted by the fact that the great powers have not as yet all ratified the the Convention'; emphasis added. MFA files record no such sentiment by Israel's officials.

[137] Robinson to Rosenne, 5 February 1951, FM-1840/2, ISA. Ch 5 provides further examples.

[138] Rosenne to Robinson, 28 February 1951, FM-1832/3, ISA.

[139] Robinson, Analysis of the Provisional Agenda, Fourth Session, [n.d.], FM-1820/8, ISA; Robinson, Report Fourth Session (n 49).

[140] UNGA Res.478 (16 November 1950).

[141] ICJ, *Reports* (1951) 21.

by others.[142] UN member states were allowed to express their position in written and oral form. The Court rendered its Advisory Opinion in May 1951.[143]

Ostensibly, this was an extension of Cold War political and ideological struggles. Advisory proceedings are not adversarial; nonetheless, in a sense the affair pitted the UK against the USSR. The reservations in question—and the objections thereto—concerned the 'compromissory clause' vesting the ICJ itself with the power to adjudicate interstate disputes arising under the Convention. Equally contentious, however, were reservations to the so-called 'colonial clause', limiting the Convention's application to the imperial metropole.[144]

In another sense, the proceedings could be seen as a plot, more-or-less coordinated, woven across Cold War division lines. British and Soviet hostility to the Convention, and obstructionism during its preparation, led Lemkin to believe that the British who had not even signed the Convention at the time 'were resorting to delaying tactics ... and trying to hold up the implementation of the convention'.[145] In his unfinished autobiography, Lemkin referred to the debate on reservations at the GA's Sixth Committee, which resulted in the ICJ referral, as 'the plan ... for the liquidation of the Genocide Convention',[146] implying that the British were behind it. The plot, if there was one, may have been directed at sabotaging US ratification—and may have contributed to that outcome.[147] For Israel, nonetheless, the World Court proceedings would come to represent an opportunity.

4.1 Israel's Written Statement

One opportunity was to make up for time lost, when more pressing foreign policy goals consumed *Yishuv* and Israeli diplomacy entirely. Here was a chance to take a late but significant role in the campaign for the Genocide Convention. This, however, was the road not taken by Israel: it was not even contemplated.[148] If there were

[142] Report of the SG, UN Doc.A/1372 (20 September 1950).

[143] ICJ, *Reports* (1951) 15. For historical analysis: Anton Weiss-Wendt, *The Soviet Union and the Gutting of the UN Genocide Convention* (University of Wisconsin Press 2017) 155–8; Alfred WB Simpson, 'Britain and the Genocide Convention' (2003) 73 Brit YB Intl L 5. For legal analysis, Schabas (n 13) 521–5; Manley O Hudson, 'The Twenty-Ninth Year of the World Court' (1951) 45 AJIL 1; Manley O Hudson, 'The Thirtieth Year of the World Court' (1952) 46 AJIL 1; Lawrence J Leblanc, 'The ICJ, the Genocide Convention, and the United States' (1987) 6 Wisconsin Intl LJ 43; Lord McNair, *The Law of Treaties* (Clarendon 1961) 163–8; Gerald Fitzmaurice, 'Reservations to Multilateral Treaties' (1953) 2 ICLQ 1.

[144] Absent notifications extending application to overseas possessions: objections by Australia and Ecuador in UN, *Multilateral Treaties Deposited with the Secretary-General* Ch IV.1, 5–6.

[145] Cooper (n 7) 216, 104, citing Lemkin to Gertrude Samuels, 12 January 1948, Lemkin Collection, P-154, Box 1/19, American Jewish Historical Society ('AJHS').

[146] Frieze (n 57) 214; Mira L Siegelberg, 'Unofficial Men, Efficient Civil Servants: Raphael Lemkin in the History of International Law' (2013) 15 J of Genocide Research 297, 315ff.

[147] Cooper (n 7) 202–3.

[148] Compare Rosenne (n 22).

opportunities in going to The Hague, these concerned the international standing and reputation of the new state—and of its representatives. The advisory proceedings, the Convention on which they turned, and its Jewish aspect were all harnessed to these ends.

Now that Israel was a UN member, Robinson and Rosenne were familiar with the Assembly debate that led to the referral to the Court. It was decided early that given potential political complications, as Rosenne suggested, 'we should remain silent'.[149] There were apprehensions, soon dispelled, that the matter might have East–West implications of the type Israel was trying to avoid in its early UN days.[150] Accordingly, Israel's involvement in the debate was scant, technical, even fastidious.[151] At first, Israel viewed the matter with apprehensive disinterest.

On 25 November 1950, the Court's Registrar formally notified Israel of the request for an advisory opinion. A week later, the MFA received the invitation to make a written submission by 20 January 1951. Time was short. Rosenne, leaning heavily on Robinson's experience, hurriedly prepared Israel's written statement.[152] Robinson chastised his younger colleague: 'a considerable portion of the [first] draft is irrelevant to the questions' before the Court, so much that 'irrelevant matters are dealt with in great detail, while the main problem ... is treated on 4 out of 42 pages'.[153]

By and by, Robinson and Rosenne became acquainted with the Convention, its provisions, and legislative history. They exchanged drafts and comments, engaging in a private, learned discourse of their own.[154] They debated theory and practice on the effects of reservations and objections. They discussed 'the proper formulation of the document' to be submitted by Israel.[155] They contemplated the 'understandings' proposed by the US Senate Foreign Relations Sub-Committee. They compiled pertinent literature. They did not hesitate to criticize the drafters for technical omissions leading to the present entanglement.[156] And the two

[149] Rosenne to Robinson, 15 September 1950, FM–1832/3 ('let the matter go by default and give no reaction ourselves to the Soviet Note'). Kerno to Sharett, 15 March 1950; Robinson to Gordon, 22 March 1950; Robinson to Rosenne, 5 May 1950; Rosenne to Robinson, 21 May 1950; Robinson to Rosenne, 1 June 1950; Rosenne to Robinson, 6 June 1950; Robinson to Rosenne, 26 June 1950, FM–1840/2, ISA.

[150] Rotem Giladi, 'Negotiating Identity: Israel, Apartheid, and the United Nations 1949–1952' (2017) 132 (No.559) English Hist Rev 1440.

[151] GAOR, Sixth Committee (10 October 1950) 46, (18 October 1950), 79–80. At first averse, Israel eventually voted for referral to the Court. It did not participate in the Plenary debate, nor explain its vote on the referring resolution: GAOR, Plenary (21 September 1950) 35–52, (16 November 1950) 384–8. For Israel's disinterest: Rosenne to Eytan, 31 August 1950, FM–1820/6; Robinson, Reservations to Multilateral Conventions, 19 December 1950, FM–1820/7, ISA.

[152] Robinson to Rosenne, 19 December 1950, FM–1832/3; Observations on S.R.'s Paper Regarding Reservations to the Convention on the Prevention and Punishment of the Crime of Genocide [n.d. *circa* December 1950], FM–1832/3, ISA, probably written by Tekoah, Rosenne's deputy.

[153] Robinson to Rosenne, 19 December 1950 (n 152), 6 February 1951, FM–1832/3, ISA (revised text 'much better than the original draft').

[154] Robinson to Rosenne, 19 December 1950 (n 152); Rosenne to Robinson, 22 December 1950, FM–1832/3, ISA.

[155] Robinson to Rosenne, 19 December 1950 (n 152).

[156] ibid; that is, the failure to list or define the contracting parties.

did allude to the 'purpose of the Convention' and speculated, in abstract terms, whether it could be 'destroyed' by this or that type of reservation.[157] Notably, they attached no particular significance to that purpose. They did not address a special role that the Jewish state, as such, was to play in the proceedings or with regard to the Convention. If any Jewish concerns animated their work, they were silent about these.

This, however, was no private exercise. Rosenne submitted Israel's written statement to the Court, on 14 January 1951, only after obtaining the approval of the Ministry's Director-General.[158] He also notified Hambro, the Court Registrar: 'I am further instructed to add that, as at present advised and subject, of course, to the wishes of the Court, it is not the intention of the Government to make an Oral Statement in this case'.[159] Israel's interest in the proceedings was, at first, limited.[160] Learning the ways of the Court—how many copies to submit, ought these be signed or unsigned, etc—was at a premium.[161] In a personal letter to the Hambro, Rosenne confided: this was 'the first occasion upon which I have had anything to do with a case actually pending before the [ICJ]'; he sought to verify that Israel's written statement was 'properly prepared'.[162] This was one new relationship he would from now on carefully cultivate.[163] There were old relationships to maintain: he sent Hersch Lauterpacht a copy of Israel's written submission.[164] He also asked Robinson to send another to Lemkin. Robinson, unenthusiastically, obliged.[165]

Israel's written statement covered twenty pages.[166] It was a highly technical, learned treatise laden with theory and citations. It made dull and dense reading. The statement briefly discussed the case history and noted significant dates. It alluded to 'certain reservations' made by unnamed 'several states'.[167] It mapped pertinent UN reports, cited scholarship, and relied on legal precedents. It interpreted phrases in the referring Assembly resolution, Convention clauses, Charter provisions, and articles of the Court's Statute. It classified categories of 'contracting

[157] ibid.

[158] Rosenne to Hambro, and handwritten draft, 14 January 1951; Rosenne to The Hague Legation, 14 January 1951; another copy he sent to the Attorney-General, who read it 'most carefully': Cohn to Rosenne, 23 January 1951, FM-1832/3, ISA.

[159] Rosenne to Hambro, and handwritten draft, 14 January 1951 (n 158).

[160] Later Rosenne wrote that if, following written statements by other governments, 'we will need to add oral arguments', this could be achieved 'without unnecessary expenditure' by appointing one of Israel's diplomats at Brussels, a licensed attorney: Rosenne to Robinson, 2 February 1951, FM-1832/3, ISA.

[161] Rosenne to Hambro, 15 January 1951; Rosenne to Robinson, 2 February 1951, FM-1832/3, ISA.

[162] Rosenne to Hambro, 15 January 1951 (n 161).

[163] Rosenne to The Hague Legation, 18 March 1951; Hague Legation to Rosenne, 30 March 1951, FM-1832/3; Rosenne to Tekoah, 5 April 1951, FM-1832/4, ISA (meeting with Hambro).

[164] Lauterpacht to Rosenne, 5 February 1951, FM-1832/3, ISA (a 'useful' and 'closely reasoned' argument; 'it was very fitting that you should submit a statement in this particular case').

[165] Robinson to Lemkin, 6 February 1950, P-154, Box 2-4, Lemkin Collection, AJHS; Robinson to Rosenne, 6 February 1951 (n 153).

[166] ICJ, *Pleadings, Oral Arguments, Documents* (1951) 195.

[167] ibid, 197.

parties' and analysed their perfect and inchoate interests. It distinguished the 'normative' from 'contractual' and 'ministerial' stipulations of the Genocide Convention.[168] It delved into the theory that reservations are contractual in nature, proposing that they would 'prima facie' be 'out of place when proposed in relation to normative … stipulations', but more apt in relation to the Convention's contractual obligations.[169] It examined various scenarios and their impact on making objections to reservations, and offered sophisticated answers to the questions put to the Court.

In all of this, not a word was written on Israel's particular interest in the Genocide Convention. The Jewish people, or the recent genocide perpetrated against Jews, likewise had no presence in the text. The statement did not mention Lemkin—or invoked the Convention's Jewish origins. Even a universal moral imperative represented by the Genocide Convention was not alluded to. Later, Robinson and Rosenne would come to regret some of the choices made: Robinson thought the statement was too 'abstract' in not drawing conclusions specific to the Genocide Convention. Rosenne, in hindsight, thought it was 'too categorical' (it was not) and suffering from 'jerkiness' that obscured its many points (which it did). 'Today I am sorry', he confessed some time later, that at first he had thought appending the full text of the Convention would be 'facetious and a waste of paper'.[170] No other written submission had included that text.

4.2 A 'Student's Moot'

In February 1951, the Registrar notified Israel of other written statements submitted to the Court—and that 'hearings for the submission of oral statements' had been fixed for 10 April. Hambro also enquired whether Israel intended to make an oral statement, and requested the name of its designated representative by 2 April.[171] The day after, Rosenne wrote to tell Robinson that he did not think 'it would be necessary to make an oral statement … simply because the British insist on their doctrine. After all we have said what we wanted to say, and there is little further we could do'. Rosenne added that, nonetheless, the written submissions by other governments would have to be read 'with an open mind'.[172] After these were received,[173] Rosenne started changing course.

[168] ibid, 201.
[169] ibid, 202–3.
[170] Robinson to Rosenne, 19 December 1950 (n 152); Rosenne to Robinson, 28 February 1951 (n 138).
[171] Hambro to Sharett, 14 February 1951, FM-1832/3, ISA.
[172] Rosenne to Robinson, 15 February 1951, FM-1832/3, ISA.
[173] Hambro to Sharett, 16 February 1951, FM-1832/3, ISA.

Rosenne now informed Robinson that only the UK and the Secretariat 'already indicated their intention' to make oral statements, with France 'still undecided'. 'Under these circumstances', he wrote, 'it behooves us to consider, as a matter of some urgency, if we intend to make an Oral Statement'.[174] In a long memorandum to Robinson, Rosenne offered his thoughts on the matter.

First, Rosenne categorized all written statements submitted to the Court—other than the 'virtually unintelligible and uncategorisable statement submitted by our cousins and neighbours on the other side of Jordan'.[175] He identified four groups: first, the 'descriptive' statements submitted by international organizations and one government (Netherlands) that specialized in the role of depositary to multilateral treaties. Here, Rosenne lamented that the contribution of the UN SG was 'inadequate and not up to the standard set' on previous occasions.[176] The SG, he thought, failed to provide 'an objective summary' of GA debate; nor did he furnish 'a full account of the drafting of the Genocide Convention itself'. Without these, how could the Court address the 'fundamental characteristics of the Genocide Convention'?[177]

Next, Rosenne noted three non-descriptive groups of written statements. One, 'proposed with vehemence' by the USSR and the Eastern bloc, advanced the sovereignty theory. This argued that no state had the right to object to any reservation. Another group included 'the United States and Israel'.[178] Here, as elsewhere, he compared Israel's statement to others favourably: '[t]hese stand for a midway sort of attitude which recognises the right of states to make reservations as well as the right of other states to make objections thereto, and attempt to synthesise between these two antagonistic rights'.[179] He disagreed with 'much in the American statement'. This was, however, 'of no importance in view of the fact that actually the American view is even more universal and liberal than our own'.[180] The last category comprised of the UK, 'standing in splendid isolation. In a statement of extreme suavity they put forward the extreme position based upon overemphasis of the role of consent'. The British position, essentially, consecrated the right of states to object to reservations—at the expense of the Convention's universality.[181]

Rosenne's memorandum now embarked on a winding path leading to an answer to the question originally posited: should Israel make an oral statement at The Hague? The answer *seemed* negative. And yet, each time Rosenne pointed in this direction, he immediately added a qualification. Thus, the written statements submitted to the Court, 'for all their partisan approach, and, generally speaking, lack

174 Rosenne to Robinson, 28 February 1951 (n 138).
175 ibid.
176 ibid.
177 ibid.
178 ibid.
179 ibid. Rosenne to Sharett, 18 March 1951, FM–1832/3, ISA (Israel's position 'very middling').
180 Rosenne to Robinson, 28 February 1951 (n 138).
181 ibid.

of doctrinal analysis', did 'cover the main ground'. Three points, nonetheless, could 'usefully be developed in far greater detail'. The first, and main, point consisted of the lack of '[a] complete and thorough analysis of the Genocide Convention itself, including a full analysis' of the preparatory work[182]—knowledge of which he had only recently acquired.

Rosenne added more reasons militating against Israel making an oral statement at the Court. First were economy, cost-effectiveness, and disinterest: from 'a utilitarian point of view, keeping in mind our throttling foreign exchange difficulties ... the conclusion must be that there is little we could add ... that would justify the expenditure of time and money'.[183] There could be one exception, however. It was the task of the UN Secretariat, Rosenne believed, to offer the Court 'a thorough analysis of the Genocide Convention'; and it may have been the task of the Jewish state to step in where the Secretariat failed:

> As they have not yet done it[,] it may be that we owe it to those, who moved by our own suffering in the War, brought about the Genocide Convention, to do our best to get it ratified by the maximum number of countries, even though the practical value in the event of another world war would be negligible.[184]

Rosenne, notably, offered a tribute neither to the victims of 'our own suffering' nor to Lemkin or the Jewish organizations engaged in advocacy for the Genocide Convention. Instead, he only acknowledged a debt to 'those, who *moved* by our own suffering in the War, brought about the Genocide Convention'[185]—namely, other nations. This seems odd. Nor was Rosenne proposing to embark on a campaign for universal ratification:[186] only to, at most, try to influence the Court to produce an advisory opinion that would not close the door on universality. For him, the question before the Court became 'academic' once the UN Secretariat had garnered the twenty ratifications, unencumbered by reservations and objections, necessary to have the Convention enter into force.[187] Israel's debt, if any, stretched only so far. Notably, Rosenne did not put much store in the universal ratification of the Convention—or in the Convention itself. Whether out of his assessment of the slim prospects of another World War, another genocide directed against Jews, or the power of law to stop atrocity, he saw in the Convention little 'practical value'.

[182] ibid; the other points concerned the distinction between the Convention's 'normative' and 'contractual' parts; and a fuller analysis of the phrase 'High Contracting Party' and the entry into force provision. Rosenne thought it was not 'necessary to say anything more about the jurisdiction of the Court', though he had things to say in that respect.

[183] ibid.

[184] ibid.

[185] ibid; emphasis added.

[186] That month, the question of Israel's involvement in such a campaign was raised; Robinson's opposition is noted above (n 137).

[187] Rosenne insisted that the question became 'academic': Rosenne to Sharett, 18 March 1951 (n 179); Rosenne to Robinson, 21 March 1951, FM-1832/3, ISA.

Later, we shall return to Rosenne's ambivalence—and low opinion of the Genocide Convention.[188] For now, this simply suggests that the justification for going to The Hague was not to be found in the Convention itself.

Next, Rosenne did identify 'weighty reasons which could justify the making of an Oral Statement'.[189] The two closely related reasons he provided were extraneous to the Convention. They were not about its import, but about benefits that may accrue from a Hague appearance:

> (a) It would be useful to obtain practical experience of work in the International Court, and as this is a case which does not excite violent political feelings, there are no political dangers inherent in this appearance. In this connexion it is important to bear in mind that our main differences are with the United Kingdom with whom our basic conception of law and its place in public life coincide.
>
> (b) Precisely because the political implications are so quiescent the proceedings in the Court can be regarded as a kind of 'student's moot'; so that if we have something to say—and I do not deny that we have—we ought to get up and say it.[190]

The proceedings, indeed, proved a 'student's moot', at low tuition fees, for Israel and for Rosenne.[191] Robinson, on his part, had already pleaded at the World Court as legal adviser for Lithuania's Foreign Ministry. Rosenne had no such experience. He had been seeking an opportunity to appear before the Court for some time. On each occasion, circumstances proved inopportune.[192] In time, Rosenne would be acclaimed as 'a leading academic authority on the Court'; his four-volume *magnum opus*[193] would be described as a 'landmark treatise' and 'an indispensable guide' to the Court, 'the first port of call for international lawyers and diplomats ... interested in the work of the principal judicial organ' of the UN. This is how the ICJ

[188] Discussed in ch 5. A few years later, Rosenne observed that the Genocide Convention was 'noted for its certain paleness'; 'there is room for great doubt if and to what extent this Convention is conclusive. Its disadvantages are many': Rosenne to UN Department, 26 January 1954, FM–2010/17, ISA.

[189] Rosenne to Robinson, 28 February 1951 (n 138).

[190] ibid.

[191] Rosenne, On the Advisory Opinion of the [ICJ] Concerning Reservations to the Genocide Convention, 13 June 1951, FM–1840/3, ISA ('Our participation ... was ... among other reasons, made with the object of gaining experience'). Israel would, a few years later, bring proceedings against Bulgaria over the shooting down of an Israeli commercial flight: ICJ, *Reports* (1959) 127.

[192] Israel could participate in advisory proceedings, following its admission, on three occasions. On all three, Rosenne had failed to convince Robinson, Eban, and Eytan that it should (Competence for Admission; Interpretation of Peace Treaties; Status of South West Africa): Robinson to Rosenne, 28 October 1949, Rosenne to Robinson, 20 November 1949, Gordon to Rosenne, 22 November 1949, FM–1822/6; Rosenne to Robinson, 30 December 1949, FM–2015/5; and various correspondence in FM–1822/8, ISA.

[193] Shabtai Rosenne, *The Law and Practice of the International Court 1920–2005* (4th edn, Martinus Nijhoff 2006).

President eulogized Rosenne in 2010, *during* proceedings, followed by a minute's silence.[194]

All this still lay in the future when Rosenne sought to offer additional, perhaps more concrete, justifications for a Hague appearance in the Reservations case. These, too, were extraneous to the Genocide Convention: 'we are of course very much interested in the problem of reservations because of our own reservations to the Geneva Conventions of 1949, and there is no doubt that this case will have an influence on the subject *in general*.'[195] Israel did have a stake in the case—or could be said to have one—after all.

Rosenne now reposed the question: '[d]oes our interest require us to go further and make our Oral Statement? On balance I feel that we should answer the question in the negative.' He was careful, still, to keep the door open. The next paragraph of his memorandum to Robinson read:

> Should it be decided—and I shall not put the matter up to higher authority here until receipt of your reply—that despite this view we should make an Oral Statement, I agree with you that the matter is too complicated to be left to Dr. Amir ... I assume therefore that you will be prepared to go to The Hague and make the statement.[196]

Rosenne immediately proceeded, however, on the assumption that Robinson—who knew of his interest in the Court—would cause him to change his mind. He admitted that preparing the written statement had taught him lessons that would 'not be lost *on me* if *I* have to make any further pleadings in the Supreme International Jurisdiction'.[197] He also outlined 'the work of preparing the statement', proposing that Robinson

> put in hand the preparations for the detailed analysis of the Genocide Convention. I am prepared immediately upon receipt of word from you to prepare the points dealing with the phrases 'High Contracting Parties' and 'the coming into force' provisions. I shall also correct one or two slight inaccuracies ... in our Written Statement.[198]

[194] President Owada (11 October 2010) https://www.icj-cij.org/public/files/case-related/124/124-20101011-ORA-01-00-BI.pdf. Malcolm N Shaw, 'Professor Shabtai Rosenne', http://legal.un.org/avl/pdf/ls/Rosenne_obituary.pdf accessed 20 January 2020 ('His writings on that Court, including a four-volume colossus, made him the foremost authority on its law and practice ... Rosenne was the accepted authority on the working of the Court').

[195] Emphasis added; Rosenne to Robinson, 28 February 1951 (n 138); Rosenne to Robinson, 10 December 1950, FM–1832/3, ISA; these concerned the use of the Red Shield of David as a protective emblem.

[196] Rosenne to Robinson, 28 February 1951 (n 138).

[197] ibid; emphases added.

[198] ibid.

In conclusion, Rosenne asked that Robinson cable him his views on: '(1) Do we make an Oral Statement? (2) Are you willing to appear? (3) Your ideas for the Oral Statement'.[199]

Was Rosenne really conflicted? For all his circumspection, he appears eager to have Israel participate in the proceedings. Did he simply avert risks, seeking to make sure that he could cite Robinson's support before raising the matter with 'higher authority here'—the Director-General or the Minister? Was he really that deferential to his much more experienced counterpart? Or was Rosenne, under a less generous reading, calculably relying on Robinson's greater sensitivity to Jewish affairs and, perhaps, on the aversion of the older, New York-based Robinson to the toll of transatlantic travel? Either way, Rosenne's attitude to the Genocide Convention was entirely instrumental. His interest in the ICJ proceedings was not related to 'our own suffering' but to Israel's UN position, its incidental legal and diplomatic interests, and his own professional development.

4.3 'We Have Done Our Duty'

Robinson did not read Rosenne's sophistries charitably: he refused to take the bait. He first cabled a succinct response on 9 March: 'Balance pros cons against oral statement except for two arguments page four which would warrant *your* appearance.'[200] These arguments, cited above, concerned 'practical experience' and 'student's moot'. But Robinson made no bones about the fact that these applied to Rosenne, not him: they would warrant 'your appearance', he wrote, not his own.

On the same day, Robinson composed a short letter to Rosenne elaborating on his reasons. Robinson would not fall into the moral duty trap: 'We have done our duty both as members of the International Community and as a State particularly interested in the Genocide Convention.' His conclusion was that there 'would therefore be hardly any justification for further action on our part except in a spirit of perfectionism'.[201] His last point was both conciliatory and rebuking: 'I fully agree with what you say on page 4 under (a) and (b) and would welcome if our Ministry would make it possible *for you* to go to the Hague. This is an experience which should be given *to any Legal Adviser* of a Foreign Office'.[202] The subtext could not be any clearer: Robinson already had been to The Hague. It was Rosenne who needed that experience, not him. If Rosenne wanted to go, Robinson would not stand in

[199] ibid.

[200] Emphasis added; Robinson to Rosenne, 9 March 1951, FM–1832/3, ISA.

[201] ibid, doubting an ICJ decision on the Genocide Convention would have 'some direct general implication'—that is, much bearing on Israel's reservations to the Geneva Conventions. While this undermined Rosenne's argument, time would prove Robinson wrong. The 'object and purpose' formula devised by the Court in the Reservations case would eventually emerge as the general yardstick for assessing reservations.

[202] ibid; emphases added.

his way. Neither would he, however, do Rosenne's job—obtaining the Ministry's approval—for him.

Rosenne got the message. Still, he tried to hoist the Jewish flag in order to get a firmer pledge of Robinson's support. He cabled Robinson: 'decided for oral statement [along] lines previously outlined also stressing Jewish aspect Genocide'. He asked Robinson to rush additional copies and materials and to write or cable his ideas for the oral statement he set out to deliver. He now acknowledged, for the first time, that Lemkin may have something to add: 'perhaps Lemkin also has viewpoint which we could express'. He concluded—was this a peace offering or one more bait?—by asking again: 'Are you willing [to] appear[?]'[203] Less than a month was left before the hearing.

Robinson refused to go: 'regret [but] no'. He advised Rosenne to lower the Jewish flag: 'Doubt appropriateness stressing Jewish aspect instead suggest emphasize [our] disinterested desire [to] create legal certainty [in this] particular field [of] interstate relations.' And he would not approach Lemkin on Rosenne's behalf: 'Doubtful Lemkin's usefulness [in] view [of] his absurd viewpoint [on the] Sec[retary]-Gen[eral's] practice [amounting to] granting USSR veto over [the] USA.' But these negatives were augmented by Robinson being 'confident [in] your success'; his promises to rush requested documents; and several points and precedents he offered for Rosenne's consideration.[204]

4.4 The 'Jewish Aspect': 'More Public Relations Than Actual Content'

Having procured the Minister's agreement,[205] Rosenne cabled Robinson: 'noted[.] Will go'. He asked for more materials and proposed lines of reasoning for Robinson's consideration. He reported that the 'whole [legal] department now engrossed [in] what must be [a] tremendous effort'. His cable to Robinson sought first, however, to clarify why he had proposed to stress the Jewish aspect of the Convention: 'Jewish aspect refers *more [to] public relations than [to] actual content*'.[206] Rosenne's attitude to the Convention now shifted to instrumental interest. From now on, he would focus on preparing his oral statement. The Jewish aspect would not be discussed again by the two; Rosenne now spent time and energy on substance and

[203] Rosenne to Robinson, 12 March 1951, FM–1832/3, ISA.

[204] Robinson to Rosenne, 14 March 1951, FM–1832/3, ISA; the context of Robinson's reference to Lemkin's position is not clear.

[205] Eytan to Hambro, 19 March 1951; Rosenne to General-Secretary, MFA, 15 March 1951; Rosenne informed the Attorney-General that 'The Foreign Minister has now decided we must participate in the oral proceedings ... and the lot fell upon myself to make an appearance there': Rosenne to Attorney-General, 18 March 1951, FM–1832/3, ISA.

[206] Emphasis added; Rosenne to Robinson, 15 March 1951, FM–1832/3, ISA.

logistics, eg whether it would be 'necessary wear legal gown bracket which dont want do unbracket'.[207]

Rosenne's instrumental interest in the Genocide Convention was expressed succinctly in a three-page brief he prepared for Minister Sharett. There, he enumerated the reasons for Israel's involvement in the proceedings: 'Since Israel has not yet appeared before the International Court, and since this affair stir no storms, and since it lacks almost entirely political factors ... and since we are also interested in the question of reservations *in general*, due to our reservations to the Red Cross Convention'.[208] He now added a new reason: 'since Israel is interested in the Genocide Convention even though it cannot be considered as universal salvation'.[209] I return to this ambivalence, and its ideological underpinnings, in the next chapter.

In anticipation of his Court appearance, Rosenne marshalled the resources he required at Israel's Hague legation. He sent Robinson sketches and drafts of the oral statement, asking for prompt comment and counsel. He tried to appease Robinson: 'I am really sorry that you cannot see your way to go to The Hague. It was due to you, after all you have done, to be the first to represent Israel there, leaving aside the fact that I have doubts about my own competence to do the job without the assistance of a more experienced leader'.[210] Robinson obliged him without rancour. He even went through the dossiers of his brother Nehemiah 'in his absence' to garner material for Rosenne.[211] Commenting on the draft, he coached Rosenne through Court practice and etiquette: 'the ideal of a pleading agent is to have his ideas accepted by the Court'. Robinson counselled the elimination of the superfluous, advocated precision, and warned Rosenne not to disturb 'the olympic serenity of the Court' by 'trying to commit its individual members to certain acts or views' expressed extra-judicially. He offered Rosenne nine pages worth of corrections, omissions, and emendations. Some were points of style, other of strategy or substance. Robinson rebuked Rosenne, however, for a sentence describing Lemkin as a person who '*claims* to have coined' the word 'genocide'. This was 'unfair to Lemkin ... There is no doubt about it'.[212] Robinson asked to see the next draft, and wished Rosenne 'complete success'.[213] His comments did not allude to the

[207] Rosenne to The Hague Legation, 15 March 1951; Levin to Rosenne, 16 March 1951 ('You may wear University or Barrister gown jacket or black suit'); Amir to Rosenne, 21 March 1951, FM–1832/3, ISA.

[208] Emphasis added; Rosenne to Sharett, 18 March 1951 (n 179).

[209] ibid, and his misgivings with the Conventions cited above (n 188). Ch 5 discusses the significance of this biblical reference.

[210] Rosenne to Robinson, 20 March 1951, FM–1832/3, ISA.

[211] Robinson to Rosenne, 21 March 1951, FM–1832/3, ISA.

[212] Emphasis added; Robinson to Rosenne, 26 March 1951, FM–1832/3, ISA. Robinson nonetheless doubted the utility of Lemkin's definition of genocide, which differed from the Convention's and that contained in UNGA Res.96(I) (n 7).

[213] ibid.

Convention's Jewish aspect; if he had any objection to Rosenne using it for public relations purposes, he kept them to himself.

Accompanied by a secretary, and having thanked Sharett for 'affording me the opportunity to be the first Israeli to appear before' the Court, Rosenne set to arrive at The Hague on 4 April 1951.[214] There, he met Hambro, Kerno, and the agents of other governments participating in the proceedings; with them, he was invited to meet the ICJ President.[215]

4.5 'Our Special Concern' in 'This ... Mostly Technical Question'

Rosenne appeared before the ICJ on 11 and 12 April 1951. He started with a reference—a stepping stone for the customary obeisance to the wisdom of the Court—to Maimonides, 'the great medieval Jewish sage, jurist and philosopher', who 'prescribed that on entering in the presence of men renowned for their knowledge one should praise the Almighty for having given of His wisdom to mortal men'.[216] Next, he expressed the appreciation of his government, 'a relative newcomer into the organised international Society', for the opportunity 'of participating in these proceedings before this august tribunal'.[217] The praise showered on the Court sitting at the Peace Palace concluded with a biblical reference, from Isaiah, alluding to the Court's own foundational ideology as an instrument of peace.[218] In a short paragraph, Rosenne bound together antiquity and modernity, pedigree and revival, the Jewish state and the World Court. There could be no question of whom he was representing—or who was speaking for Jewish interests.

The 'Jewish aspect' of the Convention also served a public relations function in Rosenne's statement at the Court. He proceeded to invoke 'our special concern for the efficacy of the Genocide Convention, because of the fact that so many Jews have so recently been victims of deliberate acts of genocide'.[219] This was new. It was not how he had grounded Israel's interest in the proceedings in internal MFA correspondence. But he also followed Robinson's proposal, asserting good UN membership as an additional reason why Israel elected to make this case the occasion of 'its first appearance before the Court': 'also to a large extent out of a disinterested desire

[214] Rosenne to Sharett, 4 April 1951, FM–2416/12; he also formulated a press release in advance: Rosenne to Levin, 2 April 1951; Rosenne to Arnon, 3 April 1951, FM–1832/4, ISA.

[215] Hambro to Rosenne, 6 April 1951; Rosenne to Robinson, 11 April 1951, FM–1832/4, ISA; the SG, France, and the UK made oral statements.

[216] ICJ, *Pleadings* (n 166) 328.

[217] ibid, 328.

[218] ibid. The day when 'nation shall not lift up sword against nation, neither shall they learn war any more' was hastened, Rosenne said, by the 'Court's contribution to the establishment of the rule of law of law among nations'. *Isaiah* 2:4 starts: 'And he shall judge among the nations, and shall rebuke many people'. For appraisal of ICJ ideology: Yuval Shany and Rotem Giladi, 'International Court of Justice' in Yuval Shany, *Assessing the Effectiveness of International Courts* (OUP 2014) 161.

[219] ICJ, *Pleadings* (n 166) 328.

to participate in the work of the Court in creating legal certainty in this particular field of international relations'.[220]

There was more. The first section of Rosenne's statement, covering twenty-nine pages of the record and two Court sessions, was dedicated to the Genocide Convention. Here Rosenne first focused on 'Genocide in the Second World War'. He concurred with the US written statement that 'practice of genocide has occurred throughout history';[221] but he set apart the twentieth century, which has 'witnessed some exceptionally revolting examples of it, more particularly during the Second World War, when the Nazis deliberately set about exterminating Jews, Russians, Poles, and members of other groups'.[222] He proceeded to remind the Court of the tally of the Jewish genocide,[223] and recalled the judicial determination that '[t]he persecution of the Jews at the hands of the Nazi Government has been proved in the greatest detail before the [Nuremberg] Tribunal'.[224] Here he tied together the Jewish Holocaust and the Convention: 'It is against this background of indescribable mass-suffering … that the problem of genocide was brought before the General Assembly.'[225] While this implied a measure of Jewish *ownership* of the Genocide Convention, lending moral authority to his own position as a representative of the Jewish state, Rosenne abstained from invoking the Convention's Jewish *authorship*: credit for the Convention he placed entirely in the universal:

> these exceptionally vile manifestations of man's inhumanity … reawakened *universal* interest and aroused *universal* concern in the problem. From this interest and concern were born the attempts to provide an adequate statement of the international legal norms of *universal* application defining the nature of the international crime, as well as to devise agreed means on its prevention and punishment. The very name 'genocide' itself dates from this modern period.[226]

Despite Robinson's rebuke, Rosenne would not acknowledge the author of 'the very name "genocide"' in the course of his Hague appearance.[227] Rather than credit

[220] ibid; Robinson to Rosenne, 14 March 1951 (n 204).

[221] ICJ, *Pleadings* (n 166) 329. This cohered with Lemkin's construction of genocide: Anson Rabinbach, 'The Challenge of the Unprecedented: Raphael Lemkin and the Concept of Genocide' (2005) 4 Simon Dubnow Institute YB 397, 409 ('a crime as old as history'), citing Lemkin Interview, [n.d.], MS-60, A-7/13, AJA.

[222] ICJ, *Pleadings* (n 166) 329.

[223] Robinson proposed using 'official [UN] sources for the numbers of exterminated Jews': Robinson to Rosenne, 26 March 1951 (n 212); Rosenne chose to cite the number 'authoritatively estimated' by Prime Minister Ben-Gurion in his UNSCOP testimony: ICJ, *Pleadings* (n 166) 329.

[224] ICJ, *Pleadings* (n 166) 329; unfamiliarity with the Nuremberg proceedings led Rosenne to request Robinson's help, who sent him a copy of Jacob Robinson, 'The Nuremberg Judgment: Crimes Against Humanity' *Congress Weekly* (25 October 1946); Rosenne to Robinson, 5 April 1951, Robinson to Rosenne, 7 April 1951, FM-1832/4, ISA.

[225] ICJ, *Pleadings* (n 166) 329.

[226] ibid; emphases added.

[227] Robinson to Rosenne, 26 March 1951 (n 212).

Lemkin, he omitted his name altogether from the final text of his statement: it remained a stranger to Lemkin and his 1944 *Axis Rule*.[228]

Rosenne's statement was equally silent on the role played by Jewish organizations in the campaign for the Convention. It treated the Jewish Holocaust as background, context, and trigger for the Genocide Convention, which, from that moment on, belonged to the universal, not the particular Jewish, sphere. Here, too, the Convention itself was not an Israeli concern. Reviewing next '[t]he drafting of the Genocide Convention', Rosenne limited his inquiry to the official, state-made drafting history at the UN, excluding the extensive unofficial campaign that pervaded the work of official channels:

> It is against this background of indescribable mass-suffering, of stern international justice and of doctrinal investigations, that the problem of genocide was brought before the General Assembly, already at the second part of its first session, in the autumn of 1946.[229]

Indeed, the Assembly's 'immediate legal task' was, according to Rosenne, not correcting past moral wrongs but instead doctrinal, even technical, in nature. Rather than preventing future genocide, it 'was—looking to the future—to prevent a repetition of the jurisdictional situation such as had existed at Nuremberg, and to respect the basic principle of law' prohibiting retroactive criminalization.[230] After invoking the Jewish aspect of the Convention to validate his own standing, Rosenne rendered that very Jewish aspect irrelevant to the Convention's purpose—and to the proceedings.

Rosenne's enquiry into the drafting history of the Convention was not aimed at finding in its 'special characteristics' restrictive rules on reservations or objections—as the Court had eventually done. In fact, he played down, not up, the uniqueness and novelty of the Genocide Convention.[231] He asserted the essentially unexceptional procedure used to prepare the Convention to suggest that the 'legislative history of this Convention contains nothing to warrant the application of special rules of treaty law'.[232] This allowed Rosenne to compare the preparatory

[228] Lemkin (n 47). When Rosenne resumed his statement in the afternoon of 11 April, he took care 'to insert in the record references to some literature which gives further analysis of the Genocide Convention'; this did not include Raphael Lemkin, 'Genocide as a Crime under International Law' (1947) 41 AJIL 145; ICJ, *Pleadings* (n 166) 339.

[229] ICJ, *Pleadings* (n 166) 331.

[230] ibid. The failure of the Nuremberg judgement to rely on the concept of genocide was central to Lemkin's drive. The day it was delivered was, he wrote, 'the blackest day' of his life: Cooper (n 7) 77.

[231] Rosenne compared, unfavourably, the Genocide Convention to the Convention on UN Privileges and Immunities and the Convention on UN Specialized Agencies: ICJ, *Pleadings* (n 166) 332. Even when praising the Convention as representing 'a great step forward', Rosenne emphasized 'all its weaknesses': ibid, 337; he also played down its novelty: 'neither Resolution 96(1) nor the Convention purported to do more than confirm existing rules of international law': ibid, 338.

[232] ibid, 332 ('this process has close similarities with the procedure at ordinary diplomatic conferences'); 333 ('it may well follow that ... conventions drafted in this way may not be found to possess

procedure to that of the 1949 Geneva Conventions. He was hoping, presumably, to obtain a general pronouncement on reservations and objections, not limited to the Genocide Convention—and outcomes favourable to Israel's own position on reservations to the Geneva Conventions.[233]

Rosenne carried on. His oral statement offered an 'Analysis of the Genocide Convention'; discussed 'General Considerations Regarding Reservations'; and countered 'Possible Challenges to the View that Only Parties to the Treaty Are Entitled to Object to Reservations Made by Other States on Their Becoming Parties to the Treaty'. It amplified, elaborated on, and added to Israel's written statement. This was a highly technical legal exercise, devoid of allusions to broader purpose or narrow Jewish interest. Years later, in a rare reference to his own involvement, Rosenne would attest that this 'was a mostly technical question, a lawyer's trial'.[234] The Jewish aspect of the Convention was not invoked in the substantive part of Rosenne's statement or in its conclusions. It was, after all, meant to serve 'more public relations than actual content'.[235]

4.6 After The Hague

The public relations exercise served its purpose. It did not bring about a substantive change in Israel's attitude to the Genocide Convention. Early in his oral statement, Rosenne invoked 'our special concern for the efficacy of the Genocide Convention' and implied a Jewish ownership now duly represented by the Jewish state. These allusions had no hold on Israel's attitude, or policy, once The Hague proceedings were exhausted. They were not meant to produce any effect beyond the courtroom: they were instrumental. They neither concerned the Genocide Convention's 'actual content'[236] nor were they designed to illustrate its idiosyncrasy. Israel's intervention in the proceedings did not seek to ensure a broad interpretation of the Convention or secure its broadest possible membership.[237] To Robinson, Rosenne reported that he had placed an 'overemphasis' on the 'nexus between the legal problems on the

those particular characteristics they are sometimes said to have and which would justify appeal to certain special rules').

233 ibid, 332, 340–53.

234 Shabtai Rosenne, *The Perplexities of International Law* (Revised & Updated Hebrew edn, Bialik 2012) 110 (Hebrew).

235 Rosenne to Robinson, 15 March 1951 (n 206).

236 ibid.

237 Rosenne reported having resisted pressure to 'intervene [in] support [of the] application [by the UN] legal dept[artment]: Rosenne to Robinson, 5 April 1951 (n 224). Later, in an academic capacity, Rosenne would use familiarity with the legislative history to promote a very narrow interpretation of the compromissory clause in Article IX, severely restricting the class of states entitled to refer a 'dispute' under the Convention to the ICJ: Shabtai Rosenne, 'War Crimes and State Responsibility' in Yoram Dinstein and Mala Tabori (eds), *War Crimes in International Law* (Nijhoff 1996) 65, 81.

one hand and the very notion of genocide and the abuses of the Second World War' on the other; the meetings he had in The Hague, only some in connection with the proceedings, seem to have been of greater concern to him.[238] Neither his final report on his Hague visit, meant for wider distribution,[239] nor a note he wrote to Robinson on 'impressions' accrued and lessons learned,[240] mentioned any Jewish aspect of the proceedings.

Rosenne's appearance garnered praise and compliments from Lauterpacht, Kerno, and his MFA colleagues.[241] When the Court delivered its opinion Rosenne thought it accepted '[m]y arguments ... [on] all major points', even if the Court's technique varied considerably from his own.[242] Later he confided to Robinson that 'if the Court did not accept our theory outright, it certainly did not reject it'.[243] Rosenne and Robinson would continue to weigh for some time the Court's decision, the dissenting opinions, and the literature that followed. A Jewish aspect would not figure in these deliberations, and the decision's impact on the fate of Genocide Convention—or its 'efficacy'—did not attract their attention.[244] Once the Advisory Opinion was published, Rosenne distributed a legal brief to all Israeli delegations abroad and all MFA departments. He justified Israel's intervention by reference to Israel being a party to the Convention 'and also because of the connexion between the Jewish suffering and the Second World War and the Convention'.[245] He was content, however, to append to that brief a review of the Opinion written by Kerno rather than offer his own commentary. He launched himself into a cordial correspondence with Eric Beckett, the British Foreign Office Legal Adviser, whose counsel he sought on Foreign Office practice on attaching reservations to international treaties.[246] He delved into the law and practice of the Court;[247] this became the topic of his 1957 doctoral thesis—and first monograph.[248]

[238] Rosenne to Robinson, 11 April 1951 (n 215); Rosenne also distributed Israel's oral statement: Rosenne to Lauterpacht, 13 April 1951, Lauterpacht to Rosenne, 20 April 1951, FM-1832/4, ISA.

[239] Report on Shabtai Rosenne's Hague Visit, 30 April 1951, FM-1832/4, ISA.

[240] Rosenne to Robinson, 29 April 1951, FM-1832/4, ISA.

[241] Rosenne to Eytan, 28 May 1951; Eytan to Rosenne, 29 May 1951, FM-1832/4, ISA ('Three cheers') and other correspondence there.

[242] Rosenne to Eytan, 28 May 1951 (n 241).

[243] Rosenne to Robinson, 11 July 1951, FM-1832/4, ISA. Still, Israel was critical of the Courts' Opinion: GAOR, Sixth Committee (8 December 1951) 81.

[244] Rosenne to Robinson, 11 July 1951 (n 243); Rosenne to Robinson, 19 February 1952, FM-1840/3, ISA; Rosenne, On the Advisory Opinion, 13 June 1951 (n 191).

[245] Rosenne, Legal Brief No 41, 11 July 1951 FM-1832/4, ISA.

[246] Beckett to Rosenne, 3 March 1952; Rosenne to Beckett, 17 March 1952; Rosenne to Robinson, 6 March 1952, 17 March 1952; Rosenne to Attorney-General, 17 March 1952, FM-1832/4, ISA.

[247] Shabtai Rosenne, 'New Tendencies in the Work of the International Court of Justice' (1952) 9 HaPraklit 78 (Hebrew).

[248] Shabtai Rosenne, *The International Court of Justice: One of the Principal Organs of the United Nations* (PhD thesis, Hebrew University of Jerusalem 19 June 1957) (Hebrew); Leo Kohn, 'Appraisal of Doctoral Thesis of Mr. Shabtai Rosenne on the [ICJ], 7 May 1957, FM-5961/8, ISA. This comprised part of Shabtai Rosenne, *The International Court of Justice* (Sijthoff 1957). By 1952, he had already tried to publish an article on reservations in the American Journal of International Law, seemingly without success: Rosenne to George A Finch, 16 March 1952; Rosenne to Robinson, 16 March 1951, FM-1832/4,

Four decades later, Rosenne again would have occasion to invoke the Jewish aspect of the Genocide Convention before the World Court. This time, however, he would limit the Convention to the Jewish particular, not the universal, sphere. When circumstances again arose, again in Europe, requiring judicial recourse to the Convention, Rosenne again took part in ICJ proceedings. Twenty years retired from government service, his statement at the Court included two personal remarks. He started with an allusion to 'the refuge granted in Bosnia and Herzegovina to ... Sephardic Jews who escaped the Inquisition and Pogroms ... in 1565'. 'I myself', he lectured the Court, 'am descended from one of those Sephardi families'. He concluded, however, by protesting references made to 'the Nazi Holocaust'—invoking its uniqueness and implying that events in the Balkans *did not* fall within the proper purview of the Genocide Convention:

> To any person who has direct knowledge of what the Holocaust was and what it was intended to achieve, such statements are nothing short of blasphemous. Nothing that has occurred since in Europe matches that unspeakable event in European history.[249]

The year was 1993. He was representing Serbia against Bosnia-Herzegovina.[250]

5. Ambivalence

The episodes accounted for in this chapter—the making of the Genocide Convention, its signature and ratification by Israel, and Rosenne's participation in the advisory proceedings—reveal Israel's ambivalence towards the Genocide Convention. Rosenne, Robinson, and their colleagues displayed a range of attitudes to the Convention. There was, at first, unfamiliar disinterest in the Genocide Convention; it represented a 'Jewish interest' yet, for that very reason, was a 'marginal problem' for Israel. As such, it could have had no place on their agenda prior to sovereignty and UN admission. Admission—attesting to the acquisition of sovereign status—made it possible for Israel's envoys to look beyond their immediate, narrow concerns, even if only in service to 'our own problems'. Admission,

ISA. Next year, he published an article on the Court: Shabtai Rosenne, '*L'exécution et la mise en vigueur des décisions de la Cour internationale de Justice*' (1953) 57 RGDIP 532.

[249] ICJ, *Bosnia-Herzegovina v Yugoslavia (Serbia and Montenegro)*, Public Sitting: Verbatim Record (2 April 1993) 11, 36–7.

[250] Rosenne, according to his son, was conflicted when approached by Yugoslavia. He enquired whether Israel's MFA would object to his involvement in the case: I thank Ambassador Robbie Sabel for this information. Rosenne represented Serbia in the preliminary phase, but later withdrew. Note also Philippe Sands, 'Shabtai Rosenne: A Personal Aspect' in James Loeffler and Moria Paz (eds), *The Law of Strangers: Jewish Lawyers and International Law in the Twentieth Century* (CUP 2019) 249.

however, also reinforced their sovereign sensibilities. These imposed on the Jewish state an 'active responsibility' to contribute to the work of the UN, repay debts accrued during the partition and admission debates, and maintain the goodwill of UN functionaries. When requested to do so, Israel's representatives identified an opportunity to harness what was expected of the Jewish state to ends of its UN stature and reputation. Visible action on the Genocide Convention allowed them to demonstrate good membership in the world organization. What drove Israel's signature and ratification of the Genocide Convention, and the law enacted to implement it domestically, was instrumental disinterest. Remarkably, Israel's ancillary reputational interests, combined with Jewish sovereign sensibilities, were enough to overcome apprehensions, expressed by Robinson and others, that ratification of the Genocide Convention might expose Israel to third-party intervention on behalf of its 'Arab minority'. Such apprehensions were raised early on in the process, but never since.

When a low-cost, risk-free opportunity to gain familiarity with the World Court and its ways presented itself, Rosenne could point to second-order, more general than concrete Israeli interests justifying participation. His involvement in the advisory proceedings dealing with the status of reservations to the Genocide Convention manifested no more and no less than Israel's as well as his own 'disinterested desire to participate in the work of the Court'. At the Court, he invoked the Holocaust to claim a special interest in the Genocide Convention and in the proceedings. This claim, however, was designed to attest to his own standing as a representative of the Jewish state, his own official Jewish voice. Israel's intervention in the proceedings—'a very middling' position, less 'universal and liberal' than the American statement—was not meant to promote the Convention or have the historical record of the Holocaust, following Nuremberg's failure to do so, rewritten through judicial commentary on a recent post-war legislative project. Once the proceedings concluded, this instrumental interest in the Genocide Convention lapsed.

And yet, Israel's envoys could not and did not deny that the Genocide Convention had a Jewish aspect. At times—to draw on the expertise of Jewish NGOs, to improve Israel's UN stature, to bolster standing before the international court—they would invoke that Jewish aspect openly. Yet they would do so, often, also in internal correspondence where such invocation served no instrumental or 'public relations' purpose. At times, they thought that the Convention's Jewish aspect imposed a 'moral duty' on the Jewish state and constrained its foreign policy choices. At others, they denied such duty or belittled what it could exact from the Jewish state. Their ambivalence was manifest, equally, in how they could both lament and critique the Convention's promise and its weakness.

All this also furnishes glimpses of aversion, even hostility, attending how Israel's early diplomats approached the Genocide Convention—and Justice Minister Rosen's own ambivalence towards it. In the *Knesset*, he announced that Israel 'as the state of the Jewish people' was 'particularly interested in' the Convention. And yet Rosen also expressed doubts as to its 'decisive practical power'. Moreover, he pronounced that the Genocide Convention was 'no solution for our dispersed people in the Diaspora'. Here he alluded to another, 'radical solution ... known to us'.[251] The following chapter turns to that 'radical solution' in search for explanations of Israel's complex attitude to the Convention: disinterest and indifference, acknowledgement and appropriation, derision and instrumentalism, aversion and hostility. It starts with Robinson's and Rosenne's aversion to the Genocide Convention and to its progenitor, Raphael Lemkin; and proceeds to demonstrate why such sentiments were owed, precisely, to the very Jewish aspect of the Genocide Convention and of Lemkin's advocacy. These sentiments, too, gave voice to Jewish ideological sensibilities and expressed Jewish political experience.

[251] Rosen (n 2) 314.

5

'A False and Perverse Doctrine'

The Genocide Convention and Jewish Nationalism

1. King Saud's Statement

In late 1953, shortly after acceding to his father's throne, King Saud told Jordanian journalists that 'the Zionist peril is like cancer, with no remedy but uprooting'. This caused Raphael Lemkin to approach Israel's United Nations ('UN') mission with a proposal to 'apply the [Genocide] Convention'. The UN Department at the Ministry of Foreign Affairs ('MFA') was unenthused: 'we have no interest in application [of the Convention] by an example of this kind'.[1] At Shabtai Rosenne's request, however, this response was not sent to New York. Like his colleagues, he opposed Israeli action on the matter, but on other grounds, which he soon elaborated. Saudi Arabia, he wrote, became a member of the Convention four months after Israel; 'formal conditions for applying the Convention in this case', he noted, were met. Rosenne, however, proceeded to offer a lengthy deprecation of the Convention: 'like any compromise, it is noted for its certain paleness'; 'there is room for great doubt if and to what extent this Convention is conclusive. Its disadvantages are many': many states refused to join the Genocide Convention, he noted, and others did so only with 'grave reservations'. Its 'practical significance' weakened as a result of various disputes; states, in consequence, 'do not know what precisely are their obligations'. In short, the MFA legal adviser observed, 'it is possible to say that its entire efficacy, legally speaking, was put into question'. Politically, 'there is no reality whatsoever in the idea that the Convention can be applied at this time'. On the facts, at any rate, he had a 'great doubt' whether King Saud's words 'constitute a violation of the provisions of the Convention'. Rosenne's conclusion, nonetheless, added nothing to that of the UN Department: 'there will be no practical utility for the state of Israel to exert an effort to apply the Convention in this case'.[2] Rosenne's intervention, and assumption of responsibility for formulating the MFA position, was therefore not quite necessary. Notably, he had nothing to say on the author of the proposal.

This was neither the first nor the last time Lemkin turned to the Jewish state. This time, however, was different. Saudi Arabia had, back in 1946, submitted the

[1] [Draft] Sidor to UN Mission, 17 January 1954, FM-2010/17, Israel State Archive ('ISA').
[2] Rosenne to UN Department, 26 January 1954, FM-2010/17, ISA.

Jews, Sovereignty, and International Law. Rotem Giladi, Oxford University Press. © Rotem Giladi 2021.
DOI: 10.1093/oso/9780198857396.003.0007

first draft of the Genocide Convention at the UN.[3] Lemkin, early in the campaign for the Genocide Convention and, later, its ratification, worked closely with Saudi, other Arab, and Muslim diplomats.[4] In his usual manner, he showered lavish praise and credit on his interlocutors for their role in advancing the cause.[5] In the early stages of the campaign, however, Lemkin also sought to avoid entangling the Convention's fate in the UN Palestine debate; he also 'rarely linked the Genocide Convention to Jewish issues at least publicly'.[6] Lemkin and involved Jewish groups, Zionist and non-Zionist alike, preferred not to enlist the diplomatic resources of first the Jewish Agency and later the Jewish state to the cause of the campaign for the drafting of the Convention. If—as James Loeffler has recently argued[7]—Lemkin had any lingering Zionist sympathies, he nonetheless was—as John Cooper notes—'playing down' the Convention's Jewish aspects in order to gain broader support.[8] The draft Convention could easily have been hijacked, then aborted, by the vagaries of the Palestine conflict.[9]

This strategy often proved successful. Sir Muhammed Zafarulla Khan, Pakistan's Foreign Minister and a future judge at the International Court of Justice ('ICJ'), early in 1948 portrayed the Convention, at the Economic and Social Council ('ECOSOC') as a Muslim cause.[10] A veteran of partition politics at home, Zafarulla Khan earned the hostile regard of members of the Jewish Agency UN mission when he 'effectively became the spokesperson for the Arab cause in Palestine' in the Partition debate. He also played a major role in the attempt to refer the 'Palestine Question' to the ICJ.[11]

[3] Hirad Abtahi and Philippa Webb, 'Secrets and Surprises in the Travaux Préparatoires of the Genocide Convention' in Margaret M deGuzman and Diane Marie Amann (eds), *Arcs of Global Justice: Essays in Honour of William A Schabas* (OUP 2018) 209, 301–5.

[4] John Cooper, *Raphael Lemkin and the Struggle for the Genocide Convention* (Palgrave-Macmillan 2008) 86, 185.

[5] Hoping to secure Finnish legislation, Lemkin wrote to Erik Castrén, the Finnish jurist-diplomat, that when 'this act will be accomplished, it could be rightly called "lex Castren"': Lemkin to Castrén, 22 March 1958, B1–F2, Raphael Lemkin Papers, Manuscripts and Archives Division, The New York Public Library ('Lemkin Papers, NYPL').

[6] Cooper (n 4) 214.

[7] James Loeffler, 'Becoming Cleopatra: The Forgotten Zionism of Raphael Lemkin' (2017) 19 J of Genocide Research 340.

[8] Cooper (n 4) 147, 96, 154; ch 4.

[9] Perlzweig to Lemkin, 29 August 1947, P–154, Box 1–18, Lemkin Collection, American Jewish Historical Society ('AJHS') ('it would have weakened the importance of the Convention to have dragged in a reference to it after rather tense discussions of the Palestine situation').

[10] Cooper (n 4) 133, 127, 185, 302ff; Douglas Irvin-Erickson, *Raphaël Lemkin and the Concept of Genocide* (University of Pennsylvania Press 2016) 170, 185; William Korey, *An Epitaph for Raphael Lemkin* (American Jewish Committee 2001) 1. Khan's 1954 ICJ election, ironically, succeeded due to Israel's absence from the vote held on *Yom Kippur*; Israel supported the Indian candidate: Kidron to Director-General, 11 October 1954, FM–1822/1, ISA.

[11] Victor Kattan, 'Decolonizing the International Court of Justice: The Experience of Judge Sir Muhammad Zafarulla Khan in the South West Africa Cases' (2015) 5 Asian J of Intl L 310, 322; (1947–48) YB of the UN 241. One Jewish Agency mission member described him as 'the most articulate opponent of the partition plan'; 'undoubtedly one of the ablest and most impressive delegates present from any country': Comay to Gering, 3 December 1947, FM–2266/15, ISA. Moshe Sharett, who had to publicly counter Khan's arguments, considered him 'a tower of strength to the Arab front ... who revealed

At other times, however, Lemkin would use Jewish organizations as middlemen to entreat with the emerging Jewish state. He did not shy from harping on both Muslim and Zionist sensibilities when the audience required such pandering. Among his papers archived at the New York Public Library is a two-page memorandum, written in the late 1950s, on *The Genocide Convention and the Moslem World*. It mentioned many Arab and Muslim delegations and diplomats, and claimed that '[t]he Genocide Convention owes much to the statesmen of the Moslem world'.[12] Lemkin's papers, however, also include an earlier memorandum addressed to an American Zionist organization. Geared towards US ratification, it asserted:

> It is superfluous to elaborate on the moral implications of this Convention especially when a memorandum is addressed to Jews. However, in connection with the situation in the Near East, the Convention acquires a special importance for Israel as a State ... Next to Arms for Israel, this Convention ranges as very important for the legal and diplomatic defense of Israel in the United Nations and in the diplomatic world at large. Many Jewish minorities are still living in unfriendly surroundings in Europe, in the Near East and in many other countries ... The Genocide Convention is the only international treaty available for the protection of the Jews in the world today.[13]

Once Israel signed and ratified the Convention, and passed legislation to implement it, Lemkin would from time to time approach its envoys, trying to enlist them to the cause of the Convention. Events in the Middle East, perhaps, estranged him from former allies; so did, likely, Lemkin's own 'slightly warped and paranoid streak'.[14] Whichever the case, for Lemkin to propose that the Jewish state run a test case against his former allies speaks volumes on his growing desperation with the fate of the Convention.[15] To have his overtures rebuffed by the Jewish state,

himself to be a brilliant jurist, sharp polemicist, and an indefatigable, profuse speaker': Moshe Sharett, *At the Threshold of Statehood: 1946–1949* (Am Oved 1958) 121 (Hebrew). For Khan's views on partition and Jewish nationalism: correspondence in FM-337/12, ISA; Faisal Devji, *Muslim Zion: Pakistan As a Political Idea* (Harvard UP 2013).

[12] The Genocide Convention and the Moslem World, [n.d.], B3–F1/2, Lemkin Papers, NYPL; though unsigned, Lemkin's style is unmistakable. Based on ratification dates mentioned, it was probably written between November 1956 and January 1959.

[13] [Raphael Lemkin], Memorandum to the American Zionist Council on the Genocide Convention, 14 June 1950, B1–F1, Lemkin Papers, NYPL; Cooper (n 4) 214.

[14] Cooper (n 4) 131, 209; Maurice Perlzweig of the World Jewish Congress ('WJC'), wrote: 'I have always done my best to back up Lemkin's efforts, but occasionally he has to be taken with a grain of salt... I found some of the allegations so remote from reality as to be startling', and 'I am one of Lemkin's most unresisting victims': Perlzweig to Petegorsky, 18 April 1951, WJC–B7/9 (World Jewish Congress Records, MS-361), American Jewish Archives ('AJA'); Robinson to Goitein, 7 February 1952, FM–341/37, ISA ('one cause *meshuga* and he sees enemies everywhere').

[15] Grossman to Sharett, 29 November 194, FM–75/7, ISA ('Lemkin is pleading').

however, reveals the existence of diverging Jewish readings of the Genocide Convention. This chapter examines these diverging readings and the ideological sensibilities underlying them.

2. Raphael Lemkin's Overtures

King Saud's 1953 statement was neither the first nor the last time that the Jewish state turned down, or disregarded, Lemkin's overtures. These, as noted, first came through others.[16] After Israel's UN admission, Lemkin sought to obtain its ratification of the Genocide Convention. In November 1949, he liaised with WJC functionaries to try and influence Israel's attitude.[17] At the same time, he also looked for ways to approach Israel's decision-making apparatus.[18] That month, he cabled Israel's Prime Minister. He first thanked David Ben-Gurion 'for the splendid co-operation' by Israel's UN mission 'in the matter [of the] Genocide Convention'.[19] This was a typical Lemkin hyperbole. There is no evidence whatsoever of pre-statehood contact between the mission, not at all involved in any UN work on the Convention, and Lemkin; the mission, as the last chapter demonstrates, was decidedly disinterested in the Genocide Convention.[20] Lemkin also informed Ben-Gurion that fourteen more ratifications were required for the Convention to enter into force. He then came to the point. Portraying the Convention as an instrument of Jewish *redemption*, Lemkin wrote that

> Ratification by Israel during [the] present United Nations Assembly [session] will spur other nations to ratify because this Convention is written with Jewish blood and therefore Israel[']s ratification will serve to the world *a symbol for greatest sufferings redeemed through justice* and new humane international law.[21]

Neither response nor action by Ben-Gurion was recorded. Israel's signature and ratification of the Convention were driven, we saw, by other considerations entirely.[22]

[16] In early 1948, Lemkin sought to enlist the support of the Chief Rabbi of mandatory Palestine: Lemkin to Herzog, 1 January 1948, P-576/4, ISA; only fragments of the letter survived.

[17] Cooper (n 4) 183; Lemkin to Kubowitzki, 5 December 1949, P-154, Box 2-2, Lemkin Collection, AJHS ('ratification by Israel... is urgently needed' intimating that 'so long as Israel did not ratify yet', this would call into question the position of Jewish organizations that 'this treaty is important to the jews').

[18] Lemkin to Kubowitzki (n 17) (proposing that 'leaders of political parties in the parliament could make a request for ratification').

[19] Rosenne to Attorney-General, 13 November 1949, with copy of Lemkin's cable [n.d.], G-5660/26, ISA; Cooper (n 4) mentions a *draft* 5 November cable to Ben-Gurion.

[20] Ch 4.

[21] Emphasis added; Rosenne to Attorney-General, 13 November 1949 (n 19).

[22] Ch 4. This contradicts Cooper (n 4) 183-5 (suggesting that Lemkin's pressure led to Israel's ratification).

When Israel's instrument of ratification was finally deposited with the Secretary-General, Lemkin again tried to engage Israel's political leadership. He immediately sent a congratulatory cable to Foreign Minister Sharett. This time, however, he also approached Israel's UN mission. Rather than meet Jacob Robinson—the mission's legal adviser, whom he had known through past correspondence—he turned to Arthur Lourie, another mission member; avoiding Robinson would become a pattern.[23] Lemkin confided to Lourie that the Arab states have 'cooled off' on the Convention and 'did not wish to have their hands tied in the event of a renewal of the assault on Israel'.[24] He now sought to enlist the diplomatic resources of the Jewish state to his cause: 'Professor Lemkin asked whether we could be of assistance [in promoting ratification] with regard to certain countries, such as the Dutch, the Danes, and the Canadians ... In particular, he wanted to know if we had any approach' to Canada's Foreign Minister Lester B Pearson, who had been closely involved in the Palestine partition debate.[25] In the absence of Abba Eban, Israel's UN Permanent Representative, Lourie would not commit this or that way. Still, some reserve was manifest in his report of the meeting with Lemkin: 'I should appreciate your instructions as to whether we should be active *at all* in canvassing other delegates on behalf of the Convention'.[26] Walter Eytan, the MFA Director-General, informed Lourie that the Ministry had 'no objection' to assisting Lemkin. He left the matter, however, to Eban's eventual discretion 'in consultation with Dr. Robinson'.[27] If Israel's UN mission engaged in any manner in the promotion of the Convention's ratification by others, following Lemkin's overture, no evidence of such engagement was recorded.

That Lemkin again would seek the assistance of the Jewish state in promoting the Genocide Convention's ratification suggests his first overture had, indeed, no effect on Israel's policy. In early 1951, he approached Israel's US Embassy. Lemkin now proposed that the date of the Genocide Convention's entry into force 'be celebrated in Israel and by Jewish organizations here'; he had prepared a two-page draft statement in Hebrew. He also requested, again, that Israel promote the Convention's ratification by other states.[28] Rosenne, at first, did not object to the latter request. He asked, however, that Robinson first be consulted.[29] Eban, however, decided in the meantime that the anniversary could be taken up by Jewish organizations, not

[23] Lemkin to Gordon, 10 January 1950, P-154, Box 2-3, Lemkin Collection, AJHS (mistakenly addressing Gordon as the MFA 'Director'); nor did Lemkin write to Rosenne.

[24] Lourie to Eytan, 22 March 1950, FM-2010/17, ISA.

[25] ibid. Eliezer Tauber, *Personal Policy Making: Canada's Role in the Adoption of the Palestine Partition Resolution* (Greenwood Press 2002); Hassan Husseini, 'A "Middle Power" in Action: Canada and the Partition of Palestine' (2008) 30 Arab Stud Quarterly 41.

[26] Emphasis added; Lourie to Eytan, 22 March 1950 (n 24).

[27] Eytan to Lourie, 4 April 1950, FM-2416/12, ISA.

[28] Herlitz to Eban, 9 January 1951, FM-1840/2, ISA.

[29] Rosenne to Herlitz, 25 January 1951, FM-341/36, ISA.

the Jewish state;[30] on promoting ratification, he noted that Israel '*may* continue to recommend ratification to any other delegation'.[31]

Robinson, however, disagreed even with this noncommittal formula. His objection was practical, personal, and principled. When made privy to that correspondence, he revealed a glimpse of a grudge towards Lemkin, Lemkin's choice of words, and his suggestion that the Jewish state had a particular stake in, or debt to, the Convention. 'I am reluctant to "celebrate" the entry into force of the Genocide Convention', he informed Rosenne, 'unless it is made a matter either for the United Nations as a whole (as has been done with regard to the Universal Declaration of Human Rights) or by a substantial number of other governments.'[32] He proceeded to record his aversion to harnessing the Jewish state to the cause of the Genocide Convention—and his hostility to the Convention:

> I wish to go one step further. I cannot see why we should become the lobbyist for the ratification of the Genocide Convention and why we should contact all these governments. We have sufficient troubles of our own and the Genocide Convention *should not be considered as a matter which gives any particular guarantee to the Jewish people against possible future acts of mass terror.*[33]

Prior to Israel's UN admission, Robinson had considered the Genocide Convention a 'marginal' problem.[34] Now he elucidated that this was not merely a matter of constrained resources and ephemeral priorities; there was something, innate in the Genocide Convention, that attracted his censure. What that defect had been is discussed later; Lemkin, at any rate, approached Israel's US Embassy again, a year later, with requests for diplomatic action.[35]

When Nationalist China sought to revise the Chinese text of the Convention,[36] Lemkin cabled Minister Sharett 'requesting [Israel's] opposition

[30] [Eban] to Herlitz, [n.d.], FM-341/36, ISA.

[31] Emphasis added; ibid. Herlitz to UN Delegation, 16 January 1951, FM-341/36, ISA. Despite Eban's use of 'continue', no evidence of such action by Israel's mission, before or after this episode, was recorded in the relevant MFA files.

[32] Robinson to Rosenne, 5 February 1951, FM-1840/2, ISA.

[33] Emphasis added; ibid. Rosenne was more conflicted: though he belittled the Convention's Jewish value, he considered it 'incumbent upon us to help Lemkin and others who put so much labour in this Convention'; still, he saw 'no need to make a special effort': Rosenne to Robinson, 15 February 1951, FM-1840/2, ISA.

[34] Robinson, Marginal Problems in the Third Regular Session of the General Assembly: Observations, 4 September 1948, FM-131/22, ISA, discussed in ch 4.

[35] Robinson to Goitein, 7 February 1952 (n 14), this time accusing Israel of '"obstructing" the [draft] Code of Offences Against the Peace and Security of Mankind' at the General Assembly ('GA'); Robinson was dismissive.

[36] Cooper (n 4) 226–7; Mary Ann Glendon, *A World Made New: Eleanor Roosevelt and the Universal Declaration of Human Rights* (Random 2002) 133–4.

[to the] Chinese revision [of the] genocide convention which he claims quote distorts international inter religious interracial character [of the] term genocide reducing it to simple murder etc unquote'. Robinson was asked, somewhat exasperatedly, to 'contact Lemkin investigate trouble act own judgment'.[37]

Rosenne and Robinson had already considered China's revision request. Their interest concerned not the implications for the Genocide Convention but the doctrinal question of what constituted a treaty's 'authentic text'.[38] They oscillated on whether the matter was important. Rosenne, at first, assumed that Israel 'had nothing to comment on this problem',[39] and that there was 'no reason to oppose' China's request as long as 'the correct method' was followed.[40] Robinson was dismissive of Lemkin's request, of his 'imaginary' assessment of the situation, and of Lemkin himself.[41] He thought Israel's position should not favour the Chinese request. Still, Robinson would not have Israel support Lemkin's request. He also took care to record that Lemkin had no effect on Israel's decision-making:

> Dr. Lemkin saw in the Chinese request one of those sinister manoeuvres which Stalin, Mrs. Roosevelt and Chang-Kai-Shek undertake jointly and severally from time to time to ruin his work. He appealed also to the Sar [Minister], the text of his cable was transmitted to us, but it could not influence our attitude which was anyway negative.[42]

China's revision request, however, did have an effect on Rosenne who soon developed an academic interest in the question of multilingual treaties. He would discuss it in a 1954 lecture course at the Hague Academy of International Law. In time, this interest would produce several publications.[43]

[37] Draft UN Department to UN Mission, 18 December 1952, FM-2010/17; Lemkin to Sharett, 15 December 1952, FM-2416/12, ISA.

[38] Robinson to Rosenne, 17 October 1951; Rosenne to Robinson, 29 October 1951, FM-1820/4; Robinson, Sixth Committee Statement, 18 December 1952, FM-1820/9, ISA.

[39] Rosenne to Robinson, 19 September 1951, FM-1820/4, ISA.

[40] Rosenne, Revision of the Chinese text of the Genocide Convention, 3 October 1951, FM-1972/7, ISA.

[41] Robinson to Goitein, 7 February 1952 (n 14).

[42] [Robinson], Request of the Government of China for Revision of the Chinese Text of the Convention on the Prevention and Punishment of the Crime of Genocide, 14 January 1953, FM-1973/10, ISA. Eventually, for reasons unrelated to the Convention, Israel abstained in the vote on the Chinese request.

[43] Shabtai Rosenne, 'United Nations Treaty Practice' (1954) 86 RdC 275, 385–90 discussed extensively 'the revision of the Chinese text of the Genocide Convention'; Shabtai Rosenne, 'The Meaning of "Authentic Text" in Modern Treaty Law' in Rudolf Bernhardt et al (eds), *Völkerrecht als Rechtsordnung, Internationale Gerichtsbarkeit, Menschenrechte: Festschrift für Hermann Mosler* (Springer-Verlag 1983) 759.

3. Sovereign Grudges

Some of Rosenne's and Robinson's hostility to the Genocide Convention took the form of a personal grudge towards Lemkin. Rosenne would not mention Lemkin in the course of the ICJ proceedings in the Reservations Case. At first, his draft statement alluded to Lemkin as one who '*claims* to have coined' the word 'genocide'. But when Robinson rebuked him that this was 'unfair to Lemkin', and that Lemkin's paternity was beyond doubt, Rosenne proceeded to omit any reference to Lemkin.[44] At the Court he would not acknowledge, let alone invoke, Jewish authorship of the Genocide Convention. Instead, he credited the making of the Convention, time and again, to the universal.[45] Rosenne, likely, did make one implicit—and rather denigrating—reference to Lemkin. He averred that the matter before the Court 'must not be approached as one of philology, but as one of the intention of the parties'—that is, sovereign states—'viewed from the angle of the actual execution of the convention'.[46] Lemkin, who coined the term 'genocide', trained as a philologist before studying law.[47]

Rosenne, never part of the Jewish advocacy scene, had no past encounters with Lemkin. Robinson, who was, harboured old resentments. One dated back to his days at the Institute of Jewish Affairs ('IJA'). In 1946, a conference convened in Paris to discuss the terms of peace with the 'satellite' states.[48] Jewish organizations were present in force;[49] reports on 'unity of action' marked the usual divisions and rivalries.[50] The American Jewish Committee ('AJC') boasted hiring Hersch Lauterpacht as its legal consultant.[51] The WJC tasked Robinson with drafting 'amendments ... to be included in the treaties with former enemy countries in order that Jewish rights and property may be safeguarded'.[52] While 'the Conference took no regard of the Jewish demands',[53] vague provisions guaranteeing the enjoyment of human rights were incorporated into the language of the peace treaties.

[44] Emphasis added; Robinson to Rosenne, 26 March 1951, FM-1832/3, ISA.

[45] Ch 4.

[46] ICJ, *Pleadings, Oral Arguments, Documents* (1951) 334.

[47] Cooper (n 4) 15.

[48] Neal H Petersen and William Slany (eds), *Foreign Relations of the United States, 1946 Paris Peace Conference: Proceedings III–IV* (Government Printing Office 1970).

[49] Nathan Kurz, 'In the Shadow of Versailles: Jewish Minority Rights at the 1946 Paris Peace Conference' (2016) 15 Simon Dubnow Institute YB 187; Nathaniel A Kurz, *'A Sphere above the Nations?': The Rise and Fall of International Jewish Human Rights Politics, 1945–1975* (PhD dissertation, Faculty of the Graduate School of Arts and Sciences, Yale University May 2015) 40–81; I am grateful to Dr Kurz for sharing a copy of his dissertation.

[50] Kurz, 'Shadow' (n 49) 197–8; Jacob Robinson, Interim Report on Our Activities at the Paris Peace Conference, 11, 13 September 1946, WJC-C133/8, AJA.

[51] Jewish Telegraphic Agency, 'Jewish Agency Asks for a Hearing at Paris Peace Conference; Points to U.N. Precedent' (8 August 1946).

[52] ibid.

[53] Kurz, *Sphere* (n 49) 35.

Robinson, already sceptical of the promise of human rights,[54] lamented that '[t]he Jews at the conference are outsiders' and that the outcomes were 'rudimentary'.[55]

It was against this backdrop that Lemkin approached Robinson, asking for help with inserting a reference to 'genocide' into the peace treaties with Nazi Germany's wartime allies. To persuade Robinson, Lemkin resorted to what he had thought was extravagant praise. His choice of words, however, was inopportune: '[s]ince *you have been the great inspiration for genocide* I don't need to convince you of the necessity to putting it in the treaty. Please help and do what you can. The matter is in your hands!'[56] Robinson, likely, did not appreciate being considered any kind of 'inspiration for genocide'. At any rate, as we shall see, he had good reason to dissociate himself from the type of protection Lemkin sought to promote.[57]

Robinson's work on the *Jewish Yearbook of International Law* also fed his aversion. The editors, Feinberg and Stoyanovsky, leaned heavily on Robinson's contacts, expertise, ideas, and the resources he commanded at the IJA. In mid-1946, they approached Lemkin through Norman Bentwich, soliciting an article on war criminals. Lemkin was asked to treat the question 'with particular reference to its [J]ewish aspects as they are now unravling [sic] themselves in the Nuremberg Trial'.[58] Like Robinson, Lemkin was present in Nuremberg during the trial of the major war criminals, though at different dates.[59] Lemkin, in response, promised to author a contribution. But he informed Bentwich 'that he would be glad to write on genocide'.[60]

Robinson, however, disparaged Lemkin's qualifications. He doubted 'whether Lemkin ... would agree to undertake writing on the Jewish aspects of the problem of war criminals which he has never dealt with scientifically (notwithstanding his credit for inventing "genocide")'.[61] Still, he joined the editors' effort to hold Lemkin

[54] Ch 3.

[55] Robinson, Interim Report, 11, 13 September 1946 (n 50) ('Jewish aspects' of the Conference 'marginal by their very nature'; he criticized 'the lack of machinery for the implementation of the provisions of Jewish interests'); Jacob Robinson, First Series of Peace Treaties: Tentative Draft, 26 February 1947, WJC-C99/9, AJA.

[56] Emphasis added; Lemkin to Robinson, and Raphael Lemkin, Memorandum on the Necessity to Include Anti-Genocide Clauses in the Peace Treaties, 28 August 1946, WJC-C14/21, AJA; no response from Robinson is contained in the file. Omry Kaplan-Feuereisen, 'At the Service of the Jewish Nation: Jacob Robinson and International Law' (2008) 8-10 OstEuropa 157, 167. Cooper (n 4) 73 accounts for Lemkin's failure to convince state representatives at the conference; Raphael Lemkin, 'The Protection of Basic Human Rights of Minorities in the Forthcoming Peace Treaties', [n.d.], P-154, Box 7-2, Lemkin Collection, AJHS.

[57] Robinson, Interim Report, 11, 13 September 1946 (n 50). The unmet Jewish demands at the Conference did not refer to 'genocide'.

[58] Feinberg and Stoyanovsky to Lemkin, 7 May 1946, Stoyanovsky to Lauterpacht, 5 April 1946, Feinberg and Stoyanovsky to Verzijl, 5 May 1946, A306\6, Central Zionist Archive ('CZA').

[59] Lemkin to Robinson, 28 August 1946 (n 56) ('I am sorry I missed you in Nuremberg').

[60] Bentwich to Feinberg, 11 April 1946, Feinberg to Guggenheim, 25 April 1946, A306\6, CZA; Lemkin to Feinberg, 20 December 1946, P-154, Box 1-18, Lemkin Collection, AJHS.

[61] Robinson to Feinberg, 8 May 1946, A306\6, CZA.

to his word. In early January 1947, Feinberg reported progress, but also that the editors

> have doubts only with regard to Dr. Lemkin's article, as he is constantly travelling and hard to get in touch with ... we may have to find in America another author in his stead. It is impossible that the yearbook will not include an article on such a grave matter as the war criminals.[62]

After all attempts to elicit an answer from Lemkin failed, Feinberg came to the conclusion that Lemkin was '"lost" to us'.[63] He cabled Robinson that the editors 'cannot obtain [L]emkin's contribution [on] war criminals' and asked him to 'arrange for other contributor'.[64] Robinson obliged: the 'Institute', he responded, 'assumes responsibility [for the] article [on] war crimes'.[65]

At this point, Bentwich reported success in contacting Lemkin, and that he had promised to send his contribution.[66] This put the editors in an awkward position: 'in the circumstances we cannot decline him'.[67] Soon, however, Lemkin again vanished, this time for good. Feinberg and Bentwich were 'perplexed'.[68] Again, alternative authors were considered. By May 1947, Feinberg reported to Robinson on the project's progress: 'last—and perhaps not necessarily the most likeable—from [L]emkin there is no sign whatsoever'.[69] The text of the Genocide Convention was reproduced in the sole volume of the *Jewish Yearbook*,[70] but no article was dedicated to that instrument—or to the question of war crimes. Instead, one IJA staff member commissioned by Robinson wrote on crimes against humanity.[71]

It is not hard to see why Robinson would in a few years be '[d]oubtful' of 'Lemkin's usefulness' and avoid approaching him in the course of Israel's preparation for the 1951 advisory proceedings.[72] This was the only time Rosenne thought Lemkin might be of service to the Jewish state.[73] Yet the reason why both approached Lemkin with hostility—or, rather, tended not to approach him at

[62] Feinberg to Robinson, 5 January 1947, Bentwich and Feinberg to Lemkin, 1 January 1947, A306\6, CZA ('Please cable when can expect promised article').

[63] Feinberg to Robinson, 24 January 1947, A306\6, CZA.

[64] Feinberg to Robinson, 17 January 1947, A306\6, CZA.

[65] Robinson to Feinberg, 22 January 1947, WJC–C16/5, AJA.

[66] Gluck to Feinberg, 23 January 1947, A306\6, CZA: 'Bentwich received a telegram from Mr. Lemkin regarding the writing of an article and that he will send it soon'; Robinson to Feinberg, 11 February 1947, WJC–C16/5, AJA.

[67] Feinberg to Robinson, 24 January 1947 (n 63).

[68] Bentwich to Feinberg, 14 April 1947, A306\6, CZA.

[69] Feinberg to Robinson, 6 May 1947, A306\6, CZA.

[70] (1948) 1 Jewish YB Intl L 300.

[71] Anatole Goldstein, 'Crimes Against Humanity—Some Jewish Aspects' (1948) 1 Jewish YB Intl L 206 made passing references to Lemkin and the Genocide Convention.

[72] In early 1947, when Lemkin proposed to assist in the compilation of a 'Master List of War Criminals', Robinson promised IJA's help but admitted that 'my scepticism still stands': Robinson to Stone, 17 February 1947, WJC–C16/5, AJA.

[73] Rosenne to Robinson, 12 March 1951, FM–1832/3, ISA.

all—drew also on their present ideological sensibilities, not merely past personal grudges.

Such sensibilities were implicit in Robinson's insistence, on the question of the Chinese revision, that Lemkin 'could not influence' the Jewish state and its policy. They were apparent in Rosenne's preoccupation with the *official* in the course of his Hague appearance. Robinson, after all, had dedicated his entire career to the welfare of the Jewish people;[74] Lemkin was a newcomer to that scene. Robinson and Rosenne were invested in international law; Lemkin, by training and experience, was a criminal lawyer.[75] Most poignantly, they were the *official* representatives of the Jewish state. Lemkin's *private* advocacy encroached on their public, official capacity and status. This was one more page in the book of Jewish representation politics.[76]

Lemkin's autobiography boasted his credentials as a 'totally unofficial' man.[77] From the perspective of our two protagonists, his private diplomacy arrogated to represent the interests of the entire Jewish people. Lemkin—like Lauterpacht in his 1950 Jerusalem lecture advocating for the individual right of petition[78]—usurped the Jewish voice. This task, however, was now appointed to the sovereign Jewish state, and to its official representatives—like Rosenne and Robinson. Such sovereign sensibilities led Robinson to lambast, in early 1951, the forms of post-1948 Jewish rights-advocacy 'as if nothing changed'.[79] Jewish sovereignty may have left, *faute de mieux*, some room for *public*, if non-governmental, Jewish advocacy;[80] it had far less tolerance for *private* Jewish advocacy. Lemkin's lack of official status, his unofficial *modus operandi*, and the apparent success of his project all encroached on the representative prerogative of the Jewish state—and undermined the standing and status of its representatives. Robinson's objection to becoming a 'lobbyist for the ratification of the Genocide Convention'[81] protested the reversal of the sovereign, and natural, order of things; Jewish sovereignty meant that private Jewish advocacy, if any, must be subordinate to public Jewish diplomacy, not the other way around. Things had changed. These same sensibilities led Rosenne to intimate to the ICJ, in April 1951, that he was speaking for the entire Jewish people. This is also why his Court statement acknowledged only the official—that is, the

[74] The Hebrew title of Rosenne's obituary of Robinson translates: 'The Great Advocate of the Jewish People': Shabtai Rosenne, 'Jacob Robinson—In Memoriam' (1978) 24 Gesher 91 (Hebrew).

[75] Cooper (n 4) 17; Irvin-Erickson (n 10) 36–9.

[76] Discussed in detail in chs 2, 3.

[77] Donna-Lee Frieze (ed), *Totally Unofficial: The Autobiography of Raphael Lemkin* (Yale UP 2013); Mira L Siegelberg, 'Unofficial Men, Efficient Civil Servants: Raphael Lemkin in the History of International Law' (2013) 15 J of Genocide Research 297; Cooper (n 4) 81.

[78] Discussed in chs 2, 3.

[79] Robinson to Rosenne, 6 February 1951, FM–1830/8; Sharett to Posner, 26 August 1948, FM–67/5, ISA.

[80] Eg the right of petition of NGOs, discussed in ch 3.

[81] Robinson to Rosenne, 5 February 1951 (n 32).

state-made—aspect of the drafting history of the Genocide Convention and credited the universal rather than the particular.[82]

Lemkin's unofficial diplomacy, moreover, was too akin to traditional Jewish Diaspora advocacy (*shtadlanut*) that was no longer consonant with the Jewish sovereign turn.[83] Following Israel's UN admission, Sharett told the *Knesset* that the transformation in the status of the Jewish people meant that Jews now no longer would have to 'chase around in corridors and cram in the galleries of convocations of governments, condemned to anonymity and silence'; they now 'sat to a table, like all others'.[84] Lemkin, by contrast, had turned chasing delegates in corridors and watching from the public gallery into a form of art.[85] Lemkin, Robinson wrote to a colleague in early 1952, was a 'one cause *meshuga* [madman]';[86] official, state-centred Jewish diplomacy entailed a broad perspective that Lemkin did not possess.

Robinson's sovereign sensibilities, and attendant aversion to Lemkin, also drew on their respective involvement with the Nuremberg trial. In late 1945, Robinson rued that IJA's role—that included establishing the factual record for the prosecution—had been limited to that of an unofficial lobbyist: 'we, those who are competent, are on the outside',[87] he wrote. Others, less competent, were on the inside. The question of Jewish representation at and exclusion from the trial highly preoccupied him and the WJC.[88] Lemkin, for his part, undoubtedly was frustrated

[82] Ch 4.

[83] On *shtadlanut* (intercession): Mirjam Thulin, 'Shtadlanut' in Dan Diner (ed), *Enzyklopädie Jüdischer Geschichte und Kultur*, vol 5 (Metzler 2014) 472; Israel Bartal, 'From *Shtadlanut* to "Jewish Diplomacy"? 1756–1840–1881' (2016) 15 Simon Dubnow Institute YB 109. I am not challenging the view that the 'practice of shtadlanut was based on a fundamental acknowledgment of the Jews' subaltern relationship to non-Jewish government', in contrast to 'modern Jewish advocacy', which 'rests upon the assumption or the demand that Jewish grievances be recognized on the basis of universal, human-rights criteria, and/or on the civic prerogatives of Jews as fellow citizens of the polity': Eli Lederhendler, 'Shtadlanut and Stewardship: Paternal Diplomacy and Leadership in American Jewry, 1860s to 1920s' (2018) 19 Jewish Culture & Hist 97. Rather, my point is that, ideologically, Jewish sovereignty tended to conflate both into a 'Diaspora' style of diplomacy.

[84] *Divrei HaKnesset* (Parliamentary Record) (15 June 1949) 717–19 (Hebrew).

[85] Frieze (n 77).

[86] Robinson to Goitein, 7 February 1952 (n 14).

[87] Robinson, General Report to the Combined Staffs of the Office on the Nuremberg War Criminals Trials, 6 December 1945, WJC-C14/16, AJA. For Robinson's Nuremberg role: Laura Jockusch, 'Justice at Nuremberg? Jewish Responses to Nazi War-Crime Trials in Allied-Occupied Germany' (2012) 19 Jewish Soc Stud 107; Michael R Marrus, 'A Jewish Lobby at Nuremberg: Jacob Robinson and the Institute of Jewish Affairs, 1945–1946' (2006) 27 Cardozo L Rev 1651, 1657; Kaplan-Feuereisen (n 56) 167; Boaz Cohen, 'Dr. Jacob Robinson, the Institute of Jewish Affairs and the Elusive Jewish Voice in Nuremberg' in David Bankier and Dan Michman (eds), *Holocaust and Justice: Representation and Historiography of the Holocaust in Post-War Trials* (Yad Vashem/Berghahn 2010) 81; Jonathan Bush, 'Nuremberg and Beyond: Jacob Robinson, International Lawyer' (2017) 39 Loyola LA Intl & Comp L Rev 259; Jacob Robinson, 'The International Military Tribunal and the Holocaust: Some Legal Reflections' (1972) 7 Isr L Rev 1.

[88] Robinson, General Report, 6 December 1945 (n 87); correspondence, WJC–C14/21, AJA; Robinson, 'Tribunal' (n 87) 3; *Resolutions: War Emergency Conference of the World Jewish Congress, Atlantic City, New Jersey, November 26–30, 1944* (WJC 1944) 20, 21 (WJC '[r]epresentatives ... shall be admitted before the tribunals set up by the United Nations for the prosecution and punishment of war

with the tribunal's judgement.[89] Yet his involvement, albeit through temporary appointment with the US War Crimes Office of the Judge Advocate-General,[90] was nonetheless far more official and on the 'inside' than Robinson's.[91] Reporting on the Nuremberg proceedings to the WJC, Robinson 'implied', as Michael Marrus noted, 'that Lemkin was some sort of unwelcome interloper in the discussions'.[92] It did not help that Lemkin's 'genocide' diluted, at Nuremberg, what Robinson considered to be unique Jewish suffering:

> parts of it [the indictment] would have looked different if not for our work and watchfulness. Suddenly the idea of 'Genocide' (Lemkin's term) came into being, and the term was inserted into the document but was not developed. As an example of the application of the concept of 'Genocide,' 'Jews and Gypsies' were cited. When I saw that I got mad, because it so reeked of the Nazi method of humiliation of Jews by putting them in a class with the gypsies. It is a doubtful source of satisfaction that the word, 'Poles,' was inserted to make the phrase read: 'Jews, Poles, and Gypsies.'[93]

And while, unlike Rosenne, Robinson would at times inform Lemkin of Israel's actions with regard to the Genocide Convention, such communications invoked the superiority of official, state action. In June 1950, he boasted the advantages of sovereign diplomacy to 'Dear Professor Lemkin', to whom he wrote with an admixture of laconicism and glee:

criminals as *amici curiae*'); Cohen (n 87) 82, 87–96 ('Robinson's insights into the dynamics of inclusion and exclusion of Jewish issues and Jewish representatives in the court').

[89] Cooper (n 4) 77.
[90] ibid, 63–4.
[91] Cohen (n 87) 89; cf Irvin-Erickson (n 10) 143. At Nuremberg, Robinson would realise that demanding observer status was 'meaningless': Robinson, General Report, 6 December 1945 (n 87). Michael R Marrus, 'Three Jewish Émigrés at Nuremberg: Jacob Robinson, Hersch Lauterpacht, and Raphael Lemkin' in Ezra Mendelsohn, Stefani Hoffman, and Richard I Cohen (eds), *Against the Grain: Jewish Intellectuals in Hard Times* (Berghahn 2013) 240.
[92] Marrus (n 91) 245.
[93] Robinson, General Report, 6 December 1945 (n 87); James Loeffler, *Rooted Cosmopolitans: Jews and Human Rights in the Twentieth Century* (Yale UP 2018) 133–4. Later, Robinson's sovereign sensibilities overrode his views on the uniqueness of the Holocaust when Rosenne planned to play down, in his ICJ statement, the Genocide Convention's idiosyncrasy and credit the making of the Convention to the universal. Robinson did not protest Rosenne's reference to the targeting of 'Russians, Poles, and members of other groups', but objected to a reference to 'Catholics': Robinson to Rosenne, 26 March 1951 (n 44). Some aversion to the Nuremberg judgement persisted in Robinson's writings. After his involvement in the Eichmann trial, he credited Lemkin for coining 'genocide' but emphasised that it 'remained a single *obiter dictum* in the records of the IMT'. He also noted it was 'never formally invoked': Robinson, 'Tribunal' (n 87) 6, 13. That article concluded with a passage analysing the Eichmann case—in terms of 'ethnocide', not Lemkin's 'genocide'—as a corrective to Nuremberg's failings: 'Ethnocide, the crime against the Jewish people, had to wait longer for its realization. In the Eichmann trial the accused appeared as responsible for the Crime against the Jewish People, not only against human rights of individual Jews, but also against the collective right of a people to existence and continuity. International law doctrine accepted the new concept approvingly'.

> Enclosed please find circular no.13 of the Legal Adviser to the Foreign Office of May 16, 1950, containing the full text of an English translation of the Crime of Genocide (Prevention and Punishment) Law, 5710–1950. I wonder whether some other countries which have ratified the Convention have already taken the necessary measures for their implementation by national legislation.[94]

4. Our 'Radical Solution'

The sovereign sensibilities driving Robinson and Rosenne's aversion to Lemkin and his project were not limited to personal grudges, difference in styles of Jewish diplomacy, or zeal with newly acquired sovereign status and voice. Their aversion ran deeper, drawing on the fundamental ideological assumptions of the Genocide Convention implicit in Lemkin's claim that the Convention was an instrument 'for the protection of the Jews in the world today'[95] or, as he wrote to Ben-Gurion, that it promised to 'redeem' Jewish suffering.[96] Like Justice Minister Rosen,[97] Robinson and Rosenne had each elected to subscribe to another, 'radical solution' to the problem of Jewish survival. Their choice, like the impetus for refuting the Genocide Convention's claim to constitute an instrument of Jewish survival, was ideological—notwithstanding any opportunity that the Convention would occasionally present to Israel's jurist-diplomats. What made that imperative even more pressing for Robinson and Rosenne was that the Genocide Convention pointed to a flaw in their own ideological credentials and threatened to undo their own transformations into sovereign Jews. Appraising their transformations, and how these affected their aversion to the Convention, requires an excursus into their respective past engagements with minority rights; into the ideological underpinnings of these engagements; and into disillusionment.

4.1 Avraham Gorali's Disillusionment

In 1952, the first ever doctoral degree conferred by Hebrew University of Jerusalem 'for a research work in international affairs' was published.[98] The point of departure of *The Jewish Minority in the League of Nations* was the evident fall of 'minority

[94] Robinson to Lemkin, 5 June 1950, B1–F20, Lemkin Papers, NYPL.
[95] [Lemkin], Memorandum to the American Zionist Council, 14 June 1950 (n 13).
[96] Rosenne to Attorney-General, 13 November 1949 (n 19).
[97] *Divrei HaKnesset* (Parliamentary Record) (26 December 1949) 313, 314 (Hebrew), discussed in ch 4.
[98] Norman Bentwich, *Preface* to Abraham Gorali, *The Jewish Minority in the League of Nations: Origin and Development of the Minorities Protection by the League of Nations and the Jewish Petitions* (Sifria Mishpatit 1952) 118 (Hebrew). The thesis, supervised by Bentwich, was approved in 1945: 'Jerusalem: Doctor of Philosophy Awarded' *Davar* (15 June 1945).

rights' into obscurity, and the new international focus on 'the rights of man as man'. 'The Universal Declaration of Human Rights adopted in the aftermath of the Second World War', wrote Abraham Gorali, a lawyer by training, 'has taken the place of the Minorities Treaties of the Versailles system'.[99]

Like the League itself, minority rights were by 1945 discredited.[100] The Genocide Convention, without resort to the term 'minorities', came into being against the post-war current. In Lemkin's words, the Convention was an extension of past 'international concern' for 'the treatment of citizens of other states by their governments' underpinning nineteenth-century 'diplomatic action' on behalf of religious or ethnic minorities and 'the minority treaties under the auspices of the League of Nations'.[101] Criminalizing genocide, then, was the swan song of minority rights.[102] As the minority system was 'laid to rest', the most extreme abuses of national, ethnic, racial, or religious groups were stamped with criminality. This led Mark Mazower to reflect that '[w]ere one unkind, one might say that [the Genocide Convention] was merely the homage paid by the United Nations to the impotence of its predecessors and to the victims of the Nazis'.[103]

Gorali's doctoral dissertation, however, recorded another type of transition—and a more particular aversion to minority rights and the Genocide Convention, their successor. In the introduction to the published thesis, Gorali wrote:

> Those who struggle to find solutions for and concern themselves with the fate of the people of Israel, after the Holocaust that has visited the European diaspora, *will do well to study and realize the extent to which international protection can assist in safeguarding the rights of Jews in the diaspora. The international Convention on the Prevention and Punishment of the Crime of Genocide* adopted by the UN Assembly on 9.12.48, its origins and roots can be understood against the backdrop

[99] The translation appears in Nathan Feinberg, *Israel and the United Nations: Report of a Study Group Set Up By the Hebrew University of Jerusalem* (Manhattan 1956) 254. The shift was noted in 1949 by Jacob Robinson, 'From Protection of Minorities to Promotion of Human Rights' (1948) 1 Jewish YB Intl L 115, 134 ('the very term "minority" almost became taboo'); Joseph B Schechtman, 'Decline of the International Protection of Minority Rights' (1951) 4 The Western Political Quarterly 1; Josef Kunz, 'The Present Status of the International Law for the Protection of Minorities' (1954) 48 AJIL 282.

[100] Jacob Robinson, Oscar Karbach, Max M Laserson, Nehemiah Robinson, and Marc Vishniak (eds), *Were the Minorities Treaties a Failure?* (IJA 1943). Historians have recently reclaimed this observation: Mark Mazower, *No Enchanted Palace: The End of Empire and the Ideological Origins of the United Nations* (Princeton UP 2009) 131–2 ('precisely as the Genocide Convention was wending its way through the various organs of the UN ... the prewar minority rights treaties were quietly and unobtrusively laid to rest'); Mira Siegelberg, 'Contending with the Ghosts of the Past: Raphael Lemkin and the Origins of the Genocide Convention' (2006) 1 Columbia Undergraduate J of Hist 30, 31–2 ('postwar climate that was no longer amenable to that agenda'); Gil Rubin, 'The End of Minority Rights: Jacob Robinson and the Jewish Question in World War II' (2012) 11 Simon Dubnow Institute YB 55; Peter Hilpold, 'The League of Nations and the Protection of Minorities—Rediscovering a Great Experiment' (2013) 17 Max Planck YB of UN L 87.

[101] Raphael Lemkin, 'Genocide' (1946) 15(2) American Scholar 227, 228.

[102] Mark Mazower, 'The Strange Triumph of Human Rights, 1933–1950' (2004) 47 The Historical J 379, 387.

[103] Mazower (100) 148.

> of the topics discussed in this book. But for the failure of the Versailles system, peoples, in the first place the Jewish people, would not have been deported or annihilated.[104]

Gorali, clearly, was disillusioned with the power of the Genocide Convention—and international law generally—to affect the protection of '*Jews in the diaspora*'. Robinson and Rosenne shared that disillusionment.[105] Robinson wrote to Rosenne that 'the Genocide Convention should not be considered as a matter which gives any particular guarantee to the Jewish people against possible future acts of mass terror'.[106] Rosenne, to justify his Hague appearance, wrote to Sharett that 'Israel is interested in the Genocide Convention even though *it cannot be considered as universal salvation*'.[107] Likewise, he had misgivings about the 'negligible' 'practical value' of the Convention 'in the event of another world war'.[108] Yet these misgivings did not concern the Genocide Convention's *universal* promise. The fault Rosenne found in the Genocide Convention concerned its *particular*, Jewish promise. The Hebrew phrase he used—'universal salvation'—referenced Jewish salvation and, specifically, salvation through a return to Zion.[109] What Rosenne had meant, as he wrote to Robinson, was that 'there was no doubt that the Convention does not safeguard the [Jewish] people against a holocaust'.[110] The fault with the Genocide Convention, then, concerned its inability to protect Jewish rights and, even more so, Jewish survival. This verdict, for Gorali, Robinson, and Rosenne, drew on recent Jewish experience and, at the same time, expressed an ideological refutation of the model of Jewish emancipation on which the Convention and, before it, minority rights were predicated.

4.2 The Genocide Convention: A Post-War Diaspora Nationalism Project

Lemkin's project did not only return, in the aftermath of the Holocaust, to protection promised by minority rights. His concept of genocide may have had numerous intellectual sources,[111] yet in Jewish terms, it drew on *fin de siècle* and interwar

[104] Emphasis added; Gorali (n 98) 7.
[105] As did Justice Minister Rosen when presenting the Convention to the *Knesset*: ch 4.
[106] Robinson to Rosenne, 5 February 1951 (n 32).
[107] Emphasis added; Rosenne to Sharett, 18 March 1951, FM-1832/3, ISA.
[108] Rosenne to Robinson, 28 February 1951, FM-1832/3, ISA.
[109] Rosenne paraphrased *Isaiah* 45:17. The King James Bible translated the Hebrew plural *olamim* as 'everlasting' (salvation). Rosenne, however, used the singular *olam*, meaning world or universe. The chapter lends itself to Zionist readings: it narrates God's words to Cyrus, and describes the King's role in the repatriation of the exiled Jews. Rosenne used the same language in a bulletin for Israel's legations, No.245, 27 March 1951, FM-1832/3, ISA.
[110] Rosenne to Robinson, 15 February 1951 (n 33).
[111] The influence of Johann Gottfried Herder and Karl Renner is often discussed in this respect: Dirk Moses, 'Raphael Lemkin, Culture, and the Concept of Genocide' in Donald Bloxham and Dirk Moses

Jewish political thought and practice. Specifically, he was influenced by the 'political vision of extra-territorial ethnic identity in the work of Simon Dubnow' (1860–1941).[112]

Dubnow's historical reading of the Jewish past and his critique of Herzl's Zionism together gave rise to a competing political vision of Jewish nationalism. The 'Autonomism'—or 'Diaspora Nationalism'—he had advocated identified the Diaspora as the proper site for Jewish national revival. 'Dubnowism'—as his political thought was sometimes known—therefore prescribed securing the maintenance of Jewish collective, autonomous, existence in the Diaspora as a form of Jewish nationalism that no longer required the territorial concentration characterizing the nation-state.[113] This model of Jewish nationalism decreed investment in the present: Autonomism, *per* Dubnow, 'recognize[s] Jewry, not only as a nation of the past or of the future, but also as a nation that is, of the present'. The writ of Autonomism became 'work of the present', or *Gegenwartsarbeit*,[114] in the Diaspora. Zionism, which Dubnow first censured as no more than modern day 'messianism' and 'fantasy', 'look[s] upon Jewry as a nation that is to be in the future'.[115] Zionism came to be associated with 'work of the future'. Critically, both versions of Jewish nationalism sought, and competed for, the guarantee of 'public law'.[116]

Programmatically, Autonomism called for '[s]triving for national rights or cultural autonomy in the Diaspora'.[117] This translated in demands for a 'national-cultural autonomy'[118] that constructed Jews as a *national* minority. A national minority, Dubnow wrote, must engage in a 'defense of its own *originality*, its language, its customs, its schools, its self-government'.[119] Dubnow's ideas drove Jewish

(eds), *The Oxford Handbook on Genocide Studies* (OUP 2010) 19, 23–4; Cooper (n 4) 91; Irvin-Erickson (n 10) 67 presents a more nuanced view.

112 Siegelberg (n 77) 314ff; Anson Rabinbach, 'The Challenge of the Unprecedented: Raphael Lemkin and the Concept of Genocide' (2005) 4 Simon Dubnow Institute YB 397, 419; Moses (111) 24; Cooper (n 4) 4, 91–4; Irvin-Erickson (n 10) 59–61. Compare, however, Loeffler, 'Cleopatra' (n 7).

113 Simon Rabinovitch (ed), *Jews and Diaspora Nationalism: Writings on Jewish Peoplehood in Europe and the United States* (Waltham 2012); Simon Rabinovitch, *Jewish Rights, National Rites: Nationalism and Autonomy in Late Imperial and Revolutionary Russia* (Stanford UP 2014).

114 Ch 1; Dmitry Shumsky, 'Gegenwartsarbeit' in Dan Diner (ed), *Enzyklopädie Jüdischer Geschichte und Kultur*, vol 2 (Metzler 2012) 402; Dmitry Shumsky, 'Zionism in Quotations Marks, or To What Extent Was Dubnow a Non-Zionist' (2012) 77 Zion 369; Israel Bartal, *Cossack and Bedouin: Land and People in Jewish Nationalism* (Am Oved 2007) (Hebrew); Marcos Silber, 'The Metamorphosis of Pre-Dubnovian Autonomism into Diaspora Jewish-Nationalism' in Minna Rozen (ed), *Homelands and Diasporas: Greeks, Jews and their Migrations* (Taurus 2008) 235; Matityahu Mintz, '"Work for the Land of Israel" and "Work in the Present": A Concept of Unity, A Reality of Contradiction' in Jehuda Reinharz and Anita Shapira (eds), *Essential Papers on Zionism* (Cassell 1996) 161.

115 Simon Dubnow, *Nationalism and History: Essays on Old and New Judaism* (Jewish Publication Society of America 1961) 157 ('Political Zionism is merely a renewed form of messianism . . . In it the ecstasy bound up in the great idea of rebirth blurs the lines between reality and fantasy'). Other editions are titled *Letters on Old and New Judaism*.

116 Ch 1.

117 Dubnow (n 115) 86.

118 ibid, 186.

119 Emphasis added; ibid, 174.

engagement with minority politics, law, and advocacy at the national level and, with the collapse of empires during the Great War, internationally.[120] By seeking to extend, if only in criminal form, 'the minority treaties under the auspices of the League of Nations',[121] Lemkin's project reasserted Dubnow's Diaspora Nationalism.

On 8 December 1941, in Riga, Simon Dubnow was murdered by the Nazis. Lemkin's carefully crafted[122] autobiography describes how he met the ageing Dubnow in Riga, in the fall of 1939, before fleeing Eastern Europe. His version of the encounter portrays, in dramaturgical terms, a scene involving the passing of the torch. No evidence appears to corroborate that it took place.[123] His writings on genocide nonetheless underscore his intellectual and ideological debt to Dubnow. Dubnow's political theory wrought, out of the particularities of Jewish history, a universal-humanist plan for protection of the existence, distinctiveness, and 'originality' of Jewish minorities.[124] Here was the blueprint for Lemkin's thought on genocide and the justification for the protection of the group. Dubnow denounced 'oppressive' nationalism: 'I would be especially ashamed of the kind of nationalism that is primarily concerned with a policy of Russification, Germanization or similar forced assimilation, that is, the annihilation of the national identity of national minorities'.[125] This was the crux of Lemkin's concept of genocide and the impetus for its criminalization.

What made, for Lemkin, groups deserving of international legal protection—what made the 'practice of genocide anywhere' worthy of criminalization—was that genocide affects 'the vital interests of all civilized people. Its consequences can neither be isolated nor localized.' This was Lemkin's answer to the question 'WHY should genocide be recognized as an international problem?'.[126] During his campaign for the Genocide Convention, he asserted that alongside economic and

[120] Oscar Janowsky, *The Jews and Minority Rights, 1898-1919* (Columbia UP 1933); Carole Fink, *Defending the Rights of Others: The Great Powers, the Jews, and International Minority Protection, 1878–1938* (CUP 2004) 193–235; Mark Levene, *War, Jews, and the New Europe: The Diplomacy of Lucien Wolf, 1914-1919* (OUP 1992); Mark Levene, 'Nationalism and its Alternatives in the International Arena: The Jewish Question at Paris, 1919' (1993) 28 J of Contemp Hist 511; Verena Dohrn, 'State and Minorities: The First Lithuanian Republic and S.M. Dubnow's Concept of Cultural Autonomy' in A Nikžentaitis, Stefan Schreiner, and Darius Staliūnas (eds), *The Vanished World of Lithuanian Jews* (Rodopi 2004) 155, 156–7; Stanislaw Sierpowski, 'Minorities in the System of the League of Nations' in Paul Smith (ed), *Ethnic Groups in International Relations* (NYU Press 1991) 13; Grit Jilek, 'Jenseits von Territorium: Jüdische Nation und Diaspora bei Simon Dubnow' (2014) 13 Simon Dubnow Institute YB 463; Anke Hilbrenner, *Diaspora-Nationalismus: Zur Geschichtskonstruktion Simon Dubnows* (Vandenhoeck & Ruprecht 2007); Victor E Kelner, 'Nation der Gegenwart: Simon Dubnow über Jüdische Politik und Geschichte' (2003) 2 Simon Dubnow Institute YB 519.

[121] Lemkin (n 101) 228.

[122] Loeffler, 'Cleopatra' (n 7).

[123] Frieze (77) 71–2; Cooper (n 4) 35; Rabinbach (112) 419–20. Dubnow's biography, written by his daughter, is silent on this meeting: Sophie Dubnov-Erlich, *The Life and Work of S. M. Dubnov: Diaspora Nationalism and Jewish History* (Indiana UP 1991).

[124] Dubnow (n 115) 174.

[125] ibid, 126. He therefore denounced policies 'based on the suppression of national minorities and on their forced assimilation with the dominant majority': ibid, 141, 174.

[126] Raphael Lemkin, 'Genocide—A Modern Crime' (1945) 4 Free World 39.

humanitarian consequences, 'the main impact of genocide is on our civilization itself. If nations are wiped out, how can they continue to make *original* contributions to world culture?'[127] This was a recurring Dubnowian theme in his writing on genocide:

> Cultural considerations speak for international protection of national, religious and cultural groups. Our whole heritage is a product of the contributions of all nations. We can best understand this when we realize how impoverished our culture would be if the peoples doomed by Germany, such as the Jews, had not been permitted to create the Bible, or to give birth to an Einstein, a Spinoza; if the Poles had not had the opportunity to give to the world a Copernicus, a Chopin, a Curie; the Czechs, a Huss, a Dvorak; the Greeks, a Plato and a Socrates; the Russians, a Tolstoy and a Shostakovich.[128]

These notions underscored the Genocide Convention and its persisting 'commitment to enshrining groups as objects of international protection'.[129] From a Jewish perspective, the Convention expressed a persistent international legal commitment to the protection of the autonomous existence of Jewish *national* minorities. For Avraham Gorali, it was too late to return to Diaspora Nationalism, *Gegenwartsarbeit*, and minority rights. So was it for Jacob Robinson and Shabtai Rosenne.

4.3 The Long-Drawn Disillusionment of Jacob Robinson

Jacob Robinson's interwar career—in political work, legal-diplomatic praxis, and scholarship—epitomizes the Jewish engagement with minority rights and autonomy.[130] After his repatriation from German captivity during World War I, he returned to independent Lithuania to participate in the founding of a Jewish education system and directed, for several years, a Hebrew Gymnasium in Virbalis. In Kovno, he served as the co-editor of a *Yiddish* newspaper, *Di Idishe Shtime* (1919–1940), that was the mouthpiece for Jewish Autonomist demands. In 1922, Robinson was elected to the *Seimas*; until its 1926 dissolution, he chaired the Jewish faction

[127] Emphasis added; [Lemkin], [Draft Letter 2], [n.d.] P–154, Box 2–5, Lemkin Collection, AJHS.
[128] Lemkin (n 101) 228.
[129] Siegelberg (n 77) 309; Lemkin (n 101) 228; and Lemkin's 1933 proposals to ban 'attacks carried out against an individual as a member of collectivity': Raphael Lemkin, 'Acts Constituting a General Danger Considered as Offenses against the Law of Nations' (1933) http://www.preventgenocide.org/lemkin/madrid1933-english.htm accessed 20 January 2020. Ana Filipa Vrdoljak, 'Human Rights and Genocide: The Work of Lauterpacht and Lemkin in Modern International Law' (2009) 20 EJIL 1163.
[130] Rubin (n 100) 56 (Robinson's 'political maturation thus coincided with the crystallization of a new agenda of Jewish nationalists in the interwar years focused on fostering the existence of Jews as a national minority'); Loeffler, *Cosmopolitans* (n 93) 33 ('one of Europe's foremost champions of minority rights'); Kaplan-Feuereisen (n 56).

and was the unofficial spokesperson for the Parliamentary minorities bloc.[131] These multiple careers all expressed Robinson's investment in the Jewish autonomous experiment in Lithuania.[132] Later, his interest extended beyond national borders: he participated in the proceedings of the Congress of National Minorities (1925–1930),[133] and wrote extensively on minority questions, including a comprehensive compendium on minorities literature.[134] Robinson, we saw, was one of those activists comprising the *Comité des Délégations Juives* and was involved, in that capacity, in the 1933 Bernheim petition to the League of Nations.[135]

It is hard to imagine an interwar career more representative of the praxis of *Gegenwartsarbeit* or a more abiding investment in the Diaspora. Robinson, fittingly, co-authored with Dubnow the entry on 'Autonomism' in the 1929 *Encyclopedia Judaica* published in Berlin.[136] He had intimate familiarity with Dubnow's historical and political writings; in May 1940, the two discussed the need for a revision of Dubnow's 'interpretation of Jewish history'.[137] In his contribution to the 1949 *Jewish Yearbook of International Law*, titled 'From Protection of Minorities to Promotion of Human Rights', Robinson professed that 'international protection of minorities was motivated' not only by the prevention of 'discrimination, but also' sought protection 'against the pressure of assimilation'. At stake was the 'fundamental right to heterogeneity'.[138] The common ground with

[131] Eglé Bendikaité, 'Politician Without a Party: A Zionist Appraisal of Jacob Robinson's Activities in the Public Life of Lithuania' in Eglé Bendikaité and Dirk Roland Haupt (eds), *The Life, Times and Work of Jokubas Robinzonas—Jacob Robinson* (Akademia Verlag 2015) 39; Dohrn (n 120) 166; Loeffler, *Cosmopolitans* (n 93) 33; Kaplan-Feuereisen (n 56) 163. On his involvement in Lithuanian Parliamentarism: 'Di fraktsye un di algemeyne un idishe minderhaytn-bavegung' ['The Jewish Faction and the General and Jewish Minorities Movement'] in *Barikht fun der idisher seym-fraktsye fun II Litvishn seym (1923–1926) [Report of the Jewish Parliament Faction of the Second Lithuanian Parliament (1923–1926)]* (1926) 77 (Yiddish).

[132] Šarūnas Liekis, *A State Within a State?: Jewish Autonomy in Lithuania 1918–1925* (Versus Aureus 2003); Marcos Silber, 'Lithuania? But Which? The Changing Political Attitude of the Jewish Political Elite in East Central Europe toward Emerging Lithuania, 1915–1919' in Vladas Sirutavičius and Darius Staliūnas (eds), *A Pragmatic Alliance, Jewish-Lithuanian Political Cooperation at the Beginning of the 20th Century* (Central European UP 2011) 119; Zvi Y Gitelman (ed), *The Emergence of Modern Jewish Politics: Bundism and Zionism in Eastern Europe* (University of Pittsburgh Press 2003).

[133] Moshe Landau, *The Disappointing Alliance: Jews and Germans in the European Minorities' Congress* (Diaspora Research Institute 1992) (Hebrew); Sabine Bamberger-Stemmann, *Der Europäische Nationalitätenkongreß 1925 bis 1938: Nationale Minderheiten zwischen Lobbyistentum und Großmachtinteressen* (Verlag Herder-Institut 2001); Kaplan-Feuereisen (n 56) 163; Shabtai Rosenne, 'Jacob Robinson—In Memoriam' (1978) 13 Isr L Rev 287; Abraham Tory, 'Jacob Robinson—In Memoriam' (1978–1979) 32 HaPraklit 125 (Hebrew).

[134] Jacob Robinson, *Das Minoritätenproblem und seine Literatur, Allgemeiner Teil* (de Gruyter 1928); 'Bibliography' in Jacob Robinson, 'Metamorphosis of the United Nations' (1958) 94 RdC 493, 495–6.

[135] Philipp Graf, 'The Bernheim Petition 1933: Jacob Robinson's Contribution to Jewish Minority Diplomacy in the Interwar Years' in Bendikaité and Haupt (n 131) 179; ch 2 discusses the *Comité* and the Bernheim Petition.

[136] Simon Dubnow and Jakob Robinson, 'Autonomie', *Encyclopedia Judaica*, vol 3 (Verlag Eshkol 1929) 749–64. Dubnow covered the past, Robinson the present: 'Autonomie in der jüdischen Gegenwart'.

[137] Robinson to Easterman, 6 January 1945, WJC-C12/1, AJA.

[138] Robinson et al, *Failure* (n 100) 119–20.

Dubnow's political thought—and with Lemkin's understanding of genocide—is patent.[139]

Robinson, however, also identified as a Zionist; he attended several Zionist Congresses and had ties to Zionist political parties in Lithuania.[140] In the interwar years, after the Zionist movement followed other Jewish political parties in Central and Eastern Europe in adopting Dubnow's Diaspora-focused programme of 'work of the present', one could be different shades of both.[141] After the Helsingfors Program, the Copenhagen Manifesto, and the Versailles settlement,[142] one could identify as a Zionist yet invest in minority politics at home—invest, that is, in Jewish national revival in the Diaspora while still professing adherence to the creed of the future National Home in Palestine. The formulae wrought at these venues made Zionism that inclusive; for some, this represented a veritable ideological synthesis of Dubnow and Herzl. For others, however, this was only a pragmatic compromise to be adopted as a political programme, an instrument, or an interim *Bildung* platform—or rejected.[143] It did not resolve the question of centre and periphery, means and ends, or priority. In 1907, Asher Ginsberg, Dubnow's close friend who shared many of his assumptions when advocating Jewish *cultural* revival in Palestine, wrote to Dubnow that 'national work in the diaspora can be of use only as a stepping stone to our national home in Palestine ... *without the centre in Palestine* this diaspora work cannot satisfy our craving for a full national life'.[144] Dubnow disagreed. So would have Robinson; his Diaspora work was an end, not merely a means.

A. 'Working for Lithuania': A National Engagement

Robinson's commitment to the imperatives of Diaspora Nationalism, by his own admission, far outweighed his adherence to Zionism: the former was the model

[139] Other affinities to Dubnow's political thought and historical analysis are apparent in Robinson's works and politics. At the first meeting of the Congress of Minorities, for example, he grounded autonomy, following Dubnow, in the historical experience of self-government of Jewish *Kehilot* (communities) before emancipation: *Sitzungsbericht der ersten Konferenz der organisierten nationalen Gruppen in den Staaten Europas im Jahre 1925 zu Genf* (Braumüller Universitäts-Verlagsbuchhandlung 1925) 47; '*Funem kongres fun di natsionalen minderhayten in Zheneve: Di rede fun doktor Robinzon*' *Der Moment* (23 October 1925) (Yiddish). Other examples are Robinson, 'Tribunal' (n 87) 13 discussed at n 93; Robinson, [Note], 15 October 1945, WJC-C14/21, AJA, discussed (n 222) below. Natan Sznaider, *Jewish Memory and the Cosmopolitan Order: Hannah Arendt and the Jewish Condition* (Polity Press 2011) 88–90 notes other affinities, including Dubnow's blueprint, written for the WJC, to what became Robinson's IJA.

[140] Bendikaitė (n 131) 39.

[141] Shumsky, 'Zionism' (n 114).

[142] Ch 1 discusses the significance of these events.

[143] Gideon Shimoni, *The Zionist Ideology* (Brandeis UP 1995) 114–15, 169; David Vital, *Zionism: The Formative Years* (Clarendon 1982) 467–75; Mintz (n 114); Jonathan Frankel, *Prophecy and Politics: Socialism, Nationalism, and the Russian Jews 1862–1917* (CUP 1981).

[144] Emphasis in original; quoted in Shimoni (n 143) 109.

of Jewish 'national self-determination' he chose to invest in.[145] Until the 1940s, Robinson's Jewish national *activism* only rarely concerned Palestine.[146]

His relationship with Zionism in interwar Lithuania was recently described, appropriately, as 'symbiosis': his ties to Zionist parties in Lithuania may have been more than nominal, but they expressed more political convenience than ideological persuasion. He often lent his name to Jewish and Zionist organizations who 'used his standing and authority for their particular purposes'[147] affording him, in turn, the necessary political and organizational platform. The best evidence of his ideological priorities was a 1943 letter to WJC leaders where he confided that:

> Since 1920 I have never attended Zionist congresses and, while faithfully fulfilling my obligations toward Zionist funds, I regarded Palestinian resettlement as secondary in importance to the protection of Jewish life in the Diaspora. As a matter of fact, I devoted two decades of my life to theoretical research and practical activity in the latter field. [148]

Robinson's faith in national revival in the Diaspora, however, came to face severe tests. First, the Jewish autonomy in Lithuania was withdrawn. A few months earlier, his pedagogic book on Jewish demography and nationhood still boasted the 'known success' of 'implementing the national autonomy' in Lithuania.[149] Now, with others, he lamented the 'destruction' of 'our autonomy' and the removal of the '*Idishen Minister*'—Jewish Minister—Shimshon Rosenbaum.[150] After the Ministry was disbanded in 1924, Rosenbaum—a veteran Zionist leader who attended the Helsingfors Conference where the synthesis between Zionism and Dubnowism was forged—immigrated to Palestine.[151] Robinson, by contrast, elected to remain in Lithuania.

[145] *Sitzungsbericht* (n 139). His political essays in Lithuania 'were mostly in close connection with his political duties and of a rather "neutral" character, dedicated to international Jewish matters, to the realia of parliamentary work or to the status of Jewish national autonomy'; by contrast, Robinson published 'on topics currently on the Zionist agenda' only '[o]n rare occasions', and 'mostly in conjunction with other leaders of the Zionist Organization': footnotes omitted; Bendikaitė (n 131) 55.

[146] His 1929 cable to the Permanent Mandates Commission, reported by Loeffler, *Cosmopolitans* (n 93) 31 constitutes a rare exception.

[147] Bendikaitė (n 131) 60.

[148] Robinson to Stephen Wise, Nahum Goldmann, 25 June 1943, WJC-C97/17, AJA, discussed in Rubin (100) 57; I thank Gil Rubin for providing me with a copy of this letter.

[149] Jacob Robinson, *Yediat Amenu: Demografyah veNatsiologyah, Sefer Limud* veIyun [*Knowledge of Our People: Demography and Nationology, A Text and Study Book*] (Ayanot 1923) 129, 140 (Hebrew) ('to this day—except for Lithuania—there is no state where the Jews enjoy full rights in matters of education and self-government').

[150] [Jacob Robinson], '*A minderhaytn-ministerium*' ['A Ministry for Minorities'] *Di Idishe Shtime* (26 June 1923) (Yiddish); Jacob Robinson, '*Der hurban undzer avtonomie*' ['The Destruction of Our Autonomy'] *Di Idishe Shtime* (23 September 1924) (Yiddish), discussed in Bendikaitė (n 131) 55ff.

[151] Arieh Rafaeli Tzentziper, '*Veidot Artziot shel Tzionei Rusia*' ['National Conferences of Russian Zionists'] in *Katzir: Kovetz LeKorot HaTenuah HaTzionit BeRussia* [*Collection on the Development of the Zionist Movement in Russia*] (Massada 1964) 76, 80 (Hebrew). Rosenbaum received his doctorate in law from the University of Vienna: Eglė Bendikaitė, 'Intermediary between Worlds—Shimshon Rosenbaum: Lawyer, Zionist, Politician' (2008) 8–10 OstEuropa 171; Eglė Bendikaitė, 'One Man's

When the May 1926 election results for the third *Seimas* restored hopes for the reinstatement of Lithuania's Jewish autonomy, Robinson moved to condemn divisions among its supporters. Previously, he had been critical of Marxist-inflected programmes for Jewish autonomy.[152] Now he took issue with the Lithuanian Jewish *Folkist* party for its theoretical detachment, narrow political base, and disregard for the fact that Zionists were, like *Folkists*, invested in Jewish self-rule in Lithuania. In a series of seven pseudonymous articles, Robinson castigated the ideological dogmatism of Lithuanian *Folkists*—'all in all a very small grouplet' that 'liberated itself of its leaders' and 'became radical'—who insisted that investment in Palestine was inconsistent with Diaspora work. He also critiqued their parochial construction of 'the Jewish community as one single unit whose authority terminates at the borders of the country', thus foregoing 'the general bonds of the Jewish nation in the world' as well as Lithuania's international obligation towards its Jewish minority.[153]

This, however, was neither rejection of Diaspora Nationalism nor its abandonment.[154] On the contrary: Robinson remained committed to 'working for Lithuania'.[155] This was, rather, an appeal for grounding Jewish autonomy work and representation politics on a broad popular consensus at home. This was his opposition to the Lithuanian *Folkist* exclusionary vision of 'autonomy without Orthodoxy, Hebraists, and Zionists, and with an absolute majority of petty bourgeoisie';[156] there was 'no contradiction', he declared in another essay, between 'Zionism and land-politik'.[157] This was, equally, a call for an international approach to Jewish minority politics. Both goals could be expressed in terms of the synthetic interwar Zionist creed, but neither entailed a shift towards or according any priority to the National Home project in Palestine.

After the December 1926 military coup dashed any remaining hope for renewal of the Jewish autonomy, the international arena became the primary stage for Robinson's persisting investment in minority rights: at the Congress of National Minorities, the *Comité des Délégations Juives* (and its successor, the WJC), and in international law scholarship. Yet at the same time Robinson's Jewish politics went

Struggle: The Politics of Shimshon Rosenbaum' (1859–1934)' (2014) 13 Simon Dubnow Institute YB 87, 90. In 1932, he published a monograph calling for the revision of the notion of sovereignty: Shimshon Rosenbaum, *Der Souveränitätsbegriff: ein Versuch seiner Revision* (Gutzwiller 1932).

[152] Loeffler, *Cosmopolitans* (n 93) 37–8.

[153] [Jacob Robinson], '*Di folkistishe atake*' ['The Folkist Attack'] *Di Idishe Shtime* (16–29 September 1926) (Yiddish), discussed in Bendikaitė (n 131) 56–60. Only in Lithuania and Latvia did Folkist parties remain active throughout the interwar years.

[154] Cf Loeffler, *Cosmopolitans* (n 93) 31, 36, 38, etc who considers Robinson a Zionist rather than a Diaspora Nationalist.

[155] Jacob Robinzon, '*Tsionizm un land-politik*' ['Zionism and Landpolitics'] *Di Idishe Shtime* (18 May 1926) (Yiddish).

[156] [Robinson], '*atake*' (n 153).

[157] Robinson, '*Tsionizm*' (n 155). Bendikaitė (n 131) 61–4 observes that Robinson became more closely involved in the Zionist organisation in Lithuania 'after his political career as a member of parliament was over'.

international,[158] his 'land-politik' investment in the Lithuanian state-building project only increased. He kept 'working for Lithuania' and its future—in his Kaunas private practice, in Lithuania's diplomatic service, and in legal scholarship.[159]

B. 'This Time of Trial': Turning International

Robinson's international engagement in minority politics, however, presented its own tests and furnished its own reasons for disenchantment. The League of Nations' guarantee for the minority obligations of the succession states was not accompanied by political will to enforce it robustly.[160] Robinson helped engineer, if reluctantly,[161] the Jewish alliance with German *auslandsdeutsche* in the Congress of National Minorities[162] and, through German 'ethnic minorities', with Weimar foreign policy.[163] That alliance, however, collapsed once the Nazis took power in Germany.[164] Jewish delegates sought to move the Congress, and the German minorities, to take a position on early Nazi anti-Jewish legislation; to that end, they planned to boycott the 1933 annual session in Berne. Robinson, who after 1930 did not attend the annual Congress sessions, criticized early attempts to reach a compromise.[165] Feinberg, whose activity in the *Comité* kept him involved in Congress work, recalled that Robinson made repeated demands on Leo Motzkin—a member of the Congress Executive, and the Executive President of the *Comité*—'to seriously consider whether it is at all desirable for the Jews to continue taking part in the Congress'.[166] Robinson proposed that the Jewish delegates attend the Congress session 'for the sole purpose of declaring their withdrawal with the strongest protest and in the most dramatic manner'.[167] His disillusionment with the Congress was explicit, and irreversible. In August 1933, he wrote to Motzkin that '[t]he Congress of Nationalities has lost its *raison d'être* for all and in particular for us in its entirety'. 'The Congress leadership', he added, 'completely failed in this time of trial

[158] Dirk Roland Haupt, 'Jacob Robinson as Writer and Practitioner in International Law' in Bendikaitė and Haupt (n 131) 123, 125.

[159] Robinson co-founded the International Law Association of Lithuania; served as legal adviser to the Lithuanian Foreign Office (1932–1934); and was Lithuania's Counsel in the Lithuanian-German Conciliation Commission and in the Memel case before the Permanent Court of International Justice (1932). His prolific writings on Lithuanian and Baltic questions, starting in the late 1920s, are listed in Robinson (n 134) 495–6; Haupt (n 158). Of note is the two-volume Jacob Robinson, *Kommentar der Konvention über das Memelgebiet* (Spaudos Fondas 1934) published also in Lithuanian, and cited by Lemkin: Raphael Lemkin, *Axis Rule in Occupied Europe* (Carnegie Endowment for International Peace 1944) 198.

[160] Fink (n 120); Janowsky (n 120); Loeffler, *Cosmopolitans* (n 93) 49–50.

[161] Loeffler, *Cosmopolitans* (n 93) 45.

[162] Bamberger-Stemmann (n 133).

[163] Christoph Kimmich, *Germany and the League of Nations* (University of Chicago Press 1975).

[164] Landau (n 133) 126–59.

[165] ibid, 129–36. Nathan Feinberg, 'On the Withdrawal of the Jewish Minorities from the Minorities Congress' in Nathan Feinberg, *Essays on Jewish Issues of Our Time* (Dvir 1980) 96, 99 (Hebrew).

[166] ibid, 101; Robinson to Motzkin, 7 August 1933, A126\50\28, A306\26, CZA. I am grateful to Philipp Graf for drawing my attention to this source.

[167] Feinberg (n 165) 101.

for European Jewry'. Robinson proceeded to recommend that the last actions of the Jewish delegates could only be '*hingehen, um wegzugehen*'—take part, in order to leave.[168] His fear—that long-drawn negotiations in search of a compromise formula would dissipate without leaving an impression on public opinion—did materialize; 'we alone' among the *Comité* leadership, he wrote to Feinberg in March 1934, 'have a completely negative approach to the question of the Minorities Congress and the rest think, seemingly, that it is necessary to continue "flirting" with the Germans'.[169]

The 1933 Bernheim affair also revealed Robinson's growing ambivalence towards minority protection, the League of Nations, and international law. Although he had urged his *Comité* colleagues to turn to the League of Nations and, specifically, to avail themselves of the individual petition procedure,[170] he was hoping, at best, only for 'a moral verdict'. 'The purpose of the action', he wrote to Feinberg, 'should perhaps be mostly didactic'; he was convinced that 'no change for the better in the situation of Germany's Jews would come'.[171] Yet unlike Feinberg, who in the aftermath of the Bernheim affair elected to practice Zionism through a return to Palestine,[172] Robinson again chose to stay in Lithuania and involve himself in the efforts to establish the World Jewish Congress. Still, around 1933, he had abandoned the preparation of the second volume of his compendium on minorities literature.[173] The unfinished manuscript, deposited in Israel's National Library in Jerusalem, hints at doubts with this path of Jewish emancipation.[174]

C. Crisis and Ambivalence: Planning Post-War Jewish Rehabilitation

Robinson's flight from Europe, at first, was not accompanied by a complete disenchantment with minority rights. His ambivalence, that is, persisted. The 'Program' of the IJA he founded in New York in early 1941 still postulated a 'vital [Jewish] interest in the future organization of the world', and in minority rights. This was grounded in the global dimensions of the Jewish crisis: '[i]n Palestine', it observed, 'the continuance of the National Home is gravely threatened', while '[i]n one country after another, *emancipation has been revoked and minority rights*

[168] Robinson to Motzkin (n 166); Philipp Graf, *Die Bernheim-Petition 1933: Jüdische Politik in der Zwischenkriegszeit* (Vandenhoeck & Ruprecht 2008) 267.

[169] Feinberg (n 165) 108ff.

[170] Robinson to Feinberg, 20 April 1933, A126\616, CZA; ch 2 discusses this affair.

[171] Robinson to Feinberg, 20 April 1933 (n 170).

[172] Feinberg first immigrated to Palestine in 1924.

[173] Robinson, *Minoritätenproblem* (n 134); apparently, in connection with the IJA study on the 'failure' of the minorities treaties, Robinson planned a third volume; in 1943, following the publication of *Were the Minorities Treaties A Failure* (n 100), he planned to have the first volume 'revised and expanded': [Brochure], Were the Minorities Treaties a Failure, [n.d.], WJC-C126/5, AJA.

[174] Jacob Robinson, *Das Minoritätenproblem und seine Literatur: Kritische Einführung in die Quellen und Literatur, Allgemeiner Teil, Band II*, RC. Ms. Var. 435, Jacob Robinson Collection, Archives Department, National Library of Israel (Jerusalem); that collection also holds a rudimentary manuscript of a volume titled 'Bibliography on the Minorities Problem, 1939–1940'.

rudely scrapped.'[175] And though the Program decried 'the decline of international law, the tacit annulment of minorities agreements, the eclipse of the League of Nations, and the transformation of anti-Semitism into an official doctrine and policy of the state',[176] it sanctioned reengagement, not disengagement, with international law. The IJA's original task—before the annihilation taking place in Nazi-occupied Europe became known—was to 'prepare [a] ... brief' on 'means ... to be devised to prevent a recurrence of what has taken place and to insure security in the future'.[177] At the same time, the Program gave voice to a positive reading of the interwar Jewish investment in minority rights: preparing for the post-war settlement, Robinson reasoned,

> is the simple lesson of experience. In the peace of 1919, the two factors which did most *to guarantee the Jewish future, viz., the recognition of minority rights in Central and Eastern Europe* and the establishment of the Mandate for Palestine, were won only after intensive effort by Jewish political bodies. The same holds good today. The Jews will have to achieve their salvation by a vigorous prosecution of just claims before the council of nations and the conscience of the world. For that, however, they will require a brief, and it is to prepare that brief that the INSTITUTE OF JEWISH AFFAIRS has been called into being.[178]

Accordingly, the IJA Program raised 'the question of Rehabilitation' of 'Jews in Nazi-dominated countries', and foresaw, on the basis of 'past experience', two principal solutions 'to be considered at the same time,—the one static and the other dynamic'. The first sought to ensure the continuation of Jewish Diasporic existence, and envisioned a revamped minority protection regime: for 'those who still remain in their old homes, or are willing eventually to return to them ... it will be necessary to devise *more adequate legal safeguards than were provided by the old-time Minorities System*'.[179]

The second solution concerned 'those millions of refugees for whom new homes will have to be found' through the examination of 'immigration possibilities'. Here Robinson professed fidelity to the Zionist creed of IJA's parent bodies, the WJC and the American Jewish Congress: '[i]n attacking this issue', he wrote, 'the Institute will take it for granted that the development of the National Home in Palestine is the primary solution of the problem of Jewish migration'. This, however, was the

[175] Emphasis added; IJA, *Institute of Jewish Affairs: Program* (American Jewish Congress/WJC 1941) 9.
[176] ibid, 10–11.
[177] ibid, 9.
[178] Emphasis added; ibid, 9.
[179] Emphasis added; ibid, 10. Ironically, Hannah Arendt—a long-time antagonist of Robinson—had already written in 1940: 'I simply do not believe in any improvement in the minority rights of Jews and to me it seems absurd to demand "better guarantees."': Hannah Arendt, 'The Minority Question' in Jerome Kohn and Ron Feldman (eds), *The Jewish Writings—Hannah Arendt* (Schocken 2007) 125, 129.

conclusion of the discussion of the question of immigration, not its starting point. Though described as a 'primary solution', in fact it was recited as secondary to rehabilitation and a return to Diaspora homes and only after detailing IJA's plans for 'a thorough examination of immigration possibilities', a study of the 'financial side', and the conduct of 'a competent survey of all countries … to determine suitable places for settlement'.[180] In another part of the Program, detailing concrete research plans for a 'thorough investigation of Jewish life during the past 25 years',[181] Robinson included 'The Minorities Question: The minority treaties, their origin, operation and tacit annulment' as well as the 'Direct and indirect causes of their "failure"'—which verdict he, evidently, was not willing to concede.[182] Palestine, the National Home, or the mandate system were not items of the detailed research programme;[183] the Institute was meant to serve the Diaspora.[184] Robinson's Zionism remained secondary to his investment in protecting Jewish existence in the Diaspora.

Robinson's reluctance to admit the failure of the minorities system persisted. In 1943, he co-authored with his IJA colleagues a monograph titled *Were the Minorities Treaties a Failure?* Robinson's original plan called for assessment with a view to prospective 'further developments'.[185] The book, as Gil Rubin recently noted, was 'finalized in mid-1942 and took an overall favorable view toward the minorities treaties'.[186] The authors took pains to exculpate the League's minorities system from responsibility for the failure of minority protection. Their conclusion acknowledged imperfections and 'difficulties', objective and subjective, but asserted the 'enormous importance' of the minorities system:[187]

> Despite all the faults and shortcomings, some inherent and others external, the experience of twenty years does not justify the condemnation of a most remarkable experiment; an experiment that could not but share the fate of the political organism in which it lived—the League of Nations itself.[188]

[180] IJA, *Program* (n 175) 10.
[181] ibid, 9.
[182] ibid, 16.
[183] ibid, 11 ('the Institute will concentrate, for the present, on the European scene, excluding Palestine and the Americas from the range of its studies').
[184] Zohar Segev, *The World Jewish Congress during the Holocaust: Between Activism and Restraint* (de Gruyter 2014) 187–8; Sznaider (n 139) 88–90 on Dubnow's involvement in conceiving IJA.
[185] Jacob Robinson, The Failure of the Minorities Treaties: Observations to the Plan, 29 January 1941, WJC-C126/5, AJA, discussed in Rubin (n 100) 59.
[186] Rubin (n 100); Jacob Robinson, *Minorities and the League of Nations* (American Council of Public Affairs 1941).
[187] Robinson et al, *Failure* (n 100) 261.
[188] ibid, 265. Rowson's review endorsed these conclusions: Shabtai Rowson, 'Were the Minorities Treaties a Failure?' *Zionist Review* (20 October 1944).

Publicly, during and after the war, Robinson continued to defend the project to which he had 'devoted two decades' of his life. In May 1943, he still considered that minority rights might play some role in the post-war settlement. In a short essay in *Free World*, he warned that excluding minority protection from post-war planning will prove 'harmful to the cause of democracy', and recommended a distinction between 'irredentist minorities' and 'minorities with legitimate aims and with honest allegiance to both their group heritage ... and to their states'.[189] Although he noted 'the distressing phenomenon that [Jews] were the least protected of all the minorities', Robinson made the case that Jews, specifically, could benefit from a post-war return to some form of minority protection.[190]

D. Defeat—and Apostasy

Yet at the same time that IJA, under Robinson's directorship, sought to attenuate history's verdict in public, in private he was grappling with his convictions and past career choices. The immediate cause was the accumulating evidence before the WJC of the systematic extermination of European Jewry.[191] This is what caused him to admit, in the aforementioned long letter to Stephan Wise and Nahum Goldmann, that previously his investment in Palestine had been 'secondary in importance to the protection of Jewish life in the Diaspora'.[192]

Robinson addressed the two precisely because both were 'leading men in both the Zionist Organization' and the WJC. Writing 'as the head of the Institute of Jewish Affairs', he warned that 'a serious conflict' between the 'philosophy and practical policy of Zionism on the one hand' and those of the WJC on the other was afoot; he felt, therefore, duty-bound to 'report ... my conclusions, however controversial they may appear *prima facie*'.[193] His analysis of the depth of the Jewish crisis and of post-war possibilities for Jewish reconstruction, and the conclusions he drew, amounted to a apostasy—and an admission of failure.[194] What supported his 'claim to be an objective observer in this matter' was precisely the fact that he had been previously invested in 'the protection of Jewish life in the Diaspora'.[195] At IJA's founding, Robinson confirmed, 'I was still dominated by the same idea'. That he now came, by 'the force of events', to conclusions that 'will certainly be classed as extreme Zionism'[196] was meant to validate the force of these conclusions. That

[189] Jacob Robinson, 'Minorities in a Free World' (1943) 5 Free World 450, 451.
[190] ibid, 453.
[191] Rubin (n 100) 59; Segev, *Holocaust* (n 184) 23–35; Yehuda Bauer, *Rethinking the Holocaust* (Yale UP 2000).
[192] Robinson to Wise, Goldmann, 25 June 1943 (n 148).
[193] Emphasis in original; ibid.
[194] Nonetheless, he continued take pride in the Jewish contribution, at Versailles, to the creation of the minorities system 'in favour of all minorities, not of Jews only. That was one of the most unselfish acts of Jewish policy ever accomplished': Robinson, Notes Submitted to the Peace Aims and Planning Committee: 'Minority Rights' as Part of Our Peace Programs, 29 June 1943, C118-8, AJA.
[195] Robinson to Wise, Goldmann, 25 June 1943 (n 148).
[196] ibid.

is, he cited his previously secondary commitment to Palestine-oriented Zionism as evidence that that solution had now become inescapable.

Robinson's analysis acknowledged 'the fact that we have been defeated by Hitler'. This, combined 'with many other factors', made the 'restoration [of Jews to their previous places] on a large scale impossible'; 'most European Jews', he wrote, became 'outlawed and uprooted'. Jews had irrevocably lost their place in Europe. Robinson proceeded to warn that the WJC must choose 'between the short-range policy of rescuing individuals and trying to bring them back to where they came from without the slightest guarantee of future security' and 'the long-range stateman-like attitude'. This required a radical shift in the WJC thinking, *modus operandi*, and structures: 'under present conditions', he observed, 'conservative methods are out of the question ... the World Jewish Congress policy must be radically different'. What was required was a drastic change of priorities, programme, tactics, *and* ideology. Most poignantly, he noted that 'a dual policy is no longer possible'. If it was not to 'degenerate into a matter of "small business"', the WJC would have to choose between the Diaspora and Palestine: 'The decisive point, in my opinion, is that the time for "both—and" has passed. Today is the time for "either—or"'. He now not only rejected the synthesis between the Diaspora and Palestine, but also chose the latter over the former. He did not see 'any possibility of doubt how Jewish policy must decide': 'Zionism', he declared, became 'a real solution to real problems'.[197] The meaning of Zionism, for him, contracted; it could no longer include Diaspora work.

Robinson's rationale for these far-reaching conclusions drew on a brutal calculus. Keeping the Jewish Diaspora as the object of investment was impossible, unnecessary, even wasteful; above all, it was *criminal*:

> The number of Jews left in Europe after the war, especially in the active age groups, will be so small that all of them will be needed for the upbuilding of either European Jewry or the Yishuv, whichever is chosen. However, under the conditions which we will find in the European countries, the reestablishment of Jews would be a crime not only against those restored, but especially against their children who will never forgive us for being deluded, in this decisive moment of Jewish history, by immediate imaginary results and neglecting to think of the future.[198]

Although he thought the time had not come 'to go into details', there could be no mistake as to Robinson's choice or that it expressed a radical ideological transformation on his part.[199] Robinson's letter acknowledged the difficulty of abandoning

[197] ibid.

[198] ibid.

[199] He thus called for a 'sound, well thought out relationship' between the WJC and the Jewish Agency—'both used not in the technical but in the ideological sense'.

old ideological commitments; to that end, he even quoted Goethe's *Faust*: '*Zwei Seelen, ach, leben in meiner Brust*'.[200] Yet the letter already expressed some of the ideological sensibilities of Palestine-oriented Zionism. Towards its end, Robinson came to present a radically Palestinocentric[201] reading of the Holocaust-as-opportunity, reminiscent of contemporaneous *Yishuv* policies and utterances by its leaders.[202] Observing that 'the great mass of Jewish settlers came [to Palestine] not because of... ideology... but because of... persecutions', he noted that '[n]ever in our history were people so psychologically prepared for change as they are now and will be at the end of this war':[203]

> We are the beneficiaries of a miracle. Palestine was preserved from the devastations of war. Whatever our interpretation of this fact—religious, philosophical, or historical—it offers new opportunities. Bu[t] the possibilities can be exploited only if the World Jewish Congress, conscious of its responsibilities, finds the proper method of cooperation with the Jewish Agency. It is not sufficient to say—'The World Jewish Congress supports the Jewish Agency,' if the policy of the World Jewish Congress itself is to be confined to short-range individualistic solutions instead of a long-range collective solution.[204]

Robinson, in effect, was calling on the WJC to harness its resources to the National Home project and make Palestine the primary, if not exclusive, focus of Jewish post-war efforts. His WJC colleagues were correct to observe that this had meant the abandonment of *Gegenwartsarbeit*, doing 'away with the specifically Jewish problems in the Galuth [Diaspora]' and, ideologically, 'the negation of the Galuth'.[205]

Approaching the crisis of the Jewish Diaspora through the prism of Palestine spelled, for Robinson, the abandonment of his investment in minority rights.

[200] 'Two souls, alas! reside within my breast, [And each withdraws from, and repels, its brother]': Johann Wolfgang von Goethe, *Faust: A Tragedy* (Bayard Taylor tr, 3rd edn, Ward, Lock & Co. 1890) 32.

[201] Chs 3, 7 discuss Palestinocentrism and its ideological dimensions: the view that the interests of first the *Yishuv*, and later the Jewish state, were paramount to any Diasporic Jewish interest.

[202] These readings continue feeding fierce historiographical debates about the *Yishuv's* attitude to the Holocaust and its survivors: Dina Porat, *An Entangled Leadership: The 'Yishuv' and the Holocaust 1942–1945* (Am Oved 1986) (Hebrew); Shabtai Beit-Zvi, *Post-Ugandan Zionism on Trial* (Beit-Zvi 1991); Yechiam Weitz, *Aware But Helpless: Mapai and the Holocaust 1943–1945* (Yad Ben-Zvi 1994) (Hebrew); Tom Segev, *The Seventh Million: Israelis and the Holocaust* (Holt 2000); Tuvia Friling, *Arrows in the Dark: David Ben-Gurion, the Yishuv Leadership, and Rescue Attempts During the Holocaust* (University of Wisconsin Press 2005); Idith Zertal, *From Catastrophe to Power: The Holocaust Survivors and the Emergence of Israel* (University of California Press 1998).

[203] Robinson to Wise, Goldmann, 25 June 1943 (n 148).

[204] ibid. Likewise, he expressed apprehension that Jewish reconstruction in Europe would mean that 'we'—that is, the *Yishuv*—'will receive all the physically and emotionally handicapped elements' from among the survivors. This paralleled selective Jewish Agency immigration preferences for and, at times, policies on 'productive elements': see the studies cited in (n 202) but compare Aviva Halamish, *A Dual Race against Time: Zionist Immigration Policy in the 1930s* (Yad Ben-Zvi 2006) 152–89, 412–48 (Hebrew).

[205] Peace Planning Committee Meeting, 10 March [1943], WJC–C118/8, AJA.

He had occasion to reflect on this choice, and on what it entailed, in a series of memoranda he prepared for the WJC Peace Aims Planning Committee and in the course of its meetings. In these, Robinson elaborated the implications of the shift from 'short-range individualistic solutions' to 'a long-range collective solution'.[206] It was there that he had concluded that if 'the right of the Jewish people to survival'[207] was to be secured, Jewish post-war demands must reflect the realization that 'the Jewish problem be considered a national problem for which there is only one solution—a national state'.[208] '*[O]ur single demand*' in the aftermath of the war, he urged, 'should be the establishment of a Jewish Commonwealth in Palestine' to solve 'the refugee and repatriation problems'.[209] This entailed calculated aloofness to the protection of Diaspora interests in the eventual post-war arrangement; he was willing, as already noted,[210] to assume that the interests of the Jewish Diaspora would be secured by the war aims of the UN and the general post-war settlement. For this reason, the dilemma as to the preferred 'form in which Jewish rights' in the Diaspora 'should be guaranteed, minority treaties ... [or] a Bill of Rights'[211] itself became, for Robinson, secondary. The primacy of Palestine meant that, like the Bill of Rights, minority rights should not be a specific WJC 'peace demand' or form part of a 'specific Jewish program'[212] but, rather, be 'allowed to fall into disuse'.[213]

The WJC rejected Robinson's 'quite revolutionary' proposals.[214] He remained in its service. This, for some time, entailed continued engagement with minority rights. In early 1945, for example, he was working 'on the problem of the transition from the League of Nations to the newly suggested World Organization, in connection with Minorities Treaties and other Multi-lateral Treaties'.[215] To that end, he examined the question of the war's impact on the validity of the minority treaties.[216] Robinson nonetheless held to his newfound faith in the dictates of

[206] Robinson to Wise, Goldmann, 25 June 1943 (n 148); Robinson, Jewish Post-War Program of the WJC, First Tentative Draft, 6 July 1943, WJC–C97/17, AJA.

[207] Robinson, An Elucidation of Preliminary Problems Concerning a Jewish Post-War Program, [n.d.], WJC–C118/8, AJA.

[208] Peace Planning Meeting, 10 March [1943] (n 205); Robinson, Jewish Peace Aims, [n.d.], WJC–C118/8, AJA ('Instead of concentrating all their efforts upon the national aim of establishing their national freedom' in the post-war arrangements, Jews 'are greatly confused, and are producing a very long catalogue of demands').

[209] Emphasis in original; Robinson, Some Fundamental Problems of Jewish Post-War Planning, [n.d.], WJC–C118/8, AJA.

[210] Ch 3.

[211] Robinson, Elucidation, [n.d.] (n 207); Robinson, The Atomistic and Collectivistic Approach to the Jewish Post-War Aims, [n.d.], WJC–C118/8, AJA.

[212] Robinson, Jewish Peace Aims, [n.d.] (n 208).

[213] Robinson, Notes Submitted, 29 June 1943 (n 194).

[214] Peace Planning Meeting, 10 March [1943] (n 205); IJA, Planning a Post-War Program: Report, 28 February 1944, WJC–C97/17, AJA; Robinson, Notes Submitted, 29 June 1943 (n 194).

[215] Robinson to Loveday, 26 March 1945, JR–4/13, Jacob Robinson Papers 2013.506.1, United States Holocaust Memorial Museum Archives, Washington DC ('USHMM'); for his ambivalent review of the Jewish experience with minority rights: Robinson, Notes Submitted, 29 June 1943 (n 194) where he noted 'the distressing fact that ... [Jews] were the least protected of all the minorities'.

[216] Robinson, The Binding Force of the Minorities Provisions During and After This War, March 1945, JR–4/13, USHMM.

'extreme Zionism'.[217] By early 1945, he came to reassess the historical experience of minority protection—and the ideology that underscored his own investment in it. When consulted on the advisability of the WJC publishing an English translation of Simon Dubnow's *Letters on Old and New Judaism*,[218] he acknowledged the '*historical* importance of the "autonomist" theory', but now offered a dim view of its achievements.[219] He had several editorial reservations that revealed the extent of his familiarity with Dubnow's writing and the fact he had discussed the need to update the historian's works with Dubnow 'as late as May 1940'. Yet he approached the question of publication, predominantly, as an ideological matter out of concern that publication might signal a return to Dubnow's 'prescriptions'. From a '*practical-political* viewpoint', he wrote, the 'importance of Dubnov's "prescriptions" to solve the Jewish problem has greatly vanished'.[220] Robinson advised, therefore, that 'from a Jewish nationalistic viewpoint' a 'revival' of Dubnow's Autonomism—'a political program not adjusted to the radically changed conditions of a new Jewish world'—would be 'utterly unrealistic and harmful'. His conclusion marked the divide that now separated Zionism and Diaspora Nationalism, and the position he now occupied in the new Jewish political geometry:

> The sound seeds of 'autonomism' have been adopted in our program but an over-emphasis on this theory now is not advisable. The publication—in whatever form—today by a political body of Dubnov's Letters, as a practical-political program would be a disservice to the cause to which we are all devoted.[221]

After 1945, Robinson's work would, from time to time, betray lingering Dubnowian thinking.[222] But in 1947, his disillusionment with Autonomism and minority protection took a definitive career turn. After a March visit to Palestine,

[217] In late 1943, IJA started looking at the validity of the 1939 British White Paper—and its compatibility with the Palestine Mandate: WJC-C132/6-9, AJA; JR-4/12, USHMM.

[218] Dubnow (n 115).

[219] Emphasis in original; Robinson to Easterman, 6 January 1945 (n 137): ('As a Jewish political program "autonomism" played an important part in the "peace planning" of 1916–1918 but was defeated by the Peace Conference which repudiated the respective demand of the Committee of Jewish Delegations. While certain constitutions proclaimed the principle of autonomy for national and religious minorities, it was practically never implemented').

[220] Emphasis in original; ibid.

[221] ibid, discussed by James Loeffler, '"The Famous Trinity of 1917": Zionist Internationalism in Historical Perspective' (2016) 15 Simon Dubnow Institute YB 211, 228–9.

[222] Contemplating war crimes in the aftermath of the Holocaust, Robinson argued that crimes against groups are greater than the sum of individual crimes. 'Collectivistic' crimes were '*qualitatively* different' from the multiplied individual crime'. This drew on a rationale of group protection that was strikingly similar to what Lemkin—following Dubnow—had propounded. Robinson argued that the 'annihilation of... human beings of certain specific characteristics is not only a manifold murder, but, in addition, a murder of a *certain species human* endowed with certain qualities and gifts, an impoverishment of humanity as a whole which is thus deprived of one of its manifold expressions. In application to the Jewish case, this approach would afford the possibility to enlarge upon the loss caused to humanity by depriving it of an untouched reservoir of human talents and energies': emphases in original; Robinson, [Note], 15 October 1945 (n 139).

the fifty-eight-year-old IJA director let Moshe Shertok—the Director of the Jewish Agency's Political Department—persuade him to lend his services to the Jewish campaign for Palestine; he was loaned to the Jewish Agency's UN mission.[223] Later, he reminded Prime Minister Sharett how he had 'defected' to start a 'new chapter'.[224] I 'had to discontinue all my work at the Institute', he informed a German correspondent in 1947; now, he explained, he would be 'serving my people'.[225] Given that he had been serving a *national* Jewish cause since the early 1920s, these words hint an acknowledgement that his previous career, and investments, might have done a disservice to his people. If so, the 'new chapter' of his career promised to offer something of a redemption.

4.4 Not 'An Asset on the National Balance Sheet': Shabtai Rosenne's Short-Lived Project

While Robinson, in New York, was coming to terms with past engagements with Jewish autonomy and becoming disillusioned with minority rights, Sefton Rowson (he had not yet changed his name), in London, embarked on a new project. He, too, was concerned with the future of the Diaspora; for answers, he turned to Simon Dubnow, Autonomism, and minority rights. For the older, East European Robinson, these questions were a matter of lived experience and personal investment. Rowson, on the other hand, could approach Dubnow as an intellectual exercise, with the benefit of hindsight and some measure of detachment. As a Western Jew, he did not require minority protection to enjoy the benefits of emancipation or individual political equality.

He did grapple with Dubnow. He, too, had undergone a transformation—more accelerated and, eventually, more complete than Robinson's.[226] Becoming Zionist, by his own testimony, at sixteen he had 'made quite a deep study of its theories and philosophies' in the decade that followed.[227] Yet he was no stranger, by dint of his family background, to the more assimilation-oriented institutes of British Jewry or to taking pride, as a British subject, in empire.[228] His Zionism still needed to be reconciled with other allegiances. The war years would change that.

[223] Later that year, he also made inquiries about a possible teaching position at the Hebrew University: Tartakower to Robinson, 14 November 1947, Feinberg to Robinson, 25 November 1947, JR–7/6, USHMM.

[224] Robinson to Sharett, 8 December 1954, JR–7/6, USHMM.

[225] Robinson to Foerster, 16 April 1947, WJC–C16/5, AJA.

[226] Rotem Giladi, 'Shabtai Rosenne: The Transformation of Sefton Rowson' in James Loeffler and Moria Paz (eds), *The Law of Strangers: Jewish Lawyers and International Law in the Twentieth Century* (CUP 2019) 221.

[227] [Sefton Rowson], Youth and Reconstruction: Speech, 18 October 1943, Shabtai Rosenne Papers ('Rosenne Papers'). Mr Daniel Rosenne kindly made available all documents from this collection, all on file with the author.

[228] Ch 1; Giladi (n 226).

In August 1942, Rowson argued that 'anyone, particularly an international lawyer who urges the establishment of a Jewish state must work out the relations between that state and the ... Diaspora.'[229] He published, in the British Zionist press, surveys and book reviews on the state of various Jewish Diaspora communities.[230] But he also perused Dubnow's works in search for a national role and justification for the Diaspora—and a new synthesis between Zionism and Diaspora Nationalism. In late 1943, he composed a long synopsis of Dubnow's *Letters on Old and New Judaism*.[231] This sought to describe, for the benefit of British Jewry, 'Dubnow's general theory of nationalism ... his theories of the nature and functions of Jewish nationalism, and finally his attitude towards Zionism.'[232] His aim was to demonstrate the persisting relevance of Dubnow's ideas: 'today', he urged, 'Dubnow's theories can offer valuable light in facing the problems of Jewish reconstruction after this war, and it is with such a hope that this and the following essays are offered.'[233] He had planned a book on the topic; parts of an incomplete manuscript survived; a few tracts were published in Zionist periodicals.

For Rowson, the writs of Autonomism presented a programme that could furnish justifications for Zionist life in the Diaspora. He noted that the old tensions between Zionism and Autonomist *programmes* had subsided. At the end of the nineteenth century, he reported, 'the conflict between' Palestine nationalists and Diaspora Nationalists

> was bitter, owing to the prevalent Zionist theory of the 'Negation of the Diaspora,' i.e., that there is no possibility for Jewish revival in the Diaspora, and its vehement denial by men like Dubnow and Zhitlovsky, etc. But, as we shall see in the course of this note, the gulf between them has so narrowed that since the last war the chief spokesmen of the two movements (though not necessarily the theorists) have been one and the same (Weizmann, Sokolow, Motzkin, Judge Mack, etc.)[234]

Ideologically, he argued, 'the old controversy concerning the possibility of Jewish national survival in the Diaspora is now largely superfluous.'[235] Dubnow's own

[229] Shabtai Rowson, 'A Plea for Justice', *Zionist Review* (20 August 1942).

[230] Shabtai Rowson, 'The Jews of Soviet Russia: Some Facts and Figures' *New Judea* (May–June 1942) 119; 'Where Stands Russian Jewry' *The Jewish Advocate* (December 1942); 'The Jews of the United States' *Zionist Review* (7 January 1944); 'Jewish Education in the U.S.A.' *Zionist Review* (21 January 1944); 'The Jewish Scientific Institute' *Zionist Review* (3 March 1944); 'New Hebrew Publications' *Zionist Review* (31 March 1944); 'Vilna' *Zionist Review* (14 July 1944); 'Preparing for Peace' *Zionist Review* (11 August 1944); etc.

[231] Dubnow (n 115).

[232] SWD Rowson, Simon Dubnow—Letters on Ancient and Modern Judaism: A Synopsis, December 1943/January 1944, Rosenne Papers.

[233] ibid; Shabtai Rowson, 'Jewish Nationalism: Simon Dubnow's Theory' *New Judea* (June–July 1944) 152.

[234] Shabtai Rowson, *Zionism in the Period of Herzl* (Zionist Federation of Great Britain & Ireland 1944) 4.

[235] SWD Rowson, Epilogue: Jewish Nationalism Today (1944) 99/242, Rosenne Papers.

'early scepticism' with 'the efficacy of Zionism as a solution [to the Jewish Question] may have been justified and indeed was shared by many sincere Zionists'.[236] Having described the history of the gulf, he proceeded to prescribed synthesis: 'Zionism would only colonize Palestine, and at the same time it would support Jewish nationalism in the Diaspora so long as the first and main aim was not prejudiced'.[237] The Jewish nation, he reasoned, still required a 'strong Diaspora'.[238]

In terms of international law, this compelled renewed engagement with minority rights, not disillusion. Reviewing Robinson's *Were the Minorities Treaties a Failure?*, Rowson urged the strengthening of the Versailles minorities system, not its abandonment:

> It has been suggested in some Jewish circles that it may be that an entirely new approach to the minorities problem will be needed after the war. Reading this book, which frankly exposes the weaknesses and defects of the Versailles system I feel that the 1919 Treaties approached the problem in the right way. They can be improved in matters of detail both as regards their substantive provisions and as regards the manner of their enforcement, but those are secondary.[239]

In August 1944, in a short essay on Dubnow's theory, Rowson still professed adherence to Dubnow's 'dream of the *political* renaissance of ten million Jews of the Diaspora!'.[240] But his project kept oscillating between Diaspora Nationalism and Palestine Zionism: in October 1943, he announced that 'the only secure future for the Jewish people is to be found in a Jewish Palestine, where a Jewish National Home is to be established in accordance with international law'.[241] He continued to preach revival of the Diaspora for some time, but now assigned it only a secondary, subservient role:[242] 'Jewish nationalism can only be centred in Palestine and not in the Diaspora'.[243] Under the force of events in Europe, Britain, and Palestine, he was shifting towards Palestine Zionism.[244] In what was to be the 'Epilogue' of his

[236] ibid, 98/241.
[237] Rowson, *Zionism* (n 234) 12.
[238] Rowson, Epilogue (n 235) 95/238 ('The duty of Jewish nationalists is to concentrate all Jewish endeavours on the rebuilding of Eretz Israel, reconstructing as strong a Diaspora as is possible, strong physically, strong economically and strong culturally on the basis of true national Judaism. Only in this way can Jewry be fully integrated in the human family and Jewish life lose its bitter misery').
[239] Rowson, 'Failure' (n 188).
[240] Emphasis added; Shabtai Rowson, 'Dubnow's Theory of Jewish Nationalism: Practical Problems' *New Judea* (August 1944) 172. This drew on earlier manuscripts: Shabtai Rowson, 'Simon Dubnow on Jewish Nationalism' (December 1943); 'Simon Dubnow's Views on Zionism and His Controversy with Ahad Ha-Am' (January 1944) Rosenne Papers.
[241] Rowson, Youth (n 227).
[242] Rowson, Epilogue (n 235) 99/242.
[243] ibid; the Diaspora, he added, would only serve 'an essential hinterland for the Yishuv' and a 'reservoir . . . [for its] reinforcements'.
[244] For background: Giladi (n 226).

work on Dubnow, he came to admit that while Dubnow's 'diagnosis ... [was] essentially correct ... the cure he prescribed, namely autonomy in the Diaspora', had failed.[245] At that point, for Rowson, the Diaspora became 'a dying force', a liability that 'cannot be included as an asset on the national balance sheet'.[246]

This transformation underscored Rowson's treatment of minority rights. They were, he observed, no writ for national life but rather an impediment, even a hazard: one of the 'objective conditions in which the nation exists' that could even 'prevent national survival'.[247] Like Robinson, he came to the conclusion that minority protection had been a bar to Jewish nationalism and testimony to the unequal, inferior status of the Jewish nation. 'The minorities Treaties of 1919', he wrote, 'did give *on paper* some measure of national rights to national minorities in some multi-national states'. But their 'inherent defect', from a Jewish perspective, was that 'they were conceived on a scale which was national not for the Jews but for the surrounding nations'.[248] Emblematic of and entrenching the Jewish nation's inequality, minority rights had to be rejected on ideological grounds.[249]

These conclusions—and Rowson's willingness to write off the Diaspora as a liability for national revival—had rendered his own book project on Dubnow redundant; he had abandoned the manuscript, and the project of intellectual reflection on Jewish nationalism. His own Negation of the Diaspora came through praxis, not essay-writing. He left the Diaspora behind, together with any lingering sympathy for minority rights, by immigrating to Palestine at the end of 1947. There, as the MFA legal adviser, Shabtai Rosenne would time and again place the Jewish state at the centre of the Jewish world and read Diaspora interests through that ideological prism.[250]

Rowson's disillusionment with minority rights, notably, preceded sovereignty. It expressed his wartime ideological radicalization born out of growing disillusionment with the promises of emancipation, the British Empire, and international law itself.[251] In particular, he became disenchanted with international law's power to affect transformation in the legal-political status of the Jewish people. By 1947, he came to argue the futility of any Jewish reliance on international law. The immediate trigger for the three-page essay he published that year under the title 'International Law and the Jewish People' was the

245 Rowson, Epilogue (n 235) 95/238.
246 ibid, 108/251.
247 ibid, 100/243.
248 Emphasis added; ibid.
249 ibid (treaties evidenced that Jews, 'being nowhere a territorial majority' were not a nation).
250 Shabtai Rosenne, 'Basic Elements of Israel's Foreign Policy' (1961) 17 India Quarterly 328, 335–6, 339–40. Rosenne consistently read Jewish interests through the ideological prism of the Jewish state and its interests: in the case of human rights (ch 3); the Genocide Convention; and, patently, the Refugee Convention (ch 7).
251 Giladi (n 226).

forthcoming Palestine Special Session of the UN General Assembly. This was his first public writing in Hebrew; it was also the first time his dual interests—Jewish affairs on the one hand, international law on the other—converged in published form.[252]

In that essay, Rowson introduced international law to laymen, noting the special meaning it assigned to the term 'nation': 'only legal-formal recognition can elevate a people to a nation possessing rights and obligations based on international law'. He proceeded to observe that 'in Palestine, neither the Jews nor the Arabs constitute "nations" from a legal viewpoint' and spell out the irrelevance, notwithstanding the League of Nations mandate, of international law: the Jews' relations with the Arabs 'or even with the English are not regulated by international law'. Not possessing a state, he averred, the Jewish people did not constitute, legally speaking, a 'nation'; and in the absence of 'nationhood', the Jewish people could not possess their own state.[253] Subjecthood was a vicious circle.

This radical reading was followed by a standard realist critique of international law: Rowson acknowledged its existence, but noted that its validity was only recognized and sustained by political force: in the absence of sanctions, international law was 'like a servant, not master' of world politics. 'In this state of affairs',[254] he observed, 'the position of the Jewish people is very weak':

> We do not constitute a recognised nation in the legal sense, and thus we have none of the rights that international law bestows on such nations. For this reason we cannot even have the right to insist that our matter be brought before an international court. And even if so brought before it, there would be no guarantee that it would agree to deal with our concerns, being devoid of authority to deal with the demands of an unrecognised nation. Moreover: we don't even have the right to appear on any international stage to defend our demands even at a time of debate on an issue so important and sacred to us as our national existence in *Eretz Israel*. Before the UN Assembly in New York, the representatives of the Jewish people appeared as 'beggars' relying on the charity of the righteous nations of the world, seeking their benevolence in order to ensure the existence of our people.[255]

By 1947, then, Rowson had come to read international law not as a vehicle of Jewish emancipation but as an obstacle to its realization. The standard against which he tested international law was Zionist ideology: the establishment of a

[252] ibid.
[253] Shabtai Rowson, 'International Law and the Jewish People' (1947) 11 Tarbut 4 (Hebrew).
[254] ibid, 5.
[255] ibid, 6; this passage echoes his future sovereign sensibilities with regard to voice and representation, a recurring theme in the diplomatic-legal practice surveyed in this book.

Jewish state in Palestine, which was to furnish the Jewish people with equal legal status. From this perspective, international law was more than a mere impediment: it attested to and affected an 'inherent defect' in the sovereign capacity of the Jewish people. Unless and until a Jewish state was established, international law entrenched the inferior legal status of Jews and their attendant voicelessness. For Rowson, in 1947, international law was part of the problem, not any solution. It lacked the power to transform the legal status of the Jewish people. The following, and final, passage prescribed Rowson's only answer to the Jewish predicament and pronounced on the futility of international law in furnishing it—including in the form of minority rights:

> It is a vital necessity for the Jewish people that its international position is made equal to the legal position of all other 'recognized' nations. As long as this has not been achieved, all rights that will be granted to Jews and to our people, whether in *Eretz Israel* under a new trusteeship instrument *or in the Diaspora under new minority treaties, would be hollow and lack any meaningful value.* Under present conditions, the Jews cannot even be assured that they would benefit from the famous 'Four Freedoms' or from the 'humane rights' that many now talk of. For this reason, in the present state of international law the Jews have no other way of securing their rights and achieving their demands than the establishment of an independent Jewish state whose international status would be equal to that of all other states.[256]

For Rowson, minority protection—and international law writ large—could liberate neither individual Jews nor the Jewish people from the trap of inequality and objecthood: minority rights could not furnish the answer to the Jewish Question. Its resolution required not 'municipal or international' legislation that 'could be no more than a semi-efficacious *palliative for a disease requiring more radical treatment*'.[257] By the time Rosenne would encounter the 1948 Genocide Convention, that 'radical treatment'—like Justice Minister Rosen's 'radical solution'[258] or Robinson's 'extreme Zionism' proposals to the WJC[259]—had already been applied. His attitude to the Convention was grounded in the ideological perspective that the disease had already been cured. This rendered the Genocide Convention redundant; even before, any international law scheme offering Jews any type of minority protection could be no more than a palliative.

[256] Emphasis added; Rowson, 'International Law' (n 253) 6.

[257] Emphasis added; SWD Rowson, [Book Review] 'An International Convention Against Antisemitism by Mark Vishniak', *Intl Affairs*, January 1947 [MS], Rosenne Papers.

[258] Rosen (n 97), discussed in ch 4.

[259] Discussed at text to n 196.

5. 'A False and Perverse Doctrine': Minority Rights, Palestine Zionism, and the Sovereign Turn

The Genocide Convention extended protection to Jews *as minorities*. When Lemkin averred that it was 'the only international treaty available for the protection of the Jews in the world today';[260] or asserted its promise to 'redeem' Jewish suffering;[261] or called, time and again, on the Jewish state to direct its diplomatic resources towards its promotion; he was, in effect, promoting a Jewish return to minority rights and to the prescriptions of Dubnowism. He was advocating, that is, a return to a model of Jewish nationalism that had already become, for Robinson and Rosenne, discredited.

Both, each in his way, had already become disillusioned with minority rights, autonomy, and Simon Dubnow's theories. Each had undergone an ideological transformation that led him to subscribe, even prior to sovereignty, to the creed of Palestine-centred Zionism. Ideologically, neither could any longer accept the claim that Jewish interests, and Jewish survival, could be protected by the Genocide Convention that reverted to treating Jews as a minority. Robinson held that it could give no 'particular guarantee to the Jewish people against possible future acts of mass terror'.[262] Rosenne, similarly, had 'no doubt that the Convention does not safeguard the [Jewish] people against a holocaust'.[263] Jewish emancipation, according to their transformed ideological outlook, could only be achieved through the 'radical solution' of a Jewish state. After its establishment, from this ideological perspective, the Convention itself was not merely redundant or anachronistic. In following Dubnow's prescriptions, it was predicated on a series of assertions and constructions that were no longer, if they ever had been, compatible with Palestine-centred Zionism; they were certainly no longer compatible with how that Zionism interpreted Jewish sovereignty. The Convention, after all, pointed to the Diaspora as a proper *locus* for Jewish national revival; yet during the Holocaust years and in its immediate aftermath, Robinson and Rosenne each came to identify the Diaspora as a liability, a bar to Jewish national revival, the problem rather than its solution. Each, for his own reasons and through a career choice, came to 'negate' the Diaspora and adopt an exclusive focus on Palestine. Investing in the Diaspora, Robinson had already concluded in 1943, would be 'a crime'.[264] In that sense, the Genocide Convention was, ideologically, a subversive proposition, an anathema to Zionism. In 1954, Rosenne found occasion to announce that '[a]s regards the rights of Jews abroad ... it is good that the minority regime was liquidated'.[265]

[260] [Lemkin], Memorandum to the American Zionist Council, 14 June 1950 (n 13).
[261] Rosenne to Attorney-General, 13 November 1949 (n 19).
[262] Robinson to Rosenne, 5 February 1951 (n 32).
[263] Rosenne to Robinson, 15 February 1951 (n 33).
[264] Robinson to Wise, Goldmann, 25 June 1943 (n 148).
[265] Minutes, 16 December 1954, FM-5850/3, ISA.

If Jewish political experience in Europe since the 1920s gave rise to disillusion with minority rights and autonomy, in Palestine it generated outright hostility towards these forms of protection of Jewish rights. Political Zionism—starting with the formulation of its original programme—displayed calculated ambiguity with regard to the final form the Jewish *polity* in Palestine would take.[266] Zionist leaders and thinkers had envisioned a variety of models to define the endgame of mandate and describe the ultimate shape of the National Home in Palestine. Some of these, before and during the mandate years, unquestionably engaged Autonomist thinking.[267] A Jewish state may have been implicit, or latent, in the 1897 Basle Program, but it was not—as Dmitry Shumsky persuasively demonstrated—the sole 'political format' that captured Zionist political imagination.[268] Full-fledged statehood—the demand for 'the same status as all the other nations', as Ben-Gurion noted in a 1944 speech[269]—became the explicit goal of the Zionist movement only after 1942.[270] Political and demographic realities in mandatory Palestine led *Yishuv* and Zionist leaders, however, to regard minority rights as an existential threat to the National Home project. For them, becoming a *majority* in Palestine, whether by the immigration provisions of the mandate instrument or by extra-legal means, was a *sine qua non* of that project.

In Palestine, hostility to minority *status* attended the very inception of the mandate. In 1922, neither Arabs nor Jews accepted the semi-proportional representative composition of the British-proposed Palestine Legislative Council. Arabs protested under-representation; Jews invoked the 'special character' of the Palestine mandate as a 'sacred trust of civilisation' on behalf of the entire Jewish people—beneficiaries, so went the interpretation, yet to arrive there.[271] In 1923, the plan was abandoned; so would be subsequent attempts to revive it. Later, Jewish resentment to minority status in Palestine would be expressed mostly in opposition to a succession of proposals to resolve the Palestine conundrum that would make

[266] Nathan Feinberg, 'Legal Significance of the Basle Program' in Nathan Feinberg, *Palestine under the Mandate and the State of Israel: Problems in International Law* (Magnes 1963) 3 (Hebrew).

[267] Dmitry Shumsky, *Beyond the Nation-State: The Zionist Political Imagination from Pinsker to Ben-Gurion* (Yale UP 2018); Bartal (n 114) 152–69.

[268] Shumsky, *Beyond* (n 267) 4 challenges the prevalent perception of 'Zionism as a movement that sought to realize self-determination for the Jews [and that] had historically always aimed for one—and only one—political format' of the nation-state.

[269] ibid, 216.

[270] Allon Gal, *David Ben-Gurion and the American Alignment for a Jewish State* (Indiana UP 1991); Yosef Gorny, *From Binational Society to Jewish State: Federal Concepts in Zionist Political Thought, 1920–1990, and the Jewish People* (Brill 2006); Tom Segev, *A State at Any Cost: The Life of David Ben-Gurion* (Farrar, Straus & Giroux 2019).

[271] Nathan Feinberg, 'The Problem of the Legislative Council—Its Legal Aspect' in Nathan Feinberg, *Some Problems of the Palestine Mandate* (Shoshani 1936) 77; Jacob Stoyanovsky, *The Mandate for Palestine: A Contribution to the Theory and Practice of International Mandates* (Longmans, Green & Co. 1928); Norman Bentwich, *The Mandate System* (Longmans, Green & Co. 1930).

Jewish immigration conditional on Arab consent, entrenching the *Yishuv's* numerical inferiority.[272]

That resentment was closely linked to the notion of the Negation of the Diaspora. It expressed an abiding conviction that Jewish Diaspora experience as a minority was the root cause of the Jewish predicament; extending minority status to Jews in Palestine would only extend the Diaspora, not overcome it. In December 1936, in connection with the Peel Royal Commission work,[273] Chaim Weizmann—President of the Zionist Organisation—told the British High Commissioner Arthur Wauchope that Britain could either decide to overcome Arab opposition to Jewish immigration or 'play false by the Jews, discard the principle of absorptive capacity and *condemn* the Jews to be a *permanent minority*'.[274] Later, fearing that opinion in London was swaying towards a single-state solution, he warned against 'the reduction of the Jews to a permanent minority status' and, therefore, a return to a new 'Jewish ghetto'.[275] Others, less moderate or pro-British than Weizmann, and who would become the architects of Israel's early foreign policy, shared the same sentiment yet could express it more bluntly. David Ben-Gurion, Chairman of the Jewish Agency Executive, considered minority status as the expression of the international legal deficiency of the Jewish people. In this reading, being classed as a minority attested to political weakness and inferiority of status;[276] minority status, he wrote in 1931, was essentially a 'lack, whether as individuals or a national collective, [of] a normal and secure basis' for 'physical and spiritual' existence.[277] Until Zionism, he wrote, under the 'extant law of nations the Jewish people have for generations suffered a denial of justice, deprived of right'.[278] As minorities, he told the Peel Commission, Jews were 'subject to the benevolence of the majority ... at any rate, always subject to the benevolence or whip of others'.[279] Rowson's 1947 critique of international law closely followed this reading.[280]

[272] Michael J Cohen, 'Secret Diplomacy and Rebellion in Palestine, 1936–1939' (1977) 8 Intl J of Middle East Stud 379; Martin Gilbert, 'The Short Life of the Peel Commission' (1979) 1 Zmanim: A Historical Quarterly 4 (Hebrew).

[273] Shmuel Dotan, *The Partition Controversy During the Mandate Period* (Yad Ben-Zvi 1980) (Hebrew); Itzhak Galnoor, *The Partition of Palestine, Decision Crossroads in the Zionist Movement* (State University of New York 1995).

[274] Emphases added; quoted in Martin Gilbert, *Exile and Return: The Struggle for a Jewish Homeland* (Lippincott 1978) 170–1.

[275] ibid, 194. In early 1938, Weizmann told a liberal politician that '[t]he one thing the Jews would and could never accept was the prospect of being in a permanent minority status in Palestine. The one thing the Jews now understood by the word *National Home* ... was some area where they had responsible self-Government and *where they were in a majority, and no longer in a ghetto status*': emphases added; ibid, 196.

[276] After the 1917 Balfour Declaration, Ben-Gurion wrote that Jews 'do ... not exist as a national-political unit. In the relations between nations, the Hebrew nations did not count. There were hated and humiliated Jews, there were useful and necessary Jews, there were also Jews who evoked compassion and received protection—but there was no Jewish people as a political factor': David Ben-Gurion, *From Class to Nation* (Davar 1933) 14 (Hebrew).

[277] David Ben-Gurion, *Us and Our Neighbours* (Davar 1931) 198 (Hebrew).

[278] ibid, 249.

[279] David Ben-Gurion, *In the Campaign*, vol 1 (5th edn, Ayanot 1955) 104 (Hebrew).

[280] Rowson, 'International Law' (n 253) 6.

The UN debate over the future of Palestine—partition or a binational federation were considered—exacerbated Zionist resentment towards minority status and, at the same time, made its repudiation part of the narrative of the sovereign transition of the Jewish people that arose out of the ensuing events. In 1947, Ben-Gurion protested to the GA's Political Committee that 'the Jews in their own historic homeland can under no conditions be made *to remain a subordinate, dependent minority as they are in all other countries in the Diaspora*'.[281] In his testimony before the UN Special Committee on Palestine, Moshe Shertok warned against condemning the *Yishuv* to the same 'fateful bane' of the Jewish homelessness, 'constituting a minority in every country in the world'.[282] He told the Security Council that 'the Jewish people in Palestine will never accept the status of a minority depending on the charity of others'—the fate of a 'frozen and shrinking minority ... *taking solace in paper guarantees*'—that is, in minorities treaties.[283] After the failure of minority rights and the Holocaust, these were no mere rhetorical allusions. Nor was that outlook limited to *Yishuv* and Zionist political leadership; in the academia, they underscored Gorali's disillusionment with minority rights.[284] Earlier, in April 1939, the Hebrew University Senate resolved that 'we shall not be reconciled to a conspiracy seeking to impose on the people of Israel to be a minority in *Eretz Israel* forever'.[285]

From this perspective, minority status, protection, and rights were, quintessentially, indicia of Jewish legal and political objecthood, markers of the ails of the Diaspora. The synthesis between the two strands of Jewish nationalism—between minority rights and the National Home; work of the present and work of the future; the Diaspora and Palestine—now became untenable. Synthesis—or compromise—could survive neither the crisis of the 1930s and the genocide of the 1940s, nor the realities of national struggle in Palestine. Zionism could no longer be inclusive of or tolerant towards Diaspora Nationalism's competing construction of Jewish political existence or the programme it prescribed. Adherents of the National Home in Palestine noted the weakness of the minority system, the failure of autonomy, the

[281] Emphasis added; David Ben-Gurion, Speech at the UNGA's Political Committee (12 May 1947) in Meron Medzini (ed), *Israel's Foreign Relations: Selected Documents, 1947–1974* (MFA 1976) 36, 38.

[282] Sharett (n 11) 142; the summary record reads: 'condemned to permanent minority status in Palestine as in all other countries': GAOR, Ad Hoc Committee on the Palestine Question (17 October 1947) 115. At the UNGA's Political Committee (12 May 1947) in Medzini (n 281) 31–2, Sharett spoke of Jews in Palestine 'who refuse to be left in a minority position under Arab domination'.

[283] Emphasis added; Sharett (n 11) 161; the UN record reads: 'the fate of a crystallized or a dwindling minority to console themselves with a paper guarantee ... will never submit to the status of a minority on sufferance': SCOR, Meetings (27 February 1948) 347. He later demanded 'collective equality, equality of status to the Jewish people, like that of all peoples': Sharett (n 11) 218; GAOR, First Committee (27 April 1948) 112–13 ('collective equality for the Jewish people as a nation', not be 'a permanent and completely isolated minority').

[284] Gorali (n 98) 7.

[285] Hedva Ben-Israel, 'Politics on Mount Scopus during the Mandatory Period' in Hagit Levsky (ed), *The History of the Hebrew University of Jerusalem: Academic Progression in a Period of National Struggle* (Magnes 2009) 3, 30 (Hebrew).

false promise of international law and institutions—and proceeded to invoke primacy and priority over all other Jewish interests.[286] Predicated all along on a prognosis of an impending catastrophe, at the core of Zionism's creed there had always inhered a critique of the Jewish Diasporic condition.[287] Events in Europe brought it again to the fore; they also furnished a terrible vindication of Zionism's predictions, its analysis of the Diaspora's ails, and its prescriptions. Its adherents, old and new, now returned to the days before the Helsingfors Program and to a principled Negation of the Diaspora that became, openly, a central tenet of the Zionist creed shared by both left and right wings of the *Yishuv* Zionist spectrum. Zeev (Vladmir) Jabotinsky, the leader of Revisionist Zionism, still celebrated in his 1936 memoire the Helsingfors Conference as the 'peak Zionist experience of my youth':

> We began negating the *galut:* that is, the idea that there is no purpose in reforming the Diaspora, there is no other cure for *galut* than exodus. However, life led us to the necessity of improving the *galut*, improving it systematically and extensively, and not merely gaining civil equality but also [equality of] national rights.[288]

In 1942, however, he recorded how in 'the peace treaties of 1919 ... special minority clauses were solemnly inserted to ensure equality, and the League of Nations was to supervise and guarantee their execution. To tell once again how all these provisions proved ineffective would be tedious.'[289]

In 1948, resentment of minority status became part of the Jewish state's foundational, and hegemonic, ideology. The very sovereign turn in Jewish history was interpreted as a transition from inferior minority status to the equal station of a majority. Minority protection, as the editors of the *Jewish Yearbook of International Law* noted in the spring of 1949, thus became irreversibly associated with the non-sovereign Jewish past—with legal and political objecthood.[290] A few weeks later, Foreign Minister Sharett told the GA that Israel's UN admission was no less than 'the consummation of a people's transition', proceeding to juxtapose its particulars. Without mentioning minority rights, status, or protection, he nonetheless recorded transition in terms long-associated with Jewish minority status, objecthood, and inferiority. That transition, he said, was 'from political *anonymity to clear identity*, from *inferiority to equal status*, from *mere passive protest to active*

[286] Shimoni (n 143); Efraim Inbar, 'Jews, Jewishness and Israel's Foreign Policy' (1990) 2 Jewish Political Stud Rev 165, 167; Beit-Zvi (n 202); Segev, *Seventh* (n 202).

[287] Ch 1; Anita Shapira, 'Did the Zionist Leadership Foresee the Holocaust' in Jehuda Reinharz (ed), *Living with Antisemitism: Modern Jewish Responses* (University Press of New England 1987) 397.

[288] Brian Horowitz and Leonid Katsis, *Vladimir Jabotinsky's Story of My Life* (Wayne State UP 2016) 89, 82.

[289] Vladmir Jabotinsky, *The War and the Jew* (Dial Press 1942) 56.

[290] 'Introduction' (1948) 1 Jewish YB Intl L v (Jews were 'the object of the international system of the protection of minorities ... At all the times they were merely the object, never the subject, of international law; nor could they have been anything else before the establishment of the State of Israel'); Bentwich (n 98) 118.

responsibility, from exclusion to membership in the family of nations.[291] Sharett proceeded to 'express deep gratitude to those nations which, *at a time when the Jews had had no voice in world councils*, had championed from the international platform ... the rights and aspirations of the Jewish people and their claim to nationhood in Palestine'.[292] Weeks later, he told the *Knesset* of UN admission:

> This was a revolutionary transformation not only in the historical, but also in the political-practical sense. In a blink of an eye, the status of our mission [to the UN] changed radically. From those who beseech help and succor for themselves, we became those required to assist others; from seekers of charity we became partners in decision.[293]

UN admission, he noted, was 'a mending of the status' of the Jewish people; it meant that the fate of the Jewish people, no longer 'prey to others', was in their own hand.[294] Jewish sovereignty—and the acquisition of majority position in Palestine through strife and war[295]—had rendered Jewish minority status a thing of the past.[296]

It was with sovereignty, then, that resentment towards Dubnow's theory could be asserted in full form. It was then that such sentiments were revealed to have been latent, all along, in Zionist thinking and that Dubnow's theory, and its investment in minority status and rights, have been exposed as what they really have been for the more radical, Palestine-exclusive strand of Zionist thought. Dubnowism was a rival ideology of Jewish nationalism. At its core, it constructed Jews as *no more* than minorities, and its prescribed solution to the Jewish Question was *no more* than the illusory promise of minority rights and autonomy in the Diaspora. That construction of status, and that prescribed solution, undermined Jewish demands for national, territorial self-determination. Zionism sought to radically transform the status of the Jewish people; minority protection—from Great Power interventions of the nineteenth century on behalf of Jewish minorities[297] to the Versailles system—manifested the endurance of their inferior status. Minority rights were

[291] Emphases added; Speech to the General Assembly by Foreign Minister Sharett, 11 May 1949 in Medzini (n 281) 119; GAOR, Plenary (11 May 1949) 332.

[292] Emphasis added; Medzini (n 281) 120.

[293] *Divrei HaKnesset* (n 84) 718.

[294] ibid, 719.

[295] Benny Morris, *The Birth of the Palestinian Refugee Problem, 1947–1949* (CUP 1989); Benny Morris, *The Birth of the Palestinian Refugee Problem Revisited* (CUP 2003).

[296] Henceforth, framing the status and rights of Palestinians in terms of minority and autonomy would serve to signify the sovereign transformation of Jews.

[297] Fink (n 120); Abigail Green, 'The Limits of Intervention: Coercive Diplomacy and the Jewish Question in the Nineteenth Century' (2014) 36 The Intl Hist Rev 473; Abigail Green, 'The British Empire and the Jews: An Imperialism of Human Rights?' (2008) 199 Past & Present 175; Abigail Green, 'Intervening in the Jewish Question, 1840–1878' in Brendan Simms and David JB Trim (eds), *Humanitarian Intervention: A History* (CUP 2011) 139; Garry J Bass, *Freedom's Battle: The Origins of Humanitarian Intervention* (Knopf 2008).

symptomatic of the Jewish problem, not its cure. Intervention may have promised humanitarian protection—but humanitarian protection, alas, also attested to an inferior political status, entrenching a defect in the sovereign capacity[298] of the Jewish people in Europe—and in Palestine. Opposition to Dubnowism, Negation of the Diaspora, rejection of the construction of Jewish existence in minority terms, mistrust of international protection—all these were part of the ideological makeup of the Zionist movement that, with the sovereign turn, crystallized into the foundational ideology of the Jewish state, part and parcel of its *raison d'être*—and of its *raison d'etat*.[299] The hostility expressed by Robinson and Rosenne towards the Genocide Convention was no more than the application of now-hegemonic ideology.

Sharett himself provided a vivid demonstration of the depth of that ideological resentment. In the late 1950s, after he was ousted from the premiership, he reminisced how he had read the first edition of Dubnow's *Weltgeschichte des Jüdischen Volkes* at age nine.[300] He also attested to the ideological fervour attending the Zionist reading of Dubnow: 'I was raised on both Dubnow the historian and on war on Dubnowism, *as a false and perverse doctrine*'.[301] Minority rights—the implementation of Dubnow's programme—were tantamount, ideologically, to idolatry. After the sovereign turn, support for minority rights was tantamount to apostasy. After 1948, any interpretation of Jews as minorities, in Palestine and elsewhere, threatened to undo Zionism's greatest achievement: internationally, equal sovereign status and, in *Eretz Israel*, a majority position. Sovereignty, that is, had already affected the 'mending of the status' of the Jewish people. A return to minority rights was a return to inferior status, voicelessness, dependence 'on the charity of others' and on international law's 'paper guarantees'.[302] That was the essential fault Robinson and Rosenne had found in the Genocide Convention: how it constructed Jews, their political-legal status, and the international legal protection they were entitled to were all at odds with the foundational ideology of the Jewish state and its

[298] Anthony Smith, 'Zionism and Diaspora Nationalism' (1995) 2 Isr Affairs 1, 15 ('minority autonomy was ultimately a matter of sufferance, not right').

[299] As late as 1980, a symposium on the 'Centrality of the State of Israel in Jewish Life' included an intervention under the Hebrew title 'Revival of Dubnovism *Will* Undermine the Unity of the Nation'. The author was a former Labour Member of *Knesset* and, at the time, a member of the quarterly's editorial board, published by the WJC's Israel Executive: Yitzhak Koren, 'The Revival of Dubnovism Could Undermine the Unity of Our People' (1980) 26 Gesher 20 (Hebrew).

[300] That would be, then, the four-volume original Russian edition.

[301] Emphasis added; Moshe Sharett, *Personal Diary: 1957–1958* (Ma'ariv 1978) 1978–9 (Hebrew). Sharett recalled bitter nocturnal arguments 'of the future of the Jewish people' between Vladimir Dubnow—who immigrated to Palestine in 1883 but returned to Russia, 'betrayed the love of his youth and identified with his brother'—and Sharett's 'loyal to Zion' father. They would wake up the children until 'mother would separate them and send each to his room, sleepless'. His father hired Simon Dubnow's brother as a Hebrew tutor to Sharett and his sister while still in Russia: Moshe Sharett, *Shall We Ever Meet Again: Letters of an Ottoman Soldier 1916–1918* (Sharett Heritage Society 1998) 33ff (Hebrew).

[302] Sharett (n 11) 161.

now-proven sovereign capacity. However implicitly, the Convention subverted its *raison d'être*, undermined its achievement, cast a doubt over its promise to be the sole guarantee of Jewish existence, and challenged its claim to alone speak for the Jewish people.

And yet, ideological refutation of the Genocide Convention also had a personal impetus. When framing the Genocide Convention as a measure that could protect Jewish survival and that should command, for that reason, the diplomatic resources of the Jewish state, Lemkin did more than contest the ideological and career choices made by Robinson and Rosenne or challenge their standing as the sovereign, and therefore exclusive, spokespersons of the Jewish voice. In advocating a return to minority rights, Lemkin and the Genocide Convention served as a reminder of their previous, now abandoned, ideological engagement with Dubnow and minority rights: a reminder, that is, that he had kept faith with a creed that Robinson and, to a lesser extent, Rosenne had abandoned. This was a reminder that they, too, once adhered to what Sharett, now their political principal, described as a 'false and perverse doctrine'. In that sense, the Genocide Convention tested their fidelity to the 'radical solution' of Jewish sovereignty and the ruling ideology of the Jewish state. The measure of their resentment of Lemkin, and the Genocide Convention, reveals the scale of the threat to their ideological credentials and to their transformation into sovereign, 'new' Jews.[303] Their common hostility to Lemkin, and to his project, had everything to do with their respective ideological conversions; it can only be fully fathomed against the backdrop of their past engagements with minority rights and a rival ideology that had insisted that these could solve the Jewish Question. The 1951 Refugee Convention, the subject of the next chapter, would present another test to the ideological credentials of Robinson and Rosenne.

***

Jewish ideological sensibilities and Jewish political experience combined to lead Robinson and Rosenne to display ambivalence towards the Genocide Convention and its progenitor, Raphael Lemkin. Their ambivalence stemmed only marginally from the Israeli-Arab conflict. For the most part, it was linked to the Convention's Jewish aspect—its ideological provenance, the political programme it drew on, and the solution it presented to the Jewish Question. For them, the sovereign turn in Jewish history had rendered the type of protection the Genocide Convention promised Jews anachronistic and redundant. It also subverted the 'radical solution'

[303] Others in the MFA did at times make recourse to minorities vocabularies when considering Jewish Diaspora communities. Consider Aubrey Eban, First Committee Statement, 12 May 1949, FM-73/17 (urging for a guarantee of minority rights for the Jewish community in Tripolitania during the 'brief transition' from trusteeship to independence). Similarly, International Organizations Division, Israel's Position on the Questions of Indians in the Union of South Africa, 1 August 1950, FM-2424/11; [Anon.], Background Review, 1 October 1952, FM-1973/1, ISA; both discussed in Rotem Giladi, 'Negotiating Identity: Israel, Apartheid, and the United Nations 1949–1952' (2017) 132 (No.559) English Hist Rev 1440.

that they were now invested in as transformed, sovereign Jews. Their patent sovereign grudges and sensibilities, mitigated by the constraints and opportunities of Israel's early foreign policy, gave rise to the myriad of attitudes they would display towards Lemkin and the Genocide Convention: disinterest and indifference, acknowledgement and appropriation, derision and instrumentalism, aversion and hostility.

Time blunted some of the edge of ideological divisions. By 1960, Jewish sovereignty was a *fait accompli*; Autonomism and minority rights, a thing of a distant past. That year, Israel captured Adolf Eichmann. His trial would assert Israel's jurisdictional ownership over the Holocaust. Time also brought, it seems, a measure of personal *rapprochement*. A year earlier, Lemkin died. Rosenne—ardent author of reviews and obituaries—wrote a short tribute to the 'Lone Fighter Against Genocide'. Lemkin's untimely death 'has removed a powerful if tragic figure from the Jewish world, and particularly from that little band of our co-religionists who were deeply concerned for the strengthening of international law and for the work of the United Nations'. Lemkin's *Axis Rule* was 'still the best account of the manner in which the Nazis made use of legal techniques for their policy of destroying European Jewry'.

Some of the old reserve, however, remained: 'It is *apparently* in this book that the word "genocide" first appeared as a legal term', wrote Rosenne. He did praise Lemkin's 'strength of will' and 'immeasurable devotion': Lemkin's effort was '[a]lmost single-handed and against the virtually universal scepticism of politicians and lawyers'. But Lemkin's achievement, he implied, was limited. And the Genocide Convention still had little practical value: universally, but even less so for Jews. Lemkin, Rosenne wrote, 'brought to the legal consciousness of the world ... a vivid awareness of the national and individual tragedy of genocide. Let us hope that circumstances will never again arise in the future which will force *any people* to have recourse the Genocide Convention. But if they do, his work will not have been in vain'.[304]

Rosenne's scepticism with the Convention and minority rights nonetheless persisted.[305] So, for that matter, did Robinson's. In a short 1990 intervention on 'The Protection of Minorities and Human Rights', Rosenne discussed the League of Nations minorities system. Nowhere did the essay even imply its Jewish aspect. He remained critical of its effects: 'the generalization or universalization of human rights ... has not had any direct beneficial effect on the various minorities around the world. If anything ... it has brought harm to the general status of minorities.'[306]

304 Emphases added; Shabtai Rosenne, 'In Memoriam: A Tribute to Dr. Raphael Lemkin, Lone Fighter Against Genocide' *Jerusalem Post* (10 September 1959), Rosenne Papers; in private, he remained hostile to Lemkin and 'doubtful of his version' and of the Convention's Jewish value: Rosenne to Golda Meir, 7 December 1958, Rosenne to Meroz, 23 October 1958, FM-5849/10, ISA.

305 Consider Rosenne's appearance in the ICJ Genocide Case, discussed in ch 4.

306 Shabtai Rosenne, 'The Protection of Minorities and Human Rights' (1990) 20 Isr YB on Hum Rts 359.

In 1971, now a Holocaust scholar, Robinson wrote that '[i]t would be exaggerated' 'to include the [Genocide Convention] ... within the code of protection of minorities, not so much because of [that Code's] complete bankruptcy in the face of genocidal mass murder' during World War II 'but because [as the ICJ has ruled] ... there was nothing ... in the Convention which was not forbidden' by international law previously.[307] If such marginalization of Lemkin's achievement was meant to signify that Robinson's sovereign transformation had been complete, it came too late—as revealed by his involvement with the 1951 Refugee Convention.

[307] Jacob Robinson, 'International Protection of Minorities: A Global View' (1971) 1 Isr YB on Hum Rts 61, 89.

PART IV
REFUGE

6

Sovereign Sensibilities and Jewish Refugees

Jacob Robinson and the Drafting of the 1951 Refugee Convention

1. *The Jewish Refugee*: Jacob Robinson's Pre-Sovereign Sensibilities

In late 1944, towards the end of the war, the Institute of Jewish Affairs ('IJA') in New York published a voluminous tome titled *The Jewish Refugee*. It was authored by two staff members who themselves had found refuge in the US.[1] The preface was composed by the Institute's Director, Jacob Robinson, who had been displaced by the war. The 'Jewish refugee problem', he wrote, was 'one of the tragedies of Jewish existence in a Gentile world'[2]—and a crucial aspect of 'the Jewish position in Europe during the Long Truce'.[3]

In early 1941, IJA's initial research plans still envisioned a post-war Jewish rehabilitation in Europe and the continuation of Jewish Diasporic existence with improved legal protection for 'those who still remain in their old homes, or are willing eventually to return to them'. IJA's 1941 Program still considered Palestine only one of the 'immigration possibilities' for 'those millions of refugees for whom new homes will have to be found'.[4] True, it recited the Zionist creed of the Institute's parent bodies when professing that IJA 'will take it for granted that the development of the National Home in Palestine is the primary solution of the problem of Jewish migration'.[5] Yet this was the conclusion of the discussion of the question of immigration, not its point of departure. In practice, the 1941 Program treated that 'primary solution' as secondary to rehabilitation and a return to Diaspora homes. It mentioned Palestine only after detailing IJA's plans to study various aspects of and

[1] Arieh Tartakower and Kurt R Grossmann, *The Jewish Refugee* (IJA 1944). The book also bore a distinctly American imprint: it was dedicated to 'Jochanan Tartakower PFC., U.S. Army Who at the Age of Nineteen Was Killed in Action in France on September 29, 1944, and Whose Sacrifice Is Typical of the Many Thousands of Jewish Refugees Who Have Given the Last Full Measure of Devotion to Their People and to the Countries That Gave Them Refuge': ibid, v.

[2] Jacob Robinson, 'Preface' in Tartakower and Grossmann (n 1) viii.

[3] ibid, vii.

[4] IJA, *Institute of Jewish Affairs: Program* (American Jewish Congress/World Jewish Congress 1941) 10, discussed in chs 3, 5; Rotem Giladi, 'A "Historical Commitment"? Identity and Ideology in Israel's Attitude to the Refugee Convention 1951–1954' (2014) 37 Intl Hist Rev 745.

[5] IJA (n 4) 10.

Jews, Sovereignty, and International Law. Rotem Giladi, Oxford University Press. © Rotem Giladi 2021.
DOI: 10.1093/oso/9780198857396.003.0008

different solutions for Jewish refugeehood.[6] In 1941, the reference to Palestine and the National Home was not much more than an ideological obeisance.[7]

The study envisioned in 1941, orchestrated by Robinson,[8] culminated in *The Jewish Refugee*. In the meantime, however, Robinson's wartime shift towards the National Home solution[9] had already led him to advocate that the '*single demand*' of the World Jewish Congress ('WJC') after the war 'should be the establishment of a Jewish Commonwealth in Palestine' to solve 'the refugee and repatriation problems'.[10] By 1944, Palestine seemed to carry a greater weight in the solution prescribed by IJA for Jewish displacement. Robinson proceeded to assert a classical Zionist claim that became even more urgent during the war years; namely, that the Jewish refugee crisis had turned from a *humanitarian* problem into a *political* solution:

> While fully alive to the humanitarian aspect of the problem, we do not stop there, but consider it in the general framework of the possibilities of Jewish survival in the modern world. Hence we link the refugee movement with the migratory movement, the migratory movement with Jewish experiments in colonization, which in turn leads inevitably to the problem of Jewish concentration in Palestine and the function of the Jewish refugee in the building of the Jewish National Home.[11]

Robinson's willingness to consider the Jewish crisis as a *political* opportunity signalled just how radical his wartime ideological shift had been. Privately, however, Robinson had already expressed even more radical, Palestinocentric views on Jewish immigration.[12]

Accordingly, Palestine was the first of 'Countries of Refuge and Settlement' to which the study dedicated a chapter.[13] In that chapter, the authors did not limit themselves to descriptive writing and analysis but strayed into the realm of contention. Here they argued that Palestine's success 'in absorbing such a great number of refugees ... leads almost automatically to the conclusion that it ought to be

[6] ibid.

[7] For similar analysis: Zohar Segev, *The World Jewish Congress During the Holocaust: Between Activism and Restraint* (de Gruyter 2014) 191.

[8] Materials in WJC–C112/2–5, WJC–C113/1–7, WJC–C119/8, WJC–H215/12 (World Jewish Congress Records, MS-361), American Jewish Archives ('AJA').

[9] Discussed in chs 3, 5.

[10] Emphasis in the original; Robinson, Some Fundamental Problems of Jewish Post-War Planning, [n.d.], WJC–C118/8, AJA.

[11] Robinson, 'Preface' (n 2) viii.

[12] Robinson to Stephen Wise, Nahum Goldmann, 25 June 1943, WJC–C97/17, AJA, where he was also apprehensive that 'we'—that is, the *Yishuv*—'will receive all the physically and emotionally handicapped elements' from among the survivors. This position and the controversy surrounding it are discussed in ch 5.

[13] Tartakower and Grossmann (n 1) 52 (the 'importance of Palestine as a country of refuge and settlement' during the war).

regarded as the haven *par excellence* for Jewish refugees'.[14] They also reproduced a *précis* of Zionist interpretations of the Palestine Mandate and its immigration provisions—as well as of Zionist critique of the immigration laws and policies of Palestine's mandatory government.

The book's last chapter, titled 'The Solution', asserted a 'close connection between the solution of the refugee problem and the establishment of a Jewish National Home in Palestine'.[15] Here the authors followed Robinson in reading opportunity into a crisis. On the one hand, they concluded that 'in all probability, the most important results of Jewish colonization in the future may also be expected in Palestine, and ... the solution of the Jewish refugee problem depends to a considerable degree on the work done in that country'.[16] On the other hand, they submitted that 'the building of the Jewish National Home' in Palestine would require the efforts of Jewish refugees.[17] Yet some ambivalence persisted. The authors also considered—echoing the 1941 IJA Program—other solutions to the problem of Jewish refugees equally acceptable, albeit not necessarily equally feasible: 'return to their homelands', enabling them 'to remain permanently in the countries where they now are', or 'final emigration to another country'. 'None of these ways', they noted, 'excludes the others'.[18] Whether for humanitarian, pragmatic, or ideological reasons, the authors would not point to Palestine as the *only* solution to Jewish refugeehood; Robinson, it would seem, fully shared the authors' broad, inclusive reading of Jewish post-war interests.[19] His wartime ideological transformation, evidently, had its limits; these would be revealed, and tested, by his work in connection with the 1951 Refugee Convention[20] and by the ideological demands presented by Jewish sovereignty.

A few years after *The Jewish Refugee* was published, now as legal adviser to Israel's United Nations ('UN') mission, Robinson was presented with an opportunity to help reform the international norms governing Jewish displacement. In August 1949, three months after Israel's admission to the UN, the Economic and Social Council ('ECOSOC') established an '*Ad Hoc* Committee on Statelessness and Related Problems' comprising a small circle of government representatives possessing 'special competence' on the subject.[21] That body was to consider, and act on, the recommendations made in the Secretary-General's ('SG') 'Study on Statelessness'.[22] Robinson was elected to serve on that body. Later, when a

[14] Emphasis in the original; ibid, 55.

[15] ibid, 518–9.

[16] ibid, 515.

[17] ibid, 526.

[18] ibid, 502.

[19] Notably, Tartakover immigrated to Palestine in 1946, where he became a professor of sociology at the Hebrew University; Grossmann, by contrast, remained in the US.

[20] Convention Relating to the Status of Refugees (28 July 1951) 189 UNTS 137.

[21] ECOSOC Res.248(IX) (8 August 1949). For the legislative history: Andreas Zimmermann, *The 1951 Convention Relating to the Status of Refugees and its 1967 Protocol: A Commentary* (OUP 2011).

[22] UN Doc. E/1112 (1 February 1949) and Add.1 (19 May 1949); prepared at the request of ECOSOC, it triggered the process that resulted in the adoption of the 1951 Convention.

Conference of Plenipotentiaries was convened to negotiate the draft Convention Relating to the Status of Refugees prepared by the *Ad Hoc* Committee,[23] Robinson was appointed to represent Israel. His familiarity with the challenges of Jewish displacement, and with the pertinent legal and institutional arrangements, was extensive. Apart from directing IJA's research on these matters, he was also closely involved with the WJC's wartime and post-war work on Jewish refugees, displaced persons, and immigration.[24] Israel's newly established foreign service could not produce a representative more qualified to contribute to the effort to reach agreement on the status and treatment of refugees. Nor could it, in all likelihood, come up with a better connected envoy.[25]

2. A Question of Representation

Robinson's work in connection with the draft Convention on the Status of Refugees appears to point to continuity: a vivid demonstration of how knowledge acquired by pre-sovereign Jewish advocacy, diplomacy, and international law engagement was placed, after 1948, at the disposal of the Jewish state that embraced, in turn, a leadership role in respect of Jewish causes. And, equally, an illustration of how such 'Jewish' knowledge would come to shape, in turn, Israel's international law outlook. Robinson certainly did place his knowledge and connections at the disposal of the Jewish state; and yet, this and the next chapter reveal that the Jewish state did not quite elect to avail itself of his pre-sovereign expertise except accidentally, belatedly, perfunctorily, instrumentally, and grudgingly. More crucially, at important junctures the Jewish state rejected, in a manner and for reasons discussed below, the pre-sovereign Jewish sensibilities underpinning Robinson's involvement in the drafting of the 1951 Refugee Convention. Israel's sovereign international law outlook on refugee status and on the Refugee Convention would stand for a radical break away from, not continuity of, any Jewish non-sovereign sensibilities held by Robinson.

Even a cursory examination of the preparatory and archival records reveals just how extensive Robinson's involvement had been in the process that would produce, in July 1951, the Refugee Convention. However, our concern here is neither

[23] UNGA Res.429(V) (14 December 1950).

[24] Segev (n 7).

[25] Robinson to Eytan, *Ad Hoc* Committee on Statelessness and Related Problems: Final Report, 21 February 1950, FM-2010/13, Israel State Archive ('ISA'). Paul Weis was one of the familiar faces Robinson would encounter in his work on the Refugee Convention. During the war, Weis had worked for the WJC's British Section. Later he joined the International Refugee Organization ('IRO'), served as legal adviser at the Office of the UN High Commissioner for Refugees ('UNHCR'), and later became Chief of its Legal Department. Weis was a key figure at the 1951 Conference: Editorial, 'Paul Weis: 1907–1991' (1991) 3 Intl J Refugee L 183; 'Paul Weis (1911–1991): A Selected Bibliography' (1991) 3 Intl J Refugee L 373.

the tally of his interventions nor the nature or effect of his contribution, overt or behind the scenes, to the Convention's making.[26] Our concern here, rather, is the extent to which Robinson was representing, in *actuality*, the views, preferences, and policies of Israel's Ministry of Foreign Affairs ('MFA'). Thus, the question at hand is not the *formal* attributes of his representative capacity;[27] the *reality* of that capacity, as we shall see, was quite another matter. This concerned, specifically, Robinson's reading of the Convention's Jewish aspects; what Jewish motives and sensibilities drove his work on the Convention were not shared by Israel's foreign policy apparatus; in this respect, he was not expressing MFA positions.

Evidence on the gulf separating Robinson's reading of Jewish matters and the MFA position draws on a rich documentary record. Though the Conference schedule was unusually hectic, Robinson scrupulously sent his MFA superiors, in lengthy instalments, detailed reports that told of initiatives and alliances, impressions and developments, amendments and statements, obstacles and achievements.[28] He did the same, earlier, in reports on the work of the *Ad Hoc* Committee,[29] and on the ensuing General Assembly's ('GA') Third Committee

[26] Robinson to International Organizations Division ('IOD'), Fifth Interim Report on the *Ad Hoc* Committee on Statelessness and Related Problems, 20 February 1950, FM-2010/13. One anecdote, however, commends some caution in any qualitative assessment of his contribution. Otherwise a keen observer, Robinson sent Rosenne, not without some pride, a copy of a short article on the draft Convention written by the chairman of the *Ad Hoc* Committee. It contained the following statement: '[t]here was Dr. Robinson, of Israel, so learned in the law that, to the bewilderment of the lay chairman, he seemed sometimes to use English only as connecting phrases for legal principles expressed in Latin': Robinson to Rosenne, 6 March 1950, FM-1830/8, ISA with a copy of Leslie Chance, 'New Convention, Protocol Drafted' *UN Bulletin* (1 March 1950) 231, 232–3.

[27] Even Robinson's accreditation to the Conference could be considered a sign of things to come: Robinson insisted on being equipped with 'the necessary credentials including, *inter alia*, the formal authority to sign on behalf of the Government of Israel the agreements which may be adopted by the Conference subject, however, to ratification': Robinson to Rosenne, 22 March 1951, FM-2010/13. At first, his credentials were 'deficient and did not contain the power to sign', but at his insistence this was later rectified, although only after the Conference's opening: Robinson to Director-General, The Conference on Refugees and Stateless Persons: First Report, 8 July 1951, FM-19/10; Robinson to Director General, 15 July 1951, FM-1847/2; Robinson to Director-General, Fourth and Final Report on the Conference of Plenipotentiaries on the Status of Refugees and Stateless Persons, Geneva, 1 August 1951, FM-19/10, FM-1847/2. See also IOD to Kahany, 12 June 1950, FM-2010/13; IOD to Kahany, 9 July 1951, and Lourie to SG, 18 June 1951, FM-19/10, ISA.

[28] Robinson to Director-General, First Report, 8 July 1951 (n 27); Robinson to Director General, 15 July 1951 (n 27); Robinson to MFA Secretary-General, Third Report on the Conference on Legal Status of Refugees, 22 July 1951, FM-19/10, ISA; Robinson to Director-General, Fourth and Final Report, 1 August 1951 (n 27).

[29] Robinson to Gordon, 19 January 1950; Robinson to IOD, First Interim Report of the *Ad Hoc* Committee on Statelessness and Related Problems, 23 January 1950; Robinson to IOD, Second Interim Report of the *Ad Hoc* Committee on Statelessness and Related Problems, 30 January 1950; Robinson to IOD, Third Interim Report on the *Ad Hoc* Committee on Statelessness and Related Problems, 6 February 1950; Robinson to IOD, Fourth Interim Report on the *Ad Hoc* Committee on Statelessness and Related Problems, 13 February 1950, FM-2010/13; Robinson to IOD, Fifth Interim Report, 20 February 1950 (n 26); Robinson to Eytan, Final Report, 21 February 1950 (n 25); Robinson to Gordon, Second Session of the *Ad Hoc* Committee on Refugees and Statelessness Persons, 21 August 1950; Robinson to IOD, Second Session of the *Ad Hoc* Committee on Refugees and Statelessness Persons: Second and Final Report, 12 October 1950, FM-2010/13, ISA.

debate.[30] Reconstructing Robinson's representative capacity also draws on his exchanges with MFA colleagues, mostly Ezekiel Gordon, the former and future UN Secretariat official now serving in the Ministry's International Organizations Division.[31] A close reading of these sources suggest that when it came to Jewish interests and concerns, Robinson was not quite expressing the MFA's position.

3. 'In Favour of Jewish Refugees': Robinson's Motives

First, then, there is the question of Robinson's motives and sensibilities. There can be no doubt that his engagement with the question of the status and treatment of refugees and stateless persons was driven by his concern for Jewish interests and by his reading of what were, in this respect, the interests of the Jewish state. This became patent early in his involvement in the work of the *Ad Hoc* Committee. Already in his first report on that body's proceedings, he observed that 'Israel's attitude' ought to be influenced by the '*plight of Jewish refugees*'.[32] Specifically, he considered that it was 'the duty of Israel to help to improve the legal status of Jewish refugees'[33] and, accordingly, worked to keep what he considered Jewish concerns on the Committee's agenda.[34] Robinson saw no reason to keep this perspective to himself or limit its circulation to official circles. In a radio broadcast, he reported to the Israeli public that Israel's participation was driven by concerns with 'the fate of tens of thousands of Jews, in the countries of Europe and outside it who are refugees ... or stateless persons ... Their legal status is not regular and can be ameliorated and improved'.[35] This would remain the crux of his approach.

Later, in connection with the Third Committee debate on the draft Convention, Robinson noted that he had 'proceed[ed] on the assumption that the Jewish world is still interested in the fate of refugees (both in those who have had this status up till now and in some new categories which may emerge in the future)'.[36] What 'important dangers' he helped avert during that debate were defined by the 'Jewish viewpoint'.[37] For him, the Jewish state was to act as guardian of Jewish interests: 'our viewpoint', he wrote, was defined by 'the interest of Israel acting for Jews in the Diaspora'.[38] Revealing a measure of his sovereign sensibilities—more on these below—he considered the Jewish state better informed and better equipped

[30] Robinson, The Problem of Refugees in the Third Committee of the General Assembly, 19 December 1950, FM-2010/13, ISA.
[31] See ch 3.
[32] Emphasis in the original; Robinson to IOD, First Interim Report, 23 January 1950 (n 29).
[33] ibid.
[34] ibid.
[35] [Robinson], Broadcast from Lake Success, 17 February 1950, FM-2010/13, ISA.
[36] Robinson, The Problem of Refugees, 19 December 1950 (n 30).
[37] ibid.
[38] ibid.

to act in favour of Jewish refugees than 'those Jewish organizations who ... are supposed to be interested in the matter'.[39] What achievements he had accomplished as Israel's representative at various UN bodies, he reported to the MFA Director-General Walter Eytan, were taken 'in favour of Jewish refugees'.[40] When the GA resolved to convene a conference to discuss and adopt the draft Refugee Convention, Robinson recommended that Israel participate, as 'part of our activities in favour of the Diaspora Jewry'.[41]

The same Jewish concerns drove Robinson's work at the 1951 Conference. He continued working to ensure that the authors of persecution would not benefit from the Convention's protection and sought, without success, to have the Conference deal with the position of stateless persons who were not, in law, refugees.[42] His concerns remained focused on the Jewish Diaspora: 'it is no secret', he reported to Eytan, 'that we are participating in the Conference in order to protect those Jewish refugees still remaining in certain European countries and whose number is not too great'.[43] Accordingly, he engaged in an effort to guard against dilution of the draft so that 'the formulation of provisions ... having special value for Jewish refugees are not changed to the worse'.[44] After the Conference, as the next chapter relates, the same Jewish concerns would drive his lobbying for Israel's ratification of the Convention. For now, our concern is that his reading of Jewish interests in the nascent Refugee Convention did not express the views and policies of the MFA.

4. A 'Certain Danger', 'Questionable' Advantage, and a Waning Interest: The Ministry of Foreign Affairs Position

Robinson's involvement in the successive phases of the drafting of the Refugee Convention could be read as evidence of an Israeli investment in the Convention owing to its Jewish aspects and, therefore, as an indication of continuity between Jewish advocacy and Israeli diplomacy.[45] A closer reading, however, compels the conclusion that this was not quite the case. The case against continuity, and

[39] Robinson to Eytan, Report on My Activities in the Fifth Session of the General Assembly, 27 December 1950, FM–2010/13, ISA.
[40] ibid.
[41] Robinson to Rosenne, 6 February 1951, FM–2010/13, FM–1830/8, ISA.
[42] Robinson to MFA Secretary-General, Third Report, 22 July 1951 (n 28).
[43] Robinson to Director-General, First Report, 8 July 1951 (n 27).
[44] ibid.
[45] For such a reading: Gilad Ben-Nun, 'The Israeli Roots of Article 3 and Article 6 of the 1951 Refugee Convention' (2014) 27 J of Refugee Stud 101; Gilad Ben-Nun, 'From *Ad Hoc* to Universal: The International Refugee Regime from Fragmentation to Unity 1922–1954' (2015) 34 Refugee Survey Quarterly 23; Gilad Ben-Nun, *Seeking Asylum in Israel: Refugees and the History of Migration Law* (Tauris 2016); James Loeffler, *Rooted Cosmopolitans: Jews and Human Rights in the Twentieth Century* (Yale UP 2018).

against the attribution of Robinson's Jewish motives to the Jewish state, starts with the very circumstances of his appointment to the *Ad Hoc* Committee. Gordon, in fact, learned of Robinson's appointment 'in the press' and 'with the greatest surprise'; the MFA had not even considered campaigning for it. It soon transpired that Menachem Kahany, Israel's Geneva representative to international organizations, uninstructed and 'without consulting us', had lobbied for the appointment. Gordon complained to Eytan, the Director-General, that Kahany had exceeded his instructions and, in fact, had acted against their spirit. Charged with representing Israel in ECOSOC's ninth session as an observer—Israel was not a member of that UN body—Kahany was to keep a low profile except, if necessary, in respect of two specific matters. Gordon therefore considered Robinson's appointment more a liability than an opportunity: he wrote to Eytan that '[t]he advantage of our presence in the *ad hoc* Committee is questionable'.[46]

Gordon's apprehensions concerned the two matters in relation to which Kahany's instructions foresaw the possibility of active involvement by Israel's representatives. Both controlled the MFA's initial approach to the UNSG 'Study on Statelessness',[47] the ensuing ECOSOC discussion, and the early work of the *Ad Hoc* Committee. For the MFA, Jewish concerns were from the start, and at best, secondary to other, more important Israeli interests.

One concern was that participation in the work of the *Ad Hoc* Committee would entangle Israel in 'the conflict which separates ... the Eastern and Western blocs'.[48] In this respect, Kahany's lobbying for Robinson's appointment went against the MFA's policy of refraining from taking sides in the Cold War. This imperative, a key component of the MFA 'orientation' strategy,[49] was strong enough to trump, time and again, the notion of '*diplomatie de présence*'—Israel's desire to be seen as a member making a regular, high-quality contribution to the UN's work.[50] Robinson's unintended appointment, however, could not be undone. Gordon proceeded to control the damage. He forwarded Robinson Kahany's unheeded instructions; these warned of the 'acute conflict between the Eastern and Western groups' and mandated that Israel's representatives 'certainly refrain from

[46] Gordon to Director-General, 14 August 1949, FM–2010/13, ISA.

[47] UN Doc. E/1112 (1 February 1949) (n 22).

[48] Gordon to Director-General, 14 August 1949 (n 46).

[49] See ch 3; Uri Bialer, *Between East and West: Israel's Foreign Policy Orientation 1948–1956* (Cambridge 2008); Avi Shlaim, 'Israel Between East and West: Israel's Foreign Policy Orientation, 1948–1956' (2004) 66 Intl J of Middle East Stud 657; Rotem Giladi, 'Negotiating Identity: Israel, Apartheid, and the United Nations 1949–1952' (2017) 132 (No.559) English Hist Rev 1440.

[50] Shabtai Rosenne, 'Jacob Robinson—In Memoriam' (1978) 13 Isr L Rev 287, 292 ('the idea that after Israel became a member of the United Nations, its delegations should make every effort to take part in all the Organization's activities and make in them a contribution based on intrinsic quality, not on mere political power'). For specific examples: UN Mission Meeting, 19 September 1949, FM–89/1; Robinson to Rosenne, 14 March 1951, FM–1832/3, ISA; Nathan Feinberg, *Israel and the United Nations: Report of a Study Group Set Up By the Hebrew University of Jerusalem* (Manhattan 1956) 30–7; Sharett, *Divrei HaKnesset* (Parliamentary Record) (15 June 1949) 717–19 (Hebrew). For a critical appraisal, see ch 4 and the Epilogue.

taking sides'.[51] Gordon also prepared a new memorandum where he tried to 'define ... what seems to me to be our "general line"'.[52] This memorandum, 'prepared at the last minute', was not meant to constitute a definitive set of instructions controlling Robinson's participation in the work of the *Ad Hoc* Committee. None at the MFA had read it—'Rosenne could not study it thoroughly'—so that even if Gordon took 'into account all the factors that guide our policy', he asked Robinson to treat the document 'as the expression of my personal views'. Gordon, nonetheless, was expressing the MFA's established policy when observing that 'our participation in the Special Committee poses a number of delicate problems ... because of the opposition that some of these problems will undoubtedly provoke between the representatives of the Eastern bloc and those of the Western countries'. Israel's policy was 'not to antagonize the Soviets and Poland'. This dictated abstention from any controversy: '[a]ccording to our general line, we must avoid, as far as possible, sharp points which would not fail to put us in opposition either with the Eastern States or with those of the West'.[53]

The other cause of Gordon's apprehensions was what he described as the matter of 'Arab refugees who left their homes in Israel and, also of the inhabitants of other parts of Palestine now under the military control of various Arab countries'.[54] Much of Israel's diplomatic and legal resources, in and outside the UN, went into denying responsibility for creating—or resolving—this problem; thwarting norms or procedures that would facilitate their return; and avoiding or at any rate controlling the opportunities of Arab states to lambast Israel on this matter in international fora.[55] A good portion of Gordon's instructions to Kahany sought to give effect to that policy. Here Israel faced, *per* Gordon, 'a very serious, if not legal, at least moral issues' and 'certain danger[s] ... at least politically', if some of the SG recommendations were to be adopted by ECOSOC. If Israel's orientation dilemma required abstention, facilitated 'by the fact that Israel is not a member' of ECOSOC, the matter of Arab refugees could compel action notwithstanding the limitations of observer status: 'our delegation should not by any means raise ... the problem of Arab refugees' but work to affect the way ECOSOC defined 'stateless persons' so as to ensure their exclusion.[56] What Gordon called 'the consequence of the end of the Mandate' for Palestine was the *ultima ratio* of his analysis: abstaining from 'raising the problem of Arab refugees' and refuting any suggestion that 'the State of Israel [may be] under a duty to bestow its nationality upon former Palestinian[s]' who

[51] Gordon, Study of Statelessness, 24 July 1949, FM-19/3, and enclosed to Gordon to Robinson, 6 January 1950, FM-2010/13, ISA (French).

[52] Gordon, Study, 24 July 1949 (n 51).

[53] Gordon to Robinson, 6 January 1950 (n 51).

[54] Gordon, Study, 24 July 1949 (n 51).

[55] Jacob Tovy, *Israel and the Palestinian Refugee Issue: The Formulation of a Policy 1948–1956* (Routledge 2014).

[56] Gordon, Study, 24 July 1949 (n 51).

became refugees or stateless persons.[57] Gordon's memorandum to Robinson advocated, on the same logic, that Israel support a 'liberal' treatment of refugees: 'Israel is particularly interested in the fact that Arab refugees in the host country enjoy a particularly liberal status, as this will reduce their desire to return to Israel (legally or by "infiltration")'.[58]

For some time, Gordon would also allude to Jewish concerns. Preparing Kahany's instructions for ECOSOC's ninth session, he proposed to read the recommendations in the SG's 'Study on Statelessness'[59] through the 'interest ... [of] the State of Israel, or for the Jewish people, or for both together'.[60] He did not elaborate, however, which interest should prevail or how to affect their synthesis. He did elaborate on certain Jewish interests and observed that Jewish 'suffering from the scourge of statelessness' commended that 'the Jewish state should ... support ... measures aimed at uprooting this evil'.[61] His memorandum to Robinson, in anticipation of the work of the *Ad Hoc* Committee, thus observed that 'persons who are guilty of certain particularly heinous crimes, such as genocide, crimes under the Nuremberg Statute, etc., must be read out of the statutory protection'. Gordon even went as far as expressing his view that 'as it is possible for Jews to invoke the benefit of the Convention, we should be *as liberal as possible*'.[62]

What was *possible* for Israel, however, was limited by its primary interests. In Gordon's actual recommendations, Jewish interests gave way to Israel's central concerns: the desire to antagonize neither East nor West and to avoid discussion of Arab refugees. Whenever these two matters could be involved, Gordon would not even consider the implications for Jewish refugees and stateless persons or for other Jewish interests. He did propose that Israel act in accordance with Jewish interests in some matters where this 'does not concern Palestinian Arabs'.[63] Yet his acknowledgement of Jewish interests went only so far. Gordon thus alluded to past Jewish statelessness as a factor compelling Israel's contribution to the UN work in this regard; yet he took care to cite Israel's disinterest in the problem. He also made it clear that whatever room the requirements of global or regional *realpolitik* left for Israeli involvement, any such involvement would be meant to *signal* Israel's

[57] ibid; here, Kahany complied with his instructions: Kahany to IOD, Ninth Session of the ECOSOC, 11 August 1949, FM–2010/13, ISA.

[58] Gordon to Robinson, 6 January 1950 (n 51) ('Israel is interested in finding a satisfactory solution to the problem of the status of Arab refugees in the neighbouring Arab States, because only such a solution will put an end to their desire to return to Israel'); Gordon to Robinson, 2 August 1950, FM–2010/13 ISA ('as you know we are interested in diverting attention from the specific problem of Arab refugees to the much larger question of refugees in general'). On 'infiltration' of Palestinian refugees: Benny Morris, *The Birth of the Palestinian Refugee Problem, 1947–1949* (CUP 1989); Benny Morris, *The Birth of the Palestinian Refugee Problem Revisited* (CUP 2003).

[59] UN Doc. E/1112 (1 February 1949) (n 22).

[60] Gordon, Study, 24 July 1949 (n 51).

[61] ibid.

[62] Emphasis added; Gordon to Robinson, 6 January 1950 (n 51).

[63] Gordon, Study, 24 July 1949 (n 51).

contribution more than promote a solution to the general, or even Jewish, problem of statelessness and refugeehood. Jewish concerns, for Gordon, occupied a residual space;[64] in his reading, even that residual space was dominated by Israel's second-order interests of diplomatic reputation. In this vein, when informing Robinson of his appointment to the *Ad Hoc* Committee, Gordon wrote:

> Israel *does not have an immediate interest* in the problem of the protection of stateless persons as all persons in that category who come to Israel are given full and equal rights. As for the Jews in that category who are as yet outside Israel, it is to be hope that by the end of IRO 1950, most of them will be settled in Israel. However, in view of the bitter experience the Jewish people have had as refugees, Israel should fully support any plan to give effective protection to stateless persons. *Without entering into a dispute over the present stateless persons*, the Israel delegation *should make it clear that its action is motivated* by the need for such protection as was shown after World War I and during the Nazi regime in Germany.[65]

As legal adviser to Israel's UN mission Robinson needed little reminder of the imperatives of Israel's policy on Arab refugees and Cold War entanglements, as Gordon readily acknowledged.[66] Throughout his work on the Refugee Convention, Robinson fully subscribed to these in principle and followed them closely in practice.[67] As an early proponent of Israel's '*diplomatie de présence*' policy, which he helped formulate,[68] he was not any less sensitive to Israel's diplomatic standing and reputation than his colleagues.[69] Just like Gordon, he measured his own work on

[64] ibid. Gordon noted the Jewish relevance of the SG's recommendation that UN member states ratify League of Nations treaties on Refugees, some of which covered Jewish refugees or were designed to address their situation. While he observed that '[f]rom a more Jewish viewpoint it should be welcome' that 'reception countries' should accede to these arrangements, he did not propose any Israeli action on the matter, only that 'there should be no objection' to this recommendation 'from the point of view of the State of Israel'. Rosenne was less than enthused on the prospect of ratifying these League-era treaties: ch 7.

[65] Emphases added; Gordon to Robinson, 19 September 1949, FM–2010/13, ISA.

[66] Gordon to Robinson, 6 January 1950 (n 51).

[67] Israel, he observed, was 'under the impact of the *cauchemar de refugies* created by the Palestine refugees': Robinson to IOD, Second Interim Report, 30 January 1950 (n 29); his actions on Arab refugees are discussed below.

[68] Discussed above, at text to n 50; Robinson to Foreign Office, 15 June 1948, FM–74/3; Robinson, Marginal Problems in the Third Regular Session of the General Assembly: Observations, 4 September 1948, FM–131/22, ISA; Rosenne (n 50) 292.

[69] Robinson to IOD, First Interim Report, 23 January 1950 (n 29) ('we have to follow faithfully our policy of cooperation with the United Nations in an effort to make the maximum contribution we are capable of'); Robinson, United Nations Conference of Plenipotentiaries on the Status of Stateless Persons, 23 March 1955, FM–1830/10, FM–1988/4, ISA ('In the first place such participation is part of our policy of *diplomatie de presénce*. As a new State we have a duty to instill [sic] on the minds of those not yet accustomed to our existence and to our possible contributions in the field of international co-operation the idea that we are here to stay and that we may be able to contribute something to problems of a general nature').

the Refugee Convention in terms of enhancing Israel's reputation within the UN.[70] And like Gordon, as we shall see, he was at times willing to assign Jewish interests limited weight relative to that of Israel's 'general' interests—or to subordinate the former to the latter. What Robinson first challenged, however, was the measure of Gordon's apprehensions on the question of Arab refugees and the Cold War issues.

On the question of 'Arab refugees', Robinson did not share Gordon's assessment of the risks posed by the work of the *Ad Hoc* Committee and the emerging regime on refugees and stateless persons.[71] Here, the MFA sought *actively* to ensure their exclusion from that regime and to ensure the Convention contained no language that 'might be construed as applying to Arab refugees'.[72] Robinson reported, however, that

> there is no need for such an exclusion since all definitions are adjusted to the problem of European refugees only. The general sentiment is to confine the operation of the Convention to the *existing* categories of protected refugees from Europe.[73]

Once the *Ad Hoc* Committee started its work, Robinson could report that both of Gordon's 'apprehensions (or expectations) did not materialize so far in any substantial way'.[74] The USSR and Poland, he reported, first 'walked out' then boycotted the *Ad Hoc* Committee in protest of the participation of (Nationalist) China.[75] Robinson proceeded to propose that the risk of Cold War entanglement proved lesser than that anticipated by Gordon: 'even if the Soviet bloc had participated in the Committee', he wrote, the 'East-West cleavage would have been a minor factor in the drafting of the Convention in view of the limited scope of the Convention'.[76]

These developments—and Robinson's evaluation—caused the MFA, after little hesitation, to lose interest in Robinson's work and in the Refugee Convention. A few days after Robinson's first report on the progress of the *Ad Hoc* Committee Rosenne—hitherto hardly involved in the matter—agreed with Gordon that 'it is useless to send additional instructions to Dr. Robinson'.[77] Up to this point, Israel's early interest in the question of statelessness and the status of refugees was, predominantly, negative. It decreed, notwithstanding Gordon's occasional allusion to Jewish concerns, that the Jewish state play not much more than a 'purely passive'[78]

[70] '[W]e are bound, as UN members, to contribute from [our] knowledge and experience to the extent that we can to humanitarian problems': [Robinson], Broadcast, 17 February 1950 (n 35).

[71] Robinson to Gordon, 19 January 1950 (n 29).

[72] Gordon to Director-General, 14 August 1949 (n 46).

[73] Emphasis added; Robinson to IOD, First Interim Report, 23 January 1950 (n 29). Robinson also disagreed with Gordon's assessment cited above (n 58) that a 'liberal' Convention might induce 'Arab refugees' to stay at host Arab countries: Robinson to Gordon, 19 January 1950 (n 29).

[74] ibid.

[75] ibid; Robinson to IOD, First Interim Report, 23 January 1950 (n 29).

[76] ibid; Robinson to IOD, Fourth Interim Report, 13 February 1950 (n 29).

[77] Gordon to Rosenne, 26 January 1950, FM–2010/13, ISA, with Rosenne's handwritten note.

[78] Gordon, Study, 24 July 1949 (n 51).

role in this UN work. From the MFA's perspective, the only possible justification for a more active role by Israeli representatives in the UN work on refugee status, barring Cold War entanglement or being called to account for the Palestinian refugees problem, could be enhancing Israel's diplomatic prestige. Once these threats proved largely immaterial, Israel's interest in the *substance* of the emerging Refugee Convention waned. Gordon's earlier observations on Jewish concerns turned out, effectively, to have reflected less 'our policy' and more his 'personal views'.[79] Robinson's assessment of reduced risks did not liberate the MFA to do more for Jewish interests; instead of seizing the opportunity, the MFA withdrew its attention from his work.[80]

The sharp decline in the MFA's interest in Robinson's *Ad Hoc* Committee work, and the concurrent shift of perspective by MFA officials who would now view this process mainly through the prism of prestige and reputation, strongly militate against the attribution of Robinson's efforts on behalf of Jewish interests to the Jewish state. Once the *Ad Hoc* Committee started its work he did not receive further instructions, and the MFA barely, and rarely, responded to his reports.[81] At the conclusion of the *Ad Hoc* Committee work (later it was reconvened, unexpectedly) Gordon offered his appreciation of Robinson's effort. On substance, his letter acknowledged, at most, the import the subject held *for Robinson*. What Gordon emphasized, rather, was how Robinson contributed to Israel's reputation. After reading Robinson's final report on the work of the *Ad Hoc* Committee, Gordon offered his 'personal heartiest congratulations' and relayed praise received 'from various friends at the Secretariat' for Robinson's 'leadership' and 'outstanding contribution'. He had 'no doubt that this achievement will be beneficial for *the prestige of Israel*'.[82] Gordon, however, had nothing to say on the substance of the draft Convention produced by the *Ad Hoc* Committee or on its service to Jewish interests.

In respect of Jewish concerns, then, Robinson was not quite representing the policy or position of the MFA. At the *Ad Hoc* Committee, or later at the Third Committee, he sought to ensure that the agenda retained items of Jewish concerns; or that Nazi criminals were excluded from protection[83] and that Jewish refugees

[79] Gordon to Robinson, 6 January 1950 (n 51).

[80] Thus, no discussion followed Robinson's report, in one meeting of Israel's UN mission, 'on the problems discussed in the committee on statelessness': UN Mission Meeting, 27 January 1950, FM–89/1, ISA.

[81] Other than routine acknowledgment of receipt: IOD to Robinson, 22 February 1950, FM–2010/13. By comparison, preparations for the 1949 Diplomatic Conference that adopted the Geneva Conventions, in which Israel had various direct and indirect stakes, included the establishment of an inter-departmental committee to propose instructions for Israel's delegation to the Conference: G–5661/11, ISA.

[82] Emphasis added; Gordon to Robinson, 3 March 1950, FM–2010/13, ISA.

[83] Robinson to IOD, First Interim Report, 23 January 1950 (n 29) ('the lack of enthusiasm on our part for improving the legal position (*nota bene*: not granting assistance nor making them eligible for IRO financed resettlement) of people with anti-Semitic background'. Here, Gordon's views were entirely in accord.

from Germany or Austria, victims of Nazi persecution, were exempt from the effective requirement of repatriation to their country of origin.[84] In this, however, he was only promoting what *he* had considered Jewish interests. He was not expressing, in *actuality*, the policies and preferences of the Jewish state. He was giving voice, at most, to views that the Jewish state permitted him, out of disinterest or in hope of reputational benefits, to express.

Further evidence supports this conclusion. Rosenne, as noted, was hardly involved, and nor was Eytan; on the rare occasion that they were, their involvement hardly touched the substance of the emerging Refugee Convention, and certainly not on its Jewish aspects. A few years later, Rosenne would furnish confirmation that the Refugee Convention was perceived as a Robinson project, not a proper MFA concern. A year after Robinson's retirement from Israel's foreign service, the UN sought to convene a conference to deal with the 'Elimination or Reduction of Future Statelessness'. Rosenne informed a senior MFA official that

> in the past the whole question of stateless persons ... and the status of European refugees was in the *exclusive charge* of Jacob Robinson ... *The truth is that in the Foreign Ministry we hardly ever dealt with this matter.*[85]

Moreover, no evidence suggests that, at the ministerial level, Moshe Sharett was even aware of the matter. Once the *Ad Hoc* Committee started its work, even Gordon's involvement became nominal—and was limited to the twin concerns relating to Arab refugees and Cold War orientation.[86]

This state of affairs persisted at the Conference of Plenipotentiaries. When the GA resolved to convene a conference to discuss and adopt the draft Refugee Convention, it was Robinson's recommendation that, as 'part of our activities in favour of the Diaspora Jewry', Israel should participate.[87] The MFA interest in the Conference, however, was limited to participation. Robinson's colleagues and

[84] Robinson to IOD, Second Interim Report, 30 January 1950 (n 29); Robinson to IOD, Third Interim Report, 6 February 1950 (n 29); Robinson to IOD, Fourth Interim Report, 13 February 1950 (n 29).

[85] Emphases added: Rosenne to Comay, 20 October 1958, FM–5849/10, ISA. On the Conference: Paul Weis, 'The United Nations Convention on the Reduction of Statelessness, 1961' (1962) 11 ICLQ 1073.

[86] On one rare occasion, Gordon made a minute 'tactical' suggestion to use an appeal by the International Committee of the Red Cross to promote the MFA's general goal of 'diverting attention from the specific problem of Arab refugees to the much larger question of refugees in general': Gordon to Robinson, 2 August 1950 (n 58). On another, he advised Eytan to instruct Robinson to 'reserve Israel's position' on the proposed definition of 'refugee' inasmuch as it covered 'recent political refugees' from the Soviet bloc, so as not to draw the USSR's ire: Gordon to Director-General, 20 August 1950, FM–2010/13. Generally, however, Robinson was free to act as he saw fit: Gordon to Robinson, 3 March 1950 (n 82) ('Of course any observations which could be made by us will be sent to you and not submitted to the Secretary-General'); Robinson to Gordon, 16 March 1950, Gordon to Rosenne, 24 April 1950, Robinson to Gordon, 26 April 1950, 30 April 1950, FM–2010/13 ISA.

[87] Robinson to Rosenne, 6 February 1951 (n 41).

superiors were content to let him decide when and how to accept the SG's invitation.[88] They were equally content to let him make the call on various questions on the Conference agenda. Robinson expected no substantive instructions and received none.[89] His lengthy, detailed reports on the progress of the Conference elicited no response from the MFA while the Conference was ongoing; his superiors and colleagues took little to no interest in the positions he presented at the Conference or in how it unfolded.[90] Other than Yugoslavia, no Soviet bloc country attended the Conference; and by the time it convened, it was clear that the Convention would not apply to Arab refugees.[91] For the MFA, the Conference was little more than one more opportunity to display Israel's contribution to the UN's work and enhance its diplomatic prestige. Robinson shared that view. At the conclusion of his work at the *Ad Hoc* Committee, he reported to Eytan that 'our reputation with the [other] delegations has been enhanced'.[92] The Conference, he reported at its close, 'undoubtedly increased our prestige in the eyes of the other nations to the dismay of the Arab delegations'.[93] At the same time, however, he considered his tasks at the Conference to also include acting 'in the interests of Jewish refugees still remaining in certain European countries' as well as 'to be present and to watch' developments 'in view of the presence of certain Arab elements in the Draft Convention'.[94] After Robinson composed his final report on the Conference, Eytan wrote to express the Foreign Ministry's

> appreciation for your brilliant personal part in the discussions . . . it is clear that you have had a crucial influence on the course of the discussion preceding the adoption and the formulation of the Convention itself. *Thus, you have not only earned respect for your name personally but have also contributed not a little to raising the prestige of Israel in the international arena.* We are all desirous that you know how much we appreciate this fact and we hope that the final outcome constitutes your payment for your enormous physical and intellectual effort during those weeks of labour.[95]

[88] Avraham to Robinson, 7 May 1951, FM-2010/13; Robinson to Rosenne, 22 March 1951 (n 27); Rosenne to Robinson, 14 January 1951, FM-2010/13, ISA; Robinson to Eytan, Fifth Session, 27 December 1950 (n 39).

[89] Robinson to Rosenne, 22 March 1951 (n 27); he did have an opportunity to confer with Rosenne and the IOD on 'mostly technical' questions during a visit to Israel: Rosenne to Eytan, 12 July 1951, FM-2379/16, ISA.

[90] For his part, Robinson rarely consulted the MFA while the Conference was at work.

[91] Robinson to Director-General, Fourth and Final Report, 1 August 1951 (n 27). He still had to stand guard on this issue: Robinson to Director-General, First Report, 8 July 1951 (n 27).

[92] Robinson to Eytan, Final Report, 21 February 1950 (n 25).

[93] Robinson to Director-General, Fourth and Final Report, 1 August 1951 (n 27).

[94] ibid.

[95] Emphasis added; Eytan to Robinson, 14 August 1951, FM-2010/13, ISA. Robinson admitted that the work of the *Ad Hoc* Committee 'was a terrible physical strain on myself, being for 5 weeks practically detached from anything else and devoted exclusively to the work': Robinson to Eytan, Final Report, 21 February 1950 (n 25); the subsequent Conference likewise was 'a great physical strain and a considerable intellectual effort': Robinson to Director-General, Fourth and Final Report, 1 August 1951 (n 27).

Eytan's letter, however, was silent on any service rendered to Jewish interests by the Refugee Convention or by Robinson's contribution to its birth.

5. Between Diaspora and 'Return': Jewish Interests and Sovereign Sensibilities

Robinson's involvement in the drafting of the Refugee Convention was driven, largely, by Jewish concerns and interests. Yet he did not quite consider the part he was playing in the legislative reform of refugee status—ostensibly on behalf of the Jewish state—as representing continuity with pre-sovereign Jewish advocacy. His sovereign sensibilities, if anything, presented a case of radical discontinuity. They were patent in his attitude to the actions—and inaction—of various Jewish organizations on the draft Convention. Robinson, as already noted, considered the Jewish state better informed and better equipped to act in favour of Jewish refugees than 'those Jewish organizations who … are supposed to be interested in the matter'.[96] Though his expertise on questions of refugeehood and statelessness was itself the product of pre-sovereign Jewish engagement, he now repeatedly disparaged the limits and deficiencies of Jewish non-sovereign advocacy. He censured Jewish NGOs for failing to attend important meetings of the *Ad Hoc* Committee, and for taking, when attending, what he had considered to be wrong positions.[97] He faulted them for failing to appraise correctly 'the best interests of Jewish refugees',[98] and for addressing matters already discussed by the Committee.[99] In particular, Robinson scorned their non-sovereign *modus operandi*. That Israel's 'participation in this Conference is part of our activities in favour of the Diaspora Jewry … is taken for granted by non-Jewish delegations', he reported, adding that this fact 'should be appreciated by the Jewish Organizations which continue their old memorandomania *as if nothing changed*'.[100] Ironically, as the IJA's director, he had previously perfected the art of writing and circulating memoranda. Now a sovereign representative, he no longer considered that method appropriate. What drew his ire most, accordingly, was the challenge to the primacy of Israel's sovereign Jewish voice posed by representatives of Jewish NGOs who addressed UN bodies 'without coordination among themselves and without consultation'[101] with Israel's envoys.[102] As the official representative of the Jewish state, he was not above

[96] Robinson to Eytan, Fifth Session, 27 December 1950 (n 39), discussed there.

[97] Robinson to Gordon, Second Session, 21 August 1950 (n 29).

[98] Robinson, The Problem of Refugees, 19 December 1950 (n 30); he excluded the WJC 'since I was in constant contact with my brother Nehemiah'.

[99] Robinson to IOD, Third Interim Report, 6 February 1950 (n 29).

[100] Emphasis added; Robinson to Rosenne, 6 February 1951 (n 41).

[101] Robinson to IOD, Third Interim Report, 6 February 1950 (n 29); Robinson to Eytan, Final Report, 21 February 1950 (n 25).

[102] Similar sensibilities, by Robinson and his MFA colleagues, on the matter of the sovereign Jewish voice, discussed in other chapters, certainly reflected the view of Robinson's political masters. Sharett

gloating. On one occasion, he noted that a WJC memorandum 'was not even circulated' to members of the *Ad Hoc* Committee;[103] on another, he derided the impracticability and irrelevance of the WJC's non-sovereign outlook: 'it is very easy for [an NGO], having no responsibilities, to object to national security measures' that may limit the protection enjoyed by refugees.[104] He also was adamant that the Jewish state, not Jewish NGOs, should receive credit for the emergent Convention.[105]

If, procedurally, Robinson presented a clear-cut reading of who had the proper capacity to represent the Jewish case in the drafting of the Refugee Convention, the substance of Jewish concerns and interests in the Convention was another matter. He was ambivalent on how these were to be defined, vacillating between two vantage points. One presented a general Jewish perspective captured by his observation that 'the *Jewish world* is still interested in the fate of refugees'[106] and stateless persons, present and future, without more. At times, his work sought to give effect to what he viewed as the interests, broadly defined, of any Jewish refugee and stateless person 'in the Diaspora'.[107] The other vantage point, however, emphasized the particularity of Jewish statehood. Robinson's reading of the Convention's Jewish aspect was shaped by what he thought were, or ought to have been, Israel's outlook on and interest in Jewish questions. At times, his involvement in the drafting of the Convention was defined, as he put it, by what he thought was '*the interest of Israel* acting for Jews in the Diaspora'.[108] This phrasing expressed, rather than resolved, the depth of his ambivalence on the Convention's Jewish aspects.

At its core, Robinson's dilemma—was the Refugee Convention a platform for addressing general Jewish concerns or a vehicle for promoting Israel's interests in Jewish matters—drew on questions about the proper role to be played by the Jewish state in the Jewish world. It therefore also drew, crucially, on an ideological interpretation of Jewish sovereignty that considered the establishment of the Jewish state as having, necessarily, brought Jewish statelessness to an end. In this reading, the Jewish state's 'historic mission'[109] vis-à-vis world Jewry was precisely

wrote to one of his subordinates: 'as to the pest of the World Jewish Congress, I entirely agree that the appearances of Congress representatives in bodies we attend must be stopped': Sharett to Katzanelson, 4 November 1949, FM–375/4, ISA.

[103] Robinson to IOD, Third Interim Report, 6 February 1950 (n 29); WJC, Memorandum submitted to the *Ad Hoc* Committee on Stateless Persons and Related Matters, 23 January 1950, FM–2010/13, ISA. At the Conference, despite having established a collaborative *modus vivendi* with Jewish NGOs, he again gloated that 'it is impossible to say that the Conference assigns any value whatsoever to these memoranda' submitted by Jewish and other NGOs: Robinson to Director-General, First Report, 8 July 1951 (n 27).

[104] Robinson to Gordon, Second Session, 21 August 1950 (n 29).

[105] Robinson thus recommended that the MFA bring information about Israel's GA achievements 'in favour of Jewish Refugees' 'to the knowledge of the Jewish public in general and in particular of those Jewish Organizations': Robinson to Eytan, Fifth Session, 27 December 1950 (n 39).

[106] Emphasis added; Robinson, The Problem of Refugees, 19 December 1950 (n 30).

[107] ibid.

[108] Emphasis added; ibid.

[109] Sharett to SG, 18 December 1950, FM–2010/13, ISA.

to provide a permanent, political solution not only to the plight of Jewish refugees but more generally to the Jewish Diasporic condition.[110] Robinson, we saw, already drew closer to this position during the Holocaust years, albeit not without some reserve.[111] The preparation of the Refugee Convention required him to reconcile his Diaspora and Zionist sensibilities on Jewish refugeehood. This ideological reading of Jewish sovereignty, however, rendered that task of reconciliation far more difficult. Israel's establishment and war of independence turned Palestine's Jewish minority—through expulsion and flight of its Arab population—into a majority.[112] It also produced among Israel's ruling elites, as the next chapter recounts, a radical reading of Jewish statehood and, attending it, a radical reading of Jewish refugeehood, statelessness, and displacement. With the advent of Jewish sovereignty, Etatist Zionism decreed that Jews would be legally allowed to immigrate to Israel and acquire, as Jews, instant Israeli nationality.[113] It also presupposed that Jews, *ideologically*, were under a duty to affect this right of 'Return' to Israel.[114] With sovereignty, the 'Ingathering of the Exiles' became a fundamental ideological principle and a policy imperative of the Jewish state, exerting direct and frequent influence on its early foreign policy.[115] Both principle and policy indicated that Jewish refugee status, and statelessness, were markers of bygone, non-sovereign times.

Given the ideological principle involved, it is hardly surprising that Robinson's ambivalence revealed itself early. At the start of his involvement in the work of the

[110] See discussion in ch 7.

[111] Noted above and in chs 3, 5.

[112] Ch 5.

[113] Law of Return—1950, 51 *Sefer HaHukim* (Laws) (5 July 1950) 159 (Hebrew); Prime Minister David Ben-Gurion described it as 'a foundation stone of the Jewish state, containing its *raison d'être* … the Ingathering of Exiles': *Divrei HaKnesset* (Parliamentary Record) (3 July 1950) 2036–7.

[114] ibid. The Explanatory Notes accompanying the Bill that became Israel's Law of Return described the Law as 'a positive expression to the will of the people to gather its exiles': 48 *Hatzaot Hok* (Bills) (27 June 1950) 189. In practice, Israel's ability to openly express this ideological imperative was constrained by objections of Jewish Diaspora constituencies, especially in the US: Charles S Liebman, 'Diaspora Influence on Israel: The Ben-Gurion-Blaustein "Exchange" and Its Aftermath' (1974) 36 Jewish Soc Stud 271; Zvi Ganin, 'The Blaustein Ben-Gurion Understanding of 1950' (2000) 15 Michael: On the History of the Jews in the Diaspora 29.

[115] Highlighted already in Sharett's UN admission speech: Speech to the General Assembly by Foreign Minister Sharett, 11 May 1949 in Meron Medzini (ed), *Israel's Foreign Relations: Selected Documents, 1947–1974* (MFA 1976) 119, 122; GAOR, Plenary (11 May 1949) 332, 335 ('the absorption of the large scale immigration currently in progress, a veritable ingathering of the exiles'). Later Sharett told the *Knesset* that notwithstanding economic constraints, '[a]bove all Israel's mission as a country of the ingathering of the exiles of the Jewish people, as its historic homeland … compels us to be represented in each country where Jewish communities live': Sharett, *Divrei HaKnesset* (15 June 1949) (n 50) 718. In December 1950, in response to a UN request for information on statelessness, Israel informed the SG that its impending legislation on 'Return' reflected the 'historic mission of the state of Israel, the "Ingathering of the Exiles", by introducing special provisions for the acquisition of citizenship by Jews who return to their homeland and take up permanent residence in Israel': Sharett to SG, 18 December 1950; Attorney-General, Information Concerning Paragraphs 6 & 7 of Resolution 319Biii (XI) of 11 August 1950 of the Economic and Social Council, [n.d.], FM–2010/13, ISA.

Ad Hoc Committee, he proposed that 'Israel's attitude' ought to be influenced by the '*plight of Jewish refugees*' even if their 'numbers are not considerable'.[116] Here, he surmised that Israel, as the Jewish state, was under a duty 'to help to improve the legal status of Jewish refugees'. At the same time, however, he was willing to see that duty constrained not only by Israel's interests in connection with the Cold War or Palestinian refugees,[117] but also by ideological imperatives and the policies giving them effect. 'This attitude'—and that duty, he concluded—'*is qualified* by our policy of in-gathering of exile and encouragement of immigration to Israel'.[118] A few weeks later, he gave public voice to these competing imperatives. To his Israeli radio audience, he conceded that 'today there is no special value, from a Diasporic-Jewish perspective, to the problem of refugees and stateless persons—the doors of the country are open to all refugees; Israeli nationality, at least potentially, is acquired easily through *Aliya*'—immigration to Israel. He nonetheless explained—or, perhaps, pleaded—that

> still the fate of tens of thousands of Jews, in the countries of Europe and outside it who are refugees ... or stateless persons ... cannot be treated lightly. Their legal status is not regular and can be ameliorated and improved [by Israel's diplomatic efforts].[119]

Robinson's ambivalence persisted. His participation in the *Ad Hoc* Committee work, the Third Committee debate, and the 1951 Conference was marked by a continuing effort to give effect to both the radical ideological imperatives of etatist Zionism and the interests, broadly defined, of Diaspora Jewry in broad refugee status and a robust refugee protection regime. There was, inevitably, some inconsistency in how he prioritized one over the other. While the Jewish, Diasporic perspective tended to dominate his actions, there were several occasions where he let Israel's immigration policy trump Jewish concerns and the interests of Jewish refugees and stateless persons.[120] His correspondence with the MFA asserted, time and again, the import of both the Jewish and Israeli perspectives.

[116] Emphasis in the original; Robinson to IOD, First Interim Report, 23 January 1950 (n 29).

[117] As when he elected to promote Jewish interests because they 'could be used in later debates on the "return" of Palestine refugees': Robinson to IOD, Second Interim Report, 30 January 1950 (n 29).

[118] Emphasis added; Robinson to IOD, First Interim Report, 23 January 1950 (n 29).

[119] [Robinson], Broadcast, 17 February 1950 (n 35).

[120] Thus, having already successfully retained a 'special Jewish clause' borrowed from the IRO constitution on 'persons who, having resided in Germany or Austria and being of Jewish origins', Robinson came to have 'some doubts as to the advisability of retaining such a clause', *inter alia*, 'in view of Israel's policy of the in-gathering of exiles': Robinson to IOD, Second Interim Report, 30 January 1950 (n 29); later the clause was 'dropped' with Robinson's blessing: Robinson to IOD, Third Interim Report, 6 February 1950 (n 29).

6. Robinson's Formula: Acquiring 'A Legal Title'

To resolve his dilemma between sovereign sensibilities and Diaspora propensities—to reconcile, one might say, his own non-sovereign past and his sovereign present—Robinson devised and made frequent recourse to a formula that sought to explain and justify the involvement of the Jewish state and his own actions, as its duly accredited representative, in the drafting of the Refugee Convention. Israel's membership in the Convention, he reasoned long before the Convention was even adopted, would 'create for us a title for intervention in case of violation of the Convention by other parties to it whenever Jewish interests will be at stake'.[121] This formula, which he repeated time and again in his reports to the MFA, drew on pre-sovereign Jewish concerns with formal voice and status[122] that therefore could also, at the same time, signify the sovereign transformation in the legal status of the Jewish people. Robinson, we saw, assigned the Jewish state the role of 'acting for Jews in the Diaspora':[123] exerting diplomatic efforts 'in favour of Jewish refugees',[124] for him, formed part of Israel's 'activities in favour of the Diaspora Jewry'.[125]

Crucially, Robinson's formula meant that acquiring a legal 'title for intervention' did not compel the Jewish state to forego the ideological credo of 'Return'. Nor did his formula oblige Israel to necessarily exert such efforts or subordinate its foreign policy to the interests of Jewish refugees or the Diaspora writ large. Rather, the formal standing Robinson wished to have the Jewish state acquire was meant to ensure only that it was equipped with the formal *capacity* to do so *in the future*. Robinson took care to note that, no less than a solution to any remaining Jewish refugees in the aftermath of the Holocaust and WWII, he was interested in providing against future Jewish displacement. His interest in 'the fate of refugees' extended to 'both [Jews] in those [categories] who have had this status up till now and [Jews] in some new categories which may emerge in the future'.[126] Reflecting, in 1955, on his involvement with the drafting of the Refugee Convention and the

[121] Robinson to Rosenne, 6 February 1951 (n 41).

[122] Such concerns, specifically in connection with Jewish immigration and refugeehood, were driven by the lessons Jewish organizations such as the WJC drew from the 1938 Evian Conference where the platform for Jewish representation was extremely circumscribed and where, '[d]espite intensive efforts and numerous attempts, the Jewish organizations had not managed to agree on a mutual position before the beginning of the conference': Martin Jost, 'A Battle against Time: Salomon Adler-Rudels Commitment at the Évian Conference' (2017) 16 Simon Dubnow Institute YB 115; Segev (n 7) 16, 132; Salomon Adler-Rudel, 'The Evian Conference on the Refugee Question' (1968) 13 Leo Baeck Institute YB 235, 255 ('The hearing was a humiliating procedure ... All left the room disheartened and disillusioned'). cf Shabtai Beit-Zvi, *Post-Ugandan Zionism on Trial* (Beit-Zvi 1991) 147–51. Specific documents expressing such WJC concerns, especially in connection with Evian, can be found in various documents in WJC–A4/20, WJC–A5/1, WJC–A6/6, WJC–A15/4, AJA; I am grateful to Martin Jost for drawing my attention to these sources.

[123] Robinson, The Problem of Refugees, 19 December 1950 (n 30).

[124] Robinson to Eytan, Fifth Session, 27 December 1950 (n 39).

[125] Robinson to Rosenne, 6 February 1951 (n 41).

[126] Robinson, The Problem of Refugees, 19 December 1950 (n 30).

subsequent 1954 UN Conference on the Status of Stateless Persons, Robinson took care to emphasize that what he had sought was entitlement to be enjoyed by the Jewish state, not a duty incumbent upon it. Once the rights of refugees and stateless persons are made the subject of treaties, he wrote,

> they become internationalized [and] they create a title for the signatories to show their interest in the way such Conventions are being implemented. Applying this principle to the particular case of Jewish stateless persons in need of improving of their status ... the fact of our membership in such a community of nations ... opens for our diplomacy new avenues of assistance to persons in need of such assistance. This does not necessarily mean that we are under an obligation to supervise the method of application of such a Convention by other states. *It suffices, however, that we are entitled to do so.* The realization by other states of the fact that Israel *may* use its contractual rights to intervene in favour of Jewish stateless persons in case they are not treated in accordance with the ... Convention may influence the behavior of ... such states.[127]

Robinson's investment in the drafting of the Refugee Convention may well have contributed to the improvement of the status of Jewish refugees and stateless persons. Yet he was fully aware that the number of Jews in need of such international legal protection was small.[128] He also worked to promote Israel's defensive policy on the question of Palestinian refugees. The need to do so, however, was rather limited. The protection regime obtained in the Refugee Convention did benefit from his efforts. Yet the impetus for his participation in this law-making process was not a *universal* vision of a robust refugee regime. It was to a large extent, rather, enhancing Israel's standing and prestige. Even when alluding to the Jewish state's ability to contribute to alleviating the general 'humanitarian problems', what he had in mind was the optic of its diplomatic standing.[129] On one occasion, he ruminated that given Israel's position as the 'only stable state in the region', it may one day—if and when 'normal relations' were to be established between Israel and its neighbours—find itself 'in the position of a country of refuge for various types

[127] Emphases added; Robinson, Conference on the Status of Stateless Persons, 23 March 1955 (n 69).

[128] Robinson to IOD, First Interim Report, 23 January 1950 (n 29) ('numbers are not considerable'); Robinson to IOD, Second Interim Report, 30 January 1950 (n 29); Robinson to Director-General, First Report, 8 July 1951 (n 27) ('in order to protect those Jewish refugees still remaining in certain European countries and whose number is not too great'); Robinson, Conference on the Status of Stateless Persons, 23 March 1955 (n 69) ('It is true that a number of Jewish stateless persons in need of international protection has diminished greatly after the Second World War and in particular after the mass migration to Israel').

[129] '[W]e are bound, as UN members, to contribute from [our] knowledge and experience to the extent that we can to humanitarian problems': [Robinson], Broadcast, 17 February 1950 (n 35); Robinson, Conference on the Status of Stateless Persons, 23 March 1955 (n 69) ('We have accumulated experience in this particular item and we owe it to the world community to contribute our experience to the solution of a problem of international dimensions').

of political, racial, and religious refugees coming from this troubled area'. This was not a 'rosy scenario'[130] expressing a moral imperative he had sought to hold the Jewish state accountable to, but a cause of concern he warned against. His conclusion was that '*[c]aution qualified by humanitarianism is therefore imperative*'.[131] Visibility, not vision, made morality important.

Israel's diplomatic prestige, then, mattered to Robinson no less than to his colleagues. He knew well that the emerging Refugee Convention was, legally, largely inapplicable to Israel. There were few, if any, persons falling within the Convention's definition of refugees in Israel.[132] He recognized that Israel was not 'a haven for refugees in general' and that Jewish immigration to Israel was 'not of the same nature as the immigration to countries like USA and Canada'.[133] He was not above directing the MFA, during the drafting of the Convention, to search the country for 'at least a few non-Jewish refugees to whom this Convention could apply'. 'The importance of having such "exhibits"', he wrote to Rosenne while preparing for the 1951 Conference, 'is obvious'.[134] Yet unlike his MFA colleagues, for him Israel's diplomatic prestige was a means to another, far more ambitious end. The 'obvious' import of 'having such "exhibits"' lay not in the display of a liberal image by the Jewish state but, rather, in entrenching Israel's *formal* standing. A few months earlier, he had prompted that 'if there are no stateless persons in Israel, who come under this Convention, we should invite a few to come to Israel and *so justify our accession and create for us a title for intervention*' to promote 'Jewish interests'.[135]

In the final analysis, Robinson's involvement in UN law-making efforts on refugees and stateless persons seemed driven by a preoccupation with formal standing. Time and again, he took care to exhort his MFA colleagues and superiors that 'only through this act [ratifying the Convention] will we acquire a legal title to help those Jewish refugees in Europe',[136] present and future. He sought to ensure, in his words, that the Jewish state would be equipped with a legal device to overcome 'the principles of sovereignty and non-intervention of domestic affairs' on which other

130 Loeffler (n 45) 180.

131 Emphasis in the original; Robinson to IOD, First Interim Report, 23 January 1950 (n 29).

132 Robinson to Director-General, Fourth and Final Report, 1 August 1951 (n 27) ('representing as I was a country which has only a few scores of refugees who may fall under the definition of Article 1').

133 Robinson to Eytan, Final Report, 21 February 1950 (n 25).

134 Robinson to Rosenne, 5 April 1951, FM–1830/8. Nor was he above mocking similar efforts by other states: 'a real hunt after non-European refugees started: one delegation suddenly discovered an Armenian who for thirty years was unaware of his right to qualify... as refugee; the other brought out of oblivion the Assyrians ... *Difficile est satiram non scribere*': Robinson to Director-General, Fourth and Final Report, 1 August 1951 (n 27). The search for 'exhibits' generated some correspondence among various government ministries eg in FM–2010/13, FM–1847/2, FM–1830/8, FM–1989/1, G–5754/14, ISA.

135 Robinson to Rosenne, 6 February 1951 (n 41).

136 Robinson to Director-General, Fourth and Final Report, 1 August 1951 (n 27).

states may rely to preclude interference in how they treated Jewish refugees.[137] He took care to clarify he was not seeking to compel it to use that right.

Robinson's focus on formal standing and legal capacity may have allowed him to reconcile the tension between his sovereign sensibilities and his concern for Diaspora Jewry. This focus, however, may well have also been aimed at influencing the MFA position and ensuring that Israel's foreign policy, despite the ideological imperative of 'Return' and the immigration policy expressing it, would have some room for Diaspora concerns. There were, from his perspective, several disconcerting signs that Gordon's early allusions to Jewish concerns in the work on the Refugee Convention—and that his own exertions in this regard—were not in fact representative of the MFA's position. Once the 'dangers' posed by the issues of Palestinian refugees and the Cold War proved largely unsubstantiated, we saw, the MFA lost interest in the substance of the draft Convention. After that, the few communications Robinson would receive from the MFA did not express any position whatsoever on his analysis of Jewish concerns. Nor did his colleagues, in fact, any longer allude in any way to Jewish interests. By framing Jewish concerns in terms of Israeli interest in formal standing, Robinson had been aiming, likely, to ensure that MFA policies would in fact—not just as a rhetorical gesture—be geared towards protecting the interests of Jews in the Diaspora. He may have also been attempting to ensure that his own work on the Refugee Convention, as the Jewish state's agent, did not stray too far from that of his principal—or, rather, that the Jewish state had not strayed too far from his own reading of its commitment to Jewish Diaspora interests.[138] His concluding report on the 1951 Conference contained a subtle reminder that he was as representing 'not only a government, but also morally the refugee as such'.[139]

Another cause for concern was presented by Rosenne. A month after the GA resolved to convene a conference to discuss the Refugee Convention, the MFA legal adviser conferred with Director-General Eytan on whether Israel should 'join' the future Convention. Rosenne reported to Robinson the conclusions of this consultation: the answer to the rather premature question would depend on 'whether there are in Israel refugees falling under the proposed Convention'.[140] Both Rosenne and Robinson knew well, however, that there were hardly any; a year before, Robinson wrote to Eytan that Israel was 'not a haven for refugees in general'.[141]

[137] Robinson, Conference on the Status of Stateless Persons, 23 March 1955 (n 69) ('It is true that a number of Jewish stateless persons in need of international protection has diminished greatly after the Second World War and in particular after the mass migration to Israel').

[138] Hence his insistence, before the 1951 Conference convened, on being credentialed to sign the Convention: Robinson to Rosenne, 22 March 1951 (n 27) discussed above.

[139] Robinson to Director-General, Fourth and Final Report, 1 August 1951 (n 27), where he reported that this was the view of the Conference President.

[140] Rosenne to Robinson, 14 January 1951 (n 88); Rosenne to Robinson, 30 March 1951, FM-2010/13, ISA.

[141] Robinson to Eytan, Final Report, 21 February 1950 (n 25); Robinson to Rosenne, 6 February 1951 (n 41); Rosenne to Robinson, 26 June 1951, FM-1830/8, ISA; Robinson to Director-General, Fourth and Final Report, 1 August 1951 (n 27).

Robinson proceeded to prompt Rosenne to canvass the country for non-Jews who might meet the Convention's definition in order to 'justify our accession'[142] to the Convention—and so acquire the desired 'title' for future interventions. Robinson, apparently, assumed that Rosenne shared his reading of the Convention's Jewish aspect or, in the very least, that his younger colleague would not hamper his efforts to persuade the MFA to include Diaspora interests in its policy calculus. If so, the matter of the ratification of the Refugee Convention by the Jewish state would prove his apprehensions entirely warranted. When the time came for the Jewish state to legally commit itself to the norms he worked hard to draft, his assumptions about Rosenne would prove entirely unfounded. The matter of ratification of the Refugee Convention would confirm how little Robinson's Jewish investment on the Convention could be said to represent Israel's foreign policy.

142 Robinson to Rosenne, 6 February 1951 (n 41), discussed above (text to nn 132–135).

7

'A Better Remedy'

Shabtai Rosenne, Ratification of the 1951 Refugee Convention, and the End of Jewish Statelessness

1. Robinson's Recommendation

Despite 'a great physical strain and a considerable intellectual effort',[1] Jacob Robinson emerged from the 1951 Conference of Plenipotentiaries with some confidence. Prior to the Conference, he had insisted on being equipped with the power to sign the Refugee Convention to be concluded at the Conference;[2] at the end of the Conference, he exercised that power. He may have had good reasons to suspect that others in the Ministry of Foreign Affairs ('MFA') were disinterested in the Convention and did not share his views on what the Jewish state owed Jewish refugees.[3] Shabtai Rosenne, the MFA legal adviser, had already signalled six months before the Conference was convened that ratification would depend on 'whether there are in Israel refugees falling under the proposed Convention'.[4] Yet Robinson's concluding report on the Conference nonetheless expressed optimism that the Jewish state would, following his signature on the Refugee Convention,[5] proceed to ratify it promptly. He took care to report that his participation in the proceedings 'undoubtedly increased our prestige in the eyes of the other nations' adding, for good measure, 'to the dismay of the Arab delegations'.[6] He also repeated, once more, the formula he had devised in the course of the Convention's making that framed Jewish concerns in the Refugee Convention as Israeli interests.[7] This was, precisely, the justification he offered when prompting Walter Eytan, the MFA Director-General, to have the Convention ratified:

[1] Robinson to Director-General, Fourth and Final Report on the Conference of Plenipotentiaries on the Status of Refugees and Stateless Persons, Geneva, 1 August 1951, FM–19/10, FM–1847/2, Israel State Archive ('ISA').

[2] The proper credentials, however, were delayed; he was only given that authority after repeated demands to the Ministry of Foreign Affairs: ch 6.

[3] Ch 6.

[4] Rosenne to Robinson, 14 January 1951, 30 March 1951, FM–2010/13, ISA.

[5] Convention Relating to the Status of Refugees (28 July 1951) 189 UNTS 137.

[6] Robinson to Director-General, Fourth and Final Report, 1 August 1951 (n 1).

[7] Ch 6.

Jews, Sovereignty, and International Law. Rotem Giladi, Oxford University Press. © Rotem Giladi 2021.
DOI: 10.1093/oso/9780198857396.003.0009

> 6. What Next? The Convention was signed by me on Wednesday, 1 August 1951, at 2 p.m. I neither made a declaration in accordance with Art.1 Section d, nor indicated any possible reservation. All this can wait till we ratify, having previously adjusted our legislation, if necessary.
>
> For reasons too obvious to elaborate on them, I recommend warmly the ratification of this convention at an early stage: only through this act will we acquire a legal title to help those Jewish refugees in Europe who have not yet made their final decision.[8]

This reasoning would prove insufficient to convince the MFA that the Refugee Convention represented a convergence of Jewish concerns and Israeli interests. The very justification he offered for ratification, as we shall see later, may well explain his colleagues' aversion to the Refugee Convention and the resulting delay in Israel's ratification of that treaty.

2. Decision Undone

Legally, Robinson's signature on the Refugee Convention was not enough to make it binding on Israel. A state wishing to be bound by its provisions needed to ratify or accede to the Convention and deposit its instrument of ratification with the United Nations ('UN') Secretary-General ('SG').[9] Before the Convention could enter into force, however, the deposit of six instruments of ratification was required.[10] Robinson's recommendation to ratify the Convention 'at an early stage'[11] aimed to have Israel included 'among the first six to ratify' so as to trigger the Convention's entry into force.[12] From his perspective, his signature and Israel's prospective early ratification of the Convention were also meant to serve a symbolic function.

Politically, however, Robinson's signature on the Convention was a routine act of foreign affairs; in Tel Aviv—the Foreign Ministry would not move to Jerusalem until 1953—and in Jerusalem, where the *Knesset* and other ministries were based, no symbolic significance was ascribed to the fact that a representative of the Jewish state fixed his signature on a UN treaty dealing with the status and treatment of refugees. Both the government and the *Knesset* habitually debated matters of foreign policy, including treaties, yet neither displayed any interest in the Convention at the time.[13] Neither, in fact, was informed that the Convention

[8] Robinson to Director-General, Fourth and Final Report, 1 August 1951 (n 1).

[9] Article 39, 1951 Refugee Convention (n 5) 178.

[10] Article 43, 1951 Refugee Convention (n 5) 182.

[11] Robinson to Director-General, Fourth and Final Report, 1 August 1951 (n 1).

[12] Robinson to Rosenne, 2 June 1953, FM–1847/2, ISA discussed below.

[13] Record of Government Meetings, 31 May, 26 September 1951; Record of *Knesset* Foreign and Security Affairs Committee, 27 July, 3 August 1951, A–7562/5, ISA; *Divrei HaKnesset* (Parliamentary Record) (20 August 1951) 1–12, 2203–6 (Hebrew).

had been concluded and signed in Geneva. The day Robinson signed the Refugee Convention, Foreign Minister Moshe Sharett had 'nothing special to announce' to the government.[14] In this and subsequent meetings, the government discussed the 'absorption' of Jewish refugees; none of the ministers mentioned the Convention.[15]

Nonetheless, Robinson's optimism at first seemed warranted. Eytan congratulated him for his effort and reported that 'the Office of the Legal Adviser takes care that the government will ratify the Convention at the earliest date possible, in accord with your proposal in the report'.[16] On his own authority, Eytan had already instructed Rosenne's deputy Yosef Tekoah—Rosenne was out of the country[17]—to 'receive government ratification of this Convention as soon as possible'.[18] Eytan did not comment on the justification offered by Robinson; given the overall tenor of his letter to Robinson, it seems most likely that 'raising the prestige of Israel in the international arena'[19] was the reason he accepted Robinson's recommendation. Tekoah, in any case, soon asked the Ministry of Justice to prioritize the Hebrew translation of the Convention so that it could be 'transmitted promptly' to government ministers; 'the Foreign Ministry', he reported, 'intends to obtain ... ratification at the earliest opportunity'.[20]

Rosenne's return to the country,[21] however, precipitated a change in the course of events. Soon, any sense of urgency evaporated: the question of ratification was dealt with routinely—and at a leisurely pace. It took Rosenne nearly two months to take any action on the question of ratification. In late September, he asked Attorney-General Haim Cohn 'whether the government could now ratify the Convention as is or by expressing reservations pursuant to Article 42, or if there is a need at first to adjust the internal law to the terms of the Convention'.[22] He did not consider it necessary to inform Cohn that there had been any urgency to the matter; nor did he mention Eytan's instruction or any MFA interest—relating to Jewish concerns or otherwise—in the Refugee Convention. All he reported was that Robinson 'who participated most actively in the abovementioned Conference [and] signed the Convention on behalf of Israel ... recommends that the Convention be ratified'.[23] Rosenne did not express any opinion on Robinson's recommendation.

In October, the Attorney-General responded that the Convention 'is incompatible with our law' in certain respects. Some of Israel's existing laws, he opined, could be amended to ensure conformity with the Convention; others, however,

[14] Record of Government Meetings, 1 August 1951, ISA.
[15] ibid; Record of Government Meetings, 15 August 1951, 26 September 1951, ISA.
[16] Eytan to Robinson, 14 August 1951, FM-2010/13, ISA.
[17] Rosenne Journal, July–August 1951, FM-5850/2, ISA.
[18] Eytan to Tekoah, [n.d.], FM-1847/2, ISA.
[19] Eytan to Robinson, 14 August 1951 (n 16).
[20] Tekoah to Gaulan, 14 August 1951, G-5754/17, ISA.
[21] Rosenne Journal, 13 September 1951 (n 17).
[22] Rosenne to Cohn, 27 September 1951, FM-1847/2, ISA.
[23] ibid.

could not. In respect of these, Cohn proposed reservations to specific Convention articles. The Attorney-General, however, also expressed concern with the 'problem of the [Arab] infiltrators':

> I do not know if you have already contemplated our position on Article 1(b)(1) of the Convention. One cannot rule out the possibility that ordinary infiltrators—who receive sophisticated legal instruction, will argue that they are refugees within the meaning of the Convention; and in light of the attitude in some of the Arab states to *Eretz Israel* refugees, such a claim may well be admitted, especially as we do not know whether such attitudes will deteriorate in the future. For such considerations, it would have been possible to limit our adherence to the Convention to Europe's refugees alone. On the other hand, I can understand that, given the role played by our delegation in the conclusion of this Convention and, considering the impression vis-à-vis the nations of the world, such a radical limitation will not be desirable.
>
> Perhaps it is possible to enter a reservation so that the Convention will not apply to refugees from Arab states as long as no peace treaties are signed between us and them?[24]

Cohn had little cause for concern; Robinson's multiple reports left little doubt that Palestinian refugees had long been excluded from the Convention's definition of 'refugee'.[25] Rosenne did not proceed to correct Cohn's misplaced concern.

Cohn's response left matters in Rosenne's hands. It also provided him with a precise roadmap on how to proceed in order to affect ratification of the Refugee Convention. Tekoah, who shared with Rosenne his thoughts on the Attorney-General's letter, proposed that there were, in fact, fewer obstacles to ratification than foreseen by Cohn. He disagreed with the Attorney-General's assessment that certain Convention articles were incompatible with Israeli law and averred that Cohn's apprehensions on Palestinian refugees were baseless. There was 'no reason to link the question of infiltrators to the question of refugees', he wrote to Rosenne.[26] Rosenne did not relay Tekoah's reasoning to the Attorney-General.

[24] Emphases in original; Cohn to Rosenne, 16 October 1951, G–5754/17, ISA.

[25] Tekoah had already transmitted Robinson's final report on the Conference to the Justice Ministry: Tekoah to Justice Ministry, 17 August 1951, FM–1847/2, ISA; Cohn, in other words, ought to have known that Palestinian refugees were so excluded.

[26] Tekoah to Rosenne, 28 October 1951, FM–1847/2, ISA ('The Convention does not apply to infiltrators returning to a territory from where they had fled. The efforts of Arab infiltrator to penetrate Israeli territory are acts which are in nature and meaning the opposite of the flight of refugees from the country of their origin. The Convention does not prohibit the expulsion of refugees from the country. Article 31 precludes the punishment of refugees who entered the state of their asylum illegally, immediately presented themselves to the authorities and supplied reasonable reasons that justify the fact of their entry and presence in the country. It is to be emphasised that expulsion for reason of national security or public order is possible under the Convention even in respect of refugees who entered the country legally').

Instead of proceeding to address the few remaining obstacles, he abstained from taking any further action on the matter. If he was not keen to see Israel ratify the Convention, he was also careful not to openly oppose Eytan's instruction. In December, Rosenne drew Eytan's attention to Israel's disinterest in the 'refugee problem': 'so far as Israel is concerned, interest in the refugee problem at large is limited, the particular Jewish aspects of the refugee problem having almost disappeared in recent years'.[27] Routine became inaction.

Robinson, for his part, was not willing to assume that his recommendation would be enough to produce ratification. He may have suspected Rosenne's disinterest when making his recommendation to Eytan or learned of it subsequently. He did raise the matter with Rosenne on a number of occasions,[28] and proposed concrete steps aimed at overcoming obstacles and expediting ratification. The two discussed the matter when they met in Paris; Rosenne again conferred with the Attorney-General. In late December 1951, he reported to Robinson that that meeting did not pave the way to a speedy ratification. 'Unfortunately', he wrote, 'I have to disagree with your opinion. Although I know that theoretically you are correct, I think that the reality here in Israel requires action more in the spirit of the A-G's proposals than in yours.'[29]

It is evident that Rosenne had, all along, little desire to see Israel ratify the Convention.[30] He now asserted the MFA's disinterest: 'we have no interest in ratifying the Convention insofar as this touches on the protection of the rights of the few scores of refugees present in the country. *Should* we ratify the Convention, we will do so only for *moral factors*'.[31] That proviso could give Robinson little comfort: he was well-aware of Rosenne's reluctance to accord weight to moral or 'symbolic considerations' in decisions on Israel's foreign policy.[32] Rosenne, nonetheless, was careful not to shut the door entirely on the prospect of ratification. He outlined two possible paths: one was to ratify the Convention at an early date while entering reservations to any provision incompatible with Israeli law. Against the possibility that this might be interpreted as a perfunctory ratification rather than a symbolic expression of genuine commitment to the Refugee Convention, he tried

[27] Rosenne to Eytan, 7 December 1951, FM–1988/5, ISA discussed below.

[28] Rosenne Journal, 3 December 1951 (n 17).

[29] Rosenne to Robinson, 27 December 1951, G–5754/17, ISA; I could not locate the proposals of either the Attorney-General or Robinson.

[30] Although he knew well that few persons falling within the Convention's definition were present in Israel, he had already in January 1951—long before the Convention was concluded—reported to Robinson, following his consultation with Eytan, that whether or not Israel will 'join' the Refugee Convention would depend on 'whether there are in Israel refugees falling under the proposed Convention': Rosenne to Robinson, 14 January 1951 (n 4) discussed in Ch 6.

[31] Emphases added; Rosenne to Robinson, 27 December 1951 (n 29).

[32] Ch 4. Report on Consultation with the Foreign Minister, 17 June 1949, FM–1976/9; discussing the prospect of joining the International Refugee Organization ('IRO'), Rosenne urged that 'our policy matters must not be influenced by symbolic considerations'; Rosenne to Eytan, 10 August 1950, FM–5850/2; Rosenne to Robinson, 18 September 1950, FM–1820/6, ISA.

to persuade Robinson that following this procedure would not 'produce a serious flaw in our ratification'.[33] The alternative, Rosenne averred, would be to 'first of all enact such amendments [to Israeli law] and later ratify the Convention'.[34] He warned Robinson, however, that this procedure 'will require a whole year before we can ratify the Convention', citing *Knesset* workload and inefficiency for his decision to prefer ratification subject to multiple reservations:

> The legislative process in the country is complicated and the truth is that the *Knesset* has not yet found the way to handle routine legislation efficiently. In addition, the *Knesset* is loaded with work and I am very much hesitant to burden it with additional work, if this can only be avoided.[35]

Rosenne was careful not to give the impression that he was dragging his feet; he preferred, after all, what he had presented as the fast track. He even sent Robinson a preliminary draft of the requisite reservations and asked for comments.[36] Yet his letter to Robinson only indicated he had made up his mind on *how* to proceed with ratification, not that he was determined to proceed. The same paragraph that contained his 'conclusion' to prefer ratification encumbered by numerous reservations also mentioned 'special circumstances for which we may ratify the Convention at all'.[37] Rosenne did not mention Eytan's early instruction to seek government ratification 'as soon as possible';[38] effectively, that instruction was undone. For the next two years, little would be done at Rosenne's office to prepare for Israel's ratification, let alone promote it; the MFA's work in connection with the Refugee Convention would now be limited, mostly, to forwarding and filing routine correspondence—including notifications received from the UN Secretariat of ratifications made by other states.

3. 'We Shall Await': Deferral, Disinterest, and Aversion

In September 1952, Israel's representative at Geneva reported to the MFA that during a meeting of the Advisory Board to UN High Commissioner for Refugees ('UNHCR'), he had expressed the hope 'that Israel ratify the Refugee Convention *before the end of this year*'. He added: 'I hope you do not blame me for this statement which I did make without being sure at all whether it was well founded'.[39]

[33] Rosenne to Robinson, 27 December 1951 (n 29); Rosenne, notably, did not proceed to propose adjusting Israeli law so as to allow the government to withdraw such reservations at a later date.
[34] ibid.
[35] ibid.
[36] ibid; I could not locate Robinson's response, if any was made.
[37] ibid.
[38] Eytan to Tekoah, [n.d.] (n 18).
[39] Emphasis in the original: Kahany to International Organizations Division ('IOD'), 23 September 1952, FM-1988/5, ISA.

Menachem Kahany had good reasons to be apprehensive. Previously, contrary to his instructions, he had lobbied the Economic and Social Council ('ECOSOC') to have Robinson elected to the *Ad Hoc* Committee on Statelessness and Related Problems.[40] This time, Tekoah delivered the reprimand:

> I regret to say that there is no certainty at all that our ratification would indeed be forthcoming before the end of this year. We have examined the question with care some time ago and have come to the conclusion that any ratification of the Convention would have to be accompanied by a rather impressive list of reservations resulting from our internal legislation. Desiring as we do to see the Convention on the Status of Refugees a success, we do not consider it wise that the first ratification of the Convention should be made subject to numerous reservations. We shall await therefore the ratification of the Convention by others before we take action in that direction ourselves.[41]

Kahany protested that he had only used qualified language that could not bind the government; but he also inquired why 'did you not take care to make … known' 'to all those concerned, including myself' a decision taken 'some time ago'.[42]

Rosenne's office had, indeed, already taken a positive decision to defer matters. In April 1952, the High Commission urged Israel—and other UN member states—to ratify the Refugee Convention 'at an early date' and asked to be 'informed of the intentions of the Government' in that respect.[43] This provided Rosenne's office with the opportunity to backtrack from the decision, communicated to Robinson in late 1951,[44] to prefer a speedy ratification through the use of multiple reservations. In May 1952, in connection with the High Commissioner's note, Tekoah advised the IOD that

> In light of the provisions of existing law we will need to ratify the Convention with a number of reservations. We decided that we should not open the list of ratifying states with a ratification that will have to be accompanied with many reservations. We shall await therefore until 4–5 ratification instruments are received from other countries.[45]

When reprimanding Kahany, Tekoah expressed a desire to see the Convention succeed. The decision made by Rosenne's office in May 1952, however, was driven

[40] Ch 6; later he was tasked with assisting Robinson during the proceedings of the 1951 Conference of Plenipotentiaries.
[41] Tekoah to Kahany, 16 October 1952, FM-1988/6, ISA.
[42] Kahany to Tekoah, 27 October 1952, FM-1988/6, ISA
[43] High Commissioner to Sharett, 23 April 1952, FM-1988/5, ISA.
[44] Rosenne to Robinson, 27 December 1951 (n 29).
[45] Tekoah to IOD, 4 May 1952, FM-1988/5, ISA.

by the desire to avoid diplomatic embarrassment. Ratifying the Convention subject to 'a rather impressive list of reservations' could well be interpreted as a *pro forma* exercise; an empty symbolic gesture was more likely to harm, not increase, Israel's diplomatic prestige both generally and in particular in connection with the work of the UNHCR Advisory Board's work.[46] Yet whatever were the motives behind the May 1952 decision, its effect was indefinite deferral. Tekoah's not did not specify what would transpire after '4–5' other countries ratified the Convention. Israel's answer to the High Commissioner, in fact, only promised to keep him 'informed of any further action taken by the Government of Israel'.[47] Rosenne would only come to express support for ratification—a rather lukewarm support, at that—in June 1954. Until then, he persistently refused to undertake that Israel would ratify the Refugee Convention. That the May 1952 decision was kept from Kahany in Geneva was, Tekoah would admit, 'regrettable'.[48] It is not clear whether it was relayed to Robinson in New York.

4. Promise Reneged?

Another year went by. In May 1953 the High Commissioner for Refugees, concerned that only Denmark and Norway had ratified the Convention, urged Kahany to have Israel included among the first six states to do so. Kahany now expressed no hope; he merely transmitted the letter to the MFA and asked to be informed as to 'what answer I shall give' the UNHCR.[49] A day later, the High Commissioner also wrote to Robinson, averring that the question of the Convention's entry into force was causing him 'some concern':

> As I know your great interest in the Convention, of which you have been one of the principle [sic] draftsmen, and am conscious of the great weight which undoubtedly your Council [sic] carries with the competent Authorities in Israel, I venture to express the hope that you will use your influence in order to achieve the desire I have expressed in the letter to Dr. Kahany, that the Convention be ratified at an early date and that Israel will be among the first six States to ratify it.[50]

[46] Israel's interest in this body is discussed below.

[47] Sharett to High Commissioner, 4 June 1952, FM–1988/5, ISA.

[48] Tekoah to Kahany, 9 November 1952, FM–1988/6, ISA.

[49] GJ van Heuven Goedhart to Kahany, 27 May 1953; Kahany to IOD, 4 June 1953, FM–1847/2. This was not the Commissioner's first appeal: High Commissioner to Sharett, 23 April 1952 (n 43). Kahany was first informed that Robinson was being consulted, and that 'when we make a final conclusion in this matter we shall be again in contact'. Office of the Legal Adviser to Kahany, 7 October 1953, FM–1847/2. He made repeated attempts to receive an answer: Kahany to IOD Director, 8 March 1954; IOD to Legal, 25 March 1954, IOD to Kahany, 25 March 1954, FM–1988/6, ISA.

[50] GJ van Heuven Goedhart to Robinson, 28 May 1953, FM–1847/2, ISA.

Robinson, in response, had to invoke constitutional and legislative 'difficulty' and 'obstacles'. These, as well as 'some other less important reasons', meant that 'the matter has been delayed'. He promised the High Commissioner, nonetheless, to write to the 'competent Ministry and suggesting some methods for the solution of these difficulties'.[51] He proceeded to urge Rosenne to 'consider one more time' and seek ways to resolve the 'legislative difficulties'. 'Morality', he exhorted Rosenne, 'demands that we be among the first six to ratify'.[52]

Rosenne was unimpressed by the moral argument. He promised to look into the matter again 'pursuant to your request', but nothing more. He also expressed hope that 'the government agrees to join the Convention on the condition that this will not prejudice the internal legal system'.[53] Robinson's urging did set in motion a slow process of MFA, then inter-departmental, review of the question of ratification. At no stage did participants in that process assume that Israel was necessarily going to ratify the Convention; nor was ratification the outcome that drove their work. The scales, in fact, were tipped against ratification. They would remain so for some time.

Rosenne tasked Itzhak Ben-Meir, a lawyer in his office, to examine once again the question of ratification. In July 1953, the High Commissioner circulated to signatory states a model travel document for refugees. Ben-Meir declined 'to offer comments on the matter as long as it is not clear to us whether or not Israel will ratify the Convention'.[54] When notified that Belgium and Luxembourg had ratified the Convention that month, bringing the overall number of ratifications to four, Rosenne routinely transmitted the UN circulars to the Justice Ministry adding that 'their contents speak for themselves'.[55] He did not mention the May 1952 decision to wait until '4–5' instruments of ratification are deposited by other signatories.[56] Silverstone, Rosenne's counterpart at the Ministry of Interior, 'assume[d] that this international treaty will have no real significance in Israel'.[57] Rosenne did not disagree.

In October 1953, Ben-Meir ventured to answer the question of ratification. The point of departure of his memorandum[58] was the Attorney-General's letter to Rosenne from October 1951;[59] in the two years separating these two documents, Rosenne's office did little to prepare the Convention's ratification. Ben-Meir rejected some of the interpretations made by the Attorney-General and Tekoah two

[51] Robinson to GJ van Heuven Goedhart, 10 June 1953, FM–1847/2, ISA.
[52] Robinson to Rosenne, 2 June 1953 (n 12).
[53] Rosenne to Robinson, 29 June 1953, FM–1847/2, ISA.
[54] Ben-Meir to IOD, 21 September 1953, FM–1988/6, and correspondence in FM–1847/2 (proposing that the MFA acknowledge receipt and notify the UNHCR that 'we shall revert to the matter when the matter is relevant after ratifying the Convention should such ratification be made by us'.
[55] Rosenne to Justice Ministry, 14 September 1953, FM–1847/2, G–5754/17, ISA.
[56] Tekoah to IOD, 4 May 1952 (n 45).
[57] Silverstone to Rosenne, 17 August 1953, FM–1847/2, ISA.
[58] Ben-Meir to Rosenne, 4 October 1953, FM–1847/2, ISA.
[59] Cohn to Rosenne, 16 October 1951 (n 24).

years earlier but embraced others. In particular, he offered a detailed analysis on the Convention's non-application to Palestinian refugees; this was a novelty. The Attorney-General's apprehensions in this respect, he wrote, were not 'sufficiently substantiated' to justify an Israeli reservation to the Convention's definition.[60] His conclusion was that the 'real difficulty' concerned a single issue: 'the conflict between Article 12 (personal status) and the laws of Israel'. Even that technical obstacle could be 'overcome by entering a reservation ... because we will be unable to adjust the law to the requirements of the Convention under the present circumstances'.[61]

Ben-Meir, nonetheless, proceeded to recommend against ratification. The language he used reveals how deep-seated had the aversion to the Refugee Convention become in Rosenne's office, and that the MFA interest in ratification was, at best, limited to considerations of diplomatic prestige:

> In light of the aforementioned, one could ask whether it is worthwhile anyway to ratify the Convention given the difficulties and the minuteness of its practical value to us. *I think not*. In his letter of 12.6.53 to us Dr. Robinson asks whether it is impossible to find a way to grant the status of refugees under the Convention in the field of private inter-national law to the dozen of refugees we have without touching the problem as a whole. In my opinion, this article is the main obstacle and I do not see how it can be overcome. If we enter a reservation to it, we will not achieve *even the modest goal* sought by Dr. Robinson.[62]

Later, Ben-Meir sent his memorandum to Robinson for comments. His accompanying letter also contained the following curious passage:

> As you know, *it was promised at the time* that Israel will not impede the Convention's entry into force and if our voice would be necessary to collect the first six ratifications in order for the Convention to enter into force, then our ratification will be forthcoming. *However, it is not yet clear to me how we can keep that promise* under the terms of today's law.[63]

Ben-Meir did not specify who made such a promise, to whom, and under what circumstances. Such a promise was, and would be, invoked by neither Robinson nor the High Commissioner when urging the MFA to ratify the Refugee Convention. It was not mentioned in Tekoah's note informing the IOD, in May 1952, of the 'decision' to defer consideration of the question of ratification 'until 4–5 ratification

[60] Ben-Meir to Rosenne, 4 October 1953 (n 58).
[61] ibid.
[62] Emphases added; ibid.
[63] Emphases added; Ben-Meir to Robinson, 8 October 1953, FM–1847/2, ISA.

instruments are received from other countries'[64] or, for that matter, in any MFA correspondence prior to October 1953. The only other mention of such a promise in the MFA or Ministry of Justice files does not shed much light on the issue. In June 1954, Rosenne wrote to the Attorney-General of 'moral considerations which we may not disparage and which moved us at the time to *solemnly promise* giving our early ratification of the Convention'.[65] Such a promise, if made, did not quite reflect Rosenne's attitude on the ratification of the Convention; nor was it consistent with Rosenne's actions. It may be that he and Ben-Meir, for whatever purpose, were referring to—and embellishing—their own May 1952 decision. Or it may be that they were alluding to Kahany's *unauthorized*—and far more vague—statement at the High Commissioner's Advisory Board.[66] At any rate, what mattered to Ben-Meir was not that a promise had been made, but the 'difficulties' involved and the Convention's minute 'practical value to us'.[67] He was content to observe that Israeli law made keeping that promise impossible.[68]

Rosenne certainly did not consider the MFA bound by any promise. In late October he reported to Ben-Meir that he had met Paul Weis, the UNHCR Jewish legal adviser.

> Weis pressured me again to be among the first six countries to ratify the Convention and if we absolutely cannot be among these—not to see ourselves exempt from the moral duty of ratifying the Convention only because it will have entered into force with the sixth ratification.[69]

Rosenne, however, denied any such 'moral duty' existed; he 'explained the difficulties and the obstacles obstructing our path and hinted that we are not very interested in ratifying his Convention as we have no need for it'.[70]

Ben-Meir's memorandum did not make the prospect of ratification more likely; nor did it expedite the decision-making process, despite proposals by Robinson on how to achieve that outcome.[71] In November 1953, Ben-Meir asked the Attorney-General to meet and discuss the question; in early December, he met the legal adviser of the Ministry of Interior.[72] Yet there was little urgency in his handling of

[64] Tekoah to IOD, 4 May 1952 (n 45).
[65] Emphasis added; Rosenne to Attorney-General, 25 June 1954, FM–1847/2, ISA, discussed below; Rosenne's account of the promise here is narrower than that reported by Ben-Meir.
[66] Kahany to IOD, 23 September 1952 (n 39).
[67] Ben-Meir to Rosenne, 4 October 1953 (n 58).
[68] Ben-Meir to Robinson, 8 October 1953 (n 63).
[69] Rosenne to Ben-Meir, 27 October 1953, FM–1847/2; Rosenne Journal, 22 October 1953, FM–5850/3, ISA (Weis 'continues to pressure us'). Ch 6 discusses Weis' background.
[70] Rosenne to Ben-Meir, 27 October 1953 (n 69).
[71] Robinson to Ben-Meir, 28 October 1953, FM–1847/2, ISA ('we could expedite the Convention's entry into force and this is worthwhile again for moral-symbolic considerations').
[72] Ben-Meir to Cohn, 12 November 1953; Silverstone to Rosenne, 22 December 1953, FM–1847/2, ISA; Silverstone tended to agree with Ben-Meir's analysis.

the matter: when West Germany became the fifth state to deposit its ratification of the Convention in December 1953, the announcement was routinely noted and filed.[73] No change of pace was recorded at Rosenne's office. Next, in January 1954, Australia became the sixth country to ratify the Refugee Convention. Once deposited, its instrument of ratification would trigger the Convention's entry into force after a ninety-day period.[74] This, too, was filed with no further action.[75] Kahany, who reported the Australian ratification, again asked for an answer.[76]

Great Britain followed in March with the seventh ratification; only then Rosenne asked Ben-Meir: 'What's with ours?'[77] In April, the Commissioner announced the Convention's entry into force; Rosenne again scribbled: 'What is the situation'?[78] If there had been any intention for Israel to be among the first six states to ratify the Convention, or a promise to that effect, it had long since dissipated.

5. 'Dr. Robinson Justly Pressures Us'

In June 1953, Rosenne promised Robinson to look again at the question of ratification.[79] A year later, Robinson had little reason to believe that any change in Rosenne's position had taken place. Rosenne's office, again, dallied. It was too late for Israel to become a member of the small club of states whose ratification triggered the Refugee Convention's entry into force; the Jewish state had lost the opportunity for that symbolic gesture in January 1954 through disinterest, inaction, and aversion. Robinson, however, still hoped for Israel to 'acquire', through ratification, 'legal title' to intervene on behalf of Jewish refugees.[80] He now identified an opportunity to press the matter again. To that end, he developed a new argument pointing to *concrete* reputational advantages to be drawn from ratification.

The opportunity concerned the question of stateless persons, a matter that the 1951 Conference of Plenipotentiaries resolved to defer. During the Conference and before, when serving on the *Ad Hoc* Committee on Statelessness and Related Problems, Robinson worked unsuccessfully to keep the matter on the agenda. In late April 1954, ECOSOC resolved to convene a Conference of Plenipotentiaries

[73] Stavropoulos to Sharett, 10 December 1953, FM-1847/2, ISA.

[74] Article 43, 1951 Refugee Convention (n 5) 182; Liang to Sharett, 5 February 1954, FM-1847/2, ISA.

[75] High Commissioner's Advisory Committee on Refugees, Conference Room Document No 12, February 1954, FM-1847/2, ISA.

[76] IOD to Legal, 25 March 1954 (n 49).

[77] UN Department of Public Information, Press Release, 11 March 1954, FM-1847/2, ISA with Rosenne's handwritten note.

[78] UN Department of Public Information, Press Release, 21 April 1954, FM-1847/2, ISA, with Rosenne's handwritten note, 3 May 1954.

[79] Rosenne to Robinson, 29 June 1953 (n 53).

[80] Robinson to Director-General, Fourth and Final Report, 1 August 1951 (n 1).

to consider a treaty on stateless persons.[81] Robinson, frustrated with his inability to affect Israel's ratification of the Convention, soon reported this development to Rosenne:

> As you know, one part of the task charged at the time on the *Ad Hoc* Committee on Statelessness, that is an agreement on the legal position of this category who are not 'refugees' within the meaning of the Convention of August 1950 [sic] was left unimplemented. In its last session, the Economic and Social Council decided . . . to convene such a conference.
>
> . . .
>
> Please discuss and decide whether we intend to participate in this conference. The fact that we have not yet decided to join the Refugee Convention (even if with reservations) diminishes our moral value. If you were to heed my advice, I'd be in favor of our participation (since there are still many Jews in the world requiring this protection, and if we will not assist them, who will?) but some time before the Conference we must ratify the Convention *so that we can appear with clean hands*.[82]

Robinson's new argument prompted Rosenne into action. He instructed Ben-Meir: 'The matter has now become urgent. Our position is to be decided *during this week*.'[83] He promised Robinson to 'make every effort to draw final conclusions about the 1950 [sic] Convention within a week';[84] he also promised to keep Robinson informed.

Rosenne did not promise to *support* the ratification of the Refugee Convention, only to 'draw final conclusions'. The week, however, soon turned into months. At the end of June, he reported to the Attorney-General that the MFA now favoured ratification. He nonetheless took care to mark Israel's disinterest in the Convention: '[a]fter further consideration and a consultation with Dr. Robinson we reached the conclusion that there is room to ratify the Convention *despite its little practical value for us*'.[85] Rosenne mentioned neither Israel's standing in the forthcoming Conference nor any time constraints. It was in this context that he alluded, instead, to a promise made about an early Israeli ratification. To justify the change in the MFA's position, after nearly three years of aversion, indecision, and stalling he now espoused Robinson's most recent formulation of 'Jewish' concerns warranting ratification, citing it verbatim:

[81] ECOSOC Res.526A(XVII) (26 April 1954).
[82] Emphasis added; Robinson to Rosenne, 2 June 1953 (n 12).
[83] Emphasis in the original; ibid, with Rosenne's handwritten note, 8 June 1954.
[84] Rosenne to Robinson, 10 June 1954, FM–1830/10, ISA.
[85] Emphasis added; Rosenne to Attorney-General, 25 June 1954 (n 65). Rosenne sent Cohn a truncated version of Ben-Meir's October 1953 memorandum; he omitted the last paragraphs expressing aversion to ratification: Ben-Meir to Rosenne, 4 October 1953 (n 58) cited (n 62).

> The main reason [for the decision to now support ratification] stems from moral considerations which we may not disparage and which at the time moved us to solemnly promise giving our early ratification of the Convention. *There are still many Jews in the world requiring this protection, and if we will not assist them, who will?*[86]

Rosenne's intimations to the Attorney-General were not entirely sincere. There was nothing new in these Jewish concerns; Robinson had been invoking these since early 1950,[87] and advocating ratification on that basis long before the Convention was concluded.[88] Rosenne, moreover, had never hitherto considered Jewish concerns as warranting ratification of the Refugee Convention. Likewise, Rosenne's allusion to the prospect of 'early' Israeli ratification was not entirely accurate: the Convention had already entered into force. Rosenne's reluctant recommendation was not driven by a sense of obligation to fulfil a past—real or fictive—promise. Nor was it meant to give effect to 'moral considerations' compelling the Jewish state to ensure that Jews outside Israel were afforded legal protection. Rosenne's reluctant recommendation, as noted below, was made *despite*, not because of, the Convention's effect on the position of Jewish refugees. Other factors, on which his letter to the Attorney-General was silent, led Rosenne to grudgingly recommend ratification.

Rosenne's ambivalence towards the Convention was patent in the practical measures he now recommended to the Attorney-General. He clarified the matter of the Convention's inapplicability to 'Arab refugees' and proposed to resolve 'the problems of legislation' by the extensive use of reservations whenever any doubt existed as to the Convention's correct interpretation, its compatibility with Israeli law, or the need for implementing legislation. Rosenne had no qualms about having Israel's ratification accompanied by multiple reservations; nor was he concerned that this might appear as a perfunctory acceptance of obligations. He even proposed novel reservations on various issues.[89] Ratification, for Rosenne, was not meant to bolster the refugee protection regime but to serve other goals.

Rosenne's slow pace led Robinson to protest that three weeks had lapsed since Rosenne had promised 'to give me an answer within a week ... the answer has not been received yet'.[90] He now honed the argument that ratification of the Refugee Convention was essential to Israel's diplomatic standing in the forthcoming

[86] Emphasis added; Rosenne to Attorney-General, 25 June 1954 (n 65); the emphasized sentence cites Robinson to Rosenne, 2 June 1953 (n 12), cited at text to n 82.

[87] Ch 6; Robinson to IOD, First Interim Report of the *Ad Hoc* Committee on Statelessness and Related Problems, 23 January 1950, FM-2010/13, ISA.

[88] Ch 6; Robinson to Rosenne, 6 February 1951, FM-2010/13, FM-1830/8, ISA.

[89] Rosenne to Attorney-General, 25 June 1954 (n 65); proposing that Israel follow Great Britain's example and enter reservations on security grounds, as well as a new reservation with regard to Arab refugees and another aimed at excluding refugees from enjoyment of Israel's social security legislation.

[90] Robinson to Rosenne, 1 July 1954, FM-1847/2, ISA.

Conference on Stateless Persons. Robinson, crucially, now abandoned the assertion that ratification was required to uphold Israel's 'moral value' or 'clean hands';[91] instead of reciting, once again, Jewish concerns or Israel's role in protecting Jewish interests, he now portrayed ratification as 'a prior condition to *effective* participation in the conference soon about to convene'.[92] Rosenne seemed receptive to arguments about Israel's standing and prestige; Robinson moved to harp on that sensibility. He was no longer content to offer advice or urge morality. Instead, he now added a thinly veiled ultimatum: 'I would like to emphasize that I do not know whether in the case of disregarding ratification I will be able to undertake representing Israel. At any rate, a substitute ought to be considered whether or not I participate.'[93] Rosenne, however, was in no hurry; three more weeks passed before he wrote to Cohn: 'Dr. Robinson justly pressures us to take a decision.' This time, he mentioned the Conference soon to be convene, but not that less than two months remained before the intended date. 'We are interested in participating ... but Dr. Robinson argues that the delay in ratification ... will put him in a difficult position.' Rosenne asked the Attorney-General to 'inform us of your decision soon', but did not urge Cohn to decide in favour of ratification. It was, he wrote, too early to decide on Israel's position for the forthcoming Conference 'until our position with regard to the Refugee Convention itself is made clear, especially since we do not know—*in case we ratify the Convention*—to which of its articles we will enter reservations'.[94] Even when recommending ratification, Rosenne was not invested in ensuring that this would be the outcome of the Attorney-General's decision.

6. Robinson's 'Last Appeal for Ratification'

Unaware of Rosenne's last letter to Cohn—or weary of delays—Robinson now took the matter, uncharacteristically, up the MFA hierarchy. On 3 August, he cabled Eytan, the MFA Director-General, directly. His frustration with Rosenne's inaction was patent:

> Opening date for UN conference statelessness finally set September 13. Our absence there from [sic] inexcusable view thousands Jewish stateless various countries whose condition may be improved by suggested protocol. Effective participation conference conditioned our previous ratification refugee convention preferably without but if impossible with reservations. Referring my 3 year old

[91] Robinson to Rosenne, 2 June 1953 (n 12) cited at text to n 82 above.
[92] Emphasis added; Robinson to Rosenne, 1 July 1954 (n 90).
[93] ibid. This was no resignation threat: cf Gilad Ben-Nun, 'The Israeli Roots of Article 3 and Article 6 of the 1951 Refugee Convention' (2014) 27 J of Refugee Stud 101, 106; Gilad Ben-Nun, *Seeking Asylum in Israel: Refugees and the History of Migration Law* (Tauris 2016) 27.
[94] Emphasis added; Rosenne to Cohn, 21 July 1954, FM-1847/2, ISA.

correspondence with Rosenne and latters [sic] with attorney general making my last appeal for ratification.[95]

Here Robinson reverted to linking Jewish concerns and Israeli interests. The former required the Jewish state to attend the impending Conference; effective participation by Israel's envoys, however, required the prior ratification of the Refugee Convention. Unlike Rosenne, Robinson was wary that a perfunctory ratification subject to multiple reservations would undermine the symbolic value of the act—and his own standing at the forthcoming Conference.

At first, Robinson's unorthodox move seemed to bear fruit. Eytan responded, by cable, that 'the Attorney-General agreed to the Convention's ratification with reservations you know. After Government decision, the instrument of ratification will be relayed to you. Legal is writing in Dip[lomatic] mail.'[96] It was Ben-Meir, not Rosenne, who reported the details to Robinson on 8 August. Cohn had 'already been prepared to write and announce his agreement to ratification, only that he was extremely preoccupied ... of late'; still, the Attorney-General 'promised to submit the Convention to government ratification soon'. Ratification, alas, would be accompanied by reservations, although Ben-Meir thought that he had persuaded Cohn that a reservation stating that the Convention 'does not apply to Arab refugees' would be redundant. The instrument of ratification, Ben-Meir promised, would be sent to Robinson immediately after the government decision.[97] As it happened, Cohn submitted the matter to the government 'with urgency' that very day.[98] Cohn reported to the Cabinet Secretary that the MFA wished to deposit Israel's instrument of ratification before the Conference on Stateless Persons convened and added, inaccurately, that 'our participation in that Conference is *conditional* upon prior ratification of the Convention'.[99]

Robinson, appeased, now wrote conciliatory personal letters to Cohn and Ben-Meir. He withdrew the threat not to participate in the Conference. At the same time, he also sought to ensure that the ratification instrument 'arrives to New York so as to enable us action in favor of thousands of Jews in the diaspora. Time is short as the Conference on Stateless Persons will open on September 13.'[100] Leaving nothing to fate, he urged Ben-Meir to hurry the Cabinet Secretary, send the ratification instrument forthwith, and furnish Robinson with proper credentials for the

[95] Robinson to Eytan, 3 August 1954, FM–1847/2, ISA.
[96] Eytan to Robinson, 6 August 1954, FM–1847/2, ISA.
[97] Ben-Meir to Robinson, 8 August 1954, FM–1847/2, FM–1830/10, ISA.
[98] Attorney-General to Cabinet Secretary, 8 August 1954, FM–1847/2; notably, the Ministry of Finance had not yet given its approval: Treasury Legal Adviser to Foreign Currency Superintendent, 13 August 1954, G–5576/10, ISA.
[99] Emphasis added; Attorney-General to Cabinet Secretary, 8 August 1954 (n 98).
[100] Robinson to Cohn, 18 August 1954, G–5754/17, ISA.

Conference.[101] He nonetheless felt confident enough to revert to his old argument that emphasized the needs of Diaspora Jews, not Israel's diplomatic standing.

Somehow, the prospect that Robinson might not attend the Conference became public knowledge. Rosenne reported from Geneva that UNHCR legal adviser Paul Weis, who expected to miss the Conference, approached him and 'pressed again for Robinson's participation ... whether or not Israel ratifies ... due to his expertise ... I promised nothing.'[102] Rosenne, moreover, did not inquire into the delay. It was Eytan who asked Ben-Meir for an update; on 22 August, Ben-Meir answered that the government may 'ratify the Convention today'.[103] It did, three years after Eytan instructed Rosenne's office to 'receive government ratification ... as soon as possible'.[104]

Government ratification, however, did not bring Robinson's tribulations to an end. Two days later, Ben-Meir assured Robinson he would receive the necessary credentials and the instrument of ratification for deposit with the UN Secretary-General 'in a week'. Ben-Meir also relayed Weis's request for Robinson's participation 'due to your expertise'.[105] The credentials were sent to Robinson on 30 August;[106] but on 8 September—a mere five days before the Conference of Plenipotentiaries was set to convene—there was no sign of Israel's instrument of ratification. Robinson now cabled the MFA: 'Rosenne. Where is ratification Refugee Convention.'[107] He was incensed with the reply from Rosenne's office: 'Convention ratified. Checking with [Attorney-General] the terms of the reservation.'[108] Exasperated, he protested that Ben-Meir already 'gave me this answer ... on August 24th'.[109]

At this juncture, Robinson once again issued an ultimatum. Previously, his threat not to participate in the Conference on Stateless Persons had been implicit, and concerned his own attendance.[110] Now he raised the stakes, cabling on 9 September an explicit ultimatum that concerned Israel's attendance:

> *We* will not be able to show up at the conference opening Monday *unless* you cable me and the [UN] Secretary-General that the Convention was ratified and that

[101] Robinson to Ben-Meir, 18 August 1954, FM-1847/2; Robinson, like in connection with the 1951 Conference of Plenipotentiaries, insisted on being equipped with full powers—'the right to participate *and sign subject to ratification*': emphasis in the original, ibid. As in 1951, at first he was equipped with unsatisfactory credentials: [Full Powers], 18 August 1954, FM-1830/10; [Full Powers], 30 August 1954, FM-1988/6, ISA.

[102] Rosenne to Legal, 20 August 1954, FM-1847/2, ISA.

[103] Ben-Meir to Director-General, 22 August 1954, FM-1847/2, ISA.

[104] Eytan to Tekoah, [n.d.] (n 18).

[105] Ben-Meir to Robinson, 24 August 1954, FM-1847/2, ISA.

[106] Robinson to Lador, 7 September 1954, FM-1847/2, ISA.

[107] Robinson to [MFA], 8 September 1954, FM-1847/2, ISA.

[108] Legal to Robinson, 9 September 1954, FM-1847/2, ISA.

[109] Robinson to [MFA], 9 September 1954, FM-1847/2, ISA.

[110] Robinson to Rosenne, 1 July 1954 (n 90) discussed at text to n 93.

ratification is on its way *and on condition that the cable is received here before the opening* [on 13 September 1954].[111]

This cable, however, was sent on a Thursday and received on the Friday; the reply came only on Monday, 13 September—the opening day of the Conference. That day, three weeks after the government ratified the Refugee Convention, Rosenne cabled the Secretary-General informing him, briefly and unceremoniously, of Israel's ratification of the Convention.[112] Robinson's blatant ultimatum, finally, yielded the outcome he had recommended three years earlier.

In the end, Israel was the tenth country to deposit its instrument of ratification. Robinson did so on 1 October, six months after the Refugee Convention entered into force.[113] After the Conference, Robinson informed—perhaps admonished—Rosenne 'just for the record' that he had 'used all opportunities during the Conference on Stateless Persons to make it known ... that the ratification took place on August 20, 1954'.[114] The civil tone would control their correspondence for some time.[115]

7. Ministers, Lawmakers, and Bureaucrats

Israel's ratification of the Refugee Convention was not the expression of concrete government policy. The political echelon was not involved in the process in any way until it was asked to formally decide on ratification.[116] The government was not informed when Robinson signed the Convention in 1951.[117] Only on 22 August 1954, at the end of a meeting lasting more than eight hours, it was asked to ratify three treaties. No explanation was given, no discussion followed, and no allusion was made to the Convention's significance, Jewish or otherwise. Unceremoniously, the government resolved 'to ratify the Convention on the Status of Refugees ... and authorize the [MFA] to implement this decision with reservations'.[118] If ratification was driven by Jewish concerns, or if the Convention held any particular Jewish significance, the ministers were not so told.

[111] Emphases added; Robinson to [MFA], 9 September 1954 (n 109).

[112] Rosenne to Secretary-General, 13 September 1954; Lador to Robinson, 14 September 1954, FM-1847/2, ISA (with note to Secretary-General detailing Israel's reservations).

[113] UN Department of Public Information, Press Release, 1 October 1954, FM-1847/2, ISA.

[114] Robinson to Rosenne, 11 October 1954, FM-1847/2, ISA.

[115] Rosenne to Robinson, 20 October 1954, FM-1847/2, ISA

[116] Cf Ben-Nun, 'Roots' (n 93) 106, Ben-Nun, *Asylum* (n 93) 27 suggest that the animosity between Prime Minister Ben-Gurion and Foreign Minister Sharett delayed Israel's ratification. I found no evidence whatsoever in the relevant files supporting this conjecture or even hinting that the two were in any way involved in the process leading up to the government decision.

[117] Record of Government Meetings, 1 August 1951 (n 14).

[118] Record of Government Meetings, 22 August 1954; Deputy Cabinet Secretary to Ministers, 23 August 1954, FM-1847/2, ISA.

The *Knesset*, for its part, was not involved. Nor did it express interest—unlike in the case of the Genocide Convention[119]—in the ratification decision.[120] The lack of parliamentary involvement was precipitated, in part, by Rosenne's strong preference to avoid any legislative amendments necessary to bring Israeli law into conformity with the Convention's obligations.[121] The *Knesset* nonetheless did not protest being bypassed, even if the press reported regularly on the making of the Convention.[122] Parliamentary record reveals a single allusion to the status of Refugees in *Knesset* debates between the time Robinson became involved in the preparation of the Convention and the government decision to ratify it—excepting debates on Palestinian refugees or, frequently linked, on Jewish refugees from Arab countries. Even that single allusion did not mention the legislative project discussed at the UN.[123]

Yet Israel's ratification of the Refugee Convention was not quite the outcome of bureaucratic preference, either. Rosenne, the MFA legal adviser, was reluctant to see Israel ratify the Convention. Through delay and inaction, he had effectively overturned the instruction his office received in August 1951 from Director-General Eytan to obtain ratification 'as soon as possible'.[124] And when he finally came to recommend ratification to the Attorney-General, he did so in terms that betrayed the depth of his reticence: 'there is room to ratify the Convention *despite its little practical value for us*'.[125] That was not the outcome of his choice.

The bureaucracy's reluctance was equally manifest in the outcome, not merely the process, of ratification. Israel's ratification evinced no more than a nominal willingness to become bound by the provisions of the Refugee Convention. By the extensive use of reservations, the act was stripped of any symbolic value that might have signified a particular interest in or special commitment to the Convention on the part of the Jewish state. While legally, in depositing its instrument of

[119] Ch 4.

[120] Ratification by the Government was mentioned neither in the plenary periodical debate on foreign policy nor in the proceedings of the *Knesset* Foreign and Security Affairs Committee: *Divrei HaKnesset* (15–17 November 1954) 64–110 (Hebrew); Record of *Knesset* Foreign and Security Affairs Committee (24 August 1954), A-7564/6, ISA.

[121] Rosenne to Robinson, 27 December 1951 (n 29) discussed above.

[122] Some reports on the UN work on the Convention mentioned the involvement of Israel's representatives: *Al HaMishmar* (28 August 1950) (Hebrew); 'Eliminating Organised Immigration' *HaTzofeh* (4 May 1951) (Hebrew); *Davar* (26 September 1951) (Hebrew). The government decision to ratify the Convention was also reported: 'Government Announcement' *Zmanim* (23 August 1954) (Hebrew); 'Official Announcement on Government Meeting' *Herut* (23 August 1954) (Hebrew).

[123] In January 1950, one *Knesset* member submitted a formal question to the relevant Minister: 'is it true that on Friday, 30 December 1949 a Christian woman from Greece ... was returned to the Greek ship "Campidoglio" because she did not possess the required documentation ... was it first checked whether or not this is a case of a political refugee which according to international usage is not to be extradited back to his country'. The Minister responded that 'there was no hint in what she said that she was a political refugee', adding that the woman, a stowaway, 'was looking for her fiancé whose name and address she does not know ... therefore she was returned abroad on the same ship': *Divrei HaKnesset* (16 January 1950) 509 (Hebrew).

[124] Eytan to Tekoah, [n.d.] (n 18).

[125] Emphasis added; Rosenne to Attorney-General, 25 June 1954 (n 65).

ratification, Israel became formally bound by the Convention subject to reservations, these very reservations, read together against the source material, were meant to produce a perfunctory, puny formal commitment to the Convention. The bureaucracy's approach to ratification, orchestrated by Rosenne, was minimalist to the last; it did the least possible to enable Israel to ratify the Convention without requiring legislative action. Whenever a tension between the Convention and Israeli law appeared to exist, the solution was entering a reservation to the offending Convention clause. Ratification sought to adapt the Convention to Israeli law, not the other way around.[126]

Avoiding legislative entanglements did not prove, despite Rosenne's prediction, the speedier procedure; it did ensure, however, that Israel would ratify the Convention at no cost. Keeping the matter in the hands of the bureaucracy is precisely what allowed Rosenne, out of disinterest and aversion, to defer its ratification.[127] In the end, Israel's ratification was both late and narrow. When the UN Secretary-General inquired in late 1954 of laws passed 'to ensure the application of this Convention', the answer was that 'in light of the reservations' entered by Israel, there was no need for any.[128] Successive Israeli governments ever since would obstruct Private Member Bills seeking to give the Convention effect in Israeli law—and invoking, typically, the moral obligation of the Jewish state to do so.[129] To this day, no Israeli legislation gives internal effect to the Convention.

Israel's ratification, then, ran against bureaucratic preference. What, in the end, surmounted the bureaucracy's disinterest and aversion were Robinson's intercessions. His campaign could eventually succeed in part because none of Israel's primary foreign policy interests was sufficiently at stake to rule ratification out.[130] In another, his campaign succeeded because he could couch his own preference in terms of secondary foreign policy interests that harped on the sensibilities of the MFA bureaucracy. By signalling his unwillingness to participate in the 1954 Conference, he had threatened to undermine Israel's diplomatic standing—that is,

[126] Cohn to Rosenne, 16 October 1951 (n 24); Rosenne to Robinson, 29 June 1953 (n 53); Tekoah to IOD, 4 May 1952 (n 45); etc.

[127] Recall that, in December 1951, Rosenne wrote to Robinson that he had decided against asking the *Knesset* to 'first of all enact such amendments' as this 'will require a whole year before we can ratify the Convention'. He cited *Knesset* workload and inefficiency: Rosenne to Robinson, 27 December 1951 (n 29). The legislative difficulties he had invoked, however, were of his own doing; he had another, prior reason to prefer keeping the *Knesset* uninvolved: see ch 4.

[128] Cohn to Rosenne, 22 December 1954, G-5754/17, ISA.

[129] Government Decision No 1129(HK/598) (23 December 2009) ('object to Refugee Convention Bill to Regulate the Status of Asylum Seekers and Refugees in Israel 2009'). Tally Kritzman and Adriana Kemp, 'The Establishment of the Refugee Regime in Israel: Between State and Civil Society' in Guy Mundlak and Mimi Ajzenstadt (eds), *Empowerment on Trial* (Nevo 2008) 55 (Hebrew).

[130] Not even the Attorney-General's misinformed apprehensions about the Convention's possible application to Arab refugees: Rosenne to Robinson, 27 December 1951 (n 29); Cohn to Rosenne, 16 October 1951 (n 24); Tekoah to Rosenne, 28 October 1951 (n 26); Ben-Meir to Robinson, 8 August 1954 (n 97). Remarkably, it took MFA lawyers three years to elaborate the correct, and simple, answer to Cohn's concerns. On the exclusion of Palestinian refugees from the Convention's definition: Alex Takkenberg, *The Status of Palestinian Refugees in International Law* (Clarendon Press 1998).

exact a concrete, positive cost from Israel's *présence* and prestige. Attending UN fora, and acquiring the reputation of a good member making a regular contribution to UN work—Israel's '*diplomatie de présence*' policy—was one of the guiding principles of Israel's UN mission.[131] This had been the one aspect of Robinson's work on the Refugee Convention that consistently drew the attention, and earned him the praise, of the MFA.[132] On questions of refugees and immigration, as we shall see, presence at UN fora also brought Israel concrete, if indirect, boons. Robinson's escalating ultimatum was well calculated; it yielded, if barely, the intended outcome. Robinson's campaign, in that sense, succeeded because he could point to instrumental Israeli interests in ratification and persuade the MFA bureaucracy to consider it a platform for routine foreign policy business. Robinson had employed such arguments, without success, for more than three years; it succeeded precisely at the moment Robinson ceased invoking 'moral considerations' compelling the Jewish state to assume the role of protecting Jewish Diaspora interests[133]—the very motive that had driven his involvement in the making of the Refugee Convention all along. Robinson's argument became persuasive enough to overcome the MFA reluctance only when he no longer linked it to the Convention's effects on the position of Jewish refugees. In that sense, Israel's ratification of the Refugee Convention came to be *despite*, not because of, the Convention's Jewish aspects.

External pressures by the UNHCR and his staff may have resonated with or bolstered Robinson's advocacy; alone, they were insufficient to overcome the bureaucracy's reluctance. This was surpassed only after three long years, and only when Robinson threatened not to participate in the 1954 Conference on Stateless Persons. He had to overcome several recommendations issued by Rosenne's office against ratification. He was operating against a prevalent sense that the Convention had little to do with the Jewish state. Such disinterest was expressed, time and again, by Rosenne, his subordinates, and his counterparts in other ministries: Rosenne told Weis that 'we are not very interested in ratifying his Convention as we have no need for it'.[134] Silverstone 'assume[d] that this international treaty will have no real significance in Israel'.[135] Ben-Meir, as late as October 1953, thought it was not 'worthwhile' for Israel to ratify the Convention 'given ... the minuteness of its practical value to us'.[136] Rosenne's eventual recommendation that there was 'room to ratify the Convention' still insisted that it had 'little practical value for us'.[137] 'We' and 'us', and often 'ours': Robinson was working, then, against some

[131] This policy and Robinson's part in expounding it are discussed throughout this book.
[132] Eytan to Robinson, 14 August 1951 (n 16); Gordon to Robinson, 3 March 1950, FM–2010/13, ISA; both discussed in ch 6.
[133] Robinson to Rosenne, 2 June 1953 (n 12) discussed at text to n 82.
[134] Rosenne to Ben-Meir, 27 October 1953 (n 69).
[135] Silverstone to Rosenne, 17 August 1953 (n 57).
[136] Ben-Meir to Rosenne, 4 October 1953 (n 58).
[137] Rosenne to Attorney-General, 25 June 1954 (n 65). After ratification, Rosenne continued to endorse a passive Israeli role in relation to the Convention eg on the question of legality of the Austrian reservation: Lador to Rosenne, 30 November 1954, and Rosenne to Robinson [n.d.], FM–1847/2, ISA.

shared understanding of the collective—Israeli, not Jewish—against whose interests and values the Refugee Convention was to be assessed. The ratification affair exposed how much he was acting against the grain of the MFA's reading of Jewish concerns and the Jewish state's role with regard to Jewish matters. With regard to ratification, just like in respect his work on the drafting of the Refugee Convention, Robinson was not expressing the MFA position or giving effect to Israel's foreign policy—notwithstanding his formal representative capacity. In substantive terms, his reading of the Convention's Jewish aspects cannot be attributed, by dint of the formal-yet-nominal act of ratification, to the Jewish state. The ratification affair revealed that Israel's legal-diplomatic bureaucracy had shared a radically different ideological reading of Jewish sovereignty and its implications for Jewish refugeehood and statelessness.

8. Robinson's Heresy: Ideology, Refuge, and 'Return'

Robinson's perspective on Palestine refugees, on Israel's Cold War orientation, or on Israel's diplomatic reputation did not diverge from the MFA positions. Nor did he offer a reading of universal values and particular interests that his colleagues had not shared.[138] The impetus for his investment in the Refugee Convention, we saw, was not a universal vision.[139] What set Robinson apart was a competing interpretation of the Jewish *particular* at the age of sovereignty. Although often framed

[138] This is the reading offered, explicitly or implicitly, by recent commentators arguing that Israel's—or, in contradistinction, Robinson's—involvement with the Refugee Convention expressed a universal or cosmopolitan vision: Ben-Nun, 'Roots' (n 93); Gilad Ben-Nun, 'From *Ad Hoc* to Universal: The International Refugee Regime from Fragmentation to Unity 1922–1954' (2015) 34 Refugee Survey Quarterly 23; Ben-Nun, *Asylum* (n 93); James Loeffler, *Rooted Cosmopolitans: Jews and Human Rights in the Twentieth Century* (Yale UP 2018). This reading resonates with the view that Israel's early foreign policy sought to promote universal values: Michael Brecher, *The Foreign Policy System of Israel: Setting, Images, Process* (OUP 1972); Charles Liebman, 'The Idea of Or Lagoyim in the Israeli Reality' (1974) 20 Gesher 88 (Hebrew). Similar claims are prevalent in present day discourse on Israel's treatment of asylum seekers: these are presented, and refuted, in Rotem Giladi, 'A "Historical Commitment"? Identity and Ideology in Israel's Attitude to the Refugee Convention 1951–1954' (2014) 37 Intl Hist Rev 745.

[139] Ch 6. Notably, universal values were hardly alluded to in MFA correspondence on the Refugee Convention. At most, Jewish experience with refugeehood and statelessness was invoked by Robinson and his colleagues alike as a factor compelling Israeli contribution to UN work—in support, that is, of Israel's diplomatic prestige: Robinson to IOD, First Interim Report, 23 January 1950 (n 87) ('we have to follow faithfully our policy of cooperation with the United Nations in an effort to make the maximum contribution we are capable of'); Robinson, United Nations Conference of Plenipotentiaries on the Status of Stateless Persons, 23 March 1955, FM–1830/10, FM–1988/4 ('our possible contributions in the field of international cooperation . . . we may be able to contribute something to problems of a general nature'; 'We have accumulated experience in this particular item and we owe it to the world community to contribute our experience to the solution of a problem of international dimensions'); [Robinson], Broadcast from Lake Success, 17 February 1950, FM–2010/13 ('we are bound, as UN members, to contribute from [our] knowledge and experience to the extent that we can to humanitarian problems'); Gordon, Study of Statelessness, 24 July 1949, FM–19/3, ISA (Jewish 'suffering from the scourge of statelessness' commended that 'the Jewish state should . . . support . . . measures aimed at uprooting this evil').

in terms of (secondary) interests, this was essentially a dispute about Israel's identity as the Jewish state, its place in the international system and, in particular, its place in the Jewish world. The dispute was ideological: ideology determined Israel's attitude towards Jewish refugeehood, which, in turn, determined its attitude towards the Refugee Convention itself.

Elements of Robinson's attitude on Jewish refugeehood and the Refugee Convention have already been presented in this and the preceding chapter. Essentially, his investment in the Refugee Convention, its making, and its ratification sought to have the Jewish state acquire status: 'legal title'[140] for 'intervention in case of violation of the Convention by other parties to it whenever Jewish interests will be at stake'.[141] Harnessing the new Jewish sovereign status to the interests of world Jewry was rooted in Robinson's pre-sovereign sensibilities; in his experience, the lack of formal standing had been the plague of the Jewish non-sovereign condition. For the veteran of Jewish legal diplomacy in the interwar and Holocaust years, this flaw in formal capacity, this absence of official voice, had hampered the efforts of Jewish organizations to find solutions for Jewish refugees at times of crises.[142] Jewish sovereignty, for Robinson, meant that the task of protecting Jewish refugees could now, appropriately, fall to the Jewish state: 'if we will not assist them, who will?'[143] He considered the Jewish state, in other words, as the *state of protection* of Jewish refugees, legally entitled to intervene on their behalf.[144] Israel's role in the world, and in the Jewish world, was to extend its protection to Jewish refugees. This reading animated his work on the Refugee Convention: in the *Ad Hoc* Committee, at the General Assembly ('GA'), in the 1951 Conference and, later, during his ratification campaign. His efforts, in his words, represented fulfilment of 'the duty of Israel to help to improve the legal status of Jewish refugees'.[145] For all the sovereign sensibilities he had displayed during his work on the Refugee Convention and at other junctures of his career at Israel's foreign service,[146] this was not an isolated attempt by Robinson to charge the Jewish state with *some* responsibility for the Diaspora. This was how he had imagined Israel's foreign policy since the early days of the MFA.[147]

[140] Robinson to Director-General, Fourth and Final Report, 1 August 1951 (n 1).

[141] Robinson to Rosenne, 6 February 1951 (n 88); ch 6 traces and analyses this formula.

[142] These sensibilities are discussed in ch 6. The preceding chapters demonstrate how prevalent was the preoccupation with standing and status in Robinson's pre-1948 Jewish advocacy and, later, in the service of the Jewish state: in inter-war minority protection, during the Holocaust, at Nuremberg, and in UN work.

[143] Robinson to Rosenne, 2 June 1953 (n 12).

[144] In 1955 he offered a more detailed legal interpretation of 'contractual rights to intervene in favour of Jewish stateless persons': Robinson, Conference on the Status of Stateless Persons, 23 March 1955 (n 139) cited and discussed in ch 6.

[145] Robinson to IOD, First Interim Report, 23 January 1950 (n 87).

[146] Ch 6 discusses Robinson's sovereign sensibilities underscoring his work on the Refugee Convention. Other instances are discussed in chs 2–5.

[147] When consulted, in June 1948, on the organization of Israel's newly established MFA he intimated to Director-General Eytan that Israel's foreign policy would have a role in catering to 'the imminent

At the same time, Robinson also considered Israel as the *state of asylum* of Jewish refugees. This was how he presented the Jewish state during the 1951 Conference. Commenting on the proposal to limit the Convention's application to events taking place 'in Europe', he chided the US representative who offered 'an otherwise exhaustive survey of the position of refugees throughout the world' for overlooking

> one country, Israel, which in the last eighteen years, first as the Jewish National Home and subsequently as the State of Israel, had absorbed more than three-quarters of a million refugees from central Europe and the Near East. It was easy to imagine what a burden that mass of people would have been for the international community had not Israel undertaken responsibility for their rehabilitation and resettlement.
>
> . . . some 200,000 refugees to Israel from Yemen, Libya and Iraq . . . had never required international assistance or protection. Moreover, under the Israeli repatriation law, every Jew automatically became a citizen of Israel from the moment of his arrival on Israeli Territory.[148]

In this statement, Robinson invoked, publicly and without reserve, the Zionist principle of 'Return' to Israel.[149] He asserted, furthermore, a perfect harmony between Zionist ideology and international policy; the latter imposed on the 'international community' a duty of alleviating the situation of refugees and remedying the unequal distribution of the 'burden' among its members. When Israel, by dint of its identity as the Jewish state and in fulfilment of its ideological vocation of 'Return', rehabilitated and resettled Jewish refugees, it was also promoting international policy. Israel, in this reading, unburdened the international community from responsibility for Jewish refugees.[150] Robinson even implied that the actions of the Jewish state went over and above its share of the collective burden: the National Home had been absorbing Jewish refugees even before Israel's establishment. The Jewish state, moreover, offered these Jewish refugees more than a transient right of asylum—which the Convention was never meant to provide refugees anyway—but a permanent solution: automatic citizenship. And if 'the Israeli repatriation law'—that is, the 'Return' principle—upheld international policy then international policy—that is, the Refugee Convention—necessarily affirmed Israel's character as the Jewish state and, as such, that it was the Jewish people's state

need of world Jewry for some international voicing of their plight and sufferings . . . We cannot neglect the Diaspora': Robinson to Eytan, 29 June 1948, FM-74/3, ISA.

[148] Conference of Plenipotentiaries on the Status of Refugees and Stateless Persons: Summary Record of the Twenty-Second Meeting, UN Doc. A/CONF.2/SR.22 (1951).

[149] Ch 6.

[150] More on this argument below.

of asylum. The Refugee Convention, for Robinson, validated the Zionist principle of 'Return' and 'Israel's policy of the in-gathering of exiles'.[151]

And yet, Robinson's own adherence to what he had preached on the conference floor was not wholehearted. His reports to the MFA betrayed some persisting ambivalence on Israel's precise role with regard to Jewish refugees and Diaspora Jewry. Early in his work on the Refugee Convention he had asserted—or, perhaps, acknowledged—that Israel's responsibility for improving the legal status of Jewish refugees was 'qualified by our policy of in-gathering of exile and encouragement of immigration to Israel'.[152] In consequence, as he informed his Israeli radio audience, the task of making 'regular' the status of Jewish refugees and stateless persons had lost some of its import because 'the doors of the country are open to all refugees; Israeli nationality, at least potentially, is acquired easily through *Aliya*'.[153] Ideology and the policy expressing it demanded that Jewish refugees 'Return' to the now-sovereign Jewish homeland. Even before Israel's establishment, Robinson had invested time and effort in defending this proposition during the UN debate on the future of Palestine.[154]

At the same time, Robinson's Diaspora sensibilities, dating back to his days at the Institute of Jewish Affairs ('IJA'), dictated that other solutions to Jewish refugeehood were not excluded, even if immigration to Israel now finally became, practically and ideologically, the preferred solution.[155] Even now, Palestine-turned-Israel was not, for Robinson, the only solution for Jewish refugeehood. Robinson's 'legal title' formula, we saw, was meant to reconcile these conflicting imperatives and resolve his own dilemma. It was also meant, however, to impress upon his MFA colleagues, disinterested in the Refugee Convention, the need to include Jewish concerns in Israel's foreign policy calculus—if need be, by highlighting the reputational benefits involved.[156] The formula was meant to persuade: hence his insistence that such legal title, and the treaty right of intervention it encapsulated, were entitlements that the Jewish state *could* exercise, not an absolute duty it was compelled to discharge.[157] The 'legal title' formula, however, failed to impress his counterparts: he was forced, time and again, to repeat this formula. His MFA colleagues

[151] Robinson to IOD, Second Interim Report of the *Ad Hoc* Committee on Statelessness and Related Problems, 30 January 1950, FM–2010/13 ISA ('Israel's policy of the in-gathering of exiles'); that policy is discussed in ch 6.

[152] Robinson to IOD, First Interim Report, 23 January 1950 (n 87) discussed in ch 6; Robinson to IOD, Second Interim Report, 30 January 1950 (n 151).

[153] [Robinson], Broadcast, 17 February 1950 (n 139) discussed in ch 6.

[154] Robinson, Jewish Immigration to Palestine, the Charter of the United Nations, and the Constitution of the International Refugee Organization, 12 May 1947, FM–2268/14 and materials in 2268/13, ISA; Robinson to Gelber, 1 December 1946, WJC–C16/2 (World Jewish Congress Records, MS–361), American Jewish Archives ('AJA').

[155] Ch 6 discusses Robinson's position, as IJA's director, on Jewish immigration issues.

[156] Ch 6 discusses that formula and its function.

[157] ibid.

never responded to his exhortations on 'Jewish' concerns,[158] notwithstanding the increasing urgency with which he reiterated it.

It was, perhaps, this urgency that led Robinson to err. His final report on the 1951 Conference contained his recommendation in favour of 'ratification of this convention at an early stage'. In justification, he offered the 'legal title' formula. Rather than Israeli interests, it accentuated needs of the Diaspora and of Jewish refugees in a manner that radically diverged from the imperative of 'Return': 'only through this act', he wrote, 'will we acquire a legal title to help those Jewish refugees in Europe *who have not yet made their final decision*'.[159] While this language implied, perhaps, that finding refuge in the Jewish state was preferable to other decisions, it also betrayed that Robinson was still willing to admit the propriety of alternative refuge destinations. For him, 'Return' was an option available to Jewish refugees, not a duty compelling them to that form of practice of Zionism. They were free to make 'their final decision' whether or not to 'Return' to the Jewish homeland.

Robinson's colleagues did not record their thoughts on Robinson's choice of words or the ideological ambivalence it attested to. They did take exception, nonetheless, to his reasoning. Their aversion to the Refugee Convention was deeply rooted: for them, the Convention suffered from a fatal flaw. Reading the Convention against the tenets of Zionist ideology portrayed it, for them, as the anathema of cardinal Zionist principles. In the first place, ideology rendered the Refugee Convention, for Robinson's colleagues, *superfluous*. It *could* be read as an affirmation of Israel's role as the state of asylum of the Jewish people and a validation of the principle of 'Return'. Ideologically, however, neither the Jewish state's role as the state of Jewish refuge nor the principle of 'Return' required—or depended on—the blessing of external authority. Both inhered in and expressed the Zionist creed itself; they were, after 1948, necessary (ideo)logical consequences of Jewish sovereignty. Israel's 1950 Law of Return[160] proclaimed but did not constitute these tenets. Presenting the Bill to the *Knesset*, Prime Minister David Ben-Gurion described the proposed enactment as 'a foundation stone of the Jewish state, containing its *raison d'être* ... the Ingathering of Exiles'. The Prime Minister proceeded to assert that 'the state does not *grant* to Jews of the Diaspora the right to Return.—This right *preceded* the State of Israel and it was [that very right] that *constituted* the State'.[161]

Robinson's colleagues preferred giving effect to the Zionist creed over invoking international norms, even where the two could be read as pointing in the same direction. For them, the Refugee Convention was redundant *on ideological* grounds.

[158] Ch 6. Briefing notes prepared by Rosenne's office after ratification did not allude to Jewish concerns addressed by the Convention: Lador to Elitzur, 23 August 1954; Lador to Press Department, 25 August 1954, FM–1847/2, ISA.

[159] Emphasis added; Robinson to Director-General, Fourth and Final Report, 1 August 1951 (n 1).

[160] Law of Return—1950, 51 *Sefer HaHukim* (Laws) (5 July 1950) 159 (Hebrew) discussed in ch 6.

[161] Emphases added; *Divrei HaKnesset* (3 July 1950) 2036–7 (Hebrew).

This is why Rosenne reluctantly 'reached the conclusion that there is room to ratify the Convention *despite its little practical value for us*'.[162] Ben-Meir used similar language when concluding a few months earlier that it was not 'worthwhile' to ratify the Convention 'given ... the minuteness of its practical value to us'.[163] Silverstone, the Ministry of Interior's Legal Adviser, assumed that the Refugee Convention—'this international treaty'—'will have no real significance in Israel'.[164] Rosenne intimated to the UNHCR's Paul Weis that Israel was 'not very interested in ratifying his Convention as we have no need for it'.[165] When asked, in late 1952, about the prospect of Israeli accession to League of Nations treaties on refugees and stateless persons, Rosenne was disinclined. Some of these instruments came into existence in response to the plight of Jewish refugees. Accession would have signalled, at no cost, Israel's investment in the protection of refugees in general, and its interest in the position of Jewish refugees in particular. Rosenne, instead, turned to invoke ideology. 'Our radical solution', he wrote, 'negates the need for our accession'.[166] Later, in connection with the Refugee Convention, he argued that 'Israel offers that Jew[ish refugee] *a better remedy* in the form of Return'.[167] In practical terms, he was not wrong: Israeli law provided Jewish refugees with instant nationality, going far beyond the transient, surrogate protection promised by the Convention.[168] Rosenne, however, was asserting an article of faith, not proffering legal analysis.[169] It was the same article of faith that drove the preference of the particular over the universal—and of the self-reliant radical solution over the charity of the universal solution.[170] These preferences expressed pre-Herzlian Zionist sensibilities that had already been formulated in Leon Pinsker's 1882 *Autoemancipation!*[171]

[162] Emphasis added; Rosenne to Attorney-General, 25 June 1954 (n 65).

[163] Ben-Meir to Rosenne, 4 October 1953 (n 58).

[164] Silverstone to Rosenne, 17 August 1953 (n 57).

[165] Rosenne to Ben-Meir, 27 October 1953 (n 69).

[166] Rosenne to Justice Minister, 17 December 1952; Cohn to Rosenne, 28 December 1952, FM-1830/9, ISA.

[167] Emphasis added; Rosenne to Attorney-General, 25 June 1954 (n 65). Similarly, when Rosenne met Jacque Vernant, author of *The Refugee in the Post-War World* (Yale University Press 1953), the conversation 'revolved mainly around the problems of Israeli citizenship: I explained the ideological notions of the Law of Return and of nationality by Return, matters that fascinated him in their originality and boldness': Rosenne Journal, 18 April 1953 (n 69).

[168] James C Hathaway and Michelle Foster, *The Law of Refugee Status* (CUP 2014).

[169] The same ideological position informs an earlier Rosenne observation: '*so far as Israel is concerned*, interest in the refugee problem at large is limited, the particular Jewish aspects of the refugee problem having almost disappeared in recent years': emphasis added; Rosenne to Eytan, 7 December 1951 (n 27). What made the 'Jewish aspects of the refugee problem' disappear was not numerical reduction but the institution of the 'Return' solution upon Israel's establishment.

[170] Elsewhere, Sharett referred to the 'paper guarantees' of international instruments: Moshe Sharett, *At the Threshold of Statehood: 1946–1949* (Am Oved 1958) 161 (Hebrew); SCOR, Meetings (1948) (27 February 1948) 347.

[171] Ch 1. In what became a canonical Zionist text, Pinsker critiqued the limits of legal emancipation and advocated instead Jewish self-emancipation as an 'act of national self-help'. Calling for a 'radical change in our position', he warned that it 'cannot be brought about by the civil emancipation of the Jews in this or that state, but only by the auto-emancipation of the Jewish people as a nation, the foundation of a colonial community belonging to the Jews, which is some day to become our inalienable home,

Ideology, however, rendered the Refugee Convention not merely superfluous. The Convention *could* be read as universal recognition of the principle of 'Return' and of Israel's 'historic mission'[172] 'as a country of the ingathering of the exiles of the Jewish people'.[173] This was, essentially, Robinson's reading. His colleagues, however, also read in the Refugee Convention propositions that threatened to subvert the Jewish state's very '*raison d'être*'.[174] Jewish sovereignty, in Zionist reading, was meant to remedy and bring to an end the Jewish Diasporic condition; it was to provide a permanent political solution not only to the plight of individual Jewish refugees but to Jewish statelessness itself—the essence of the non-sovereign condition.[175] The establishment of the Jewish state, as Ben-Gurion wrote in 1952, meant precisely that Jews would no longer require the protection of 'a "Nansen" passport';[176] these League of Nations travel documents may have helped interwar individual Jewish refugees, yet at the same time attested to their inferior, non-sovereign political position.[177] The Jewish state represented an end to Jewish statelessness and refugeehood;[178] it made Jews, Ben-Gurion wrote, in 'our own State ... citizens of the world of full and equal status'.[179] International protection was a marker of deficient, inferior, non-sovereign status; Israel's establishment obviated Jewish recourse to such international protection. All this was captured by a single paragraph of Israel's Declaration of Independence that proclaimed Jewish statelessness and Jewish sovereignty mutually exclusive:

> The recent holocaust, which consumed millions of Jews in Europe, provided fresh and unmistakable proof of the necessity of solving the problem of the *homelessness and lack of independence* of the Jewish people by re-establishing the Jewish State which would fling open the gates of the fatherland to every Jew and *would endow the Jewish people with equality of status within the family of nations.*[180]

With Israel's establishment, *Aliyah*—immigration to Israel—was consecrated as the *only* solution to the Jewish refugee problem.[181] This position also drew on

our fatherland'. Aubrey S Eban (ed), *Auto-Emancipation by Leo Pinsker* (Federation of Zionist Youth 1939) 40.

[172] Sharett to Secretary-General, 18 December 1950, FM–2010/13, ISA.
[173] Sharett, *Divrei HaKnesset* (15 June 1949) 718 (Hebrew).
[174] *Divrei HaKnesset* (3 July 1950) (n 161).
[175] Ch 6.
[176] David Ben-Gurion, 'Israel Among the Nations' in State of Israel, *Government Yearbook* (1952) 1, 44.
[177] Officially known as 'Stateless Persons Passports', they were issued to stateless refugees between 1922 and 1938 by the League of Nations High Commissioner for Refugees Fridtjof Nansen.
[178] Efraim Inbar, 'Jews, Jewishness and Israel's Foreign Policy' (1990) 2 Jewish Pol Stud Rev 165.
[179] Ben-Gurion (n 176) 44.
[180] Emphases added; Declaration of the Establishment of the State of Israel (14 May 1948) in (1948) 1 Jewish YB Intl L xii, xiii.
[181] Inbar (n 178) 169 ('Israel has been obviously interested in Jewish immigration (aliyah) from all possible sources ... but they were expected to be on their way to Israel').

prior political experience. It was the extension of the *Yishuv*'s post-war demand, itself rooted in 'ideological attitude', to have all Holocaust survivors brought to *Eretz-Israel*.[182] The prospect that Holocaust survivors may be rehabilitated at their countries of origin 'was conceived not only as a possibility that must be rejected outright, vehemently and blatantly, but also as a real nightmare'; equally detestable was the possibility that they immigrate elsewhere: 'The main goal of the Zionist strategy toward [Holocaust survivors] was to cause that [they] come to Eretz-Israel alone.' Accordingly, 'efforts to protect Jewish rights in the Diaspora' were seen as a contradiction of the Zionist project.[183] Only a Jewish state, so went the argument, could resolve in totality the problem of Jewish displacement after the Holocaust.[184] Advocating the rehabilitation of Jewish life in their countries of origin 'was perceived as a non-Zionist position that had to be fought vigorously'. Rehabilitation in Europe, for Ben-Gurion, was no more than a 'false solution'.[185] After independence, ideology and experience converged to cause the Jewish state to perceive itself as the only appropriate solution to the problem of Jewish refugees, the only legitimate place of their asylum.[186] Israel's foreign policy gave frequent voice to this self-perception.[187]

Robinson's error was to seek ratification of the Refugee Convention in order 'to help those Jewish refugees in Europe *who have not yet made their final decision*'.[188] His choice of words unwittingly drew attention to the ideological flaw of the Refugee Convention. How could Jews be considered refugees if they forever have an available asylum in the form of 'Return' to Israel? And, more importantly, how could the establishment of the Jewish state as the permanent place of refuge for Jews be justified if Jewish refugees were at liberty to go elsewhere and require the protection of international law? And yet, if they sought refuge in the state of asylum of the Jewish people, how could they be considered refugees at all? This was

[182] Dalia Ofer, 'Immigration and Aliyah: New Aspects of Jewish Policy' (1995) 75 Cathedra 142, 145 (Hebrew).

[183] Yechiam Weitz, 'From Holocaust to Rebirth: The D.P. Question in Zionist Policy' (1990) 55 Cathedra 162, 168, 171 (Hebrew).

[184] Walter Eytan, *The First Ten Years: Diplomatic History of Israel* (Simon and Schuster 1958) 132 ('The Zionist movement drew some of its postwar strength from the world's readiness to help the Jewish D.P.s in the concentration camps, for whose future it was able to formulate a constructive solution the establishment of a Jewish state').

[185] Weitz (n 183) 166.

[186] Daniel J Elazar, 'The "Noshrim": Jewish Emigres from the Soviet Union Who Avoid Israel' (1978) 16(2) Tefutsot Israel 5, 7 ('the Zionist position, becoming the norm after 1948, that with the exception of extraordinary cases Jews who seek new homes with the assistance of world Jewry ought to be settled in Israel alone').

[187] Eytan (n 184) 132; Anon., Reasons for Israel's Possible Inclusion as Member of the Advisory Board of the High Commissioner, 7 August 1951, FM-1988/5. In 1949, when Arab states criticised IRO for assisting the relocation of Jewish displaced persons to Israel, one MFA representative to the GA's Third Committee retorted that 'the only way of settling the survivors of the Hitlerite extermination is moving them to the very place they wanted and where they were wanted—the same place that was … meant to be, by accord of organised mankind, the place of the Jewish National Home': Katzanelson, Jewish and Arab Refugees, 12 November 1949, FM-2015/7, ISA.

[188] Emphasis added; Robinson to Director-General, Fourth and Final Report, 1 August 1951 (n 1).

the source of Rosenne, Ben-Meir, and Silverstone's hostility to the Convention. In their reading, Jews no longer were or could be stateless after 1948; nor could they properly be considered 'refugees'. For Israel's legal bureaucracy, the possibility that Jews may be considered refugees in the Jewish state was an (ideo)logical fallacy.[189] Though he identified no *legal* problem with that scenario, Silverstone protested that

> this possibility, that a Jewish person who immigrated here will be considered a refugee in the state of Israel *contradicts the whole idea of Return*. In my . . . opinion, the State of Israel must not recognize this possibility, *from a principled viewpoint*, when joining the Convention.[190]

Robinson's assumption that Jews may require international protection and seek refuge elsewhere—and his suggestion that it was the task of the Jewish state to ensure they could do so—were equally fallacious. They were, furthermore, subversive. Before and during the interwar period, one could profess Zionism yet remain in the Diaspora. One could even invest, as a Zionist, in improving the conditions of Jews in the Diaspora. In parallel, however, more Palestinocentric readings of Zionism had argued that building the National Home must take precedence.[191] Their adherents considered that the proper *practice* of Zionist faith required one to immigrate—in Hebrew, 'ascend'—to Palestine.[192] Early in the twentieth century, Zionist thought may have become more inclusive and willing to accommodate Diaspora causes; the notion of the 'Negation of the Diaspora'—postulating that the Diasporic condition is the prime cause of Jewish political inferiority, not in any way its solution—was central enough to Zionist thought to persist notwithstanding pragmatic alignments and ideological adjustment.[193] The Jewish crisis of the 1930s brought that notion back to the fore.[194] The *Yishuv* could invoke it vis-à-vis both Diaspora Jews and the increasingly restrictive immigration policies of Palestine's

[189] Under the Convention, the acquisition of a new nationality terminated refugee status. Accordingly, the UNHCR considered Jewish refugees in Israel no longer within its mandate: Louise W Holborn, *Refugees, A Problem of Our Time: The Work of the United Nations High Commissioner for Refugees 1951–1972* (Scarecrow Press 1975) 807; Gordon to Robinson, 19 September 1949, FM-1830/8, ISA.

[190] Emphases added; Silverstone to Rosenne, 22 December 1953 (n 72). By contrast, the possibility that non-Jews would seek asylum in Israel, when contemplated, seemed simply like an oddity: correspondence in FM-1847/2, FM-1830/8, FM-1989/1, and G-5754/14, ISA.

[191] Ch 3 discusses Palestinocentrism: the view that *Yishuv*'s—and later Israel's—interests took precedence over any Diasporic Jewish interest.

[192] For appraisal of the ideological aspect of *Aliyah* in Zionist thought, consider eg Aviva Halamish, *A Dual Race Against Time: Zionist Immigration Policy in the 1930s* (Yad Ben-Zvi 2006) 9–14 (Hebrew).

[193] Eliezer Schweid, 'Rejection of the Diaspora in Zionist Thought: Two Approaches' in Jehuda Reinharz and Anita Shapira (eds), *Essential Papers on Zionism* (Cassell 1996) 133; Zeev Sternhell, *The Founding Myths of Israel: Nationalism, Socialism and the Making of the Jewish State* (Princeton UP 1998) 47–52. Chs 3, 5 note fluctuations in the idea of the 'Negation of the Diaspora'.

[194] On the Jewish Agency's Palestinocentric position during the Evian Conference, see Dan Diner, *Beyond the Conceivable: Studies on Germany, Nazism, and the Holocaust* (University of California Press 2000) 91–2.

mandatory government. The Holocaust, perceived as a confirmation of Zionism's catastrophic prediction on the future of Jews in Europe, furnished the notion of the Negation of the Diaspora with a terrible validation. Israel's establishment—Zionism's ultimate triumph over competing ideological prescriptions for Jewish survival in the modern world—only produced a more radical and more forcefully argued opposition to investment in the Diaspora. This doctrine now insisted, as a matter of state ideology, that Jews were under an obligation to immigrate to Israel.

Legally and politically, Israel could only offer Diaspora Jews a right of 'Return'. The limits of sovereignty precluded the Jewish state from imposing any legal duty, let alone its nationality, on the nationals of other states.[195] And even if Israel could boast sovereign status and primacy, it still was in crucial need of the political and financial support of Jewish Diaspora communities, especially in the US. In the aftermath of the Holocaust, powerful Western Jewish constituencies that hitherto insisted that Jews were individuals, not a nation, and that civil and political emancipation in the Diaspora was the key to Jewish survival, found it no longer tenable to oppose Zionism and the establishment of a Jewish state. Shifting from an anti-Zionist to a non-Zionist stance, nonetheless, did not dispel the apprehensions of organizations such as the American Jewish Committee ('AJC') that the Jewish state's establishment might call their national allegiance into question or otherwise undermine their equality and political position in American public life. Openly calling on American Jews to immigrate to Israel, or even implying that they were under an obligation to do so, was bound to lead—as it did—to open conflict between the Jewish state and the AJC.[196] Yet the 'Negation of the Diaspora' was so deeply embedded in Israel's foundational ideology that Jews who elected to remain in the Diaspora despite having the option of becoming sovereign Jews were deemed to suffer from a deficiency. They remained, that is, 'Diasporic': 'old Jews' that continued to suffer and embody the ailments of the Diaspora.[197]

Robinson's efforts to secure 'legal title' to help Jewish refugees whether or not they intended to immigrate to Israel not only placed him in the position of a one-man minority within Israel's foreign service;[198] they also marked his ideological

[195] Presenting the Law of Return to the *Knesset*, Ben-Gurion acknowledged: 'The State of Israel has no dominion but over those residing in it, Jews in the Diaspora, citizens of their country, who want to stay there—they have no legal and civic nexus to the State of Israel and the State of Israel does not represent them in any legal sense': *Divrei HaKnesset* (3 July 1950) (n 161) 2035.

[196] As well as other, even Zionist, Jewish organizations: Zvi Ganin, 'The Blaustein Ben-Gurion Understanding of 1950' (2000) 15 Michael: On the History of the Jews in the Diaspora 29; Charles S Liebman, 'Diaspora Influence on Israel: The Ben-Gurion-Blaustein "Exchange" and Its Aftermath' (1974) 36 Jewish Soc Stud 271. Other factors restrained Israel from asserting this doctrine vis-à-vis Soviet bloc countries: Inbar (n 178).

[197] Anita Shapira, *New Jews Old Jews* (Am Oved 1997) (Hebrew); Daniel Boyarin, 'The Colonial Drag: Zionism, Gender and Mimicry' in Fawzia Afzal-Khan and Kalpana Seshadri-Crooks (eds), *The Pre-Occupation of Post-Colonial Studies* (Duke UP 2000) 234; Amnon Raz-Krakotzkin, 'Exile Within Sovereignty: Toward a Critique of the Negation of Exile in Israeli Culture' (1994) 4 Theory and Criticism 25, and 5 Theory and Criticism 113 (Hebrew).

[198] Outside government circles, a few others shared Robinson's perspective. A Jewish Agency representative—another veteran of Jewish immigration causes—wrote to tell him that 'from a Jewish

deviation. Jewish sovereignty, ideologically read, rendered anachronistic his goal of improving the legal status of Jewish refugees and stateless persons and his vision of Israel as the state of protection of Jewish refugees. That role had already been rejected, on ideological grounds, by the Jewish Agency well before Israel's establishment. That rejection was a direct consequence of Zionism's focus on Palestine. On the occasion of the nineteenth Zionist Congress convened in Lucerne in 1935, Moshe Shertok—later Sharett—then the Director of the Jewish Agency's Political Department, refused to assume the 'burden' of protecting the Jewish Diaspora:

> The Executive of the [Jewish] Agency cannot *burden itself with the role of protecting Jewish minorities the world over*; ... this is a Zionist Congress, this is a Zionist Organisation, that chooses a Zionist Executive; and the Zionist Executive is an institution that prepares and focuses the energies of the Jewish people towards the building of *Eretz Israel*, towards the creation of a large, free *Yishuv* in *Eretz Israel*... Zionism says: the solution is *Eretz Israel*, and the method is actions and measures for *Eretz Israel* (Emphases in original).[199]

Even Robinson's attempt to reconcile Diaspora concerns and Israeli interests was anachronistic. His campaign gave voice to his Diasporic, pre-sovereign sensibilities; it therefore, necessarily, appeared as a remnant of old, Diasporic Jewish diplomacy that attested to Jewish political inferiority, dependence, and subordination.[200] His willingness to entertain the liberty of Jewish refugees to choose their immigration destinations subverted Israel's immigration policy and the ideological imperative underpinning it. His very suggestion that Jews may, in the present or *future*,[201] again require international protection constituted no less than a heresy. Like the Refugee Convention, it cast a doubt over the future of the project of Jewish sovereignty and so undermined Zionism's achievement.[202] Robinson's ideological deviation may have been tolerated—such was his value to Israel's early

point of view [it] is my conviction that the creation of the State of Israel does not mean a complete solution of the Jewish refugee problem... These Jewish refugees will be in need of help and assistance until they will be able to leave Germany or Austria... for Israel or any other country of resettlement': Adler-Rudel to Robinson, 15 August 1951, FM-1988/5, ISA.

199 Quoted in Halamish (n 192) 439.

200 Mirjam Thulin, 'Shtadlanut' in Dan Diner (ed), *Enzyklopädie Jüdischer Geschichte und Kultur*, vol 5 (Metzler 2014) 472; Israel Bartal, 'From *Shtadlanut* to "Jewish Diplomacy"? 1756–1840–1881 (2016) 15 Simon Dubnow Institute YB 109; Carole Fink, *Defending the Rights of Others: The Great Powers, the Jews, and International Minority Protection 1878–1938* (CUP 2004).

201 Robinson, recall, acknowledged the small numbers of Jews requiring protection as refugees, yet sought it for 'those who have had this status up till now and in some new categories which may emerge in the future': Robinson, The Problem of Refugees in the Third Committee of the General Assembly, 19 December 1950, FM-2010/13, ISA.

202 In future years, the MFA would object to the US grant of asylum to Jews leaving the USSR: Inbar (n 178) 169. When, in the 1990s, Canada granted asylum to Russian Jews who first immigrated to Israel, Israel protested vehemently: 'Canada' (1996) 96 American Jewish Yearbook 196–7.

foreign policy apparatus—but it did leave his ideological credentials blemished. A few years later, he would come to pay the cost of deviation.[203]

9. Ambivalence and Exemption

Zionist ideology provided Rosenne and others in government service several reasons for disinterest in and hostility towards the Refugee Convention. Yet these sentiments were constrained by factors that precluded them from asserting their aversion openly, outside the sanctum of internal, official correspondence. Denying outright any 'general' Jewish interest in the status and treatment of refugees a mere few years after the Holocaust—vis-à-vis Robinson or the world at large—seemed beyond the power of the representatives of the Jewish state. Another constraint was presented by Israel's second order interests, reputation in particular. Only at the very moment these led Rosenne to finally and grudgingly recommend ratification did he also acknowledge, finally and grudgingly, the Jewish interest in the Convention. Until that moment, he had been consistently averse towards the Convention and the prospect of its ratification, denying its '*value for us*'.[204] Before, he had effectively overturned the MFA's Director-General August 1951 express instruction to obtain its ratification 'as soon as possible'[205] and had, time and again, delayed and obstructed the ratification process. Now, constrained to recommend ratification, he did more than acknowledge that there was, from a Jewish perspective, some value in the Convention. Having repeatedly ignored Robinson's allusions to Jewish moral considerations, and having rebuffed Paul Weis' suggestion that the Jewish state was under a 'moral duty' to ratify the Convention,[206] Rosenne grounded his decision to recommend ratification in the very same 'moral considerations'. 'The main reason' animating his recommendation to now ratify the Convention, he reported to Attorney-General Cohn, 'stems from moral considerations which we may not disparage'. Rosenne's *volte face* went further. He not only reproduced, as already noted, Robinson's formula assigning the Jewish state the role of assisting Jewish refugees;[207] he also moved to acknowledge, then *understate*, the tension between the Refugee Convention and 'the notion of Return'. This sophistry, ostensibly, qualified the principle of 'Return'; effectively, it reasserted the primacy of the 'radical solution' it offered Jewish refugees. It both attested to and dismissed the value of the Convention for Jewish refugees:

[203] See Epilogue.
[204] Rosenne to Attorney-General, 25 June 1954 (n 65).
[205] Eytan to Tekoah, [n.d.] (n 18).
[206] Rosenne to Ben-Meir, 27 October 1953 (n 69) discussed at text to n 70.
[207] 'There are still many Jews in the world requiring this protection, and if we will not assist them, who will?': Rosenne to Attorney-General, 25 June 1954 (n 65) discussed at text to n 86.

> I am of course aware of the question raised by Mr Silverstone ... concerning the relationship between the status of Jewish refugee in Israel on the one hand and the notion of Return on the other hand ... yet I do not consider this possibility of the existence of a Jewish refugee in Israel a matter that detracts from the value or import of the notion of Return, but an additional remedy, less radical, that aims at enhancing the status of the Jewish refugee as such. Even if Israel offers that Jew a better remedy in the form of 'Return', his stay here as a refugee should be permitted. I do not consider, therefore, that there is any principled contradiction and yet practically it is clear that a Jew who enters Israel specifically as a refugee not only will he not be treated as merely a refugee ... it is doubtful that in his own view there will be any special import to that status.[208]

Rosenne could have elected to follow Robinson's reasoning and simply consider the Refugee Convention as sanctioning the principle of 'Return' and according international recognition to Israel's character as the state of asylum for the Jewish people. This would have rendered his attempt to reconcile the tension between Zionist ideology and international norms far more simple. He chose, instead, to accentuate the separate, autonomous standing of the principle; in this case, rather than reconciling ideology and norm, Rosenne sought to entrench the primacy of the former over the latter.

In other settings, however, the argument that Israel's role as the Jewish people's state of asylum was internationally, and legally, sanctioned had its appeal and use. At such junctures, Rosenne did not hesitate to make that argument himself—and help turn it into a regular feature of the rhetorical arsenal of Israel's diplomatic service. Alongside hostility and aversion, Israel's attitude to the Refugee Convention—and the larger refugee regime—consisted also, at times, of instrumental interests that were linked but not limited to prestige and reputation. Ambivalence towards the Refugee Convention could, on occasion, be constructive.

It was Robinson who first demonstrated the utility of reading Israel's immigrating policies and the principle of 'Return' as rendering service to international policy. At the 1951 Conference, we saw, he asserted that by absorbing 'more than three-quarters of a million refugees', Israel had effectively alleviated a burden that otherwise would have fallen on 'the international community'. By assuming the 'responsibility for their rehabilitation and resettlement', he argued, the Jewish state obviated the need for them to rely on 'international assistance or protection'.[209]

This very logic allowed Israel's early diplomats to reaffirm the Jewish state's notional commitment to the global refugee regime by constructing Israel as a particular exception to it. Under this construction, the very existence of the Jewish

[208] Rosenne to Attorney-General, 25 June 1954 (n 65).
[209] A/CONF.2/SR.22 (1951) (n 148) quoted and discussed there.

state constituted the performance of Israel's part, as a member of the world community, in the solution of the global refugee problem.[210] By implication, Israel's very existence, its Law of Return, and its immigration policy represented *complete performance* of Israel's obligations under the Refugee Convention. Keeping 'open the gates of the fatherland to every Jew'—this commitment was proclaimed in Israel's Declaration of Independence[211]—to Jewish refugees past, present, and future exhausted Israel's international legal obligations. This was fidelity not to the law's letter, but to its higher spirit.

In practice, this construction served—rhetorically, practically, and politically—to justify various forms of exemption. It allowed Israeli diplomats to demonstrate that Israel alleviated the burden falling on the UN High Commissioner. On one occasion, during a debate at the GA Third Committee, Kahany sought to deflect the criticism of Arab representatives by asserting that Israel treated refugees in its territory far better than its neighbours:

> in our country, there are no refugees still under the mandate of the High Commissioner ... a Jewish refugee reaching the soil of Israel ceases to be a refugee, because my Government has no reason to extend, be it even for a moment, his status as a refugee.[212]

In the same vein, Kahany could even boast that the Jewish state succeeded 'in absorbing the Jewish refugees without any help whatsoever from the United Nations High Commissioner for Refugees'. Israel, he submitted, 'though wholly entitled to do so—has never appealed to the High Commissioner for assistance of any kind'.[213] A year later, upon his election to the Chairmanship of the UNHCR Advisory Board, Kahany reported that this diplomatic achievement was tantamount to UN confirmation of Israel's 'contribution to the solution of the refugees problem ... even if we have no refugees falling under the High Commissioner's authority and despite the fact that we make no financial contribution' to the UNHCR.[214] This helped Israel's perception and presence and, concretely, its ability to shape the debate on questions of Arab refugees.[215] Indeed, Israel's UN representatives could deploy

[210] Aspects of this reading can be found in Robinson to Eytan, *Ad Hoc* Committee on Statelessness and Related Problems: Final Report, 21 February 1950, FM–2010/13, ISA ('On one hand, we are an immigration country of a particular nature. In fact, we are not an immigration country but a repatriation country. On the other hand, we are not a haven for refugees in general. I certainly did not boast by our policy of unlimited immigration since it is obvious that this immigration is not of the same nature as the immigration to countries like USA and Canada').

[211] Declaration of the Establishment of the State of Israel, 14 May 1948 (n 180) xiii.

[212] Statement by Dr Menahem Kahany of Israel before the Third Committee, 19 October 1953, G–1234/3, ISA.

[213] ibid. While technically this statement may have been accurate, this was not the case in respect of IRO, the UNHCR predecessor, as noted below.

[214] Kahany to IOD Director, 8 December 1954, FM–2406/11, ISA.

[215] Ch 6 discusses Israel's position in this respect.

such arguments to retort to criticism by Arab diplomats by comparing Israel's progressive (Jewish) refugee policies to its neighbours' treatment of (Palestinian) refugees. Such arguments accentuated Israel's role in the solution of the *global* refugee problem over its role in the creation of the *particular* Palestinian refugee problem.[216]

Arguing that the particularity of Israel's identity and immigration policy alleviated the UNHCR's task had, additionally, an important financial aspect for the new state that had to institute a radical austerity regime to allow it to absorb mass Jewish immigration.[217] One Israeli envoy argued that IRO assistance in the transportation of Jewish refugees to Israel 'helped, more than it burdened, the funds of [IRO]'.[218] Later iterations of this argument transformed it into a plea of exemption from financial liabilities—a firm line of defence against demands for contribution to the international refugee regime. Kahany, having emphasized that Israel had 'never appealed' to 'any kind' of UNHCR assistance,[219] added that this was the very reason why

> Israel does not appear among the countries to which international refugee assistance is extended and this also explains and justifies the fact that Israel does not figure on the list of countries contributing to the emergency fund of the High Commissioner.[220]

UNHCR appeals for financial contributions were received by Israel as a signatory state, even before it ratified the Refugee Convention.[221] Asked for his opinion, Rosenne formulated the elements of what soon became a boilerplate response designed, in his words, to 'save a lot of trouble in the future':

> I think we need not contribute. Not because the goal is not respectable but because we are poor, absorb a large *Aliyah* of refugees etc. etc. All will understand our argument and there is no reason to be shy about it.[222]

Rosenne's advice, and formula, was fully endorsed by the MFA. Kahany was first told that 'we shall probably decide not to contribute on the grounds that we are in

[216] Gordon to Robinson, 2 August 1950, FM-2010/13 ISA ('we are interested in diverting attention from the specific problem of Arab refugees to the much larger question of refugees in general').
[217] Orit Rozin, *The Rise of the Individual in 1950s Israel: A Challenge to Collectivism* (Brandeis UP 2011).
[218] Katzanelson, Refugees, 12 November 1949 (n 187).
[219] Kahany Statement, 19 October 1953 (n 212) quoted there.
[220] ibid.
[221] UNHCR to Sharett, 18 February 1952, FM-1832/14; UNHCR to Sharett, 6 June 1952, FM-1988/5, ISA.
[222] Rosenne, handwritten note, [10 March 1952], FM-1832/14; Kahany to IOD, 7 June 1952, FM-19/15; Sharett to UNCHR, 4 May 1954, FM-1988/6, ISA.

any case spending millions on the absorption of refugees'.[223] A week later he received express instructions:

> We will be unable to contribute in cash to the Emergency fund . . . for reasons . . . such as . . . the tremendous burden already weighing upon us as a result of the immigration of the masses of refugees seeking a new life in Israel . . . This . . . must not however appear as a simple refusal, and we therefore ask you to emphasize that, *in fact, we are contributing continually and not inadequately by the tremendous undertaking of resettling and rehabilitating refugees* (Emphasis added).[224]

In time, a similar formula was communicated to the UNHCR: 'the task of absorbing hundreds of thousands of Jewish refugees in Israel' precluded an additional 'contribution to be made at present by the Government of Israel to the funds of Your Excellency's Office'.[225] When the UNHCR staff then requested to meet Kahany to discuss Israel's negative response, he did not rule out collaboration between Israel and the UNHCR, 'similar to those undertaken in former years with the help of the IRO', if action was required 'in favour of a certain group of Jewish refugees under the UNHCR mandate, who are fit and willing to emigrate to Israel'. But when it came to monetary contribution, Kahany

> repeatedly stated that Israel did and continues to make one of the relatively biggest contributions to the solution of the world problem of refugees by absorbing so great numbers of Jewish refugees. They all recognized our great contribution and let me understand that they do not expect from us more than a quite symbolic goodwill gesture.[226]

Two years later, Israel again refused to make a contribution to UNHCR funds. Again it was implied that its difficulties were only temporary. This time, however, it also argued it was absorbing 'Jewish and Arab refugees' alike:

> Since the creation of the State, Israel has absorbed hundred [sic] of thousands of Jewish and Arab refugees and has taken full responsibility for their resettlement which constitutes a heavy burden on the country's financial resources.
>
> Consequently, the Minister, though realizing the urgent necessity for finding a solution to the financial difficulties as far as the U.N.R.E.F. is concerned, sincerely

223 Kidron to Kahany, 13 March 1952, FM-19/13, ISA.

224 Tekoah to Kahany, 21 March 1952; Kahany to Tekoah, 17 April 1952, FM-19/14, ISA.

225 Kidron to UNCHR, 5 July 1952, FM-19/16; absorption of Jewish immigration 'requires the concentration of all the available resources of the country for that purpose': Kidron to UNCHR, 21 July 1952, FM-1988/5, ISA.

226 Kahany to IOD, 7 June 1952 (n 222).

> regrets that the Government of Israel is at present unable to respond to the High Commissioner's appeal for a contribution.[227]

Only considerations of diplomatic presence led the MFA in 1955 to relent. There was the prospect that Israel may not be re-elected to the UNHCR Advisory Board;[228] the MFA also received reports of a 'growing impression in UN circles that Israel is interested in that institution only inasmuch as it can milk it'.[229] The MFA now sought the funds, outside its regular budget, for a symbolic, one-off contribution.[230]

Other UNHCR requests for the assistance of specific groups of refugees were rejected on the same ground. Here, too, the absorption of Jewish refugees proved a useful shield. One request concerned a small number of remaining 'institutional', or 'hard core' cases long-stranded in Shanghai. The High Commissioner asked that Israel accept fourteen such individuals 'over and above those refugees to whom you are already generously giving asylum'.[231] The MFA replied that Israel had already received thousands of Shanghai refugees evacuated in 1949–1950 by IRO, many of whom were 'a permanent charge for welfare institutions'. The crux, however, was that the absorption of Jewish refugees in Israel precluded that of others: the list submitted by the High Commissioner did 'not appear to include persons whose hospitalization and acclimatization could be suitably effected in this country'. At the same time, Israel was attending to 'a continuous stream of immigrants coming to Israel, most of whom are obliged to leave their countries of present residence because of the particular conditions prevailing there'.[232] Israel's share of the refugee burden was limited to Jewish refugees.

Finally, the logic of exemption—implicit in Israel's role as the asylum of Jewish refugees—also underscored successful Israeli claims to compensation and indemnification for Israel's expenditure on the absorption of various categories of Jewish refugees. Eytan estimated that the Jewish Agency had received millions of dollars from IRO, the UNHCR's predecessor.[233] Israel's agreements with IRO were explicitly based on this reasoning: in 1949, for example, IRO agreed to indemnify Israel for the transport cost of 6,000 persons in 'recognition of the substantial contribution thus made by the Government of Israel to the solution of the international problem of refugees and displaced persons under' IRO's mandate.[234] On the

[227] Sharett to UNHCR, 4 May 1954 (n 222).

[228] IOD Director to Kahany, 1 April 1955; Kidron to IOD, 10 March 1955, FM–1988/9, ISA.

[229] ibid.

[230] Eytan to Loker, 21 March 1955; IOD to Kahany, 1 April 1955 (n 228).

[231] UNHCR to MFA, 31 May 1955, FM–1988/9, ISA.

[232] Cider to UNHCR, 26 June 1955, FM–1988/9; Doron to IOD, 11 March 1952, 28 February 1952, FM–1976/7; and documents in FM–1976/9, ISA.

[233] Eytan to Loker, 21 March 1955 (n 230). Israel's request for IRO's assistance emphasises the burden assumed by Israel in justification: Sharett to [IRO], 1 July 1949, FM–19/3, ISA.

[234] Agreement between the Government of Israel and the International Refugee Organization Concerning Permanent Provision in Israel for Institutional Care of Refugees, 28 October 1949, FM–1976/9; Eytan to Kingsley, 30 May 1950, FM–1988/4, ISA.

occasion of IRO's final session, Israel's representative added that the Jewish state's efforts in the absorption of six hundred and fifty thousand displaced persons from Europe placed it third among those states 'opening their doors to those homeless' and acknowledged that some of the costs of this 'burden' were defrayed by IRO.[235] Israel and the Jewish Agency, he wrote elsewhere, 'drew important material benefit from "IRO" funds'.[236]

What worked multilaterally had purchase, too, in bilateral relations. Israel's identity as the state of asylum for Jewish refugees from Nazi persecution supplied one basis of its reparations claims from the Federal Republic of Germany.[237] The preamble to the 1952 Luxembourg Agreement between Israel and West Germany accepted this claim—and its underlying rationale:

> WHEREAS the State of Israel has assumed the heavy burden of resettling so great a number of uprooted and destitute Jewish refugees from Germany and from territories formerly under German rule and has on this basis advanced a claim against the Federal Republic of Germany for global recompense for the cost of the integration of these refugees.[238]

Robinson, by dint of expertise acquired as the IJA director in the service of the World Jewish Congress, was the MFA lawyer tasked with drafting this Israeli-German agreement;[239] it is quite likely that he was responsible for inserting that formula into the 1952 agreement.

When the ruling Labour Party's Political Committee met to discuss the extremely controversial agreement, Sharett invited Robinson to attend. Israel's Foreign Minister took care to certify Robinson's expertise and trustworthiness—and that these trumped his faulty ideological credentials. 'Dr Jacob Robinson', he told senior Labour members, 'is our chief legal adviser in the matter of German reparations, and I invited him out of complete trust *even if he is not a member of our*

[235] Doron to IOD, 11 March 1952 (n 232) ('In spite of the tremendous efforts entailed in this project my Government has taken upon itself the added heavy burden of providing shelter for ten thousand "Hard core cases" of aged, sick, and handicapped [sic] Jewish refugees. This undertaking, who would form a constant liability to the state, could be carried out only through the generous help extended' by IRO).

[236] Doron to IOD, 28 February 1952 (n 232); other documents in this file and in FM-1976/9, mention the sums involved; see also FM-2458/15, ISA.

[237] Nana Sagi, *German Reparations: A History of the Negotiations* (Magnes 1986); Richard M Buxbaum, 'A Legal History of International Reparations' (2005) 23 Berkeley J Intl L 314.

[238] Agreement between the State of Israel and the Federal Republic of Germany (10 September 1952) (1953) 162 UNTS 205, 206.

[239] Nicholas Balabkins, *West German Reparations to Israel* (Rutgers UP 1971); Sagi (n 237); Nahum Goldmann, 'Introduction' in Nehemiah Robinson, *Ten Years of German Indemnification* (Conference on Jewish Material Claims Against Germany 1964) 7–11; Shabtai Rosenne, 'Jacob Robinson—In Memoriam' (1978) 8 Isr L Rev 287, 293–294. Jacob's brother Nehemiah, who also attended the Israel-German negotiations, had a cardinal role shaping IJA and WJC expertise on indemnification: Nehemiah Robinson, *Indemnification, Reparations: Jewish Aspects* (IJA 1944); Ronald W Zweig, *German Reparations and the Jewish World: A History of the Claims Conference* (Routledge 2014) 8.

party'.[240] The 1951 Refugee Convention, we saw, revealed Jacob Robinson's ideological deviation yet, at the same time, allowed Shabtai Rosenne to profess fidelity to a radical interpretation of Jewish sovereignty. As the Epilogue notes, it was the 1952 Reparation Agreement that would put Rosenne's own ideological credentials to the test, calling into question the sovereign transformation of Robinson's younger colleague.

[240] Emphasis added: Yaacov Sharett (ed), *Moshe Sharett and the German Reparations Controversy* (Moshe Sharett Heritage Society 2007) 712.

PART V
CREED

Epilogue
Revolutionaries, Torchbearers, and Imperfect Subjects
The Zionist Creed and the Test of Sovereignty

1. International Law, Ambivalence, and the Test of Creed

The future that the editors of the *Jewish Yearbook of International Law* would not prophesize in the spring of 1949, mere weeks before Israel's admission to the United Nations ('UN'), would be highly ambivalent. At the core of Robinson and Rosenne's reading of international law in the few years that followed the sovereign turn was a deep-seated ambivalence expressing sensibilities that were rooted in the period preceding Jewish sovereignty. Their attitude towards concrete post-war international law reforms was ambivalent because of, not despite, the Jewish aspect of each of these projects: the right of petition in the draft Human Rights Covenant, the 1948 Genocide Convention, and the 1951 Refugee Convention. In all three cases, these jurist-diplomats approached international law predominantly through the prism of ideology. That is, they tested international law through the prism of the creed of Jewish nationalism. Their vantage point on international law was determined by Zionism, its interpretation of the modern Jewish condition, and its prescriptions for resolving the Jewish Question.

Zionist ideology was the principal yardstick against which our protagonists tested international law on matters they deemed to involve some Jewish aspect. At times, ideology impelled their investment in international law and institutions or could, in the very least, furnish justifications for such investment when (secondary) interests required it. In most instances, however, ideology decreed disinterest, aversion, and hostility towards the right of petition and the human rights project at large, the Genocide Convention and its progenitor, and the Refugee Convention and the international refugee regime. The ideological sensibilities that led Robinson and Rosenne to invest in, reject, or grudgingly accept these post-war international law reforms predated the sovereign turn; the sovereign turn only rendered these sensibilities more radical. All sensibilities, in some way, drew on pre-sovereign Jewish objecthood and expressed newly acquired Jewish subjecthood. The terms of Israel's early engagement with international law thus embodied both continuity and change.

Jews, Sovereignty, and International Law. Rotem Giladi, Oxford University Press. © Rotem Giladi 2021.
DOI: 10.1093/oso/9780198857396.003.0010

Some of these sensibilities took the form of preoccupation with Jewish standing, status, and voice: that preoccupation had already been expressed in Leon Pinsker's 1882 *Auto-Emancipation*[1] and it underscored Theodor Herzl's struggle to resolve the conundrum of the Jewish national movement's legal incapacity to represent and entreat while excluded from the sovereign club of civilized states.[2] Such sensibilities were compounded, moreover, by Jewish representation politics—that is, by Zionism's need to contend with competing Jewish voices working to promote alternative visions of Jewish emancipation. Other sensibilities underlying Robinson and Rosenne's ideological reading of international law expressed foundational assumptions of the Zionist creed and its core doctrines. One was the Zionist negation of the Diasporic condition as the root cause of the modern Jewish predicament. Another, in consequence, was a principled prioritization of the needs and interests of the *Yishuv*, then Israel, over those of Diaspora communities—in a word, Palestinocentrism. A third, related, sensibility involved the very nature of Zionism's prescription for overcoming Jewish objecthood, achieving Jewish subjecthood, and protecting Jewish rights and existence: the establishment of a *majority* Jewish polity in Palestine open to all Jews. This prescription entailed resentment towards other, competing models of Jewish emancipation that challenged Zionism's reading of the modern Jewish condition, not merely the path it identified for overcoming it. Such resentment fed off disenchantment with Emancipation's promise to protect Jews as individual, apolitical subjects and international law's promise to protect Jews, its perennial others, as a minority—an inferior kind of subject, in reality an object. Often, such resentment and disenchantment were expressed in terms of an ethos of Jewish national self-reliance drawing, again, on Pinsker's *Auto-Emancipation*.

These ideological sensibilities drove both Zionist disengagement from and engagement with international law. Engagement, disengagement, and re-engagement underscored Zionist, and early Israeli, ambivalence towards international law. Engagement was grounded in ideology no less than disengagement: the Zionist creed, after 1949, preserved more than an echo of the progressive, even utopian aspects of Herzlian thought that had claimed that Jewish subjecthood and inclusion in the family of nations would not only remedy the Jewish condition but also mend the world itself—that the Jewish state would have, that is, a universal vocation.[3]

The Zionist creed expressed by Robinson and Rosenne in their reading of the right of petition, the Genocide Convention, and the Refugee Convention was not static. The overlapping, mutually reinforcing, and at times conflicting sensibilities

[1] Leon Pinsker, *Autoemancipation!: Mahnruf an seine Stammesgenossen von einem russischen Juden* (W Issleib 1882); ch 1.
[2] ibid.
[3] ibid.

it encompassed inhered in Zionist ideology, were produced by Zionism's contestation with competing models of Jewish emancipation, and were confirmed by the political experience of the Zionist movement. The sources of ambivalence were shaped and reshaped by the force of events in Europe and Palestine; some of these shifts in Zionism's *weltanschauung* are recorded in this book in some detail; often, they left palpable marks on the ideology, lives, and careers of our two protagonists. Israel's establishment and its UN admission, in turn, produced—or reverted to—a radical version of Zionism that became the Jewish state's foundational ideology. More often than not, the sensibilities comprising the Zionist creed in the age of Jewish sovereignty qualified Israel's international law engagement in Jewish matters; disinterest, aversion, and hostility were the dominant products of the ideological test Robinson and Rosenne applied in their reading of the right of petition, the Genocide Convention, or the Refugee Convention. A measure of investment in these international law reforms, however, persisted: often, as noted, such investment was the product of a calculus of second-order interests, such as diplomatic presence and prestige; nonetheless, that investment was also grounded in the Zionist creed.

These findings, in turn, raise a number of questions. One concerns my choice to focus on two jurist-diplomats. Was Robinson and Rosenne's attitude to international law representative? To what extent did their ambivalence reflect that of their peers and superiors at Israel's Ministry of Foreign Affairs ('MFA')—or that of other departments in the executive and other branches of government?

2. Revolutionaries, Torchbearers: Envoys and Ideology

One answer is that together—even when they diverged on how to read, ideologically, the Refugee Convention[4]—Robinson and Rosenne were the engines of Israel's early international law diplomacy. Their reading of international law had determined, to a large extent, Israel's attitude towards and actual practice on the right of petition, the Genocide Convention, and the Refugee Convention. Other forces no doubt also shaped that practice: at times, Robinson and Rosenne required the approval of political superiors in New York, Tel Aviv, and Jerusalem. At others, foreign policy preferences or constitutional constraints limited the purchase of their influence. Such was the case with Eban's insistence to have the Genocide Convention signed, then ratified, in order to earn the new UN member diplomatic prestige.[5] In another instance, it was the *Knesset*'s involvement in the ratification of that instrument, to Rosenne's chagrin.[6] Such constraints, nonetheless, only served

[4] Chs 6–7.
[5] Ch 4.
[6] ibid.

to highlight Robinson and Rosenne's ambivalence and the conflicting ideological impulses underlying Israel's foreign policy practice. They also help measure our protagonists' fealty to ideological creed: when electing or compelled, by dint of second-order interests, to affect or demonstrate Israel's international law investment, our protagonists would record their ideological reserve—and, at the same time, proceed to ground investment in ideological terms. It is that investment in reading international law through the lens of Zionist ideology that renders their attitude expressive and illustrative; and so, representative.

This bears emphasis: Robinson and Rosenne did not limit their service to the foreign policy of the Jewish state to legal or political advice. They elected to serve as torchbearers of the Zionist creed; their self-appointed task was to affect Jewish subjecthood—to interpret, that is, Jewish sovereignty in light of the demands of the Zionist creed. In that, they sought to give effect to a now-hegemonic set of sensibilities expounded by their political masters. That creed demanded their own adherence—but also that of their peers in the MFA and outside it. They gave voice to shared sensibilities about the contents and contours of a 'radical solution' to the problem of Jewish objecthood: voicelessness, protection, and statelessness. Their peers shared faith in that 'radical solution'. Theirs was a generation of revolutionaries who had witnessed and took part in the sovereign turn in Jewish history: the radical transformation—'a total, fundamental revolution'[7]—of Jews from mere 'objects' into a 'subject' of international law.

Yet more than revolutionaries, our two protagonists elected to act as the of bearers of the torch of ideology. More than any of their peers, they had made a consistent and explicit recourse to the Zionist creed when weighing on Israel's foreign policy choices; on most occasions, their ideological reading of international law had been the most radical. And while their investment in elaborate interpretations of the demands of the sovereign turn stands out, they were not alone reading international law through the prism of the Zionist creed. Others, we saw, approached the human rights project, the Genocide Convention, or the Refugee Convention through the prism of Zionism's 'radical solution'—and with the same ambivalence. Why the members of the legal profession—and these two jurist-diplomats in particular—would assume the role of ideological guardians of creed is a question I consider below. For present purposes, it suffices that what made their international law outlook representative is their self-appointed role as torchbearers seeking to give voice to shared, foundational sensibilities. Their ambivalent reading of international law became so central to Israel's approach to international law precisely because it expressed shared sensibilities.

[7] In the words of one reviewer of the *Jewish Yearbook of International Law*, a Ministry of Justice official: Uri Yadin, 'The Jewish Question in the Eyes of International Law' (1949) 7 BeTerem: A Quarterly for Policy, Social Affairs and Critique 63 (Hebrew).

3. Terms of Engagement: Zionism, Ambivalence, and Cosmopolitanism

Another question concerns this book's *conceptual* point of departure: the ways we think of the meeting point between international law and Jewish history and of the terms of Jewish engagement with international law.[8] Here, the record presented in the preceding chapters reveals that the terms of Jewish *national* engagements with international law following, but also prior to, the sovereign turn not only merit further study but also require a re-evaluation of the story of Jews and the international legal discipline. Future research, I hope, will find of value the conceptual framework devised in this book for approaching the study of Jewish engagements with international law[9] and the findings to which it points: legal objecthood as a key concept for the recovery of the terms of Zionist—and other Jewish national—engagements with international law, and Jewish representation politics and the contestation over the Jewish voice as a key arena where these terms might be usefully examined.

In regard to the need to re-evaluate the story of Jews and international law, it is patent that the nature, provenance, and prevalence of the ambivalence displayed by Robinson and Rosenne all furnish a corrective to a common reading of Jewish international law scholars and practitioners as agents of cosmopolitanism invested in some vision of universal redemption.[10] These factors also, at the same time, militate against James Loeffler's recent critique of that reading. Seeking to reclaim the national investment of Jewish international law protagonists, Loeffler argues that rather than tensions between a cosmopolitan and a particularist *weltanschauung*, the lives and works of Jewish international lawyers demonstrate a synthesis of visions, one universal and the other defined by Jewish particularism. Loeffler's groundbreaking study argues, accordingly, that we should think of Jewish historical agents in the field of human rights or international law as '*rooted* cosmopolitans, braiding together the ethnos and ethical in a distinctively Jewish model of universalism'.[11] Yet rather than synthesis and coherence of values and vantage points, the evidence on how Robinson—one of Loeffler's protagonists—and Rosenne approached the right of petition, the Genocide Convention, or the Refugee Convention tells that the dominant vantage point from which they surveyed international law was the particular, not the universal. That is, they read international law as Jews driven by the Jewish Question *and guided by the prescriptions of its national solution* rather than as advocates of any world vision—liberal, 'distinctively-Jewish', or otherwise. Even when invested in ostensibly cosmopolitan projects—consider Robinson's

[8] Ch 1.

[9] ibid.

[10] For that reading see the Introduction and chs 1–3.

[11] Emphasis in original; James Loeffler, *Rooted Cosmopolitans: Jews and Human Rights in the Twentieth Century* (Yale UP 2018) xv.

involvement in the drafting of the Refugee Convention[12]—what drove their investment and defined their perspective was the Jewish particular.[13] Even where he departed from a narrow reading of what the principle of 'Return' required, Robinson was driven by a broader reading of Jewish interests, not any liberal vision of overcoming global refugeehood and statelessness. His and Rosenne's cosmos was defined and delimited by the Jewish particular. Their interest—often, disinterest—in post-war legislative projects concerned the respective 'Jewish aspect' of such projects far more than any 'general' impact or liberal effect these would have on world order or on the position of the individual, in the abstract, under international law. For them, eschewing the promise of the human rights project, likewise, went beyond its association with the assimilationist solution to the Jewish Question; it was required by the base assumptions and fundamental doctrines of Zionism. Their vehement reaction to Lauterpacht's Jerusalem advocacy for the right of petition attests just how profound was their rejection of cosmopolitanism and how embedded it was in their *national* Jewish reading of human rights.[14]

Rather than synthesis entwining the particular with the universal, the terms on which our protagonists engaged international law before and after 1949 were dominated by a principled, ideological scepticism of the international, hostility towards the universal, and rejection of the cosmopolitan. The sensibilities these attitudes expressed, after all, inhered in the Zionist ideology, stemmed from Zionism's contestation with competing models of Jewish emancipation, and were entrenched by the political experience of the Zionist movement. They were embedded, likewise, in Robinson and Rosenne's own professional experience; we may recall, as patent evidence, Rowson-Rosenne's 1947 assertion of the futility of Jewish—that is, Zionist—reliance on international law.[15] A few years earlier, discussing post-war Jewish reconstruction, he had revealed his misgivings towards '[i]nternationalism'; it was 'a red herring to distract the mind from the real issues' facing Jews. Being citizens of the world, he averred, 'must not become an excuse for our failing in our duty to our own kind and kin'. Internationalism was a luxury that the Jewish people could not afford.[16] Robinson's career, dotted with disenchantment with the international, led him to decry the need to camouflage Jewish interests and demands with the cloak of universal vernacular. His scathing critique of the cosmopolitan vision and language of the 1944 'Declaration on Human Rights' issued by the

[12] cf the suggestion that Robinson's work on the Refugee Convention represents Israel's investment in legal universalism: Gilad Ben-Nun, 'The Israeli Roots of Article 3 and Article 6 of the 1951 Refugee Convention' (2014) 27 J of Refugee Stud 101. The evidence cited in chs 6–7 challenges such readings.

[13] Chs 6–7.

[14] Chs 2–3.

[15] Shabtai Rowson, 'International Law and the Jewish People' (1947) 11 Tarbut 4 (Hebrew) discussed in chs 3, 5; Rotem Giladi, 'Shabtai Rosenne: The Transformation of Sefton Rowson' in James Loeffler and Moria Paz (eds), *The Law of Strangers: Jewish Lawyers and International Law in the Twentieth Century* (CUP 2019) 221, 241–4.

[16] [Sefton Rowson], Youth and Reconstruction: Speech, 18 October 1943, Shabtai Rosenne Papers ('Rosenne Papers') discussed in Giladi (n 15) 241.

assimilationist American Jewish Committee gave voice to Zionist sensibilities: '[o] nce more', he wrote, 'an attempt is being made to disguise Jewish demands under the mask of general ones. This is not only a self-deception but also shows a lack of dignity and self-respect'.[17] Jewish political realism demanded a particularist, not cosmopolitan, investment; misgivings with the cosmopolitan and aversion towards international law were not born with Jewish sovereignty; they have been, rather, constitutive aspects of the struggle to obtain it.

That particularistic struggle for Jewish national subjecthood nonetheless required, as a pragmatic matter, investment in the international sphere and engagement with the universal. Such engagement was, likewise, grounded in how Zionism had approached, all along, the Jewish Question and in the means and ends it prescribed for its solution.[18] The Zionist creed, therefore, furnished Rosenne and Robinson with various ideological justifications for engagement with the universal. The universal vocation of the Jewish state, asserted by Zionism long before its establishment, meant that Jewish sovereignty now required, ideologically, the Jewish state's 'active responsibility'[19] in the form of international law investment, support for the UN's 'lofty, exalted goals',[20] contribution to its work, and bolstering its 'campaign for world peace'.[21] Rosenne's allusions to the universal in the course of his appearance at the International Court of Justice ('ICJ') in the Reservations case,[22] or Robinson's human rights work, undoubtedly were meant to promote concrete Israeli interests; that these investments in the universal were couched in ideological terms does not attest to cosmopolitanism: these were the terms of a national ideology. Even the highly ambivalent investment Rosenne and Robinson made in cosmopolitan projects was, in the final analysis, particularistic. Their involvement in such projects does not render their actions or worldviews, before or after 1949, cosmopolitan.

If, today, Israel's early diplomatic practice gives the impression of cosmopolitan investment at the origin, that impression may be largely rooted in the present—a point to which I will return shortly. That impression, however, also stems from the foundational period of Israel's legal diplomacy: it was deliberately cultivated. At diplomatic arenas, Rosenne, Robinson, and their peers did not hesitate to claim credit, on behalf of the Jewish state, for the Genocide Convention's making—notwithstanding their disinterest in and hostility towards it, and even though

[17] Robinson, Memorandum, 30 October 1944, WJC–B86/2, World Jewish Congress Records, MS-361) American Jewish Archives ('AJA') discussed in Loeffler (n 11) 86.

[18] Ch 1.

[19] Speech to the General Assembly by Foreign Minister Sharett, 11 May 1949 in Meron Medzini (ed), *Israel's Foreign Relations: Selected Documents, 1947–1974* (MFA 1976) 119; GAOR, Plenary (11 May 1949) 332.

[20] Rosen, *Divrei HaKnesset* (Parliamentary Record) (26 December 1949) 313 (Hebrew) discussed in ch 4.

[21] Eytan to Sharett, 5 September 1950, FM–2015/5; Eytan to Sharett, 26 June 1950, FM–1820/6, Israel State Archive ('ISA') and examples discussed in ch 4.

[22] Ch 4.

sensibilities and preoccupations with the question of the Jewish voice led Rosenne, at The Hague, to discount the Jewish aspects of the Convention's paternity. Indeed, at the Court, Rosenne took care to present a universal reading of the Convention; this reading and the allusions his oral statement did make to the particular 'Jewish aspect' of the Convention[23] were, as he wrote to Robinson, exercises in 'public relations'.[24] Israel's diplomatic standing and prestige at the UN arena required the appropriation of Jewish investment in international law, cosmopolitan or otherwise.

The appropriation of the Jewish aspect, and paternity, of international law projects by the Jewish state's representatives was not limited to the case of the Genocide Convention: for all their censure of Zionist and non-Zionist non-sovereign Jewish voices, and for all their ideological aversion to the international law investments by Jewish individuals and organizations, Rosenne, Robinson, and their peers did not hesitate to display, to external audiences, what passed as Jewish cosmopolitan sensibilities when such display could support *some* foreign policy goal. The Jewish aspect of the right of petition, the Genocide Convention, and the Refugee Convention was the cause of disinterest and aversion but, at the same time, it could be invoked by Israel's diplomats to signify the Jewish state's cosmopolitan investment even where none existed.

The impression of such cosmopolitan investment on the part of the Jewish state was forged not merely *ad hoc*, whenever the need arose at The Hague, New York, or Geneva. Nor was its use limited to Rosenne's polemic with Lauterpacht over the right of petition,[25] to his assertion of sovereign standing and authoritative representation of Jewish interests at the World Court,[26] or to fending off calls on Israel to bear part of the burdens of the international refugee regime.[27] When the opportunity presented itself to produce an enduring impression of the Jewish state's investment in international law and institution, Rosenne seized it. His participation as the anonymous *rapporteur* of the Hebrew University 'Study Group' that produced a report on 'Israel and the United Nations'—and his success in forcing the MFA's rendering of Israel's diplomatic practice on the Group's academic members—ensured that the impression of Israel's cosmopolitan investment could boast scientific authority.[28]

The story of the report cannot be told here in full.[29] It was commissioned in 1952, by the Carnegie Endowment for International Peace, to look into public attitudes

[23] Chs 4–5.
[24] Rosenne to Robinson, 15 March 1951, FM–1832/3, ISA.
[25] Chs 2–3.
[26] Ch 4.
[27] Chs 6–7.
[28] Nathan Feinberg, *Israel and the United Nations: Report of a Study Group Set Up By the Hebrew University of Jerusalem* (Manhattan 1956).
[29] Rotem Giladi, 'At the Sovereign Turn: International Law at the Hebrew University Law Faculty Early Years' in Yfaat Weiss and Uzi Rebhun (eds), *The History of the Hebrew University in Jerusalem*, vol 5 (forthcoming Magnes 2021) (Hebrew).

towards the international organization with a view to a prospective revision of the UN Charter. Nathan Feinberg, now the former dean of the Law Faculty, chaired the 'Study Group' but Rosenne, as the *rapporteur*, drafted the different versions of the report on the basis of MFA materials other members had no access to. Many of those who were asked to comment on the drafts saw an awkward attempt 'to promote the official viewpoint', 'in sharp contradiction to any principle of academic research'.[30] The work involved acrimonious, and *ad hominem*, clashes of perspectives and pitted political authority against scientific objectivity. Rosenne insisted that the report 'needs be a diplomatic document even if it would appear under unofficial auspices'; he also rejected 'the possibility of Olympian academic treatment of ongoing foreign policy problems' by those lacking official 'responsibility or access to the facts'; the report was to be a product of the MFA in content—but not in name.[31] Robinson agreed: 'only those who bear the burden have the authority to decide ... and the others are compelled by national discipline to accept the verdict'.[32] The quarrel was about content—but it was also about capacity, standing, and voice: it was another extension of Jewish representation politics, another test of sovereignty.

With the weight of the MFA behind him, Rosenne's efforts to turn the report into a public relations exercise in the service of Israel's foreign policy and prestige succeeded. The report presented an idealized account of Israel's support, as the Jewish state,[33] for UN work and told of the unique contribution it made to the promotion of UN purposes.[34] While the report offered subtle evidence on some ambivalence towards the UN and international law, its account of Israel's attitude towards human rights, the Genocide Convention, and the Refugee Convention[35] did not cohere with the evidence, contained in MFA files, presented in this book. The report gave Israel's diplomatic practice the most liberal interpretation possible, but revealed none of the disinterest, aversion, and hostility that dominated how Rosenne and Robinson had approached these 'Matters of Jewish Concerns'[36] and other items on the UN agenda.[37] Instead, it presented selections of Israeli diplomatic practice and statements that told of an investment in the universal as a matter of tradition,

[30] Nahumy to Feinberg, 18 December 1953; Ben-Aharon to Feinberg, 23 November 1953, P-1035/6, ISA.

[31] Rosenne to Robinson, 9 April 1954, FM-5850/3, ISA.

[32] Robinson to Rosenne, 20 April 1954, FM-5850/3, ISA.

[33] Feinberg (n 28) 37–41.

[34] ibid, 8, 31–7.

[35] ibid, esp 173–80.

[36] This was the heading of the chapter presenting the flattering interpretation of Israel's practice on concrete agenda items: Feinberg (n 28) esp. 173; these were the same agenda items that Rosenne and Robinson classified as 'marginal problems' and whose 'Jewish aspect' attracted their ideological critique.

[37] Compare Rotem Giladi, 'Negotiating Identity: Israel, Apartheid, and the United Nations 1949–1952' (2017) 132 (No.559) English Hist Rev 1440; to Feinberg (n 28) 213, 255.

ideals, and interests.[38] Furthermore, in the report, as on subsequent occasions,[39] Rosenne portrayed the Jewish state as successor to past cosmopolitan investments by Jewish organizations[40] and a present-day partner to non-governmental organs of Jewish advocacy at the UN arena.[41] Little of the pervasive sovereign aversion of the Jewish state's envoys towards competing Jewish voices was visible in the report; the public relation exercise required the appropriation of their work.

The report, at any rate, did produce an enduring impression of Israel's universalist outlook and cosmopolitan investment: it became a major source for first-generation studies of Israel's foreign policy.[42] The report misrepresented the terms of Israel's early international law engagement; backed by academic credentials, the account it placed on public record could hardly be challenged; archival evidence on the scope and depth of the Jewish state's ambivalent, and hostile, attitude towards international law remained occluded by prolonged restrictions on access to the relevant State Archive files.

4. Legacies of Ambivalence

Another matter requiring reflection concerns any long-term or present-day implications of my findings. In tracing the roots of Israel's ambivalence, this book sketches something of a *longue durée*, albeit incomplete, perspective on Zionist international law engagement. This timeframe contrasts with the short span of events comprising the three case studies. My intent here is not to revisit the justifications for this temporal limitation—1949 to 1954—but, rather, ask how persistent was ambivalence, and how enduring was continuity. To what degree did the ambivalence of our protagonists survive their terms of their tenure at the MFA and what instruction can the findings on Israel's early attitude offer for the understanding of Israel's current international law perspective and record?

Part of the answer is that to examine the endurance of ambivalence, it is to be studied. A *longue durée* perspective on Israel's attitude towards international law requires the study of other episodes spanning the decades that followed the first few formative years and reliance on materials that are, often, still restricted. Relating the present to the past also compels inquiries into causation, circulation,

[38] ibid, 253 ('Israel is deeply concerned with the problem of human rights and their protection by appropriate international procedures. Proper respect for human rights is seen to be an essential requirement of national policy . . . not only because of [Israel's] own minorities but also because of its concern for the Jewish people all over the world. In this respect, Israel is inspired by the ideals which guided the Jewish organizations in 1919–20 when they advanced the cause of minorities in the Paris Peace Conference').

[39] Shabtai Rosenne, 'Book Review' (2009) 39 Isr YB Hum Rts 379 discussed in ch 4.

[40] Feinberg (n 28) 253.

[41] ibid, 175 ('on many occasions the government of Israel has taken steps side by side with the Jewish organizations' working at the UN).

[42] Eg Michael Brecher, *The Foreign Policy System of Israel: Setting, Images, Process* (New Haven 1972).

and reception. The task of bringing an understanding of the past to bear on the present, besides, presents historians with particular pitfalls and demands particular modes of circumspection. Not having conducted such research I can only offer a few preliminary, tentative observations and leave the readers, pending future research, to exercise their own judgement.

One observation concerns the entrenchment of the Zionist creed. Israel today continues to define itself as a Jewish state; its foreign policy is still defined by reference to that self-perception. And, notwithstanding far-reaching transformations in Israeli society and politics and in Israel's regional and global circumstances, the Zionist creed that served Rosenne and Robinson as the yardstick for testing international law retains its role as Israel's foundational ideology—and as a key factor in the Jewish state's external outlook. Time and circumstances, no doubt, made some of the sovereign sensibilities, patent and ubiquitous in the years that immediately followed the sovereign turn, lose some of their salience or edge. The practical need for the Jewish state to contend with competing models of Jewish emancipation waned: Diaspora Nationalism became a thing of the past; assimilationist institutions in the West had to account for the fact of Jewish sovereignty. With time, Israel's sovereign standing blunted the preoccupation of its representatives, at international arenas, with competing Jewish voices.

Yet how Zionism read the Jewish crisis of modernity and the remedy it prescribed for its solution remain unaltered. Leon Pinsker's writ of *Auto-Emancipation*[43] may not be alluded to explicitly, yet it continues to define Israel's ethos of self-reliance in both the military and diplomatic realms. Theodor Herzl's reading of European anti-Semitism and his investment in and critique of liberal internationalism remain central to Israel's self-perception as to how the Jewish state conceives its own role in Jewish affairs and in the world. And echoes—often, more than echoes—of the ideological sensibilities underscoring Robinson and Rosenne's ideological outlook in the first few years that followed the sovereign turn are still heard today in public, governmental, parliamentary, judicial, diplomatic, and academic discourses and arenas. Recent court cases that decided the fate of Franz Kafka's literary estate and the Vienna Jewish community archives gave effect to a reading of Israel as the heir to Diasporic Jewish cultural property;[44] that reading was given voice, decades earlier, by Robinson when formulating the basis of Israel's reparations claims from the Federal Republic of Germany.[45] Contemporary scholarly reflections on Israel's jurisdiction to try Adolf Eichmann, or the 1994 legislative expansion of Israel's prescriptive extra-territorial jurisdiction, continue to draw on the view that it was, and remains, 'the sole sovereign representative of the Jewish people, as well as the

[43] Pinsker (n 1).

[44] Administrative Appeal Request 6251/15, Hoffa v Cassouto et al (7 August 2016, Israel Supreme Court); Civil Appeal 9366/12, Israelitische Kultusgemeinde Wien v Central Archives for the History of the Jewish People (30 June 2015, Israel Supreme Court).

[45] Ch 7.

nation where many of the victims [of the Holocaust] took refuge'.[46] The affinity of that view to earlier Palestinocentrism, or to sensibilities on standing and voice, is patent, even if expressed more vehemently by Rosenne and Robinson in the first decade of sovereignty; recall here Rosenne's retort to Lauterpacht's voice.[47] Jewish voicelessness—Jewish objecthood writ large—may not command the preoccupation of the makers of Israel's foreign policy makers today, or preoccupy their legal advisers; yet the interpretation of Jewish subjecthood in the world, affected by Robinson and Rosenne in the early days of Israeli diplomacy, remains trenchant and ubiquitous.

Yet if ideologically driven ambivalence—not merely a repertoire of sensibilities—remains embedded in how Israel approaches international law today, I suspect it has most purchase and is most manifest at moments and arenas where Israel's international law record falls short of the standard or is made the subject of censure. At times, ideological ambivalence is patent in the logic of exemption underscoring how Rosenne approached the Refugee Convention and how Israel continues to approach it today. For Rosenne, the very existence of the Jewish state as the state of asylum for Jewish refugees past, present, and future represented complete performance of Israel's obligations under the Refugee Convention.[48] Contemporary official and public discourse—and Israel's treatment of asylum seekers—suggests that that logic of exemption continues to have legal, political, and diplomatic currency.[49]

At other times, ambivalence takes the form of a moral-historical, rather than normative, shield. It is here that an ideological reading of international law's futility and its patent failure to protect Jews—the Holocaust looms large here as conclusive evidence and ultimate justification for the existence of a Jewish state and its *raison d'être*—is brought to bear on legal-diplomatic practice. It is here that the Jewish state's universal vocation, binding together Herzl's thought and the circumstances of Israel's UN birth, is cited to mark international law's promise. Next comes indignation at what had become of that promise: the authoritarian composition and skewed agenda of the Human Rights Council; the prospects of politicization of the International Criminal Court (and the crimes enumerated in its Statute) and abuse of its powers; or the uneven effort to ensure implementation of the Fourth Geneva Convention. Indignation requires ownership, and ownership requires appropriation in the form of allusions to original, seminal Jewish investments in the human rights project, in early international criminal law, or in the international refugee

[46] Eugene Kontorovich, 'The Piracy Analogy: Modern Universal Jurisdiction's Hollow Foundation' (2004) 45 Harvard ILJ 183, 197. In 1994, Israel prescribed jurisdiction over offences committed outside Israel against 'the life, person, health, freedom or property of any Jew as such or the property of any Jewish institution as such': Section 13, Penal law (Amendment No 39) (Preliminary Part and General Part) (1994), 1481 *Sefer HaHukim* (Laws) (25 July 1994) 348 (Hebrew).

[47] Ch 3.

[48] Ch 7.

[49] Rotem Giladi, 'A "Historical Commitment"? Identity and Ideology in Israel's Attitude to the Refugee Convention 1951–1954' (2014) 37 Intl Hist Rev 745.

regime. Such appropriation marks not only just how far international law had deviated from its promise but also vexed protests that it is now turned against the heirs of its authors. Ambivalence, it would appear, persists; its manifestations may take other forms, but it continues to draw on, and express, the Zionist creed.

This calls attention, again, to appropriation of Jewish engagements and to the claim to cosmopolitan investment—and to irony. Rosenne and Robinson were ambivalent towards the right of petition, the Genocide Convention, and the Refugee Convention because of, not despite, their Jewish aspect: when hostile, it was because the norm in question did not pass the test of the Zionist creed; when invested, they sought to justify their investment as consonant with its teachings. For them, it was precisely the Jewish aspect of cosmopolitan legal projects that offended their ideological sensibilities at the dawn of the age of sovereignty. Today, however, the Jewish aspects of international law—of these and other post-war projects, in particular—are invoked in Israeli public discourse to call the Jewish state to return to a liberal, cosmopolitan, humanist tradition of its early days when its Jewish investment in international law drew on and expressed universal values. Yet as this book demonstrates, no such golden age had ever existed. Whatever had been its impact on Israel's attitude towards international law, the 1967 occupation of Palestinian territories did not bring to an end or corrupt an earlier universalist outlook and engagement by the Jewish state. If evidence attesting to the existence of a foundational Israeli liberal tradition or cosmopolitan investment in international law and human rights can validate such liberal nostalgia, that evidence is to be found outside the record of the MFA and its lawyers. The irony here is not that the critique of government policy impels nostalgic demands to return to a golden age and the renewal of Israel's original loyalties that are historically fallacious; rather, it is that they affect the appropriation, by the Jewish state, of the work of Jewish individuals and institutions no less than Rosenne had done in the preparation of the Carnegie Report.[50]

5. Centre and Margin: Jewish Sensibilities and Palestinian Exigencies

And then, there are the conundra raised by the question of absence and presence of Palestinians. In committing UN agenda items involving Jewish questions to the margins of their engagement in that arena, Robinson and Rosenne offered commentary on how peripheral such international law projects—'marginal problems', for them—had been to Israel's diplomatic investment. The record of their work in those years leaves no doubt that their principal preoccupation at the UN, before or

[50] Feinberg (n 28).

after Israel's admission, was with other agenda items—matters directly concerned with and arising out of the Middle East contestation and conflict. We may certainly consider the marginalization of Jewish matters as the embodiment of sovereign claims: disinterest signified sovereign status that obviated—again, in ideological terms—the need to strive for standing or secure the protection of international law. This, nonetheless, does not resolve any conundrum: the hold of ideology—that is, of the Jewish prism—on how Rosenne and Robinson read international law belies the 'marginal' character they ascribed to such Jewish items on the UN agenda. So does the measure of the time and toil they came to spend on legal projects in which they professed only marginal interest. This self-contradictory evidence appears as one more manifestation of ambivalence.

It remains evident, at the same time, what little role was played by the 'Arab Question' in how our protagonists weighed in on the right of petition, the Genocide Convention, or the status and treatment of refugees. It is not that Palestinians—in Israel or outside it—were altogether absent from internal exchanges expressing reserve towards the right of individual petition, disinterest in signing the Genocide Convention, or disinclination towards ratifying the Refugee Convention. Yet their presence in these exchanges tended to be ephemeral, marginal, and on the whole inconsequential. They could be invoked to justify aloofness or objection; but such sentiments drew mainly on other, Jewish, sensibilities predating the sovereign turn.

Self-perception mattered: it was important for Robinson and Rosenne to signify Jewish concerns as marginal; yet doing so also signified the importance of these marginalia. When it came to matters Jewish, Israel's international law outlook was couched in and conditioned by Jewish terms and pre-sovereign objecthood; this also made possible, I suspect, treating core concerns of Israel's early diplomacy, albeit pressing and critical, as somehow or somewhat trivial. Accounting for Palestinian presence and absence may require, then, accounting for the interchangeability of core and margin and for how Jewish and Palestinian concerns could relate to one another. Undoubtedly, Rosenne and Robinson's ambivalent international law engagement in Jewish matters—their displays of disinterest, aversion, and resentment towards international legislative projects as well as the measure of their investment in these very projects—served to signify the sovereign transformation of Jews, their legal subjecthood vis-à-vis other, non-sovereign Jews. Palestinian presence and absence, and the reversal of roles between core and periphery, hint that ambivalence towards international law, expressed in 'Jewish' terms, may have also served to signify another transformation affected by Jewish subjecthood: the othering of Palestinians who, as surrogates, would now take the place Jews had occupied under international law before the sovereign turn; in the words of the editors of the *Jewish Yearbook of International Law*, 'merely the *object*, never the subject, of international law'.[51] If so, then the terms of international law

[51] Emphasis added; 'Introduction' (1948) 1 Jewish YB Intl L v.

engagement affected by Robinson and Rosenne in the service of the Jewish state lend themselves to another reading of continuity and change.

6. Imperfect Subjects: Robinson, Rosenne, and the Sovereign Test

Last, there is the question of Rosenne and Robinson's own subjecthood. What invites reflection here is the tension underlying their agency: on the one hand, epistemological sensibilities as international law professionals and, on the other, sovereign sensibilities as nationally emancipated Jews that underscored their investment in and recourse to national ideology. Why did these jurist-diplomats assume the role of torchbearers of the Zionist creed, appoint themselves to interpret the sovereign turn by reference to its demands, and elect to give voice, more than any of their colleagues, to ambivalence towards international law—the very body of knowledge that grounded their professional credentials? Why did they turn to the Zionist creed to gauge the valence of international law—and to find it, time and again, lacking? What was their perception of the role they had played in the transition of Jews from objects to subjects of international law?

It might be that ambivalence towards international law, inherent in Zionist ideology and embedded in Zionist experience, undermined the ideological credentials of those possessing the professional aptitude to express it. If so, ideology had served as a trap: the very professional qualifications that equipped our protagonist with the necessary epistemological credentials to interpret Jewish sovereignty also undermined the ideological credentials required to do so. This, however, is only a conjecture: the evidence supporting it is circumstantial and contextual.

Other, more direct evidence cited throughout this book suggests, however, that concerns with their own subjecthood as Jews, not their agency as lawyers, drove Rosenne and Robinson's preoccupation with the Zionist creed and precipitated their choice to act as its guardians. Time and again, Rosenne and Robinson would stake a claim to Jewish subjecthood and sovereign standing by faulting the ideological credentials and lacking standing of other, non-sovereign Jews marked, thereby, as outsiders. That was the crux of Rosenne's censure of Hersch Lauterpacht following the latter's reproach of the Jewish state's antagonism towards the individual right of petition.[52] Rosenne's aversion towards crediting Lemkin, at the ICJ, with fathering the Geocide Convention played a similar role.[53] Robinson, for his part, marked his own sovereign *locus standi* by deriding the non-sovereign *modus operandi* of the Jewish organizations he had, prior to 1947, worked for and disparaging the unofficial voice of their representatives—his former colleagues.[54]

[52] Ch 3.
[53] Ch 4.
[54] Robinson to Rosenne, 6 February 1951, FM–1830/8, ISA.

What drove, in turn, their preoccupation with their own subjecthood was a fault in their own ideological credentials. Robinson could claim Zionist credentials going back to his Lithuania days; yet, for a long time, his predominant ideological investment was in *Gegenwartsarbeit*—'work of the present' aimed at ameliorating the condition of Jewish minorities in the Diaspora, not the building of the future Jewish National Home in Palestine. The creed he had followed was, for Moshe Sharett, 'a false and perverse doctrine':[55] it considered the Diaspora, not Palestine, as the proper site of Jewish national revival. Robinson's ideological transformation—his conversion from Dubnow's teachings and Diaspora Nationalism to the 'radical solution' of a narrow, exclusive version of Zionism[56]—was not quite complete. Robinson's struggle to reconcile the Zionist imperative of Return with his pre-state Diasporic sensibilities on Jewish statelessness and refugeehood marked, as chapter 7 recounts, an ideological deviation. This deviation revealed that the fault in his credentials had lingered past the sovereign turn. Interpreting the requirements of Jewish sovereignty did not, evidently, come easily: in late 1949 he openly acknowledged 'our difficulty in ridding ourselves of the discrimination and inferiority complex. We continue to think in terms of a minority looking for protection against discrimination and transfer the same mentality into the United Nations'.[57] Jewish subjecthood demanded sovereign Jews, envoys of the Jewish state, to shed any vestige of Diasporic 'mentality' and abandon any sensibility expressing past Jewish objecthood.

Robinson's failure to do so—his outsiderness—was apparent to Moshe Sharett, Israel's Foreign Minister. A few years earlier, persuaded by Sharett, Robinson 'defected' from the world of Jewish advocacy to start a 'new chapter' as legal adviser of the state in the making.[58] Sharett would, in later years, record Robinson's 'invaluable aid' in tutoring Israel's budding diplomatic service in the ways of multilateral diplomacy and the 'operation of the new international organisation'.[59] In late 1951, however, he had occasion to record Robinson's ideological deficiency. In a letter to Prime Minister David Ben-Gurion, Sharett requested that David HaCohen—a prominent Labour *Knesset* member lent to Israel's UN mission but then recalled to serve on a Parliamentary Commission of Inquiry—return to New York help the mission's work at the General Assembly. One of the reasons compelling HaCohen's return was his 'unique value', stemming from the fact that

[55] Ch 5.
[56] ibid.
[57] Robinson, Convocation of International Conferences by the Economic and Social Council, 8 December 1949, FM-1823/7, ISA.
[58] Robinson to Sharett, 8 December 1954, JR-7/6, Jacob Robinson Papers 2013.506.1, United States Holocaust Memorial Museum Archives, Washington DC ('USHMM').
[59] Moshe Sharett, *At the Threshold of Statehood: 1946–1949* (Am Oved 1958) 63 (Hebrew).

> most members of the delegation are essentially good people but they lack *Eretz Israel* tenure, lacking all *Yishuv* experience and bereft of any roots in the living reality of Israel ... I find it hard, alone ... to impose on this group, good and precious as it is, the authority of our fundamental conceptions.[60]

First among those named by Sharett as deficient in national credentials and lacking 'our fundamental conceptions' was Jacob Robinson.

Reading the right of petition and the Genocide and Refugee Conventions through the prism of the Zionist creed, Robinson and Rosenne tested, as self-appointed guardians of creed, international law's compatibility with Jewish national ideology; often, on that basis, they found it lacking. At the very same time, the revolution in Jewish legal-political history that they had witnessed, affected, and sought to interpret also put their own subjecthood to the test. At stake was their own adherence to the demands of the Zionist creed, their own transformation into new, sovereign Jews free of Diasporic sensibilities, 'mentality', and complexes. Try as they had, at times they were found lacking.

No less than any effort to shed lingering Diasporic sensibilities or his past investment in Diaspora Nationalism, it was Robinson's lack of 'any roots in the living reality of Israel'[61] that marred his ideological credentials, attested to the incompleteness of his sovereign transformation, and signified his less-than-full fidelity to the Zionist creed. Unlike Rosenne, he would never practice the prime imperative that Zionism demanded of its adherents. He never immigrated to Israel. And so, upon his retirement from MFA service, his credentials and standing were challenged in the public arena. In 1957, at sixty-eight years of age and suffering from chronic ailments and recent personal tragedies,[62] Robinson informed his superiors that his decision to retire from Israel's foreign service was final—but also that alongside his new career, as a Holocaust scholar, he would continue to render advice and assistance to the MFA.[63] Only days after his resignation came into effect, a daily Israeli newspaper published a short article under the title *The Retiree*. The Hebrew word used, however, also denotes one who breaks rank. The unsigned article reported the resignation, adding that Robinson was 'not returning to the country. He is staying in the USA, having also received American citizenship.' The anonymous author recognized Robinson's advocacy for the 'rights of the Jewish minority in Lithuania', and professed that it was Robinson's 'private affair' to 'decide to settle in America'. Instead, he faulted Robinson's foreign service superiors: 'how

[60] Sharett to Ben-Gurion, 2 December 1951, G–5577/14, ISA.

[61] ibid.

[62] Eban to Golda Meir, 25 July 1957, FM–5935/66, ISA.

[63] Eban to Robinson, 27 June 1957, Robinson to Eban, 2, 5 July 1957; he intended to resign earlier: Robinson to Eban, September 1956, 1 October 1956, JR–7/6, USHMM; 'Preface', in Sharett (n 59) 8 expressed 'special gratitude to my friend Dr. Jacob Robinson, whose erudition and wisdom continue to constitute a valuable national asset even after his retirement from state service'. Later, he joined the prosecution team in the trial of Adolf Eichmann.

could it be possible that a Jew who is a citizen of the USA, who holds on to that citizenship'—and who was, besides, notoriously 'pro-American'—'could have during all those years represented us at the UN, and take part in critical decisions'? The article used Robinson to target the government: Robinson's case, the author argued, only demonstrated that foreign service appointments were made on the basis of expertise, not 'the principal standard of first loyalty to Israel and devotion to the vocation of this young state'. Robinson's failure to abide by that standard—his decision not to immigrate to Israel—was only proof that the government had not properly considered 'the composition of our foreign service . . . from a practical *and ideological* standpoint'.[64]

Eban's retort, published in the same newspaper after an exchange with the editor,[65] decried the 'shocking criticism' directed at Robinson. It also reported the 'wrath of protest' felt by Robinson's colleagues when reading it. Eban, Robinson's direct superior at Israel's UN mission, attested to Robinson's professional stature and marked his contribution to Israel's diplomacy. Eban denounced the 'malignant faulting of the integrity and the very national loyalty' of public servants and Israel's envoys, insisting that personal circumstances justified Robinson's decision to retire. He did not, however, offer anything to answer the charge, levelled against Robinson, of ideological failings. Framed as a defence of Robinson's professional standing and grounded in personal circumstances—not of the foreign service or the government—Eban's response intimated that Robinson's ideological credentials were indeed deficient.[66]

Rosenne, by contrast, already fulfilled Zionism by immigrating to Palestine a few months before the termination of the British Mandate. His investment in Diaspora Nationalism was short-lived—and far less significant than Robinson's; still, his explorations of Dubnow's teachings were on public record in the form of various essays he had published in the London Jewish and Zionist press in the 1940s.[67] And while his investment in Zionism had begun at adolescence, his family background and past association with assimilationist institutions of British Jewry[68] may have played a role in the fervour he would display when professing fidelity, as the MFA legal adviser, to the Zionist creed. If Robinson struggled, at times, to reconcile sovereign sensibilities and Diaspora concerns, Rosenne tended to give voice, explicitly ideological and often blatant in terms, to a radical reading of Jewish sovereignty and its demands. Often, he would signify his own official, sovereign standing and ideological credentials by marking the deficiency of others and their position as outsiders: over the question of the right of petition, he denounced Lauterpacht's

[64] Emphasis added; 'HaPoresh', *Ma'ariv* (9 September 1957); Disatnik to Herman, 19 September 1957, FM-5935/66, ISA.

[65] Correspondence in FM-5935/66, ISA.

[66] Aba Eban, *Ma'ariv* (16 October 1957), in JR-7/6, USHMM.

[67] Ch 5.

[68] ibid.

'extreme non-Zionist' stance and assimilationist sensibilities;[69] when his plans to have the MFA take over the *Jewish Yearbook of International Law* met the editors' resistance, he castigated Feinberg's professional capacity;[70] and, in order to ensure that the Carnegie Report served as a diplomatic public relations exercise, he rejected 'the possibility of Olympian academic treatment of ongoing foreign policy problems' by those, like Feinberg, lacking official 'responsibility or access to the facts'.[71] Even Rosenne's persisting reticence towards the ratification of the Refugee Convention, thwarting Robinson's recommendation and efforts, asserted his ideological fealty over that of his older colleague.[72] In later years, he would describe Lauterpacht and Robinson as his mentors; Feinberg, as the Hebrew University's first (and, for a long time, only) professor of international law, was by necessity the academic counterpart of MFA lawyers—and would soon serve as Rosenne's doctoral supervisor. Staking his claim to ideological credentials, even at the risk of impairing professional relationships, was paramount for Rosenne.

For all his effort Rosenne, too, would struggle with the test of sovereignty. The verdict on his defective subjecthood was delivered, again, by Sharett, though it was Rosenne's own eagerness to display his ideological credibility that put him on trial and gave Sharett the occasion to find fault in his legal adviser's ideological reading of Jewish sovereignty. In early September 1952, unprompted, Rosenne sent a 'secret', 'personal' letter to Sharett. He had been little involved in the negotiations that led to the conclusion of the highly controversial Reparations Agreement between Israel and the Federal Republic of Germany;[73] Robinson was the legal adviser of the Israeli delegation to the talks. Neither was Rosenne asked to weigh in on the matter of signature; the government had already resolved that Sharett, as Foreign Minister, would sign the treaty on Israel's behalf.

Begging Sharett to 'forgive me very much for the candour', Rosenne confessed that he was 'deeply worried by the idea that it is to be you who will ... sign the Reparations Agreement. I consider this a matter beneath the dignity of Israel's Foreign Minister, and which may in years to come tarnish the name of Moshe Sharett'. Rosenne reasoned that the rank of the signor will not 'affect the performance of the agreement' and so concluded: '[i]t is therefore my duty to you', he wrote, 'to request that you reconsider the whole matter again'.[74]

[69] Ch 3.
[70] Prologue.
[71] Rosenne to Robinson, 9 April 1954 (n 31).
[72] Ch 7.
[73] Agreement between the State of Israel and the Federal Republic of Germany (10 September 1952) (1953) 162 UNTS 205, 206; Jacob Tovy, *Destruction and Accounting: The State of Israel and the Reparations from Germany 1949–1953* (Bar-Ilan UP 2015).
[74] Rosenne to Sharett, 1 September 1952, FM-2417/6, ISA; translations of Rosenne's letter and Sharett's reply appear in Yaacov Sharett (ed), *Moshe Sharett and the German Reparations Controversy* (Moshe Sharett Heritage Society 2007) 343–5; here I use, however, my own translation.

Sharett's response was swift and brutal. A day later, he thanked Rosenne for the concern for his good name: 'it is very dear to me, as are your alert and sensibility to Israel's ... moral quality'. But he also admonished Rosenne for the lateness of his intervention: 'the matter has already been decided, communicated to the other party, and published in the press without any denial'. In this state of affairs, 'no self-respecting government would recant', in particular since a retraction would compel West Germany 'to reconsider the entire matter'. Rosenne's letter was 'at least ten days late'; and his assumption that repudiating the agreed procedure would have no political implications was 'extremely odd'.[75]

Having questioned Rosenne's political judgement, Sharett proceeded to the merits. First, Sharett refuted the argument that it would be beneath his dignity 'to sign an agreement with Germans': he denied 'the morality of this argument with all the power of persuasion I am capable of'. If claiming reparations from Germany was moral, so was, necessarily, the negotiation, conclusion, and signing of the agreement. If so, there was no moral dimension to the question of the rank and identity of the signor. Sharett's involvement had already been such, he wrote, that a signature by another would not 'mitigate my sentence' in case 'history ever pass a condemning verdict on the whole Reparations affair'. Sharett also 'wholly rejected' Rosenne's implication that he could abdicate his own responsibility by leaving it to 'loyal friends' to negotiate or sign the agreement—and assume the moral blame.[76]

Next, however, came a far graver reproach. For Sharett, Rosenne's warning was predicated on a false interpretation of the demands of Jewish sovereignty. The crux of Rosenne's objection was that it would be inappropriate for the Foreign Minister of the sovereign Jewish state to contract 'with Germans', a few years after the Holocaust, and to the end of securing a remedy for the wrong against the Jewish people. Sharett, however, vehemently rejected Rosenne's reading as a remnant of Diasporic mentality expressing sensibilities of Jewish objecthood, not sovereign subjecthood; the fault with Rosenne's objection was ideological—the same one he had, on other occasions, found in others:

> I can only conclude from your position one or the other: either that your heart is not at ease with the whole matter, or that you are flawed, in your attitude towards it, with the vice of fastidiousness, that to me is not at all sovereign but patently a residue of Diasporic sentimentalism.[77]

That was not the end of Rosenne's trial. Sharett insisted that his own signature was essential for securing Konrad Adenauer's signature, and that the ageing

[75] Sharett to Rosenne, 2 September 1952, FM–2417/6, ISA; Yehoshua Freundlich (ed), *Documents on the Foreign Policy of Israel: 1952*, vol 7 (ISA 1992).
[76] ibid.
[77] ibid.

Chancellor's involvement could prove crucial for the treaty's performance. His own signature, moreover, was meant to do Adenauer justice: it was to Adenauer's credit that Germany was willing, without precedent, to acknowledge its responsibility for unprecedented evil. Here Sharett delivered the *coup de grâce*, intimating that Rosenne's residual 'Diasporic sentimentalism' was no isolated aberration but, in fact, proof of Rosenne's failure to understand, appraise, and *internalize* the sovereign transformation of the Jewish people:

> You may be surprised to hear from me such considerations obligating respect and reciprocity—even a duty of chivalry—towards a German Prime Minister. Well, in my opinion, only this could be the approach of the independent State of Israel which, historically and morally, was founded upon the ruins of the Nazi regime and redeemed the dignity of the Jewish people profaned by that regime. *The fear of conducting our relations with Germany in such a manner causes us to revert to a status that is now a thing of the past*—the status of a people devoid of sovereign remedies and exempt from sovereign considerations, secluding itself in its four corners, mourning its past, praying for its future and resolving its present relations with other nations by only detesting them in its heart. A sovereign nation looks to the future, and its present relations impose on it a burden of practical obligations that are an honour to be bound by for others are bound by these obligations towards it.
>
> We need educate the nation to this new conception of our dignity, *yet first we need educate ourselves.*[78]

Like the nation, and others under Sharett's charge, Rosenne required ideological instruction; Sharett proceeded to ensure that their correspondence was circulated, as a didactic measure, to all MFA units—laying bare to all the fault with Rosenne's ideological credentials and attesting to the fact that his transformation from Jewish objecthood to subjecthood was not—like Robinson's—quite complete. For all their efforts to bear the torch of the Zionist creed, affect the national revolution in Jewish history, and give voice to sovereign sensibilities, they remained imperfect subjects of international law.

[78] Emphases added; ibid.

Select Bibliography

Abtahi, Hirad and Webb, Philippa, *The Genocide Convention: The Travaux Préparatoires* (Martinus Nijhoff 2008)

Adler-Rudel, Salomon, 'The Evian Conference on the Refugee Question' (1968) 13 Leo Baeck Institute Yearbook 235

Alroey, Gur, *Zionism Without Zion: The Jewish Territorial Organization and Its Conflict with the Zionist Organization* (Wayne State UP 2016)

Altman, Alexander (ed), *Studies in Nineteenth-Century Jewish Intellectual History* (Harvard UP 1964)

American Jewish Committee, *In Vigilant Brotherhood* (AJC 1965)

Anderson, Benedict, *Imagined Communities: Reflections on the Origins and Spread of Nationalism* (rev edn, Verso 2006)

Anghie, Antony, *Imperialism, Sovereignty and the Making of International Law* (CUP 2005)

Arendt, Hannah, *The Origins of Totalitarianism* (Meridian 1961)

Avineri, Shlomo, *Herzl's Vision: Theodor Herzl and the Foundation of the Jewish State* (Bluebridge 2014)

Bamberger-Stemmann, Sabine, *Der Europäische Nationalitätenkongreß 1925 bis 1938: Nationale Minderheiten zwischen Lobbyistentum und Großmachtinteressen* (Verlag Herder-Institut 2001)

Bar-Yosef, Eitan, 'Spying Out the Land: The Zionist Expedition to East Africa, 1905' in Bar-Yosef, Eitan and Valman, Nadia (eds), *'The Jew' in Late-Victorian and Edwardian Culture: Between the East End and East Africa* (Palgrave-Macmillan 2009) 183

Bar-Yosef, Eitan, 'Bonding with the British: Colonial Nostalgia and the Idealization of Mandatory Palestine in Israeli Literature and Culture after 1967' (2017) 22 Jewish Social Studies 1

Bartal, Israel, *Cossack and Bedouin: Land and People in Jewish Nationalism* (Am Oved 2007) (Hebrew)

Bartal, Israel, 'From *Shtadlanut* to "Jewish Diplomacy"? 1756–1840–1881' (2016) 15 Simon Dubnow Institute Yearbook 109

Bass, Garry J, *Freedom's Battle: The Origins of Humanitarian Intervention* (Knopf 2008)

Bauer, Yehuda, *Rethinking the Holocaust* (Yale UP 2000)

Beatson, Jack and Zimmermann, Reinhard (eds), *Jurists Uprooted: German-Speaking Emigré Lawyers in Twentieth Century Britain* (OUP 2004)

Becker Lorca, Arnulf, *Mestizo International Law: A Global Intellectual History 1842–1933* (CUP 2015)

Beit-Zvi, Shabtai, *Post-Ugandan Zionism on Trial* (Beit-Zvi 1991)

Ben-Gurion, David, *Us and Our Neighbours* (*Davar* 1931) (Hebrew)

Ben-Gurion, David, *From Class to Nation* (*Davar* 1933) (Hebrew)

Ben-Gurion, David, 'Israel Among the Nations' in State of Israel, *Government Yearbook* (1952) 1

Ben-Gurion, David, *In the Campaign* (5th edn, Ayanot 1955) (Hebrew)

Ben-Gurion, David, *From Class to People* (Ayanot 1955) (Hebrew)

Ben-Nun, Gilad, 'The Israeli Roots of Article 3 and Article 6 of the 1951 Refugee Convention' (2014) 27 Journal of Refugee Studies 101

Ben-Nun, Gilad, 'From *Ad Hoc* to Universal: The International Refugee Regime from Fragmentation to Unity 1922–1954' (2015) 34 Refugee Survey Quarterly 23

Ben-Nun, Gilad, *Seeking Asylum in Israel: Refugees and the History of Migration Law* (Tauris 2016)

Bendikaitė, Eglė and Haupt, Dirk Roland (eds), *The Life, Times and Work of Jokubas Robinzonas—Jacob Robinson* (Akademia Verlag 2015)

Bentwich, Norman, *The Mandate System* (Longmans, Green & Co 1930)

Bentwich, Norman, 'The League of Nations and Racial Persecution in Germany' (1933) 19 Transactions of the Grotius Society 75

Bentwich, Norman, 'The Limits of the Domestic Jurisdiction of the State' (1945) 31 Transactions of the Grotius Society 59

Bialer, Uri 'Top Hat, Tuxedo and Cannons: Israeli Foreign Policy from 1948 to 1956 as a Field of Study' (2002) 7 Israel Studies 1

Bialer, Uri, *Between East and West: Israel's Foreign Policy Orientation 1948–1956* (Cambridge 2008)

Birnbaum, Pierre and Katznelson, Ira (eds), *Paths of Emancipation: Jews, States, and Citizenship* (Princeton UP 1995)

Boyarin, Daniel, 'The Colonial Drag: Zionism, Gender, and Mimicry' in Afzal-Khan, Fawzia and Seshadri-Crooks, Kalpana (eds), *The Pre-Occupation of Post-Colonial Studies* (Duke University Press 2000) 234

Boyarin, Jonathan, *Storm from Paradise: The Politics of Jewish Memory* (University of Minnesota Press 1992)

Boyarin, Jonathan, *The Unconverted Self: Jews, Indians, and the Identity of Christian Europe* (University of Chicago Press 2009)

Brecher, Michael, *The Foreign Policy System of Israel: Setting, Images, Process* (New Haven 1972)

Brenner, Michael, Caron, Vicki, and Kaufmann, Uri R (eds), *Jewish Emancipation Reconsidered: The French and German Models* (66 Schriftenreihe wissenschaftlicher Abhandlungen des Leo Baeck Instituts, Mohr Siebeck 2003)

Broude, Tomer and Noam, Gilad, 'Parliamentary Involvement in Treaty-Making Processes: Understanding the Knesset's Past Record and Its Future Potential' (2008) 9 Law and Business 175 (Hebrew)

Bruegel, Johann W, 'The Right to Petition an International Authority' (1953) 2 International and Comparative Law Quarterly 542

Bruegel, Johann W, 'The Bernheim Petition: A Challenge to Nazi Germany in 1933' (1983) 17 Patterns of Prejudice 17

Bush, Jonathan, 'Nuremberg and Beyond: Jacob Robinson, International Lawyer' (2017) 39 Loyola of Los Angeles International and Comparative Law Review 259

Clavin, Patricia and Sluga, Glenda (eds), *Internationalisms: A Twentieth-Century History* (CUP 2017)

Cohen, Boaz, 'Dr. Jacob Robinson, the Institute of Jewish Affairs and the Elusive Jewish Voice in Nuremberg' in Bankier, David and Michman, Dan (eds), *Holocaust and Justice: Representation and Historiography of the Holocaust in Post-War Trials* (Yad Vashem/Berghahn 2010) 81

Cohen, Uri, *The Mountain and the Hill: The Hebrew University of Jerusalem During Pre-Independence Period and Early Years of the State of Israel* (Am Oved 2006) (Hebrew)

Cooper, John, *Raphael Lemkin and the Struggle for the Genocide Convention* (Palgrave-Macmillan 2008)
Davidson Kalmar, Ivan and Penslar, Derek Jonathan (eds), *Orientalism and the Jews* (Brandeis UP 2005)
Devji, Faisal, *Muslim Zion: Pakistan As a Political Idea* (Harvard UP 2013)
Diner, Dan, *Beyond the Conceivable: Studies on Germany, Nazism, and the Holocaust* (University of California Press 2000)
Diner, Dan, *Gedächtniszeiten: Über jüdische und andere Geschichte* (CH Beck 2003)
Dotan, Shmuel, *The Partition Controversy During the Mandate Period* (Yad Ben-Zvi 1980) (Hebrew)
Dubnov, Arie M, 'Jewish Nationalism in the Wake of World War I: A "State-in-the-Making" or The Empire Strikes Back?' (2016) 24 Israel: Studies in Zionism and the State of Israel 5 (Hebrew)
Dubnov, Arie M, 'On Vertical Alliances, Informal Imperialism, and "Perfidious Albion": Reflections on the Balfour Declaration Centennial' (2017) 49 Theory and Criticism 177 (Hebrew)
Dubnov-Erlich, Sophie, *The Life and Work of S. M. Dubnov: Diaspora Nationalism and Jewish History* (Indiana UP 1991)
Dubnow, Simon, *Nationalism and History: Essays on Old and New Judaism* (Jewish Publication Society of America 1961)
Eban, Abba, *An Autobiography* (Random 1977)
Eban, Abba, *Personal Witness: Israel Through My Eyes* (Jonathan Cape 1993)
Eilath, Eliahu, *The Struggle for Statehood: Washington 1945–1948* (Am Oved 1982) (Hebrew)
Elon, Amos, *Herzl* (Holt, Rinehart & Winston 1975)
Eyffinger, Arthur, *T.M.C. Asser (1838–1913): In Quest of Liberty, Justice, and Peace* (Brill 2019)
Eytan, Walter, *The First Ten Years: Diplomatic History of Israel* (Simon & Schuster 1958)
Fassbender, Bardo and Peters, Anne (eds), *The Oxford Handbook of the History of International Law* (OUP 2012)
Feinberg, Nathan, *La Question Des Minorités à la Conférence de la Paix De 1919–1920 et l'action Juive en faveur de la Protection Internationale Des Minorités* (Rousseau & Cie 1929)
Feinberg, Nathan, *La Juridiction de la Cour Permanente de Justice Internationale dans le Systeme des Mandats* (Rousseau & Cie 1930)
Feinberg, Nathan, *La juridiction de la Cour Permanente de Justice Internationale dans le systeme de la protection internationale des minorites* (Rousseau & Cie 1931)
Feinberg, Nathan, '*La pétition en droit international*' (1932) 40 *Recueil de cours de l'académie de droit international* 525
Feinberg, Nathan, *Some Problems of the Palestine Mandate* (Shoshani 1936)
Feinberg, Nathan, '*La juridiction et la jurisprudence de la Cour Permanente de Justice Internationale en matire de mandats et de Minorités*' (1937) 59 *Recueil de cours de l'académie de droit international* 591
Feinberg, Nathan, 'The Recognition of the Jewish People in International Law' (1948) 1 Jewish Yearbook of International Law 1
Feinberg, Nathan, *Israel and the United Nations: Report of a Study Group Set Up By the Hebrew University of Jerusalem* (Manhattan 1956)
Feinberg, Nathan, *The Jewish Struggle Against Hitler in the League of Nations (The Bernheim Petition)* (Bialik Institute 1957) (Hebrew)
Feinberg, Nathan (ed), *Studies in Public International Law in Memory of Sir Hersch Lauterpacht* (Magnes 1961) (Hebrew)

Feinberg, Nathan, *Palestine Under the Mandate and the State of Israel* (Magnes 1963) (Hebrew)
Feinberg, Nathan, *The Jewish League of Nations Societies: A Chapter in the History of the Struggle of the Jews for Their Rights* (Magnes 1967) (Hebrew)
Feinberg, Nathan, 'The International Protection of Human Rights and the Jewish Question: A Historical Survey' (1968) 3 Israel Law Review 487
Feinberg, Nathan, *Essays on Jewish Issues of Our Times* (Dvir 1980) (Hebrew)
Feinberg, Nathan, *Reminiscences* (Keter 1985) (Hebrew)
Feinberg, Nathan and Stoyanovsky, Jacob (eds), *Jewish Yearbook of International Law*, vol 1 (1948)
Feldstein, Ariel L, *The Gordian Knot, David Ben Gurion, the Zionist Organization, and US Jewry* (Ben-Gurion Institute 2003) (Hebrew)
Fink, Carole, *Defending the Rights of Others: The Great Powers, the Jews, and International Minority Protection, 1878–1938* (CUP 2004)
Frankel, Jonathan, *Prophecy and Politics: Socialism, Nationalism, and the Russian Jews, 1862–1917* (CUP 1981)
Frankel, Jonathan, *The Damascus Affair: 'Ritual Murder', Politics, and the Jews in 1840* (CUP 1997)
Frieze, Donna-Lee (ed), *Totally Unofficial: The Autobiography of Raphael Lemkin* (Yale UP 2013)
Friling, Tuvia, *Arrows in the Dark: David Ben-Gurion, the Yishuv Leadership, and Rescue Attempts During the Holocaust* (University of Wisconsin Press 2005)
Gal, Allon, *David Ben-Gurion and the American Alignment for a Jewish State* (Indiana UP 1991)
Galchinsky, Michael, *Jews and Human Rights: Dancing at Three Weddings* (Rowman & Littlefield 2008)
Galnoor, Itzhak, *The Partition of Palestine, Decision Crossroads in the Zionist Movement* (State University of New York 1995)
Ganin, Zvi, *An Uneasy Relationship: American Jewish Leadership and Israel, 1948–1957* (Syracuse UP 2005)
García-Salmones Rovira, Mónica, *The Project of Positivism in International Law* (OUP 2013)
Giladi, Rotem, 'A "Historical Commitment"? Identity and Ideology in Israel's Attitude to the Refugee Convention 1951–4 (2014) 37 International History Review 745
Giladi, Rotem, 'Not Our Salvation: Israel, the Genocide Convention, and the World Court 1950–1951' (2015) 26 Diplomacy and Statecraft 473
Giladi, Rotem, 'Negotiating Identity: Israel, Apartheid, and the United Nations 1949–1952' (2017) 132 (No.559) English Historical Review 1440
Giladi, Rotem, 'The Phoenix of Colonial War: Race, the Laws of War, and the "Horror on the Rhine"' (2017) 30 Leiden Journal of International Law 847
Giladi, Rotem, 'Shabtai Rosenne: The Transformation of Sefton Rowson' in Loeffler, James and Paz, Moria (eds), *The Law of Strangers: Jewish Lawyers and International Law in the Twentieth Century* (CUP 2019) 221
Giladi, Rotem, 'At the Sovereign Turn: International Law at the Hebrew University Law Faculty Early Years', in Weiss, Yfaat and Rebhun, Uzi (eds), *The History of the Hebrew University in Jerusalem*, vol 5 (forthcoming Magnes 2021) (Hebrew)
Gilbert, Martin, *Exile and Return: The Struggle for a Jewish Homeland* (Lippincott 1978)
Gitelman, Zvi Y (ed), *The Emergence of Modern Jewish Politics: Bundism and Zionism in Eastern Europe* (University of Pittsburgh Press 2003)
Glendon, Mary Ann, *A World Made New: Eleanor Roosevelt and the Universal Declaration of Human Rights* (Random 2002)

Gluzman, Michael, 'The Zionist Body: Nationalism and Sexuality in Herzl's *Altneuland*' in Brod, Harry and Zevit, Shawn Israel (eds), *Brother Keepers: New Perspectives on Jewish Masculinity* (Men's Studies Press 2010) 89

Golani, Motti, *The End of the British Mandate for Palestine, 1948: The Diary of Sir Henry Gurney* (Palgrave MacMillan 2009)

Gong, Gerrit W, *The Standard of 'Civilization' in International Society* (Clarendon 1984)

Gorali, Abraham, *The Jewish Minority in the League of Nations: Origin and Development of the Minorities Protection by the League of Nations and the Jewish Petitions* (Sifria Mishpatit 1952) (Hebrew)

Gorny, Yosef, *From Binational Society to Jewish State: Federal Concepts in Zionist Political Thought, 1920–1990, and the Jewish People* (Brill 2006)

Graetz, Michael, *The Jews in Nineteenth Century France: From The French Revolution to the Alliance Israelite Universelle* (Stanford UP 1996)

Graf, Philipp, *Die Bernheim-Petition 1933: Jüdische Politik in der Zwischenkriegszeit* (Vandenhoeck & Ruprecht 2008)

Graf, Philipp, 'The Bernheim Petition 1933: Probing the Limits of Jewish Diplomacy in the Interwar Period' (2016) 15 Simon Dubnow Institute Yearbook 167

Green, Abigail, 'The British Empire and the Jews: An Imperialism of Human Rights?' (2008) 199 Past and Present 175

Green, Abigail, 'Intervening in the Jewish Question, 1840–1878' in Simms, Brendan and Trim, David JB (eds), *Humanitarian Intervention: A History* (CUP 2011) 139

Green, Abigail, 'The Limits of Intervention: Coercive Diplomacy and the Jewish Question in the Nineteenth Century' (2014) 36 International History Review 473

deGuzman, Margaret M and Amann, Diane Marie (eds), *Arcs of Global Justice: Essays in Honour of William A Schabas* (OUP 2018)

Halamish, Aviva, *A Dual Race against Time: Zionist Immigration Policy in the 1930s* (Yad Ben-Zvi 2006) (Hebrew)

Hathaway, James C and Foster, Michelle, *The Law of Refugee Status* (CUP 2014)

Heian-Engdal, Marte, Jensehaugen, Jørgen and Waage, Hilde Henriksen, '"Finishing the Enterprise": Israel's Admission to the United Nations' (2013) 35 International History Review 465

Herzl, Theodor, *Der Judenstaat: Versuch einer modernen Lösung der Judenfrage* (M Breitenstein's Verlags-Buchhandlung 1896)

Herzl, Theodor, *Altneuland: Roman* (Hermann Seemann Nachfolger 1902)

Herzl, Theodor, *The Jewish State: An Attempt at a Modern Solution for the Jewish Question* (Maccabæan 1904)

Herzog, Chaim, 'Sir Hersch Lauterpacht: An Appraisal' (1997) 2 European Journal of International Law 299

Hilbrenner, Anke, *Diaspora-Nationalismus: Zur Geschichtskonstruktion Simon Dubnows* (Vandenhoeck & Ruprecht 2007)

Holborn, Louise W, *Refugees, A Problem of Our Time: The Work of the United Nations High Commissioner for Refugees 1951–1972* (Scarecrow Press 1975)

Horowitz, David, *HaEtmol Sheli* (Schocken 1970) (Hebrew)

Humphrey, John P, *Human Rights and the United Nations: A Great Adventure* (Transnational 1984)

Inbar, Efraim, 'Jews, Jewishness and Israel's Foreign Policy' (1990) 2 Jewish Political Studies Review 165

Irvin-Erickson, Douglas, *Raphaël Lemkin and the Concept of Genocide* (University of Pennsylvania Press 2016)

Jabotinsky, Vladmir, *The War and the Jew* (Dial Press 1942)

Jackson, Simon and O'Malley, Alanna (eds), *The Institution of International Order: From the League of Nations to the United Nations* (Routledge 2018)

Janowsky, Oscar, *The Jews and Minority Rights, 1898–1919* (Columbia UP 1933)

Jilek, Grit, '*Jenseits von Territorium: Jüdische Nation und Diaspora bei Simon Dubnow*' (2014) 13 Simon Dubnow Institute Yearbook 463

Jockusch, Laura, 'Justice at Nuremberg? Jewish Responses to Nazi War-Crime Trials in Allied-Occupied Germany' (2012) 19 Jewish Social Studies 107

Jost, Martin, 'A Battle against Time: Salomon Adler-Rudels Commitment at the Évian Conference' (2017) 16 Simon Dubnow Institute Yearbook 115

Kaplan, Eran and Penslar, Derek J (eds), *The Origins of Israel 1882–1948: A Documentary History* (University of Wisconsin Press 2011)

Kaplan-Feuereisen, Omry, 'At the Service of the Jewish Nation: Jacob Robinson and International Law' (2008) 8–10 OstEuropa 157

Karch, Brendan, 'A Jewish "Nature Preserve": League of Nations Minority Protections in Nazi Upper Silesia, 1933–1937' (2013) 46 Central European History 124

Karlip, Joshua, 'In the Days of Haman: Simon Dubnow and His Disciples at the Eve of WWII' (2005) 4 Simon Dubnow Institute Yearbook 531

Karlip, Joshua M, *The Tragedy of a Generation: The Rise and Fall of Jewish Nationalism in Eastern Europe* (Harvard UP 2013)

Kattan, Victor, 'Decolonizing the International Court of Justice: The Experience of Judge Sir Muhammad Zafarulla Khan in the South West Africa Cases' (2015) 5 Asian Journal of International Law 310

Katz, Ethan B, Leff, Lisa Moses, and Mandel, Maud S (eds), *Colonialism and the Jews* (Indiana UP 2017)

Katz, Jacob (ed), *Toward Modernity: The European Jewish Model* (Transaction 1987)

Katz, Shaul and Heyd, Michael (eds), *The History of the Hebrew University of Jerusalem: Origins and Beginnings* (Magnes 1997) (Hebrew)

Kaufman, Menahem, *An Ambiguous Partnership: Non-Zionists and Zionists in America, 1939–1948* (Magnes 1991)

Keidar, Nir, *Mamlakhtiyut: David Ben-Gurion's Civic Thought* (Ben-Gurion UP 2009) (Hebrew)

Kelner, Victor E, '*Nation der Gegenwart: Simon Dubnow über Jüdische Politik und Geschichte*' (2003) 2 Simon Dubnow Institute Yearbook 519

Kohn, Jerome and Feldman, Ron (eds), *The Jewish Writings—Hannah Arendt* (Schocken 2007)

Korbin, Rebecca and Teller, Adam (eds), *Purchasing Power: The Economics of Modern Jewish History* (Pennsylvania UP 2015)

Korey, William, *An Epitaph for Raphael Lemkin* (American Jewish Committee 2001)

Kornberg, Jacques, *Theodor Herzl: From Assimilation to Zionism* (Indiana UP 1993)

Koskenniemi, Martti, *The Gentle Civilizer of Nations: The Rise and Fall of International Law 1870–1960* (CUP 2001)

Kritzman, Tally and Kemp, Adriana 'The Establishment of the Refugee Regime in Israel: Between State and Civil Society' in Mundlak, Guy and Ajzenstadt, Mimi (eds), *Empowerment on Trial* (Nevo 2008) 55 (Hebrew)

Kubowitzki, A Leon, *Unity in Dispersion: A History of the World Jewish Congress* (WJC 1948)

Kurz, Nathan, 'In the Shadow of Versailles: Jewish Minority Rights at the 1946 Paris Peace Conference' (2016) 15 Simon Dubnow Institute Yearbook 187

Kurz, Nathaniel A, '*A Sphere above the Nations?*': *The Rise and Fall of International Jewish Human Rights Politics, 1945–1975* (PhD Dissertation, Faculty of the Graduate School of Arts and Sciences, Yale University May 2015)

Lahav, Pnina, 'The Jewish Perspective in International Law' (1993) 87 Proceedings of the American Society of International Law 331

Landau, Moshe, *The Disappointing Alliance: Jews and Germans in the European Minorities' Congress* (Diaspora Research Institute 1992) (Hebrew)

Lapidoth, Ruth, 'Nathan Feinberg: A Tribute' (1985) 20 Israel Law Review 113

Lauterpacht, Elihu (ed), *International Law, Being the Collected Papers of Hersch Lauterpacht* (CUP 1975, 1977)

Lauterpacht, Elihu, *The Life of Hersch Lauterpacht* (CUP 2010)

Lauterpacht, Hersch, *The Function of Law in the International Community* (Oxford 1933)

Lauterpacht, Hersch, 'The Law of Nations, the Law of Nature and the Rights of Man' (1943) 29 Transactions of the Grotius Society 1

Lauterpacht, Hersch, *An International Bill of the Rights of Man* (Columbia UP 1945)

Lauterpacht, Hersch, 'The Universal Declaration of Human Rights' (1948) 25 British Yearbook of International Law 354

Lauterpacht, Hersch, *International Law and Human Rights* (Stevens & sons 1950)

Lavsky, Hagit (ed), *The History of the Hebrew University of Jerusalem: A Period of Consolidation and Growth* (Magnes 2005) (Hebrew)

Lederhendler, Eli, 'Shtadlanut and Stewardship: Paternal Diplomacy and Leadership in American Jewry, 1860s to 1920s' (2018) 19 Jewish Culture and History 97

Leff, Lisa Moses, *Sacred Bonds of Solidarity: The Rise of Jewish Internationalism in Nineteenth Century France* (Stanford UP 2006)

Leiblich, Eliav and Shachar, Yoram, 'Cosmopolitanism at a Crossroads: Hersch Lauterpacht and the Israeli Declaration of Independence' (2014) 84 British Yearbook of International Law 1

Lemkin, Raphael, *Axis Rule in Occupied Europe* (Carnegie Endowment for International Peace 1944)

Lemkin, Raphael, 'Genocide—A Modern Crime' (1945) 4 Free World 39

Levene, Mark, *War, Jews, and the New Europe: The Diplomacy of Lucien Wolf, 1914–1919* (OUP 1992)

Levene, Mark, 'Nationalism and its Alternatives in the International Arena: The Jewish Question at Paris, 1919' (1993) 28 Journal of Contemporary History 511

Liebman, Charles S, 'Diaspora Influence on Israel: The Ben Gurion-Blaustein "Exchange" and its Aftermath' (1974) 36 Jewish Social Studies 271

Liekis, Šarūnas, *A State Within a State?: Jewish Autonomy in Lithuania 1918–1925* (Versus Aureus 2003)

Likhovski, Assaf, 'Peripheral Vision: Polish-Jewish Lawyers and Early Israeli Law' (2018) 36 Law and History Review 235

Loeffler, James, '"The Conscience of America": Human Rights, Jewish Politics, and American Foreign Policy at the 1945 United Nations San Francisco Conference' (2013) 100 Journal of American History 401

Loeffler, James, '"The Famous Trinity of 1917": Zionist Internationalism in Historical Perspective' (2016) 15 Simon Dubnow Institute Yearbook 211

Loeffler, James, 'Becoming Cleopatra: The Forgotten Zionism of Raphael Lemkin' (2017) 19 Journal of Genocide Research 340

Loeffler, James, *Rooted Cosmopolitans: Jews and Human Rights in the Twentieth Century* (Yale UP 2018)

Loeffler, James and Paz, Moria (eds), *The Law of Strangers: Jewish Lawyers and International Law in the Twentieth Century* (CUP 2019)

Marrus, Michael R, *The Politics of Assimilation: A Study of the French Jewish Community at the Time of the Dreyfus Affair* (Clarendon 1971)

Marrus, Michael R, 'A Jewish Lobby at Nuremberg: Jacob Robinson and the Institute of Jewish Affairs, 1945–1946' (2006) 27 Cardozo Law Review 1651

Mazower, Mark, 'The Strange Triumph of Human Rights, 1933–1950' (2004) 47 The Historical Journal 379

Mazower, Mark, *No Enchanted Palace: The End of Empire and the Ideological Origins of the United Nations* (Princeton UP 2009)

McNair, Arnold, [Tribute to Sir Hersch Lauterpacht] (1961) 10 International and Comparative Law Quarterly 3

Mendelsohn, Ezra, *Zionism in Poland: The Formative Years, 1915–1926* (Yale UP 1981)

Mendelsohn, Ezra, Hoffman, Stefani, and Cohen, Richard I (eds), *Against the Grain: Jewish Intellectuals in Hard Times* (Berghahn 2013)

Mendes-Flohr, Paul, *Divided Passions: Jewish Intellectuals and the Experience of Modernity* (Wayne State UP 1991)

Mendes-Flohr, Paul, *German Jews: A Dual Identity* (Yale UP 1999)

Mendes-Flohr, Paul and Reinharz, Jehuda (eds), *The Jew in the Modern World: A Documentary History* (3rd edn, OUP 2011)

Mermelstein , Ari, Saker Woeste , Victoria, Zadoff , Ethan, and Galanter , Marc (eds), *Jews and the Law* (Quid Pro 2014)

Möller, Jakob T, 'Petitioning the United Nations' 1 Universal Human Rights (1979) 57

Morris, Benny, *The Birth of the Palestinian Refugee Problem, 1947–1949* (CUP 1989)

Morris, Benny, *The Birth of the Palestinian Refugee Problem Revisited* (CUP 2003)

Moses, Dirk 'Raphael Lemkin, Culture, and the Concept of Genocide' in Bloxham, Donald and Moses, Dirk (eds), *The Oxford Handbook on Genocide Studies* (OUP 2010) 19

Moskowitz, Moses, *Human Rights and World Order: The Struggle for Human Rights in the United Nations* (Oceana 1958)

Moyn, Samuel, *Human Rights and the Uses of History* (Verso 2014)

Mufti, Amir R, *Enlightenment in the Colony: The Jewish Question and the Crisis of Postcolonial Culture* (Princeton UP 2007)

Nikžentaitis, A, Schreiner, Stefan, and Staliūnas, Darius (eds), *The Vanished World of Lithuanian Jews* (Rodopi 2004)

Normand, Roger and Zaidi, Sarah, *Human Rights at the UN: The Political History of Universal Justice* (Indiana UP 2008)

Ofer, Dalia, 'Immigration and Aliyah: New Aspects of Jewish Policy' (1995) 75 Cathedra 142 (Hebrew)

O'Malley, Joseph J (ed), *Marx: Early Political Writings* (CUP 1994)

Oppenheim, Lassa, *International Law: A Treatise*, vol 1 (1st edn, Longmans, Green & Co 1905)

Orford, Anne (ed), *International Law and its Others* (CUP 2006)

Pawel, Ernst, *The Labyrinth of Exile: A Life of Theodor Herzl* (Farrar, Straus & Giroux 1992)

Paz, Moria, 'A Non-Territorial Ethnic Network and the Making of Human Rights Law: The Case of the Alliance Israelite Universelle' (2009) 4 Interdisciplinary Journal of Human Rights Law 1

Paz, Reut Yael, *A Gateway between a Distant God and a Cruel World: The Contribution of Jewish German-Speaking Scholars to International Law* (Brill 2012)

Pedersen, Susan, *The Guardians: The League of Nations and the Crisis of Empire* (OUP 2015)

Penslar, Derek J, 'Declarations of (In)Dependence: Tensions within Zionist Statecraft, 1896–1948' (2018) 8 Journal of Levantine Studies 13

Penslar, Derek, *Theodor Herzl: The Charismatic Leader* (Yale UP 2020)

Pinsker, Leon, *Autoemancipation!: Mahnruf an seine Stammesgenossen von einem russischen Juden* (W Issleib 1882)

Porat, Dina, *An Entangled Leadership: The 'Yishuv' and the Holocaust 1942–1945* (Am Oved 1986) (Hebrew)

Prost, Antoine and Winter, Jay, *René Cassin and Human Rights: From the Great War to the Universal Declaration* (CUP 2013)

Rabinbach, Anson, 'The Challenge of the Unprecedented: Raphael Lemkin and the Concept of Genocide' (2005) 4 Simon Dubnow Institute Yearbook 397

Rabinovitch, Simon (ed), *Jews and Diaspora Nationalism: Writings on Jewish Peoplehood in Europe and the United States* (Waltham 2012)

Rabinovitch, Simon, *Jewish Rights, National Rites: Nationalism and Autonomy in Late Imperial and Revolutionary Russia* (Stanford UP 2014)

Raz-Krakotzkin, Amnon, 'Exile Within Sovereignty: Toward a Critique of the Negation of Exile in Israeli Culture' (1994) 4 Theory and Criticism 25; 5 Theory and Criticism 113 (Hebrew)

Reimer, Michael J, *The First Zionist Congress: An Annotated Translation of the Proceedings* (SUNY Press 2019)

Reinharz, Jehuda, *Chaim Weizmann: The Making of a Zionist Leader* (OUP 1985)

Reinharz, Jehuda (ed), *Living with Antisemitism: Modern Jewish Responses* (University Press of New England 1987)

Reinharz, Jehuda, *Chaim Weizmann: The Making of a Stateman* (OUP 1993)

Reinharz, Jehuda and Shapira, Anita (eds), *Essential Papers on Zionism* (Cassell 1996)

Reinharz, Jehuda and Shavit, Yaacov, *Glorious, Accursed Europe: An Essay on Jewish Ambivalence* (Brandeis UP 2010)

Renton, James, *The Zionist Masquerade: The Birth of the Anglo-Zionist Alliance, 1914–1918* (Palgrave MacMillan 2007)

Robinson, Jacob, *Yediat Amenu: Demografyah veNatsiologyah, Sefer Limud veIyun [Knowledge of Our People: Demography and Nationology, A Text and Study Book]* (Ayanot 1923) (Hebrew)

Robinson, Jacob, *Das Minoritätenproblem und seine Literatur, Allgemeiner Teil* (de Gruyter 1928)

Robinson, Jacob, *Kommentar der Konvention über das Memelgebiet* (Spaudos Fondas 1934)

Robinson, Jacob, *Minorities and the League of Nations* (American Council of Public Affairs 1941)

Robinson, Jacob, 'Minorities in a Free World' (1943) 5 Free World 450

Robinson, Jacob, *Human Rights and Fundamental Freedoms in the Charter of the United Nations: A Commentary* (IJA 1946)

Robinson, Jacob, 'From Protection of Minorities to Promotion of Human Rights' (1948) 1 Jewish Yearbook of International Law 115

Robinson, Jacob, 'Metamorphosis of the United Nations' (1958) 94 *Recueil de cours de l'académie de droit international* 493

Robinson, Jacob, 'International Protection of Minorities: A Global View' (1971) 1 Israel Yearbook on Human Rights 61

Robinson, Jacob, 'The International Military Tribunal and the Holocaust: Some Legal Reflections' (1972) 7 Israel Law Review 1

Robinson, Jacob, Karbach, Oscar, Laserson, Max M, Robinson, Nehemiah, and Vishniak, Marc (eds), *Were the Minorities Treaties a Failure?* (IJA 1943)

Robinson, Nehemiah, *Indemnification, Reparations: Jewish Aspects* (IJA 1944)

Robinson, Nehemiah, *The United Nations and the World Jewish Congress* (IJA/WJC 1956)

Robinson, Nehemiah, *The Universal Declaration of Human Rights: Its Origin, Significance, Application, and Interpretation* (IJA/WJC 1958)
Robinson, Nehemiah, *The Genocide Convention: A Commentary* (IJA 1960)
Robinson, Nehemiah, *Ten Years of German Indemnification* (Conference on Jewish Material Claims Against Germany 1964)
Rosenne, Shabtai, 'International Law and the Municipal Law of the State of Israel' (1950) 7 HaPraklit 258 (Hebrew)
Rosenne, Shabtai, 'New Tendencies in the Work of the International Court of Justice' (1952) 9 HaPraklit 78 (Hebrew)
Rosenne, Shabtai, 'L'exécution et la mise en vigueur des décisions de la Cour internationale de Justice' (1953) 57 *Revue Générale de Droit International Public* 532
Rosenne, Shabtai, 'United Nations Treaty Practice' (1954) 86 *Recueil de cours de l'académie de droit international* 275
Rosenne, Shabtai, *The International Court of Justice: One of the Principal Organs of the United Nations* (PhD Thesis, Hebrew University of Jerusalem, 19 June 1957) (Hebrew)
Rosenne, Shabtai, *The International Court of Justice* (Sijthoff 1957)
Rosenne, Shabtai, 'Basic Elements of Israel's Foreign Policy' (1961) 17 India Quarterly 328
Rosenne, Shabtai, 'Jacob Robinson—In Memoriam' (1978) 8 Israel Law Review 287
Rosenne, Shabtai, 'The Meaning of "Authentic Text" in Modern Treaty Law' in Bernhardt, Rudolf et al (eds), *Völkerrecht als Rechtsordnung, Internationale Gerichtsbarkeit, Menschenrechte: Festschrift für Hermann Mosler* (Springer-Verlag 1983) 759
Rosenne, Shabtai, 'The Protection of Minorities and Human Rights' (1990) 20 Israel Yearbook on Human Rights 359
Rosenne, Shabtai, *An International Law Miscellany* (Martinus Nijhoff 1993)
Rosenne, Shabtai, 'War Crimes and State Responsibility' in Dinstein, Yoram and Tabori, Mala (eds), *War Crimes in International Law* (Nijhoff 1996)
Rosenne, Shabtai, *The Law and Practice of the International Court 1920–2005* (4th edn, Martinus Nijhoff 2006)
Rosenne, Shabtai, 'Book Review' (2009) 39 Israel Yearbook on Human Rights 379
Rosenne, Shabtai, *The Perplexities of International Law* (rev & updated Hebrew edn, Bialik 2012) (Hebrew)
Rosensaft, Menachem Z (ed), *Voice of a People: The World Jewish Congress, 1936–2016* (WJC 2017)
Rovner, Adam, *In the Shadow of Zion: Promised Lands Before Israel* (NYU Press 2014)
Rowson, Shabtai, 'International Law and the Jewish People' (1947) 11 Tarbut 4 (Hebrew)
Rozin, Orit, *The Rise of the Individual in 1950s Israel: A Challenge to Collectivism* (Brandeis UP 2011)
Rubin, Gil, 'The End of Minority Rights: Jacob Robinson and the Jewish Question in World War II' (2012) 11 Simon Dubnow Institute Yearbook 55
Sagi, Nana, *German Reparations: A History of the Negotiations* (Magnes 1986)
Sands, Philippe, *East West Street: On the Origins of Genocide and Crimes against Humanity* (Knopf 2016)
Schabas, William A, *Genocide in International Law: The Crimes of Crimes* (2nd edn, CUP 2009)
Schachner, Nathan, *The Price of Liberty: A History of the American Jewish Committee* (AJC 1943)
Schneer, Jonathan, *The Balfour Declaration* (Random House 2010)
Segev, Tom, *The Seventh Million: Israelis and the Holocaust* (Holt 2000)
Segev, Tom, *A State at Any Cost: The Life of David Ben-Gurion* (Farrar, Straus & Giroux 2019)

Segev, Zohar, *The World Jewish Congress during the Holocaust: Between Activism and Restraint* (de Gruyter 2014)
Shachar, Yoram, 'Jefferson Goes East: the American Origins of the Israeli Declaration of Independence' (2009) 10 Theoretical Inquiries in Law 589
Shapira, Anita, *Land and Power: The Zionist Resort to Force, 1881–1948* (Stanford UP 1992)
Shapira, Anita, *New Jews, Old Jews* (Am Oved 1997) (Hebrew)
Shapira, Anita, *Israel: A History* (Brandeis UP 2012)
Sharett, Moshe, *At the Threshold of Statehood: 1946–1949* (Am Oved 1958) (Hebrew)
Sharett, Moshe, *Personal Diary: 1957–1958* (*Ma'ariv* 1978) (Hebrew)
Sharett, Moshe, *Shall We Ever Meet Again: Letters of an Ottoman Soldier 1916–1918* (Sharett Heritage Society 1998) (Hebrew)
Sharett, Moshe, *The London Days: Letters 1923–1925* (Moshe Sharett Heritage Society 2008) (Hebrew)
Sharett, Yaacov (ed), *Moshe Sharett and the German Reparations Controversy* (Moshe Sharett Heritage Society 2007)
Sheffer, Gabriel, *Moshe Sharett: Biography of a Political Moderate* (Clarendon 1996)
Shimoni, Gideon, *The Zionist Ideology* (Brandeis UP 1995)
Shimoni, Gideon and Wistrich, Robert (eds), *Theodor Herzl: Visionary of the Jewish State* (Magnes 1999)
Shlaim, Avi, 'Israel Between East and West: Israel's Foreign Policy Orientation, 1948–1956' (2004) 66 International Journal of Middle East Studies 657
Shumsky, Dimitry, 'Leon Pinsker and "Autoemancipation!": A Reevaluation' (2011) 18 Jewish Social Studies 33
Shumsky, Dimitry, 'Zionism in Quotations Marks, or To What Extent Was Dubnow a Non-Zionist' (2012) 77 Zion 369 (Hebrew)
Shumsky, Dimitry, *Beyond the Nation-State: The Zionist Political Imagination from Pinsker to Ben-Gurion* (Yale UP 2018)
Siegelberg, Mira, 'Contending with the Ghosts of the Past: Raphael Lemkin and the Origins of the Genocide Convention' (2006) 1 Columbia Undergraduate Journal of History 30
Siegelberg, Mira L, 'Unofficial Men, Efficient Civil Servants: Raphael Lemkin in the History of International Law' (2013) 15 Journal of Genocide Research 297
Silber, Marcos, 'The Metamorphosis of Pre-Dubnovian Autonomism into Diaspora Jewish-Nationalism' in Rozen, Minna (ed), *Homelands and Diasporas: Greeks, Jews and their Migrations* (Taurus 2008) 235
Silver, Matthew M, *In the Service of the West: A New Look at Modern Jewish History* (HaKibbutz HaMeuchad 2014) (Hebrew)
Simpson , Alfred WB, *Human Rights and the End of Empire: Britain and the Genesis of the European Convention* (OUP 2001)
Simpson , Alfred WB, 'Britain and the Genocide Convention' (2003) 73 British Yearbook of International Law 5
Sirutavičius, Vladas and Staliūnas, Darius (eds), *A Pragmatic Alliance, Jewish-Lithuanian Political Cooperation at the Beginning of the 20th Century* (Central European UP 2011)
Smith, Anthony, 'Zionism and Diaspora Nationalism' (1995) 2 Israel Affairs 1
Steinberg, Jacob (ed), *Kitvei Haim Arlosoroff* [The Works of Haim Arlosoroff]: *A Glass Wall*, vol 1 (Stybel 1934) (Hebrew)
Sternhell, Zeev, *The Founding Myths of Israel: Nationalism, Socialism and the Making of the Jewish State* (Princeton UP 1998)
Stoyanovsky, Jacob, *The Mandate for Palestine: A Contribution to the Theory and Practice of International Mandates* (Longmans, Green & Co 1928)

Sznaider, Natan, *Jewish Memory and the Cosmopolitan Order: Hannah Arendt and the Jewish Condition* (Polity Press 2011)

Takkenberg, Alex, *The Status of Palestinian Refugees in International Law* (Clarendon Press 1998)

Tartakower, Arieh and Grossmann, Kurt R, *The Jewish Refugee* (IJA 1944)

Tory, Abraham, 'Jacob Robinson—In Memoriam' (1978–1979) 32 HaPraklit 125 (Hebrew)

Tovy, Jacob, *Israel and the Palestinian Refugee Issue: The Formulation of a Policy 1948–1956* (Routledge 2014)

Tovy, Jacob, *Destruction and Accounting: The State of Israel and the Reparations from Germany 1949–1953* (Bar-Ilan UP 2015)

Vital, David, *Zionism: the Formative Years* (Clarendon 1982)

Vital, David, *A People Apart: A Political History of the Jews in Europe 1789–1939* (OUP 2001)

Wasserstein, Bernard, *The British in Palestine: The Mandatory Government and the Arab-Jewish Conflict 1917–1929* (2nd edn, Basil Blackwell 1991)

Weiss, Yfaat, *Ethnicity and Citizenship, German and Polish Jews 1933–1940* (Magnes 2000) (Hebrew)

Weiss, Yfaat, '"*Nicht durch Macht und nicht durch Kraft, sondern durch meinen Geist": Die Hebräische Universität in der Skopusberg-Enklave*' (2015) 14 Simon Dubnow Institute Yearbook 59

Weiss-Wendt, Anton, *The Soviet Union and the Gutting of the UN Genocide Convention* (University of Wisconsin Press 2017)

Weitz, Yechiam, 'From Holocaust to Rebirth: The D.P. Question in Zionist Policy' (1990) 55 Cathedra 162 (Hebrew)

Weitz, Yechiam, *Aware But Helpless: Mapai and the Holocaust 1943–1945* (Yad Ben-Zvi 1994) (Hebrew)

Weizmann, Chaim, *Trial and Error: The Autobiography of Chaim Weizmann* (Harper 1949)

Wendehorst, Stephan EC, *British Jewry, Zionism, and the Jewish State, 1936–1956* (OUP 2012)

Wheatley, Natasha, 'Mandatory Interpretation: Legal Hermeneutics and the New International Order in Arab and Jewish Petitions to the League of Nations' (2015) 227 Past and Present 205

Yegar, Moshe, *The History of the Political Department of the Jewish Agency* (The Zionist Library 2011) (Hebrew)

Zertal, Idith, *From Catastrophe to Power: The Holocaust Survivors and the Emergence of Israel* (University of California Press 1998)

Zimmermann, Andreas, *The 1951 Convention Relating to the Status of Refugees and its 1967 Protocol: A Commentary* (OUP 2011)

Zuijdwijk, Ton JM, *Petitioning the United Nations: A Study in Human Rights* (St Martin's 1982)

Zweig, Ronald W, *German Reparations and the Jewish World: A History of the Claims Conference* (Routledge 2014)

Index

For the benefit of digital users, indexed terms that span two pages (e.g., 52–53) may, on occasion, appear on only one of those pages.